Advances in Information Security

Volume 87

The purpose of the *Advances in Information Security* book series is to establish the state of the art and set the course for future research in information security. The scope of this series includes not only all aspects of computer, network security, and cryptography, but related areas, such as fault tolerance and software assurance. The series serves as a central source of reference for information security research and developments. The series aims to publish thorough and cohesive overviews on specific topics in Information Security, as well as works that are larger in scope than survey articles and that will contain more detailed background information. The series also provides a single point of coverage of advanced and timely topics and a forum for topics that may not have reached a level of maturity to warrant a comprehensive textbook.

Alexander Kott
Editor

Autonomous Intelligent Cyber Defense Agent (AICA)

A Comprehensive Guide

 Springer

Editor
Alexander Kott
United States Army Research Laboratory
Adelphi, MD, USA

ISSN 1568-2633   ISSN 2512-2193   (electronic)
Advances in Information Security
ISBN 978-3-031-29271-2   ISBN 978-3-031-29269-9   (eBook)
https://doi.org/10.1007/978-3-031-29269-9

This Springer imprint is published by the registered company Springer Nature Switzerland AG
The registered company address is: Gewerbestrasse 11, 6330 Cham, Switzerland

Contents

1 Autonomous Intelligent Cyber-defense Agent:
Introduction and Overview 1
Alexander Kott
   1   Introduction 1
   2   AICA as an Agent 2
   3   AICA's Environment 4
   4   AICA's Roles 5
   5   AICA's Architecture.................................... 7
   6   AICA's Risk and Trust.................................. 9
   7   Preview of This Book................................... 11
   8   Summary and Conclusions 14
   References.. 15

2 Alternative Architectural Approaches 17
Paul Theron
   1   Introduction 17
   2   The Architecture of Autonomous Intelligent
        Cyber-Defence Agents.................................. 20
   3   AICAs Are Themselves Multi Agent Systems:
        Our Initial Assumption.................................. 21
   4   The Decision-Making Paradigm of AICAs Has a Key
        Influence on AICAs' Architecture 22
   5   The MASCARA Architecture of AICAs 25
   6   The General Functional Model of the MASCARA Architecture .. 26
   7   The Detailed Functional Model of the MASCARA Architecture .. 28
   8   The Technical Implementation of a MASCARA-Based AICA.... 31
   9   Beyond Prototypes, the Rationale of AICAs' Architecture:
        Required Aptitudes and Benefits 35
   10   And Now, What? Further Areas of Research and Technology..... 40
   11   Summary and Conclusions 43
   References.. 44

3   Perception of the Environment 47
      Martin Drasar
      1   Background 47
      2   From Percepts to the World Representation. 50
      3   Power and Bandwidth Constraints......................... 51
      4   Trusting the Perception 52
      5   Developing a Perception Model for AICA 53
             5.1   Environment – The Objective Reality 55
             5.2   First Approximation – Taking Inputs Verbatim 56
             5.3   Second Approximation – Elimination of (Semi)static
                      Observations 57
             5.4   Approximation Detour – The Interplay Between
                      Request and Responses 57
             5.5   Third Approximation – Indexing of Large Domains 58
             5.6   Fourth Approximation – State Restructuring............ 58
             5.7   Fifth Approximation – Explicit Activity History......... 59
             5.8   Sixth Approximation – Additional Transformations
                      Within the Perception. 60
      6   Summary and Conclusions 60
      References.. 61

4   Perception of Cyber Threats 63
      Kevin Kornegay, Kofi Nyarko, Jeffrey S. Chavis, and Ahmad Ridley
      1   Introduction 63
      2   Simplified Hierarchical Cyber-Defense Agents for Threat
             Perception 66
      3   Autonomous Hierarchical Agents for Anomaly Detection 69
      4   Honeypot Agents 74
      5   Perception of Threat Applications 75
      6   Experimentation... 77
      7   In Conclusion: Further Research Areas 78
      References.. 78

5   Situational Understanding and Diagnostics 83
      Steven Noel and Vipin Swarup
      1   Introduction 83
      2   Background and Challenges 84
      3   Synthesis and Analysis................................... 85
      4   Abstraction and Generalization 90
      5   Illustrative Examples 92
      6   Summary and Conclusions 102
      References.. 103

6   Learning About the Adversary 105

Azqa Nadeem, Sicco Verwer, and Shanchieh Jay Yang

　1　Introduction: "Know thy Enemy" 105

　　1.1　Learning from Observable Data. 106

　　1.2　Definitions 108

　2　Challenges for Data-Driven Autonomous Cyber Agents......... 109

　　2.1　Evolving and Adversarial Threat Landscape 109

　　2.2　Data Availability and Quality. 110

　　2.3　Modeling Adversary Behavior. 111

　　2.4　Modeling Context 112

　　2.5　Interpretable Approaches. 112

　　2.6　Open-World Evaluation 113

　3　Approaches and Advancements. 114

　　3.1　Use Case 1: Attack Model Synthesis (ASSERT). 114

　　3.2　Use Case 2: Attacker Strategy Extraction (SAGE) 118

　　3.3　Use Case 3: Attack Campaign Discovery (HeAT). 123

　4　Thoughts and Future Opportunities. 125

　5　Summary and Conclusions 128

　References. 129

7   Response Planning 133

Scott Musman and Lashon Booker

　1　Overview of Cyber Response Planning. 133

　　1.1　Matching Wits with a Hacker 133

　　1.2　Defeating an Email Worm 134

　　1.3　Topics Covered in This Chapter. 135

　2　Response Planning Problem Characteristics and Requirements ... 135

　　2.1　Representing System State and Function. 136

　　2.2　Managing Uncertainty and Risk 139

　3　Projecting Possible Futures 141

　4　Approaches to Cyber Response Planning 142

　5　Toward Fully Automated Cyber Response Planning. 145

　　5.1　Efficiently Managing Uncertainty in Cyber Response 146

　　5.2　Simulating the Cyber Terrain and Attacker/Defender

　　　　 Interactions. 148

　　5.3　Experimental Tests of an ARCR Prototype 151

　　5.4　Steps Toward Deployment for Real Applications 153

　6　Summary 153

　References. 155

8   Recovery Planning   159
Meiyi Ma, Himanshu Neema, and Janos Sztipanovits
   1   Introduction   159
   2   Recovery Planning Overview   161
         2.1   Definition of Recovery Planning   161
         2.2   Different Components in the Recovery Plan   161
         2.3   Techniques for Recovery Planning   163
   3   Problem Formulation   166
   4   System Overview   166
   5   Recovery COA Generation   167
   6   Simulation and Prediction with Uncertainty   169
         6.1   Introduction to the SURE Platform   169
         6.2   Simulation of Different Attack Scenarios   171
         6.3   Simulation for Prediction with Uncertainty   173
   7   Recovery COA Verification   174
   8   Recovery Scenarios   176
         8.1   Recovery Scenario 1   177
         8.2   Recovery Scenario 2   179
   9   Summary and Conclusion   180
   References   181

9   Strategic Cyber Camouflage   183
Christopher Kiekintveld, Aron Laszka, Mohammad Sujan Miah,
Shanto Roy, and Nazia Sharmin
   1   Introduction   183
   2   Implementing Camouflage   184
         2.1   Obfuscation Techniques   184
         2.2   Decoy Technologies   185
   3   Optimizing Camouflage Strategies   186
         3.1   Optimizing Decoy Resource Allocation   187
         3.2   Optimizing Feature Obfuscation   188
   4   Example Methods for Optimizing Camouflage   188
         4.1   Disguising Network Attributes   189
         4.2   Feature Selection Game   191
         4.3   Two-Sided Feature Deception Using Adversarial
                 Learning   193
   5   Evaluating Camouflage   194
         5.1   Theoretical Evaluation   194
         5.2   Experimental Evaluation   196
   6   Summary and Conclusions   198
   References   199

10 Adaptivity and Antifragility................................... 203

Anton V. Uzunov, Bao Vo, Hoa Khanh Dam, Charles Harold,
Mohan Baruwal Chhetri, Alan Colman, and Saad Sajid Hashmi

1   Introduction 203

       1.1   S* Agents....................................... 204

       1.2   AICA Systems and Agents......................... 204

       1.3   Relation Between S* and AICA Agents 205

       1.4   Agent Communication............................ 205

2   Self-* Properties....................................... 206

       2.1   Definitions 206

       2.2   Realization Approaches 207

3   S* Multi-Agent Systems for Adaptivity & Antifragility 208

       3.1   S* Agent Reference Architecture
(Conceptual Framework, Part 1) 208

       3.2   S* Multi-agent System Design Concepts
(Conceptual Framework, Part 2) 211

       3.3   Generic Self-Management and Self-Improvement
(S-M/I) Approach................................ 212

       3.4   Reifying the S* Conceptual Framework and Generic
S-M/I Approach 215

4   The AWaRE Framework................................. 216

       4.1   AWaRE Principles 216

       4.2   AWaRE Concepts................................ 217

       4.3   AWaRE Architecture 218

       4.4   AWaRE 3.0 – Micro-service Integration 220

       4.5   Applicability of AWaRE to AICA 222

5   Challenges and Recommendations 222

       5.1   Learning and Self-Improvement 222

       5.2   Agent Teaming and Negotiation 224

6   Summary and Conclusions............................... 225

References.. 226

11 Collaboration and Negotiation............................. 229

Samrat Chatterjee, Arnab Bhattacharya, Ashutosh Dutta,
Aowabin Rahman, Thiagarajan Ramachandran,
Satish Chikkagoudar, and Ramesh Bharadwaj

1   Background and Objective............................... 229

2   AICA Agent Levels 231

3   AICA Agent Properties for Secure Communication 233

       3.1   Active Learning 234

       3.2   Safety Verification 237

       3.3   Stealthiness 238

4   Algorithmic Approaches for Multi-agent Coordination.......... 240

5   Representative Multi-agent Navigation and Communication
        Simulation Example..................................... 242
        5.1   Algorithmic Approach........................... 243
        5.2   Simulation Environment 246
        5.3   Discussion 246
6   Summary and Conclusions................................ 248
References... 249

12   Human Interactions 253
Eric Holder, Jessie Y. C. Chen, Kristen Liggett, Phillip Bridgham,
Neil Briscombe, Thomas Eskridge, Marco Carvalho,
and Lavinia Burski
1   Introduction 253
2   Human Interaction Considerations and Techniques............. 255
        2.1   Trust and Transparency 255
        2.2   Transparency-Based Approaches to Human-Agent
                Interaction 256
        2.3   Human Factors Design Process 259
3   An Example Approach for AICA Applications 262
        3.1   Applying Lessons Learned for Human Interactions
                in AICA-Relevant Systems 262
        3.2   Implementation Strategies Aligning Human
                and Agent Mental Models 262
        3.3   An Implementation Strategy Applied
                to the AICA Reference Architecture (AICA RA) 264
        3.4   Example 1: Applying the OODA Trace Method
                as a Web Interface 266
        3.5   Example 2: Applying to OODA Trace Method
                to Natural Language Interfaces 267
4   Evaluating AICAs' Operational Effectiveness................. 268
5   Future Interaction Considerations 271
6   Summary and Conclusions................................ 272
References... 273

13   Testing and Measurements................................. 275
Toby J. Richer and Maxwell Standen
1   Introduction 275
2   Background 276
        2.1   Robustness..................................... 277
        2.2   The Reality Gap................................. 277
        2.3   The CIA Triad 278
        2.4   Reliability...................................... 278
        2.5   Resilience...................................... 280
3   Existing Test Systems................................... 280

4 Case Study: CybORG 282
    4.1 CybORG Design 282
    4.2 Scenarios 282
    4.3 Simulation 283
    4.4 Emulation.................................. 284
    4.5 Experiment One: Reality Gap Test 284
    4.6 Experiment 2: CAGE Challenge One 287
    4.7 Analysis of Measurement in CybORG 290
5 Future Work 290
6 Summary and Conclusions............................. 291
References... 292

14 **Deployment and Operation** 295
Benjamin Blakely, William Horsthemke, Daniel Harkness,
and Nate Evans
1 Introduction 295
2 Advantageous Scenarios 296
    2.1 Interacting with an Adversary 296
    2.2 Dynamic Threat Environments 297
    2.3 Human-in-the-Loop 298
3 Learning and Cooperation 298
    3.1 Federated Machine Learning 298
    3.2 Swarm Intelligence 299
4 Deployment Environments.............................. 300
    4.1 Dichotomies as Environmental Classifications 301
    4.2 Unmanned Aircraft Systems (UAS)................. 302
    4.3 Power Grids 303
    4.4 Orbital or Deep-Space Platforms.................. 305
    4.5 Large-Scale Computational Arrays 307
5 Summary and Conclusions............................. 308
References... 309

15 **Command in AICA-Intensive Operations** 311
Arne Norlander
1 Introduction and Challenges: The AICA-Inhabited Operational
   Environment Is Contested, Nonlinear, and Dynamic............ 311
2 Developing AICA Command Capabilities: A Command Layer
   of the AICA Architecture............................... 313
3 Joint Cognitive Systems............................... 314
4 Complex Adaptive Systems (CAS) 315
5 Intelligent Collaboration: An Emergent Feature of Artificial
   and Human Agents.................................... 316
    5.1 A Functional Perspective on Intelligent Collaboration ... 316
    5.2 Standardized Automation Concepts Do Not Capture
        Intelligent Collaboration 317

6   Cognitive Systems and Autonomous Agents: Learning
      from Experience and Adapting to Circumstances   318
7   Executing High-Risk Missions with AICAs as Part
      of High-Reliability Organizations   321
8   Command Characteristics for AICA-Enabled Capabilities   322
      8.1   Command in AICA-Intensive Operations Requires
              an Agility Mindset That Embraces Uncertainty.   322
      8.2   Studies on Command, Systems Safety, Agents, Network
              Theory and Learning: A Foundation for AICA-Enabled
              Capabilities   326
9   Defining Command in AICA-Intensive Operations.   329
10   Recommendations: Developing an Essence of Command
      for AICA-Intensive Operations   334
11   Summary and Conclusions.   336
References.   337

16   **Risk Management**   341
      Alexandre K. Ligo, Alexander Kott, Haley Dozier, and Igor Linkov
      1   Introduction   341
      2   Types of Risks Introduced by AICA   342
      3   Consequences of Risks Introduced by AICA.   343
      4   Human-Centric Approaches with Real-Time Cooperation   344
      5   Human-Centric Approaches with Data-Driven Intervention   345
      6   Human-Centric Approaches Based on Algorithm Design   347
      7   Simulation of Strategies.   348
      8   Software-Centric Strategies: Constraints to AICA Algorithms   350
      9   Summary   351
      References.   352

17   **Policy Issues**   353
      Samuel Sanders Visner
      1   Introduction – AICA and the Changing Information Technology
            Eco-System   353
      2   The Changing Concepts of Cyber-Defense   355
      3   Existing Policies and Considerations.   357
            3.1   Wartime Policy Considerations – Some Examples   358
            3.2   AICA in the "Grey Zone"   361
            3.3   US National and Economic Security Policy   362
            3.4   Consumer Privacy   362
            3.5   Constitutional Protections   364
      4   Policy Issues for the Future   364
            4.1   National Security   364
            4.2   Homeland Security and Privacy.   365
      5   Summary and Conclusions.   366

18 AICA Development Challenges 367
Shouhuai Xu
  1   Chapter Motivation 367
  2   AICA Engineering Ecosystem 368
  3   AICA Engineering Challenges 370
       3.1   Challenges on AICA Design 370
       3.2   Challenges on AICA Implementation 371
       3.3   Challenges on AICA Individual Test & Certification 372
       3.4   Challenges on AICA Composition 373
       3.5   Challenges on AICA Composite Test & Certification 373
       3.6   Challenges on AICA Deployment 374
  4   AICA Research Ecosystem 375
  5   ACIA Research Challenges 377
       5.1   Challenges on AICA Models 377
       5.2   Challenges on AICA Architectures 379
       5.3   Challenges on AICA Defense Mechanisms 382
       5.4   Challenges on AICA Testing and Certification 385
       5.5   Challenges on AICA Operations 386
       5.6   Challenges on Social, Ethical, and Legal Aspects 388
  6   Mapping Between the Engineering Ecosystem
       and the Research Ecosystem 389
  7   Summary and Conclusions 390
  References 391

**19 Case Study A: A Prototype Autonomous Intelligent Cyber-Defense
     Agent** 395
Benjamin Blakely, William Horsthemke, Nate Evans,
and Daniel Harkness
  1   Introduction 395
  2   Related Work 395
       2.1   Frameworks and Methodologies 395
       2.2   Moving Target and Proactive Defenses 397
       2.3   Application Libraries 398
  3   Guiding Principles for Prototype Development 399
  4   Technical Details of Prototype 400
  5   Demonstration Scenario and Results 402
  6   Future Capabilities 404
  7   Summary and Conclusions 406
  References 407

20 Case Study B: AI Agents for the Tactical Edge 409
Pierre Trepagnier and Allan Wollaber
  1   Introduction to the Tactical Edge 409
       1.1   Network Characteristics 410
       1.2   Computing Resources 411

2   AI Agents at the Tactical Edge............................. 412
    2.1   AI Characteristics Relevant to the Tactical Edge........ 414
    2.2   Tactical Edge Conditions and Resultant Needs......... 414
    2.3   Discussion 415
3   Technical Illustration: AI Agents for Blue Force RF Situational
       Awareness (BFSA)................................... 416
    3.1   Introduction 416
    3.2   State of the Art Prior to AI........................ 417
    3.3   Program Goal.................................... 417
    3.4   Architecture 418
    3.5   Software Methodology............................. 420
    3.6   Tactical Edge Issues.............................. 420
    3.7   Technical Illustration Recapitulation................. 422
4   Thoughts and Recommendations........................... 422
    4.1   Thoughts on Future Evolution....................... 422
    4.2   Concluding Remarks 423
References... 423

21   Case Study C: Sentinels for Cyber Resilience 425
       Peter A. Beling, Tim Sherburne, and Barry Horowitz
1   Introduction 425
2   How Sentinels Detect Attacks 428
    2.1   Changing Control Input........................... 428
    2.2   Resource Introspection............................ 429
    2.3   Attestation Using TPM 429
3   What Sentinels Do After Detecting an Attack 431
    3.1   Example Sentinel Pattern: Diverse Redundant
             Controller...................................... 431
    3.2   Example Sentinel Pattern: Path Diversity 431
    3.3   Example Sentinel Pattern: Protected Restore 432
4   Where to Place Sentinels 434
5   How to Test Sentinels................................... 435
6   Silverfish Case Study 437
    6.1   Pre-resilience Architecture......................... 437
    6.2   MA – Cyber Tabletop 438
    6.3   MA – Resilience Analysis 441
    6.4   MA – Requirements Elicitation..................... 441
    6.5   Post-Resilience Architecture 443
7   Conclusions 444
References... 444

Contributors

Peter A. Beling is a professor in the Grado Department of Industrial and Systems Engineering and director of the Intelligent Systems Division in the Virginia Tech National Security Institute. Dr. Beling's research interests lie at the intersections of systems engineering and artificial intelligence (AI) and include AI adoption, reinforcement learning, transfer learning, and digital engineering. He has contributed extensively to the development of methodologies and tools in support of cyber resilience in military systems. He serves on the Research Council of the Systems Engineering Research Center (SERC), a University Affiliated Research Center for the Department of Defense.

Ramesh Bharadwaj is a senior systems researcher at the Navy's Center of Excellence in High Assurance Systems. He conducts research in rigorous engineering methods and tools for the specification, design, and construction of mission-critical software-intensive systems to ensure their safety, reliability, and trustworthiness. Tools, methods, guidelines, and standards being developed as part of this research will ensure dependability of fielded autonomous unmanned systems employing machine learning (ML), more specifically deep learning (DL), and provide better protection against adversarial attacks. Dr. Bharadwaj serves as an adviser to organizations such as DARPA, ONR, PEO-IWS, and USC, to address future research challenges.

Arnab Bhattacharya is an operations research scientist in the Optimization and Control Group at U.S. Department of Energy's Pacific Northwest National Laboratory (PNNL). His research interests lie at the intersection of stochastic modeling and optimization, predictive control, and reinforcement learning. He has led multiple DOE-sponsored projects on advanced building control, co-design of cyber-physical systems, infrastructure network resilience, and cyber-physical security. Dr. Bhattacharya has co-authored more than 35 peer-reviewed journal and conference articles and is a recipient of multiple awards, including the IISE Best PhD Dissertation Poster (2017) and Best Paper Award at IEEE Modeling, Estimation, and Control Conference (2021). He is a member of IEEE, INFORMS, and SIAM.

Benjamin Blakely PhD, CISSP, CISM, is a cybersecurity and machine learning researcher at Argonne National Laboratory and assistant teaching professor at Iowa State University. He has over 20 years of experience in the private, public, and education sectors in operational and research aspects of cybersecurity. He has served as a subject matter expert in cybersecurity for the United States Departments of Energy, Homeland Security, and Defense. He holds PhD and BS degrees from Iowa State University and Certified Information Systems Security Professional (CISSP) and Certified Information Security Manager (CISM) certifications. His research interests span the topics of machine learning methods for cybersecurity enhancement, psycho-socioeconomic issues in cybersecurity risk management, and the development of systems that can intelligently defend themselves.

Lashon Booker is a senior principal scientist in MITRE's Artificial Intelligence and Autonomy Innovation Center. Dr. Booker received his PhD in Computer and Communication Sciences from the University of Michigan in 1982. Dr. Booker has published numerous technical papers in the areas of machine learning, probabilistic methods for uncertain inference, and distributed interactive simulation. He currently serves on the editorial board of the journal *Evolutionary Intelligence*. Dr. Booker has previously served as an associate editor of the journal *Adaptive Behavior*, on the editorial boards of the *Machine Learning* journal, the *Evolutionary Computation* journal, and the *Journal of Machine Learning Research*, and regularly serves on program committees for conferences in these areas. He has also served as a member of the Advisory Council for the Howard University Cybersecurity Research Center and the Steering Committee for the IAPR Technical Committee on Computational Forensics. He is a life member of the IEEE and a member of the Association for the Advancement of Artificial Intelligence.

Phillip Bridgham is a senior cognitive software engineer, technical fellow, and design-science researcher for Northrop Grumman Corporation. As principal investigator and researcher, Dr. Bridgham performs research efforts to tackle emerging challenges in cyber operations, cybersecurity, and cyber survivability. With a focus on shared situational understanding and human-machine teaming, he applies cognitive solution designs, model-based and semantic knowledge management, information fusion, complex event processing, and novel user interface designs. Dr. Bridgham holds a Doctor of Computer Science degree and is currently researching model-driven cognitive solutions to enhance cyber survivability.

Neil Briscombe is a senior principal engineer with over 30 years' experience directing Cybersecurity, Communications Simulation and Agent-Based research for UK Government, the European Commission (EC) and Industry. He is internationally known for communications and security-related decision support, situational awareness, and simulation systems, especially those incorporating various forms of Artificial Intelligence. Highlight projects related to the chapter on which some work is published include: TROOPER's automated Cybersecurity information sharing between various CSOC roles, SERSCIS' Cybersecurity simulation systems used to validate the EC's SWIM air traffic management Decision Support systems in degraded/attacked networks, and D3C's automated risk management of complex, mixed-trust, networked computer systems. Neil also led the UK contributions to Northrop Grumman's Cyber Academy Security Architecture course used by various US Government agencies and projects.

Lavinia Burski is currently a technology consultant at AECOM specializing in projects relating to connected autonomous vehicles and future transport solutions. She has previously worked within the Aerospace/Defense sector and was involved in the delivery of research projects and growth strategies related to autonomy and unmanned air vehicles. She has a PhD from Heriot Watt University in Edinburgh and a background in Computer Science. Her research involved analyzing specifications and checking their correctness in order to improve the safety of high integrity systems.

Marco Carvalho is a tenured professor in Computer Sciences and experienced researcher with a demonstrated history of working in the research industry and academia. He is an accomplished leader with executive level management experience in both industry and academia, currently serving as executive vice president and provost. He is a strong research professional skilled in cybersecurity, engineering, communications, AI and machine learning.

Samrat Chatterjee is a senior data/operations research scientist and team lead with the Data Sciences and Machine Intelligence Group at U.S. Department of Energy's Pacific Northwest National Laboratory (PNNL). He serves as PI/PM and key technical staff on national security and computational science research efforts in support of multiple sponsors (DHS, DOE, and DoD) and has over 12 years of experience in cyber and physical infrastructure network resilience modeling and simulation, risk and decision optimization under uncertainty, and graph and data analytics. Dr. Chatterjee is an affiliate professor at Northeastern University-Boston and has authored two books, four book chapters, and over 75 peer-reviewed journal articles, conference papers, and technical reports, and received multiple best paper and poster awards. He is a senior member of IEEE and a member of SRA and MORS.

Jeffrey S. Chavis is a member of the principal professional staff at the Johns Hopkins University Applied Physics Laboratory (APL) and teaches in Johns Hopkins University's Engineering for Professionals programs in both the software engineering and the information systems engineering. He serves as the vice chair for the Baltimore Chapter of the Association of Computer Machinery and is a senior member of IEEE. He was recognized with the Black Engineer of the Year Award (BEYA) for Professional Achievement at the BEYA STEM Global Competitiveness Conference in 2016. Dr. Chavis earned a BS in Electrical Engineering from Howard University, an MS in Electrical Engineering from the University of Maryland, College Park, and a DEng degree from Johns Hopkins University.

Jessie Y.C. Chen is a senior research scientist (ST) for Soldier Performance in Socio-Technical Systems with U.S. Army DEVCOM Army Research Laboratory. She received a PhD in Applied Experimental and Human Factors Psychology from University of Central Florida, an MA from University of Michigan (Ann Arbor), and a BA from National Tsing-Hua University in Taiwan. Her research interests include human-autonomy teaming, agent transparency, human-robot interaction, and human supervisory control. Dr. Chen is an associate editor for IEEE Transactions on Human-Machine Systems and IEEE Robotics and Automation – Letters. She also co-chairs the International Conference on Virtual, Augmented, and Mixed Reality (VAMR), which is a parallel conference under the International Conference on Human-Computer Interaction.

Mohan Baruwal Chhetri is a senior research scientist with the Distributed Systems Security Group at CSIRO's Data61, Australia, and an adjunct research fellow at Swinburne University of Technology. Prior to joining CSIRO, he worked as a lecturer at Swinburne University. He holds a Master of Information Technology (MIT) and a Doctor of Philosophy (PhD) from Monash University and Swinburne University of Technology, respectively. His main research interests are in developing intelligent solutions to facilitate decision support, decision automation, and decision optimization in cyber-physical-social ecosystems.

Satish Chikkagoudar is a senior researcher at the Navy's Center of Excellence in High Assurance Systems in Naval Research Laboratory (NRL). He has a decade of research experience tackling complex cybersecurity problems. At NRL, Dr. Chikkagoudar leads C5ISR projects in the areas of mission assurance, computer network defense, and infrastructure protection. Over the past decade, he has led and co-led several DoD funded mission assurance research efforts to model complex system dependencies and interdependencies. Dr. Chikkagoudar's research portfolio includes devising novel resilience methods for interdependent and interconnected infrastructure networks, especially in the presence of compound extreme events for a DoD SERDP effort.

Alan Colman is currently a research scientist in the Distributed Systems Security Group at CSIRO's Data61. He holds a PhD in Software Engineering (2007) and Master of Information Technology (MIT) in Human-Computer Interaction (1998) from Swinburne University of Technology, Australia. His research focuses on self-adaptive service-oriented systems and software architectures. He has more than 150 publications in top ranking journals and conference proceedings, which have over 2600 citations.

Hoa Khanh Dam is an associate professor in the School of Computing and Information Technology, University of Wollongong (UOW) in Australia. He is associate director for the Decision Systems Lab at UOW, heading its Software Analytics research program. His research interests lie primarily at the intersection of software engineering and artificial intelligence (AI). He develops AI solutions for project managers, software engineers, QA, and security teams to improve software quality/cybersecurity and accelerate productivity. His research also focuses on methodologies and techniques for developing AI/IoT-based autonomous systems.

Haley Dozier is a computer scientist at the Information Technology Laboratory (ITL) of the US Army Corps of Engineers, Engineering Research and Development Center (ERDC). Dr. Dozier received her PhD in Computational Science with an emphasis in Mathematics from the University of Southern Mississippi in 2019. There her research focused on numerical methods for time-dependent partial differential equations, specifically Krylov Subspace Spectral Methods. At the ITL, Dr. Dozier specializes in machine learning research as well as rapid response data analytics that provides state-of-the-art innovation for the defense community.

Martin Drasar is the head of Research and Innovation Group at Computer security incident response team of Masaryk University (CSIRT-MU) in Czechia. He received his PhD on the topic of behavioral detection of distributed dictionary attacks but later shifted his focus to autonomous cybersecurity. He is mainly interested in autonomous stealthy collaborative adversarial behavior. Recognizing the lack of suitable tools for complex simulations of cybersecurity interactions, needed for efficient training of autonomous cybersecurity agents, he led the development of the CYST simulation engine. This engine incorporates his experience with penetration testing, adversarial behavior, as well as defensive and analytic techniques, which he gained in the course of his work.

Ashutosh Dutta is a postdoctoral research associate in the Applied Statistics and Computational Modeling Group at the U.S. Department of Energy's Pacific Northwest National Laboratory (PNNL). His research interest focuses on developing autonomous frameworks for network security and resilience, cybersecurity automation, and control decision-optimization, applying formal modeling, deep learning, game theory, and reinforcement learning. Dr. Dutta earned his PhD in Computing and Information Science from UNC Charlotte in 2021. His research projects have been funded by DHS, NSA, NRL, NSF, and DOE. He has co-authored seven peer-reviewed conference articles and served as technical staff on multiple commercially launched R&D projects.

Thomas Eskridge is an associate professor in Computer Science and Human-Centered Design at the Florida Institute of Technology. He conducts research into human-aware artificial intelligence in the domains of human-agent teamwork, knowledge work, and cybersecurity in FIT's L3Harris Institute for Assured Information. He received bachelor and master's degrees in Computer Science from Southern Illinois University, Carbondale, and the PhD in Philosophy from Binghamton University. He has published over 80 papers and holds 18 patents.

Nate Evans PhD, CISSP, is the cyber program lead at Argonne National Laboratory and the Autonomous Intelligent Cyber Defense Agent International Working Group (AICA-IWG) president. Dr. Evans has a variety of patents and has won two R&D 100 awards for his work in proactive defense mechanisms. He received his PhD in Computer Engineering from Iowa State University. He is also an adjunct professor at the University of Chicago and Moraine Valley Community College and has spent time teaching for the African Institute of Mathematics and Sciences as part of the Next Einstein program. Dr. Evans also leads the Department of Energy's CyberForce Competition®.

Daniel Harkness performs cybersecurity research at Argonne National Laboratory, where he is the group lead for the Cyber Operations Research and Situational

Awareness group in the Strategic Security Sciences Division. He has spent over a decade helping to shape cyber threat information sharing and promoting automated solutions to cyber defense. His research interests include speeding up the creation of and increasing the usefulness of cyber threat intelligence, helping critical infrastructure operators ensure cybersecurity of their OT environments, and ensuring the safe use of artificial intelligence and machine learning technologies. He is a CISSP and holds BS degrees in Computer Engineering and Computer Science and an MS degree in Computer Engineering and Information Assurance from Iowa State University.

Charles Harold currently works as a research engineer at Swinburne University of Technology, where he is responsible for the implementation of novel concepts in resilient self-adaptive systems. Prior to joining Swinburne University, he worked as an engineer in physical metrology for one of the largest equipment retailers in Australia. He holds a bachelor degree in Mechatronics Engineering with first class Honors (2018) from Swinburne University of Technology, Australia. His research interests include self-adaptive systems, computability theory, and resilient decentralized algorithms for multi-agent decision-making.

Saad Sajid Hashmi received his PhD degree in Computer Science from Macquarie University (Australia, 2020), MSc degree in Computer and Software from Hanyang University (Rep. of Korea, 2015), and BSc degree in Software Engineering from GIK Institute (Pakistan, 2011). He is currently working as a research fellow at the School of Computing and IT, University of Wollongong (UOW). His current research interests include solving measurement-driven analytical problems in the domain of cyber resilience, human-centric privacy, machine learning, and self-adaptation.

Eric Holder is Human Factors professional who received his PhD in experimental psychology (Human Factors) from Texas Tech University in 2003 and his BA in Psychology (Engineering Psychology) from the University of Illinois at Urbana-Champaign in 1999. He specializes in qualitative and quantitative data collection and analysis, user-centered design and evaluation, human performance, and task and workload analysis. He has more than 18 years of experience in human-centered research, development, and design. His current position is with the U.S. Army Research Laboratory's Human Research and Engineering Directorate (HRED) stationed at Ft. Huachuca, AZ. Example projects include research on human autonomy teaming (HAT), explainable artificial intelligence, computer vision support to imagery analysis workflows, and advanced manufacturing of mission-adaptable 3D printed drones among other themes. He is also an officer and the program chair for the Human Factors and Ergonomics Society's Human-AI-Robot-Teaming Technical Group.

Barry Horowitz held the Munster Professorship in Systems Engineering at the University of Virginia, prior to his retirement in May 2021. His research interests include system architecture and design.

William Horsthemke PhD, CISSP, is a computer scientist at Argonne National Lab, currently focused on cyber resilience. His research has included computer-aided diagnosis of medical images, interactive visual simulation of military deployments, freight-train control systems, atmospheric data acquisition and analysis, and metropolitan-scale surveillance video distribution. He holds a PhD in Computer Science from DePaul University.

Christopher Kiekintveld is an associate professor at the University of Texas at El Paso (UTEP). His research is in the area of intelligent systems, focusing on multi-agent systems and computational decision-making. He is also interested in applications of artificial intelligence to security, trading agents, and other areas with the potential to benefit society. He received his PhD in 2008 from the University of Michigan for thesis work on strategic reasoning, including applications in designing a champion trading agent for the TAC SCM competition. He has authored more than 80 papers in peer-reviewed conferences and journals (e.g., AAMAS, IJCAI, AAAI, JAIR, JAAMAS, ECRA). He has received several best paper awards, the David Rist Prize, and an NSF CAREER award.

Kevin Kornegay received a BS degree in electrical engineering from Pratt Institute, Brooklyn, NY, in 1985, and the MS and PhD degrees in electrical engineering from the University of California at Berkeley in 1990 and 1992, respectively. He is currently the Eugene Deloatch Endowed Chair in IoT and director of the Cybersecurity Assurance and Policy (CAP) Center for Academic Excellence in the Electrical and Computer Engineering Department at Morgan State University in Baltimore, MD. His research interests include secure autonomy, trustworthy AI, hardware assurance, reverse engineering, secure embedded systems, side--channel analysis, and differential fault analysis. Dr. Kornegay serves or has served on the technical program committees of several international conferences, including the IEEE Symposium on Hardware Oriented Security and Trust (HOST), USENIX Security, the IEEE Physical Assurance and Inspection of Electronics (PAINE), and the ACM Great Lakes Symposium on VLSI (GLSVLSI). He is the recipient of multiple awards, including the NSF CAREER Award, IBM Faculty Partnership Award, National Semiconductor Faculty Development Award, and the General Motors Faculty Fellowship Award. He is currently a senior member of the IEEE, Eta Kappa Nu, Sigma Xi, and Tau Beta Pi engineering honor societies.

Alexander Kott serves as the U.S. Combat Capabilities Development Command Army Research Laboratory's chief scientist. Dr. Kott is also the army senior research scientist (ST) for Cyber Resilience. Prior to becoming the chief scientist of ARL, Dr. Kott was the chief of the Network Science Division at ARL. Earlier, Dr. Kott served as a program manager at Defense Advanced Research Projects Agency (DARPA). Kott's earlier positions included director of Research and Development at Carnegie Group, Pittsburgh, PA. Dr. Kott earned his PhD in Mechanical Engineering from the University of Pittsburgh, Pittsburgh, PA, in 1989, where he researched AI approaches to invention of complex systems. He received the

Secretary of Defense Exceptional Public Service Award. He published over 100 technical papers and served as the co-author and editor of 12 books.

Aron Laszka is an assistant professor in the Department of Computer Science at the University of Houston. His research interests revolve around the applications of artificial intelligence and machine learning to cybersecurity and societal-scale cyber-physical systems. His recent work has been funded by the National Science Foundation, the Department of Energy, and the Department of Transportation. Previously, he was a research assistant professor at Vanderbilt University from 2016 to 2017, and a postdoctoral scholar at the University of California, Berkeley, from 2015 to 2016. He graduated summa cum laude with a PhD in Computer Science from the Budapest University of Technology and Economics in 2014.

Kristen Liggett is a principal Human Factors engineer at the Air Force Research Laboratory's Human Performance Wing at Wright-Patterson AFB, OH. She has been conducting research for 35 years, determining how to apply the science of human factors design to a variety of Air Force applications. Her current focus is on the design and evaluation of information visualizations, user interfaces, and cognitive work aids for a range of cyber operators. Dr. Liggett received her BS in Human Factors Engineering (1989) from Wright State University, MS in Engineering Management (1994) from the University of Dayton, and PhD in Engineering (2000) from Wright State University.

Alexandre K. Ligo is a senior research scientist with the Risk and Decision Science team at the Army Engineer Research and Development Center and is also affiliated with the Engineering Systems Department at the University of Virginia. He holds a PhD in Engineering and Public Policy from Carnegie Mellon University, USA, an MS in Business from Fundação Getúlio Vargas, and a BS in Electrical Engineering (automation and control) from the University of São Paulo, Brazil. His research interests include policy and resilience of socio-economic and cyber-physical systems. He has over 20 years of experience in research and consulting with the US government, academia, and industry on COVID-19 economic and public health recovery, wireless communications, transportation, energy, and other areas.

Igor Linkov is a senior scientific technical manager with the U.S. Army Engineer Research and Development Center and adjunct professor of Engineering and Public Policy at Carnegie Mellon University. He has managed multiple risk and resilience management projects in the areas of environmental management, cybersecurity, critical infrastructure, climate change, pandemics, and systems vulnerability. He is currently developing resilience assessment and management approaches for infrastructure and cyber systems. He has published over 14 books and 250 peer-reviewed papers and book chapters. Dr. Linkov is Society for Risk Analysis Fellow and recipient of 2005 Chauncey Starr Award for exceptional contribution to Risk Analysis and 2014 Outstanding Practitioner Award.

Meiyi Ma is an assistant professor in the Department of Computer Science at the Vanderbilt University. Dr. Ma received PhD in Computer Science from the

University of Virginia. Her research interest lies at the intersection of machine learning, formal methods, and cyber-physical systems. Specifically, her work develops rigorous and robust AI by integrating formal methods and machine learning and applies new integrative solutions to build safe and reliable cyber-physical systems, with a focus on smart city and healthcare applications.

Mohammad Sujan Miah is a PhD student in Computer Science at the University of Texas at El Paso. His research interest lies between game theory and adversarial machine learning areas. His main research focuses on the application of game theory in cyber defense. Particularly, he has been exploring deceptive strategies using the game-theoretic model. He received a Bachelor of Science in Computer Science and Engineering from the University of Dhaka, Bangladesh. After graduation, he worked as a software engineer at a Samsung Electronic research center for a few years. He also had professional experience working as a software engineer at other leading software companies in Bangladesh.

Scott Musman is a principal engineer at the MITRE Corporation. He has a BSc(Hon) in Electrical Engineering from the University of Sussex in the UK and an MSc in Computer Science from Johns Hopkins University. In addition to working in other domains that usually involve decision support and complex decision making in uncertain environments, he has been working cybersecurity problems since the mid-1990s, acting as director of R&D for Integrated Management Services Inc. and head of Enterprise Security Research for Alphatech/BAE Systems-AIT. At MITRE he has focused on mission assurance, cyber mission impact assessment, response planning and employing quantitative methods for managing cybersecurity risk, resilience and return on investment decision-making. He has applied these skills to a variety of customer and research focused projects.

Azqa Nadeem is a PhD candidate and junior lecturer in the Intelligent Systems Department (Cyber Analytics Lab) at Delft University of Technology in the Netherlands. She has a master's in Computer Science with an emphasis on Data Science and Cybersecurity from Delft University of Technology, and a BS in Computer Science from the National University of Science and Technology, Pakistan. Her research interests include cyber-attack modeling, data analytics, network security, explainable machine learning, and sequence models. Applications include intrusion alert driven attack graph generation, and the behavioral profiling of malware samples.

Himanshu Neema is a research assistant professor of Computer Science at Vanderbilt University. Dr. Neema received MS and PhD in Computer Science from Vanderbilt University. Dr. Neema researches in model-based design of cyber-physical systems and their integrated co-simulations with hardware and humans. His other research interests include system-of-systems, secure and resilient systems, design automation, design space exploration, machine learning, constraint programming, planning and scheduling, smart cities, and transactive energy. Dr. Neema has 24 years of experience in research and development and has co-authored more than 75 publications. He is the creator of Cyber-Physical Systems Wind Tunnel – a model-based simulation integration and experimentation framework that has been transitioned to the US National Institute of Standards and Technology (NIST).

Steven Noel is a principal cybersecurity scientist at the MITRE Corporation. Before joining MITRE, Dr. Noel worked at George Mason University for 13 years, the Naval Surface Warfare Center for 8 years, and the University of Houston–Clear Lake for 5 years. His research interests include cyber situational understanding and resiliency optimization. He led the development of technology transitioned to numerous government organizations, Federally Funded Research and Development Centers (FFRDCs), and industry partners, and is the basis of two startup companies. He has published over 80 papers and holds 10 patents. He has PhD and MS degrees in Computer Science from the University of Louisiana at Lafayette and a BS degree in Electro-optics from the University of Houston–Clear Lake.

Arne Norlander is the founder and CEO of NORSECON, a consulting firm offering science and technology foresight, innovation leadership, and policy development. He holds a master's degree in Mechanical Engineering and Computerized Automation and a doctoral degree in Industrial Ergonomics from Linköping University, Sweden. In 2018 Dr. Norlander retired after over 30 years of service as an Air Force staff officer, Strategic Defence R&D program manager, senior scientist at the Swedish Defence Research Agency, and research director at the Swedish Defence Staff. Dr. Norlander is an IEEE senior member and an internationally recognized scientist with over 70 peer-reviewed publications. Dr. Norlander and his research fellows received the 2014 NATO Scientific Achievement Award. Dr. Norlander chairs the Science and Technology Committee of the Swedish Security and Defence Industry Association and serves as an independent expert for the European Commission and the European Defence Agency.

Kofi Nyarko is a tenured professor in the Department of Electrical and Computer Engineering at Morgan State University. He serves as the director of the Center for Equitable Artificial Intelligence and Machine Learning. He also serves as director of the Data Engineering and Predictive Analytics (DEPA) Research Lab. Under his direction, he has acquired and conducted research from the Department of Defense, Department of Energy, Army Research Laboratory, NASA, and Department of Homeland Security and Purdue University's Visual Analytics for Command, Control, and Interoperability Environments (VACCINE), a DHS Center of Excellence. Dr. Nyarko's expertise lies in automating complex systems through computer vision and machine learning as well as scientific/engineering simulation and visualization, predictive visual analytics, complex computer algorithm development, and computer network security. In 2020, he was a recipient of the US Black Engineer HBCU STEM Innovation Award for contributions to innovation that furthered economic development and entrepreneurship at Morgan State University. He also holds two US patents in the area of building occupant localization via visible light communication.

Aowabin Rahman is a postdoctoral research associate in the Optimization and Control Group, Electricity and Building Infrastructure Division (EIBD) at the

U.S. Department of Energy's Pacific Northwest National Laboratory (PNNL). His research efforts include data-driven approaches for resilient cyber-physical systems, scientific machine learning, and building energy modeling and simulation and have experience serving as technical staff on projects funded by DOE and NASA. Dr. Rahman earned his doctoral degree in Mechanical Engineering from University of Utah in 2018 and has co-authored 14 peer-reviewed journal articles, conference papers, and technical reports. He has received multiple awards, including a best paper award at ASME 2015 Energy Sustainability Conference.

Thiagarajan Ramachandran is an electrical engineer in the Optimization and Control Group at the U.S. Department of Energy's Pacific Northwest National Laboratory (PNNL). His research background is in control and optimization of distributed systems, and his current research interests are adaptive control and optimization, machine learning for control, co-design of cyber-physical systems, and cyber-security. He has co-authored over 25 peer-reviewed journal and conference papers and is a member of IEEE and INFORMS.

Toby J. Richer leads the Autonomous Cyber Operations Discipline at the Defence Science and Technology Group, Department of Defence, Commonwealth of Australia. Before joining the Defence Science and Technology Group, Dr. Richer conducted postdoctoral research in Particle Swarm Optimisation at Goldsmiths College, University of London. He received a Bachelor of Science (Mathematical and Computer Sciences) in 1999 and a Bachelor of Engineering (Computer Systems) in 2000 from the University of Adelaide. In 2005, he received a PhD in biologically inspired robotics from the University of South Australia. His current research interest is in the application of artificial intelligence techniques to the cybersecurity domain.

Ahmad Ridley is a senior applied research mathematician at the National Security Agency (NSA) Laboratory for Advanced Cybersecurity Research. He completed his PhD in Applied Mathematics from the University of Maryland, College Park (UMCP), in 2004, where he applied stochastic fluid and diffusion processes to the optimization of telecommunication queueing models. Since joining NSA, Dr. Ridley has performed research at the intersection of artificial intelligence (AI), stochastic optimization, reinforcement learning (RL), and cybersecurity. His current research interests include the development of RL-based, autonomous cyber-defense systems, where he collaborates with a cross-disciplinary group of academic, industry, and government researchers. Recently, Dr. Ridley has served on the organizing committees for several workshops focused on strengthening the collaboration between the AI and cybersecurity research communities, including the 2021 AI/ML for Cybersecurity (*SIAM Data Mining Conference*), 2021 Adaptive Cyber Defense (IJCAI), 2022 AI for Cyber Security (AAAI Conference), and 2022 Machine Learning for Cyber Defense (ICML Conference).

Shanto Roy joined the Resilient Networks and Systems Lab as a PhD student in the fall 2019 semester. His research interest is in Cybersecurity, Privacy, Data Analytics, Machine Learning, Cloud-IoT ecosystem, etc. Earlier, he earned his BSc and MSc in Information Technology from Jahangirnagar University, Bangladesh, in 2015 and 2016, respectively. Later, he served as a lecturer in the Department of Computer Science at the Green University of Bangladesh from 2016 to 2019. In the meantime, he contributed to several cloud-IoT ecosystem security and optimization projects. Currently, his research work focuses on Cyber Deception, an approach to minimize significant damages in an enterprise network by deceiving and misdirecting adversaries.

Nazia Sharmin is a computer science PhD student at the University of Texas at El Paso. She received an MS and a bachelor's degree in Physics from the University of Texas, El Paso, and the University of Dhaka, respectively. Her research interest includes cybersecurity and machine learning, particularly in the application of machine learning to the existing threat in the network.

Tim Sherburne is a research associate in the Intelligent System Division of the Virginia Tech National Security Institute. Sherburne was previously a member of the systems engineering staff at the University of Virginia supporting Mission Aware research through rapid prototyping of cyber-resilient solutions and model-based systems engineering (MBSE) specifications. Prior to joining the University of Virginia, he worked at Motorola Solutions in various Software Development and Systems Engineering roles defining and building mission critical public safety communications systems.

Maxwell Standen is a researcher at Defence Science and Technology Group and a PhD candidate at the University of Adelaide. Maxwell received a Bachelor of Engineering (Electrical and Electronic) with first class honors and a Bachelor of Mathematical and Computer Science from the University of Adelaide in 2018. In that same year, he joined Defence Science and Technology Group as a cybersecurity and AI researcher. Maxwell began his PhD candidature at the University of Adelaide in 2021. His current research interests include multiagent reinforcement learning and adversarial machine learning for the purpose of cybersecurity.

Vipin Swarup is a distinguished engineer for Cyber Resiliency at the MITRE Corporation. Currently, he leads MITRE's moonshot project in adaptive cyber resiliency. Previously, as chief scientist and innovation area leader for Cybersecurity, Dr. Swarup created MITRE's corporate cybersecurity research strategy and spawned numerous high-impact innovations including MITRE ATT&CK. His research interests include resiliency optimization, adversary emulation, and cybersecurity experimentation. He has led several large research projects as principal investigator and has published extensively. He received his bachelor's degree in Computer Science and Engineering from the Indian Institute of Technology Bombay, and his master's and doctoral degrees in Computer Science from the University of Illinois at Urbana-Champaign.

Janos Sztipanovits is currently the E. Bronson Ingram Distinguished Professor of Engineering at Vanderbilt University and John Von Neumann Professor of the Budapest University of Technology and Economy. He is founding director of the

Institute for Software Integrated Systems. Between 1999 and 2002, he worked as program manager and acting deputy director of DARPA Information Technology Office. He was member of the US Air Force Science Advisory Board between 2006 and 2010 and the Board on Army RDT&E, Systems Acquisition, and Logistics (BARSL) between 2019 and 2021. He co-authored two books and over 350 papers in model-based design, model-integrated computing, design automation for cyber-physical systems, security and autonomous systems. He is fellow of the IEEE and external member of the Hungarian Academy of Sciences.

Paul Theron PhD, in Computing Science (University of Glasgow), founded and was the first chair of the Autonomous Intelligent Cyber-defence Agents International Work Group (AICA IWG). He has been the co-lead of NATO's IST-152 Research Task Group on Intelligent, Autonomous and Trusted Agents for Cyber Defense and Resilience. He has been Thales' co-director of the Aerospace Cyber Resilience (Cyb'Air) research chair sponsored by the French Air Force, Dassault Aviation and Thales. He defined the Multi-Agent Systems Centric AICA Reference Architecture (MASCARA) and led its first implementations. He was also a member of the European Network and Information Security Agency's Permanent Stakeholders Group and a European Expert on behalf of EU's DG CNECT, EU's EASA and French DGAC, and EU's DG Joint Research Centre where he led the research group who produced the IACS Cybersecurity Certification Framework (ICCF) that inspired the EU's 2019 Cyber Act on cybersecurity certification.

Pierre Trepagnier is a member of the technical staff in the Cyber-Physical Systems Group at MIT Lincoln Laboratory. His current areas of research are concentrated in the interaction of the cyber and radio-frequency domains and in offensive cyber operations. In the context of the former research interest, he has been interested in applying artificial intelligence and machine learning techniques to the stressing environment of the tactical edge. Prior to that at Lincoln, he has worked on many projects centered around data-driven techniques for cyber vulnerability ranking and mitigation utilizing latent features. Prior to joining Lincoln Laboratory, Dr. Trepagnier had a long career in industry, including work in optics and machine vision. He holds 14 US patents.

Anton V. Uzunov leads the Intelligent Agents discipline within the Cyber and Electronic Warfare Division (Contested Communications Branch, IWC2) of Australia's Defence Science and Technology Group, which develops technologies for next-generation autonomous software systems operating in contested, edge-oriented computing environments. He holds a PhD in Computer Science, an honors degree in Pure Mathematics, and a bachelor degree in Maths and Computer Science, all from the University of Adelaide. His current research interests span the areas of software architecture, autonomic/self-adaptive computing for cyber resilience, and distributed AI/multiagent systems.

Sicco Verwer is an associate professor at Delft University of Technology in machine learning for cybersecurity. He is the head of the TU Delft Cyber Analytics Lab where he works on understandable AI for intrusion detection and software understanding. His team won several AI challenges including ones on learning software models, automated reverse engineering, and adversarial machine learning. He received many grants and awards for his research, including prestigious VENI and VIDI grants from NWO, and a test-of-time award from ECMLPKDD for his pioneering work on discrimination-free classification.

Samuel Sanders Visner is currently a tech fellow at the MITRE Corporation and vice chair of the Board of Directors of the Space Information Sharing and Analysis Center, focused on the security and resilience of Space Systems. He is also an adjunct professor of cybersecurity at Georgetown University and has led two cybersecurity businesses, ICF Cybersecurity and Resilience (2014–2017) and CSC Global Cybersecurity (2008–2014). Mr. Visner has also served as chief of Signals Intelligence Program at the National Security Agency (2001–2003) and is currently a member of the Intelligence Community Studies Board of the National Academy of Sciences and the Board of Directors of the Oak Ridge Associated Universities.

Bao Vo received the BSc, MSc, and PhD degrees from the University of Dalat (Vietnam), Asian Institute of Technology (Thailand), and University of New South Wales (Australia), respectively. He is the director of the Intelligent Software Systems Lab, Swinburne University of Technology, where he is an associate professor of Artificial Intelligence. His research interests include intelligent agent technologies and multiagent systems and automated negotiation. His current projects include autonomic-resilient agent-based systems and antifragility and agent-enabled technologies for smart grids and smart cities.

Allan Wollaber is a technical staff member in the Artificial Intelligence (AI) Technology Group at MIT Lincoln Laboratory. He is an accomplished computational scientist with a broad skill set in mathematical modeling, numerical analysis, artificial intelligence, and software development for high-performance computing applications. His current research interests lie in building evidence-driven, computationally tractable models and software technologies that enhance situation awareness, understanding, and decision-making under uncertainty, as well as the intersection of scientific computing and machine learning. At Lincoln, he has worked on multiple projects leveraging machine learning for cybersecurity, including classification, regression, semi-supervised learning, Bayesian inference, and genetic optimization problems.

Shouhuai Xu is the Gallogly Chair Professor in Cybersecurity, Department of Computer Science, University of Colorado Colorado Springs (UCCS). He pioneered a systematic approach, dubbed Cybersecurity Dynamics, to modeling, analyzing, and quantifying cybersecurity from a holistic perspective. His research has won several awards, including the 2019 worldwide adversarial malware classification challenge organized by the MIT Lincoln Lab. He co-initiated the International Conference on Science of Cyber Security (SciSec) and is serving as its Steering Committee Chair. He has served as program committee co-chair for several international conferences. He is/was an associate editor of three top-tier journals (IEEE TDSC, IEEE T-IFS, IEEE TNSE). More information about his research can be found at https://xu-lab.org.

Shanchieh Jay Yang is a professor in the Department of Computer Engineering and director of Global Outreach for Global Cybersecurity Institute at Rochester Institute of Technology. He received his MS and PhD degrees in Electrical and Computer Engineering from the University of Texas at Austin in 1998 and 2001, respectively. His research focuses on cyber-attack modeling, machine learning, and simulation to enhance cyber situational awareness and anticipatory cyber defense. He was a NSF Trusted CI fellow in 2019 and a NSF Trusted CI TTP fellow in 2020. He was recognized in 2019 with IEEE Region 1 Outstanding Teaching in an IEEE Area of Interest Award – for outstanding leadership and contributions to cybersecurity and computer engineering education.

Chapter 1
Autonomous Intelligent Cyber-defense Agent: Introduction and Overview

Alexander Kott

1 Introduction

This book is based on the premise that the future of cyber-defense and cyber resilience will depend largely on autonomous, artificially intelligent (AI) agents. Such an agent will reside on a system that includes one or more computing devices and be responsible for defending the system from cyber compromises. If a compromise occurs, the agent will then be responsible for response and recovery of the system, usually autonomously. To refer to such a class of agents, we use the term Autonomous Intelligent Cyber-defense Agent (AICA). In this book, we explore how AICA will be designed and how it will operate.

Experience shows that even well-protected computing systems are likely to be successfully attacked and infiltrated by hostile malware. There is no reason to believe this will be any different in the future. Today, when a compromise occurs, response, mitigation and recovery depend largely on human cyber-defenders. This approach is becoming increasingly untenable. With an ever-growing number of computerized, automated and even autonomous systems in our society, human-based cyber-defense must be replaced by autonomous cyber-defenders such as AICA.

Similarly to the current generation of cyber-defense tools, AICA will detect malicious signatures, patterns and anomalies; it will also classify, characterize and diagnose what it observes within its environment, traffic and host. However, unlike the current generation of cyber-defense tools, AICA is a doer, not merely a watcher. It will have to plan and then decisively execute responses to attacks and perform recovery actions.

A. Kott (✉)
US Army DEVCOM Army Research Laboratory, Adelphi, MD, USA
e-mail: alexander.kott1.civ@army.mil

© The Author(s), under exclusive license to Springer Nature Switzerland AG 2023
A. Kott (ed.), *Autonomous Intelligent Cyber Defense Agent (AICA)*, Advances in
Information Security 87, https://doi.org/10.1007/978-3-031-29269-9_1

AICA will be an active fighter in maintaining a system's resilience (Kott & Linkov, 2019) against cyber threats. This means that the agent's capabilities should include a significant degree of autonomy and intelligence for the purposes of rapid response to a compromise – either incipient or already successful – and rapid recovery that aids the resilience of the overall system. Often, the response and recovery efforts need to be undertaken in absence of any human involvement, and with intelligent consideration of the risks and ramifications of such efforts.

The cyber-defense technology community is beginning to recognize the potential and even necessity of autonomous, AI-supported cyber-defenses. In particular, the vision of AICA is a product of a NATO-based research project that took place from 2016 to 2020. The research yielded an AICA Reference Architecture (Kott et al., 2018). Later, an international working group formed to continue work on AICA (see https://www.aica-iwg.org/). The authors of this book are grateful to the AICA research community.

In the remainder of this chapter, we discuss what it means for AICA to be an agent, what environments that agent will face, what roles the agent will perform, how these roles will be supported by the internal architecture of the agent, and the inevitable concerns regarding the risks and trust associated with such an autonomous technology. The chapter concludes with a preview of each chapter of the book.

2 AICA as an Agent

We call AICA an agent. What does it mean? The term "agent" refers to software or collection of software that resides and operates on one or more computing devices, perceives and comprehends its environment, and plans and executes purposeful actions on the environment (and itself) to achieve the agent's goals.

Autonomy, complete or partial, is an important characteristic of an agent. AICA will have to be capable of autonomous planning and execution of complex, multi-step activities. These activities will pursue the key goal of the agent – defeating or degrading malware while anticipating and minimizing any resulting side effects. It will have to be capable of adversarial reasoning (Kott & McEneaney, 2006) to battle against thinking, adaptive malware. To defend itself against the malware, AICA should keep itself and its actions as undetectable as possible, and thus will have to use deceptions and camouflage.

The autonomy of such an agent is a necessity, not luxury. Today, much of cyber-defense is based on remote monitoring and remote mitigation and recovery (Kott & Arnold, 2013). However, today's reliance on human cyber-defenders, whether local or remote, will be untenable in the future for a number of reasons.

One reason is the growing scarcity of human cyber-experts to defend systems, either remotely or onsite. This is further exacerbated by the proliferation of robots, such as self-driving cars, where a local cyber-defender is unlikely to be found by definition – these systems are intended to operate with little or no human involvement (Kott & Stump, 2019). There is an ever-growing number of critically needed software systems, all of which present tempting targets for malicious cyber actors and require cyber-defenders in ever-growing – unsupportable – quantities.

Remote cyber-defense, i.e., remote monitoring, mitigation and recovery, is further complicated by the growing sophistication of malware. One of the first actions sophisticated malware may do is degrade or spoof the communications of a system that uses a remote monitoring center. This means that the system must possess local defenses that do not depend on communicating with the remote service. If a local human defender is not available, as will most often be the case, the system will need to rely on a local autonomous agent, AICA.

Let's take a more detailed look at the features and characteristics that should be exhibited by any autonomous intelligent agent (Théron et al., 2018). These are helpful as we consider the comparable features and characteristics of AICA.

A proper agent should be assigned a specific mission, with corresponding goals and constraints. It should possess the key competencies to execute that mission, such as the ability to perceive the environment in which the agent is deployed, detect attacks, plan and assess the required countermeasures, and adapt rapidly to successes or failures when executing its plan.

The agent should be proactive and autonomous, which means it should not rely on an external source to initiate or control its activity. On its own, the agent should be able to assess the situation, and make decisions and execute actions, without being controlled by another program or a human operator. To do so, the agent typically needs a base of knowledge, memories of what the agent has done before, and in many cases, even a degree of self-learning from experience.

Safety is another important characteristic. The agent should not harm the friendly systems it defends. For that, the agent should be able to anticipate the ramifications of its actions and attempt to minimize the risk of causing harm. In exceptional cases, considerations of safety may require the agent to contact a remote human controller, activate a fail-safe mode or even self-destruct when no other possibility is available. Similarly, the agent should be trustworthy, e.g., it will not deceive other friendly agents or human operators.

Finally, let's consider robustness and resilience to various threats and abnormal circumstances. Doing this requires the agent to possess a means of defending itself and recovering its own operations when degraded by a threat.

To achieve all of these characteristics, should an agent be a monolithic piece of software? That can be one implementation option. In general, however, an agent's modules should be distributed over multiple processes or devices, or implemented as a team of agents or subagents.

If implemented as a multi-agent system, a number of additional considerations must be addressed. These include the manner in which the multiple, potentially heterogenous agents are coordinated, self-organize, admit (or not) new members and deal with emergent behaviors.

3   AICA's Environment

AICA operates within its environment, i.e., everything that surrounds the agent and that the agent can perceive. This includes the computer hardware and software where the agent operates; the physical entity controlled by the computers, e.g., a self-driving car; the malware; the humans who communicate with the agent or with surrounding hardware and software; and other agents that the agent can find and with whom it can communicate.

To make our discussion more concrete and focused, let's consider a single physical item or platform, such as a vehicle or industrial robot, with one or more computers residing on the platform connected to sensors and actuators. We assume that, at any given time, one or more computers are compromised by malware. The compromise is either established as a fact or is suspected. We further assume that, in general, the platform's communications with any remote operators or a monitoring center is compromised as well; malware has disabled or is spoofing the communications.

As mentioned earlier, with compromised communications, conventional centralized cyber-defense is often infeasible. Here, by "conventional centralized cyber-defense," we mean an architecture where local sensors send cyber-relevant information to a central location where highly capable cyber-defense systems and human analysts detect the presence of malware and initiate corrective actions remotely. It is unrealistic to expect that the human cyber-defenders will reside on the platform, for example, a self-driving vehicle, or that they would have the necessary skills or time available to perform cyber-defense functions locally on the vehicle even if present.

Furthermore, many situations demand much faster responses than human responders may be able to provide. Criminals or irresponsible pranksters are able to take control of cars traveling at high speed or planes in the air, which may constitute a mortal threat to the vehicle's passengers and others interacting with those systems. In such cases, waiting for a human incident response team will not do. Instead, such systems need an onboard intelligent autonomous agent capable of taking the necessary response and recovery actions, with response times on the order of seconds or even less (Kott & Théron, 2020). In short, AICA operates in an environment where it must act autonomously.

But how did AICA find itself in this environment? We assume here that the agent resides on a computer where it was originally installed by a human controller or an authorized process. We do envision a possibility that an agent may move itself (or a replica of itself) to another computer. Such propagation is assumed to occur only under exceptional and well-specified conditions, and takes place only within a friendly network – from one friendly computer to another friendly computer. Granted, this type of action might seem very close to the controversial idea of a "good virus" (Muttik, 2016). However, AICA is not a virus, because it does not propagate except under explicit conditions within authorized and cooperative nodes.

4 AICA's Roles

Having considered the demanding environment of AICA, let's explore its roles within that environment.

Unlike most of today's cyber-defense tools, AICA is a doer, not merely a watcher (Kott & Théron, 2020). Most of today's tools are largely watchers: they monitor traffic and events; check packets and files; detect malicious signatures, patterns and anomalies; and classify and characterize what they watch. In some respects, such tools can also be classified as doers: they issue alerts, stop suspicious packets and connections, and remove or quarantine suspected malware.

Still, such tools are very constrained and limited in what they do. In the face of a sophisticated and ongoing attack by a capable, stealthy malware, today's tools do little to plan, assess options, and execute a sophisticated, multi-step response.

Further, when malware succeeds in degrading a friendly system, today's tools do little to plan and execute recovery activities. The critical activities of response and recovery after a successful cyber-attack are left to the human cyber analysts, incident responders and system administrators. As just discussed, these human actors are unlikely to be available in the environments where AICA operates. AICA has to perform these activities, and do so autonomously.

Granted, AICA has to be a competent watcher too. The agent must be able to observe the state and activities within the system it is asked to defend. Using these observations, AICA must be able to diagnose the situation, understand what is happening and project the future, i.e., the likely actions of the malware and how those actions would affect the state of the system.

Having assessed the situation and formed a vision of anticipated future states if the malware is unopposed, AICA must create a plan of action, or generally, several alternative plans. All such plans have a degree of uncertainty, and AICA should anticipate possible adaptations of its plans as well.

With one or more plans available, the agent should assess the risks and benefits involved (Kott et al., 2017) and make its decisions accordingly. Needless to say, all this deliberation must be performed very rapidly. In cases when time is lacking and immediate action is needed, instead of engaging in such reasoning, AICA may have to resort to simple but fast "condition-action" rules.

Once a plan is selected, AICA executes the actions. Some of the actions might be benign, e.g., gathering additional information. Other actions, however, may have destructive impacts, such as destroying, degrading or quarantining certain software and data – autonomously – or inhibiting certain actions of the malware. This may involve stopping or starting certain processes, installing or reinstalling software, or initiating or terminating connections. In executing such actions, AICA must observe the specified rules of engagement and continually assess risks (Ligo et al., 2021a, b).

One of the major risks facing AICA is being destroyed by the enemy malware. In the case where the enemy malware knows that an agent is likely to be present on the computer, the malware will seek to find and destroy the agent. Therefore, a key responsibility of AICA is self-defense and self-preservation. The agent must possess techniques and mechanisms for maintaining a certain degree of stealth, camouflage and concealment. More generally, the agent must take measures that reduce the probability that the enemy malware would detect it.

On the other hand, AICA may find it advantageous to communicate with other friendly agents that might reside on other computers and systems. For example, AICA may need to ask another agent to terminate a certain connection or send software to AICA. Such a collaboration entails risks because it potentially reveals the presence and activities of AICA to the malware. In cases where the communications may be impaired or observed by the malware, the agent may have to eschew collaboration and operate alone. Nevertheless, in general, the agent should be able to collaborate with other friendly agents when a need arises and conditions permit. Thus, collaboration schemes and negotiation mechanisms are needed for that.

Finally, a friendly agent with a particularly important role is the human operator. Typically, these operators would be the personnel of a remote operations center who deploy, monitor and control AICA, to the extent that communication channels permit. The agent, whenever requested and when conditions permit, reports its situation, activities and related data to the external controller. This information helps the controller to make inferences about the trustworthiness of the agent, measure the effectiveness of the agent (Kott & Linkov, 2021) and determine whether AICA needs to receive updates.

More generally, we envision a degree of role distribution between AICA and a remote cyber-defense control center (Kott et al., 2021). Their roles are not incompatible and may coexist. Both have their strong and weak points. As discussed, relying primarily on remote monitoring and response may be risky or impossible if the sophisticated malware takes over the communication channels. If remote mitigation of a cyber compromise cannot be provided rapidly, the compromised system will find itself at extreme risk. This is when AICA is necessary, even if it is less capable then the comprehensive cyber-defense capabilities of a competent remote center.

Similarly, reliance only on AICA comes with its own risks. For example, if the malware is able to overcome the capabilities – inevitably limited – of AICA, external intervention will be a necessity. Such coexistence should be carefully orchestrated. In particular, a clear protocol should be established for the handover of responsibilities between AICA and the remote center, and back. If both need to operate simultaneously, a coordination protocol should ensure that their respective actions do not produce undesirable interference.

5   AICA's Architecture[1]

The sophisticated roles and responsibilities of AICA demand appropriate internal functions. Let's consider the functional capabilities the agent must possess within its architecture (Kott et al., 2018; Théron et al., 2020). Figure 1.1 depicts the functional components of the agent.

The AICA Reference Architecture (Kott et al., 2018; Théron et al., 2020) defines five main functions:

- Sensing and world state identification
- Planning and action selection
- Collaboration and negotiation
- Action execution
- Learning and knowledge improvement

Sensing and world state identification allows a cyber-defense agent to acquire data from the environment in which it operates as well as from itself in order to understand the current state of the world. This sensing and world state identification function relies upon the "world model," "current world state and history," "sensors" and "world state identifier" components of the functional architecture. Current world state descriptors are captured by the agent's sensing function, while the world state identification draws from (1) processed current world state descriptors and (2) learned world state patterns. Having identified a problematic current world state

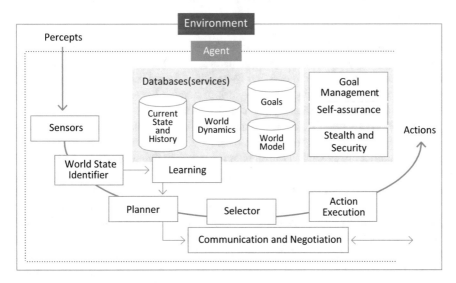

Fig. 1.1 Functional components of an agent

---

[1]This section is based in part on a book chapter. Théron et al. (2020).

pattern (e.g., a cyber compromise), the world state identification function triggers the planning and action selection function.

The planning and action selection function allows AICA to formulate one or several action proposals and then submit them to the action selector. The latter decides on the action or a set of actions to execute in order to resolve the problematic world state pattern previously identified by the world state identifier function. This function relies upon the "world dynamics" and should include knowledge about the "actions and effects," "goals," "planner-predictor" and "action selector" components of the functional architecture. The planning function operates based on (1) the problematic current world state pattern and (2) a repertoire of response actions. The action selector function operates based on (1) the proposed response plans, (2) the agent's goals and (3) execution constraints and requirements, such as the environment's technical configuration. The proposed response plan is analyzed by the action selector in the light of the agent's current goals as well as any execution constraints and requirements. The proposed response plan is then trimmed of elements that do not fit the situation at hand and augmented with prerequisite, preparatory, precautionary or post-execution complementary actions. The action selector thus produces an executable response plan, which is then submitted to action execution, after collaboration and negotiation if needed.

The collaboration and negotiation function enables AICA to (1) exchange information with other agents or a central cyber command and control (C2), for instance, when one of the agent's functions cannot reach satisfactory conclusions on its own and (2) negotiate with its partners the details of a consolidated conclusion or result. Collaboration and negotiation operate based on (1) the outgoing data sets sent to other agents or to a central C2, (2) incoming data sets received from other agents or a central cyber C2, and (3) the agents' own knowledge (i.e., produced through its function of learning and knowledge improvement). When an agent (including possibly a central cyber C2) develops conclusions, it shares them with other (selected) agents, usually including the one that issued the original request for collaboration. Once this response is received, the network of involved agents starts negotiating to develop a consistent, satisfactory set of conclusions.

The action execution function enables AICA, based on the action selector's executable response plan, to monitor its execution and its effects, and provides the means to adjust the execution of the plan (or possibly dynamically adjust the plan) as needed. This function relies upon the "goals" and "action execution" components of the functional architecture. Action execution includes four subfunctions: (1) action effector, (2) execution monitoring, (3) effects monitoring and (4) execution adjustment. Taking into account the environment's technical configuration, the action effector function executes each planned action within the executable response plan in the scheduled order. The execution monitoring function uses the executable response plan in concert with plan execution feedback to monitor each action's execution status. Any status apart from "done" triggers the execution adjustment function. The effects monitoring function operates on the basis of the executable response plan and environment's change feedback, leading to execution adjustment as needed. Should warning signs be identified by one of the two previous functions, the execution adjustment function will either adapt the actions' implementation to circumstances or modify the plan.

The learning and knowledge improvement function allows AICA to use its experience in order to improve progressively its efficiency. This function relies upon the learning and goals modification components of the functional architecture. The learning function operates based (1) feedback data from the agent's functions and (2) feedback data from the agent's actions. This function analyzes the reward function of the agent (the distance between goals and achievements) and their impact on the agent's knowledge database. Results are fed to the knowledge improvement function. The knowledge improvement function merges the results (propositions) from the learning function with the current elements of the agent's knowledge.

Like any reference architecture, this proposed AICA Reference Architecture is merely a step toward a structured solution and a set of common vocabulary with which to discuss possible implementations. Actual implementations of AICA may differ dramatically. Several chapters in this book describe case studies of implementations of AICA-like agents and illustrate the diversity of possible approaches.

6 AICA's Risk and Trust

The architecture discussed in the previous section prompts at least two observations. One is that it is necessarily complex. In a complex software system, much can go wrong and ensuring highly reliable operation of such a system is difficult and expensive. Second, the entire architecture is aimed at actively doing things, i.e., making changes in AICA's environment. We already mentioned that in order to fight the malware that has infiltrated the friendly computer, the agent may have to take destructive actions, such as deleting or quarantining certain software. Granted, such destructive actions should be carefully controlled by the appropriate rules of engagement and are allowed only on the computer where the agent resides. Needless to say, developers of AICA will strive to design its actions and planning capability to minimize the risk to the system (Ligo et al., 2021a, b).

Nevertheless, in general, such risk cannot be fully eliminated. Nothing can guarantee that AICA will always preserve the availability or integrity of the functions and data of the computer the agent is trying to defend. It is not entirely improbable that the agent will "break" the friendly computer, disable important friendly software, or corrupt or delete important data. AICA's actions may have harmful consequences of a functional, safety, security or ethical nature.

To be sure, this is nothing new. Every technology comes with risk. Any artifact may cause unintended harm. The reason to accept AICA, as with any technology, is for the users to determine that the advantages of using the technology outweigh the risk that comes with it. In case of AICA the risk that the agent's action will harm a friendly computer must be balanced against the losses that might occur if the agent does not act.

This is a not fully comforting answer. Can we do better than that? Can we find other ways to manage the risk? Well, a natural reaction to a risky machine is to have a human supervise the machine. Perhaps, we should create a human-AICA team, where the human could intervene in AICA's operations as needed? Unfortunately, this is unlikely to produce positive outcomes.

Let's consider an analogy. Given AICA is an autonomous agent, a suitable analogy is an autonomous, self-driving car. When a dangerous situation arises on a road, e.g., a pedestrian suddenly appears in the middle of a street, should the human passenger take over the controls and try to swerve around? Or should the human let the autonomous driving system execute its collision-avoidance routine? The answer probably depends on who is more likely to avoid the collision – the human or autonomous agent. Chances are quite high that the human – who has been driving less since buying the autonomous car – is not as alert or capable as the autonomous driving system. If so, the best course of action (COA) is for the human not interfere with the agent's driving.

The case of cyber-defense is even more unfavorable for the human. Car driving, after all, was initially specifically designed for human drivers. It has become relatively natural for humans to drive a car. Many are quite good at driving. In the world of cyber-defense, little if anything was designed for humans. The extremely high volume of information, the extremely short durations of events and so on are inconsistent with human cognitive abilities. Thus, the chances of a human successfully interfering with an autonomous decision of AICA are even lower than in case of a human driver taking over the controls of an autonomous car.

Still, other ways exist for a human to influence AICA. At the stage of AICA's software development, human designers determine the goals of the agent and populate the knowledge base of the agent. They decide on decision algorithms and decision criteria. If AICA's knowledge base is formed through machine learning, human designers select the data samples for training and guide the learning process. At the validation stage, human developers create an ensemble of test cases, assess the correctness of the agent's behavior and measure its effectiveness (Ligo et al., 2021a, b). In these multiple ways, humans shape the behavior of AICA before it begins its actual operation.

Then, once AICA is placed in operation, human supervisors can observe the agent's behavior and determine whether its behavior meets the desired criteria. If the behavior needs adjustments, a human supervisor can take action. As already discussed, it would be unwise to intervene into the agent's fast-paced operation directly. Instead, the human supervisor, in a deliberate fashion, can modify the goals, criteria and constraints of AICA, or offer additional examples for the agent's learning process. All this can be done without taking AICA offline, while it continues its operations.

Trust is closely related to risk. Whenever a technological artifact is perceived as associated with risk, human users have difficulties trusting the artifact. Undoubtedly, human users will build their trust of AICA only gradually, by observing its behavior over a period of time, in multiple events. As they observe the agent's behavior, they will interpret its behavior, i.e., try to determine what exactly AICA did and for what reasons. Eventually, the human users will accumulate enough evidence that AICA appears to do the right things, for the right reasons. AICA's designers can help this trust-building process by providing the agent a means to communicate to the human users what the agent is doing, the decision process involved, and the information used as inputs into its decision and eventual actions (Linkov et al., 2020).

7 Preview of This Book

The next chapter "Alternative Architectural Approaches" describes an approach to AICA and considerations about the rationale of the design of AICA's architecture. Further, the Multi Agent System Centric AICA Reference Architecture (MASCARA) is presented with regard to the three layers of its definition: general, detailed and technical. From the early prototyping experience, lessons for the future are drawn.

Next, the "Perception of Environment" chapter describes how AICA continually perceives (obtains information about) its environments (network, host computer(s) hardware and software, broader systems such as a vehicle on which AICA resides, etc.). Perception in AICA is best considered a pipeline consisting of four main parts: physical sensors, logical sensors, transformers and the world state. This chapter addresses the complexity surrounding its perception, providing guidelines and state-of-the-art examples.

Because AICA exists to fight against a cyber-adversary, it needs a means to perceive/sense the presence and characteristics of hostile agents (malware) and their actions and effects, as well as recognize when appropriate active sensing may be engaged. The "Perception of Threat" chapter discusses key use cases and methods of obtaining threat intelligence, fingerprinting, characterizing threats, passive threat detection, anomalous activity detection, the use of honeypots and threat hunting.

Given the perception of its environments and threats, AICA attempts to assess and characterize the situation. In "Situational Understanding and Diagnostics," we discuss situational understanding (SU) inputs from sensors, the dependencies of SU on the knowledge base, updating the knowledge base as needed for SU, and logical formalisms supporting knowledge and reasoning. We also discuss the means of using abstraction and generalization, through which agents can better manage model complexity, using illustrative examples.

The "Learning about the Adversary" chapter considers how an agent can gain insights about the behaviors and intents of the adversary (human-directed attack or automated malware). We argue that the evolving nature of cyber-adversary tactics and techniques and system configurations and vulnerabilities makes it difficult for autonomous agents to rely on supervised learning or, in general, much a priori expert knowledge. We review alternative approaches and recent advancements in the field.

Having examined the perception of the environment and threat, and the overall assessment of the situation, in "Response Planning," we discuss how AICA plans a COA, or multiple COAs, intended to defeat the malware and/or minimize the malware's damage to the system. We explore ways to include an adversary model into the defender's decision making, to understand how observations differ from the known adversary model and hence require a different type of response than what worked last time. We also consider the challenges of integrating host-based response systems and network-based systems.

Even when the threat has been neutralized or is otherwise no longer active, AICA must attempt to return the system to adequate working condition. In the "Recovery Planning" chapter, we introduce and demonstrate a recovery planning system that evaluates the impact of system degradation and generates COAs for recovery. The system evaluates these COAs through integrated heterogeneous simulations that account for unavoidable uncertainty and formally verify recovery COAs with confidence guarantees.

Given that hostile malware will give high priority to finding and disabling AICA, AICA must stay as undetectable as possible. In "Cyber Camouflage," we review the common techniques of adversarial reconnaissance, and methods for formally modeling reconnaissance activities and belief formation. We discuss common techniques such as honeypots, deceptive or obfuscated traffic, and deceptive responses to probes, and then propose new techniques based on adversarial machine learning to create more effective deceptive objects.

The "Adaptivity and Antifragility" chapter stresses the need to make cyber-defense agents adaptive and antifragile. A resilient system can survive attacks by autonomously adapting and managing its own functionality. An antifragile system can also enhance its capabilities and become more resilient as a result of endogenous and exogenous stressors. We present a concrete example of a self-improving system and middleware framework for antifragility.

When conditions permit, AICA may collaborate with other friendly agents. Conflicts may arise due to incompatible plans and objectives of the agents. Negotiations to jointly identify and execute a COA require building consensus under distributed and/or decentralized multi-agent settings with information uncertainties. The "Negotiation and Collaboration" chapter presents algorithmic approaches for enabling the collaboration and negotiation function. The strengths and limitations of potential techniques are identified, and a representative example is illustrated.

Humans are a special type of friendly agent, with special privileges. When conditions permit, human operators will oversee, approve or modify the actions of AICA. In the "Human Interactions" chapter, we explore knowledge acquisition to understand the user groups and use cases, as well as iterative design and feedback with users. Human trust in intelligent systems can be supported by transparency-based approaches, using metrics/frameworks to assess system transparency and explanation effectiveness.

The performance characteristics of AICA, including quality of defenses, resilience, reliability, probability of undesirable effects, etc., must be tested in measured in a consistent, quantitative and rigorous manner, under a broad range of conditions. The "Testing and Measurements" chapter draws upon real-world examples to present potential metrics for performance; reviews existing work in the field, e.g., several testbeds for testing autonomous cyber defense algorithms; and offers a detailed case study.

In "Deployment and Operation," we analyze several scenarios to consider the types of threats such agents might be expected to encounter and what actions would potentially be beneficial for them to take in response. These scenarios include an unmanned automated system (UAS, or "drone"), solo or as part of a swarm; an electrical distribution grid; an orbital or deep-space communication network; and a large-scale computational array (such as offered by a cloud vendor or high-performance computing).

Operations that involve a significant number of AICA-like agents comprise complex, intractable and risk-laden tasks. The "Command in AICA-intensive Operations" chapter explores how such operations would be commanded. A central part of managing these challenges is recognizing and accepting complexity. Additionally, success in AICA-intensive operations requires highly capable SU. Finally, the turbulent environment in which these units operate stresses the need for organizational agility, ensuring internal operations match the degree of turmoil in external environments.

AICA is essentially a robot that, by necessity, must be given a chain saw. As such, it presents a host of risks. In the "Risk Management" chapter, we argue that human intervention in real time during AICA operation may increase the harm. We propose other options for human-centered strategies that allow humans to shape AICA behavior before it chooses a COA: providing labeled data for supervised learning of AICA, offering a choice of machine learning algorithms, and/or devising algorithmic rules that constrain AICA actions.

Active autonomous systems like AICA face a host of policy issues, ethical concerns, governance concerns, societal impact concerns and legal concerns. In the "Policy Issues" chapter, we explore how the ever-changing concepts of cyber-defense reflect changing policies and review existing policies, including wartime policy considerations with examples. We note that, in some cases, AICA may fall into the "gray zone" of policy and explore how this relates to US national and economic security policy, consumer privacy and matters of constitutional protections.

In "Development Challenges," we divide development challenges into two areas: engineering and research. The engineering ecosystem has six components: design, implementation, individual test and certification, composition, composite test and certification, and deployment. The research ecosystem includes models, architectures, mechanisms, testing and certification, operations, and social, ethical, and legal aspects. We show connections between these two ecosystems by describing how tackling challenges in the research ecosystem would contribute to tackling the challenges encountered when engineering AICAs.

The "Case Study A: The AICAproto21 Prototype" chapter describes a prototype system that encompasses a number of AICA features. This prototype was built using open-source software components in a containerized manner to allow for a quick time-to-completion with maximum flexibility for future capabilities. It demonstrated the ability of the agent to respond to an indicated attack with a defensive action. The chosen approach provided an easy-to-scale solution that is likely to work well cross-platform.

In chapter, "Case Study B: Tactical Edge Agent," we focus on aspects characteristic of deploying agents at the "tactical edge." Here the environment for an AI cyber-defense agent is vastly different from its classic habitat, the enterprise-scale network. We discuss our approach to overcoming the challenges of austere conditions, low availability of computing power, poor to nonexistent connectivity to enterprise-scale resources, and porous borders between the cyber domain (as conventionally considered) and the physical and electronic warfare (EW) domains.

A different type of resilience-support agents called sentinels are described in the "Case Study C: The Sentinel Agents" chapter. A sentinel agent is connected to the system interfaces from which it receives the data to support its monitoring function. The sentinel then conditions the diverse sets of collected data so that they can be integrated and analyzed, and performs the specific analyses required for detecting a cyber attack and determining the location within the protected system that is under attack.

8   Summary and Conclusions

AICA is an agent, i.e., a software that resides and operates on one or more computing devices, perceives and comprehends its environment, and plans and executes purposeful actions on the environment (and on itself) to achieve the agent's goals. AICA is local to a system and is responsible for defending the system from cyber compromises. If a compromise occurs, the agent is responsible for response and recovery of the system, usually autonomously. The autonomy of the agent is a necessity because of the growing scarcity of human cyber-experts who could defend systems, either remotely or onsite, and because sophisticated malware may degrade or spoof the communications of the system using a remote monitoring center. The agent can be distributed over multiple processes or devices, or could be implemented as a team of agents or subagents.

AICA observes the state and activities within the system it is asked to defend, diagnoses the situation and projects the future state of the system. AICA creates a plan of action, assesses the risks and benefits involved in the plans of actions and makes its decisions accordingly. Because AICA is responsible self-defense and self-preservation, it must practice stealth, camouflage and concealment. An AICA Reference Architecture has been proposed and defines five main functions: sensing and world state identification, planning and action selection, collaboration and negotiation, action execution and learning and knowledge improvement.

As AICA is intended to make changes in its environment, there is a risk that the agent's action could harm a friendly computer. This risk must be balanced against the losses that might occur if the agent does not act. To manage the risk, when able to communicate with the agent, the human supervisor could modify the goals, criteria and constraints of AICA or offer additional examples to improve the agent's learning process.

New technologies are often perceived as being associated with risk, thus human users have difficulties trusting the artifact. AICA's designers can help the trust-building process by providing the agent with a means to communicate to the users what the agent is doing, the decision process involved, and the information it used as inputs into its decision and eventual actions.

References

Kott, A., & Arnold, C. (2013). The promises and challenges of continuous monitoring and risk scoring. *IEEE Security and Privacy, 11*(1), 90–93.

Kott, A., & Linkov, I. (Eds.). (2019). *Cyber resilience of systems and networks*. Springer.

Kott, A., & Linkov, I. (2021). To improve cyber resilience, measure it. *IEEE Computer, 54*(2), 80–85.

Kott, A., & McEneaney, W. M. (2006). *Adversarial reasoning: Computational approaches to reading the opponent's mind*. Chapman and Hall/CRC.

Kott, A., & Stump, E. (2019). Intelligent autonomous things on the battlefield. In *Artificial intelligence for the internet of everything* (pp. 47–65). Academic.

Kott, A., & Théron, P. (2020). Doers, not watchers: Intelligent autonomous agents are a path to cyber resilience. *IEEE Security and Privacy, 18*(3), 62–66.

Kott, A., Ludwig, J., & Lange, M. (2017). Assessing mission impact of cyberattacks: Toward a model-driven paradigm. *IEEE Security and Privacy, 15*(5), 65–74.

Kott, A., Théron, P., Drašar, M., Dushku, E., LeBlanc, B., Losiewicz, P., Guarino, A., Mancini, L., Panico, A., Pihelgas, M., & Rzadca, K. (2018). *Autonomous intelligent cyber-defense agent (AICA) reference architecture*. Release 2.0. arXiv preprint arXiv:1803.10664.

Kott, A., Golan, M. S., Trump, B. D., & Linkov, I. (2021). Cyber resilience: By design or by intervention? *Computer, 54*(8), 112–117.

Ligo, A. K., Kott, A., & Linkov, I. (2021a). Autonomous cyberdefense introduces risk: Can we manage the risk? *Computer, 54*(10), 106–110.

Ligo, A. K., Kott, A., & Linkov, I. (2021b). How to measure cyber-resilience of a system with autonomous agents: Approaches and challenges. *IEEE Engineering Management Review, 49*(2), 89–97.

Linkov, I., Galaitsi, S., Trump, B. D., Keisler, J. M., & Kott, A. (2020). Cybertrust: From explainable to actionable and interpretable artificial intelligence. *Computer, 53*(9), 91–96.

Muttik, I. (2016). *Good viruses. Evaluating the risks*. Talk at DEFCON-2016 Conference. https://www.defcon.org/images/defcon-16/dc16-presentations/defcon-16-muttik.pdf

Théron, P., Kott, A., Drašar, M., Rzadca, K., LeBlanc, B., Pihelgas, M., Mancini, L., & Panico, A. (2018). Towards an active, autonomous and intelligent cyber defense of military systems: The NATO AICA reference architecture. In *2018 international conference on military communications and information systems (ICMCIS)* (pp. 1–9). IEEE.

Théron, P., Kott, A., Drašar, M., Rzadca, K., LeBlanc, B., Pihelgas, M., Mancini, L., & de Gaspari, F. (2020). Reference architecture of an autonomous agent for cyber defense of complex military systems. In *Adaptive autonomous secure cyber systems* (pp. 1–21). Springer.

Chapter 2
Alternative Architectural Approaches

Paul Theron

1 Introduction

In order to thrive peacefully, organisations and their systems need to be resilient to cyber-threats. Cyber Resilience results from building cybersecurity (cyber-attack prevention) and Cyber-defence (cyber-attack response & resolution) into systems, organisations and people. Cyber Resilience is the aptitude of an asset, i.e. an organisation or a system, to keep thriving in the face of cyber threats. It is required because despite efforts on cybersecurity to prevent cyber-attacks the latter will happen because of the growing complexity of systems and of attackers' smart strategies and capacities.

Cyber resilience is implemented through six mechanisms (Theron, 2013) (Fig. 2.1):

Cyber-attack avoidance (**Cybersecurity**) mechanisms seek to reduce the likelihood of attacks:

- **Identify cyber-threats** = knowing of threats & planning cyber risk management strategies,
- **Prevent cyber-threats** = eliminating cyber-threats at source or deterring attackers,
- **Protect & Prepare** = mitigating residual cyber-threats & preparing Cyber-defence.

P. Theron (✉)
Founder of the AICA IWG, Former Head of the Cyb'Air Chair, AICA Lab France, Valence, France

© The Author(s), under exclusive license to Springer Nature Switzerland AG 2023
A. Kott (ed.), *Autonomous Intelligent Cyber Defense Agent (AICA)*, Advances in Information Security 87, https://doi.org/10.1007/978-3-031-29269-9_2

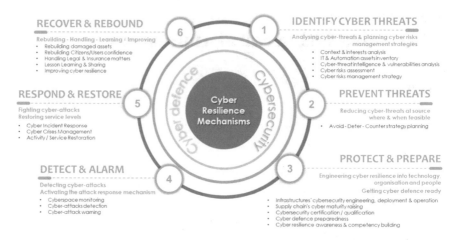

Fig. 2.1 The 6 mechanisms of cyber resilience (P3R3 model)

Cyber-attack response (**Cyber-defence**) mechanisms seek to fight, and learn from attacks:

- **Detect & Alarm** = detecting attacks and alarming response/crisis teams or cyber-defence agents,
- **Respond & Restore** = containing and resolving attacks and continuing or restoring activities,
- **Recover & Rebound** = lesson learning, rebuilding, adapting, handling consequences.

If we take the case of protective features, for instance, one should engineer them into all kinds of Information technology (IT) and operations technology (OT) assets: Endpoints (workstations for instance, mobile terminals, etc.), communications & connectivity, data; servers, cryptographic keys… Securing a system's endpoint, for instance, requires protecting its various components against attacks: Hardware (processor, memory, peripherals); system boot process (like BIOS); operating system, hypervisor and separation kernels; application software and APIs; runtime environment and containers; user access and connections, etc. To that end, cybersecurity engineers would implement a combination of good practices and solutions that make cyber-attacks more difficult to perform, easier to detect, absorb or deflect, or easier to analyse.

As for cyber-defence solutions, they rely typically, today, on growingly intelligent sensors and detection systems, driven by AI or fed by Cyber Threat Intelligence, on sophisticated attack analysis and countering toolboxes, and on highly skilled specialists (Incident responders, Malware reverse engineers, Forensics specialists, cyber crisis managers, etc.).

Today, humans stand at the centre of the cyber-defence (as defined above) of IT and OT systems.

Autonomous Intelligent Cyber-defence Agents (AICA) are a new, alternative, technological proposition. And it has a strong rationale.

IT and OT systems are now evolving towards autonomy and higher levels of connectivity and complexity, both in the civil and military domains. The future looks like an intricate combination of highly contested and safety-critical environments, growingly abundant autonomous vehicles, billions of objects connected through the Internet of [Military or Civil] Things, 6G networks, software-defined networks and radios, AI and cloud computing, edge systems, storage, and much more.

To quote (Kott, 2018), in the Internet of Battlefield Things, Intelligent Things will fight Intelligent Things. Which, in turn, means that in the Internet of [Battlefield/Civil] Things, Intelligent Autonomous Goodware will fight Intelligent Autonomous Malware (Theron & Kott, 2019).

A number of fundamental assumptions have thus progressively emerged from seminal research on AICA.

Many factors can shape AICAs' architecture, which is a "trade-off" in response to multiple requirements. There is not necessarily an ideal, universal form of architecture for AICAs.

In the context depicted above, the speed, scale, complexity and constraints of IT/OT operations, as well as the new cyber-attack strategies that will match the expected maze of new technologies, will overwhelm human SOC operators and will leave them powerless in the face of cyber-attacks (Theron et al., 2020a, b).

A bio-inspired autonomous, intelligent and trustworthy cyber-defence technology, embedded into every system, must do the job for us, at speed and scale. We assume that AICAs will cyber defend our friendly systems and infrastructures on their own, on our behalf, i.e. without humans in the loop.

To act intelligently, autonomously, and before the malware inflicts serious damage on our friendly systems, AICAs will monitor systems in their perimeter, detect attacks, plan an appropriate response and pilot its execution against the enemy malware that itself will not stand passive, and, when needed and possible, AICAs will interact with humans, and they will also learn as-they-walk, and they will protect themselves.

To make "intelligent" decisions, AICAs will need to handle, and to adapt to, a wide variety of adverse situations, and this implies significant progress in Artificial Intelligence (AI) or the way it is used. Learning from experience in this context will be a necessity, and the acquired knowledge and experience, successful and not so successful, will have to be stored in AICAs' memory and used.

We also assume that AICAs can themselves be conceived as Multi Agent Systems, and that AICAs will likely work together in swarms, distributed across software and hardware components.

These initial assumptions have a direct impact on AICAs' architecture. They have generated a number of initial thoughts about what we present here. This chapter stems from research work carried out within both the AICA International Work Group (AICA IWG) and the French Cyb'Air research chair (Aerospace Cyber Resilience) since 2015.

2   The Architecture of Autonomous Intelligent Cyber-Defence Agents

The architecture of an agent describes the arrangement of its components and their relations.

Literature describes many types of agent architectures. For instance, one type of architecture is the layered architecture in which each layer is a function seeking to achieve specified goals. The different layers complement each other in achieving certain behaviours. Another type, cognitive architectures, implements a theory of the human mind and its cognitive functions and allows to carry out a succession of reasoning steps, each step achieving a part of the decision-making process under the drive of some sort of principle such as the BDI (Belief – Desire – Intention).

NATO IST-152's final report on AICA (Kott et al., 2019) proposed an initial – cognitive – architecture for AICAs, itself derived from (Russell & Norwig, 1995) (Fig. 2.2):

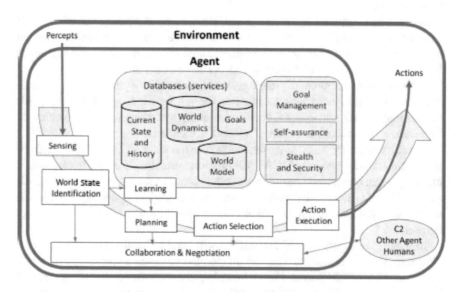

Fig. 2.2 IST-152's cognitive agent model inspired by Russell and Norwig

Kott et al. (2019), p. 18) classify AICAs' functions into:

Classes of components	Functional & non-functional components
Core components	Sensing
(Decision-making functions)	World state identification/situation awareness
	Action planning
	Action selection
	Action execution

Classes of components	Functional & non-functional components
Support functions	Collaboration and negotiation
	Learning
	Goals management
	Self-assurance
	Stealth and security
Data services	World model
	Current state and history
	World dynamics
	Goals

3 AICAs Are Themselves Multi Agent Systems: Our Initial Assumption

Besides possibly working in a team/swarm, (Kott et al., 2019) indicated that AICAs might be implemented as a "society of agents" in which each of its components would be an agent.

In the work carried out between 2016 and 2021 within both the AICA International Work Group (AICA IWG) and the French Cyb'Air research chair of the French Air Force, we have assumed that each AICA would itself be conceived as a Multi Agent System (MAS). First specified in 2019–2020, the MASCARA (MAS-Centric AICA Reference Architecture) architecture was the conceptual driver of a number of initial research projects.

Multi agent systems' architectures have been largely discussed in manifold publications, as well as a series of workshops such as ATAL and AAMAS since the mid-90s (https://link.springer.com/conference/atal) (Muller et al., 1999), for instance, define an agent's architecture as the set of functional components of the agent and how they are working together towards its goals.

Multi-Agent Systems work collectively toward a common goal, and therefore make decisions together and individually, from the most basic ones to the most sophisticated.

Multi-Agent Systems implementation architectures reflect the way their decision-making process is conceived. For instance (Palau et al., 2019) refer to the context of industrial equipment's failure prediction. The authors recapitulate and discuss four types of implementation architectures:

- **Centralised**: A master agent (social platform (Palau et al., 2019)) makes decisions from data supplied by slave agents (sensors) that themselves have a role limited to collecting data from the system's environment and sending data to the master agent. The master agent controls communications between agents and it holds a data repository and a data analytics function.
- **Hierarchical**: Basic agents (sensors) collect data from the system's environment. They transmit those data to intermediate agents that aggregate them and

make some parts of decisions: situation awareness (diagnosis & prognosis). Intermediate agents hold a communications manager, a data repository and a data analytics engine. They transmit their elaborate data to the master agent. Intermediate agents do not collaborate with each other. The master agent holds higher-order functions and finalises or/and communicate decisions to the system of human operator endpoints.

- **Heterarchical**: This type of architecture is similar to the hierarchical architecture except that intermediate agents exchange data between them and collaborate with one another to produce more elaborate situation awareness data.
- **Distributed**: All agents are decision-making agents that receive basic data collected by low-level agents (sensors). Decision-making agents can collaborate with one another and they communicate their decisions to either machines or human operator endpoints.

This crosses with (Dorri et al., 2018) who identify the following types of MAS architectures:

(a) **Flat**: Agents work all on a single level of hierarchy and can collaborate with one another based on needs and purpose.
(b) **Hierarchical**: As previously described.
(c) **Holonic**: This architecture presents several layers of "holons", i.e. groups of agents clustered on the foundation of their functionality. Lower-level agents or holons can be required by higher-order ones to perform specific tasks that deliver data then consolidated at the upper level.
(d) **Coalition**: Agents cluster on the foundation of a goal they all share.
(e) **Team**: Agents cluster on the foundation of a global collective goal to reach.
(f) **Matrix**: Agents are administered by at least two upper-level agents that themselves pursue different goals or see a common goal from different perspectives like the production of some result on one hand and the efficiency of the production process on the other hand.
(g) **Congregation**: Agents require each other's resources to achieve their own goal.

Preliminary research projects carried out in France with ESISAR MSc students and ESEO MSc students in 2019, 2020 and 2021, confirmed that an AICA can be implemented technically as a MAS (Theron et al., 2020a, b). This choice drove the development of the AICAproto21 prototype (Theron et al., 2021) co-sponsored by NCIA, Argonne National Laboratory and Masarik University.

4   The Decision-Making Paradigm of AICAs Has a Key Influence on AICAs' Architecture

Agents' Decision-Making is a key to their trustworthiness. But Artificial Decision-Making is still today at a very early stage of development (Heinl, 2014). Machine learning (ML) and reinforcement learning are regularly advocated as a pathway to the future, e.g., in (Ridley, 2018), but reduce Decision-Making to a well-rehearsed, goal-focused process. Out of a given data vector, the algorithm is trained to conclude to a certain type of results.

The issue with this is that in cyber battles between goodware and malware, AICAs will face complex, highly varied situations. They will then need to make "smart decisions", not just implement an ML algorithm to process a constantly similar type of data to yield a constantly similar type of results.

And smart decisions will not consist in an immediate reaction to a single state of the defended system. The adversary makes many moves and reacts to our response to his moves. In a tactical cyber battle, a smart decision is one that will win the battle, not one that will only respond to a single adversary move and thus ignore potential later malware retaliation that might entail further hardship and damage. The notion of value, of gain, will become more sophisticated.

As human beings, we constantly make smart decisions. Human Decision-Making is smart because it helps us overcome the ever-showing difficulties of life, every minute of our life. It is smart because it builds on vigilance, vision, knowledge, experience, anticipation, wisdom, goals, constraints, margins of manoeuvre, deliberation, emotion, simulation… It is smart because it is dynamic, i.e. because it has "plasticity". Plasticity is the capacity of the mind to adjust our cognitive process to the necessities, the appraisal or the uncertainties of each situation to which we have to react. And plasticity stems from metacognition. Metacognition both ensures the continuity of our thoughts and actions and monitors the shortages of information about situations, their risks, our difficulties to understand. At each step of the cognitive process of decision-making, metacognition evaluates our cognition and orients it in ways that best satisfy our existential needs.

Several strands of work support this idea, not mentioning Brain Sciences, which are beyond the scope of this chapter. Instance-Based Learning Theory (IBLT) showed that five mechanisms are at play in Dynamic Decision-Making (Gonzalez et al., 2003): instance-based knowledge, recognition-based retrieval, adaptive strategies, necessity-based choice, and feedback updates. (Blakely & Theron, 2018; LeBlanc et al., 2017) showed that for agents, making the right decision requires the integration of a variety of approaches. The model of Decision-Making in Action (Theron, 2014) depicted the patterns of Decision-Making in Action and explored some potential factors of their variability, or plasticity, and its adaptive response to situations' characteristics or uncertainty (Fig. 2.3).

The process of Decision-Making in Action (DMA) unfolds as depicted here:

- Some stimuli are brought to the subject's attention (acquired by consciousness).
- Possibly at this early step, information received is incomplete and new pieces are requested.
- That set of information is then analysed and interpreted (judgement), and potential consequences are anticipated.
- At this step, either the situation of which the subject is now aware is appraised as stressful (or traumatic sometimes) and then emotion takes over and entails an urge to act, or not, in which case a deliberative process starts that considers what

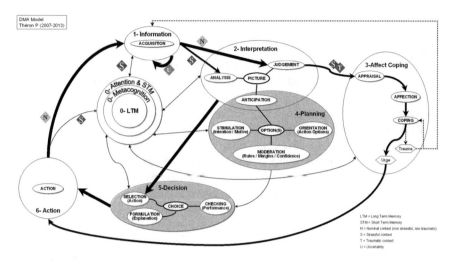

Fig. 2.3 The DMA (Decision-Making in Action) model (most frequent trajectories shown as bold arrows)

    stimulates us (our intentions/motives) as well as moderators of our reaction, such as rules by which we abide, our margins of manoeuvre such as time or safety, or our trust in ourselves or in our envisaged course of action. And all this helps us to come up with one or several options for action.

- This/These option(s) are then evaluated (by way of mental simulation) and a course of action is selected for its superior potential, and orders are given to our various body parts or to people or systems involved in the execution of our decision.
- Actions are then executed.
- And the loop, again, restarts in the next present moment.
- Our short-term memory and vigilance are constantly mobilised.
- Long-term memory, whether semantic or episodic, feeds every step of the process.
- Learning consolidates our lived experience into our semantic and episodic memory.
- Metacognition supervises the cognitive process.

At each step, deviations from the main trajectories occur, under the influence of some factors not yet well-known. Also, emotion and deliberation interact. Hundreds of cognitive operations as well as very diverse patterns of the cognitive process can be found in human subjects' cognition.

    The architecture of this metacognitively controlled cognitive process entails a sophisticated architecture of the human mind. Brain Sciences have shown, out of brain imagery, the multiple subcortical and cortical areas of the brain that are activated in the course of our cognitive activity.

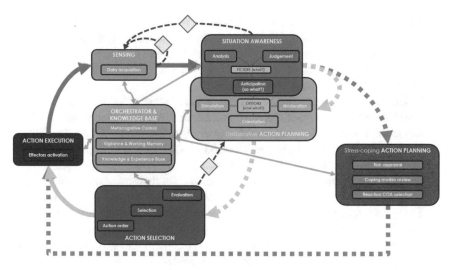

Fig. 2.4 General diagram of the Deep Decision-Making process in AICAs

Deep Decision-Making (DDM) assumes that AICAs' Decision-Making can be up to the challenge of making smart decisions in the course of fast-paced tactical cyber battles only if their cognitive process is organised in a human-like, plastic way (Theron, 2020) as suggested by the DMA model.

In AICAs, under the DDM paradigm, decision-making would then be a metacognitively controlled, algorithm-fed, multi-step process. Each DDM cognitive function, as in the DMA model, would implement a combination of non-AI and AI/ML techniques (e.g., genetic algorithms and classifiers or neural networks, game theory, …) and would call upon other steps/functions to resolve reasoning challenges due to the unlimited variety, complexity and uncertainty of situations at hand.

Metacognitive control would then require a specific function/component in charge of monitoring, driving and optimising the decision-making process. At this stage, we assume that AI and a formal knowledge base will be used to optimise AICAs' cognitive process, to feed it and adjust it to the necessities of situations at hand.

The AICA is therefore primarily a metacognitive agent. Inspired by the DMA model, it would resemble the following diagram (Fig. 2.4):

5   The MASCARA Architecture of AICAs

The assumed MASCARA architecture (Multi Agent System Centric AICA Reference Architecture) was inspired by:

- Naturalistic Decision Making (NDM) studies: This research, begun in the 1990s, aimed at studying the pattern of cognitive processes underlying experts' decision-making in real-life situations, in the face of events to which they had to react. This is illustrated by the DMA model that shows the functions of an individual's cognitive process in a variety of circumstances (unchallenging, stressful, and traumatic) and some of the factors that may explain the complex variation of its pattern (Theron, 2014).

- Russell & Norwig's description of a cognitive software agent (Russell & Norwig, 1995) shows that the functions of an individual's cognitive process are the foundation of the cognitive engine of an intelligent software agent. The NATO Science and Technology Organization (ST & O)'s IST-152 report on the architecture of AICAs (Kott et al., 2019) depicts how Autonomous Intelligent Cyberdefence Agents can make decisions to defend, on their own, our networks and systems against enemy malware in the safety-critical context of the battlefield. The speed, spread, and complexity of enemy malware attacks in a battlefield would overwhelm human operators who would need to monitor the cybersecurity of those systems and networks, understand them, devise countermeasures, evaluate their potential reward and activate them.
- Multi-Agent Systems that provide a way to create a "network" of cooperating software entities. Each one possesses its own functional capacities to provide answers to the requests they process. It is to be noted that Multi Agent System standards such as FIPA (Foundation for Intelligent Physical Agents, @ www. fipa.org) did not yet influence our research on AICA's architecture.

Given these preliminary considerations, the MASCARA architecture can be described in three levels:

- A General Functional Model;
- A Detailed Functional Model;
- A Technical Model.

6   The General Functional Model of the MASCARA Architecture

The highest-level, general, functional description of MASCARA stands in the following diagram (Fig. 2.5):

An AICA is embedded within the host system it defends. An AICA is a set of functions and resources that together deliver countermeasures in response to a cyber-attack actually taking place within a defended host system or network. Besides, an AICA can work either on its own, or collectively i.e. within groups (swarms, cohorts…) of AICAs.

The outside world of operation of an AICA may include, not mentioning the host system or network itself:

- Other AICAs (case of swarms or cohorts of agents);
- A Cyber Command & Control (C2) server/application (Cyber C2, or CC2) that may pilot AICAs if the latter were to be used in a not-fully autonomous mode;

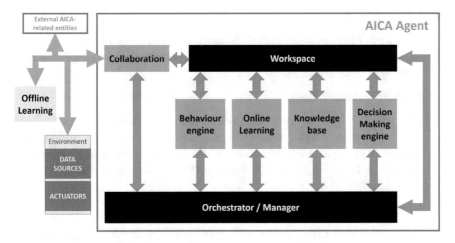

Fig. 2.5 AICA's general functional architecture

- Human operators who might be willing or requested to cooperate with AICAs in circumstances were the latter's concept of operation would request it, especially if AICAs are unable to make decisions on their own and need humans to provide sense or directions;
- Data sources like IDS (Intrusion Detection Systems) that provide data to AICAs for making decisions;
- Actuators like a honeypot for instance that would receive orders from the AICA to deflect or analyse the enemy malware;
- Offline learning systems that may be loaded with data accumulated by AICAs during their "missions" within defended systems. They serve for learning from the agent's experience in action, and increase the intelligence and capacity of autonomy of agents. Knowledge bases provide AICAs the information they need to inform their missions.

An AICA's internal components are, on a global level:

- A Decision-Making Engine

    - Its goal is to collect data, decide on the countermeasures to oppose to enemy malware, to communicate those decisions to the actuators who will perform those countermeasures, and to pilot tactically their execution, i.e., to adjust planned countermeasures to the tactical evolution of the situation.
    - It is made of five key functions: Sensing (data collection), Situation Awareness (sense making), Action Planning (proposition of possible countermeasures), Action Selection (choice of the set of countermeasures promising best gains/benefits), Action Activation (transmission/dispatch of detailed orders to outside actuators).

- A Knowledge Base

  - Its goal is to record and deliver the agent's knowledge and experience as the AICA acts and to supply all AICA components with the knowledge they need to make smart decisions.

- An Online Learning Engine

  - Its goal is to help the agent increase its intelligence: its capacity to disable the enemy malware and maximise its own utility. This requres deriving new knowledge from actions performed by the agent as a whole or by its components, or from the global experience of the team/swarm in which the AICA participates.

- An Agent Behaviour Engine

  - Its goal is to specify, regulate, and control the rights and limits of the agent to act upon its environment.

- An Orchestrator (or Manager)

  - Its goal is to organise and optimise the way the agent's components work together. The Orchestrator manages or coordinates the messages exchanged between the components of the agent.
  - It also manages incoming and outgoing messages and data exchanges between the agent and the outside world.

- A Workspace

  - Its goal is to allocate the working memory resources required by the agent's components.

- A Collaboration interface

  - Its goal is to enforce and control the rules of information and data exchange between the interior and the exterior of the AICA, or between AICAs in the case of a swarm or cohort of AICAs.

- An Internal Communication Protocol between the agent's functions

  - Its goal is to provide interoperability between the components of an AICA.

7   The Detailed Functional Model of the MASCARA Architecture

MASCARA can be described in more details by the following Detailed Functional Model (Fig. 2.6):

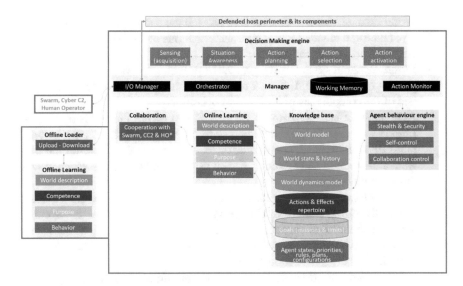

Fig. 2.6 Detailed functional model of an AICA

This second-level diagram presents the sub-components of:

- The Orchestrator (Manager) component

  - Orchestrator: Its goal is to organise and optimise how the agent's components work together. In particular, the Orchestrator manages the exchange of messages between the components of the agent.
  - Working Memory: Its goal is to provide, manage, and control the working memory resources of the agent.
  - I/0 (Input/Output) Manager: Its goal is to manage and control all incoming and outgoing data exchanges between the agent and its outside world of operation, including queues/piles and priorities management, interoperability, or portability services.
  - Action Monitor: Its goal is to watch the execution of actions plans communicated to outside actuators.

- The Collaboration component

  - Cooperation with Swarm, CC2 & HO: Its goal is to "translate" outgoing and incoming messages destined to or originating from external entities such as other AICAs (working in swarm), a cyber Command & Control system (CC2) or Human Operators (HO). This includes the semantics and formatting of exchanged messages.

- The Knowledge Base component

  - World Model: Its goal is to provide the agent's components an up to date ontology of the agent's world of operation and of itself. This includes the relations between the elements of those ontologies.

- World State & History: Its goal is to provide the agent's components with an up to date and detailed log of all transformations of the agent itself and of its outside world of operation.
- World Dynamics Model: Its goal is to provide the type of "if... then..." clauses characterising the track record of transformations of the agent itself and of the components of its world of operation.
- Actions & Effects Repertoire: Its goal is to provide the Decision-Making Engine with knowledge about the type of causal "if... then..." clauses about plans of, or individual, countermeasures, the impacts they have on the malware and on defended systems, as well as the reward/benefit associated with those countermeasures.
- Goals (Missions & Limits): Its goal is to inform the agent's components, and especially the Decision-Making Engine, about the mission the agent is assigned, the rules of engagement it must abide by, and the actions not to take as well as the rewards/benefits (negative vs. positive, immediate vs. long-term, for instance) they should seek or avoid.
- Agent's states, priorities, rules, plans, configurations: Its goal is to supply the agent's components with any further elements of knowledge that can help regulating, controlling, securing, optimising the agent's behaviour, decisions, self-resilience, etc.

- The Online Learning component

  - It identifies 4 classes of knowledge that an agent can generate in the course of its missions: World Description, Competence, Purpose, and Behaviour. Those 4 classes correspond to the Knowledge Bases previously seen.

- The Agent Behaviour Engine component

  - Stealth & Security: Its goal is to provide the agent's components with the rules of behaviour to apply when the agent faces adversity, such as during attacks, when tracked by the enemy malware, or when the agent's operating conditions degrade. Those rules aim to improve the AICA's resilience to the threats it faces.
  - Self-control: Its goal is to provide the agent with the rules it must/should apply to manage itself in a variety of circumstances. This would help the agent adapt or reorganize its internal functioning or how the agent is deployed across the components of the defended host system/network.
  - Collaboration Control: Its goal is to monitor, control. and possibly enforce the agent's goals, priorities, and rules of behaviour.

- The Offline Learning component

  - Offline Loader: Its goal is to download from agents the data they have collected during their "missions" for the purpose of learning, and to upload into agents the knowledge bases they need to perform their duties during their missions.

– Offline Learning: Its goal is to perform learning activities in "times of rest" i.e. in the context of a data science/AI laboratory, on the foundation of the data collected by agents during their "missions" (time of operation) in order to improve their performance. It identifies 4 classes of knowledge that an agent requires in the course of its missions: World Description, Competence, Purpose, Behaviour. Those 4 classes correspond to the Knowledge Bases previously seen.

8 The Technical Implementation of a MASCARA-Based AICA

The idea of implementing cyber-defence solutions in the shape of Multi Agent Systems is not new. Collaborative Intrusion Detection Systems (CIDS) have been developed[1,2] for the past decade or so. Their principle is to implement multiple layers of sensors/monitors from which a master/manager/analyst agent draws data, consolidates them and via ML-based data analytics algorithms detects an attack.[3] They can be seen as Multi-Agent Systems, possibly combined with an artificial immune systems paradigm.[4] There are developments in the area of Vehicle ad-hoc network (VANETs)[5] and mobile ad hoc networks (MANETs).[6]

As for AICAs, there will be many ways to implement the MASCARA architecture technically. So far, some generic principles have been identified and have driven its technical implementation:

• AICAs are themselves Multi Agent Systems made of a set of MicroAgents (MA).
• A MicroAgent is a "functional capsule", a "container" of methods, algorithm(s) or data, altogether processing input data to deliver output data, under the regulation of some form of process control parameters, and with the help of some resources.
• All components/functions of an AICA, such as those described in the functional architecture described above, are implemented as "MicroAgents".
• MicroAgents interact with one another as needed.

An initial implementation was made in 2019–2021 in the context of the Cyb'Air research chair. It relied on Java and was presented by (Théron et al., 2020) at the 2020 NATO-AICA IWG Technical Workshop on AICA.

---

[1] https://ieeexplore.ieee.org/document/1254328

[2] https://core.ac.uk/download/pdf/161257409.pdf

[3] https://www.researchgate.net/publication/276205397_Taxonomy_and_Survey_of_Collaborative_Intrusion_Detection

[4] https://www.sciencedirect.com/science/article/abs/pii/S0952197614001444

[5] https://ieeexplore.ieee.org/abstract/document/9119934

[6] https://ieeexplore.ieee.org/abstract/document/6209126

The AICAproto21 project's team created a more elaborated technical prototype of an AICA that relies on Docker containers (Theron et al., 2021). The project built the technological "shell" of AICAs, in a fashion that allows a) its reuse under an LGPL licence and b) the progressive development of AICA components' non-ML and ML-based decision-making and learning features.

Besides, the project developed a demonstration/visualisation environment based on CYST (https://dl.acm.org/doi/abs/10.5555/3451906.3451908; https://muni.cz/go/565e43).

The project did not implement AI functionalities, only rule-based reasoning.

The development considered a simple use case situated within a Command, Control, Communications, Computers (C4) Intelligence, Surveillance and Reconnaissance (C4ISR) system. This system included personal computers (PCs) and servers connected via a local area network (LAN). The use case's topology comprises the following nodes:

- A central router, taking care of routing the traffic within a LAN;
- A targeted server, the primary target of the attacker;
- A vulnerable server, not specifically targeted by the attacker;
- A high interaction honeypot, where the attacker is routed after successful detection;
- Two PCs, not specifically targeted by the attacker;
- An IDS monitoring the traffic;
- One AICA agent set on separate node;
- An infected machine containing the attacker.

In the scenario, the AICA resides on an isolated secure device and receives reports from the Intrusion Detection System (IDS). The AICA has no defensive capabilities. In response to intrusions, the AICA triggers response actions performed by other systems:

- Activating the honeypot;
- Rerouting specific traffic to the honeypot.

The goal of the AICA is to isolate the malware and study its behaviour. The expected chain of actions is as follows:

- The AICA monitors the IDS reports of attacks;
- The attacker scans the network and its actions are detected by the IDS;
- The AICA selects an appropriate action and redirects the attacker to the HoneyPot;
- The HoneyPot receives all attacking traffic for further analysis.

The AICAproto21 project's team implemented a MASCARA-based AICA as a containerized environment (Fig. 2.7).

The implementation uses Docker Compose. It:

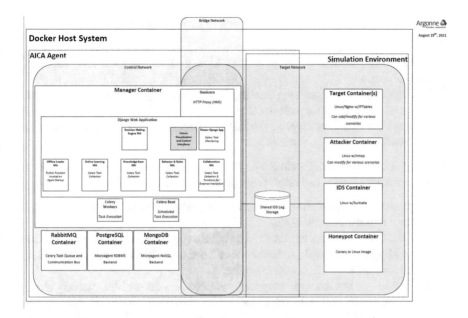

Fig. 2.7 AICA implemented in a Docker-based containerized environment

- Enables the creation of a lightweight, cross-platform, easy-to-replicate and share, and highly flexible environment that can be deployed on any Linux, Mac, or Windows system using only Docker, Python, and Make.
- Allows the full encapsulation of all systems that comprise an AICA, as well as the ability to encompass a simulation/demonstration environment with minimal additional overhead and no external dependencies.
- Enables the use of a wide variety of services that can be easily instantiated freely and publicly available from dockerhub.com with minimal required configuration.

Within this architecture, the AICA is a collection of containers (described below), and the MicroAgents are tasks running within a Celery Task Management system managed by Django, a common Python web application framework:

- This design permits for easily extending AICA to add human-machine interaction (HMI) components with minimal additional coding, parallelization of the MicroAgents' operations, and scalability to encompass large numbers of workers to process tasks, as system load requires.
- This design allows developers to add easily new types of tasks. All of this functionality lives within a primary container named the "Manager".
- The Manager exposes the Flower frontend to allow for monitoring of the state of running and scheduled Celery tasks, and the RabbitMQ management interface to monitor the state of task queues.

As for backend systems, the Manager leverages multiple other containers providing standard services:

- A RabbitMQ container supports the Celery Task Queues and inter-task communication;
- A PostgreSQL container supports the Django web application and any other relational-schemas as they are developed;
- A MongoDB container supports the storage of document objects such as lists and dictionaries in a NoSQL database.

MicroAgents consist of collections of Python functions comprising Celery tasks to implement MicroAgents and allow them to communicate:

- Upon start-up of the Manager container, the Django application calls the Offline Loader's initialization function.
- After the Offline Loader has finished its bootstrapping tasks, it calls the Decision Making Engine's main loop (the "monitor" method). This, in turn, calls the poll_ dbs function of the Collaboration Engine.
- For initial demonstration purposes, database-based or Structured Threat Information eXpression (STIX)/Trusted Automated Exchange of Intelligence Information (TAXII)-based communications with the intrusion detection system (described below) were not used. Instead, a shared Docker volume was used to allow both the IDS and Manager to access Suricata log files in real-time.
- The poll_dbs function monitors the communication channel with the IDS (in this case, the shared log file). If it detects an alert, it notifies the Decision Making Engine. The Decision Making Engine consults with the Knowledge Base to identify what actions can be taken, then determines the action to take. It then makes any necessary calls to other MicroAgents to update its world-state, and the Collaboration Engine to take any external actions, such as redirecting specific network traffic to a honeypot.
- Because all of these functions (exception the Offline Loader's initialization function) are Celery Tasks, they can be run asynchronously and simultaneously and can scale as required to meet demand.
- Communications between them are handled either by direct Python function calls, or instantiation of new Celery Tasks with any necessary parameters and return values communicated via the RabbitMQ message bus.

In addition to tasks initiated by other tasks, the use of Celery Beat allows for tasks to be set to run on a periodic schedule. This can support routine loading of external data, polling of systems where real-time communication is not necessary, saving status to an external location, etc.

The AICAproto21 prototype was released at the end of November 2021. Its capabilities have reached a "Minimum Viable Product" (MVP) state, meaning that they are operational and provide a basic level of functionality.

The containerized environment built using Docker Compose, the Manager Container, including the Flower monitoring application, Celery Workers and Scheduler, Django web framework (and gunicorn proxy), Offline Loader

MicroAgent, Collaboration MicroAgent, and the remaining MicroAgents, only provides a "shell" that can be filled in with functionality.

This is true for the RabbitMQ Container, the PostgreSQL Container, the MongoDB Container, the Target Container, the Attacker Container, the IDS Container and updated community rulesets, the Honeypot Container, shared Suricata logfile monitoring between the IDS container and Collaboration MicroAgent, and Secure Shell (SSH) communication between the Collaboration MicroAgent and the Target container.

With the capabilities completed to date, one can currently build and start the AICA environment (this takes 5–10 min and is fully automated using the included Makefile), start a shell on the Attacker, scan the Target, and confirm that the Collaboration Agent becomes aware of the scan.

Machine learning capabilities, the incorporation of or contribution to external threat feeds, and the interaction with systems outside the containerized simulation environment were not part of the project.

9   Beyond Prototypes, the Rationale of AICAs' Architecture: Required Aptitudes and Benefits

As said earlier, there will be multiple ways to implement AICAs technically. A variety of considerations will guide future AICA developers' choices. And designing the architecture of an AICA will equal to finding the right trade-off between its various requirements.

(a) General aptitudes required for AICAs

AICAs' architecture will be shaped by requirements such as:

- Functional interoperability: It is the aptitude of AICAs, or of their internal components, to operate together, and to exchange information that they can mutually interpret and process.
- Technical Interoperability: It is the aptitude of AICAs, or of their internal components, to resolve their possible differences in terms of technical standards or protocols. Technical interoperability in a sine qua non condition of functional interoperability.
- Portability: It is the aptitude of AICAs, or of their internal components, to function in a native way in a specified variety of technical environments (OS, protocols, formats…).
- Protection of AICAs' resources' confidentiality: It is the aptitude of AICAs, or of their internal components, to guarantee that their data, code, and specifications will not be disclosed to unauthorised agents, applications, software, users.
- Flexibility of AICAs' organisation: It is the aptitude of AICAs to adapt their implementation or internal architecture to a specified variety of factors.

- Resource consumption optimisation: It is the aptitude of an AICA to minimise the computing power, communication load & memory that it consumes within its host system.

The following table presents some of the consequences these requirements entail:

Aptitudes	Design principles
Functional interoperability	MicroAgents, as well as AICAs themselves, must be able to exchange data and to address requests from and to one another A messaging control mechanism should be engineered into AICAs to interpret and translate the format and semantics of incoming messages or to adapt those of outgoing messages Common messaging standards will be required to allow AICAs created by different suppliers or teams to interoperate functionally The Orchestrator MicroAgent manages the communication between all MA at the application/data level
Technical interoperability	MicroAgents, as well as AICAs themselves, must be able to communicate in heterogeneous technical environments that include different Operating Systems, protocols, data formats, languages and APIs, etc. A technical abstraction mechanism should be engineered into AICAs to deal with a variety of operating systems, communication protocols, etc. Such a mechanism should be implemented in a function of the AICA dedicated to the agent's collaboration with other entities The I/O MicroAgent manages the communication between all MicroAgents at the system level
Portability	AICAs must be deployed at no extra-cost indifferently on any IT or OT platform The use of vastly used high-level languages (Java, Python…) or/and of Containers (Docker…) should help making the agents portable The AICA (I/O MicroAgent) interfaces system-level protocols in heterogeneous technical environment
Security (confidentiality)	AICAs' data, code and specifications should not be violated and their details leaked to attackers Confidentiality protective measures should be implemented within AICAs and their operating environment. Encryption and trust-checking (0-trust) are eligible approaches
Resilience	AICAs will become key targets of enemy malware MicroAgents could be cloned to maximise the AICA's resilience Mirror MicroAgents with data synchronisation could be an eligible technique Stealth should help MicroAgents and their communications to remain undetected by the enemy malware
Flexibility of the agent's organisation	Whatever the technical and operational constraints, multiple configurations/organisations of AICAs must be deployed easily within host systems or networks Handling communications between all MicroAgents, keeping memory of MicroAgents' locations and cooperation rights as well as of optimal patterns of the cognitive process, the Orchestrator MicroAgent will assure an important level of flexibility of the agent's deployment

Aptitudes	Design principles
Resource consumption optimisation	The engineering of AICAs must take this requirement into account in the context of agents' future operating environments and their technical constraints Thus, AICAs installed within powerful systems may benefit from a large computing power and extended memory resources But when embedded into mere sensors, and in general within devices that have limited technical resource, their consumption must be reduced to a bear minimum In this latter case, for instance, online/ongoing learning may reveal too resource-greedy and therefore knowledge bases needed by the AICA to make decisions should be of a small size, embedded at the Factory stage, and upgraded only by the AICA "factory"

(b) Other factors that may shape an AICA's architecture

For instance, we identified 13 research & technology (R & T)[7] challenges, grouped into four classes:

- Building and qualifying AICAs: Infrastructure, Architecture, Engineering, testing, simulation and certification challenges;
- Making decisions and learning: Individual & Collective Decision Making challenges;
- Facing attacks on AICAs themselves: Stealth & Resilience challenges;
- Framing AICAs: Societal limits, Law, ethics, doctrines of use, rules of engagement (Fig. 2.8).

Such R & T challenges may influence AICAs' architecture, and this remains to be studied. For instance:

- **Agents' engineering & certification**: AICAs need to be built according to recognised standards that might imply specific architectural choices.
- **Testability & At-scale Simulation**: AICAs' internal activity and data should be made accessible, without disturbance to their functioning, for tests and simulation purposes.
- **Implementation and compatibility technologies**: AICAs might be implemented in a variety of ways. One is a single, full agent that hosts all the functions and data required to detect and beat malware. Another is a swarm of full agents that will develop superior capacities to those of a single one. Another way might be to have a community/society of specialised agents working together in swarms, such as, but not necessarily as described, a detection agent, another interpreting data, a third making decisions about countermeasures, etc. Finally, some agents might be hardware and some software, some might be elements of the host environment itself while its "colleagues" would be full or specialised agents. Such choices could be influenced by the computing, memory and

[7] Research Challenges – Autonomus Intelligent Cyberdefence Agents International Work Group (aica-iwg.org).

Fig. 2.8 13 Research & technology challenges that shape AICAs' architecture

communication capacities of the host system to defend. The second aspect is about AICA agents' compatibility with host systems, at the present moment not designed to accept AICAs within, especially if those are to patrol networks and systems, constantly moving from one spot to another. It is likely that the engineering of host systems itself might be impacted. Finally, the third aspect is about agents' compatibility with cybersecurity systems and devices. As of today, agents would be stopped by the first firewall or detected as carrying out adverse activities by an IDS. AICA agents must be able to function despite cybersecurity devices, software and procedures or they will not operate at all. Like host systems, cybersecurity devices and processes may have to evolve in order to allow AICAs to function.

- **Autonomous self-engineering and self-assurance**: AICAs will be embedded into systems in which they might be operating for very long periods of time, may be without [sufficient] communications or maintenance through which their knowledge base or their algorithms could be updated. To prevent a decline in their efficiency, AICAs could then be equipped with capacities to self-develop their functions, to adapt to new conditions of operation, to reassess their own performance as well as their own reliability, integrity, etc.

- **Agents' individual decision making**: AICAs, by their very name, are autonomous and intelligent.

    - Derived from the Greek Auto (self) and Nomos (law), the word "autonomous" means that agents, whether purely software or software-driven hardware, act on their own towards goals set by their designers or users, on the basis of underlying rules and "cognitive" processes that generate decisions in the pursuit of these goals. However, agents' autonomy is limited by rationality, situatedness and sociality (Castelfranchi, 1995).
    - Derived from the Latin Intelligere (to understand), the word "intelligent" means that agents have a cognitive faculty to understand their environment and circumstances, whether internal (their current state or its variation for instance) or external (events occurring outside of them for instance), as well as the actions they should take in reaction. This faculty confers agents the capacity to make smart, well-adapted decisions that resolve the problems at hand, however complex they may be (at least in theory).
    - (Castelfranchi, 1995) suggests that autonomy frames an agent's architecture by requiring it includes all due cognitive functional components.

- **Collective intelligence & decision making**: For swarms or communities of AICA agents to bring superiority over single full AICA agents, they need to make collective decisions that are more effective than single agents. To that end, agents will need sharing and exchanging data, which also raises the issue of trust and of its mechanisms.
- **Learning, loading, sizing**: AICA agents will learn "on-the-fly" (if computing capacities permit) or else off-line. Their size, and components will be influenced accordingly. And in case of off-line learning, knowledge uploading will require components external to AICAs themselves.
- **Agents cooperation with other entities**: AICA agents may have to cooperate with other agents, a cyber C2 or human operators, implying specific functionalities, protocols, data flows, data flows, ergonomics, security and continuity in case of disturbances.
- **Agents' stealth and resilience**: To do what they are meant reliably, AICAs need to be protected and defended against attacks from the enemy. Protective and defensive mechanisms must be embedded into AICAs.
- **Friend of foe? Ping, trust and social dynamics**: When two agents "meet", or when an unknown agent knocks on the door, AICAs must discriminate good agents from bad ones. To defend themselves against intruders, they might have to reconfigure their cooperation liaisons and trust mechanisms must be included in agents and between agents.
- **Law, ethics, doctrines and society**: The implementation of AICAs, along with the emergence of a similar technology for cyber-attacks, will have societal,

philosophical and legal implications. Similarly to debates of the UN's Lethal Autonomous Weapon Systems (LAWS) committee, AICAs will appear as a "dangerous" technology and mechanisms to limit, for instance their degree of autonomy, will have to be embedded into agents.

10   And Now, What? Further Areas of Research and Technology

This chapter aimed at opening-up the discussion about AICAs' architecture. As we understand, a Multi-Agent System approach is likely to be an interesting way forward. Alternatives might be either to make an AICA a single software agent, which would entail coding hardships probably, or making very light agents, meaning that they would embark a reduced set of functionality (if that is possible) and a small dataset (again if that makes sense).

And as we speak today, research on AICA's architecture (and other challenges) is still in its infancy. It is a vast endeavour that will probably require a good 15 years before operational AICAs start being embedded into real IT and OT systems.

From what we said earlier, AICAs' architecture poses many research questions. To quote only a few:

- What is the optimal technical internal architecture and collective organisation of AICAs?
- How can we embed AI and non-ML algorithmic solutions within an AICA in ways compatible with the resource constraints of host systems?
- What technical standards do we need to make AICA agents implementable in host systems, interoperable, and resilient?
- How can we help heads of military and civil organisations understand the AICA technology and the part it needs to play in future technological developments?

Research about Deep Decision-Making and the MASCARA architecture should build on several currents of work such as, for instance:

- Cognitive Architectures (Lebiere & Anderson, 1993) and their use for computer games (Smart et al., 2016);
- Naturalistic Decision-Making (Lipshitz, 1997) and Decision-Making in Action (Theron, 2014) to explore the micro-cognitive processes, resources, metacognitive control of expert Decision-Making, its circumstances and the factors that determine the transition between consecutive cognitive operations; Brain sciences also as they study cortical synchronisations and the transition between them and will help understanding the control of the transition between cognitive operations;
- Instance-Based Learning Theory for Dynamic Decision-Making (Gonzalez et al., 2003);
- Agent-based modelling and simulation of cyber battles (Kotenko et al., 2012);

- Cyber-attack graphs and models (Jajodia & Noel, 2010), (Noel et al., 2015) as they seek to provide formal models of adversarial cyber battles, along with game theory, AI and ML and its current refinements such as reinforcement learning.

Such research will help to refine and optimise the architecture of the cognitive and metacognitive process within single AICAs, and likely so as well within swarms of AICAs.

Existing technical standards for Multi-Agent Systems such as those listed below should be analysed for their capacity to help the development of the AICA architecture with a view to assure interoperability among other required aptitudes:

- IEEE's FIPA (Foundation for Intelligent Physical Systems) standards:[8] They are founded on the principle that an agent is a physical device that is to cooperate with other physical devices.
- IEEE P2660.1/D1/D2/D3, May 2020 – IEEE Draft Recommended Practices on Industrial Agents: Integration of Software Agents and Low-Level Automation Functions.[9]
- OMG's MASIF/MAF (Mobile Agent System Interoperability Facility)[10] & CORBA:[11] This standard is about interoperability between agent systems written in the same language, but potentially by different vendors and systems that are expected to go through many revisions within the lifetime of an agent.
- W3C's Web Services Architecture:[12] Inspired by and built on MAS concepts WSA provides a standard means of interoperating between different software applications, running on a variety of platforms and/or frameworks.

AICA simulation, testing and demonstration environments are very much in need to help decision-makers to understand the AICA technology. They are needed also by scientists and engineers to evaluate AICA technologies and performances in a wide variety of adverse and technological scenarios. And the creation of testing datasets of reference is also a necessity to support and systematise basic testing and benchmarking requirements.

Simulation environments will need to scale up to the size of actual deployments, such as the Internet of Battlefield Things. This is due to the necessity to understand the phenomena that will take place within those complex environments and how AICAs act and perform in the face of real-life complex attack scenarios.

Testing Multi-Agent Systems, and AICAs especially in the near future, is difficult because agents exhibit a complex behaviour. The testing of Multi-Agent Systems,[13] for instance of BDI (Belief-Desire-Intentionality) agents, has been the

---

[8] http://www.fipa.org/repository/componentspecs.html

[9] https://ieeexplore.ieee.org/document/9093227

[10] https://www.omg.org/spec/MOBFAC/About-MOBFAC/

[11] https://www.omg.org/spec/CORBA/About-CORBA/

[12] https://www.w3.org/TR/ws-arch/

[13] https://link.springer.com/chapter/10.1007/978-3-319-50983-9_12

object of various research[14,15,16] as well as the verification and validation of Multi-Agent Systems.[17]

There are multiple development & simulation research,[18] methods, languages and platforms. They need to be assessed in the light of AICAs' requirements and specificities. As part of development and simulation technologies, we can cite a few, for instance:

- Agent Oriented Software Engineering (AOSE)[19,20] methodologies.
- JADE (Java Agent Development Framework):[21] This language and its associated development allow to create agents and their behaviours and communications.
- JACK and C BDI platforms,[22] meant for developing intelligent (Beliefs, Desires and Intentions) agents.
- GAMA,[23] MATLAB,[24] F#,[25] agentscript,[26] CoSMoSim,[27] DEVS-Suite Simulator,[28] Evoplex,[29] Flame[30] & Flame GPU,[31] or else JaCaMo[32] for programming multi-agent systems including the agents (with Jason), the environment (with Cartago) and agents' organisation (with Moise).
- Prometheus (Padgham & Winikoff, 2004), meant for developing intelligent agents.
- GAIA[33] (Wooldridge et al., 1999), which is not meant for *open systems in which system components may join and leave at run-time, and which may be composed of entities that a designer had no knowledge of at design-time.*

[14] https://link.springer.com/article/10.1007/s11219-017-9392-4

[15] https://www.jair.org/index.php/jair/article/view/10903

[16] https://link.springer.com/article/10.1007/s10458-016-9356-2

[17] https://arxiv.org/abs/1210.3640

[18] https://dl.acm.org/doi/abs/10.1145/3310013.3322175

[19] https://dl.acm.org/doi/10.1145/2980258.2982111

[20] https://www.researchgate.net/publication/282392089_Understanding_Agent-Oriented_Software_Engineering_methodologies

[21] http://jade.tilab.com/

[22] http://www.agent-software.com/

[23] https://gama-platform.github.io/

[24] https://fr.mathworks.com/products/matlab.html

[25] https://fsharp.org/

[26] https://github.com/backspaces/agentscript

[27] https://sourceforge.net/projects/cosmosim/

[28] https://sourceforge.net/projects/devs-suitesim/

[29] https://evoplex.org/en/

[30] http://flame.ac.uk/

[31] http://www.flamegpu.com/home

[32] https://sourceforge.net/projects/jacamo/

[33] https://www.cs.ox.ac.uk/people/michael.wooldridge/pubs/jaamas2000b.pdf

- Quviq QuickCheck[34] that supports property-based testing of software written in Haskell.[35]
- MASH[36] that was designed to test jointly software agents and their hardware environment.
- CYST that is developed for the lightweight simulation of cybersecurity agents[37,38]

AICA's certification is also an important line of progress. No research has been done yet, it seems, about the certification of Multi-Agent Systems, either from a functional, technical or cybersecurity perspective. However, for instance, Europe's Cybersecurity Act of 2019 will make cybersecurity certification mandatory for all connected objects, which includes agents such as AICAs. This is an urgent area of work.

One last consideration, as we need to close this discussion, is about the education and training of future scientists and engineers. The early research works that we have piloted have clearly shown that students, to handle AICA research and technology, need a vast background: Cybersecurity and cyber-defence, Multi Agent Systems, Embedded systems, Artificial Intelligence, Artificial Decision-Making both individual and collective, MAS certification methods, etc.

Creating AICA architectures for the future requires that we invest today in focused MSc and PhD research and education programmes.

11   Summary and Conclusions

Autonomous Intelligent Cyber-defence Agents (AICA) represent a future of the cyber-defence of infrastructures, networks, systems and devices. They are particularly needed where systems will be highly complex or autonomous and potentially disconnected from their supervisor. Embedded within these various items, they will substitute to human cyber operators who will not be in a position to monitor cybersecurity in missions and environments too complex and too fast-paced for their limited cognitive abilities.

The architecture of AICAs responds to a range of requirements. Among others, AICAs' architecture must ensure that these agents can be embedded within a variety of host systems, from very large to very small. AICAs must function whatever the host operating systems, communication protocols, data formats implemented in their environment. And they must run fast enough and consume as little computing resource as feasible.

---

[34] www.quviq.com/products/

[35] www.haskell.org

[36] https://hal.archives-ouvertes.fr/hal-00804650

[37] https://ieeexplore.ieee.org/document/9213690

[38] https://gitlab.ics.muni.cz/98998/simulation-engine-public

On the other hand, what will structure AICAs' architecture is the cognitive process that will make them smart enough to become autonomous. Where current ML algorithms deliver an interpretation of an input vector of data, like recognising a pattern of a cyber-attack, AICAs need more than this. Their decision making process is articulated around several steps/functions that complement each other, as in the model of Decision-Making in Action (DMA): data acquisition (sensing), data interpretation (situation awareness), elaboration of response plan options (action planning), the selection of the best option (action selection), and the activation of the selected action plan (action activation). Action planning can be either deliberative or stress-handling driven. Each of these steps involve a wide variety of cognitive operations that follow one another in a complex fashion.

AICAs' architecture must give them the capacity to implement a highly-plastic cognitive process to adapt to extremely varied situations, attacks, configurations of host systems and uncertainty.

Beyond, AICAs' architecture must also include the functions that guarantee the agent's resilience to failures and to the attacks that will be directed against them. It must also include the functions that will keep agents' actions within the limits set by their doctrine of use.

The MASCARA architecture is probably only one of the possible approaches to the set of challenges that the AICA faces.

Its first implementations have, however, shown that a Multi-Agent System architecture was a viable solution. It has to be tested and discussed further. The AICAproto21 prototype, depicted in this book, was created under the AICA IWG's auspices by a small consortium (Théron, Argonne National Laboratories, Masaryk University and Stag). Under an LPGL licence, ANL is currently developing and testing it further.

The way forward for the science of AICA requires, at this moment, that such prototypes blossom and be evaluated. This was the very reason for creating the AICA IWG (www.aica-iwg.org).

References

Blakely, B., & Theron, P. (2018). *Decision flow-based agent action planning.* Prague, 18–20 October 2017. https://export.arxiv.org/pdf/1804.07646

Castelfranchi, C. (1995). Guarantees for autonomy in cognitive agent architecture. Lecture notes on artificial intelligence, intelligent agents. In *890(ECAI-94 workshop on agent theories, architectures, and languages*, Amsterdam, the Netherlands August 8–9, 1994 proceedings) (pp. 56–70).

Dorri, A., Kanhere, S. S., & Jurdak, R. (2018). Multi-agent systems: A survey. *IEEE Access, 6,* 28573–28593.

Gonzalez, C., Lerch, J. F., & Lebiere, C. (2003). Instance-based learning in dynamic decision making. *Cognitive Science, 27*(2003), 591–635.

Heinl, C. H. (2014). Artificial (intelligent) agents and active cyber Defence: Policy implications. In P. Brangetto, M. Maybaum, & J. Stinissen (Eds.), *6th international conference on cyber conflict* (pp. 53–66). NATO CCD COE Publications.

Jajodia, S., & Noel, S. (2010). *Advanced cyber attack modeling, analysis, and visualization.* AFRL/RIGA – George Mason University.

Kotenko, I., Konovalov, A., & Shorov, A. (2012). Agent-based simulation of cooperative defence against botnets. *Concurrency and Computation. Practice and Experience, 24*(6), 573–588.

Kott, A. (2018, October 12). Bonware to the rescue: The future autonomous cyber defense agents. In *Conference on applied machine learning for information security (CAMLIS),* Washington, DC

Kott, A. et al. (2019). *Autonomous intelligent cyber-defense agent (AICA) reference architecture. Release 2.0.* NATO/STO/IST-152 RTG: ARL-SR-0421, https://arxiv.org/abs/1803.10664

Lebiere, C., & Anderson, J. R. (1993). A connectionist implementation of the ACT-R production system. In *Proceedings of the fifteenth annual conference of the cognitive science society* (pp. 635–640). Institute of Cognitive Science University of Colorado-Boulder.

LeBlanc, B., Losiewicz, P., & Hourlier, S. (2017). *A program for effective and secure operations by autonomous agents and human operators in communications constrained tactical environments.* NATO IST-152 workshop.

Lipshitz, R. (1997). Naturalistic decision making. Perspectives on decision errors. In C. E. Zsambok & G. A. Klein (Eds.), *Naturalistic decision making.* Lawrence Erlbaum Associates.

Muller, J. P., Singh, M. P., & Rao, A. S. (1999). *Intelligent Agents V. Agent Theories, Architectures, and Languages. 5th international workshop proceedings/ATAL'98, Paris, France, July 4–7, 1998* (Lecture notes in computer science, Vol. 1555). Springer.

Noel, S., Harley, E., Tam, K. H., & Gyor, G. (2015). Big-data architecture for cyber attack graphs representing security relationships in NoSQL graph databases. In *IEEE symposium on technologies for homeland security.* Greater Boston, Massachusetts.

Padgham, L., & Winikoff, M. (2004). *Developing intelligent agent systems: A practical guide* (Wiley Series in Agent Technology) (p. 2004). Wiley.

Palau, A. S., Dhada, M. H., & Parlikad, A. K. (2019). Multi-agent system architectures for collaborative prognostics. *Journal of Intelligent Manufacturing, 2019*(30), 2999–3013.

Ridley, A. (2018). Machine learning for autonomous cyber defense. *The Next Wave, 22*(1), 7–14.

Russell, S. J., & Norwig, P. (1995). *Artificial intelligence – A modern approach: The intelligent agent book* (Prentice Hall series in artificial intelligence). Prentice Hall.

Smart, P. R., Scutt, T., Sycara, K., & Shadbolt, N. R. (2016). Integrating ACT-R cognitive models with the unity game engine. In J. O. Turner, M. Nixon, U. Bernardet, & S. DiPaola (Eds.), *Integrating cognitive architectures into virtual character design* (pp. 35–64). IGI Global.

Theron, P. (2013). ICT resilience as dynamic process and cumulative aptitude. In P. Theron & S. Bologna (Eds.), *Critical information infrastructure protection and resilience in the ICT sector* (pp. 1–35). Hershey.

Theron, P. (2014). *Lieutenant A and the rottweilers. A pheno-cognitive analysis of a fire-fighter's experience of a critical incident and peritraumatic resilience*, PhD thesis. University of Glasgow, Scotland. Available at https://theses.gla.ac.uk/view/creators/Theron=3APaul=3A=3A.html

Theron, P. (2020, November 30). Making AICA agents intelligent: The paradigm of deep decision making. 1st NATO – AICA IWG Virtual Technical Workshop on Autonomous Cyber Defence, NCIA – AICA IWG.

Theron, P., & Kott, A. (2019). When autonomous intelligent Goodware will fight autonomous intelligent malware: A possible future of cyber defense. In *Proceedings of the military communications conference, MILCOM-2019, Norfolk, VA* (p. arXiv:1912.01959). Available from https://arxiv.org/abs/1912.01959

Théron, P. et al. (2020, November 30). *A first prototype of the multi agent system centric AICA reference architecture (MASCARA).* 1st NATO – AICA IWG virtual technical workshop on autonomous cyber defence, NCIA – AICA IWG.

Theron, P., et al. (2020a). Reference architecture of an autonomous agent for cyber defense of complex military systems. In S. Jajodia et al. (Eds.), *Adaptive autonomous secure cyber systems* (pp. 1–21). Springer Nature Switzerland AG.

Theron, P., et al. (2020b). *2020 AICA IWG – NCIA report on autonomous cyber defence. State of the art, gaps and 2021 roadmap*. AICA International Work Group.

Theron, P., Evans, N., Drasar, M., & Guarino, A. (2021). *Autonomous intelligent cyber-defence agent prototype 2021 – Project report*. NATO: NATO Communications & Information Agency (NCIA), VISTA Portal.

Wooldridge, M., Jennings, N. R., & Kinny, D. (1999). A methodology for agent-oriented analysis and design. In *Proceedings of the third international conference on autonomous agents (Agents 99), Seattle, WA* (pp. 69–76).

Chapter 3
Perception of the Environment

Martin Drasar

1 Background

Perception is a critical component of AICA and one of the few that cannot be omitted. Perception provides information about the environment, communicates the results of the agent's actions, and shapes and influences the agent's reasoning. While it may be possible to consider only the raw data gathered from sensors as the perception, this narrow view does not appreciate the complexity involved and only defers the issues of percept processing to other parts of AICA, such as the decision-making engine.

Perception in AICA is as multifaceted concept as it is in biological systems. Even though the artificial systems have the benefit of not being required to copy nature, many of the constraints and drivers are universal. The raw percepts or stimuli go through a lot of preprocessing and transformations before they can be subjected to the reason. Consider the optical illusion in Fig. 3.1. Our brain is hardwired to identify real-world objects, so we get thrown off because they are not there. Moreover, it takes actual willpower to treat this image as just an image. The perception mechanisms shape how we think about our environment, and the same goes for AICA.

There are multiple ways to conceptualize the perception in AICA. One possible way is in the context of the DIKW pyramid, which conceptualizes the relation between data, information, knowledge, and wisdom (Ackoff, 1989). This is depicted in Fig. 3.2, where the perception occupies the two lower tiers of the pyramid (data and information) but can sometimes venture up to the knowledge tier due to its close relation with AICA's world model. Another way we will adopt in this chapter is a pipeline, as shown in Fig. 3.3, consisting of four main parts: physical sensors, logical sensors, transformers, and the world representation.

M. Drasar (✉)
CSIRT-MU, Institute of Computer Science, Masaryk University, Brno, Czechia
e-mail: drasar@ics.muni.cz

© The Author(s), under exclusive license to Springer Nature Switzerland AG 2023
A. Kott (ed.), *Autonomous Intelligent Cyber Defense Agent (AICA)*, Advances in
Information Security 87, https://doi.org/10.1007/978-3-031-29269-9_3

Fig. 3.1 An optical illusion

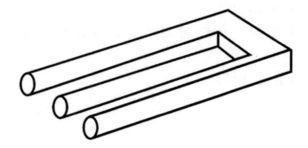

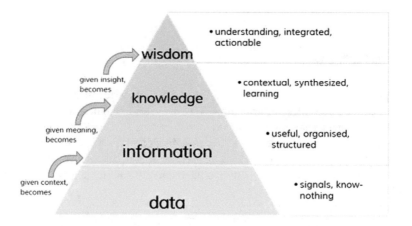

Fig. 3.2 DIKW pyramid. (Baldasarre, 2017)

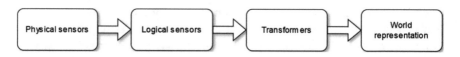

Fig. 3.3 A simple perception pipeline

Physical sensors: are primarily out of the scope of AICA. Physical sensors process non-virtual stimuli reaching the agent from the environment. Each of these sensors has specific operation capabilities, requirements, and physical domain, but they all share the need for power. Therefore, AICA using physical sensors must very carefully manage its power envelope.

Physical sensor examples: Temperature or pressure sensors and noise detectors could be employed by AICA tasked with maintaining physical security inside a building. Perimeter sensors could be used in outside deployment. Gyroscopes and lidars may be used within the context of unmanned vehicles.

Logical sensors: in the context of this chapter, they are understood as a counterpart to the physical ones. That is any source of data that rests within the software. A vast range of data can be fed to AICA in this way. Ranging from its internal state measurements, host diagnostics, and network measurements to open-source intelligence readings and even news feed. The only common attribute of this data is that there is nothing in common. The data provided by logical sensors is heterogeneous, with many dimensions, and can potentially require a large bandwidth to process. These attributes go counter to the current reinforcement learning algorithms, so there is a need for data reduction.

Logical sensor examples: Reading of running processes to gather information about the state of AICA and the infrastructure it operates in. Network probe to gather information about traffic within a guarded infrastructure. A periodic download of the CVE (MITRE) database to provide updates to AICA's knowledge base.

Transformers: provide means to reduce data complexity, dimensionality, and size. They ensure the move from the data tier of the DKIW pyramid up to the information tier. They can provide additional semantics to the data and serve as a heuristic that offloads a part of the logic that we do not want the machine learning (ML) algorithms to discover. There are many different types of processors, arguably more than types of data. The selection of transformers ultimately dictates how an agent perceives the environment and how it can reason about it.

Transformer examples: Statistical aggregation and transformation of observed network traffic (from packet traces to flows). Anomaly detection (from flows to events). Application of ML-driven tools (from events to patterns).

World representation: is AICA's representation of itself and of the environment it operates in. A model of the world as it is being perceived. It is the foundation on which the agent chooses its actions and against which their impact is evaluated.

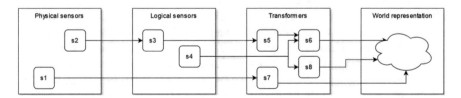

Fig. 3.4 A complex perception pipeline

Currently, there exist no firm guidelines for the design of state representation. If anything, it is considered an art by some because the representation influences which algorithms can be used, how demanding the agent's training will be, and ultimately, what the agent can achieve.

Even though a pipeline is a fitting and easy-to-grasp concept, it gives an illusion of serial data processing. However, the sensors are usually independent, and the same mostly holds for transformers. As the data is being processed in parallel, delays, time skews, and interval differences are bound to happen, as illustrated in Fig. 3.4. The impact of these irregularities strongly depends on the agent's mode of operation and choice of algorithms. Passive observing agents are largely unaffected because they can evaluate snapshots of the world state as the data comes in. However, for active agents, this de-serialization can impact AICA's efficiency by providing only partial observations over a longer time, thus impacting both learning and acting.

This chapter addresses the complexity surrounding the perception and provides readers with guidelines and state-of-the-art examples. It does not present definite solutions, as many of these problems are still open and subject to research, but all the presented approaches have either been peer-reviewed or tested in attempts to develop a functional AICA.

2 From Percepts to the World Representation

AICAs will always operate in a partially observable environment. In fact, the observations provided by sensors will usually cover only a sliver of the environment. AICA will not observe, among other things, triggers that make other actors behave the way they do. Therefore, to enable rational and sensible actions, AICA must construct its belief state to be as close to the objective world state as possible. Through a sensible world representation, perception can go a long way to enable AICA to do just that. Conversely, choosing a suboptimal world representation will widen the gap between the belief and the objective state.

The world representation, as constructed from observations, can be split into three categories depending on their complexity and expressive power – atomic, factored, and structured (Russel & Norvig, 2020). With the atomic representation, states are indivisible and without an internal structure. This is the equivalent of perception playing no role in shaping the agent's understanding and providing only raw inputs to the decision-making engine. With the factored representation, incoming percepts are processed and represented as collections of attributes. These attributes may be primary, where parts of raw inputs are given their semantics, or secondary, where raw inputs are transformed into higher-level representations encoding some knowledge. With structured representation, attributes also encode their relation to other attributes. Going from atomic, over factored to structured representation leads to a sharp increase in expressiveness, where the world representation can concisely describe a complex environment and its interactions.

However, this increase in expressiveness causes an inevitable increase in complexity, impacting reasoning and learning. Real-world AICA thus may be forced to combine representations of all three categories, carefully balancing the upsides and downsides.

Orthogonal to complexity, nevertheless with a considerable impact on creating a sensible world representation, is the matter of how perception deals with time. While analog sensors may measure continuously and provide an uninterrupted stream of stimuli, perception in AICA is inevitably discrete, with processing being done in independent time slices (Russel & Norvig, 2020). Meanwhile, sensors are unlikely to be synchronized, and their readings (or transformations) arrive at various intervals. It is then bound to happen that percepts related to one event will be split between two or more time slices. This, in turn, can impact the decision-making because the responses to AICA's actions may be incomplete. Three strategies can be used to counter this effect: slice extension, multi-slice perception, and contextual perception. Slice extension, as the name suggests, extends the time frame when percepts are collected. The problem persists, but the frequency of occurrence decreases, and the impact could be considered acceptable at some point. The downside is that an acceptable interval may be long enough to hamper AICA's speed of reaction to the point of jeopardizing its mission. With multi-sliced perception, the percepts are sampled in parallel with different interval lengths. Perception then produces multiple state updates, and AICA needs to have a strategy to cope with that, either on the perception level or at the decision-making level. With contextual perception, the percepts are still sampled; however, 1 to N neighboring samples are inspected, and the completeness of percepts is evaluated in relation to AICA's actions. This approach is the most complex one, as it requires the perception to have a clear model of which percepts occur and when. As with the complexity issue above, real-world AICA will likely have to combine all three approaches, carefully balancing the trade-offs.

The last consideration when designing the perception mechanism of AICA is the distinction between active and passive sensors, which can also be viewed as a distinction between the pull and the push model. Active sensors (pull) gather percepts as a result of their interaction with the environment. Passive sensors (push) receive stimuli from the environment and do not exert control over when and how it happens. As such, active sensors can be set in such a way to diminish the impact of the aforementioned sampling issue. However, this usually comes with considerably increased power or bandwidth requirements, as mentioned in the following text.

3 Power and Bandwidth Constraints

A naïve wisdom would suggest that the more sensors and the more sensory inputs, the better. After all, every new sensor can shorten the gap between the world representation and the world's objective state. New sensors can provide new auxiliary readings, additional details to already present sensors, and even wholly new percepts enabling the AICA to understand the world around itself. However, with each added sensor, there is a trade-off (Theron et al., 2020). On the pure hardware level, each enabled sensor equates to energy expenditure. Whether this is a problem is a matter of AICA's deployment. Large stationary installations would probably be unaffected; however, AICAs on mobile platforms, personnel, or autonomous devices will have a strict power envelope, and the decision which sensors to use and when will rest on many factors, which are also shared with sensors on the software level. These usually do not have such stringent power limitations; rather, their issue is bandwidth. With pull-based sensors, too short sampling rate or too broad data collection can easily overwhelm the ability of AICA to process and reflect on the data.

When designing an AICA, one has to balance several sensor properties and prioritize sensors providing maximum utility for AICA's operation.

- Sensors (or their percepts) should be ordered by their importance for the decision-making process. This entails understanding how the percepts are transformed into the world representation and how the representation influences the decision-making. This can either be achieved through methods of explainable AI or by extensive testing, evaluating the importance of each sensor.
- If the hierarchy is established, a base set of sensors should be selected, and AICA should activate the rest on demand.
- Especially for power-constrained environments, there should be a strategy to limit sensor function with the smallest possible impact on decision making, e.g., turning off sensors, prolonging sampling intervals, switching from pull to push mode, etc.
- AICA's decision-making should also be fortified against sensor impairment or partial sensor subversion.

4 Trusting the Perception

One common theme in the literature is that the sensors provide objective input to agents' systems. Whether they are physical or logical sensors, it is taken for granted that the percepts they are producing are forming the world representation that is a clear reflection of the objective world state. This, however, need not hold in deployment settings. In fact, unintentional or deliberate fault of sensors can widen the gap between AICA's belief and objective state so much that the actions of an agent will go contrary to its goals.

Attacks against physical sensors have been studied in the literature (Nasralla et al., 2020; Man et al., 2020). Recently, the interest has been in the area of autonomous cars (Yan et al., 2016; Liu & Park, 2021); however, for any potential AICA deployment where physical sensors may play a role, the same concepts apply. While the faults cannot be eliminated, there are ways to build fault tolerance into the system, namely into data acquisition and data processing. For data acquisition, that can take the form of active probing of the environment against a known baseline

(Shoukry et al., 2015). For data processing, a simple sensor redundancy, fault-tolerant approaches researched in the area of sensor networks, and others can be used (Modarez et al., 2020). Regardless of the chosen approach, there will be incurred costs stemming from the need to increase the number of physical sensors, both as a procurement cost and increased power envelope.

For attacks against the logical sensors, mostly the same holds as for the physical ones. Active probing and sensor redundancy can be employed with the same expected results; however, some measures may be unattainable. Consider the example of the AICA measuring the state of the machine it is on. If the adversary managed to hide itself via hijacking certain syscalls, no amount of sensor redundancy would help because ultimately, every probe or every query would end up calling said syscalls, and the adversary would remain hidden. In such a case, only indirect information may hint at the presence of an adversary. One may argue that the time when an adversary hijacks syscalls is the time when the machine is effectively lost, but the same principle applies in different scenarios, where there is only one ultimate source of information for logical sensors, which is susceptible to subversion.

Considering the previous paragraphs, the perception cannot and should not be fully trusted, and the possibility of its subversion should be taken into account, especially when AICA is being built as a resilient solution operating in an adversarial environment. However, the price to maximize the trust in perception may be too high, and alternative solutions may have to be employed. Aside from fault-tolerant decision making, multi-agent setups of AICA allow for perception sharing. In such a case, the setup can be considered a sensor network, and all the approaches, issues and limitations apply.

Finally, the perception may not only be a victim of an external adversary but also of wrong expectations. The purpose of perception is mapping sensory inputs to possible real-world states, with the key word being "possible" here. Most sensors come with expectations about the domain of possible values or their combination. However, the vast history of program faults caused by unexpected inputs should be treated as a cautionary tale. With physical sensors, the domain of percepts is bound by physical laws, but with logical sensors, all bets are off. That is why we have a lot of provably secure bridges and not many provably secure programs.

5   Developing a Perception Model for AICA

Perception models, i.e., world representations and associated transformations, are being extensively researched in the areas of autonomous cars, planes, and robots, where correct processing of environmental stimuli is of paramount importance. A similar situation is in natural language processing, where approaches to word embedding for encoding semantic similarity between words can also be considered a perception model for natural languages (Mikolov et al., 2013).

However, perception models for fully virtual entities like AICA are not extensively researched. As mentioned earlier, sensory inputs are treated as objective, and the creator of such a virtual entity is left to develop the perception model on their own, despite there being no solid guidance in the literature. Even the seminal work of Russel and Norwig, which provides probably the most complete exploration of the field of artificial intelligence, only skirts over this topic and rather focuses on the transformations of visual and physical stimuli. However, the book at least presents three essential properties which a good world representation should have (Russel & Norvig, 2020):

- it contains enough information for the agent to make good decisions,
- it is structured so that it can be updated efficiently,
- it is natural in the sense that it corresponds to the real world.

These are essential properties but not as easy to use as a starting point.

Modeling the cybersecurity domain, i.e., creating a perception model that is a good representation of the environment and satisfies the three properties above, is not an easy task. Unlike the scenarios that are being used across the literature, the cybersecurity domain in its entirety is highly dynamic, ever-expanding, and complex. The model has to reflect this to provide actionable information to the agent. Nevertheless, with such complexity, one can easily run into the so-called curse of dimensionality, when the total number of states that an agent can encounter is only a tiny fraction of states that exist in a world representation. And the agent would be wasting scarce resources to try and work with it. At the same time, it is not possible to simply resort to methods reducing the dimensionality of the representation, such as low-dimensional embedding via unsupervised learning (Saul & Roweis, 2003) or principal component analysis. While these methods are perfectly applicable in a technical sense, lowering the dimension count risk going counter to one of the aforementioned properties – that the representation is natural. If AICAs are ever to be used as a replacement for human cybersecurity experts or trusted with control over infrastructure, a key requirement will be full auditability in the form of explainable AI. However, if sensor inputs are non-linearly transformed into compact representation, AICAs and humans lose a shared vocabulary for explanation.

Currently, the only way to create satisfactory perception models is to handcraft them together with required heuristics (transformations) and painstakingly evaluate their efficiency. The author is aware of research in the area of unsupervised dimensionality reduction, which preserves explainability; however, that research is still in too early phase to be useful to the reader.

As there do not seem to be guidelines for creating perception models in an area as complex as cybersecurity, the following text will present a couple of use cases, which should help readers gain insights useful for building their own models. These use cases were taken from real-life attempts to create autonomous attackers driven by reinforcement learning algorithms.

Each of these use cases was realized within the CYST cybersecurity simulation engine, which is, to our knowledge, the currently most complex cybersecurity simulator that is freely available. (Drašar et al., 2020) CYST is a multi-agent discrete-event simulator based on message passing and tailored for cybersecurity applications. Given its complexity, only the parts relevant to the topic of perception are introduced in the following text. However, this chapter is accompanied by a code repository where the presented use cases are implemented, and readers are welcome to try and tinker with the ideas presented here.

5.1 Environment – The Objective Reality

The environment observed by the AICA is the environment simulated by CYST and defined by its simulation model. To minimize the cognitive load on the reader, this text uses only the bare minimum needed to execute and understand the presented use cases. However, if the reader is so inclined, they can further explore the simulation model in the relevant paper or the CYST's documentation (Drašar, CYST, 2022).

The infrastructure where AICA resides consists of simulated machines on which services are running. These machines are connected via a simulated network that replicates an ethernet network without networking details. The network is partitioned utilizing active network devices called routers. AICA is just one of the services running on one or more simulated machines. AICA communicates with or influences the environment through messages. These messages are also the only mechanism through which AICA can observe the environment.

The messages used in CYST come in two types: requests and responses. One request-response pair represents an entire exchange related to one AICA's action. The fragmentation related to, e.g., packets or even TCP sessions, is treated as an implementation detail; thus, the perception is fully realized through observing one response to each request. Messages are a collection of attributes, some of whom have a factually finite domain, some have a technically finite domain, and the domain for some is infinite. The following table summarizes the attributes and their function:

Message	
id	Unique identifier of a message. The id is the same for request and response in a pair
type	Request or response
src_ip, dst_ip	Source and destination IP addresses of the message (IPv4 or IPv6)
src_service, dst_service	Source and destination service (in simulation treated as a string, technically a port number)
ttl	Message time to live (used to prevent routing cycles)
metadata	Observable statistical properties, such as packet count, flow length, etc.
authentication/ authorization	Authentication or authorization token (multi-factor authentication intricacies are purposefully omitted)
session	The persistent connection between two services

Request (in addition to all Message attributes)	
Action	An effect that AICA wants to achieve (for the purpose of this text, a string from a finite domain, otherwise a much more complicated structure)

Response (in addition to all Message attributes)	
Status	Structured description of the effect of the request. Contains origin (network, node, service, system), value (success, failure, error), and detail (an enumeration of possible values).
Content	Currently, unstructured data sent in response.

Session	
Start	A tuple containing an originating IP address and a service of the session
End	A tuple containing a destination IP address and a service of the session

These attributes are the variables that AICA can observe for the purpose of this text. The number of variables is higher within the CYST simulation, but these were omitted for clarity as the added complexity does not affect the proposed approaches. Also, despite the previously expressed concern about trust in perception, the presented use case treats all these observed attributes as trustworthy and reflecting the objective state, because CYST does not currently support fabrication of wrong percepts.

The following text presents several potential approximations of the objective state, which is perceived from the attributes of incoming responses. These approximations are largely independent, and their ordering rather reflects a thought process when developing the perception model than some kind of hierarchy.

5.2 First Approximation – Taking Inputs Verbatim

The first and probably the most straightforward way to represent the objective state is based on responses being the only percept that the AICA has. The world representation is constructed as a set of all possible response values.

Size: The size is 2^n, where n is the number of bits in each response. If we take a compact representation of the response structure above (and give ourselves a bit of leeway in limiting the infinite domain attributes and set the strings at most 256 bits long), we will reach the n over 1500.

Pros: This representation is very easy to make. Just take the incoming response and pass it to the decision-making engine to process.

Cons: This is a clear case of the curse of dimensionality. States that are to be encountered during an AICA's run will represent only a minuscule portion of the entire state space, and the burden of data filtering and turning it into a reasonable belief state will be left to the decision-making engine, which will have to expend disproportional amount of energy.

5.3 Second Approximation – Elimination of (Semi) static Observations

As mentioned before, the number of states that could effectively be encountered is disproportionate to the size of the world representation. One of the reasons is that many observations are static or semi-static within the context of AICA's operation. Consider the type of message. It can be either a request or a response; however, the perception only processes the responses. This attribute is static and can be freely omitted without any loss of precision. The same goes for source IP addresses and services of both message and its session, as these are fixed for the AICA. Destination IP addresses can be considered semi-static if all AICAs activities happen within specific subnets. In such a case, it is not necessary to process the entire range of IP addresses, and only a subset can be a basis for world representation.

Size: The size is still 2^n, where n is the number of non-static bits in each response.
Pros: This representation is still as easy as the first approximation to make and requires only limited analysis.
Cons: The actual reduction in world representation size depends on the nature of observations, and there is no easy way to specify a fixed upper bound.

5.4 Approximation Detour – The Interplay Between Request and Responses

The selection of actions is not a responsibility of the perception, as it belongs to the decision-making engine. However, unlike many scenarios that can be seen in the literature, in cybersecurity, an action may have a similar complexity as a response. That is, not some tightly packed domain or one or more real numbers, but a complex structure dependent on the observed percepts. AICA thus must be able to use the data from the observation and must be able to use them accordingly.

Approximations of the objective state may reduce precision, especially the ones in the following text. Yet, AICA's actions may require precise attributes for their correct execution. Therefore, any lossy approximation or transformation must be accompanied by supplementary data to enable the reconstruction of the attributes within the decision-making engine.

5.5   Third Approximation – Indexing of Large Domains

Among the attributes in the responses, some expand the world representation unreasonably, at least considering the total number of states the AICA can encounter. For such large domains, it is better to keep a dictionary of encountered values and map them to an index that is used in the world representation.

Size: This approximation enables almost arbitrary size reduction of the world representation by specifying a fixed index size.

Pros: The size reduction does not come with a loss of information and benefits larger domains more. The approximation is still comparatively easy to implement. Using a fixed index with a reasonable eviction strategy can enable AICA to forget superfluous observations.

Cons: Using the index can hamper the transferability of the algorithms because the mappings of attribute values may not be static. This non-static property can also harm the learning algorithms, where a change in mapping between runs may lead to wrong transition function inference. Fixed index sizes risk unintended consequences in case of overflow. This is further exacerbated if AICA is trained in diverse and fluctuating environments, where diversity of percepts will fuel the index overflow.

5.6   Fourth Approximation – State Restructuring

There is a distinct difference between the objective state as was described earlier, and the contents of responses. AICA's version of this objective state – its belief state – is pieced from small probes of request-response pairs. However, there is no reason why the perception should not be modeled closer to the objective state as it is being understood.

This is one of the possible versions of world representation:

Machine			Machine			
IP	Services	Sessions	IP	Services	Sessions	...

The perception is centered around the information about possible targets. For each target, an IP address, the running services, and active sessions are retained. All this information can be index-mapped, especially the services, as their domain is finite, and many services are likely to be shared among different machines. There would probably be a limit on the number of machines the AICA had in its operating memory.

Size: is likely to be similar to the third approximation. In this approximation, information is only restructured and not necessarily changed.

Pros: this heuristic approach removes the burden of understanding the world from AICA's decision-making, and it can focus more on the higher-level strategic decisions. It also provides a more natural representation that AICA's operator can understand.

Cons: depending on the restructuring, this approximation can help or hinder the decision-making process. It is thus very dependent on the capabilities of the person doing the restructuring.

5.7   Fifth Approximation – Explicit Activity History

Operations in the cybersecurity domain naturally have complex dependencies on past events. The decision-making process thus has to keep track of what was done by AICA, how the counterparty reacted, how the infrastructure evolved, and so on. While these considerations can be technically modeled as a k-order Markov process, the k would be very large.

Current decision-making algorithms tackle these dependencies, e.g., through the use of LSTM neural networks, Gated Recurrent Units, and similar. However, training and imprinting these memories to be correctly used over disjoint response-request pairs can be resource-consuming or currently infeasible.

The alternative is for perception to act as an explicit memory that is (partially) taking the role of decision-making processes. In the presented use case, this could mean adding new attributes to the world representation by means of also observing the requests. The potential representation for a service can then look like this:

Service				
Name	Version	Vulnerable	Exploitation attempts	Time since the last exploitation

In this case, *name* and *version* are taken from responses, *vulnerable* is evaluated by consulting the list of vulnerable services (CVE or such), *exploitation attempts*, and *time* are taken from requests.

Size: each new attribute expands the world representation; however, this expansion can be limited by carefully choosing an appropriate domain.

Pros: this approach, which is the first strong application of transformers into the perception pipeline, provides several guarantees that the dependency on LSTM and such do not. The memory over which the decision is being made is explicit, precise, and does not rely on gradual imprinting into a neural network. This explicitness also supports better explainability.

Cons: Some important information may be hidden from the decision-making process if the attributes are not chosen carefully.

5.8   Sixth Approximation – Additional Transformations Within the Perception

This final approximation is an umbrella one for every other conceivable transformation that can be added to the perception pipeline. In principle, each new transformation moves the logic away from the decision-making engine through heuristics application. The goal is to let the decision-making engine concentrate on high-level decisions while automating the things that are possible to be automated. Today, this approach seems the most viable one to achieve notable results.

6   Summary and Conclusions

Perception is a key component of AICA, strongly shaping and influencing decision-making. This chapter introduced perception as a pipeline that acquires, transforms, and stores the raw percepts into a form that benefits the decision-making engine the most. The extent of this benefit depends on several important decisions taken when developing a perception model of AICA:

- What are the intended complexity and expressive power of the world representation?
- How should the perception deal with time?
- Should it be actively polling the percepts or waiting for their arrival?
- What power or bandwidth constraints are there for percepts' processing, and what is the importance of specific sensors?
- How can perception be trusted in the adversarial environment?

This chapter discussed these questions and presented trade-offs associated with various decisions. It then delved deeper into developing an actual perception model for AICA. Because the cybersecurity domain where AICA operates is much more complex than the traditional environments used in the literature, it introduced CYST, a cybersecurity simulation engine whose simulation model was used as an objective reality on which the world representation building approaches were demonstrated. In total, six approaches to approximating the objective state were presented, and their properties were explored:

- Passing the raw percepts to the decision-making engine.
- Eliminating (semi)static observations.
- Using indexing to eliminate the impact of percepts with large domains.
- Restructuring the world state to a form useful for the decision-making engine.
- Keeping an explicit activity history.
- Including additional transformations within perceptions.

Because these approaches were developed in the context of CYST, which is freely available, users are welcome to try implementing them and experiment with their implementation.

References

Ackoff, R. (1989). From data to wisdom. *Journal of Applied Systems Analysis, 16*, 3–9.

Baldasarre, M. (2017). Think big: learning contexts, algorithms and data science. *Research on Education and Media*, stránky 69–83.

Drašar, M. (2022). *CYST*. Načteno z. https://muni.cz/go/cyst/

Drašar, M., Moskal, S., Yang, S., & Zaťko, P. (2020). Session-level adversary intent-driven cyber-attack simulator. In *2020 IEEE/ACM 24th International Symposium on Distributed Simulation and Real Time Applications (DS-RT)*.

Liu, J., & Park, J.-M. (2021). "Seeing is not always believing": Detecting perception error attacks against autonomous vehicles. *IEEE Transactions on Dependable and Secure Computing*, stránky 2209–2223.

Man, Y., Li, M., & Gerdes, R. (2020). GhostImage: Remote perception attacks against camera-based image classification systems. In *RAID 2020*.

Mikolov, T., Corrado, G. S., Chen, K., & Dean, J. (2013). Efficient estimation of word representations in vector space. In *Proceedings of the International Conference on Learning Representations*.

MITRE. (nedatováno). *CVE*. Načteno z. https://cve.mitre.org/

Modarez, H., Kiumarsi, B., Lewis, F. L., Frank, F., & Davoudi, A. (2020). Resilient and robust synchronization of multiagent systems under attacks on sensors and actuators. *IEEE Transactions on Cybernetics*, stránky 1240–1250.

Nasralla, M. M., García-Magariño, I., & Lloret, J. (2020). Defenses against perception-layer attacks on iot smart furniture for impaired people. *IEEE Access*, stránky 119795–119805.

Russel, S., & Norvig, P. (2020). *Artificial intelligence: A modern approach* (4th ed.). Pearson.

Saul, L. K., & Roweis, S. T. (2003). Think globally, fit locally: Unsupervised learning of low dimensional manifolds. *Journal of Machine Learning Research*, stránky 119–155.

Shoukry, Y., Martin, P., Yona, Y., Diggavi, S., & Srivastava, M. (2015). PyCRA: Physical challenge-response authentication for active sensors under spoofing attacks. In *CCS '15: Proceedings of the 22nd ACM SIGSAC conference on computer and communications security* (stránky 1004–1015).

Theron, P., Kott, A., Drašar, M., Rzadca, K., LeBlanc, B., Pihelgas, M., …, de Gaspari, F. (2020). Reference architecture of an autonomous agent for cyber defense of complex military systems. V *Adaptive Autonomous Secure Cyber Systems* (stránky 1–21).

Yan, C., Xu, W., & Liu, J. (2016). Can you trust autonomous vehicles: Contactless attacks. *DEF CON, 24*.

Chapter 4
Perception of Cyber Threats

Kevin Kornegay, Kofi Nyarko, Jeffrey S. Chavis, and Ahmad Ridley

1 Introduction

An important aspect of cyber threat perception is reducing the uncertainty level represented by the large volumes of cyber events collected from host-based and network-based sensors (Shakut et al., 2020). By automating the collection, filtering, and aggregation of these events in real-time, threat perception can be improved. In addition, cyber alerts generated from such context can enable the prioritization of threat alerts and, ultimately, efficient and effective responses to threats. Autonomous Intelligent Cyber-Defense Agents (AICA) can identify and prioritize cyber threats faster, and in an increasing number of scenarios, better than human cyber defenders, motivating their inclusion in the cyber threat analysis process (Muser & Garriott, 2021).

K. Kornegay (✉)
Cybersecurity Assurance & Policy (CAP) Center, Morgan State University,
Baltimore, MD, USA
e-mail: kevin.kornegay@morgan.edu

K. Nyarko
Electrical and Computer Engineering, Morgan State University, Baltimore, MD, USA
e-mail: kofi.nyarko@morgan.edu

J. S. Chavis
Asymmetric Operations Sector, The Johns Hopkins University Applied Physics Laboratory,
Laurel, MD, USA
e-mail: Jeffrey.Chavis@jhuapl.edu

A. Ridley
Laboratory for Advanced Cybersecurity Research, National Security Agency (NSA),
Laurel, MD, USA
e-mail: adridle@uwe.nsa.gov

© The Author(s), under exclusive license to Springer Nature Switzerland AG 2023   63
A. Kott (ed.), *Autonomous Intelligent Cyber Defense Agent (AICA)*, Advances in
Information Security 87, https://doi.org/10.1007/978-3-031-29269-9_4

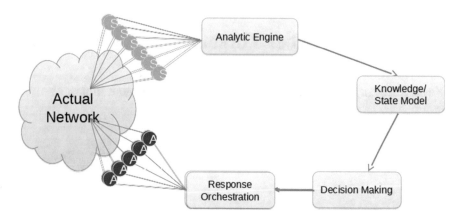

Fig. 4.1 Cyber-defense monitoring and decision-making feedback loop

Cyber threats can vary depending on the type of network being monitored. Figure 4.1 below provides an abstract view of a closed-loop monitoring and decision-making system. The sensors, S, collect cyber data from hosts and network devices. The data is processed by fixed, rules-based, or machine learning-based analytics, producing results such as cyber alerts about potentially compromised network devices. The analytic engine results are aggregated to create a current overall network state, which provides a context about the security or availability of the network. Based on this state of information, AICA decide how to respond to potential threats. Any response is implemented on the network using actuators, A. The sensors continue collecting data, initiating the next phase of the monitoring loop, providing feedback to the agents about the impact of their decisions.

The type of threats against an Internet-connected, open network will differ from a closed network with no internet access. Agents monitoring these open networks must continuously detect threats originating from internal and external sources, while agents monitoring closed networks are probably more concerned about threats originating from internal sources. Another example of cyber threat diversity involves the homogeneity of hardware and software on a network. The cyber threats to the homogenous enterprise networks of Windows workstations and servers vary from threats to an industrial control system (ICS) network. Furthermore, the spectrum of threats encountered by an agent monitoring a heterogeneous enterprise network containing a combination of Internet of Things (IoT) devices, Windows- and Linux-based workstations, servers, routers, and iOS- and Android-based mobile devices can be extremely large, and complex. Nguyen and Reddi (2021) provide specific examples of these types of network environments that can be monitored by AI-based agents. AICA have the ability to either quickly detect threats or adapt to various threats encountered across these diverse network environments.

One specific type of automated agent is a defensive cyber deception agent. A decoy environment consists of realistic, lightweight decoy agents that appear to be real systems running real services from an attacker's perspective performing actions, such as IP address scanning, on the network (Walter et al., 2021). These decoy agents are deployed on a real network alongside real systems to maximize the probability of detecting and quickly mitigating threats from cyber-attackers. A high number of false systems helps provide an asymmetric advantage for cyber defenders by distracting an attacker from the real assets. This forces an attacker to take additional actions, increasing the likelihood of revealing themselves and the defender detecting the threat in its early attack stage. Leveraging deceptive AICA for improved threat perception can be effective in reducing the inherent cyber-attacker advantage (Muser & Garriott, 2021).

Since authorized network users usually do not interact with decoys, these agents can provide an early warning, high-confidence threat signal to defenders about an attacker's presence (Walter et al., 2021). In contrast to light-weight baits, honeypots are a different type of high-fidelity deception system. These high-interaction fake systems are connected to but located outside the real network. Once an attacker enters a honeypot, defenders can gain insight about cyber-attack threats, such as goals and severity level, through further attacker interactions with the deceptive honeypot agents. Ferguson-Walter et al. (2019) describe how the impact of cyber deception can be extended further, leading an attacker towards a specific incorrect belief.

However, there exists a full spectrum of AICA, from automated (i.e., static, expert-driven rules) agents to autonomous (i.e., adaptive, Artificial Intelligence (AI)-based rules) agents, which can be used to improve cyber threat perception. Although automated agents created by human expert-based rules and logic can be beneficial, autonomous, artificial intelligence (AI)-based agents evolve. Muser and Garriott (2021) describe the potential short- and long-term benefits of AICA, and how AICA can adapt to detect changing cyber threats. For example, as network administrators add new machines to a network, new hardware and software attack surfaces are introduced. The time required for administrators to manually update the security rules/policies that guide automated agents would potentially leave the network vulnerable to the speed and scale of new and existing cyber threats. AI-based agents that efficiently learn to defend the new attack surface autonomously can mitigate this speed and scale challenge better than automated agents.

AICA have been employed to defend against cyber-attacks. Such agents have been trained using supervised and unsupervised methods to perform automated and autonomous cyber-defense tasks, such as intrusion detection, malware detection, and data privacy protection (Shakut et al., 2020). Recently, reinforcement learning (RL) has been increasingly used to autonomously detect (and respond) to cyber-attacks (Nguyen & Reddi, 2021). Unlike other ML methods, like supervised learning from labeled input-output examples, an RL-based agent learns its behavior from interacting directly with the environment. It is a trial and error approach that attempts to imitate the basic manner in which humans learn. Given a state of the environment and a reward signal indicating how good or bad an action is, the agent learns a sequence of good actions to achieve a goal (Shakut et al., 2020). For cyber threat perception, an RL agent can learn from which host or network device to gather additional data to reduce the uncertainty of cyber threats. These RL-based AICA

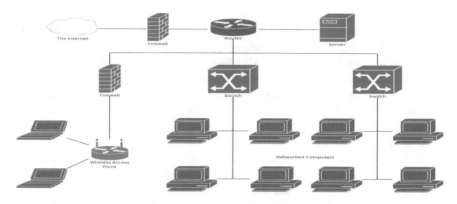

Fig. 4.2 Sample enterprise computer network

can also be leveraged to adapt the capabilities of decoy agents to maintain the effects of cyber-deception (Ferguson-Walter et al., 2019). Both ML- and RL-based AICA provide increased ability to detect threats hidden among large amounts of cyber event data.

Different AICA agent hierarchies can be implemented for improved cyber threat perception. For example, a single agent can be effective in monitoring a small, homogenous enterprise network. The single agent would collect cyber data from each devices or aggregated data across each device to perform malware detection. For larger, heterogenous network monitoring, this agent structure would be inefficient. A decentralized hierarchy of multiple agents is more practical and generalizes across multiple cyber environments, such as Internet of Things, Cloud Computing, and 5G Networks (Nguyen & Reddi, 2021).

Individual agents located on each network device, e.g., the switches, routers, and computers shown in Fig. 4.2, provide local monitoring and report their results to higher-level agents performing global monitoring. The higher-level agents use these results to monitor different network segments, e.g., the wireless and wired segments. Teaming and cooperation among agents can provide additional benefit in reducing uncertainty about the nature of a cyber threat.

Finally, in the remaining sections, we will discuss the potential impact of AICAs in a hierarchical, decentralized agent structure in perceiving complex cyber-attacks within various, dynamic cyber environments.

2 Simplified Hierarchical Cyber-Defense Agents for Threat Perception

As discussed in previous chapters, in general terms, a software agent can be defined as a software entity that functions continuously and autonomously in a particular environment and can carry out activities flexibly and intelligently that are responsive to changes in the environment (Bradshaw, 1997). Ideally, an agent that functions continuously would be able to learn from its experience and inhabit an environment with other agents and processes collaboratively and cooperatively, moving from place to place as needed (Bradshaw, 1997). In this chapter, the hierarchical agent architecture (Palau et al., 2019) is further explored for the purpose of conceptualizing the implementation of threat perception in AICA. More specifically, cyber-defense agent may be considered as software processes that perform specific monitoring and offensive and defensive functions via individualized configurations that may be duplicated or migrated across multiple operating environments. Hence, these agents are autonomous because they are independently-running entities, individuated by their configuration profiles that govern how they sense, adapt, and affect their local environment. Due to the agent's independent nature, they can be added, removed, and reconfigured without altering other components of the operating environment.

In general, a Cyber-defense agent system should provide the following characteristics: (1) continuous operation, (2) fault tolerance, (3) ability to resist subversion, (4) minimal overhead, (5) dynamic reconfigurability, (6) adaptability, (7) scalability and (8) graceful degradation of service (Spafford & Zamboni, 2000). Regarding continuous operation, a collection of agents may form a group that performs simple or complex coordinated functions that the individual agent can not achieve. The collective agent system can be designed to run continuously if some agents are taken off-line, purposely or through malicious intent, thereby providing continuous cyber-defense functionality.

When agents are deployed hierarchically, they can capture higher-level system states and be able to adapt to changes in global behavior. This hierarchical structure enables agents to be inherently scalable. One bottleneck that agents deployed in this fashion may face lies in the agents' communication mechanism. But there are various methods of circumventing these bottlenecks by minimizing communication between components (Cen et al., 2014). If the service for one or more agents is disabled, the damage is restricted to just those sets, and perhaps those directly depend on their service. Thus, if the agents are correctly organized in mutually independent sets, service degradation will be gradually proportional to the number of agents that stop functioning (Spafford & Zamboni, 2000). The ability to start and stop agents independently enables the possibility of reconfiguring dynamically. This, in turn, allows other agents or processes to migrate agents by overwriting current configurations with configurations from other agents that have demonstrated improved effectiveness at a task in a given environment. Because an agent can be reconfigured arbitrarily, it can obtain its data from an audit trail, probing the system it is running, capturing packets from the network, or capturing data through physical sensors. Thus, cyber-defense activities can be supported across traditional boundaries between the physical system, the operating system host, and networks. Furthermore, since agents are implemented as separate processes on a host, each agent can be implemented in the programming language best suited for the task and the host (e.g., light-weight drone vs. enterprise system).

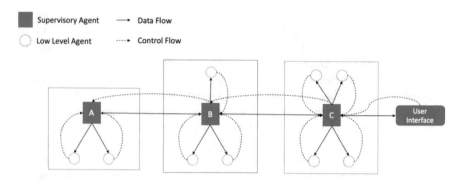

Fig. 4.3 Simplified hierarchical agents

As illustrated in Fig. 4.3, a simplified agent system architecture could consist of generic agent profiles that can be adapted for various functionalities based on their configuration. Besides specific task-based functionalities, agents can be configured in one of 2 primary types: low-level and supervisory. Low-Level agents are distributed over any number of hosts, where they either monitor for specific events or perform task-specific actions. Each agent can persist in its state for a certain period of time defined by its configuration, which enables the detection of long-term attacks. Each low-level agent is configured to monitor for one or more events and report detected events to a supervisory agent, where one such agent exists per host. The supervisory agent oversees all operations of the low-level agents on that host. These agents can start/stop low-level agents and send new configurations as needed. Supervisory agents exist in a hierarchy in which each one may communicate with several parent supervisory agents, where each one monitors and controls several child supervisory agents. This architecture provides redundancy and resistance to the failure of one or more supervisory agents. These agents have access to network-wide data and can thus perform higher-level correlations and detections across several hosts. By combining reports from multiple agents, they can build a unified picture of the status of their host. Supervisory agents at the highest level of the architecture will employ capabilities to interface with users; this may be through a graphical user interface, terminal commands, or physical input/output interfaces on embedded systems. There are several methods by which agents can communicate securely and in a distributed manner, such as through asymmetric encryption over TLS/SSL with publish/subscribe (pub/sub) messaging (Farmer et al., 1996).

Low-level agents consume host/network data via another kind of process called filters (Spafford & Zamboni, 2000). These filter processors are responsible for acquiring specific host/network data types and feeding the filtered data to one or more agents. One efficient process by which agents could receive these data streams is through a pub/sub messaging implementation. A low-level agent would generate a notification when an event is detected on the subscribed data provided by one or more filters based on its current configuration. The agent doesn't have the authority to trigger an alarm or action directly. Hence it sends its event to one or more supervisory agents on the same parent hierarchical level. These agents combine events received across child agents and communicate across sibling supervisory agents to determine the appropriate course of action. Depending on the deployed system architecture, the right course of action may be to generate alerts sent further up the hierarchy to parent supervisory agents or to directly trigger an alarm or action event. Action events are sent across or down the hierarchy to agents capable of executing the actions, where the activities may change the host's communication, state information, or physical posture.

Agents may evolve over time based on their function and information obtained from their environment. For example, suppose the agent utilizes reinforcement learning to detect malicious activity on its local host. In that case, it may evolve to better detect behavior based on communication with, and feedback from, supervisory hosts. This evolution would be captured in its configuration parameters, such as current learned weights of its neural network. If the agent successfully detects desired events, supervisory agents may clone its configuration to other agents on other hosts.

3 Autonomous Hierarchical Agents for Anomaly Detection

Anomaly detection in a complex system of systems can be performed on two primary levels, communication network and application, including environment and system state sensing. These systems often have some aspect of mobility where network nodes wander freely and can join and leave a given network arbitrarily. These network dynamics impose further complications on effective anomaly detection. With traditional centralized solutions, the scale of these types of networks would be an issue since anomaly detection solutions would have to factor in load-balancing and fault tolerance. However, an agent architecture inherently addresses these factors with intelligent autonomous agents.

In the AICA architecture, low-level agents disbursed across fixed and mobile network nodes detect anomalies by analyzing the events on the systems where a data instance designates each event. The data instance possesses defining features (i.e., attributes) (Xie et al., 2011), such as a packet's source/destination address, length, and time at which it was sent for the case of network-level anomaly detection. Features are crucial for distinguishing normal behavior from anomalous behavior. A given communication network typically provides many features per a given data instance, yet they are not necessarily all equally informative (Bhuyan et al., 2014). Low-level agents can be configured independently to observe varying features based on their location within the network and on the systems in which they reside. For example, some agents can be configured to use information-theoretic approaches to help distinguish informative features (Cen et al., 2014; Ham & Choi, 2013; Mas'ud et al., 2014). In this approach, Information Gain (IG) (Mitchell, 1997) and chi-squared (Sharma, 2005) methods can be utilized to select the most informative features.

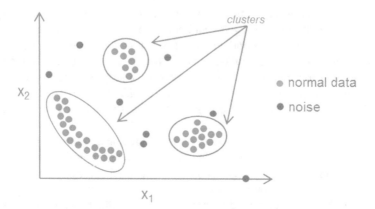

Fig. 4.4 Example of a point anomaly

Similarly, other agents could be configured to choose features and perform anomaly detection based on the Fisher score, the ratio of inter-class variance to the intra-class variance for a given feature, assuming that normal instances form a class and anomalous instances form another class (Crowley et al., 2003). Agents can also be configured to perform a similar method through machine learning (Guyonand & Elisseeff, 2003). In the simplest incarnation, agents can be configured based on hand-pick informative features to help detect anomalies (Al Marakeby et al., 2010).

Low-level agents can detect anomalies by observing data instances (i.e., point anomalies). However, point anomalies do not fit the situations where anomalous behavior is an aggregate of data instances, or when anomalies are associated with given contexts, as shown in Fig. 4.4. In some cases, the anomalous behavior is defined within a context; thus, a given data instance is not anomalous unless it happens within a predefined context (Chandola et al., 2009). In this case, Low-level agents would not conclusively detect anomalies since they may lack the broader context of the state of relevant parts of the network or system. Hence, when the right conditions are met, they send alerts to the supervisory agents that consider all incoming alerts to facilitate the detection of anomalous contextual activity. In contextual anomalies, the data instance has to have some features about the context, whether temporal (i.e., time-relevant), spatial (i.e., location-relevant), or a different kind of context per the problem domain, as shown in Fig. 4.5.

Agents can be configured to detect anomalies through methods that are either signature-based (Migliardi & Merlo, 2013) or behavioral (Bhuyan et al., 2014). Signature-based solutions operate by applying a set of hardwired patterns, signatures, or rules against given behavior(s). An anomaly is detected if a given behavior matches either one of the hardwired signatures. Otherwise, the agent will not tell whether or not the designated behavior is anomalous. While these agents are potentially more efficient in terms of computational cost, which is a practical consideration when deployed on power-constrained platforms, these solutions fail to identify new or previously unseen anomalies.

Fig. 4.5 Example of contextual anomaly

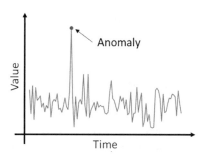

On the other hand, behavioral agents can learn the normal and/or anomalous behavior(s) of a network and, thus, have the potential to identify whether new or previously unseen behavioral patterns are anomalous (Mitchell, 1997). These agents are typically supervisory and may experience longer computational times and utilize more computational resources. Hence, its best for these agents to be deployed on near-edge platforms or systems.

Individuated agent configurations enable hybrid methods to detect anomalies and activities across an entire network. The following are some common approaches that an agent can be configured to utilize:

The spectral approach: In some situations, the dimensions of the data instances (i.e., features) are inherently dependent. Thus, combining the dependent dimensions both improves the classification accuracy and reduces the computational complexity; the application of such a combination transforms the original data instances into new instances with only the independent dimensions, formally referred to as dimensionality reduction (Wang, 2012). One popular dimensionality reduction technique is the Principal Component Analysis (PCA) algorithm which gets applied to a matrix of the original instances and generates a set of orthogonal vectors. The first k vectors capture the highest variance and designate normal activity, while the last m vectors represent anomalous activity. Hence if a data instance is projected into the anomalous subspaces, it can be considered anomalous (Chandola et al., 2009)

The Information-Theoretic Approach: Data instances can be a set of symbols generated by the network or system, whereas each instance is generated independently with a certain probability. Thus, one would seek to measure the average amount of information conveyed by each instance. This approach utilizes the concept of entropy that assumes anomalies distort the information content of the network's data instances. Hence, the anomaly detection technique needs to split the data instances into subsets that minimize the entropy (Cen et al., 2014; Ham & Choi, 2013; Shabtai et al., 2012; Cuadra-Sanchez et al., 2014)

The Machine Learning Approach: Machine learning (ML) agents improve their ability to distinguish normal behavior from anomalous behavior with experience (Mitchell, 1997). These agents typically provide a mapping that adapts to unseen network anomalies (Wang, 2012) by utilizing a set of data instances that resemble the instances within a given system network; this set is referred to as a training dataset. Supervised ML algorithms learn the mapping function by utilizing labeled training sets. On the other hand, Unsupervised ML algorithms utilize training sets of totally unlabeled instances. The two approaches are mixed into the semi-supervised learning hybrid approach in some cases. The algorithm is trained with most unlabeled instances and a minority of labeled instances. A machine learning algorithm starts by learning the mapping function from the training dataset, then proceeds to the testing phase. It examines "other" data instances collectively referred to as the testing set and computes the label for each instance using the mapping function learned. Once trained, an agent's configuration would include the desired ML architecture and associated trained weight vectors. ML algorithms can be further categorized into: (1) Classification-based, (2) Nearest-neighbor algorithms, (3) clustering.

The main goal of classification-based ML algorithms is to assign each data instance to either one of pre-set classes based on their features. Some examples include:

Classification-oriented neural networks: A neural network loosely mimics the human neuronal structure and comprises a set of highly interconnected processes that operate asynchronously on their local data (Chandola et al., 2009). A neural network is trained on normal data instances. After that, it is presented with unseen cases. Here, the network applies a test on the test data instance; it gets accepted as a typical instance if it passes. Otherwise, it is considered anomalous. Feed-forward networks are neural networks typically used in classification, like multilayer perceptron networks (Cuadra-Sanchez et al., 2014). Depending on the labeling of the data, neural networks can be used for both supervised and unsupervised learning.

Bayesian networks: A Bayesian network is a graphical model that encodes probabilistic relationships among variables of interest (Thottan et al., 2010). Bayesian networks are supervised learning algorithms based on the well-known Bayes Theory (Mitchell, 1997). They operate by estimating the posterior probability of an event given some pre-condition. A particular class of Bayesian networks is referred to as Naïve Bayesian networks used for univariate categorical data instances (Mitchell, 1997). Here, for a given data instance, the network estimates the posterior probability of detecting a class label from a set of normal and anomalous class labels. The class label with the most considerable posterior probability is selected as the class to which the data instance belongs. Multivariate data instances are handled via generalizing the univariate model, as the posterior probability for each attribute is estimated. The estimated probabilities get combined to assign the data instance to a given class (Chandola et al., 2009)

Support Vector Machines (SVM): SVMs are supervised learning algorithms that represent the training data instances in a multi-dimensional plane and then determine a hyperplane that splits the data instances into two disjoint groups while maintaining the maximum margins around the separating hyperplane (Nigrin, 1993). One-class SVM algorithms are trained only with normal data. Thus, upon receiving a test data instance, they predict whether it belongs to the normal data class or not. SVMs are well-defined as they stem from a solid mathematical background in statistical learning theory (Nigrin, 1993). An SVM algorithm is considered a linear classifier when it uses a line to split the data instances into normal and anomalous. To perform non-linear classification, SVM algorithms use kernel functions (Gardner & Dorling, 1998).

Rule-based machine learning algorithms: These supervised learning algorithms learn the rules that capture the expected behavior of a data instance. Thus, it is considered anomalous when all the rules fail to capture a data instance during testing. Decision trees and Association Rule Mining (ARM) techniques, among other rule-based methods, are used to learn the rules from the training data instances (Crosbie & Spafford 1995; Hofmeyr 1999). Each rule is assigned a weight proportional to the ratio of the number of training data instances the rule classified correctly to the total number of training instances covered by the rule. The rule that best captures the test instance for a given test data instance is sought. Here, the anomaly score is the inverse of the weight associated with the best rule. Random forests are constructed from several decision trees; a random forest reports the mode of classifying all individual decision trees as the overall classification result (Heckerman, 2008).

Nearest-neighbor algorithms use distance-based or density-based functions to measure the distance between a given data instance and its nearest neighbor (Chandola et al., 2009) This distance designates the anomalous score of that instance. The assumption is that normal instances occur in dense groups, unlike anomalous instances. These algorithms can operate in supervised or unsupervised fashions based on whether labels are used in training data instances.

Clustering algorithms are unsupervised learning algorithms that operate by trying to identify groups (i.e., clusters) of closely located (or similar) training data instances. Anomalies may form sparse clusters or belong to no cluster at all. Self-Organizing Maps (SOM) (Karnin et al., 2012), Expectation-Maximization (EM) (Kecman & Brooks, 2010), k-means clustering (Elbasiony et al., 2013), and Density-Based Spatial Clustering of Applications with Noise (DBSCAN) algorithms (Kohonen, 1990) are classical clustering algorithms.

Based on the anomaly detection techniques discussed, agents can be imbued with the ability to perform network-level and application/system level detection effectively. For network-level detection, low-level agents analyze the headers and/or the payloads of the messages exchanged in the network and send filtered alerts to supervisory agents for correlation and detection. For application/system-level detections, low-level agents analyze the application or system specification and/or examines its behavior during runtime and then report significant events to supervisory agents for further action. Generally speaking, agents can tackle anomaly detection using several techniques belonging to different disciplines. One approach to anomaly detection uses either parametrized or non-parametrized statistical methods to model the network and/or devices behavior and measure the deviation of anomalous behaviors from normal ones. Alternatively, machine learning techniques can be used to learn the normal and/or abnormal behaviors and then try to classify or cluster unseen behaviors accordingly. In addition, information-theoretic and spectral techniques provide different perspectives to help measure how an anomalous behavior differs from normal behaviors.

4   Honeypot Agents

Another class of general agents is one where each agent is designated to collect crucial, accurate, concise high-quality information about malicious activities (Yegneswaran et al., 2005). These agents facilitate the configuration of computer resources to serve as honeypots whose value lies in being probed, attacked, or compromised (Ester et al., 1996). With the help of these resources, agents can spot zero-day attacks and give insights into attackers' actions and motivation. Supervisory agents can receive log data from honeypot agents for analysis from the systems on which they are deployed. The general objective of a computer resource configured as a Honeypot is either to distract attackers from their actual target or to gather information about the attackers and attack patterns, such as a set of popular target hosts and the frequency of requests-responses (Yegneswaran et al., 2005). For the AICA architecture, the primary purpose of honeypot agents is to configure systems to gather information about the attackers. Once a system has been configured and deployed, these agents are responsible for actively monitoring log data (e.g., applications, services, design) for known text patterns or anomalous patterns for essential events. When these events are detected, honeypot agents send alerts to supervisory agents for further analysis, resulting in alerts sent up the agent hierarchy or actions sent down the order to appropriate agents for execution.

While the AICA architecture includes general agents configured to detect malicious activities through various techniques, this task is often complicated on production systems because the attacks are submerged in vast amounts of production or mission-critical activity. Honeypot agents can simplify the detection process since the systems they configure have no production activity, and thus all connections to the honeypot system are suspect by nature. Therefore, unauthorized probes, scans, or attacks are easily detected with fewer false positives and negatives (Yegneswaran et al., 2005).

Reaction to attacks can be accelerated with the help of honeypots. Because attack data is not mingled with production activity data, supervisory agents' analysis of potential attacks is greatly simplified. In addition, honeypot systems can be taken offline entirely for further forensic examination. Insights from this analysis can be used to reconfigure the honeypot agents for increased effectiveness and help supervisory agents develop appropriate countermeasures against threats.

For example, an organization that deploys the AICA architecture can redirect incoming traffic to unused IP addresses to a virtual machine (VM) configured as an SSH honeypot and spun up by a honeypot agent. Agents on the honeypot VM identifies the attackers by IP addresses and then send this information to supervisory agents that develop filters to block the access to mission-critical systems. The functionality of the honeypot agents on the VM can be limited, as it only has to recognize the traffic and its source. A more complex honeypot agent configuration might help determine which dictionaries were used to guess the passwords. This information would be sent to a supervisory agent, which would then use the information to update a rule relating to password strength, which would then be sent to the human analyst as an alert. This type of agent configuration would require the analysis of extensive log records with SSH credentials.

In general, honeypot agent configurations may be classified in terms of the level of interaction (Leita et al., 2008) or the direction of interaction (Spitzner, 2003). In terms of the level of interaction, the honeypot agents consider low-interaction, medium-interaction, or high-interaction configurations. Low-interaction configurations simulate only a small set of services, such as SSH or FTP, and do not allow the attacker to access the operating system. These configurations would be suitable for recognizing peaks in the number of requests. Medium/High-interaction configurations provide more simulated services with increasing sophistication that offer higher levels of attacker interactions but may still limit access to the operating system. These systems would produce reasonable replies to attackers in the hope of triggering follow-up attacks. The difference between medium and high levels of interactions is based on the levels of risk of compromise, information levels, and level of access to the operating system. For honeypot agents configured based on the direction of interaction, they fall primarily into server or client-based configurations. Server-based honeypot configurations are entirely passive; therefore, all incoming requests form an anomaly and are, by definition, an attack. Client-based honeypot configurations actively search and contact communication partners. Thus, client honeypots must discern which communications comprise an anomaly. Heuristics usually verify this by looking after uncommon modifications.

In summary, honeypot agents enable data collection that is not polluted with noise from production activities and is usually of high value. This makes the data sets they process smaller and less complex, which reduces their workload and, by extension, the supervisory agents to which they communicate their findings. Furthermore, honeypot agents deployed on configured VMs only need to process traffic directed at them or originates from them. This means that they are independent of the workload of their parent process. Additionally, these agents capture everything used against them, which means unknown strategies and zero-day-exploits will be identified. It should be noted that any activity with server-honeypot configurations is an anomaly, which should be considered an attack. On the other hand, client-honeypot configurations verify attacks by detecting system state changes, reducing false positives and false negatives (Yegneswaran et al., 2005).

5   Perception of Threat Applications

One approach to applying automation to the cybersecurity problem is Integrated Adaptive Cyber Defense (IACD). IACD is a research effort jointly funded by the US Department of Homeland Security (DHS) and the US National Security Agency (NSA), in collaboration with The Johns Hopkins University Applied Physics Lab (JHU/APL) and industry. Integrated Adaptive Cyber Defense (IACD) aims to shorten the timeline and effectiveness of cyber defense via integration, automation, orchestration, and sharing of machine-readable cyber threat information. IACD defines a strategy and framework to adopt an extensible, adaptive, commercial off-the-shelf (COTS)-based approach (IACD, 2016).

Since 2014, IACD has been a jointly sponsored government, industry, and Trusted agent (JHU/APL) initiative. IACD is an effort to get humans from 'in the loop' to 'on the loop' (Sparrell, 2019). Human-in-the-loop aspects of cybersecurity include disgruntled employees, human errors, awareness and training, access controls and certifications. Human-on-the-loop, deals with the lack of Situation Awareness (SA) or a Common Operating Picture (COP), increased cognitive load and stress that contribute to lower attention span, and the difference in speed between technology and human cognition processes (Sundararajan et al., 2018).

Automated Cyber systems like IACD seek to create an ecosystem to alter the timeline and efficacy of cyber defense through integration, automation, and information sharing. IACD seeks to decouple functions and standardize interfaces between functions to and defines the following security functions:

- Sensing: gathering all the data
- Sense-making: correlating and analyzing data, transforming it into information, knowledge, and intelligence
- Decision-making: deciding what to do
- Acting: sending the actual commands.
- Socializing: Sharing threat data among interested, trusted parties.

One of the more prevalent forms of attacks that are particularly suited for Automated cyber defense is effects-based courses of action. Effects Based Operations (EBO) are "actions taken against enemy systems, designed to achieve specific effects that contribute directly to the desired military and political objectives" (Caroli et al., 2004).

Effects-Based Courses of Action Cybersecurity attacks increase volume, scale, and complexity. To address the growing threats, cybersecurity solutions are also becoming more complex. To help manage this complexity, Security Orchestration, Automation, and Response (SOAR) technology can be used to coordinate the actions of multiple security tools. SOAR technology seeks to create a need to ensure that the correct information is exchanged between products to provide the necessary context to achieve a coordinated response. SOAR platforms enable the Observe and Act functions of cyber defense required to Observe, Orient, Decide, & Act, more commonly known as the OODA loop, for decision-making and operations.

Now, many security vendors are adding artificial intelligence (AI) and/or machine learning (ML) capabilities to their products, which could be used to address and improve decision-making functions for cyber security. This division of labor between AI/ML solutions and SOAR platforms could help manage cybersecurity solutions' complexity, speed, and scale: AI/ML solutions can be applied to find patterns and decide faster and at scale. In contrast, SOAR can be applied to act faster and at scale. Integrated Adaptive Cyber Defense (IACD) demonstrated how to bridge these technologies while maintaining human control using effects-based courses of action (COAs).

An effects-based COA is a set of response actions to a cyber-attack, selected based on the desired high-level cyber affect – the goals of the response – rather than having to specify the exact steps to be executed via a course of action. In a traditional COA workflow, a SOAR platform starts the workflow, gathers additional data/evidence, selects an appropriate COA, and performs its execution – covering all the functions of the OODA loop within that single platform. With an effects-based COA workflow, an AI capability can be used to gather additional data/evidence and select an appropriate COA based on that data and the desired cyber effect. Then the SOAR platform can be used to automate and orchestrate the actions required of various security products to achieve that desired response and outcome.

6 Experimentation

IACD conducted an experiment to demonstrate the benefits of combining AI and SOAR technologies using effect-based COAs. The experiment used the DarkLight AI expert system to provide sense-making and decision-making capabilities, corresponding to the Orient and Decide functions of the OODA loop. IACD used the Cortex XSOAR platform to control response actions, corresponding to the Act function. The figure below depicts the workflow for an effects-based COA, where DarkLight performed the first few decision-making functions, and Cortex XSOAR performed the remaining response actions.

In the experiment, The automated system successfully demonstrated the combination of DarkLight AI and the Cortex XSOAR platforms to select and execute effects based COAs in the face of different attack scenarios, all with a human monitoring "on the loop" instead of a human having to decide and act "in the loop." DarkLight made sense of two different attack scenarios – malware conducting data exfiltration versus ransomware – and selected an appropriate effects-based COA response for the attack. DarkLight then triggered Cortex XSOAR to execute the proper COA for the attack, and Cortex XSOAR orchestrated the response actions of the enterprise security products.

Throughout the process, a human monitored the performance of both the AI and SOAR components via metrics and summaries of the actions taken. The human had specific criteria defined for situations where he/she would take over control. The human was available for decision escalation in cases where the AI could not decide with a certain threshold level of confidence. The effects-based COA experiment successfully demonstrated the ability to coordinate the activities of an AI/ML product and a SOAR platform, allowing each to perform functions of the OODA loop to which each is best suited while enabling human monitoring and control.

Leveraging automation in IT systems has been shown to provide measurable improvements in cyber security. Several organizations have used automation with their systems, as shown below:

- JHU/APL did studies on their network comparing various automation scenarios with their current manual scenarios. The most significant finding was that the attacks were stopped two orders of magnitude faster, resulting in significantly less damage (Peters, 2017).

  - Phantom Cyber, a security orchestration vendor, published similar savings in combating phishing. Their customer reduced phishing incident response costs by 98% and saved $1.06 M annually (Royer, 2016)

- Zepko, a managed security service provider in the United Kingdom, used OpenC2 to increase the efficacy of their Security Operations Centre (SOC) by 25–30% (Bradbury, 2016).

Automation solutions like IACD are not a cure-all for solving cybersecurity challenges, but they provide a mechanism to respond to the threat at the speed of the threat and not at human speed. Moving forward, much work is needed to evolve automation systems to recognize, react and respond to threats as they evolve and to deploy solutions to systems in a timely and effective fashion.

7   In Conclusion: Further Research Areas

This chapter aimed to discuss the potential benefits of applying AICA to improve the perception of cyber threats for effective mitigation of cyber-attacks. Research on applications of different types of AI/ML algorithms and architectures has been performed to evaluate AICA. As mentioned in other chapters, the practical use of AI-based AICA is still relatively new. More research experiments are required to answer the following questions and motivate AICA adoption into commercial cyber-defense solutions:

- What combination of cyber data, e.g., host, network, cyber threat intelligence, is required for optimal AICA performance?
- How do we curate representative cyber datasets for AICA training and testing?
- How do we design and evaluate more realistic simulated and emulated cyber environments to train AICA for real-world threat perception?
- What cooperative and competitive multi-agent AI methods can be leveraged to evaluate AICA architectures for cyber threat perception?
- How do we mitigate adversarial AI/ML attacks on AICA reasoning and decision-making processes?

References

"2021 Trends Show Increased Globalized Threat of Ransomware | CISA." https://www.cisa. gov/uscert/ncas/current-activity/2022/02/09/2021-trends-show-increased-globalized-threat-ransomware. Accessed 5 Mar 2022.

Al Marakeby, H., Zaki, M., & Shaheen, S. (2010, November). A generalized object detection system using automatic feature selection. In *Proceedings of the 10th international conference on intelligent systems design and applications (ISDA'10), Cairo, Egypt* (pp. 839–844).

Bhuyan, M., Bhattacharyya, D., & Kalita, J. (2014). Network anomaly detection: Methods, systems and tools. *IEEE Communication Surveys and Tutorials, 16*(1), 303–336.

Bradbury, A. (2016, September 29). *OpenC2 and OrchID – Using OpenC2 is a managed security services provider*. OpenC2 Forum.

Bradshaw, J. M. (1997). Chapter 1: An introduction to software agents. In J. M. Bradshaw (Ed.), *Software agents* (pp. 3–46). AAA1 Press/MIT Press.

Cen, L., Gates, C., Si, L., & Li, N. (2014). A probabilistic discriminative model for android malware detection with decompiled source code. *IEEE Transactions on Dependable and Secure Computing, PP*(99), 1–1.

Chandola, V., Banerjee, A., & Kumar, V. (2009). Anomaly detection: A survey. *ACM Computing Surveys, 41*(3), 15:1–15:58. [Online]. Available http://doi.acm.org/10.1145/1541880.1541882

Crosbie, M., & Spafford, E. (1995, October). Defending a computer system using autonomous agents. In *Proceedings of the 18th National Information Systems Security Conference*.

Crowley, J. L., Piater, J. H., Vincze, M., & Paletta, L. (Eds.). (2003, April). *Proceedings of the 3rd international conference on computer vision systems (ICVS'03), Graz, Austria*. Springer.

Cuadra-Sanchez, A., Aracil, J., & Ramos de Santiago, J. (2014, June). Proposal of a new information-theory based technique and analysis of traffic anomaly detection. In *Proceedings of the 2014 international conference on smart communications in network technologies (SaCoNeT'14), Vilanova i la Geltru, Spain* (pp. 1–6).

Elbasiony, R. M., Sallam, E. A., Eltobely, T. E., & Fahmy, M. M. (2013). A hybrid network intrusion detection framework based on random forests and weighted k-means. *Ain Shams Engineering Journal, 4*(4), 753–762. [Online]. Available: http://www.sciencedirect.com/science/article/pii/S2090447913000105

Ester, M., Peter Kriegel, H., Sander, J., & Xu, X. (1996). A density-based algorithm for discovering clusters in large spatial databases with noise. In *Proceedings of the 1996 knowledge discovery and data mining conferences (KDD'96), Portland, Oregon, USA* (pp. 226–231). AAAI Press.

Farmer, W. M., Guttman, J. D., & Swarup, V. (1996, October). Security for mobile agents: Issues and requirements. In *Proceedings of the 19th national information systems security conference* (Vol. 2). National Institute of Standards and Technology.

Ferguson-Walter, K. J., Fugate, S. J., Mauger, J., & Major, M. M. (2019, March). Game theory for adaptive defensive cyber deception. In *ACM hot topics in the science of security symposium (HotSoS)*.

Gardner, M., & Dorling, S. (1998). Artificial neural networks (the multilayer perceptron) – A review of applications in the atmospheric sciences. *Atmospheric Environment, 32*(14–15), 2627–2636. Available http://www.sciencedirect.com/science/article/pii/S1352231097004470

Guyonand, I., & Elisseeff, A. (2003). An introduction to variable and feature selection. *Journal of Machine Learning Research, 3*, 1157–1182.

Ham, H.-S., & Choi, M.-J. (2013, October). Analysis of android malware detection performance using machine learning classifiers. In *Proceedings of the 2013 international conference on ICT convergence (ICTC'13), Jeju Island, Korea* (pp. 490–495).

Heckerman, D. (2008). A tutorial on learning with Bayesian networks. In D. Holmes & L. Jain (Eds.), *Innovations in Bayesian networks* (Studies in computational intelligence) (Vol. 156, pp. 33–82). Springer. [Online]. Available https://doi.org/10.1007/978-3-540-85066-33

Hofmeyr, S. A. (1999, May). *An immunological model of distributed detection and its application to computer security*. PhD thesis, University of New Mexico.

"IACD Spirals 1 to 22 graphic". H. B. J. Caroli, D. Fayette, N. Koziarz, and T. Stedman, "Tools for effects based course of action development and assessment."

Karnin, Z., Liberty, E., Lovett, S., Schwartz, R., Weinstein, O., Mannor, S., Srebro, N., & Williamson, R. C. (2012). Unsupervised SVMs: On the complexity of the furthest hyperplane problem. *Journal of Machine Learning Research, 23*, 1–18.

Kecman, V., & Brooks, J. (2010, July). Locally linear support vector machines and other local models. In *Proceedings of the 2010 international joint conference on neural networks (IJCNN'10), Barcelona, Spain* (pp. 1–6). IEEE.

Kohonen, T. (1990). The self-organizing map. *Proceedings of the IEEE, 78*(9), 1464–1480.

Leita, C., Pham, V., Thonnard, O., Ramirez-Silva, E., Pouget, F., Kirda, E., & Dacier, M. (2008). The leurre.com project: Collecting internet threats information using a worldwide distributed honeynet. In *Information security threats data collection and sharing, 2008. WISTDCS'08. WOMBAT workshop on* (pp. 40–57). IEEE.

Mas'ud, M., Sahib, S., Abdollah, M., Selamat, S., & Yusof, R. (2014, May). Analysis of features selection and machine learning classifier in android malware detection. In *Proceedings of the 2014 international conference on information science and applications (ICISA'14), Seoul, Korea* (pp. 1–5).

Migliardi, M., & Merlo, A. (2013). Improving energy efficiency in distributed intrusion detection systems. *Journal of High Speed Networks, 19*(3), 251–264.

Mitchell, T. M. (1997). *Machine learning* (1st ed.). McGraw-Hill, Inc.

Micah Muser and Ashon Garriott (2021) Machine learning and cybersecurity: Hype and reality. Center for Security and Emerging Technology (CSET), Georgetown University. https://cset.georgetown.edu/wp-content/uploads/Machine-Learning-and-Cybersecurity.pdf

"NCCIC CYBER INCIDENT SCORING SYSTEM", "Integrated adaptive cyber defense, IACD." https://www.iacdautomate.org/. Accessed 5 Mar 2022.

Nguyen, T. T., & Reddi, V. J. (2021). Deep reinforcement learning for cybersecurity. *arXiv:1906.05799v4 [cs.CR]*. https://arxiv.org/pdf/1906.05799.pdf

Nigrin, A. (1993). *Neural networks for pattern recognition*. MIT Press.

Peters, W. (2017, March 23). *IACD overview and IACD framework*. IACD Community Day, Laurel, Maryland.

Royer, P. (2016, September 29). *Orchestration and automation*. OpenC2 Forum.

Shabtai, A., Kanonov, U., Elovici, Y., Glezer, C., & Weiss, Y. (2012). Andromaly: A behavioral malware detection framework for android devices. *Journal of Intelligent Information Systems, 38*(1), 161–190. [Online]. Available https://doi.org/10.1007/s10844-010-0148-x

Shakut, K., Luo, S., Varadharajan, V., Hameed, I. A., & Xu, M. (2020). A survey on machine learning techniques for cyber security in the last decade. *IEEE Open Access Journal*. https://doi.org/10.1109/ACCESS.2020.304195

Sharma, A. K. (2005). *Text book of chi-test and experimental designs* (1st ed.). Publishing House.

Spafford, E. H., & Zamboni, D. (2000). Intrusion detection using autonomous agents. *Computer Networks, 34*(4), 547–570.

Sparrell, D. (2019). Cyber-safety in healthcare IoT. In *11th academic conference ITU kaleidoscope: ICT for health: Networks, standards and innovation, ITU K 2019*. https://doi.org/10.23919/ITUK48006.2019.8996148

Spitzner, L. (2003). The honeynet project: Trapping the hackers. *IEEE Security and Privacy, 1*(2), 15–23. [Online]. Available: https://doi.org/10.1109/MSECP.2003.1193207

Staniford-Chen, S., Cheung, S., Crawford, R., Dilger, M., Frank, J., Hoagland, J., Levitt, K., Wee, C., Yip, R., & Zerkle, D. (1996, October). GrIDS: A graph-based intrusion detection system for large networks. In *Proceedings of the 19th national information systems security conference* (Vol. 1). National Institute of Standards and Technology.

Sundararajan, A., Khan, T., Aburub, H., Sarwat, A. I., & Rahman, S. (2018). A tri-modular human-on-the-loop framework for intelligent smart grid cyber-attack visualization. In *SoutheastCon 2018* (pp. 1–8). https://doi.org/10.1109/SECON.2018.8479180

Thottan, M., Liu, G., & Ji, C. (2010). Anomaly detection approaches for communication networks. In G. Cormode & M. Thottan (Eds.), *Algorithms for next generation networks* (Computer communications and networks) (pp. 239–261). Springer. [Online]. Available https://doi.org/10.1007/978-1-84882-765-311

"US-CERT Year in Review 2012", "Battle against cybercrime continues." https://blog.checkpoint.com/2021/10/06/as-battle-against-cybercrime-continues-during-cybersecurity-awareness-month-check-point-research-reports-40-increase-in-cyberattacks/. Accessed 5 Mar 2022.

Verizon. *2016 data breach report*. Available https://www.verizonenterprise.com/resources/reports/rp_DBIR_2016_Report_en_xg.pdf

Walter, E. C., Ferguson-Walter, K. J., & Ridley, A. (2021). Incorporating deception into CyberBattleSim for autonomous defense. In *IJCAI 2021 international workshop on adaptive cyber defense. arXiv:2108.13980v1 [cs.CR]*. https://arxiv.org/pdf/2108.13980.pdf

Wang, J. (2012). *Geometric structure of high-dimensional data and dimensionality reduction*. Springer.

White, G. B., Fisch, E. A., & Pooch, U. W. (1996). *Cooperating security managers: A peer-based intrusion detection system* (pp. 20–23). IEEE Network.

Xie, M., Han, S., Tian, B., & Parvin, S. (2011). Anomaly detection in wireless sensor networks: A survey. *Journal of Network and Computer Applications, 34*(4), 1302–1325. Advanced Topics in Cloud Computing. [Online]. Available http://www.sciencedirect.com/science/article/pii/S1084804511000580

Yegneswaran, V., Barford, P., & Paxson, V. (2005). Using honeynets for internet situational awareness. In *Proceedings of the fourth workshop on hot topics in networks (HotNets IV)* (pp. 17–22). Citeseer.

Chapter 5
Situational Understanding and Diagnostics

Steven Noel and Vipin Swarup

1 Introduction

Given percepts from the environment, an autonomous cyber-defense agent must gain the understanding needed to characterize and assess a given situation. For effective decision making, this understanding needs to span the agent itself, the system that the agent defends, any threats within the agent's sphere of operations, and the context of the organizational mission. Situational understanding is crucial to effective operations not only within cyberspace, but also across all warfighting domains (air, land, maritime, space, and cyberspace) as part of multi-domain operations.

The core functions of situational understanding are to diagnose the underlying nature of a situation, project possible future states, and assess associated risks. This includes understanding the scope of adversarial presence, any exploitable vulnerabilities and potential adversarial movement within the defended system, and the way in which mission elements depend on assets within that system. To perform this function, situational understanding needs to employ general models of entity and relationship classes within the world, which can be instantiated through parametrized templates for a given situation. As situations dynamically evolve, a cyber-defense agent must continuously maintain situational understanding and keep its domain knowledge updated accordingly.

Given the uncertainties and myriad of concerns in contested environments, situational understanding can apply lower-fidelity modeling and analysis for managing

S. Noel (✉)
Cyber Resiliency Department, The MITRE Corporation, McLean, VA, USA
e-mail: snoel@mitre.org

V. Swarup
Cyber Solutions Innovation Center, The MITRE Corporation, McLean, VA, USA
e-mail: swarup@mitre.org

© The Author(s), under exclusive license to Springer Nature Switzerland AG 2023
A. Kott (ed.), *Autonomous Intelligent Cyber Defense Agent (AICA)*, Advances in
Information Security 87, https://doi.org/10.1007/978-3-031-29269-9_5

complexity. For example, it can make more conservative (worst case) assumptions about adversarial capabilities. Then, once a threshold level of assessed threat is reached, the cyber-defense agent can trigger response and recovery planning for more nuanced and multi-faceted treatment in formulating courses of action. To prepare for this planning, situational understanding functionality needs to characterize the available defensive options, both passive and active. This includes options for reacting to threat situations, as well as options for proactively mitigating system weaknesses in advance of attack.

Overall, a cyber-defense agent needs to understand the current situation, what the situation should be, and characterize the differences. Furthermore, the agent needs to project the current state into potential future situations. When the level of risk associated with a situation reaches a threshold level, the agent can trigger response planning. This includes analyzing how defensive response actions (alone and in combination) affect potential adversary actions and impact mission functionality. After the planning and action selection functions decide on a course of action and that action is carried out, the resulting effects are perceived through the agent's sensing function, which becomes new input to situational understanding.

In the next section, we provide background material for this topic and outline the challenges to be met. The Synthesis and Analysis section explains how an agent processes its sensed information, updates its knowledge base, and assesses a given situation. The Abstraction and Generalization section shows ways in which an agent can manage complexity and adapt to previously unseen situations. The Illustrative Examples section considers various practical concerns for the application of situational understanding and diagnostics. The Recommendations section shares insights about potential future directions for research and development in this area.

2   Background and Challenges

Situational awareness is conventionally held to be the perception of entities in an environment, the understanding of their meaning, and the projection of their future states (Endsley, 1995). The relationship between understanding and knowledge is analogous to that between learning and memorizing. From an epistemological standpoint, understanding is distinct from knowledge, and has been acknowledged as the main goal of cognitive systems (Baumberger, 2014).

Understanding is the ability to reason over gained knowledge and to apply that reasoning in flexible ways (Perkins, 1998). Intelligent systems are said to possess understanding if they can synthesize new knowledge from previous information and knowledge (Ackoff, 1989). Understanding can thus be characterized as the mechanism for transitioning from data to information to knowledge to wisdom (Bellinger et al., 2004), with understanding providing explanations of what has already occurred and wisdom illuminating what is best to undertake for the future.

Situational awareness seeks to understand meaning, which lies within the purview of semantics. In this view, meaning is a relationship between an entity and the kind of thing that the entity signifies. Semantic memory is seen as general world knowledge, stored as an abstract structure that applies to a wide variety of experiential objects (Yee et al., 2013). One example is a semantic network (Sowa, 1992), which is a graph structure for representing knowledge as interconnected nodes and edges, e.g., stored in a graph database.

For situational understanding, considering individual events and data elements in isolation provides limited value. The low-level elements need to be assessed within the full context of the operational environment. Analysis of the interrelationships among the individual entities provides the insight needed for truly informed decision making. The performance of situational understanding can be assessed in terms of identifying activities in the cyber domain, including dimensions such as confidence, purity, cost utility, and timeliness (Tadda, 2008). Effectively managing a wide range of concerns within situational understanding requires methods such as hierarchical rollups with relative importance weighting at each level of the hierarchy (Noel & Jajodia, 2017).

Military doctrine acknowledges that situational awareness is a key capability for all phases of cyberspace operations (U.S. Joint Chiefs of Staff, 2018). Doctrine also recognizes that because of the complexity and scope of cyberspace, the ability for humans to achieve and maintain cyber situational understanding is often lacking, and methods are needed for mitigating the risks of such inadequate understanding. With regards to the emerging doctrine of multi-domain operations, currently no capabilities exist for integrated situational understanding spanning all domains (Nettis, 2020). Such trends as the convergence of warfighting domains and increased warfighter mobility (Buckland, 2021) will accelerate the need for cyber situational understanding by intelligent agents.

3   Synthesis and Analysis

Figure 5.1 shows the functional elements and interfaces for Situational Understanding and Diagnostics within a cyber-defense agent. The Sensing function provides the percepts needed for building an understanding of the current state of the agent itself, the system it is defending, and other entities in the world. If Situational Understanding and Diagnostics exposes a threat posing a risk, then Planning is invoked for responding to the threat, and if needed, to recover the agent or defended system to a working condition.

Sensing synthesizes raw data into information (including deduplication, normalizing, tagging, etc.), yielding processed descriptors about the current state. Sensing includes information about the agent itself (to ensure its own operational integrity), the defended system (system resources, network connectivity, etc.), previous actions taken by the agent on behalf of the defended system, and activities from the environment at large (including threats and mission dependencies), i.e., that are external to the agent and its defended system. Sensing spans all host machines that comprise the defended system, including logs from the host operating systems and relevant

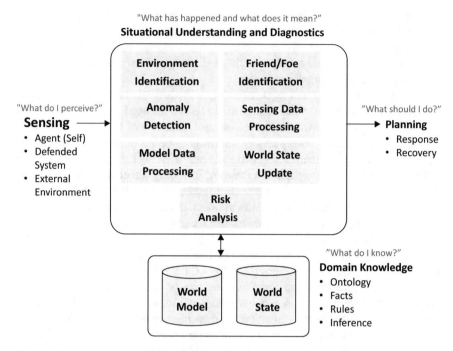

Fig. 5.1 Situational understanding and diagnostics for a cyber-defense agent

applications, as well as network traffic among the hosts. It includes other relevant security information such as vulnerability scan reports, authentication system configuration, access control policy, placement of deceptive elements, intrusion detection system alerts, etc.

In addition to Sensing, Situational Understanding and Diagnostics for a cyber-defense agent depends on the agent's Domain Knowledge Base. This knowledge base abstracts reality to provide semantics (meaning) of perceived information. For understanding threats (with corresponding risks or impacts), the agent can extract patterns from the knowledge base and compare patterns for current sensed percepts against corresponding baseline (goal) patterns. The Domain Knowledge Base is itself intelligent, in the sense that it includes ontologies as common vocabulary to accelerate information sharing, facts (truth statements), rules (facts with logical conditions that make them true), and an engine that can infer new facts.

The Domain Knowledge Base for a cyber-defense agent is comprised of a World Model that describes the entities and their relationships within the domain, along with behavioral rules within the domain for inferring possible future states (dynamics). The World State describes the world as understood by the agent at the current time (Current State), as well as the state of the world as it existed in previous times (State History). The functions for model building within the cyber-defense agent leverage shared domain ontology so that consistency is maintained throughout the Domain Knowledge Base.

The World Model includes the cyber-defense agent itself, the system that the agent defends, and the external environment in which the agent and system operate (including cyber threats and mission dependencies). It is based on a logical theory of world models in the context of cyber defense, expressed through formal descriptive language. Data sources for building the World Model include system descriptors, cyber threat intelligence, and mission planning information.

The World Model contains knowledge about the agent configuration, e.g., agent architecture, communication, collaboration links, processes, and performance indicators. It contains knowledge about the configuration of the defended system (for all host and network elements comprising the system) such as known vulnerabilities, security mechanisms, and network connectivity requirements. Knowledge about cyber threats include the MITRE ATT&CK knowledge base of adversary tactics and techniques (The MITRE Corporation, 2015–2021) and standardized enumerations and languages under MITRE's Making Security Measurable effort (The MITRE Corporation, 2007–2022), such as Common Attack Pattern Enumeration and Classification (CAPEC) (The MITRE Corporation, 2007–2021), Malware Attribute Enumeration and Characterization (MAEC) (The MITRE Corporation, 2020) and Common Vulnerabilities and Exposures (CVE) (The MITRE Corporation, 1999–2022).

The dynamical aspect of the World Model captures the behavioral rules and possible future states of the agent, its defended system, and other entities in the domain (such as adversaries and affected elements of a mission). World dynamics can be categorized in terms of the entities (internal versus external) taking actions and the effects (either internal or external) of the actions taken. Here, internal entities are the cyber-defense agent and its defended system, and external entities are cooperating agents, threats, mission elements, etc.

World dynamics include ways in which cyber adversaries can exploit multiple interrelated vulnerabilities to incrementally penetrate a network (attack graphs), e.g., from tools such as MITRE's CyGraph (Noel et al., 2016, 2017) and other approaches (Kordy et al., 2014; Kaynar 2016; Noel 2018). World dynamics also include the potential defensive response actions that the agent can take, as well as knowledge about cyber resources in a mission context via methods such as MITRE's Cyber Mission Impact Assessment (CMIA) tool (Musman & Temin, 2015) and other approaches (Bodeau et al., 2013; Schulz et al., 2015; Guion & Reith, 2017; Heinbockel et al., 2016).

The processing and tempo of knowledge updates need to match that of the systems or agents providing the data (extracted as information through Sensing). For example, vulnerability scans (showing detected vulnerabilities on host machines) might be done weekly, ingest of CVE data (showing details for reported vulnerabilities) might be done daily, or network flow records might be available hourly.

Given a current operational state, the cyber-defense agent needs to analyze the situation and compare those results to the analytic results for a goal state. For that, the agent needs to continually update its Current State by processing new percepts from Sensing within the context of the World Model and its dynamics. To analyze risks more completely, a cyber-defense agent can project possible future states, map likely end states to impacts on dependent mission elements, and then measure the risks and potential impacts in that larger context.

The State History for a cyber-defense agent is a time-ordered track of world state descriptors. A logical framework for autonomous agent reasoning about dynamical systems is called situation calculus. In the predominant formulation of situation calculus (Reiter, 1991), a dynamic world is modeled as progressing through a series of situations through various actions. Situation calculus represents changing scenarios as first-order logic formulas to express (1) actions that the agent can perform in the world, (2) fluents (properties) that describe the state of the world, and (3) situations (sequences of agent actions).

This situation calculus framework (as opposed to state-based ones) favors logical sentences about what is true of the domain and the causal laws in effect, rather than explicitly enumerating states and their transition functions. The State History is then comprised of the historical record of situations (action sequences) and fluents. Under Markovian (memoryless) reasoning, in which decisions depend on the current state only, the current world state represents the resulting state after the sequence of actions (situation) have been applied to an initial state.

Figure 5.2 shows the processing flow within a cyber-defense agent for Situational Understanding and Diagnostics. Percepts (from Sensing) that pertain to the entities and relationships in the world (regardless of their current state) are processed by the Model Data Processing function to update the World Model in the agent's Domain

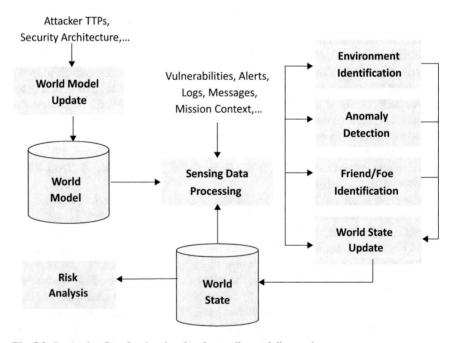

Fig. 5.2 Processing flow for situational understanding and diagnostics

Knowledge Base. Other Percepts (also from Sensing) involving the evolving state of the world are processed by the Sensing Data Processing function.

After processing its sensor data, a cyber-defense agent performs these three functions:

1. Environment Identification assesses any changes about the environment in which the agent itself is deployed (physical host, virtual machine, container, etc.). This function also identifies the actions that are possible for mitigating cyber risks and responding to attacks.
2. Anomaly Detection identifies potentially anomalous behavior in sensed data and produces indicators of compromise (or at least indicators of concern).
3. Friend/Foe Identification function identifies any potential adversaries and produces indicators of compromise (e.g., host processes and files) as needed for delineating the scope of response actions.

Then, in the World State Update function, the results from these three functions are combined with the processed sensor data to update the World State in the agent's Domain Knowledge Base.

Given an updated (current) World State, the Risk Analysis function assesses risks associated with that state. An initial phase of Risk Analysis should consider the immediate risk, based on factors such as the scope (friend versus foe), severity (kernel, operating system, application, container, privilege level, etc.), and likelihood (e.g., from the Anomaly Detection function) of the attacker presence. This phase of analysis identifies the impact that an attacker could potentially inflict on the compromised resources. Then, relying on knowledge in the World Model about mission dependencies on cyber resources, the Risk Analysis function can measure risk in the context of mission elements such as critically important functionality or organizational units.

Risk Analysis can also consider possible future states, independent of any planned actions that the cyber-defense agent might eventually take. This provides a conservative assessment as a baseline, i.e., the worst-case outcome that could result given the current state. For this, the agent can apply knowledge of entity dynamics stored in its World Model, e.g., attack graph models. In particular, the agent can apply these models to simulate multi-step attacks in which the attacker incrementally increases presence within the defended system.

Such attack simulation starts with knowledge about the scope, severity, and likelihood of the current attacker presence, which provides initial conditions as input parameters to risk models. This modeling and simulation can also include presumed attacker capabilities and how they can be applied within the defended system, given the knowledge of existing vulnerabilities. For this, vulnerabilities are to be considered in the broad sense of any system or network properties that contribute to attack success, not just vulnerabilities in the sense of software flaws. For example, the presence of password hashes cached on a system represents a kind of vulnerability in the sense that they could potentially be stolen and used for authenticated access to other systems.

Then, as such attack modeling and simulation progresses, the Risk Analysis function can continually measure risk in the context of mission elements. For this, it can apply a potential future state (with updated properties for attacker scope, severity, and likelihood) as input to the risk scoring algorithms. These simulated attacks can also be constrained to consider only those attack paths that reach assumed attack goals (such as mission-critical resources within the defended system), thus reducing the space of attack paths to be analyzed.

In some situations, an attacker presence might not be identified by the Anomaly Detection function. The cyber-defense agent could still perform an analysis of risk that is independent of a known or assumed attacker. Measures such as the number of connected components in an attack graph (not constrained by assumed attack starts and goals) could be applied in such cases. In considering weakly connected components (i.e., ignoring graph edge directionality), the intuition is that it is better to have an attack graph comprised of disconnected parts rather than a connected whole. Then strongly connected components take edge directions into account, yielding sets of nodes such that if an attacker compromises any node in the component, every other member of the component can be reached.

Graph diameter can also be applied in situations that ignore attack starts and goals. The intuition in this case is that it is better to have an attack graph that is deeper rather than shallower. For shallower attack graphs, an attacker can directly reach more targets from a given node, saving effort on establishing an environment (attacker tools, reconnaissance, etc.) on each new attack platform.

Attack graph distances (numbers of potential attack steps) can be applied in other ways for situational understanding. This includes handling false negatives (missed detections) by inferring missing attack steps to bridge gaps in reconstructed attack sequences. Attack graph distances or numbers of walks can also be applied for estimating adversary effort for achieving certain attack ends.

At any point in this Risk Analysis process, either from the initial attacker presence, any potential attack presence in future states, or for proactive mitigations in advance of detecting actual attacks, the cyber-defense agent can trigger response planning to consider courses of action to handle the situation.

4 Abstraction and Generalization

In practice, a World State model for a cyber-defense agent can be large and complex. Just as humans seek to reason about what really matters for effective decision making, intelligent agents need to identify invariants, salient features, and general characterizations of phenomena in the world. Through abstraction and generalization techniques, cyber-defense agents can better manage model complexity and produce models that can adapt properly to previously unseen situations. Both classes of techniques seek to derive simpler models while maintaining the validity of diagnostic results.

Abstraction emphasizes the qualities and properties of entities in a domain rather than their actual values, i.e., it suppresses irrelevant details. A concrete entity can be considered a superset of an abstract one, in the sense that the concrete entity can contain additional properties not shared by other members of that abstract class. Abstraction characterizes what an entity is or what it does, rather than how it is represented or how it works. It is therefore the primary way of managing complexity in large models.

Generalization broadens processing to encompass a set of entities of a certain type, characterizing trends or common patterns to emphasize the similarities between entities. A specific entity can be considered a subset of a general one, in the sense that generalization formulates general concepts or rules from specific instances. Generalization therefore manages complexity by collecting individuals into groups and providing a representation that serves to specify any individual of the group.

Figure 5.3 illustrates some aspects of model abstraction and generalization for situational understanding in cyber defense. Fig. 5.3a shows the inferred state for a current situation, which is represented as an attack graph with intrusion alerts, potential exploitation paths, and mission dependencies on cyber assets (Noel et al., 2021a, b). As an example of model abstraction, in Fig. 5.3b a decision is required for whether a particular security patch should be applied. For cases in which there are multiple servers that are candidates for patching, an agent might reduce this to a single decision, i.e., to apply the patch or not, for all vulnerable servers rather than on a per-server basis. Such reductions (along with certain approximations) can result in decision making that scales linearly with the size of the attack graph (Albanese et al., 2012).

As part of situational understanding, cyber risk analysis needs to consider the functional failure modes of software systems (Thieme et al., 2020), both from the

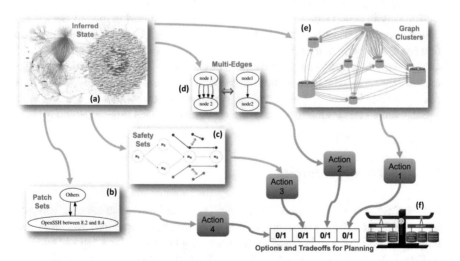

Fig. 5.3 Some aspects of cyber-defense model abstraction and generalization

standpoint of cyberattack impacts as well as attack mitigations. As illustrated in Fig. 5.3c, the correct functioning of an application requires network connectivity between two pairs of hosts (two graph edges) rather than connectivity between a single pair (one graph edge) for a given function. Such a set of edges constitutes a safety set (in the sense of correct functioning), so that blocking any single edge in the set renders the function unsafe. In Fig. 5.3c, there are two such safety sets, with one edge in common (i.e., when blocked would render two functions unsafe. Thus, situational understanding needs to abstract these safety sets as a compound entity.

Figure 5.3d considers abstraction from the standpoint of a collection of potential attack vectors that have a common set of preconditions (conditions needed for exploitation) and postconditions (results of exploitation). In this case, there are four potential exploits (represented as graph edges) from one host (graph node) to another. As a lower level of abstraction, one could represent each potential exploit as a separate edge, yielding a multigraph. Figure 5.3d shows the mapping to a higher level of abstraction by representing the entire set of four potential exploits as a single edge. In terms of situational understanding, this is a worst-case assumption since the same outcome would result regardless of which of the four exploits were successful.

Another form of abstraction cyberattack models is to partition the elements of the model into clusters according to some invariants or similarities in their properties, and then treat each cluster as a single entity. In Fig. 5.3e, the host nodes in an attack graph are clustered according to a common property. In the resulting clustered graph, situational understanding needs only to consider exploitation edges between each cluster, with edges within each cluster abstracted from consideration. The edges from one cluster to another could be considered individually (a cluster-level multigraph) or as a single unit (a cluster-level simple graph). Such cluster-based analysis can be done hierarchically (through multiple levels), based on the applicable semantics at each level (Noel & Jajodia, 2004).

The way in which entities and relationships are abstracted in models determines how a cyber-defense agent can reason about situations. An agent's planning function has the responsibility for formulating agent actions in response to threats. Still, analytic results (knowledge gained) from situational understating can be applied to evaluate the risks associated with given response actions. Conceptually, the application of a sequence of response actions simply represents a new situation for the agent, which it can evaluate as it does for any situation. This is depicted in Fig. 5.3e.

5   Illustrative Examples

Model clustering can be applied for distributing situational understanding concerns across multiple cyber-defense agents that cooperate in defending a system of systems. This is illustrated in Fig. 5.4. In this example, Nodes 1.x support Defended System 1, Nodes 2.x support Defended System 2, etc. Thus, there are four defended systems, each with a dedicated cyber-defense agent. Together, these four systems constitute a larger system of systems. In this model, each edge represents the set of

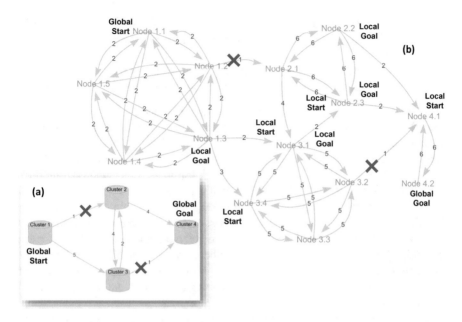

Fig. 5.4 Distributing situational understanding concerns across cyber-defense agents

all exposed vulnerabilities reachable from one host to another. Each edge is labeled with a weight showing the importance (according to some measure) of that edge to mission readiness.

Now, consider a situation in which an adversarial presence is detected on Node 1.1, which is part of System 1. In this situation, the given defensive goal is to prevent the adversary from reaching Node 4.2 (e.g., to protect critical data), which is part of System 4. As shown in Fig. 5.4a, the situation can be first considered at the system-to-system (rather than node-to-node) level, e.g., by a fifth cyber-defense agent dedicated to the overall system of systems. In this case, assume that the fifth agent's planning module has chosen to block the edge(s) from System (Cluster) 1 to System (Cluster) 2, as well as the edge(s) from System (Cluster) 3 to System (Cluster) 4. Thus the remaining edges need to be monitored as potential paths of adversarial exploitation.

This information can be shared with the cyber-defense agents for each defended system. Each agent need only be concerned with its local viewpoint of the situation, i.e., the situation after the global (entire system of systems) agent has taken its actions. Thus, we have the following local situations for each (individual system) agent:

- Agent 1 (protecting System 1): Adversarial has a presence on Node 1.1. Prevent the adversary from either reaching or leaving Node 1.3.
- Agent 2 (protecting System 2): Adversary will potentially reach Node 2.3 (from Node 3.1). Prevent the adversary from either reaching or leaving both Node 2.1 and Node 2.3.

- Agent 3 (protecting System 3): Adversary will potentially reach either Node 3.1 or Node 3.4 (from Node 1.3). Prevent the adversary from either reaching or leaving Node 3.1.
- Agent 4 (protecting System 4): Adversary will potentially reach Node 4.1 (from either Node 2.1 or Node 2.3). Prevent the adversary from reaching Node 4.2.

As cyber-defense agents have the responsibility for defending larger environments, the ability to effectively manage complexity becomes especially important. Partitioning graph-based security models in this way has been shown to provide a $(1/k)^2$ reduction in computational complexity, for k clusters (Sabur et al., 2022). For example, to better understand trends in network traffic, an agent could cluster hosts according to similarities in their traffic patterns, as shown in Fig. 5.5.

The agent begins with a current state having network traffic flows as shown in Fig. 5.5a. In this case, there are about 75 host machines. From the input flows, the agent builds features (e.g., Jaccard index) for inbound and outbound hosts using network addresses, protocols, and port numbers, as shown in Fig. 5.5b. The agent then applies the features to compute similarities (in an abstract space) between each pair of hosts, as shown in Fig. 5.5c. Hosts having relatively more inbound and outbound edges in common are thus deemed more similar.

In Fig. 5.5d, the agent applies a clustering algorithm (e.g., single-linkage agglomerative clustering) to compute a cluster hierarchy. This hierarchy represents a sequence of nested clustering results (clusters of clusters). The cluster hierarchy is parameterized by a threshold value of host similarity, using the host-to-host similarity values computed as in Fig. 5.5c. A chosen value of similarity then defines a particular clustering result (partitioning of hosts into clusters), such that each pair of hosts in a cluster have similarity within the threshold value.

Applying the approach in Fig. 5.5, the cyber-defense agent can generalize the entire set of observed network flows into patterns that apply at the cluster level. For

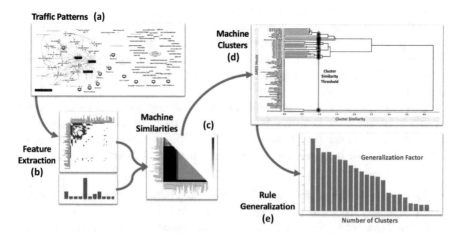

Fig. 5.5 Analyzing commonality in host traffic patterns

example, a straightforward rule is to consider the union of all inbound or outbound flows for a cluster (for a period of observation time) as the nominal behavior for all cluster members. Then for anomaly detection, any flows into or out of a cluster that are not within such a union set could be considered anomalous.

In this approach, the similarity threshold applied to the cluster hierarchy is a tuning parameter that allows the agent to select the amount of generalization. At one extreme (largest similarity threshold), there is a single cluster containing all hosts, so that nominal behavior is the union of all inbound and outbound flows observed for the network. At the other extreme (smallest similarity threshold), each host is in its own cluster, so that nominal behavior is restricted to only those previously flows (i.e., no union operations occur). That tuning is illustrated in Fig. 5.5e, using the total number of rules (inbound and outbound) for the entire network divided by the average number of rules per cluster as a generalization measure.

To assess cyberspace risks in the context of organizational missions, situational understanding can leverage mappings from mission-critical functions and systems to the cyber assets on which they depend. This is illustrated in Fig. 5.6.

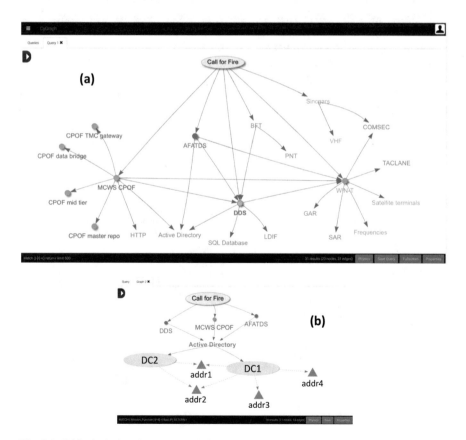

Fig. 5.6 Critical mission elements at risk from malware attack

Figure 5.6a shows notional dependencies for a "call for fires" mission function (use of weapons systems to create effects on a target). Here, the graph edges represent dependencies of mission elements, i.e., the warfighting function (call for fires) depends on certain weapon systems, which depend on other systems, which depend on certain network services.

In Fig. 5.6b shows the dependency graph augmented with certain hosts and observed flows (dashed lines) from a red/blue team exercise network. Here, there are four hosts (triangle nodes) that have been infected by malware. In this example, given the confirmed presence of malware on these four hosts, a cyber-defense agent would seek to trace which other hosts have been communicating with the infected ones, especially those hosts providing mission-critical roles. In this case, the infected machines have communicated with the domain controllers, which provide critical functionality for three of the systems that support the "call for fires" warfighting function, thus putting that function at high risk.

For situational understanding, performing analysis from a threat perspective (versus a pure vulnerability perspective) provides a more complete picture. Such threat-oriented analysis also needs to consider the defended system's configuration and security posture. Matching threats against vulnerabilities within an operational environment focuses the analysis on what is most relevant for understanding the situation. Figure 5.7 shows an example of this kind of analysis.

In this example, the network is protected from the internet by an external firewall, and an internal firewall protects critical servers. The client has two vulnerabilities (a remote buffer overflow and a local credentials exposure), although they are blocked by the firewalls. The database back-end server has a vulnerability (SQL injection), blocked by the internal firewall. The DNS server in the DMZ is vulnerable to a cache-poisoning attack, exposed through the external firewall.

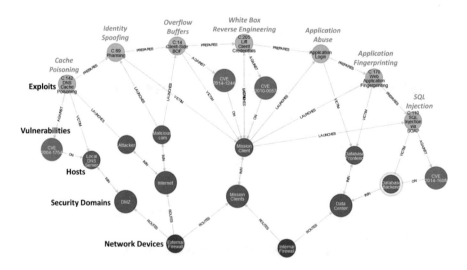

Fig. 5.7 Matching attack patterns with host vulnerabilities and network configuration

The nodes at the bottom of Fig. 5.7 are network devices, i.e., the firewalls that filter traffic according to specified access policy rules. The nodes above the firewalls are security domains (e.g., subnets) that are separated by firewalls, with edges of type ROUTES showing which domains have their traffic routed through which firewalls. The nodes above the domains are hosts, with edges of type IN (oriented in both directions) showing which hosts are in which domains. So, for example, traffic between the local DNS server and the attacker (coming from the Internet) is filtered by the external firewall, e.g., being allowed via misconfigured firewall rules. While this view of the operational domain does not show which connections are allowed through the firewall, there are other available views of the model to show that (Noel et al., 2015).

In Fig. 5.7, the chain of nodes along the top (connected by edges of type PREPARES) is a sequence of interdependent attack patterns (potential exploits) relevant to a certain network environment. Each attack pattern is labeled with its CAPEC identifier. For example, the first attack pattern in the chain is CAPEC-142 (DNS Cache Poisoning). The CAPEC-142 attack pattern includes a CanPrecede field that references CAPEC-89 (Pharming). This indicates that in terms of an attack chain, successful execution of CAPEC-142 (DNS Cache Poisoning) provides postconditions that fulfill preconditions for CAPEC-89 (Pharming). In this case, a fraudulent record in a Domain Name System (DNS) server can misdirect traffic to a malicious domain, e.g., for serving malware to client hosts.

In Fig. 5.7, an edge from a host to a CAPEC attack patterns (of type LAUNCHES) indicates the host from which the attack can be launched, and an edge from an attack pattern to a host (of type VICTIM) indicates the potential victim host. An edge from an attack pattern to a vulnerability (of type AGAINST) gives the reported vulnerability on the victim (edge of type ON) that is susceptible to the attack pattern. Here, each vulnerability node is labeled by CVE identifier. For example, the local DNS server in the defended environment has vulnerability CVE-2004-1754 (cache poison via malicious DNS server).

In Fig. 5.7, the vulnerabilities reported in CVE are presumably detectable by detected by cyber-defense agent sensors, either potentially exploitable (via vulnerability scanning) or exploited (via intrusion detection). Thus, those elements of the attack chain are observable. Other attack patterns (i.e., those without corresponding CVE vulnerabilities in the figure) could be unobservable (e.g., pharming or application fingerprinting). In the case of the Application Login, that event is not considered an attack pattern per se. Rather, it is a standard operation (logging in) that is done for malicious purpose. Such events require other sensor data sources, e.g., application logs. Since adversaries are often able to morph their attacks to evade detection, some attacks might still be missed by intrusion detection. The kind of threat-oriented analysis as shown in Fig. 5.7 can help fill in such missing information.

For this network, an attack graph based solely on vulnerability scan data and analysis of firewall rules would show four vulnerabilities, with only one of them exposed to the outside (cache poising on the DNS server). Augmentation with threat knowledge as shown in Fig. 5.7 gives a more complete understanding of the situation:

- The DNS cache poisoning vulnerability (CVE 2004–1754) is associated with DNS cache poisoning (CAPEC-142), which is a pre-cursor to pharming (CAPEC-89), in which the poisoned DNS cache directs a web client to a malicious web site.

  This is followed by the malicious web site exploiting the client's buffer overflow vulnerability (CAPEC-14 against CVE 2014–1244), which bypasses the firewall as an outbound connection, and then stealing the client's credentials needed for permitted access to the database front-end web service (CAPEC-205 against CVE 2010–0557).
- The adversary then uses the stolen credentials to authenticate as a regular user on the database front-end user interface.
- The execution of CAPEC-170 Web Application Fingerprinting represents the adversary abusing the database access to discover the SQL injection vulnerability (CVE 2014–1608), which is exploited via CAPEC-110 SQL Injection through SOAP Parameter Tampering.

There is in fact a vulnerable path from an outside adversary leading to critical database compromise, while the basic model concludes that no such path exits. This is because associations between CAPEC attack patterns fill in gaps between known vulnerabilities.

CAPEC includes detailed descriptions of how each attack pattern is carried out. An attack pattern is organized as a series of individual steps, with each step preparing for the next. The attack steps are grouped into three phases: exploration, experimentation, and exploitation. Within each phase, details are provided for each attack step, including the criteria for attack success/failure and indicators of attack activity. CAPEC also serves an ontological role for attack patterns, being decomposed into a hierarchy of attack patterns at different levels of abstraction. In Fig. 5.7, the parent (more abstract) attack pattern appears above each CAPEC node, e.g., CAPEC-142 (DNS Cache Poisoning) is a child of CAPEC-141 (Cache Poisoning). A significant portion of the content in CAPEC is expressed as natural language text, which can be mined for enhanced agent situational understanding (Noel, 2015).

Once adversaries have a foothold in an environment, they can leverage the inherent capabilities of the entities that they control. This means that they can perform operations that benign users would perform, such as system logins or accessing file shares. Such operations are not exploitation of vulnerabilities in the usual sense, i.e., the software components are not flawed. Rather, they are working as intended, but are being abused for malicious purposes.

Key operations that adversaries perform for lateral movement (such as logins to remote systems) are of particular interest for situational understanding. Such operations typically require authentication and are enforced through access policy rules. A predominant service for this is Windows Active Directory. Effective situational understanding for cyber-defense agents therefore requires understanding how adversaries can abuse Active Directory to achieve their aims (Binduf et al., 2018).

Figure 5.8 shows key aspects of an Active Directory configuration for an operational network. This model is built from the outputs of SharpHound, which collects

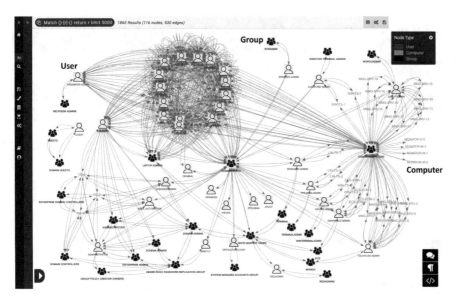

Fig. 5.8 Relationships within a windows active directory configuration

data as part of the BloodHound tool (Robbins et al., 2016–2019). This model has entities in a Windows domain as graph nodes, i.e., users (single-person icon), user groups (three-people icon), and computers (text label only). Graph edges show users as members of groups. Edges between computers and users or groups show which users are allow to login to which computers. The model has other properties (such as privilege levels) that further determine potential adversary capabilities.

Of particular interest for situational understanding is to assess risks associated with attacker techniques such as identity snowball attacks (Dunagan et al., 2009). In such attacks, an adversary who has gained access to a victim host steals the credentials of legitimate users on that host and uses the stolen credentials to launch new attacks, via "pass the hash" or other techniques (Jungles et al., 2014). That process can be repeated on new hosts in a "snowball" fashion.

To model such risks, a cyber-defense agent needs to model not only the configuration aspect of Active Directory (who can log in where), but also the state of cached credentials for hosts across the network (who has logged in where). Agent sensing therefore needs to include logs of user logins. For a complete picture of potential lateral movement through snowball attacks, the cyber-defense agent needs to correlate Active Directory configuration, cached credential state, and firewall effects. That is, all these aspects are preconditions for remote access (logins, file shares, etc.) leveraging credential theft.

Figure 5.9 illustrates such a combined model. Here, each node in the graph model is a network host. An edge from one host to another represents the ability to remotely log in to the remote host via Secure Shell. The remote access edges include the fact that the connection is allowed over the network (enforced via

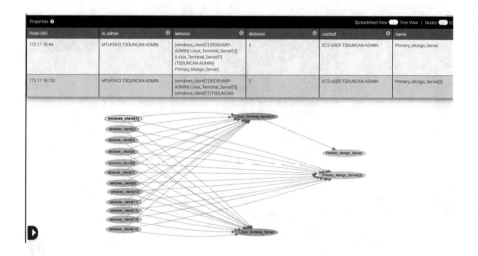

Fig. 5.9 Understanding combined effects of authentication events and firewall policy

transport-layer rules), and an adversary could traverse the network (from a particular starting point) to have the needed credentials at that point in the attack. A certain traversal path provides the "witness" (third column of the table in Fig. 5.9) as being sufficient to carry out that portion of the attack.

Assessing a cyber-defensive situation usually involves multiple concerns that are at odds with one another, constituting a multi-objective optimization problem (Noel et al., 2021a, b). For a particular situation, various numerical measures are possible to characterize the various security concerns. Informed situational understanding by a cyber-defense agent should consider the array of such measures, including tracking them over time to analyze temporal trends.

Figure 5.10 illustrates a set of measures that characterize a certain attack/defense situation in cyberspace. In this situation, there is an observed adversarial presence in a network. The primary goal of the cyber-defense agent is to prevent the adversary from reaching a particular set of hosts containing mission-critical information. The various measures in Fig. 5.10 characterize different aspects of the situation, i.e., to what extent each aspects support the agent's goal. The measures are oriented from top to bottom as least benefit (bottom) versus most benefit (top) to defense.

In Fig. 5.10, each column represents a certain measure assessing the situation (11 measures total). For assessing the measures in a methodical way, they fall under two main categories: those that characterize thwarting the adversary, and those that characterize legitimate access to mission-critical resources. In Fig. 5.10, this is represented by the Attack and Mission measures (respectively). These high-level measures are combined (according to relative weights reflecting the current level of threat) to form the Overall measure that characterizes the situation. The remaining

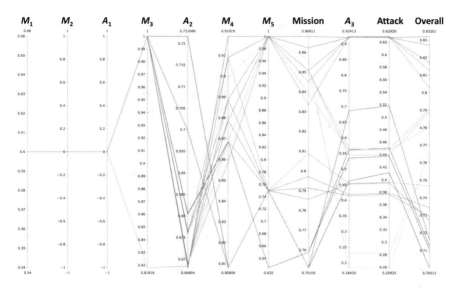

Fig. 5.10 Various measures assessing a cyber-defense situation

measures (8 of them) fall under either the Attack or Mission high-level measures. For example, measure A_3 (under Attack) estimates the adversary effort for the attack/defense scenario, i.e., the number of available walks through the attack graph that result in attacker success. Measure M_4 (under Mission, a complement measure so that fewer flow losses are ranked as higher values) characterizes access to mission-critical resources across the network.

Such multi-faceted situational understanding provides the context needed for effective response planning. In Fig. 5.10, each segmented line (running horizontally) assesses a given set of response actions according to the 11 assessment measures. For this situation (and range of potential response actions), the Overall measure ranks response sets according to overall benefit to the defender. For example, the response sets with Overall measure above 0.8 all have a maximal value of Attack measure (just over 0.62), and a range of Mission measures that are all still above 0.83. On the other hand, the three leftmost measures (M_1, M_2, A_1) are the same for all potential response sets, so those measures can be disregarded in this situation.

This example underscores an important characteristic of modern conflict in cyberspace. Defenders must be prepared for adversaries already having a presence within their environment. We must assume there is generally considerable overlap between reachability to mission-critical resources and reachability that supports adversarial aims. This requires a careful analysis of the various factors when evaluating cyberattack situations.

6 Summary and Conclusions

This chapter examines situational understanding and diagnostics for autonomous cyber-defense agents. It explains how an agent processes its sensed information, keeps its knowledge base continually updated, and assesses a given situation. It shows ways that agents can manage complexity and adapt to new situations. It also considers practical concerns for operational contexts.

This chapter focuses on the core functions of situational understanding: diagnosing the nature of a situation, projecting possible future states, and assessing associated risks. It examines how situational understanding must consider adversarial presence, exploitable vulnerabilities, potential adversarial movement, and how missions depend on defended cyber assets. It describes world models that can be instantiated for a given situation, spanning the agent, the defended system, threats within the sphere of operations, and the mission context. It also explains how an agent can characterize available defensive options and trigger response/recovery planning when it encounters a threshold level of assessed threat.

For new research and development in support of situational understanding for cyber-defense agents, a particularly important area to pursue is richer capabilities for shared threat knowledge that enable automated building of risk models (e.g., based on attack graphs). One example is standard ways of defining attack patterns in terms of preconditions and post conditions, so that chains of attack patterns can be readily formed. Another example is more direct and complete enumerations that associate known vulnerabilities (e.g., reported by vulnerability scanning tools) with commonly understood attack patterns. Much of the valuable information in such vulnerability and threat reports is provided as natural language descriptions rather than in formal knowledge, which impedes progress. Another area of needed improvement is the application of formal specifications for mission dependency models as a routine stage of system development.

Another challenge for situational understanding is the limited view of the world that an agent might have, i.e., limited by the data that can be collected by its sensors. For this, multi-agent collaboration could help, although communication with friendly agents could be limited in contested environments. Research is also needed in ways of integrating situational understanding results across agents, e.g., for defending systems of systems. Methods of measuring risks from attack graph models are also relatively unexplored.

Situational understanding depends heavily on the agent's domain knowledge (world model, dynamics, and state). Thus, limitations in the collection, curation, and representation of domain knowledge can reduce the effectiveness of situational understanding and diagnostics. A key challenge is developing the appropriate theory, expression languages, ontology, and reasoning needed for such knowledge bases. This is especially challenging in resource-constrained environments such as tactical military platforms.

References

Ackoff, R. L. (1989). From data to wisdom. *Journal of Applies Systems Analysis, 16*, 3–9.
Albanese, M., Jajodia, S., & Noel, S. (2012). *Time-efficient and cost-effective network hardening using attack graphs*. IEEE Computer Society.
Baumberger, C. (2014). Types of understanding: Their nature and their relation to knowledge. *Conceptus, 40*(98), 67–88.
Bellinger, G., Castro, D., & Mills, A. (2004). *Data, information, knowledge, and wisdom*. [Online] Available at: https://www.systems-thinking.org/dikw/dikw.htm. Accessed 8 Feb 2022.
Binduf, A., et al. (2018). *Active directory and related aspects of security*. IEEE.
Bodeau, D., Graubart, R., & Heinbockel, W. (2013). *Mapping the cyber terrain – Enabling cyber defensibility claims and hypotheses to be stated and evaluated with greater rigor and utility* (Technical Report MTR130433). The MITRE Corporation.
Buckland, J. (2021). Brigade and battalion mobile tactical operations centers. *Infantry*, Summer, pp. 15–17.
Dunagan, J., Zheng, A. X., & Simon, D. R. (2009). *Heat-ray: Combating identity snowball attacks using machine learning, combinatorial optimization and attack graphs*. ACM.
Endsley, M. (1995). Toward a theory of situation awareness in dynamic systems. *Human Factors Journal, 37*(1), 32–64.
Guion, J., & Reith, M. (2017). *Cyber terrain mission mapping: Tools and methodologies*. IEEE.
Heinbockel, W., Noel, S., & Curbo, J. (2016). *Mission dependency modeling for cyber situational awareness*. NATO Science and Technology Organization (STO).
Jungles, P., et al. (2014). *Mitigating pass-the-hash and other credential theft*. Microsoft Corporation.
Kaynar, K. (2016). A taxonomy for attack graph generation and usage in network security. *Journal of Information Security and Applications, 29*, 27–56.
Kordy, B., Piètre-Cambacédès, L., & Schweitzer, P. (2014). DAG-based attack and defense modeling: Don't miss the forest for the attack trees. *Computer Science Review, 13–14*, 1–38.
Musman, S., & Temin, A. (2015). *A cyber mission impact assessment tool*. s.n.
Nettis, K. (2020, March 16). Multi-domain operations: Bridging the gaps for dominance. *Wild Blue Yonder*, pp. 1–9.
Noel, S. (2015). *Interactive visualization and text mining for the CAPEC cyber attack catalog*. ACM.
Noel, S. (2018). A review of graph approaches to network security analytics. In *From databases to cyber security* (Lecture Notes in Computer Science) (pp. 300–323). Springer.
Noel, S., & Jajodia, S. (2004). *Managing attack graph complexity through visual hierarchical aggregation*. ACM.
Noel, S., & Jajodia, S. (2017). A suite of metrics for network attack graph analytics. In *Network security metrics* (pp. 141–176). Springer.
Noel, S., Harley, E., Tam, K. H., & Gyor, G. (2015). *Big-data architecture for cyber attack graphs: Representing security relationships in NoSQL graph databases*. IEEE.
Noel, S., et al. (2016). CyGraph: Graph-based analytics and visualization for cybersecurity. In *Cognitive computing: Theory and applications* (Volume 35 of Handbook of Statistics) (pp. 117–167). Elsevier.
Noel, S., Bodeau, D., & McQuaid, R. (2017). *Big-data graph knowledge bases for cyber resilience*. NATO Science and Technology Organization (STO).
Noel, S., et al. (2021a). Graph analytics and visualization for cyber situational understanding. *Journal of Defense Modeling and Simulation, Volume Impact Analysis for Cyber Defense Optimization*, 1–15.
Noel, S., Swarup, V., & Johnsgard, K. (2021b). Optimizing network microsegmentation policy for cyber resilience. *Journal of Defense Modeling and Simulation, Volume Impact Analysis for Cyber Defense Optimization*, 1–23.

Perkins, D. (1998). What is understanding? In *Teaching for understanding: Linking research with practice* (pp. 39–57). Wiley.

Reiter, R. (1991). The frame problem in the situational calculus: A simple solution (sometimes) and a completeness result for goal regression. In *Artificial intelligence and mathematical theory of computation: Papers in honor of John McCarthy* (pp. 359–380). Academic.

Robbins, A., Vazarkar, R., & Schroeder, W. (2016–2019). *Bloodhound: Six degrees of domain admin*. [Online]. Available at: https://github.com/BloodHoundAD/BloodHound. Accessed 15 Jan 2022.

Sabur, A., Chowdhary, A., Huang, D., & Alshamran, A. (2022). Toward scalable graph-based security analysis for cloud networks. *Computer Networks, 206*, 1–20.

Schulz, A., Kotson, M., & Zipkin, J. (2015). *Cyber network mission dependencies* (Technical Report 1189). Lincoln Laboratory.

Sowa, J. F. (1992). Semantic networks. In N. J. Hoboken (Ed.), *Encyclopedia of artificial intelligence* (2nd ed., pp. 1–25). Wiley.

Tadda, G. (2008). *Measuring performance of cyber situation awareness systems*. s.n.

The MITRE Corporation. (1999–2022). *CVE® – Common vulnerabilities and exposures*. [Online]. Available at: https://cve.mitre.org. Accessed 25 Jan 2022.

The MITRE Corporation. (2007–2021). *CAPEC™ – Common attack pattern enumeration and classification*. [Online]. Available at: https://capec.mitre.org. Accessed 25 Jan 2022.

The MITRE Corporation. (2007–2022). *Making security measurable™*. [Online]. Available at: https://makingsecuritymeasurable.mitre.org. Accessed 25 Jan 2022.

The MITRE Corporation. (2015–2021). *MITRE ATT&CK®*. [Online] Available at: https://attack.mitre.org. Accessed 25 Jan 2022.

The MITRE Corporation (2020). *Malware attribute enumeration and characterization (MAEC™)*. [Online]. Available at: http://maecproject.github.io Accessed 25 Jan 2022.

Thieme, C., Mosleh, A., Utne, I., & Hegde, J. (2020). Incorporating software failure in risk analysis – Part 1: Software functional failure mode classification. *Reliability Engineering and System Safety, 194*, 1–13.

U.S. Joint Chiefs of Staff. (2018). *Cyberspace operations* (Joint Publication 3-12). U.S. Department of Defense.

Yee, E., Chrysikou, E. G., & Thompson-Schill, S. L. (2013). Semantic memory. In *The Oxford handbook of cognitive neuroscience* (Volume 1: Core Topics) (pp. 353–374). Oxford University Press.

Chapter 6
Learning About the Adversary

Azqa Nadeem, Sicco Verwer, and Shanchieh Jay Yang

1 Introduction: "Know thy Enemy"

Understanding the capabilities of an adversary is one of the first principles of warfare (McFate, 2005). It allows to categorize adversaries based on their capabilities, and thus help with designing effective and targeted countermeasures. Attacker modeling aims to quantify the risks associated with an adversary. Specific abuse cases can be designed using these models and security guarantees can be provided. To this end, several threat assessment models have been proposed. For example, the Capability, Opportunity, Intent (COI) model, also referred to as the Capability, Opportunity, Motivation, Behavior (COM-B) model is one of the most widely used threat assessment models in psychology, business management, and military defense (Michie et al., 2011; Steinberg, 2005, 2007). "Capability" is defined as an attacker's capacity to undertake the task at hand. "Opportunity" refers to the presence of an operating environment that enables the attacker to perform the task, and "Intent" refers to the brain processes that make the attacker act upon the task. A "behavior" is an act of performing the task itself, and is directly influenced by the attacker's capability, opportunity and intent (Michie et al., 2011). Risk can be measured as a product of the attacker's intent and capability.

Tactics, Techniques and Procedures (TTP) describe the abilities and behavior of a cyber adversary. TTPs are usually an expression of an attacker's training, and thus

A. Nadeem (✉) · S. Verwer
Department of Intelligent systems, Delft University of Technology,
Delft, Zuid Holland, Netherlands
e-mail: azqa.nadeem@tudelft.nl; s.e.verwer@tudelft.nl

S. J. Yang
Department of Computer Engineering, Rochester Institute of Technology,
Rochester, NY, USA
e-mail: jay.yang@rit.edu

© The Author(s), under exclusive license to Springer Nature Switzerland AG 2023
A. Kott (ed.), *Autonomous Intelligent Cyber Defense Agent (AICA)*, Advances in
Information Security 87, https://doi.org/10.1007/978-3-031-29269-9_6

are extremely difficult to alter, once detected. TTPs relate to an adversary's capability of employing a strategy to obtain their objectives. These strategies are often visible in observable data generated by a targeted system, e.g., network traffic and intrusion alerts. A vulnerability in the target system presents as an opportunity for the adversary, while the adversary's intent is often implicitly inferred through their actions via observables.

1.1   Learning from Observable Data

Obtaining threat intelligence regarding TTPs from observables is extremely difficult, as indicated by the Pyramid of Pain (Bianco, 2013). The Pyramid of Pain describes the difficulty of obtaining various kinds of Indicators of Compromise (IoCs), where the difficulty increases as one goes up the pyramid, see Fig. 6.1. Lockheed Martin's Cyber Kill Chain (Hutchins et al., 2011) and MITRE's ATT & CK (Strom et al., 2018) are two of the most popular frameworks to study the structure of a cyber-attack in terms of tactics and techniques. The Cyber Kill Chain, shown in Fig. 6.2, models the attack process as a sequential chain of seven steps that an attacker must complete in order to obtain their objective, and thus implementing countermeasures to break the chain may be a useful defense strategy. ATT & CK is a popular behavioral model for the TTPs used by cyber adversaries. Though extremely comprehensive, the attack types in ATT & CK cannot be easily linked to observable signatures. Recently, Moskal et al. (Moskal & Yang, 2020) have developed an Action-Intent framework (AIF) based on the ATT & CK framework that links attacker intent with intrusion alert signatures.

There are two main approaches to building adversary behavioral models: expert-knowledge-driven and data-driven approaches. Expert-knowledge based approaches rely on human expertise curated over several decades' worth of experiences, which makes them largely manual and time-consuming in nature. Many existing techniques are expert-knowledge driven. Consequently, these models must be updated periodically to accurately reflect the evolving threat landscape. For example,

Fig. 6.1 The Pyramid of Pain (Bianco, 2013) shows the difficulty of obtaining various levels of Indicators of Compromise (IOCs)

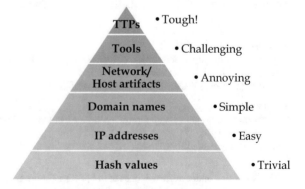

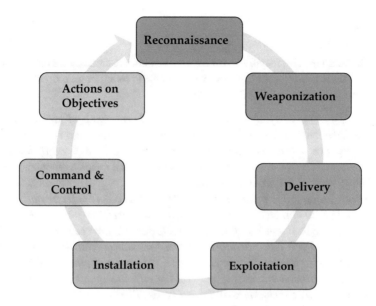

Fig. 6.2 The Cyber Kill Chain categorizes a cyber-intrusion in seven phases, starting with scanning for reconnaissance and ending with actions on objectives

malware detectors often use handcrafted template-based signatures, which are straightforward to evade, as indicated by several studies (Afianian et al., 2020; Marpaung et al., 2012). Attack graphs are another example of adversary behavioral models. Traditional attack graphs are based on Topological Vulnerability Assessment (TVA), which correlates extensive expert input and system vulnerabilities (Noel et al., 2009). As such, the process of constructing such attack graphs is labor-intensive, and it is ineffective to constantly rely on vulnerability scanning to accurately capture the threat landscape, since not all vulnerabilities are known in advance (Jha et al., 2002).

Data-driven approaches can be automated since they utilize observable artifacts collected from intrusion alerts, network traffic, software code, or shared threat intelligence feeds. In recent years, there has been an explosion of data-driven approaches for malware detection (Nadeem et al., 2022a; Souri & Hosseini, 2018), malware analysis (Ucci et al., 2019; Piplai et al., 2020; Nadeem et al., 2021a), attacker strategy extraction (Alsaheel et al., 2021; Moskal & Yang, 2021a; Nadeem et al., 2022b), and intrusion detection (Buczak & Guven, 2016; Rimmer et al., 2022), among other tasks. Although quite promising, building effective and reliable data-driven agents is difficult: The challenges are related to the quality and availability of the observable data, the assumptions on the used models, and the interpretability and robustness of these models. For example, reconstructing adversary behavior from intrusion alerts would only be successful for actions that generated alerts: the actions for which the attackers managed to evade detection cannot be observed in the data, and consequently cannot be modeled.

1.2 Definitions

In this chapter, we primarily focus on data-driven autonomous cyber defense agents because of their life-long ability to learn without too much human involvement.

For clarity, we define the following terms:

- Cyber adversary: *A cyber adversary is a single or group of human actors or automated agents that intend to perform malicious actions that harm other cyber resources. The actions can also have physical aspects, e.g., as in the case of social engineering attacks. The risk associated with a cyber adversary is related to their perceived capabilities and intent.*
- Adversary behavior: *A behavior is a learnt abstraction (model or pattern) from observable data that can be interpreted and transferred to other systems.*
- Adversary intent: *Intent is defined as the relationship between an adversary and their action, which lends insights into the motivations that lead to an attack. Intent is inferred through observed actions. A framework such as ATT & CK or Action-Intent framework aims to connect the intended attack stage with the corresponding tactics, techniques and procedures (TTPs).*
- Observables: *Autonomous cyber defense agents extract observables from data sources (via sensing) to learn about adversary behavior. These include, but are not limited to, software logs (network traffic, intrusion alerts, system logs), software code (malware binaries decompiled or otherwise), threat intelligence (feeds shared among organizations, collected through open source threat intelligence (OSINT)). "Features" are attributes derived from observables that model the adversary behavior. Note that obtaining real-world and usable observables is one of the biggest challenges in constructing autonomous cyber defense agents, as described later in the chapter.*

In addition, we define an autonomous intelligent cyber defense agent (AICA) as being an autonomous, data-driven software agent that learns contextually meaningful cyber adversary behaviors.

- Autonomous: *A white box machine learning based semi-supervised or unsupervised agent (model) that does not require frequent human intervention for (re-) learning. The white box model enables a human-in-the-loop setting where a security analyst can debug and understand the inner-workings of the agent.*
- Data-driven: *An agent (model) that learns from observable data artifacts.*
- Contextually meaningful: *An agent (model) that produces contextually meaningful output by correlating several temporally-linked observables from different modalities in order to provide a holistic view of the threat landscape, instead of viewing a single observable in vacuum. The output must also be multi-faceted and adjusted according to the operator's level of understanding.*

In the rest of the chapter, we describe the challenges of designing effective data-driven autonomous agents, followed by detailed illustrations of three state-of-the-art data-driven autonomous cyber defense agents. We specifically focus on agents that learn from traffic induced data. We close with recommendations and future research directions for R & D practitioners who are looking to get into developing and utilizing data-driven autonomous cyber defense agents.

2   Challenges for Data-Driven Autonomous Cyber Agents

Data-driven autonomous agents utilize some form of machine learning to extract patterns from observables in order to learn cyber adversary behaviors, and to detect and analyze nefarious activities. Several challenges need to be addressed in order to design an effective agent. These challenges are related to the learning environment captured by the threat landscape, the availability of observable data, the assumptions that go into modeling cyber adversary behavior, and the open-world evaluation of said agent. We briefly describe these challenges below:

2.1   Evolving and Adversarial Threat Landscape

In cybersecurity, there is a continual arms-race between attackers and defenders, which causes the threat landscape to evolve rapidly, making it near-impossible for autonomous agents to rely on supervised learning, or much of a priori expert knowledge. An autonomous agent is expected to perceive the changing adversary behaviors and relearn along with them. This can be done by detecting the changing data distributions (also known as Concept Drift). Change detection is commonly utilized in anomaly detection agents to keep up with the evolving systems. An anomaly detector typically models the normal state of a system in order to detect deviations from it. Over time, the system behavior may evolve, either due to system upgrades or new features, which may trigger the anomaly detector to raise false alarms for normal behavior that no longer fits its criteria of normality (Hammerschmidt et al., 2016; Jordaney et al., 2017. Hence, the agent must detect when the data distribution has changed sufficiently and relearn what the 'new' normal behavior looks like.

Cyber adversaries also actively try to evade detection by obscuring their activities. An autonomous agent must expect such evasion attempts and proactively defend against them. For instance, malware authors often evade detection by obfuscating malware (e.g., by encoding or encrypting it). Malware detector agents can fail if the attributes (features) used to model the malware are based on its appearance rather than its behavior. Behavioral features are shown to be more resilient to obfuscation attempts (Cai et al., 2019).

With the recent rise of adversarial machine learning for offensive security, a new breed of evasive attacks has surfaced that challenge the fundamental laws of machine learning. Deep learning models have shown to be particularly brittle to this kind of evasion attempts. Firstly, evasive malware samples can be crafted by either perturbing an existing malware sample to look like goodware, or by perturbing it to the extent that it no longer belongs to the training data distribution (a phenomenon known as "Out Of Distribution" sample detection). In a study, Kolosnjaji et al. were successful in fooling several state-of-the-art classifiers by altering less than 1% of the malware code (Kolosnjaji et al., 2018). Secondly, the data on which an agent learns can be poisoned so it no longer performs as expected (Chen et al., 2018). Thirdly, backdoors may be planted in a trained model so it becomes blind to adversary-chosen targets (Severi et al., 2021). These troubling results were followed by the proposal of several robust/hardened classifiers that include adversarial examples in the training process in order to identify and eliminate the so-called "blind spots" of the malicious domain. Despite recent advances, many classifiers are unable to provide robustness guarantees, making their use and deployment in the real-world tricky.

2.2 Data Availability and Quality

The concerns regarding the quality and availability of observable data to train autonomous agents is a known problem with multiple facets (Du et al., 2018; Nadeem et al., 2022a). Industry practitioners are hesitant, and are often contractually not allowed to share observables since they may contain sensitive information about their clients. It takes significant efforts and resources to make datasets publicly available. However, open source datasets quickly become obsolete due to the rapidly evolving threat landscape. Besides, open source data is often collected in isolated lab environments that do not accurately capture reality. For example, the well-known CTU-13 dataset (García et al., 2014) contains network traffic collected by running botnet-infected virtual machines, where the source IP and source port number are highly indicative of malicious hosts. Thus, using these features alone results in almost perfect classification. Such a situation almost never occurs in reality. Moreover, seamlessly incorporating real (benign) traffic into synthetic malicious traffic is non-trivial, since the differences in underlying network properties makes certain features unusable. For example, timestamps are generally unusable for such synthetically generated datasets, while in reality, these are among the most critical factors for threat intelligence and are indicative of attacker behavior.

Furthermore, open source datasets often have noisy ground truth labels. For example, the malware family names linked to open source malware datasets have repeatedly been shown to be noisy and unreliable. To partially resolve this issue, VirusTotal (VT) executes multiple Anti-Virus vendors and aggregates their results to determine whether a binary is indeed malicious. AVClass (Sebastián et al., 2016) was developed specifically to determine the true malware family label among the (many) VT labels. This unreliable nature of ground truth makes supervised learning very challenging, since the model is learning from faulty labels. Recent works have proposed learning from noisy labels as a potential countermeasure (Croft et al., 2022), though it is unclear how such methods fare when deployed in the real-world. Semi-supervised and unsupervised learning techniques appear to be more suitable paradigms for training autonomous cyber defense agents. For instance, Nadeem et al. have utilized unsupervised learning to construct network behavioral profiles of malware samples to characterize them, instead of relying on noisy family labels (Nadeem et al., 2021a).

Finally, open source datasets are often not at the desired granularity required for a specific task. For example, threat intelligence feeds are often too generic to be useful (Sauerwein et al., 2017; Schaberreiter et al., 2019. In addition, the majority of the traces in network induced observables, such as intrusion alerts and network traffic, often reflect benign behavior, while those related to malicious activities are rare. Thus, it is often easier to perform anomaly detection on network traffic, rather than multi-class classification of the anomalies themselves. Learning with infrequent data remains an open problem in the machine learning community (Lu et al., 2020). A solution for obtaining good quality experimental data is to use honeypots. Honeypots are bogus, deceptive systems that lure adversaries into attacking it, and enable security practitioners to investigate how a particular threat actor operates. Honeypots have been used occasionally to collect granular observables (and threat intelligence) in order to understand an adversary's TTPs (Alata et al., 2006). Though, the design of realistic and robust honeypots is an open area of research (Surber & Zantua, 2022).

2.3 Modeling Adversary Behavior

The Pyramid of Pain (Fig. 6.1) shows the various levels of Indicators of Compromise (IOCs) that can be extracted from observables. As one moves up the pyramid, the IOCs get harder to extract. The IOCs regarding adversary behavior and strategy (the TTPs) are at the very top of the pyramid. Extracting insights regarding adversary strategies is difficult due to a multitude of reasons, one of them being the noisy nature of the observables, and another being the arbitrary nature of human actions.

When designing an autonomous agent, one must determine whether to model an attack or the attacker, since the former is relatively simpler to model. For example, a botnet detector that models the periodicity between network requests is more likely to succeed in its objective (Eslahi et al., 2015), compared to an autonomous agent that models the time it takes a human adversary to complete a task, which can be arbitrarily difficult. As such, autonomous threat actors, e.g., malware are much more deterministic than human actors. Thus, the observable features that characterize malware and human actors must be different. For example, in order to characterize a malware, observable features regarding its functionality are chosen, while to characterize a malware's author, features related to the code writing style are chosen, such as a function's name, or length of added comments (Nadeem et al., 2022a). Ultimately, it is important to borrow insights from clinical psychology and criminology to understand the role certain features play in order to effectively model adversary behavior.

2.4   Modeling Context

The context (or semantics) of observables is crucial to accurately model adversary behavior. In order to comprehend an attacker's intent, it is paramount to view the observable data in the context of different perspectives. For example, one can assess a) temporal anomalies such as a host becoming excessively active during early morning or weekend hours, when less traffic is observed typically, b) irrational access attempts with mismatched port numbers, c) correlated increase in activity from multiple sources, and d) unexpected outbound traffic from specific internal hosts. An effective autonomous cyber defense agent is expected to learn such contextually meaningful adversary behaviors.

Additionally, investigating multiple data sources is important to establish confidence in an agent's judgment. For example, if an agent detects a data exfiltration attempt, only investigating an intrusion alert with data exfiltration signature does not provide sufficient evidence. Instead, the corresponding host's system logs should be cross correlated to see if a sensitive file was accessed and transmitted over the network. This is known as multimodal learning, i.e., learning from different data sources. Multimodal learning is a highly coveted property of autonomous agents, but presents a few challenges: (1) Data from different modalities often exist in different dimensionalities that must be brought to a common representation before learning, e.g., consider diverse data sources like threat intelligence feeds and network traffic. (2) Aligning and reasoning over semantically-linked events from different modalities is often not straightforward, e.g., a network packet that causes a denial of service attack may not have a corresponding entry in the system logs at the same timestamp since the system was unresponsive for the duration of the attack. Nevertheless, some of the challenges also present as opportunities: (1) Co-learning, or transferring what is learnt from one modality across different modalities is a promising avenue to handle the unlabeled nature of some modalities, e.g., Knowledge graphs can be used as a domain knowledge-rich modality to model adversary behavior from intrusion alerts. (2) Translating one modality to another could prove useful for creating synthetic anonymized observables that can be easily shared with the research community.

2.5   Interpretable Approaches

Although repeated human intervention is not required to train an autonomous cyber defense agent, removing a human analyst entirely from the loop makes it difficult to understand what the agent is learning (Sejnowski, 2020). This is more so the case for the recently proposed deep learning models and complex ensembles of machine learning pipelines that turn the whole agent into a black box. Metrics alone cannot adequately capture the performance of such a black box. Without a qualitative analysis, the metrics may give a false sense of how well an agent is actually working.

For example, in a recent study, it was observed that a highly performant "Wolf vs. Husky" image classifier in fact did not learn the distinguishing features of the two animals, but rather looked at the image background to make its decision (Ribeiro et al., 2016). As it turned out, the training data contained all wolf images in snowy backgrounds, while husky images in non-snowy backgrounds. This is known as the "Clever Hans phenomenon" (Samhita & Gross, 2013). Machine learning models can easily learn such biases if the training data contains them, and it becomes extremely difficult to debug them if they are black boxes (Rudin, 2019). Aside from ethical and moral repercussions, these biases may be exploited by adversaries in their favor.

Recent studies show that there does not necessarily have to be a trade-off between explainability and performance, i.e., interpretable models can sometimes even achieve better performance (Letham et al., 2015). In fact, when a model is interpretable, it allows humans to learn from it, which ultimately also elevates human performance. The cybersecurity field has placed a renewed focus on designing interpretable and explainable autonomous agents in recent years. There are several approaches that attempt to explain the inner workings of a black box model, e.g., by learning a simpler surrogate model (Szczepański et al., 2020), or by providing feature importance (Apruzzese et al., 2020), to name a few. While promising for verifying the correctness of black box models, the fidelity and trustworthiness of these explanations themselves can be subjected to attacks (Slack et al., 2020). Therefore, there is an increasing emphasis on interpretable by-design models for decision support, where human analysts are kept in the loop. These approaches enable the debugging and auditing of an agent to ensure that it learns exactly what it is intended to learn. For example, a recent study proposed a multi-step explanation system to make network intrusion detection systems more interpretable (Liu et al., 2021). Their system explains the model internals, its decisions, and also provides explanations based on the level of expertise of the operator. These types of autonomous agents are more likely to be deployed and used by security operators since they keep the human in the loop and allow them to intervene when necessary.

2.6   Open-World Evaluation

The evaluation of an autonomous cyber defense agent must be designed with care. For instance, when dealing with datasets that have noisy ground truth, matching predicted labels with true labels is an unreliable and dangerous evaluation technique. Similarly, for unsupervised tasks such as clustering, the traditional definition of a true positive does not hold since data may be assigned to arbitrary clusters in different executions. Thus, a pair-wise co-occurrence method that looks at whether data items from one class are placed in the same cluster is a more suitable choice (Manning et al., 2010).

Furthermore, the choice of certain metrics may lead security practitioners to misleading conclusions (Jordaney et al., 2016). For example, an anomaly detector trained on a highly imbalanced dataset may not detect even a single anomaly, while still achieving impressive accuracy. This is why it is imperative that practitioners do not rely entirely on metrics, and attempt to understand the inner workings of the autonomous agent. One way to achieve this is by explaining a detected anomaly. Li et al. (Li et al., 2019) explain network anomalies using a local explanation method that ranks the most important features that led to a network flow being classified as an anomaly. These insights not only help security operators generate effective preventative policies, but also enable them to debug the anomaly detector, if necessary.

Finally, open-world studies investigating the generalizability of autonomous agents are imperative to get a glimpse of whether such an agent behaves as expected when deployed. Any number of reasons may cause the agent's performance to decline, including incorrect assumptions, mishandled edge cases, data quality, concept drift, and evasion attempts. Recognizing the unique challenges that emerge when machine learning meets cybersecurity is the first step towards the solution. Sethi et al. (Sethi & Kantardzic, 2018) coin this crossroads between cybersecurity, machine learning, and streaming data mining as "Dynamic Adversarial Mining", which considers the combined problems of streaming data mining and adversarial learning in order to build generalizable autonomous cyber defense agents.

3   Approaches and Advancements

Below, we describe three cutting-edge cyber defense agents that model contextually meaningful adversary behavior with little to no ground truth labels, namely ASSERT (use case 1), SAGE (use case 2), and HeAT (use case 3). Although they are not fully autonomous, these approaches are certainly pushing the boundary of what can be learnt from observables. Note that these use cases specifically design agents that learn from traffic induced data, such as intrusion alerts.

In typical enterprise networks, intrusion detection and prevention systems (IDS) act as gatekeepers for adversaries, and raise alerts if any malicious activity is detected. Intuitively, intrusion alerts can provide insights into the attacker intent and it should be possible to reverse engineer attacker behavior from them. However, it is a challenging task for supervised learning, since intrusion alerts are rarely accompanied by ground truth labels. In this section, we describe three autonomous cyber-defense agents that extract insights about adversary behavior and attack campaigns from intrusion alerts.

3.1   Use Case 1: Attack Model Synthesis (ASSERT)

In this example, Yang et al. (2021; Okutan & Yang, 2019) aim to monitor the evolving threat landscape by continuously synthesizing and updating emerging attack behavior models. To this end, they develop ASSERT – an unsupervised information theoretic learning framework that analyzes an endless stream of intrusion alerts to either dynamically generate a new model when an emerging attack is identified, or to update existing models if attack behaviors change. These models aggregate numerous related alerts to describe the "type of host" an adversary is targeting, "how" they are doing it, and the "intended outcome" they are trying to accomplish. Analysts can utilize their time more efficiently by focusing on critical attack models instead of the overwhelming streaming alerts. The overall component diagram of ASSERT is shown in Fig. 6.3.

ASSERT is an information theoretic, unsupervised, continual learning system that consumes streaming alerts to synthesize statistical attack models in near real-time without requiring expert knowledge. It takes intrusion alerts generated by Suricata (https://suricata.io/) and produces attack models, with both the I/O pipelines in JSON format. ASSERT analyzes aggregated intrusion alerts as non-parameterized data distributions in order to identify and separate emerging attack models. There are three main components in the core engine of ASSERT: (a) alert transformation into attack action aggregates, (b) unsupervised information theoretic synthesis of attack models, and (c) interpretation of attack models.

The first component aims to transform heterogeneous alert attributes into a set of contextually meaningful attack features. Specifically, ASSERT focuses on the following attack action dimensions:

- Attack Intent Stages (AIS) (Moskal & Yang, 2020): a condensed version of MITRE's ATT & CK categories to imply the intended consequences of an observed attack action. A Pseudo Active Transfer Learning (PATRL) (Moskal & Yang, 2021a) approach has been developed to automatically transform alert signatures into AIS.

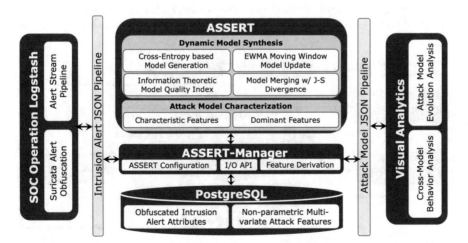

Fig. 6.3 The system architecture of ASSERT. It takes intrusion alerts as input and produces visual representations of attack behavior models. (Adapted from Yang et al., 2021)

- Targeted Services: Contextually, the targeted services, as implied by the port numbers, are one of the most indicative characteristics for an attacker's behavior. This is done through a regularly updated mapping of port numbers to known services or labels indicating reserved or other uses of TCP and UDP ports.
- Attack Maneuver: This is a mapping of IP addresses to categorical maneuvers, reflecting both, the direction of the observed action (i.e., inbound, outbound, internal) and the change(s) in source and destination IPs between consecutive alerts (e.g., the src IP of the new alert is the dst IP of the last alert, or the new alerts has the same src IP but a different dst IP) in the same alert stream.
- Attack Speed: This feature is derived based on the time elapsed between consecutive alerts in the same alert stream. The time is discretized in a logarithmic manner to reflect the significant variation (from nano-secs to mins or hours) in attack speed.
- Attack Source: This feature reflects the "region" and the "blacklistness" of the source of the attack based on the IP address(es). Note that the source can be the source or destination IP, depending on which one is external to the targeted network and the type of attack actions. For example, the external destination IP of a data exfiltration attack would be the attack source, instead of blindly treating all the IPs in the src-IP field as the attack source.

The second component is the main algorithm that enables the unsupervised attack model synthesis process. Figure 6.4 shows the high-level process, where X is an aggregate of attack actions transformed from intrusion alerts by processing small batches of alerts, and $Q*$ is the best attack model that matches the characteristics exhibited by X. The $H()$ function represents the cross-entropy between the two distributions, P_X and P_Q, and serves as a proxy of Kullback-Leibler divergence (KLD) since $H(P_X)$ is the same in the argmin process. The use of H_{max} threshold provides a computationally efficient and effective heuristic to determine whether the new aggregate sufficiently resembles the best-matched model or should be used to create a new model. The Model Quality Index (MQI) measures the overall quality of

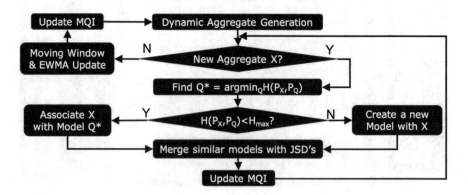

Fig. 6.4 The unsupervised attack model synthesis process of ASSERT. (Adapted from Yang et al., 2021)

model separation in the joint attack feature space, by integrating Jensen-Shannon divergence (JSD) and the notion of Wemmert-Gancarski Index (WGI).[1]

The final component of ASSERT aims to provide an interpretable set of characteristics for each attack model. Continuing the information theoretic framework, the characteristic feature for each attack action dimension of model Q is as follows:

$$x_Q^* = \arg\max_{x \text{ in } \bar{Q} \neq Q} \left(p_{Q(x)} \log p_{\bar{Q}(x)} \right)$$

where $p_{Q(x)}$ and $p_{\bar{Q}(x)}$ are the probabilities of the feature x in Q and $\bar{Q}$ (all other models that are not Q), respectively. Intuitively, this finds the feature that is prominent (not necessarily the most) in Q but very rare or non-existent in any other model. The characteristic features provide an intuitive way for the analysts to comprehend and differentiate the attack models.

The authors worked with a real-world Security Operations Center (SOC) to process streaming Suricata alerts and to synthesize attack behavior models. Over a month of continuously running ASSERT, the system maintains approximately 20 to 25 attack models even with tens of millions of intrusion alerts. Fig. 6.5 shows a cropped screenshot from ASSERT output. In this case, there were 21 unique attack models. One of the attack models drew the analyst's attention: It shows a potential critical persistent code execution attack through Kerboros authentication. This is a persistent attack because most of the observed actions are inbound traffic with no change on the source or target IPs. There are other malicious activities observed in

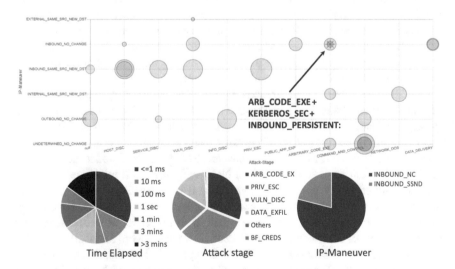

Fig. 6.5 (Top) A screenshot of attack models produced by ASSERT with a persistent arbitrary code execution through Kerberos. (Bottom) The pie charts show the model's attack features in Attack Speed, Attack Intent Stage, and Attack Maneuver. (Adapted from Yang et al., 2021)

---

[1] https://cran.r-project.org/web/packages/clusterCrit/vignettes/clusterCrit.pdf

this persistent attack, including privilege escalation and data exfiltration. Recognizing this critical attack model by using the autonomous ASSERT helps the analysts to focus on the relevant intrusion alerts and system logs, and determine effective remediation to treat the vulnerabilities, and to defend against the adversary.

3.2   Use Case 2: Attacker Strategy Extraction (SAGE)

In this example, Nadeem et al. (Nadeem et al., 2022b; Nadeem et al. 2021b) propose a data-driven attack graph approach to extract attacker strategies without a priori expert input. Attack graphs (AG) are well-known models of attacker strategies that assess pathways utilized by a cyber adversary to penetrate a network. Existing techniques to construct attack graphs are based on Topological Vulnerability Assessment (TVA), which requires significant expert input to correlate system vulnerabilities. However, it is expensive and ineffective to constantly rely on expert input and vulnerability scanning in real-world operations. Meanwhile, SOC analysts often investigate millions of intrusion alerts on a daily basis. Alert correlation techniques help to reduce the overall load of intrusion alerts by aggregating alerts that originate from the same attacker action. While useful in its own right, alert correlation does not show attack progression and attacker strategies. Instead, in this study, the authors define a novel adversary behavioral model, i.e., an "Alert-driven Attack Graph", that learns attacker strategies directly from intrusion alerts without a priori expert input.

The authors develop SAGE – an interpretable sequence learning pipeline that constructs attack graphs from the actions observed through intrusion alerts, without a priori expert knowledge. SAGE utilizes an unsupervised statistical model, known as a suffix-based probabilistic deterministic finite automaton (S-PDFA) to learn attacker strategies from intrusion alerts, and display them in the form of attack graphs. The authors discuss two application scenarios for alert-driven attack graphs: (1) SAGE is designed to augment existing intrusion detection systems for triaging critical attack scenarios that might require urgent attention. Thus, instead of investigating thousands of tabular alerts, SOC analysts can visualize attacker strategies, and investigate only a selection of intrusion alerts relevant to a critical attack path. They can use these AGs to understand how an attack transpired, and to extract threat intelligence about adversaries based on historically observed malicious activities. (2) Alert-driven attack graphs can monitor and rank red-teaming exercises. For instance, AGs can be reviewed after a training exercise to determine which team member(s) managed to find the shortest path to an objective, or to find redundant paths indicative of communication problems between the team members.

The overall component diagram of SAGE is given in Fig. 6.6. SAGE consumes Suricata alerts in JSON format as input, and generates images of the resulting attack graphs as output. The steps for learning alert-driven attack graphs are given as follows:

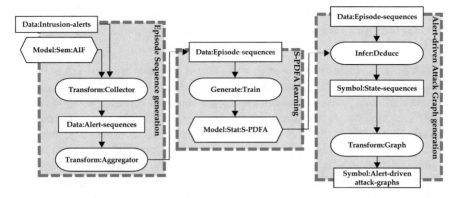

Fig. 6.6 An overview of SAGE. It aggregates intrusion alerts into episode sequences, which are used by the S-PDFA to learn temporal and probabilistic relationships between them. Alert-driven attack graphs are extracted from the S-PDFA for each victim host and exploited objective. (Adapted from Nadeem et al., 2022b)

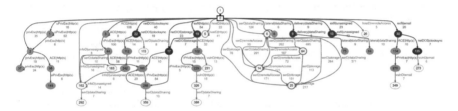

Fig. 6.7 The S-PDFA learnt from over a million intrusion alerts collected through the Collegiate Cyber Defense Competition. The states (vertices) are colored according to severity: the darker the color, the more critical the attacker action is. The edges describe an episode as a combination of the attack stage and the targeted service. (Adapted from Nadeem et al., 2022b)

- Intrusion alerts are pre-processed and augmented with the Attack Intent Stages (AIS) from the Action-Intent Framework (Moskal & Yang, 2020). Similar to the previous use case, the attack stages indicate the intended consequence of an attacker action.
- The alerts are aggregated into "Episodes" (Moskal et al., 2018) such that an episode characterizes an attacker action.
- The episodes are arranged in sequences for each attacker-victim IP pair.
- The episode sequences are partitioned for each attack attempt. The start of a new attack attempt is indicated by observing a low-severity episode followed by a high-severity episode. These episode subsequences form the training data for the S-PDFA.
- An S-PDFA is learnt using the FlexFringe automaton learning framework (Verwer & Hammerschmidt, 2017). An example of the S-PDFA learnt from over a million alerts is given in Fig. 6.7.
- The episode subsequences are replayed through the S-PDFA. This step augments the episodes with their respective contextual information (i.e., state identifiers).

- Finally, the augmented subsequences are transformed into attack graphs, where one attack graph is generated for every objective exploited on each of the victim host(s).

Nadeem et al. identify three design challenges for learning alert-driven attack graphs: (1) Alert-type imbalance: Severe or critical alerts are infrequent, while non-severe alerts (e.g., related to network scans) are common. Frequency-analysis methods discard infrequent events as noise, thus making most machine learning methods unsuitable for this application. (2) Modeling context: The same alert signature may be involved in different strategies. This is indicated by the neighboring alerts, which can be used to model an alert's context so as to distinguish between similar attacker strategies. (3) Interpretable model: SOC analysts are often contractually obligated to investigate all alerts, making black box models inherently unsuitable since it is often not possible to reverse engineer the alerts behind a classifier decision.

The S-PDFA is responsible for addressing the design challenges: (1) A suffix-based model is specifically chosen to highlight infrequent episodes, without discarding any low-severity episodes. Since severe episodes always appear at the end of the episode subsequences, a suffix-based model is a natural choice. (2) The state identifiers of the S-PDFA model capture an episode's context. Using the Alergia heuristic (Carrasco & Oncina, 1994) for state merging, states having similar futures and pasts are merged, while those leading to significantly different outcomes are not. (3) The Markovian property of the S-PDFA, together with Sink states make the model components interpretable. Sinks are states that occur too infrequently to learn from. The authors remove low-severity sinks from the S-PDFA, making the model cleaner and easier to follow. Additionally, the Markovian property ensures that the input transition symbols of a state are unique, making it easier to interpret the meaning of a state. In this case, the states represent milestones achieved by an attacker. Overall, the S-PDFA shows a bird's eye view of all the attacker strategies that can be observed in an alert dataset. The deterministic nature of the S-PDFA makes it algorithmically-transparent. The parameters of the model are selected through trial-and-error of visualizing the S-PDFA until it matches the authors' intuition about the data, making it design-transparent (Roscher et al., 2020).

A notional alert-driven attack graph is shown in Fig. 6.8. The root node of an alert-driven attack graph shows the IP address of a victim host and the objective exploited on that host. The graph shows all the attempts made by the attackers to reach the objective. The vertices reflect actions (characterized by episodes) taken by the attackers to obtain the objective, while the edges are annotated with timestamps. All adversaries that achieve the objective are shown in the same graph to aid strategy comparison. The authors compare the complexity of the attack graphs (in terms of vertices and edges) against several baselines, and find that SAGE generates the most succinct graphs.

The authors learn attacker strategies used by participating teams in the Collegiate Penetration Testing Competition (CPTC) (Munaiah et al., 2019), and the Collegiate Cyber Defense Competition (CCDC) from 2018. The CPTC alert dataset is composed of 330,270 Suricata-based alerts generated by 6 participating teams, while the

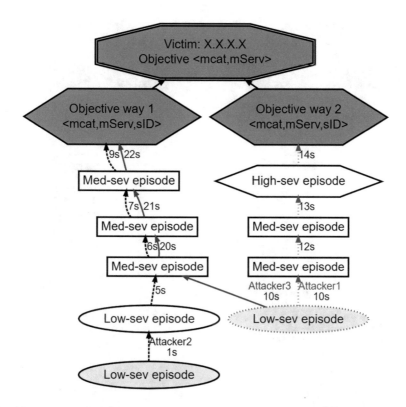

Fig. 6.8 A notional alert-driven attack graph showing paths towards an objective. Each vertex represents an episode. The vertex labels are <mcat, mServ, sID>, reflecting the AIF attack stage, targeted service, and state identifier from S-PDFA. The vertex shape indicates the episode severity. The root nodes reflect the attacker's objective and the victim host. The dotted vertices reflect the sink states. The edges show attack progression and are annotated with the time since the first alert was captured. The attacker's IP address is stated next to the first action in an attack path. (Adapted from Nadeem et al., 2021c)

CCDC dataset is composed of over one million alerts. SAGE compresses all the CPTC alerts into 93 attack graphs, and all the CCDC alerts into 139 attack graphs. These graphs show the strategies employed by the various attackers to obtain their objectives. By visualizing the alert-driven attack graphs, the authors observe several insights regarding attacker strategies: First, the attackers seem to follow shorter paths to re-exploit objectives in 84.5% of the cases, which also appeals to common sense, since an attacker does not necessarily need to go through reconnaissance and scanning when they already know how to exploit a vulnerability. Second, they discover potentially scripted attacks by observing identical attack graphs for several hosts. The intuition is that the automated nature of a scripted attack targets several hosts simultaneously, which results in identical attack graphs for these hosts. An example of a potentially scripted data exfiltration attempt is given in Fig. 6.9 that shows identical attack graphs for two different victim hosts. In addition, the authors

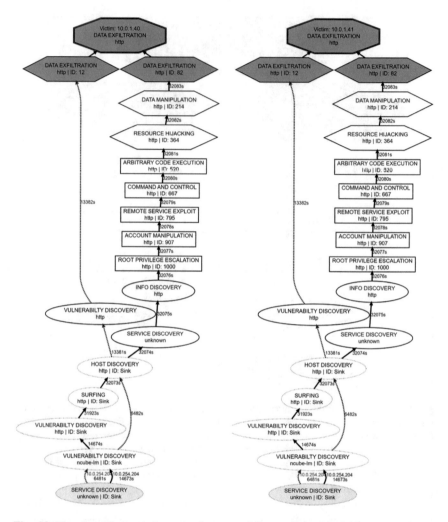

Fig. 6.9 The alert-driven attack graphs from two different victim hosts. They show that two attackers attempt to exfiltrate data over the HTTP service on both hosts, where one team takes significantly more actions to obtain the objective than the other. Both the attack graphs are identical in terms of the attacker actions and their timestamps, indicating a potentially scripted attack attempt. (Adapted from Nadeem et al., 2022b)

posit that the rarity of certain attack paths can serve as fingerprints for attacker re-identification. They also propose a metric based on weighted average percentage to rank the participating teams based on the fraction of observed critical actions. This metric can provide a faster and cheaper alternative to manually ranking teams. Finally, by comparing the S-PDFA models of different alert captures, the authors conclude that it might be easier to break the cyber kill chain, and to place countermeasures in some network infrastructures, depending on the reachability of critical milestones.

3.3   Use Case 3: Attack Campaign Discovery (HeAT)

In this example, Moskal et al. (Moskal & Yang, 2021b) aim to reverse engineer an attack campaign, given a critical intrusion event. They develop HeAT – a semi-supervised learning system that incorporates analyst domain knowledge regarding the contribution of intrusion alerts to an attack campaign in a so-called "Alert Episode HeAT" value. For a given critical event, prior alerts are grouped into alert episodes and each alert episode is given a HeAT value estimating its contribution towards the critical event. A HeAT value of 0 indicates no contribution, and a higher value indicates increasing contribution towards the critical event. This way, HeAT sorts out the relevant alert episodes and gives an estimated progression of how past malicious activities have led to the critical event. HeAT tries to mimic and automate the triaging process of human analysts by learning their emphasis on particular features (such as port-service, attack intent stages, and IP addresses) to reconstruct an attack campaign. The system overview of HeAT is shown in Fig. 6.10.

Moskal et al. define an "Attack Campaign" as a sequence of attacker actions showing how an attacker(s) gained initial access to the network and eventually obtained their objectives. In other words, an attack campaign enumerates multi-stage actions leading up to a critical event, by taking into consideration the network's context (e.g., services running, IP subnets) and the relationship between prior alerts and the critical event, similar to that used for ASSERT (Use case 1). An "Alert Episode HeAT" is a numeric value between 0 and 3 that captures the analyst opinion about the contribution of a given alert episode to a critical event. To this end, the authors curate a small labeled dataset composed of intrusion alerts and their

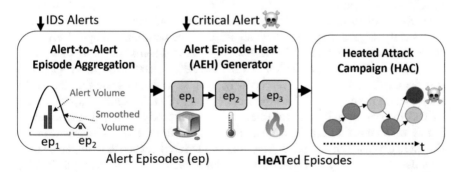

Fig. 6.10   The system overview of HeAT. It aggregates intrusion alerts into episodes, and extracts features from them. These features are used in a tabular model to predict their corresponding episode's HeAT value. Given a critical event, the episodes with high HeAT values are used to reconstruct an attack campaign. (Adapted from Moskal & Yang, 2021b)

corresponding HeAT values that are manually assigned by security analysts. They train a tabular model on this labeled dataset to predict HeAT values of other unseen alerts.

The process of attack campaign extraction is as follows:

- Intrusion alerts are aggregated into episodes using a Gaussian smoothing approach on a per-attack stage basis. Note that the concept of an episode is similar to that of SAGE (Use case 2) with a different implementation.
- Several network agnostic features are used to characterize the timing-related, IP-related, and action-related differences between two episodes. These network agnostic features allow to uncover similar attack campaigns across different network infrastructures.
- The features are given to the tabular model to predict the HeAT values. Naturally, the HeAT values are predicted for alerts that had appeared before a selected critical alert.
- Finally, the alerts with non-zero HeAT values are used to reconstruct the attack campaign.

The authors also propose an entropy-based "HeAT-gain" metric to evaluate the quality of extracted attack campaigns. This metric is based on the diversity and completeness of attack stages in the attack campaign, the reduction of irrelevant alerts in the attack campaign, and the overall coherence between analyst opinions and the predicted HeAT values for the alerts in the attack campaign. The authors envision that HeAT-gain can also be used to prioritize attack campaigns.

The authors extract attack campaigns from the Collegiate Penetration Testing Competition (CPTC) (Munaiah et al., 2019), and the Collegiate Cyber Defense Competition (CCDC) from 2018. They observe that the CodeRed exploit appears several times in both datasets. Specifically, in the CPTC dataset, they present an example of two different types of adversaries that exploit CodeRed in significantly different ways, i.e., a script kiddie and a calculated adversary. The authors find 144 episodes showing that the script kiddie targets multiple different hosts with approximately uniform time between attempts, indicating a scripted attempt. On the contrary, there are 19 episodes related to the calculated adversary, showing that they consistently target a single host with significant time between attempts. HeAT succeeds in discarding a remarkable amount of irrelevant alerts for this exploit in the given time-frame, i.e., a reduction of 71% and 92% episodes for the script kiddie and the calculated adversary, respectively. They also demonstrate that the HeAT values learnt from the CPTC dataset can be used to identify similar exploits in the CCDC dataset, which was collected in a significantly different environment. Figure 6.11 shows an attack campaign extracted from the CCDC dataset for the CodeRed exploit. The authors find striking similarities between the campaigns from both datasets. Namely, the adversary found a vulnerable SMB share that enabled them to deliver malware to the victim host. POP and IMAP are targeted due to a vulnerability in the mail server, which is used to gain initial access to the victim host. They also use the Shellshock vulnerability and SMTP verification of root access to gain further access to the victim host. Even though this attack campaign is

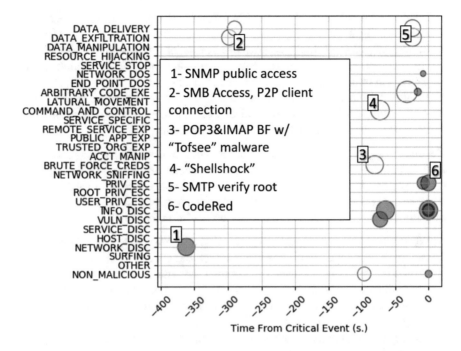

Fig. 6.11 HeATed attack campaign for the CodeRed exploit from the CCDC dataset. (Adapted from Moskal & Yang, 2021b)

not exactly identical to the ones found in the CPTC dataset, the authors demonstrate that HeAT generalizes to other network infrastructures and enables analysts to find similar attack campaigns.

4   Thoughts and Future Opportunities

The three cyber defense agents described in Sect. 3, namely ASSERT (use case 1), SAGE (use case 2), and HeAT (use case 3) actively address the challenges listed in Sect. 2:

- The three agents are designed specifically to help security analysts manage the rapidly evolving threat landscape. Particularly, ASSERT continuously creates and updates attack behavior models as new intrusion alerts come in. All three agents use several open source unlabeled experimental datasets that resemble real-world operations.
- They also conduct extensive qualitative analysis since they operate in either semi-supervised or unsupervised settings. The three agents model adversary behavior differently, i.e., ASSERT builds attack models with an emphasis on continual learning, HeAT reconstructs attack campaigns with an emphasis on

forensic analysis, and SAGE models attacker strategies with an emphasis on threat intelligence.

- In addition, they all model contextual information using some combination of temporal and statistical features. SAGE particularly also discovers probabilistic patterns in intrusion alerts to model their semantics.
- Finally, the three agents utilize visual analytics to communicate their findings with security analysts. SAGE specifically uses an interpretable model, and has a detailed explainability analysis of all its components.

Needless to say, developing a data-driven autonomous cyber defense agent is a challenging task. When designed carefully, such an agent can increase the productivity of security analysts by tenfold. However, it is not always straightforward to realize when an agent works as expected. Below, we list a few recommendations for R & D practitioners and researchers who are getting started in this field:

- While observable data reveals a lot about an adversary, it does not show the full picture: It requires carefully selected data sources to form a reliable picture of an adversary's behavior, and even then, putting those data sources together is not so straightforward (recall the challenges from, e.g., Multimodal learning). Oftentimes, the ideal dataset is not even available, and one must make do with noisy and unlabeled datasets.
- Beware of spurious and undesired correlations learnt by autonomous agents: First, if there is bias in an observable dataset, it will likely be learnt by the autonomous agent, making it behave unexpectedly, especially for minority classes. Second, an autonomous agent will find patterns even when there are none in the training dataset. For example, a clustering algorithm will always find clusters, even when the dataset does not have any. Therefore, it is important to run an autonomous agent on drastically different use cases and verify its output, whenever possible.
- Be prepared to handle a lot of false positives, but also be on the lookout for false negatives: Autonomous agents will likely never achieve a 100% accuracy in modeling adversary behavior, owing to the complexity of the real world and the noise in observables. These errors can either appear as false positives (false alarms) or false negatives (missed opportunities). False alarms are often investigated manually. In real-world SOC operations, even 0.1% of false alarms can be too much to handle on a daily basis (Axelsson, 2000). False negatives can be even more dangerous because they give a false sense of security. These could either refer to adversary behaviors not picked up by the autonomous agent, or not yet executed by the adversary in the first place. While there is little that can be done about the latter, the former is a big problem since there are typically insufficient traces in the observables to learn about them. Infrequent pattern mining is currently an open area of research.
- Beware of misleading metrics: It is convenient to choose from several autonomous agents when their performance can be quantified in terms of metrics. Metrics like accuracy, F1 score, Area Under the Curve (AUC) are widely used in the machine learning world. However, metrics can mislead if not correctly cho-

sen: It is easy to obtain impressive accuracy on highly imbalanced datasets when the autonomous agent does not even work. Qualitative studies, although time-consuming and frequently subjective, provide much deeper insights into how an agent actually works, and whether it works as expected.

- Choose interpretable models: It is understandable to get swept away by the giant state-of-the-art models. However, understanding how they actually reach their decisions is extremely difficult. When practitioners are able to understand the model internals, they can debug and fine-tune those models for further performance optimizations. Spotting bugs in interpretable models is much easier than debugging a black box model. The recent emphasis on explainable AI and interpretable models by-design has given evidence that white box models achieve competitive performance compared to their deep learning counterparts. It is also easier to trust the decisions of an interpretable model over a black box model, even when post-hoc explanations are provided, which themselves can be manipulated. Besides, adversaries are known to exploit weaknesses in cyber defenses. Recent studies have also shown that robust models are more interpretable since they provide more human intelligible explanations (Ross & Doshi-Velez, 2018).
- Multi-faceted explanations: An intuitive explanation that does not accurately explain an agent's behavior is more dangerous than a poor explanation. The faithfulness of an agent and its explanations are both equally important. Multi-faceted explanations from different perspectives can help identify any discrepancies between an agent's decision and an analyst's intuition. For example, finding indicators of compromise from multiple data sources can ensure that an intrusion alert is not a false alarm. To understand why an agent assigns a particular label to an observable, it can be helpful to investigate the labels of similar observables that receive a different label. This is known as contrastive explanations, and it can help answer "what-if" questions about the agent's reasoning.
- Realistic assumptions: Having unrealistic expectations of what an autonomous agent may be able to do can set one up for failure. Despite recent advances, it is important to understand that machine learning can only do so much, especially with noisy observables. Instead, it is better to identify the key strengths of autonomous agents. For example, we know that autonomous agents are much better at monotonous tasks, and can browse through large volumes of observables much faster than human analysts. Realizing this strength, Holder et al. (Holder & Wang, 2021) design an autonomous cyber defense agent to serve as a junior 'support' analyst for human security analysts. The autonomous agent takes over the repetitive and time-consuming jobs, such as scouring the Internet for resources, correlating patterns in large volumes of intrusion alerts, and presenting them to their human counterparts. The human analysts are then free to spend their time doing more complex tasks, such as investigating critical attacks and threat hunting.

Given the increasing number of cyber-attacks in recent times, autonomous cyber defense agents will become a necessity in dealing with large volumes of observables. However, there is still much to be done regarding the adversarial robustness and effectiveness of these agents. We discuss a few prominent research directions below:

- Learning from temporal features is challenging since features are often out-of-sync. Although temporal features provide a lot of contextual cues, it is not always apparent how to represent and learn from them effectively. There are two interesting problem classes: Picking an event at present and looking backwards in time can provide forensic and provenance analysis capabilities, while looking forward can provide threat intelligence and predictive capabilities.
- Learning from infrequent observables that reflect the rare adversary behaviors is an important open problem.
- We expect that multimodal learning and multi-faceted explanations will play a key role in designing trustworthy and robust cyber defense agents that learn contextually meaningful adversary behaviors.
- Incorporating concise reporting and visualization tools that reduce the cognitive load on security analysts is important for effective communication between analysts and autonomous cyber defense agents.
- Cyber defense agents with threat prioritization capabilities that can present their findings at the right level of abstraction (based on an analyst's expertise) are important for usability and deployability.

5 Summary and Conclusions

This chapter discusses how an autonomous cyber defense agent can gain insights into the behaviors and intents of cyber adversaries. The popular Capability, Opportunity, and Intent (COI) model helps categorize various types of adversaries, while the Cyber Kill Chain and ATT & CK frameworks describe the tactics, techniques and procedures (TTPs) of cyber adversaries. Specifically, the Action Intent Framework (AIF) is derived from MITRE ATT & CK that infers the intent of cyber adversaries from traffic induced observable data.

The rapidly evolving threat landscape and adversary TTPs have made it near-impossible for autonomous agents to rely on a priori expert knowledge. Instead, the emphasis should be on the design and deployment of data-driven autonomous agents that learn contextual meaningful adversary behaviors from observable data. Although enticing, designing effective and reliable data-driven agents is difficult due to:

- The evolving and adversarial threat landscape that requires proactive and robust machine learning models,
- The unavailability of good quality observable data with corresponding ground truth that makes supervised learning paradigm unsuitable,
- The unpredictable nature of cyber adversaries and their tactics that require context modeling to adequately capture their behavior,

- The challenges of open world evaluation of black box machine learning models to ensure that the agent behaves as expected.

This chapter illustrates three state-of-the-art use cases for autonomous cyber defense agents that learn adversary behavior from traffic induced observables in order to assist security analysts in defending against the adversary in a timely manner.

- ASSERT is an unsupervised continual learning system that synthesizes and updates emerging attack behavior models from intrusion alerts in a streaming setting without expert input. The behavior models provide a statistical summary of the various attacks conducted by cyber adversaries.
- SAGE follows a two-step approach to reconstruct attacker strategies from intrusion alerts by first learning an unsupervised interpretable model that discovers temporal and probabilistic patterns in intrusion alerts, and then representing the discovered attacker strategies as targeted attack graphs, without any expert input. The attack graphs provide a dynamic view of the network by showing how specific attacks transpired, and enable visual analytics regarding attacker behavior dynamics.
- HeAT is a semi-supervised learning system that integrates analyst domain knowledge and reverse engineers multi-stage attack campaigns given a critical intrusion alert. This system helps analysts in uncovering the chain of actions that led to a critical alert while discarding thousands of irrelevant alerts.

A brief discussion of how the use cases address the aforementioned challenges is given, together with some words of caution for practitioners getting started in the field, pertaining to observable data, spurious correlations, misleading metrics, and interpretable approaches. Finally, a few prominent future research directions are provided with respect to learning paradigms and reporting techniques.

References

Afianian, A., Niksefat, S., Sadeghiyan, B., & Baptiste, D. (2020). Malware dynamic analysis evasion techniques. *ACM Computing Surveys, 52*, 1–28.

Alata, E., Dacier, M., Deswarte, Y., et al. (2006). Collection and analysis of attack data based on honeypots deployed on the internet. In *Quality of protection* (pp. 79–91). Springer.

Alsaheel, A., Nan, Y., Ma, S., et al. (2021). ATLAS: A sequence-based learning approach for attack investigation. In *30th USENIX security symposium (USENIX security 21)* (pp. 3005–3022).

Apruzzese, G., Andreolini, M., Marchetti, M., et al. (2020). Deep reinforcement adversarial learning against botnet evasion attacks. *IEEE Transactions on Network and Service Management, 17*, 1975–1987. https://doi.org/10.1109/TNSM.2020.3031843

Axelsson, S. (2000). The base-rate fallacy and the difficulty of intrusion detection. *ACM Transactions on Information and System Security, 3*, 186–205. https://doi.org/10.1145/357830.357849

Bianco, D. (2013). *The pyramid of pain*. Enterprise Detection & Response.

Buczak, A. L., & Guven, E. (2016). A survey of data mining and machine learning methods for cyber security intrusion detection. *IEEE Communications Surveys Tutorials, 18*, 1153–1176. https://doi.org/10.1109/COMST.2015.2494502

Cai, H., Meng, N., Ryder, B., & Yao, D. (2019). DroidCat: Effective android malware detection and categorization via app-level profiling. *IEEE Transactions on Information Forensics and Security, 14*, 1455–1470. https://doi.org/10.1109/TIFS.2018.2879302

Carrasco, R. C., & Oncina, J. (1994). Learning stochastic regular grammars by means of a state merging method. In *Grammatical inference and applications* (pp. 139–152). Springer.

Chen, S., Xue, M., Fan, L., et al. (2018). Automated poisoning attacks and defenses in malware detection systems: An adversarial machine learning approach. *Computers & Security, 73*, 326–344. https://doi.org/10.1016/j.cose.2017.11.007

Croft, R., Ali Babar, M., & Chen, H. (2022). Noisy label learning for security defects. *arXiv* [cs.SE].

Du, P., Sun, Z., Chen, H., et al. (2018). Statistical estimation of malware detection metrics in the absence of ground truth. *IEEE Transactions on Information Forensics and Security, 13*, 2965–2980. https://doi.org/10.1109/TIFS.2018.2833292

Eslahi, M., Rohmad, M. S., Nilsaz, H., et al. (2015). Periodicity classification of HTTP traffic to detect HTTP botnets. In *2015 IEEE Symposium on Computer Applications Industrial Electronics (ISCAIE)* (pp. 119–123).

García, S., Grill, M., Stiborek, J., & Zunino, A. (2014). An empirical comparison of botnet detection methods. *Computers & Security, 45*, 100–123. https://doi.org/10.1016/j.cose.2014.05.011

Hammerschmidt, C., Marchal, S., State, R., & Verwer, S. (2016). Behavioral clustering of nonstationary IP flow record data. In *2016 12th International Conference on Network and Service Management (CNSM)* (pp. 297–301).

Holder, E., & Wang, N. (2021). Explainable artificial intelligence (XAI) interactively working with humans as a junior cyber analyst. *Human-Intelligent Systems Integration, 3*, 139–153. https://doi.org/10.1007/s42454-020-00021-z

Hutchins, E. M., Cloppert, M. J., Amin, R. M., & Others. (2011). Intelligence-driven computer network defense informed by analysis of adversary campaigns and intrusion kill chains. *Leading Issues in Information Warfare & Security Research, 1*, 80.

Jha, S., Sheyner, O., & Wing, J. (2002). Two formal analyses of attack graphs. *Proceedings 15th IEEE Computer Security Foundations Workshop. CSFW-15.*

Jordaney, R., Wang, Z., Papini, D., et al. (2016). *Misleading metrics: On evaluating machine learning for malware with confidence.* Tech Rep.

Jordaney, R., Sharad, K., Dash, S. K., et al. (2017). Transcend: Detecting concept drift in malware classification models. In *26th USENIX security symposium (USENIX security 17)* (pp. 625–642).

Kolosnjaji, B., Demontis, A., Biggio, B., et al. (2018). Adversarial malware binaries: Evading deep learning for malware detection in executables. In *2018 26th European Signal Processing Conference (EUSIPCO)* (pp. 533–537).

Letham, B., Rudin, C., McCormick, T. H., & Madigan, D. (2015). Interpretable classifiers using rules and Bayesian analysis: Building a better stroke prediction model. *aoas, 9*, 1350–1371. https://doi.org/10.1214/15-AOAS848

Li, H., Wei, F., & Hu, H. (2019). Enabling dynamic network access control with anomaly-based IDS and SDN. In *Proceedings of the ACM international workshop on security in software defined networks & network function virtualization* (pp. 13–16). Association for Computing Machinery.

Liu, H., Zhong, C., Alnusair, A., & Islam, S. R. (2021). FAIXID: A framework for enhancing AI explainability of intrusion detection results using data cleaning techniques. *Journal of Network and Systems Management, 29*, 40. https://doi.org/10.1007/s10922-021-09606-8

Lu, Y., Richter, F., & Seidl, T. (2020). Efficient infrequent pattern mining using negative Itemset tree. In A. Appice, M. Ceci, C. Loglisci, et al. (Eds.), *Complex pattern mining: New challenges, methods and applications* (pp. 1–16). Springer.

Manning, C., Raghavan, P., & Schütze, H. (2010). Introduction to information retrieval. *Natural Language Engineering, 16*, 100–103.

Marpaung, J. A. P., Sain, M., & Lee, H.-J. (2012). Survey on malware evasion techniques: State of the art and challenges. In *2012 14th International Conference on Advanced Communication Technology (ICACT)* (pp. 744–749).

McFate, M. (2005). *The military utility of understanding adversary culture*. OFFICE OF NAVAL RESEARCH ARLINGTON VA.

Michie, S., van Stralen, M. M., & West, R. (2011). The behaviour change wheel: A new method for characterising and designing behaviour change interventions. *Implementation Science, 6*, 42. https://doi.org/10.1186/1748-5908-6-42

Moskal, S., & Yang, S. J. (2020). Cyberattack action-intent-framework for mapping intrusion observables. *arXiv* [cs.CR].

Moskal, S., & Yang, S. J. (2021a). Translating intrusion alerts to cyberattack stages using pseudo-active transfer learning (PATRL). In *2021 IEEE conference on communications and network security (CNS)* (pp. 110–118).

Moskal, S., & Yang, S. J. (2021b). Heated Alert Triage (HeAT): Network-agnostic extraction of cyber attack campaigns. In *Proceedings of the conference on applied machine learning for information security*.

Moskal, S., Yang, S. J., & Kuhl, M. E. (2018). Extracting and evaluating similar and unique cyber attack strategies from intrusion alerts. In *2018 IEEE international conference on intelligence and security informatics (ISI)* (pp. 49–54).

Munaiah, N., Pelletier, J., Su, S.-H., et al. (2019). A cybersecurity dataset derived from the national collegiate penetration testing competition. In *HICSS symposium on cybersecurity big data analytics*.

Nadeem, A., Hammerschmidt, C., Gañán, C. H., & Verwer, S. (2021a). Beyond labeling: Using clustering to build network behavioral profiles of malware families. In M. Stamp, M. Alazab, & A. Shalaginov (Eds.), *Malware analysis using artificial intelligence and deep learning* (pp. 381–409). Springer.

Nadeem, A., Verwer, S., Moskal, S., & Yang, S. J. (2021b). Enabling visual analytics via alert-driven attack graphs. In *Proceedings of the 2021 ACM SIGSAC conference on computer and communications security* (pp. 2420–2422). Association for Computing Machinery.

Nadeem, A., Verwer, S., & Yang, S. J. (2021c). SAGE: Intrusion alert-driven attack graph extractor. In *2021 IEEE symposium on visualization for cyber security (VizSec)* (pp. 36–41).

Nadeem, A., Rimmer, V., Joosen, W., & Verwer, S. (2022a). Intelligent malware defenses. In L. Batina, T. Bäck, I. Buhan, & S. Picek (Eds.), *Security and artificial intelligence: A crossdisciplinary approach* (pp. 217–253). Springer.

Nadeem, A., Verwer, S., Moskal, S., & Yang, S. J. (2022b). Alert-driven attack graph generation using S-PDFA. *IEEE Transactions on Dependable and Secure Computing, 19*, 731–746. https://doi.org/10.1109/TDSC.2021.3117348

Noel, S., Elder, M., Jajodia, S., et al. (2009). Advances in topological vulnerability analysis. In *2009 cybersecurity applications technology conference for homeland security* (pp. 124–129).

Okutan, A., & Yang, S. J. (2019). ASSERT: Attack synthesis and separation with entropy redistribution towards predictive cyber defense. Cybersecurity.

Piplai, A., Mittal, S., Joshi, A., et al. (2020). Creating cybersecurity knowledge graphs from malware after action reports. *IEEE Access, 8*, 211691–211703.

Ribeiro, M. T., Singh, S., & Guestrin, C. (2016). "Why should I trust you?": Explaining the predictions of any classifier. *arXiv* [cs.LG].

Rimmer, V., Nadeem, A., Verwer, S., et al. (2022). Open-world network intrusion detection. In L. Batina, T. Bäck, I. Buhan, & S. Picek (Eds.), *Security and artificial intelligence: A crossdisciplinary approach* (pp. 254–283). Springer.

Roscher, R., Bohn, B., Duarte, M. F., & Garcke, J. (2020). Explainable machine learning for scientific insights and discoveries. *IEEE Access, 8*, 42200–42216. https://doi.org/10.1109/ACCESS.2020.2976199

Ross, A., & Doshi-Velez, F. (2018). Improving the adversarial robustness and interpretability of deep neural networks by regularizing their input gradients. *AAAI, 32*.

Rudin, C. (2019). Stop explaining black box machine learning models for high stakes decisions and use interpretable models instead. *Nature Machine Intelligence, 1*, 206–215.

Samhita, L., & Gross, H. J. (2013). The "clever Hans phenomenon" revisited. *Communicative & Integrative Biology, 6*, e27122.

Sauerwein, C., Sillaber, C., Mussmann, A., & Breu, R. (2017). Threat intelligence sharing platforms: An exploratory study of software vendors and research perspectives. In *Wirtschaftsinformatik 2017 proceedings*.

Schaberreiter, T., Kupfersberger, V., Rantos, K., et al. (2019). A quantitative evaluation of Trust in the quality of cyber threat intelligence sources. In *Proceedings of the 14th international conference on availability, reliability and security* (pp. 1–10). Association for Computing Machinery.

Sebastián, M., Rivera, R., Kotzias, P., & Caballero, J. (2016). AVclass: A tool for massive malware labeling. In *Research in attacks, intrusions, and defenses* (pp. 230–253). Springer.

Sejnowski, T. J. (2020). The unreasonable effectiveness of deep learning in artificial intelligence. *Proceedings of the National Academy of Sciences of the United States of America, 117*, 30033–30038. https://doi.org/10.1073/pnas.1907373117

Sethi, T. S., & Kantardzic, M. (2018). When good machine learning leads to bad security. *Ubiquity, 2018*, 1–14.

Severi, G., Meyer, J., Coull, S., & Oprea, A. (2021). Explanation-guided backdoor poisoning attacks against malware classifiers. In *30th USENIX security symposium (USENIX security 21)* (pp. 1487–1504).

Slack, D., Hilgard, S., Jia, E., et al. (2020). Fooling LIME and SHAP: Adversarial attacks on post hoc explanation methods. In *Proceedings of the AAAI/ACM conference on AI, ethics, and society* (pp. 180–186). Association for Computing Machinery.

Souri, A., & Hosseini, R. (2018). A state-of-the-art survey of malware detection approaches using data mining techniques. *Human-centric Computing and Information Sciences, 8*, 1–22. https://doi.org/10.1186/s13673-018-0125-x

Steinberg, A. N. (2005). An approach to threat assessment. In *2005 7th international conference on information fusion* (p. 8).

Steinberg, A. (2007). Predictive modeling of interacting agents. In *2007 10th international conference on information fusion* (pp. 1–6).

Strom, B. E., Applebaum, A., Miller, D. P., et al. (2018). *Mitre att & ck: Design and philosophy*. Tech Rep NAVTRADEVCEN.

Surber, J. G., & Zantua, M. (2022). Intelligent interaction honeypots for threat hunting within the internet of things. *CISSE, 9*, 5–5. https://doi.org/10.53735/cisse.v9i1.147

Szczepański, M., Choraś, M., Pawlicki, M., & Kozik, R. (2020). Achieving explainability of intrusion detection system by hybrid Oracle-explainer approach. In *2020 international joint conference on neural networks (IJCNN)* (pp. 1–8).

Ucci, D., Aniello, L., & Baldoni, R. (2019). Survey of machine learning techniques for malware analysis. *Computers & Security, 81*, 123–147. https://doi.org/10.1016/j.cose.2018.11.001

Verwer, S., & Hammerschmidt, C. A. (2017). Flexfringe: A passive automaton learning package. In *2017 IEEE international conference on software maintenance and evolution (ICSME)* (pp. 638–642).

Yang, S. J., Okutan, A., Werner, G., et al. (2021) Near real-time learning and extraction of attack models from intrusion alerts. *arXiv* [cs.CR].

Chapter 7
Response Planning

Scott Musman and Lashon Booker

1 Overview of Cyber Response Planning

Given a perception of the environment and threat, and the overall assessment of the situation, cyber response planning is invoked to generate a course of action (COA) or multiple COAs intended to defeat the threat and minimize damage to the system. A variety of computational techniques can be employed toward this end. Before discussing how automated agents can begin to address these challenges, we will start by reviewing two historical examples of cyber response planning to highlight issues associated with cyber response planning problems.

1.1 *Matching Wits with a Hacker*

In the book the Cuckoo's Egg (Stoll, 2005), Cliff Stoll describes a cyber-attack by a foreign hacker and the steps that were taken to respond to that attack. Despite the years since the cuckoo's egg incident occurred, it illustrates many issues that remain relevant. First, note that the attacker was detected unexpectedly while investigating

Portions of this technical data were produced for the U. S. Government under Contract No. FA8702-19-C-0001 and W56KGU-18-D-0004, and is subject to the Rights in Technical Data-Noncommercial Items Clause DFARS 252.227-7013 (FEB 2014).

S. Musman (✉)
Cyber Infrastructure Protection Innovation Center, MITRE Corp, McLean, VA, USA
e-mail: smusman@mitre.org

L. Booker
AI & Autonomy Innovation Center, MITRE Corp, McLean, VA, USA
e-mail: booker@mitre.org

what was thought to be an accounting error. For new, novel attacks, often what will be detected first is a side effect of the compromise, such as a mission impact, rather than the compromise itself. Stoll's book then explains the steps taken to perform forensics on the breach, monitor for additional activities, the setting of traps, and his decision process related to response actions and when they should occur. His decision making involved attempts to gather information about the attacker, and to back-trace the source of the attack. Partly this was to identify the perpetrator and their target(s), but also to understand how the attacker was able to move through the system. Response options were not taken immediately because Stoll did not want to tip off the attacker that they had been detected. The concern was that the attacker would just come back via some other means that may bypass his ability to monitor them. When he finally responded, the response actions taken included distributed ones that had to be coordinated to try and ensure that when the attacker was disconnected there was some confidence that reentry and access avenues were no longer available.

1.2   Defeating an Email Worm

The defensive strategies used to defeat the Morris worm (Orman, 2003) also illustrate some important aspects of cyber response planning. The Morris worm was the first worm that infected and propagated across the internet. Response planning required correlation across multiple servers to identify the problem, find common elements pointing to the compromised components, and then formulate a remediation plan. Initial remediation plans were not effective, so additional information was gathered and a more complex multi-step remediation plan had to be developed.

The Survivable Autonomous Response Architecture (SARA) (Lewandowski et al., 2001) was designed to make it possible for autonomous agents to protect a network. The test problem being solved with the SARA prototype was to protect a network against an email worm (Musman, 2010). Once an infection was detected, a simple solution is to shut down the mail server. This action, however, would incur a significant impact on the ability to perform mission functions that rely on email exchanges. Consequently, a significant portion of the response decision making involved attempts to only block email messages with worm payloads. Knowledge gained from an analysis of the tainted emails was used to develop blocking signatures, to identify targeted hosts containing messages that may have been sent but had not been triggered yet, or to find any other hosts with the same infection symptoms as the known infected hosts.

Approaches to detecting, tracking and blocking emails include analysis of email subject lines (which are crafted to entice a victim to open the message), the email message content, characteristics of the payload itself (even if it's a URL), and some of the symptoms that are found present on an infected host. To devise effective blocking signatures that have minimal impact on legitimate messages, this defense requires significant domain knowledge about how these emails and payloads are crafted. To support this analysis, a corpus of "normal" email traffic was collected to estimate the mission impacts of blocking actions, and a specialized email anomaly detector was developed (Gupta & Sekar, 2003). A significant challenge in responding to worm attacks is that because infection growth is exponential, a failure to take action in timely manner can cause a system to be overrun by infection.

Long term response planning also needs to account for the possibility of an arms race between defenders and attackers. As defenders become more sophisticated, the attackers will correspondingly make their attacks more sophisticated. Early worms did little to hide their targeting actions or vary their digital signatures merely because, at the time, they had no need to do so. But as defenders got better, the attacks correspondingly became more complex. Considering that an email worm is just one of a multitude of attack types to potentially defend against, it should be apparent how complex a general-purpose response planner must be.

1.3 Topics Covered in This Chapter

As these two examples illustrate, cyber response planning brings together many of the capabilities described in the other chapters of this book. A response planner must represent the system being defended. It must also understand the capabilities of the attacker. It must represent the system processes and functions, and understand how changes to the system state can result in operational impacts. And it must represent how the set of response actions affect the state of the system and/or the ability of an attacker to compromise components. The timeframe over which planning and decision making needs to occur must also be accounted for. Does the plan outcome need to be the best choice over the next 10 seconds, 10 minutes, 10 hours, 10 days, or months? Sometimes the best action for one timeframe can be a bad option for the others.

The remainder of this chapter is organized as follows. The next section describes the characteristics of cyber response planning problems and discusses how those characteristics affect the solution requirements. That discussion is followed by a section describing various planning methods that have been proposed and implemented and discuss how they relate to the requirements we identified. Finally, the chapter concludes with a discussion of the prospects for fully automating cyber response planning and a description of an implemented system that points the way toward that goal.

2 Response Planning Problem Characteristics and Requirements

Perhaps the simplest way to think about cyber response planning is in terms of reactive plans. Stimulus-response pairs are a straightforward way to characterize cyber response plans – i.e., as rules that match defensive actions with observed situations – and some early attempts to automate response planning (e.g.,

Ballasubramaniyan et al., 1998; Lindqvist & Porras, 1999; Musman & Flesher, 2000) pursued this approach. It soon became apparent, however, that this approach had fundamental limitations as a general-purpose solution for cyber response planning. First, simple reactive plans lack a formal model of system function that characterizes how response actions might impact the functions that the system being defended is trying to perform. Without an explicit representation of system function, response interactions with intended system function or purpose must be represented implicitly, making the decisions brittle and hard to generalize across different systems. Second, simple reactive plans lack the ability to handle the uncertainties inherent in sensing the cyber environment. Sensing in cyberspace is far from perfect, often only providing the ability to detect some attacks, but not others, or detect some steps in an attack but not others. One must also consider whether a sensor detects the actions of the attacker, or the effects caused by the attacker. These are different things. Even detectable attacks can suffer from limitations in terms of poor detection rates and false alerts. Response actions also usually incur some cost, such as taking a useful service offline to thwart an ongoing attack. That cost must be weighed against the cost of the impacts that may occur if the defender does nothing. Thus, when evaluating if – and when – to respond, defenders must make a risk-based cost/benefit decision as to when and where a response is warranted. Thirdly, reactive approaches have no ability to consider the malicious attackers potential next actions when choosing their response. Not only is it critical to consider the consequences of attack responses, it is also important to anticipate how attacker/defender response sequences will unfold over time and what that implies for the eventual mission success or failure of the system being defended.

The remainder of this section discusses these three critical aspects of cyber response planning problems in more detail.

2.1   Representing System State and Function

From a cyber defense perspective, the state of a system is a heterogenous collection of information spanning multiple levels of resolution both in terms of physical attributes as well as time. The set of potentially relevant details include the hardware, software and architectural elements associated with networks, network components (i.e., switches, routers, firewalls), hosts on the networks, user groups accessing hosts, peripherals, applications, services, as well as the various access and trust relationships among all these entities. Other elements of state might include things like mission functions and objectives, and constraints imposed by cybersecurity policies. Clearly, no approach to planning a cyber response is feasible without making some choices about how much of the system state to explicitly represent, yet still have a tractable cyber defense problem to solve.

One way to begin defining representations of system state is to consider representing the factors that enable an attacker to misuse or subvert a system and create mission effects. Insights about the types of details associated with cyber attacks on real systems can be found in information collections that provide structured information about cyber attacks such as the Common Vulnerability Enumeration (CVE) and the Common Attack Pattern Enumeration and Classification (CAPEC) (MITRE Corporation, 2013). More recently, the MITRE ATT&CK (MITRE Corporation, 2019) framework has provided a more operational mapping of the tools, tactics and techniques used by malicious cyber actors. These information resources provide a starting point for representing the system state relevant to cyber defense, but there are a staggering number of exploits and cyberattack methods to account for. For example, CVE has over 170,000 entries and CAPEC enumerates over 500 cyber attack patterns. To avoid having to reason about every possible attack instance, it is clearly more efficient to reason about the possible effects of successful attacks rather than the attack instances themselves. Even when specific attack instance actions are detected, it may not be known if the attack succeeded. For this reason, attack instance detection is not always an indicator of system state.

Semantic representations of the relationships between the cyber and physical domains (de Barros Barreto et al., 2012), along with abstractions characterizing various types of cyber incident effects affecting the state of the system cyber resources, can be very helpful tools in reducing the amount of detail in a system state representation. Abstractions are often based on cyber asset security attributes such as confidentiality, integrity, and availability. However, even given these incident abstractions, a cyber response planner still faces some difficult questions about how to comprehensively reason about all the cyber incidents and potential responses that are possible. Formal ontologies provide a class of tools that planners and reasoners in many domains have used to organize and represent semantic information about entities, their properties, and their interrelationships. The Unified Cyber Ontology (UCO, 2022) is an ongoing effort to provide an ontological foundation for modeling the cyber domain, offering definitions for classes of cyber objects and their interrelationships. Another relevant ontology in the cyber domain is Camus (D'Amico et al., 2009) which ties cyber entities to mission elements.

To represent and reason about complete cyber attacks, a cyber response planner must identify and defend against multi-step attacks where an attacker achieves a foothold and then takes subsequent steps using other cyber assets as pivot points to reach one or more cyber targets. Because of the interconnectedness of cyber systems, attackers can exploit seemingly non-critical cyber components to bypass security controls and other defenses. An individual compromise may cause no impact on its own but can be a vital stepping stone for follow-on attacks. Therefore, a cyber response planner needs to be primarily concerned with intrusion tolerance rather than fault tolerance. Fault tolerance assumes that faults are independent, whereas intrusion tolerance must consider that an attacker might cause multiple faults when it suits their goal. This means that a planner also needs to consider how combinations of incidents and non-critical system IT components contribute to risks.

Graphical models (Kordy et al., 2014) are a straightforward approach that a planner can leverage to represent and reason about multi-step attacks and their potential consequences. Attack graphs (Ammann et al., 2002) are graphical models that facilitate the analysis of attacker action sequences targeting some goal. These representations can help a planner consider responses in the context of a larger attack sequence and make cost-based assessments given that context. Service dependency graphs (Kheir et al., 2009) can be used to model how different computing components rely on each other. These representations can be used to model actions in terms of their consequences, and reason about the ways different consequences can propagate through system components and result in some impact.

Understanding how a system is vulnerable to cyber attacks requires an analysis of both micro and macro details, where capturing micro level details makes it possible to identify the multitude of factors that enable an attacker to misuse, subvert a system and create mission effects. For example, inspecting the MITRE ATT&CK matrix[1] provides insights into the types of details that would be needed to notice that a process may have been hollowed,[2] that operating systems can be compromised by rootkits,[3] or to recognize the multiple ways attackers can achieve persistent access.[4] Representing a system with a high degree of detail is not necessarily practical, however, especially when considering that a complete cyber attack is better represented as an attack graph of complete moves to reach one or more cyber targets, all being done within the access and trust relationships provided by the system or enabled by the attack. Finding a tractable way to account for all these potentially relevant factors is what makes crafting a good representation of cyber system state such a challenge. There is no consensus on how much detail is appropriate or necessary for representing the state of cyber systems.

Representing time in cybersecurity response planning has similar challenges. At one extreme, cyber attacks can occur at machine speed, meaning that responses must be quick. On the other hand, some attack actions take significant amounts of time (e.g. brute forcing) or there can be long delays between attacker actions, meaning a subsequent attacker move can occur in seconds, days or even weeks later. The speed at which attacker actions occur, and the duration of the incident associated with those actions, will affect the decision cycle timeframe for a response planner. If a planning cycle takes too long, it may allow an attack to succeed without interference. This was an important consideration, for example, in the need for a timely response to worm attacks mentioned previously. Impacts may also be delayed, not occurring at the time of an incident. Additionally, impacts may stem from follow-on cascading effects that propagate through a system and cause impacts elsewhere in the mission. These details matter if one wants a coherent way to compare catastrophic impacts that are time sensitive with incidents that are an accumulation of minor impacts that can occur at any time. Accordingly, it is imperative that a cyber response planner be capable of reasoning about time: as it relates to attacker activity, as it relates to the time available to make a decision, and as it relates to the timing associated with the anticipated completion of its own actions.

---

[1] https://attack.mitre.org

[2] https://attack.mitre.org/techniques/T1055/012/

[3] https://attack.mitre.org/techniques/T1014/

[4] https://attack.mitre.org/tactics/TA0003/

2.2 Managing Uncertainty and Risk

Every assessment of system state needs to consider sources of uncertainty in the evidence supporting the assessment. Sensing in cyberspace is often imperfect, with both false positive and false negative reports that need to be accounted for. Moreover, not all response actions will succeed 100% of the time. As previously noted, many of the failures in the early attempts to develop response planners were due to an inability to manage uncertainty.

It is important to recognize that there are distinct aspects of uncertainty, each of which needs to be handled differently in a response planner. One key consideration is whether a sensor detects some property of asset state (e.g. when an asset is unavailable, or the asset has been modified from its desired state, or when an attacker is making unauthorized use of a compromised asset), or whether a sensor detects a state transition event. State transition sensors tend to be useful only when their false alarm rate is very low, and when they are used in conjunction with sensors that detect asset state properties associated with the outcomes of the state transition. Another consideration is the approach used to model uncertainty in sensors. The classic model treats each sensor as a Bernoulli random variable, meaning that sensor observations can be viewed as a sequence of independent stochastic Bernoulli trials. While this model is attractive because it is theoretically and computationally tractable, a response planner will likely require additional inference machinery to determine an appropriate level of confidence in assertions about the true state of an asset and the causal link (if any) between the asset state and attacker actions, when, for example, a sensor detects attack actions 100% of the time but for only some fraction of the attack instances. Lastly, sequences of cyber alerts, whether they are composed of true detections or false alarms, may include lags or bursty behavior. This means that a time sequence of sensor returns may not have a stationary distribution even if an asset stays in the same state. For a probability model that uses only first order probabilities, this kind of variable behavior over time can be problematic.

There is almost always uncertainty regarding what is known about the attacker and their capabilities. Attacker actions, goals and strategies can also evolve as they acquire more information about the target system. When a defender is uncertain about whether all the attacker's actions have been detected, even if nothing is apparently wrong, it may be possible that the attacker is a single step away from causing a serious impact without the defender knowing it. These uncertainties highlight the risk of using information-gathering response actions that are designed to help reduce uncertainty about the state of the system or the adversary. These actions take time that the adversary might utilize for advantage, so information gathering actions often may need to be combined with risk mitigation actions such as quarantining or disabling certain types of access from suspect assets. Uncertainty about the adversary may also make it difficult for the planner to even know what response options to consider. For example, we may know of 10 different techniques attackers can use to compromise a host and only be able to detect 7 of them. Planning responses to handle the 3 techniques that cannot be detected adds additional complexity to the planning problem. It may be possible to compare what has been detected with what was expected and use any discrepancy to try and determine if an attack using some unexpected or new technique is underway. If these newly observed attack capabilities are then incorporated into the planner's ability to look ahead, this will enable the response planner to adapt dynamically as new attacker capabilities are discovered (see Chap. 6).

As discussed in Chap. 16, cyber risk does not depend only on uncertainty and probabilities. Typical formulations of risk (National Bureau of Standards, 1979) include the damage (loss) caused by an unfavorable event in addition to an estimate of how often the event may happen in a period of time (likelihood). This means cyber response planning must be mindful of costs. Cost in response planning isn't necessarily just action cost. It is a combination of action cost with operation gain, and can be further conditioned by other operational preferences (e.g. a requirement to choose stealthy actions). When there is uncertainty associated with outcomes, costs should be conditioned probabilistically. This raises issues about confidence levels for risk assessments and tradeoffs in response decisions. For example, some cyber incidents (such as a loss of information confidentiality) can have high impact and can't be recovered from. In such situations, it is often necessary to have a high degree of confidence in both the state and action outcome. For example, recovering a compromised service on a host is a relatively low cost response but is only effective if that is the only part of the host that has been subverted. On the other hand, recovering the whole host is a more costly response, but will also recover the compromised service and will work even when there are undetected subverted aspects of the host.

The underlying importance of costs and risks is ultimately tied to considerations of how an attack affects mission outcomes. The change in mission performance measures caused by some cyber incident is often referred to as mission impact. When computing mission impacts, many factors must be considered. First, impacts can be different depending on the type of cyber incident effect. For example, an interruption of an ICT resource may lead to minor losses, whereas the modification of that same resource could lead to catastrophic losses. Secondly, impact can depend on incident timing, incident duration, and whether impacts are immediate or delayed. For example, an incident affecting an ICT asset after it is no longer needed, causes no impact. Thirdly, system risks and hence, risk assessments, can change over time (e.g., as new vulnerabilities are discovered).

Finally, it is worth noting that any dynamic response action that incurs no cost (i.e. a firewall rule that blocks hosts that don't ever need to communicate with each other from connecting) or has an acceptable long term cost is something that is worth implementing as a policy. For example, in response to the code-red virus in the 1990's, which attacked only web servers, an effective solution was to stop web servers from connecting out to other hosts, since at the time there was no functional need for most web servers to do so. Later, the idea of rate-limiting the number of connections from one host to other hosts was shown to be an effective way to slow down scanning worms. Both ideas started off as response actions to a specific threat, and later became widely available standard policy options.

3 Projecting Possible Futures

Actions in a dynamic cyber response arsenal incur some cost that one might only be willing to accept if the situation warrants it. This means cost-benefit tradeoffs are a key driver for response planning decisions. If, for example, the cost of preventing a compromised state is prohibitively expensive, a response planner may conclude that it is better to just take actions that clean up the consequences of the compromise and operate through it. A different cost profile could lead to a different decision. For example, a response planner may decide it is better to head off some potential compromise before it occurs because it is cheaper to take an action now, than incur a larger impact later. Decisions like this are not possible without knowing the current state of the system, or at least the plausible states the system might be in, and being able to project forward from those states a prediction of what might occur next. Figure 7.1 illustrates this distinction.

The need to identify potential future states implies at least three capabilities that a response planner must have. The first is to be able to project what is likely to occur if no action is taken. Since impacts may not always occur immediately, it is sometimes necessary to be able to know that an impact will occur in the future if no action is taken. This capability is a requirement for situation awareness (see Chap. 5). The second capability is to understand how response actions can alter the state of the system to possibly recover from or block impacts given the assessed state of the system. The third capability addresses the likelihood that response actions may be observable to the attacker and the attacker may adapt their actions based on what they see. Since some response actions may be easily circumvented by attackers as they see them, the response planner may need to anticipate how attackers may react to different response choices.

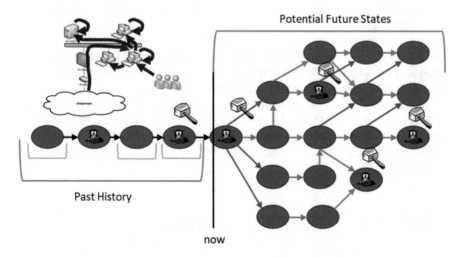

Fig. 7.1 Notional depiction of the difference between understanding and projecting system state

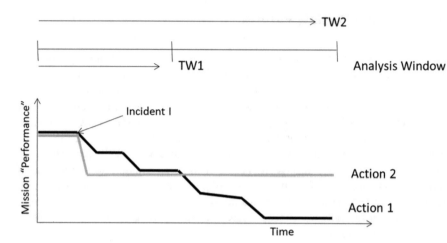

Fig. 7.2 Decision timeframe

Finally, note that there is always a timeframe over which response decisions are most appropriate. That timeframe can be explicit or implicit. Figure 7.2 shows a notional example where the timeframe associated with a decision matters. If one cares about performance in the short term, action 1 is better, while if one cares about a longer term outcome then action 2 is the better choice. It is also worth referring back to the issues raised in Fig. 7.1 and considering the number of cyber moves that can occur during the selected decision timeframe. The number of alternative courses of action for the defender can grow exponentially the further ahead in time and moves a response planner looks. This means that, practically speaking, cyber response planning can usually only consider modest levels of lookahead, over a somewhat bounded timeframe. Because of these practical limitations of planner lookahead, and uncertainty associated with the state of the system, a planner may need to manage decisions at several timescales simultaneously. There may be short timeframe decisions associated with stopping catastrophic situations from occurring (e.g. apply a tourniquet to buy time), along with a longer timeframe planning cycle is used to make decisions enabling the system to operate through or, as described in Chap. 8, to reach a recovered state.

The graphical methods mentioned in the previous discussion about state representations are a starting point for projecting states into the future. What must be added, however, are reasoning processes that can predict how attacker and defender actions will interact with each other over time and affect the states represented in those graphs.

4   Approaches to Cyber Response Planning

Many early approaches to automating cyber response tended to be tightly coupled with intrusion detection systems (Stakhanova et al., 2007; Shameli-Sendi et al., 2014; Inayat et al., 2016) and used the presence or absence of alerts to represent the state of the system being defended. These approaches often relied on detecting known signatures, or even anomalous signals (Somayaji & Forrest, 2000), to trigger static responses. This reactive approach to response planning has wide applicability and is still commonly used today; for example, anti-virus software automatically quarantines files it suspects are malicious. While such approaches to cyber response can be effective, they also have several shortcomings which were discussed earlier. Accordingly, these cyber response systems tend to only be used in situations where predefined and specific playbook style responses are sufficient.

Other lines of work sought to address these shortcomings by looking for ways to provide more flexible responses across a variety of scenarios a system might encounter. The idea was to provide a dynamic response where decisions are made based on conditional logic (Porras & Neumann, 1997), or on case-based reasoning that can map the current situation to past situations where response actions were successful previously (Musman & Flesher, 2000; Borges et al., 2015). There have also been attempts to augment reactive response plans with strategic plans (Thayer et al., 2013). Even with this added flexibility, however, it is difficult to generalize approaches like these to apply across different systems. A key limitation is that specific logical predicates and descriptions of past situations tend to rely on implicit knowledge about the specific system and its use. Consequently, decisions based on this implicit information are often only applicable for a specific system. A reasoning approach designed work across a variety of different systems will require explicit models of the system, domain, and mission in order to differentiate between circumstances where a response is suitable on one system, but not another.

Several lines of research have explored different representations to implement such reasoning methods. Many approaches start with the attack graphs (Ammann et al., 2002) or service dependency graphs (Kheir et al., 2009) mentioned earlier in the discussion about representations. For example, Kanoun et al. (2007) show how to use attack graphs to strategically disrupt an anticipated attack sequence or deny potential attack opportunities. Many of these attack and service dependency graphs are based on currently known vulnerabilities and as such are often "full knowledge" representations, where the models do not account for uncertainty about the current system state and the attacker goals. Bayesian attack graphs (BAGS) (Liu & Man, 2005; Poolsappasit et al., 2011; Musman & Turner, 2018) extend the approach to incorporate the uncertainty associated with attack steps, but usually tend to assume a known system state from which the actions are projected. αLADS (Kreidl & Frazier, 2004) handles sensor uncertainty and uncertainty in the current state, but had to run a sample of representative attacks to collect training data on the system to be defended in order to empirically estimate the probability of future states. Other work (Wang et al., 2013) explores future attacker actions, building on the underlying attack graph model by converting it into a hidden Markov model, better capturing attack consequence as a probabilistic outcome. Interestingly, several lines of work have acknowledged the insufficient ability of attack graphs to encode uncertainty from the *attacker*'s point of view (e.g., see Hoffmann, 2015).

Much of the literature on automated response (and automated attacking) does not consider the dynamic interplay between the attacker and the defender, where the agents execute actions in response to one another. To address this issue, several authors have proposed using *attack-defense* (Kordy et al., 2010) or *attack-response* trees (ART) (Zonouz et al., 2014) to model the relationship between attacker and defender more realistically. In these trees, alternating layers in the tree represent attacker and defender actions, respectively. This approach offers much better insight into the interplay between the attacker and defender, although it quickly becomes computationally intractable to compute. Other efforts (Roy et al., 2012) propose mechanisms to scale the tree to make solutions more computationally feasible. ARTs, due to their dueling-agents formulation, have also lent themselves well towards game theoretic solutions (Musman & Turner, 2018) wherein the optimal action selection policy can be explicitly computed as a problem of finding the Nash equilibrium. Many other approaches leveraging ARTs have been proposed and analyzed as well, with varying degrees of specificity, uncertainty, and strategy. See Kordy et al. (2010) for an overview of these approaches.

Once knowledge characterizing the system, domain and mission models is gathered, a variety of approaches to classical automated planning (Hendler et al., 1990) can be used to generate a sequence of cyber responses. For example, the relevant knowledge in the models can be translated into logical predicates that a planner using forward heuristic search techniques could use to generate a cyber course of action (Boddy et al., 2005). It is also possible to work with an attack graph directly, for instance by combining it with a partial-order planner to recognize attack plans based on sensor observations (Amos-Binks et al., 2017). Planning approaches like this can be effective if the number of predicates and actions is small. This is problematic in realistic cyber problems though. There is a tension between the level of detail required to capture cyber nuances (e.g. like a OS library load path that most people don't realize is even there that can be modified to point to a trojan library) and a level of detail that is more practical to model, yet which still captures the essence of the cyber problem. Classical planning approaches are extremely knowledge intensive. Applying these techniques at scale requires a costly effort to collect the detailed knowledge and heuristics needed, and then to represent it symbolically in a language the planner can work with. Boddy et al. (2005) provides details about many of the challenges.

Though classical planning is good for generating action sequences to achieve some goal, it is less adept at capturing, dynamically assessing, and selecting among different strategies for generating actions. This requires the consideration of costs and uncertainty, capabilities that are available with decision-theoretic planning techniques (Boutilier et al., 1999). One of the earliest examples of applying decision-theoretic planning to cyber response was the Response and Recovery Engine (RRE) (Zonouz et al., 2009; Zonouz et al., 2014). RRE used ARTs as a primary state representation technique and showed how cyber defense could be modeled as a game-theoretic variant of a Partially Observable Markov Decision Process (POMDP). This system was successful at defending small-scale networks that generate ART trees with about 900 nodes. More recently, Miehling et al. (2018) showed how to use a variant of an attack graph to define a POMDP with limited scope whose solution reduces the probability that an attacker reaches their goal(s), while minimizing the negative impact of defender actions on availability. While decision-theoretic planning approaches like these have shown promise on problems of limited size or scope, they are not yet able to address the large cyber response problems associated with most real-world systems of interest.

Work applying reinforcement learning to cyber security is still in its infancy. See Nguyen and Reddi (2021) for an overview of the research in this area. The reinforcement learning work has not yet impacted developments in cyber response planning because reinforcement learning algorithms need large amounts of training data to characterize all the relevant cybersecurity interactions. This chapter has discussed the many reasons why collecting such training data is problematic for cyber response planning. Generating synthetic data using simulations is one way to address this issue (Molina-Markham et al., 2021; Musman & Turner, 2018; Microsoft Defender Research Team, 2021), but that raises other concerns about whether capabilities developed using simulations can be reliably applied to real world events, and can adapt when aspects of the defended system change (e.. new vulnerabilities are identified).

In the next section we describe ongoing work that has taken significant steps toward satisfying the various requirements we have identified.

5   Toward Fully Automated Cyber Response Planning

The previous sections in this chapter have characterized the key challenges that must be addressed by any technical approach to cyber response planning. Many approaches to automating cyber response planning are focused on helping human analysts manage these challenges, or on automating some limited aspect of the response planning problem. There is a case to be made, though, that even with automated support, current approaches to cyber security might be overwhelmed by a new generation of AI-enabled attacks. Future cyber-attackers are likely to increasingly exploit advances in AI to achieve faster, stealthier, and more impactful attacks. Many of these effects will be achieved at a speed and scale that makes a human-in-the-loop defense paradigm unlikely to be effective. Consequently, future systems will have to rely to some extent on fully automated planning and automated responses – with humans on the loop or out of the loop – to ensure mission success and continuously adapt to an evolving adversary.

This section describes an approach to fully automating cyber response planning that is designed with this goal in mind. The Automated Reasoning about Cyber Response (ARCR) project (Musman et al., 2019; Booker & Musman, 2020) uses a technical approach based on the premise that, from an AI perspective, it is advantageous to frame the cyber response problem as a sequential decision-making problem under uncertainty. From this starting point, ARCR shows how to bring together state-of-the-art techniques for anytime online planning in large state spaces with a simulation of the system being defended to efficiently achieve fully automated cyber response. The remainder of this section provides more details about the ARCR technical approach and empirical results illustrating how well it works.

5.1 Efficiently Managing Uncertainty in Cyber Response

ARCR views automated reasoning about cyber responses as a form of game-playing where the defender and attacker are each afforded an opportunity to make a move. One way to account for the uncertainty about the system state and future projections is to address the cyber response problem directly as a partially observable stochastic game (e.g. as a partially observable competitive Markov decision process (Zonouz et al., 2014)). However, suitable state-of-the-art solution techniques for these games are only capable of solving relatively small games that must be fully specified in advance.

An alternative to a pure game-theoretic solution is to focus on resolving the defender's uncertainty about how to respond, rather than trying to solve the complete stochastic game. When the opponent's policy is fixed (either known or estimated from data), we can model a partially observable stochastic game as a partially observable Markov decision problem (POMDP) from the perspective of the protagonist (Oliehoek et al., 2005). The adversarial aspects of the stochastic game are incorporated into the transition function of the POMDP. This is an attractive option because recent advances in POMDP solution techniques make it possible to solve large-scale POMDPs in real time. Additionally, POMDP solvers can find policies that exploit opponent weaknesses. For these reasons, our research tackles the cyber response challenges using the formal framework of partially observable Markov decision problems.[5]

Formally, a POMDP can be expressed as a tuple $(\mathbf{S}, \mathbf{A}, \mathbf{Z}, \mathbf{T}, \mathbf{O}, \mathbf{R})$ where $\mathbf{S}$ is a set of states, $\mathbf{A}$ is a set of actions, $\mathbf{Z}$ is a set of observations, $\mathbf{T}(s, a, s')$ is a transition function giving the probability $p(s' \mid s, a)$ of transitioning to state s' when the agent takes action a in state s, $\mathbf{O}(s, a, z)$ is an observation function giving the probability $p(z \mid s, a)$ of observing z if the agent takes action a and ends in state s, and $\mathbf{R}(s, a)$ is a reward function giving the immediate reward for taking action a in state s. The goal of the decision maker is to maximize the expected reward accrued over a sequence of actions. Since the states in a POMDP are not fully observable, the only basis for decision making is the sequence of prior actions and subsequent observations. A sufficient statistic summarizing the probability of being in a particular state, given a history of actions and observations, is called a belief, and a probability distribution over all states is called a belief state. Solving a POMDP is a planning problem that involves finding an optimal policy which maps belief states to actions.

---

[5] Note that a POMDP approach can compute the kind of general-purpose conservative solution one would expect from a game-theoretic approach if we formulate the POMDP to assume a robust adversary like a min-max opponent.

Clearly, any search involving probabilistic belief states and arbitrarily long histories of actions and observations quickly becomes computationally intractable (Pineau et al., 2003). Although state-of-the-art offline methods for solving POMDPs have made great strides, they are not yet powerful enough to address the challenges of real-world cyber response problems. Fortunately, there are approaches available to (sometimes approximately) solve POMDPs online in real time that appear to be suitable for cyber response planning problems.

An alternative to offline planning is to select actions online, one at a time, using a fixed-horizon forward search (Ross et al., 2008; He et al., 2011). Here, the key to making this idea effective for real-world problems relies on sampling the belief space, rather than fully exploring it. In particular, great efficiencies can be achieved[6] by using a black-box simulation of the problem to generate samples of possible action outcomes. The DESPOT algorithm (Ye et al., 2017) is a widely used approach that leverages simulation in this way. Moreover, DESPOT is an anytime algorithm for POMDP planning that avoids the worst-case behavior of other widely used online solution methods.

Theoretical results show that, given a suitable number of scenarios to work with, the DESPOT algorithm can reliably find near optimal policies with a regret bound that depends on the size of the optimal policy. This approach has been successfully applied to compute solutions to complex POMDP planning problems for autonomous vehicles in real time. Its performance characteristics, and its characteristics as a decision-theoretic planner (Boutilier et al., 1999), make this algorithm a good choice as the starting point for building a POMDP planner to address cyber response problems.

The state representation for the POMDP used in ARCR is a bit string consisting of bits for each state attribute for each asset, where these state attribute bits are set via probabilistic intrusion detection system (IDS) alert predicates. This is a common choice for cyber planning approaches based on this formalism. One or more security sensors monitor the state attributes associated with each asset, and each sensor reports the binary status of an asset state attributes as either compromised or uncompromised. The current implementation of ARCR assumes that these sensors operate independently, and that sensor reliability is characterized using a false negative rate and a false positive rate. Observations for the defender are in the form of binary strings showing the (possibly noisy) sensor returns for the state of each asset represented in the system.

---

[6] A state-of-the-art algorithm like POMCP (Silver & Veness, 2010) can solve POMDPs with state spaces as large as 10^{56} with only a few seconds of computation.

5.2 Simulating the Cyber Terrain and Attacker/ Defender Interactions

The black box simulator needed for the online planning approach used in ARCR is provided by a modified version of the Cyber Security Game (CSG) (Musman & Turner, 2018). CSG is a coarse-grained simulation of attacker and defender interactions in cyberspace. The original implementation of CSG focused on assessing defensive architectures and deploying static cyber defenses. CSG uses a cyber mission impact assessment (CMIA) model (Musman et al., 2010; Musman & Temin, 2015) to translate the occurrence of incidents in cyberspace into mission outcome impacts that relate to the state of the system's cyber assets. CSG's defensive cyber decision-making focuses primarily on defending the mission that the cyber assets are intended to support. This mission focus helps reduce the scope of the cyber defender's problem since often only a subset of the system's cyber assets is relevant at any given time.

To avoid having to reason about every possible attack instance, CSG reasons about the *effects* of successful attacks, rather than the attack instances themselves. The effects of cyber compromises are represented by the set of incident effects in the DIMFUI (Temin & Musman, 2010) taxonomy. These effects are summarized in Table 7.1. The DIMFUI effects provide a robust representation of cyber incidents. They can account for every successful cyber compromise that exists in CVE, and which is described by a CAPEC attack pattern, as well as the more operational mapping of the techniques used by malicious cyber actors found in the MITRE ATT&CK framework. All but one of the DIMFUI effects correspond to simple binary states of a cyber asset. This makes DIMFUI a useful abstraction that allows a cyber defender to reason only about binary representations of cyber incidents derived from the impact of six DIMFUI incident effects per asset, rather than hundreds or thousands of attack instances. To this set of effects, we also consider whether compromises are persistent (e.g. they survive a reboot), since different response actions are often needed for clearing persistent effects. Moreover, when replacing Degradation with Persistence, the resulting PIMFUI representation aligns nicely with our approach to representing cyber state using bit strings.

CSG incorporates a cyber mission impact assessment (CMIA) model that maps PIMFUI incident effects on the cyber assets that support mission functions into mission impacts. In addition to the CMIA model, CSG also uses models of the cyber terrain and the capabilities of the attacker and defender. An example of a cyber terrain model used in CSG is shown in Fig. 7.3. It consists of networks, network components (i.e. switches, routers, firewalls), hosts on the networks, user groups having access to the hosts, peripherals, applications, services and interactors that run on the host, and information used in the performing mission function. The representation of user groups, that may have access to multiple assets in the network, provides a way to simulate how compromised user credentials can be used to access and pivot through hosts.

Table 7.1 The DIMFUI taxonomy

DIMFUI	Explanation	Typical Attacks
Degradation	1. Reduction in performance or capacity of an IT system	1. Limited-effect DoS
	2. Reduction in bandwidth of a communication medium	2. Zombie processes using up CPU and slowing server
	3. Reduction in data quality	3. Transfer of non-mission related data over a link that slows the transfer of mission data
		4. Dropped packets cause an image to have less resolution
Interruption	IT asset becomes unusable or unavailable	1. Ping of Death
		2. Wireless Jamming
		3. Wipe disk
Modification	Modify data, protocol, software, firmware, component	1. Change or corrupt data
		2. Modify access controls
		3. Modify/Replace system files
Fabrication	Attacker inserts information into a system or fakes components	1. Replay attacks
		2. DB data additions
		3. Counterfeit software/ components
Unauthorized Use	Attacker uses system resources for illegitimate purposes. Related and often a precondition for other DIMFUI	1. Access account or raise privileges in order to modify/degrade/ interrupt the OS
		2. Subvert service to spawn a program on remote machine
		3. Bandwidth used surfing for porn degrades mission critical exchanges
Interception	Attacker gains access to information or assets used in the system	1. Key logger
		2. SQL injection
		3. Crypto key theft
		4. Man-in-middle attacks
		5. Knowledge of component or process that is meant to be secret

CSG was originally designed to represent a fully-observable, probabilistic outcome, zero-sum game for assessing the employment of static defenses. In order to use CSG with the online planner in ARCR, it was modified to support queries from an external agile defender with partial and uncertain knowledge of the game state.

Figure 7.4 illustrates aspects of the ARCR state vector representation, and how security analytics map to the state attributes of the assets captured in the state model. The state vector consists of different segments associated with different types of assets: precursor assets (e.g. assets that cause minimal impact); target assets (assets that cause impact); the availability of network connections that are needed to

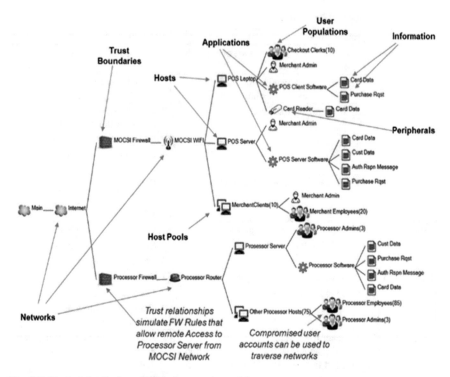

Fig. 7.3 Typical details for a CSG cyber terrain model

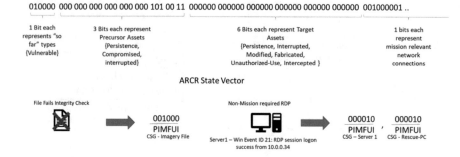

Fig. 7.4 Example of ARCR State Representation

support mission function; and asset types that represents assets believed to be vulnerable to attack at any given moment. An important aspect of this state representation is that it needs to be sufficiently expressive and self-contained enough to enable the CSG simulator to completely instantiate the state of the simulation and be able to play forward hypotheticals from that state, given only the state vector.

5.3 *Experimental Tests of an ARCR Prototype*

ARCR uses the Approximate POMDP Planning (APPL) toolkit[7] to build an online planner that employs the DESPOT algorithm. This toolkit makes it possible to implement a customized planner that includes problem-specific heuristic bounds on forward search, arbitrary representations for POMDP states, beliefs, actions and observations, and a clearly defined interface for the black-box simulator.

Ongoing work is applying the ARCR planner to realistic cyber defense problems. One series of simulated experimental scenarios is illustrated in Fig. 7.5. Figure 7.5a shows a simple use case involving an information fusion mission. Business transaction agents (not shown) generate Sales and Inventory files that are placed in File Shares A and B respectively being served from Server 1. A client agent accesses paired Sales and Inventory files, performs some (unspecified) fusion operation on them and produces a combined status update file as an output, which is placed in Shared Folder C being served on Server 2. It is presumed that there is mission value to generating the combined status files in a timely fashion, while maintaining their integrity and confidentiality.

Experiments with this use case assumed a persistent greedy attacker that selects the highest payoff path to a target. In the first scenario (Fig. 7.5b), the attacker steals a user credential on its foothold, then uses that credential to move laterally from the foothold to Server 1. Once on Server 1, the attacker modifies the Sales or Inventory data, thereby causing adverse impact to the mission. Assuming the available sensors do not detect that credentials are stolen but do detect the lateral move, the easiest defensive response is to eject the attacker and prevent impact by taking an action (RX) to restore the compromised host to a known good state. While this response defends against the attack, it does not eliminate the threat and the attacker can simply go after the host again. If the defender is provided with an action that can disable a user account (DA), the planner can determine that the DA action completely blocks the attacker from performing the lateral move, hence preventing any damage. Consequently, this is the preferred solution (unless disabling the account is too costly or adversely impacts the mission). Note that because the planner is using a model-driven lookahead search, it can consider such response options and block a vulnerable credential pathway even without reliable sensor input. We are not aware of any other approach to automating cyber defense that can provide this capability in the presence of probabilistic outcome assessments and sensor noise.

It is more complicated to determine the correct defensive response when more than one credential pathway exists. The scenario in Fig. 7.5c shows an attack that, in addition to the compromised user account enabling access to Server 1, also includes a compromise of the Server 2 admin account, giving the attacker access to Server 2 and the combined files. Using lookahead search, the planner correctly recognizes that that if one of the credentials are not (preemptively) disabled right at the

---

[7] http://bigbird.comp.nus.edu.sg/pmwiki/farm/appl/

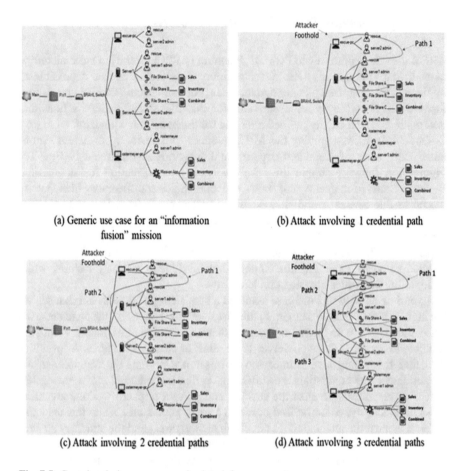

(a) Generic use case for an "information
fusion" mission

(b) Attack involving 1 credential path

(c) Attack involving 2 credential paths

(d) Attack involving 3 credential paths

Fig. 7.5 Generic mission use case and cyber defense scenarios

beginning of this scenario, the defender will be forced to take a much more costly
action later to avoid adverse mission impact.

The final scenario shown in Fig. 7.5d illustrates the importance of having an
appropriate model of the problem in order to be successful. Here, the attacker manages to grab three user credentials. Because there are now three paths to targets, but
only two attacker moves needed to compromise one of them, the planner identifies
that a target may get compromised and need to be reset before the credential that
accesses it can be disabled. This dilemma is a consequence of a choice to model the
actions that disable user accounts individually, with only one of those actions executable for a given defender move. A more effective approach gives the planner an
action that disables all compromised accounts, easily handling the need for concurrent primitive model actions in a manner consistent with the POMDP formalism.

The experimental results from testing the ARCR planner have demonstrated several of its abilities: (a) to select mission sensitive responses that are less impactful
on the mission when possible; (b) to appropriately respond even with unobserved

attacker actions; (c) to respond appropriately even with false sensor alerts; (d) to appropriately sequence atomic actions when they're needed to block multiple avenues of attack; (e) to use lookahead to identify preemptive actions when they are needed; and (f) to leverage observed attacker capability to adapt its response and avoid playing whack-a-mole (e.g. where an attacker stimulates the defender to perform the same response repeatedly). These capabilities fulfil many of the requirements for cyber response planning identified earlier in this chapter.

5.4 Steps Toward Deployment for Real Applications

While there is still more to be learned about the ARCR approach, the project goal is to deploy ARCR in real systems. Toward that end, current work uses a test harness on virtual machines that includes an automated adversary emulator (Applebaum et al., 2016) to generate attacker behavior and a streaming sensor (Damodaran et al., 2021) for CAR analytics (MITRE Corporation, 2022) to provide the observations ARCR requires. This makes it possible to test ARCR performance on real machines for the use cases described above and many others.

The test results for the ARCR prototype to date have demonstrated it can perform efficiently for problems of moderate[8] complexity. Work is also underway on modifications to ARCR to demonstrate its ability to handle larger scale problems. Representations for abstract states and actions in the planner will facilitate significant reductions in the branching factor of the lookahead belief tree. These new representations also provide the starting point for converting the planner into a hierarchical POMDP solver (Vien & Toussaint, 2015; Bai et al., 2016), which should significantly speed up the search of the belief tree.

The concept of operations for using ARCR in an application is shown in Fig. 7.6. ARCR can be applied to any cyber system and repertoire of tactics that can be modeled in the modified version of CSG. Being model-based, the simulator models can be maintained and updated to reflect the latest threats, and changes to the system or mission. The progress to date on the ARCR project suggests that this technical approach provides a promising path toward computing automated, tractable, on-line solutions to complex cyber response problems in real-world scenarios.

6 Summary

This chapter has described the characteristics of the cyber response planning problem and the requirements for implementing a response planner. A response planner must represent the system being defended. It must also understand the capabilities

---

[8] In simple use cases for systems with 1024 assets, the ARCR planner can compute a defensive response in less than 10 s on a standard laptop. When there are 512 assets, response time is under 2 s.

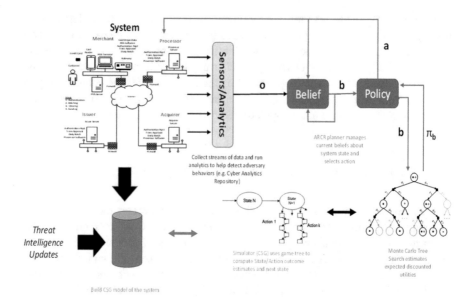

Fig. 7.6 Concept of operations for ARCR

and potential strategies of the attacker. It must represent the system processes and functions, and understand how changes to the system state can result in operational impacts. And it must represent how the set of response actions affect the state of the system and/or the ability of an attacker to compromise components. Since response planning integrates and leverages the capabilities described in the other chapters of this book, it is difficult to view a response planner as a standalone entity. All of these capabilities must work together seamlessly.

While many technical approaches are available to address the broad range of challenges in cyber response planning, there are still several areas where improvements are needed. A response planner that doesn't consider how an adversary will react and adapt when they perceive response actions will make it easy for an attacker to side step or leverage those observed actions for their own advantage. Despite this, it's only recently that defenders have started incorporating adversary models into their decision making. Incorporating adversary capability and strategy considerations into response planning brings a variety of challenges that can make the problem computationally intractable. Response planners will need to address these challenges by devising system representations that are suitably expressive but practical to implement, and decision-making strategies that strike a suitable balance between satisficing and optimizing.

Additional complications arise from the adversarial nature of cyber response planning. As attackers develop new strategies and capabilities, a response planner may need to adapt both in the short term and over the long term. This remains an area for additional work. It is also important for response planners to explicitly consider how an adversary may evolve. Planning approaches with this capability are still being developed.

Approaches that can plan effectively for large scale systems, especially across multiple time scales, are not yet available. Historically, host-based based response systems have been autonomous and work independently of other host-based systems. Network-based systems have been centralized. Work on collaboration and coordination among these various types of agents is still an emerging capability.

Finally, it should be noted that it is difficult to "glue" cyber security and response agents into/onto a system in a secure manner. Once an attacker has subverted the operating system, information reported by sensors that drive the cyber response system may no longer be trustworthy. It is also necessary to protect the cyber defense agent itself. If its response actuators can delete users, files, etc., then attacking it becomes a primary goal for an attacker. If multiple collaborative cyber defense agents are distributed, then it is especially difficult to secure them (see Chap. 18).

References

Ammann, P., Wijesekera, D., & Kaushik, S. (2002, November). Scalable, graph-based network vulnerability analysis. In *Proceedings of the 9th ACM conference on computer and communications security* (pp. 217–224).

Amos-Binks, A., Clark, J., Weston, K., Winters, M., & Harfoush, K. (2017, July). Efficient attack plan recognition using automated planning. In *2017 IEEE symposium on computers and communications (ISCC)* (pp. 1001–1006). IEEE.

Applebaum, A., Miller, D., Strom, B., Korban, C., & Wolf, R. (2016, December). Intelligent, automated red team emulation. In *Proceedings of the 32nd annual conference on computer security applications* (pp. 363–373).

Bai, A., Srivastava, S., & Russell, S. J. (2016). Markovian state and action abstractions for MDPs via hierarchical MCTS. In *Proceedings of the twenty-fifth international joint conference on artificial intelligence* (pp. 3029–3039).

Ballasubramaniyan, J. S., Garcia-Fernandez, J. O., Isaco, D., Spafford, E., & Zamboni, D. (1998). *Aafid-autonomous agents for intrusion detection* (Coast Technical Report 98/05). Coast Lab, Purdue University, West Lafayette.

Boddy, M. S., Gohde, J., Haigh, T., & Harp, S. A. (2005). Course of action generation for cyber security using classical planning. In S. Biundo, K. Myers, & K. Rajan (Eds.), *Proceedings of the fifteenth international conference on automated planning and scheduling (ICAPS 2005)* (pp. 12–21). AAAI Press.

Booker, L. B., & Musman, S. A. (2020). A model-based, decision-theoretic perspective on automated cyber response. The AAAI-20 workshop on Artificial Intelligence for Cyber Security (AICS). *arXiv preprint*, arXiv:2002.08957.

Borges, J., Martins, J., Andrade, J., dos Santos, H. & Militar-Cinamil, A. (2015, July). Design of a case-based reasoner for information security in military organizations. In *ECCWS2015-proceedings of the 14th European conference on cyber warfare and security* (Vol. 2015, p. 26).

Boutilier, C., Dean, T., & Hanks, S. (1999). Decision-theoretic planning: Structural assumptions and computational leverage. *Journal of Artificial Intelligence Research, 11*, 1–94.

Damodaran, S., Moffitt, R., Lamourine, R., & Guttman, J. (2021). *US patent application: "Systems and methods for analyzing distributed system data streams using declarative specification, detection, and evaluation of happened-before relationships"*. US Patent App. 16/824,166, https://patents.google.com/patent/US20210294805A1/en

de Barros Barreto, A., Costa, P.C.G. and Yano, E.T., (2012). A semantic approach to evaluate the impact of cyber actions on the physical domain. In *7th international conference on semantic Technologies for Intelligence, defense, and security (STIDS 2012)*. CEUR-WS.org.

Gupta, A., & Sekar, R. (2003, September). An approach for detecting self-propagating email using anomaly detection. In *International workshop on recent advances in intrusion detection* (pp. 55–72). Springer.

Goodall J. R., D'Amico A., & Kopylec J. K. (2009). Camus: Automatically mapping Cyber Assets to Missions and Users. Proceedings of the 2009 IEEE Military Communications Conference, 1–7.

He, R., Brunskill, E., & Roy, N. (2011). Efficient planning under uncertainty with macro-actions. *Journal of Artificial Intelligence Research, 40*, 523–570.

Hendler, J. A., Tate, A., & Drummond, M. (1990). AI planning: Systems and techniques. *AI Magazine, 11*(2), 61–77.

Hoffmann, J. (2015, April). Simulated penetration testing: From "Dijkstra" to "Turing Test++". In *Proceedings of the international conference on automated planning and scheduling* (Vol. 25, pp. 364–372).

Inayat, Z., Gani, A., Anuar, N. B., Khan, M. K., & Anwar, S. (2016). Intrusion response systems: Foundations, design, and challenges. *Journal of Network and Computer Applications, 62*, 53–74.

Kanoun, W., Cuppens-Boulahia, N., Cuppens, F., & Autrel, F. (2007, October). Advanced reaction using risk assessment in intrusion detection systems. In *International workshop on critical information infrastructures security* (pp. 58–70). Springer.

Kheir, N., Debar, H., Cuppens-Boulahia, N., Cuppens, F., & Viinikka, J. (2009, June). Cost evaluation for intrusion response using dependency graphs. In *2009 international conference on network and service security* (pp. 1–6). IEEE.

Kordy, B., Mauw, S., Radomirović, S., & Schweitzer, P. (2010). Foundations of attack–defense trees. In P. Degano, S. Etalle, & J. Guttman (Eds.), *International workshop on formal aspects in security and trust* (pp. 80–95). Springer.

Kordy, B., Piètre-Cambacédès, L., & Schweitzer, P. (2014). DAG-based attack and defense modeling: Don't miss the forest for the attack trees. *Computer Science Review, 13*, 1–38.

Kreidl, O. P., & Frazier, T. M. (2004). Feedback control applied to survivability: A host-based autonomic defense system. *IEEE Transactions on Reliability, 53*(1), 148–166.

Lewandowski, S. M., Van Hook, D. J., O'Leary, G. C., Haines, J. W., & Rossey, L. M. (2001, June). SARA: Survivable autonomic response architecture. In *Proceedings DARPA information survivability conference and exposition II. DISCEX'01* (Vol. 1, pp. 77–88). IEEE.

Lindqvist, U., & Porras, P. A. (1999, May). Detecting computer and network misuse through the production-based expert system toolset (P-BEST). In *Proceedings of the 1999 IEEE symposium on security and privacy (Cat. No. 99CB36344)* (pp. 146–161). IEEE.

Liu, Y., & Man, H. (2005, March). Network vulnerability assessment using Bayesian networks. In *Data mining, intrusion detection, information assurance, and data networks security 2005* (Vol. 5812, pp. 61–71). SPIE.

Microsoft Defender Research Team. (2021). *CyberBattleSim*. https://github.com/microsoft/CyberBattleSim. Accessed 28 Mar 2022.

Miehling, E., Rasouli, M., & Teneketzis, D. (2018). A POMDP approach to the dynamic defense of large-scale cyber networks. *IEEE Transactions on Information Forensics and Security, 13*(10), 2490–2505.

MITRE Corporation. (2013). *Making security measurable.* [Online] Available at: https://making-securitymeasurable.mitre.org. Accessed 1 Nov 2019.

MITRE Corporation. (2019). *ATT&CK.* [Online] Available at: https://attack.mitre.org/. Accessed 1 Nov 2019.

MITRE Corporation (2022). *Cyber analytics repository.* [Online] Available at: https://car.mitre.org/. Accessed 30 Mar 2022.

Molina-Markham, A., Miniter, C., Powell, B., & Ridley, A. (2021). Network environment design for autonomous cyberdefense. *arXiv preprint*, arXiv:2103.07583.

Musman, S. (2010). Using parallel distributed reasoning for monitoring computing networks. In *2010-MILCOM 2010 Military Communications conference* (pp. 417–422). IEEE.

Musman, S., & Flesher, P. (2000, January). System or security managers adaptive response tool. In *Proceedings DARPA information survivability conference and exposition. DISCEX'00* (Vol. 2, pp. 56–68). IEEE.

Musman, S., & Temin, A. (2015). A cyber mission impact assessment tool. In *2015 IEEE international symposium on Technologies for Homeland Security (HST)* (pp. 1–7). IEEE.

Musman, S., & Turner, A. (2018). A game theoretic approach to cyber security risk management. *The Journal of Defense Modeling and Simulation, 15*(2), 127–146.

Musman, S., Temin, A., Tanner, M., Fox, D., & Pridemore, B. (2010). Evaluating the impact of cyber attacks on missions. *Proceedings of the 5th international conference on information warfare and security* (pp. 446–456).

Musman, S., Booker, L., Applebaum, A., & Edmonds, B. (2019, May). Steps toward a principled approach to automating cyber responses. In *Artificial intelligence and machine learning for multi-domain operations applications* (Vol. 11006, p. 110061E). International Society for Optics and Photonics.

National Bureau of Standards. (1979). *Guideline for automatic data processing risk analysis* (FIPS PUB 65). National Bureau of Standards, US Dept of Commerce.

Nguyen, T. T., & Reddi, V. J. (2021). Deep reinforcement learning for cyber security. *IEEE Transactions on Neural Networks and Learning Systems*. https://doi.org/10.1109/TNNLS.2021.3121870. [arXiv:1906.05799v1, 2021, https://arxiv.org/abs/1906.05799v4]

Oliehoek, F., Spaan, M. T., & Vlassis, N. (2005). Best-response play in partially observable card games. In *Proceedings of the 14th annual machine learning conference of Belgium and the Netherlands* (pp. 45–50).

Orman, H. (2003). The Morris worm: A fifteen-year perspective. *IEEE Security & Privacy, 1*(5), 35–43.

Pineau, J., Gordon, G., Thrun, S. (2003, August). Point-based value iteration: An anytime algorithm for POMDPs. In *Proceedings of the 18th international joint conference on artificial intelligence (IJCAI'03)* (Vol. 3, pp. 1025–1030).

Poolsappasit, N., Dewri, R., & Ray, I. (2011). Dynamic security risk management using Bayesian attack graphs. *IEEE Transactions on Dependable and Secure Computing, 9*(1), 61–74.

Porras, P. A., & Neumann, P. G. (1997). EMERALD: Event monitoring enabling response to anomalous live disturbances. In *Proceedings of the 20th national information systems security conference* (Vol. 3, pp. 353–365).

Ross, S., Pineau, J., Paquet, S., & Chaib-Draa, B. (2008). Online planning algorithms for POMDPs. *Journal of Artificial Intelligence Research, 32*, 663–704.

Roy, A., Kim, D. S., & Trivedi, K. S. (2012). Attack countermeasure trees (ACT): Towards unifying the constructs of attack and defense trees. *Security and Communication Networks, 5*(8), 929–943.

Shameli-Sendi, A., Cheriet, M., & Hamou-Lhadj, A. (2014). Taxonomy of intrusion risk assessment and response system. *Computers & Security, 45*, 1–16.

Silver, D., & Veness, J. (2010). Monte-Carlo planning in large POMDPs. In *Advances in neural information processing systems, 23* (pp. 2164–2172).

Somayaji, A., & Forrest, S. (2000). Automated response using system-call delay. In *9th USENIX security symposium (USENIX security 00)* (pp. 185-197).

Stakhanova, N., Basu, S., & Wong, J. (2007). A taxonomy of intrusion response systems. *International Journal of Information and Computer Security, 1*(1–2), 169–184.

Stoll, C. (2005). *The cuckoo's egg: Tracking a spy through the maze of computer espionage.* Simon and Schuster.

Temin, A., & Musman, S. (2010). *A language for capturing cyber impact effects* (MITRE technical report MTR 100344, PR 10-3793). The MITRE Corporation.

Thayer, J. T., Burstein, M., Goldman, R. P., Kuter, U., Robertson, P., & Laddaga, R. (2013, September). Comparing strategic and tactical responses to cyber threats. In *2013 IEEE 7th international conference on self-adaptation and self-organizing systems workshops* (pp. 35–40). IEEE.

UCO. (2022). *Unified cyber ontology*. [Online] Available at: https://github.com/ucoProject/UCO. Accessed 30 Mar 2022.

Vien, N. A., & Toussaint, M. (2015). Hierarchical Monte-Carlo planning. In Proceedings of the *twenty-ninth AAAI conference on artificial intelligence* (pp. 3613–3619).

Wang, S., Zhang, Z., & Kadobayashi, Y. (2013). Exploring attack graph for cost-benefit security hardening: A probabilistic approach. *Computers & Security, 32*, 158–169.

Ye, N., Somani, A., Hsu, D., & Lee, W. S. (2017). DESPOT: Online POMDP planning with regularization. *Journal of Artificial Intelligence Research, 58*, 231–266.

Zonouz, S. A., Khurana, H., Sanders, W. H., & Yardley, T. M. (2009). RRE: A game-theoretic intrusion response and recovery engine. In *2009 IEEE/IFIP international conference on dependable systems & networks* (pp. 439–448). IEEE.

Zonouz, S. A., Khurana, H., Sanders, W. H., & Yardley, T. M. (2014). RRE: A game-theoretic intrusion response and recovery engine. *IEEE Transactions on Parallel and Distributed Systems, 25*(2), 395–406.

Chapter 8
Recovery Planning

Meiyi Ma, Himanshu Neema, and Janos Sztipanovits

1 Introduction

Despite the rapid development of cybersecurity, recovery, as a core element of cyber resilience, is often left to human decision-makers, e.g., cyber analysts, incident responders, and system administrators and operators (Kott & Theron, 2020). However, in many scenarios in the real world, e.g., executing missions, operating smart cities, autonomous vehicles or vehicle fleets, due to the issues of safety, time constraints, communication, and complexity, recovery efforts need to be undertaken with only restricted human involvement and with intelligent consideration of the risks and ramifications of such efforts. Therefore, an autonomous intelligent cyber defense agent (AICA) responsible for planning rapid recovery to a compromise state of the system is highly demanded. When the threat has been neutralized or deactivated, AICA will attempt to return the system to adequate working conditions through the most appropriate courses of actions (COAs).

However, generating and obtaining the optimal recovery COAs in practice are very **challenging** and complex. First, multiple recovery COAs must be produced by various algorithmic techniques, all of which must be evaluated for possible influences and side effects. However, the requirements and objectives in applications such as smart cities are often expressed vaguely in natural language. Defining them formally and measuring the influences quantitatively on different systems and their environments is an open question. Secondly, these COAs may not be compatible or be in conflict with each other that may further harm the system and environment. It is extremely important yet challenging to obtain the optimal set of COAs to execute. Thirdly, there are uncertainties in the system's state and environment, human

M. Ma (✉) · H. Neema · J. Sztipanovits
Computer Science, Vanderbilt University, Nashville, TN, USA
e-mail: meiyi.ma@vanderbilt.edu; himanshu.neema@vanderbilt.edu;
janos.sztipanovits@vanderbilt.edu

© The Author(s), under exclusive license to Springer Nature Switzerland AG 2023
A. Kott (ed.), *Autonomous Intelligent Cyber Defense Agent (AICA)*, Advances in
Information Security 87, https://doi.org/10.1007/978-3-031-29269-9_8

behaviors, and the impact of the resolutions (in time and space). It is challenging to simulate various attacks and predict future performance with recovery COAs under uncertainty. System degradation may occur due to security attacks and operational disruptions (e.g., a city's road traffic may be disrupted due to national festivals, football games, road constructions, highway closures, etc.). Security attacks include cyber-attacks (e.g., DOS, Data corruption), physical attacks (e.g., lane closures, traffic jamming), and hardware attacks (e.g., controller overrides, sensor damage/hacking). Fourthly, the scale of smart cities or complex mission operations also make it challenging to search for an optimal resolution due to an enormous solution space.

Targeting these challenges, we introduce and demonstrate a system for recovery planning using simulation-based predictive monitoring in this chapter. We build the system in the context of a smart city, but the solution is generalizable for other Cyber-Physical System (CPS) applications. The goal is to recover the system from attacks (cyber, physical, or hardware) and/or disruptions. The system is extended from CityResolver (Ma et al., 2018), a decision support system for conflict resolution among smart services in smart cities. It uses a novel Integer Linear Programming (ILP) based method to generate a small set of candidate resolution options. It then simulates and verifies the city's future performance under each option against city requirements and computes the degree of satisfaction to support decision making. Targeting the unique challenges in recovery planning, we extend CityResolver by (1) incorporating a powerful simulation integration platform to evaluate secure and resilient CPS (SURE) (Koutsoukos et al., 2018; Neema et al., 2018); (2) defining and formalizing security and safety requirements using Signal Temporal Logic with Uncertainty (STL-U) (Ma et al., 2021) in smart cities for recovery planning; and (3) verifying the predicted performance of multiple recovery COAs with confidence guarantees.

In summary, the main **contributions** of this chapter on recovery planning include,

- A comprehensive overview of existing techniques for recovery planning
- Method for evaluating impact of system degradation
- Method and tool for generating recovery COAs efficiently
- Method and tool for evaluating of recovery COAs through integrated heterogeneous simulations considering uncertainty
- Studying and formalizing security and safety requirements using STL-U
- Verifying recovery COAs with confidence guarantees

Organization For the rest of the chapter, we first discuss the overview of recovery planning in Sect. 2. Then, we formalize the problem in Sect. 3 and present an overview of our system in Sect. 4. Next, we discuss the details of three key components of the system, viz. recovery COA generation, simulation and prediction with uncertainty, and recovery COA verification in Sects. 5, 6, and 7, respectively. At last, we show two recovery scenarios using simulation-based predictive monitoring in a smart city in Sect. 8 and summarize the chapter with a discussion on the insights and future directions in Sect. 9.

2   Recovery Planning Overview

2.1   Definition of Recovery Planning

In general, recovery is the process that an entity or system uses to quickly resume its functions from some unplanned, degraded state created by an incident, such as malicious attacks. In the scope of AICA, it includes recovery of corresponding physical systems as well as the recovery of software systems' functions. Recovery planning is defined as the process of designing a structured approach for the recovery. As a basic example, recovery plans can be a manually designed document that lists all the steps in a recovery process from some cyber-attacks. In an advanced view of recovery planning, the recovery plans are automatically generated by composing the steps using available recovery tasks and actions in various ways and evaluating and choosing the composed recovery plans for optimal recovery goal. The goal is to optimize the recovery plan according to system state and resources, with the help of AI systems.

2.2   Different Components in the Recovery Plan

An AICA is assumed to reside on a physical platform and then protect the integrity of all vulnerable parts of the platform against cyber-attacks. Such platform is a mixture of physical and software systems, which increases the complexity of the recovery planning task. Before we introduce our system, we briefly review the recovery techniques for each of these components for general IoT applications, including device recovery, communication system recovery, and data recovery.

Device Recovery   For the recovery of the platform, one key part is to make sure the physical devices of the platforms (e.g., sensors and actuators) are correctly functioning, that is, ensure both the availability and operational integrity of devices. While the maintenance of the physical systems often requires human support, for the purpose of recovery planning the AICA should be able to diagnose the problem and notify the maintenance team when necessary. A second requirement for device recovery is to make sure the devices are trustworthy – not controlled by a malicious party.

In the practice of CPS systems, the device availability and trustworthiness are often guaranteed by exchanging messages between the device to the server/controller via secure communication protocols. For example, Sridhar and Smys (2017) gives a unique ID to every device in the system, and lets each device send message along with the device ID within the crypto protocol. Therefore, when a DoS attack, eavesdropping attack, or man-in-the-middle attack is present, the attack can be detected and subsequently an efficient recovery can be made. Li et al. (2017) propose a lightweight mutual authentication protocol to efficiently exchange messages between components in a smart city.

Communication Recovery Communication is essential to IoT services, especially during the recovery process. Therefore, continued operation could be very severely degraded or disrupted when communication is disrupted. A common practice is to set up an alternative communication path before the attack. This back-up communication should be secure against cyber-attacks. As an example, the state of Indiana set up redundant WAN connectivity (Indiana State Government, 2021) between Indianapolis and Bloomington for their IoT devices to reduce the disaster recovery time. The framework proposed by Woo et al. (2018) design a two-layer network structure, such that for each layer gateways are connected with a daisy chain. When at most two gateways have failed, the secure communication can still be maintained.

As a specific example, Kim et al. (2021) designs a CPS framework that is resilient and able to recover from the pole-dynamic attack (PDA). PDA is an attack that targets physical devices of a system in an unstable region by corrupting specific sensors' measurements. In this case, the system may still assume that the physical devices are functioning normally, but they may already be stuck. To recover from such PDA attack, Kim et al. proposes a three-step recovery plan powered by a network manager. After identifying the attack's location in the detection step, their network manager isolates the attacker from the existing CPS network by closing the connection toward adjacent nodes. The network manager then finds a new connection route in the network to connect the physical and the computing systems again, thus regaining the function of the IoT device. The three-step recovery process is shown in Fig. 8.1.

Data Recovery Recently, the application of AI techniques highlights the importance of the data in an IoT application. Data is thus another target for the adversary, as missing/corrupted data can greatly reduce the performance of IoT applications or even make them unusable.

A common approach to data recovery is to have redundancy in data storage, e.g., by setting up redundant array of inexpensive disks (RAID) for the data. If the redundancy is set prior to the attack and the damage on the data is within a certain limit of the redundancy, the data can then be efficiently recovered. As an example, the state of Indiana (Indiana State Government, 2021) stores the IoT data with NAS and keeps a replication of the data in Bloomington. The data is aimed to be recovered within 6 h.

Researchers also target how to recover the data in an approximate way without physical redundancy. Analytical redundancy is an effective approach for recovering

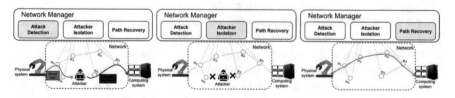

Fig. 8.1 Three-step recovery for PDA attack. (Source: Kim et al. 2021)

lost sensor data if they are observations of interacting physical processes with at least partially known underlying models. This is frequently the case in IoT applications with dense sensor coverage. The computational approach is based on minimizing residual error relative to the underlying models that are derived from first principles or from observations using ML methods. For example, Fekade et al. (2018) proposes an approach based on probabilistic matrix factorization, a Bayesian machine learning approach. Other machine learning techniques, such as SVM (Min & Han, 2005) or deep neural networks (Christakou et al., 2007) can also be applied to the problem.

Specifically, in Fekade et al. (2018), the authors first start with a random matrix R′, and try to optimize R′ so that the matrix R′ at the *remaining* positions match the original data matrix R. This difference is measured by an inconsistency loss, which is then minimized with an optimization algorithm, The completion process is shown in Fig. 8.2.

Data integrity during communication is another issue, which requires that the data to be received has not been altered or modified during communication. In case of detection and reconstruction of tampered data, error correction mechanisms such as Cyclic Redundancy Checks (CRC) and checksum functions have been used.

2.3   Techniques for Recovery Planning

Simulation In recovery planning, there are usually multiple possible recovery COAs to take, each having a different future impact on the system. How shall we pick the best recovery option? Simulation offers one possible approach.

For the purpose of evaluating the performance of IoT-based systems, many simulation tools have been proposed. For example, simulators NS2 (Issariyakul & Hossain, 2012) and Cooja (Österlind et al., 2006) can be used to evaluate the

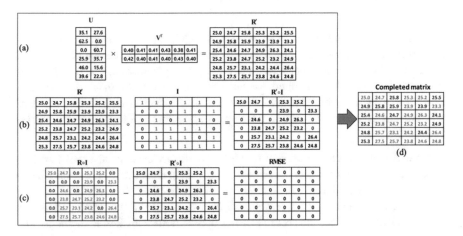

Fig. 8.2 Data recovery. (Source: Fekade et al. 2018)

performance of sensor networks, traffic simulator SUMO (Krajzewicz et al., 2012) can be used to evaluate performance of traffic planning, and simulator DPWSim (Han et al., 2014) can be used to evaluate the performance of IoT applications.

As an example of simulation-based evaluation, in Al-Hamadi and Chen (2017), the authors present a decision-making protocol for health IoT systems. The protocol, which is designed robust to malicious attack, decides whether a user should visit a place/environment for health reasons. To evaluate the protocol, the authors use network simulator to simulate scenarios when a fraction of the nodes in the network are malicious. The authors then test the protocol and show that within a certain time period, most malicious nodes are identified, and the protocol returns correct result confidently. With the simulation result, the authors conclude that their proposed decision-making protocol is effective.

Prediction with Machine Learning With recent development in machine learning, predictions with machine learning algorithms are widely applied to different IoT applications, even for making crucial decisions. For example, Piccialli et al. (2020) uses an unsupervised learning method on IoT data to support the decision-making process of the stakeholders of a museum. They gather visitors' tracks during the museum visit and perform a clustering to understand users' behavior, and also compare them with historical results (i.e., previous month and year), to support the decision-making process of the museums' owner, e.g., for deciding whether or not more audio guide should be added.

Specifically, the concept of *predictive analytics* (PAs) refers to the method that predict future events based on current patterns and then make analysis based on the potential future events. As an example, in Akbar et al. (2017), the authors propose a framework (shown in Fig. 8.3) that collects IoT data to predict future events and use those to infer complex patterns. The framework utilizes open-source machine learning components for event prediction. The proposed method is adaptive, such that its prediction horizon is adjusted dynamically with the data stream. The framework is successfully applied to perform predictive analytics on intelligent transportation systems.

Formal Methods In general, *Formal Methods* (FM) is the approach that uses logical and mathematical description to specify system behaviors (Chong et al., 2016), so that reliable conclusions can be drawn about those behaviors. Since 1970s, formal methods have been applied for enforcing the safety of industrial systems. Specifically, by describing the system and a class of adversaries with formal methods, one can give a certification that the system is secure to all possible adversaries in the class.

Formal methods can be applied to a lot of hardware systems and software systems, including IoT applications. For example, Zhang et al. (2015) proposes a hardware specification language SecVerilog that specifies the security of the information-flow between processors. Mohsin et al. (2017) proposes IoTSAT, a framework that enforces the security of IoT applications with formal methods. The

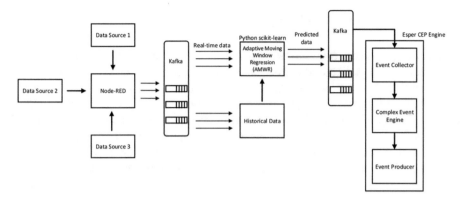

Fig. 8.3 Predictive analytics system for IoT application proposed by Akbar et al. (Source: Akbar et al. 2017)

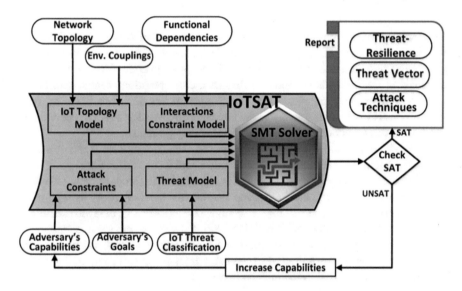

Fig. 8.4 Formal verification based secure IoT framework proposed by Mohsin et al. (Source: Mohsin et al. 2017)

framework models IoT behavior and defines certain threats on IoT applications. After that the system try to verify whether adversaries can yield an unsafe state in the model. If the verification is successfully completed, the framework concludes that the IoT framework is resilient to the adversaries. The process is shown in Fig. 8.4.

3 Problem Formulation

Assuming a system S and its environment E is compromised by attacks and the threat has been neutralized or deactivated, a set of recovery COAs $A = \{a_1, ..., a_n\}$ are produced by various agents and services to mitigate the impact of attacks. Services and agents have dynamic priorities $P = \{p_1, ..., p_m\}$ under different contexts. The system and its environment have important safety and security requirements $R = \{r_1, ..., r_i\}$. The problem is to find the optimal subset of recovery COAs $A' \subseteq A$ that guarantees the satisfaction of requirements in set R with the highest degree of satisfaction under confidence level c considering the dynamic priorities and uncertainty.

4 System Overview

We discuss the recovery planning system in the context of a city operation center which would oversee all services and provide recovery COAs that aim to best mitigate the impact of these attacks. Figure 8.5 shows an overview of our envisioned architecture that extends the functionality of a city operations center with attack detector and recovery planner. Recovery planner makes decisions based on real-time city states. We refer readers to the previous chapters for attack detection and limit our focus on addressing challenges of recovery planning.

As shown in Fig. 8.6, our system includes four key components, which are COA generator, simulator, requirement formalization, and COA verification.

When a compromise is detected, it follows the following steps to obtain the optimal recovery COA. First, the COA generator derives a set of COAs incorporating different services and agents. It may also suggest alternatives or delayed executions of COAs. Thus, the number of potential resolution options grows exponentially with the number of action requests and locations. Considering context factors and constraints, it returns a small subset of COAs using Integer Linear Programming (ILP). We will describe the ILP-based method in Sect. 5.

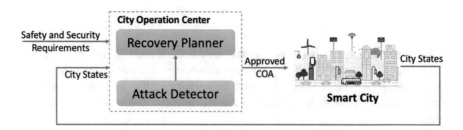

Fig. 8.5 Overview of security attack detection and recovery in a smart city

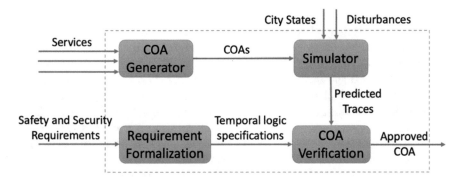

Fig. 8.6 System overview

The second step is to simulate the execution of these resolution options to predict the effect of choices on the city. We use a powerful simulation integration platform for secure and resilient CPS (SURE) (Koutsoukos et al., 2018; Neema et al., 2018). The simulator reproduces the same scenario after the attack (e.g., half the number of the sensors down), then simulates the city's future performance with COA options. Multiple simulations may be instantiated in parallel to simulate the execution of smart city processes under different COA options. By considering the uncertainty and disturbance, the simulator returns sequences of city states as flowpipes (representing sequences of distributions). We will show the details of the simulation in Sect. 6.

The next step is to verify if each option's simulated traces of city states satisfy various safety and security requirements. We develop an approach to formalize city requirements as Signal Temporal Logic with Uncertainty (STL-U) specifications and compute the satisfaction degree of different resolution options on multiple specification objectives via STL-U verification. We will show the study of safety and security requirements, their formalization, and verification with confidence guarantees in Sect. 7.

5   Recovery COA Generation

In this section, we present an Integer Linear Programming (ILP) based method to generate a small set of COA options, which corresponds to the "COA Generator" module in Fig. 8.6.

Suppose that there are m ongoing service actions executing in the smart city. For example, the traffic service redirects some vehicles to a new route to reduce traffic congestion, and an accident service blocks a lane due to a traffic accident. After attacks happen, the operation center receives n new COA requests agents that try to mitigate the influence from the attacks. Next step is to evaluate the safety of these

$m + n$ actions. One strategy to obtain resolutions is to only accept some of the new actions while rejecting others in a way that there is no safety violation. To achieve this, it may also be necessary to suspend some ongoing actions. Thus, the number of possible COA choices is at least 2^{m+n}. If we consider a more complex resolution strategy, such as suggesting alternative actions to the requested actions, the solution space of possible resolutions becomes even larger. Checking all these resolution choices' impact against requirements within the short time frame is very challenging. Thus, we present a method to select a small number of candidate COA options based on the intuition that a good set of COAs should (1) accept as many actions as possible, (2) not allow safety violations, and (3) account for priorities of agents.

We formulate the problem as an integer linear program. Given a set A of smart service actions causing conflicts, we define a binary variable $\mu \in \{0, 1\}$ for each action $a \in A$ to track if the action is chosen by a candidate resolution option. Each action a is associated with a weight value $w \in Z$ representing the action priority determined by current, state-dependent importance policies. For simplicity, we assume that action weights are given as constants at time t. We denote a set C of contradicting action pairs and a set D of dependent action pairs. We also group an action and its alternatives into a set $\theta \subseteq A$. The resulting ILP problem is

$$\underset{w_i \in Z,\ \mu_i \in \{0,1\}}{maximize} \sum_{1 \leq i \leq A} w_i \times \mu_i \tag{8.1}$$

Subject to

$$\forall \left(a_i, a_j\right) \in C : \mu_i + \mu_j \leq 1 \tag{8.2}$$

$$\forall \left(a_i, a_j\right) \in D : \mu_i - \mu_j = 0 \tag{8.3}$$

$$\forall a_i \in \theta \subseteq A : \sum \mu_i \leq 1 \tag{8.4}$$

The objective function (8.1) is to maximize the number of accepted COAs in the recovery planning based on their priority weights. The constraint (8.2) guarantees a resolution does not accept a pair of contracting actions. The constraint (8.3) ensures that dependent actions are both accepted or rejected at the same time. Finally, the constraint (8.4) requires that at most one action from a set of alternative actions is chosen by a resolution. Transforming the problem to ILP and solving it with the Gurobi tool (Gurobi, 2021) do not necessarily find the best solution when the number is very large, but it can give the solution in polynomial time, which is very important for runtime decision making system in cites. We illustrate the usage of the ILP solution in Sect. 8.

6 Simulation and Prediction with Uncertainty

6.1 Introduction to the SURE Platform

CPS involves close coupling of physical and cyber components in various ways to achieve their desired functions. However, these systems are vulnerable to attacks that can span physical and cyber spaces and impact the functionality of even deeply rooted system components. In addition, with the advancements in network connectivity, computational environments, and process control, modern CPSs are continually becoming more distributed, which further increases their attack surfaces. Therefore, it is highly important to design these systems such that they are not only resilient to cyber-attacks but can also "recover" once under an attack. This requires a comprehensive experimentation and evaluation framework. The SecUre and REsilient Cyber–Physical Systems (SURE) platform (Koutsoukos et al., 2018; Neema et al., 2018) incorporates: (1) realistic models of cyber and physical components and their interactions; (2) cyber-attack models that focus on the impact of attacks to CPS behavior and operation; and (3) operational scenarios that can be used for evaluation of cybersecurity risks. Further, it allows the evaluation of performance impact and assessment of resilient monitoring and control algorithms. In the SURE approach, research processes and results are documented as executable software models, simulations, and generated data that support cybersecurity analysis and design in a quantifiable manner.

In general, there are two approaches to building resilience: *passive and active resilience*. Passive resilience refers to 'resilient by construction' where the system is designed by taking into account the operational uncertainties encountered. This is accomplished using redundant and overperforming components while balancing the cost with resilience. On the other hand, active resilience refers to the ability of a system to quickly restore its operation when faced with cyber-attacks and/or physical disruptions. This requires the use of *monitors* to actively look for abnormal system behavior, *detectors* to find causes for the abnormal behavior (e.g., a cyber-attack), and *responders* that implement cause-dependent solutions to restore system operations. The main issue with active resilience is that it is difficult to implement for complex systems and may not be feasible with respect to time and resources it might require. The SURE platform provides tools for both passive and active resilience.

As shown in the Fig. 8.7, the SURE platform provides a web-based and cloud-deployed architecture. Analysts interact with SURE for modeling the systems and attacks in an online multi-user modeling environment based on WebGME (Maróti et al., 2014) and the modeled experiments are run in the cloud backend with results reported back on the front-end both as live charts during the experiment execution and aggregate results when the execution has completed. In the cloud backend, the experiments are designed to run using Vanderbilt's CPSWT framework (Neema & Karsai, 2018; Neema et al., 2019) that supports multi-domain integrated simulation experiments along with cyber scenarios through courses-of-action modeling. The

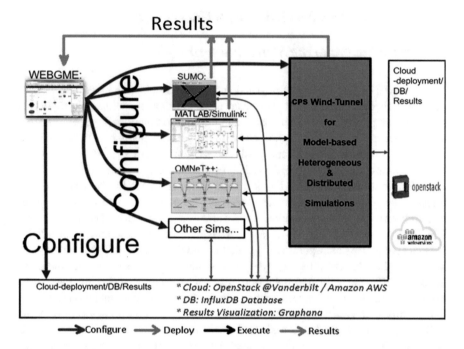

Fig. 8.7 Architectural overview of the SURE platform

CPSWT framework relies on the IEEE High-Level Architecture (HLA) (IEEE Std 1516-2010, 2010) standard for integrating various simulation engines such as MATLAB/Simulink (Matlabworks), OMNeT++ (Varga, 2019), CPNTools (Westergaard & Kristensen, 2009), and SUMO (Krajzewicz et al., 2012). It also has a reusable Cyber-Attack Library (Neema & Karsai, 2018; Neema et al., 2018) and capability of modeling and evaluating COAs (Maróti et al., 2014; Neema et al., 2018, 2019) which is utilized by the SURE platform for designing Cyber COAs. The framework is also capable of performing cyber-gaming experiments, where different cyber-attacks and their combinations can be evaluated against different combinations of available security mechanisms. Using the web-based architecture, the SURE platform allows multiple users to work on the same model at the same time and maintains and provides full history of model edits (like the distributed version control system Git (Spinellis, 2012)). The online and multi-user nature of the platform makes it suitable for shared modeling and analysis. The cloud deployment of the experiment executions enables it to execute multiple experiments in parallel and scale to the needs of scenarios being evaluated.

It is important to note that even though the SURE platform targets the domain of networked sensing and control of road traffic, the components, and technologies it is built upon are modular and reusable for direct reuse in many different CPS application contexts.

6.2   Simulation of Different Attack Scenarios

The ability of simulating various attacks within the context of CPS operational scenarios is important for both passive and active resilience methods. The SURE platform supports three different attack categories – cyber-attacks, physical attacks in the road traffic network, and Hardware-In-the-Loop (HIL) attacks on physical devices in the system (e.g., traffic lights and controllers). These different attack categories and the supported attacks within each category are listed in Table 8.1. The table also provides a description for each of the attack types supported.

These attacks from the attack libraries in SURE are modular and reconfigurable. For example, for a Denial-of-Service (DOS) attack, the modeler can specify the network node on which the attack will be deployed, the simulation time at which the attack will be initiated, and the simulation time at which the attack was over/mitigated, if any. It is important to note that these attacks do not represent the physical mechanisms through which these attacks are carried out in the real-world but rather represent the impact such attacks achieve when deployed. For example, the network delay attack ensures that the messages between network components are delayed by the amount of delay specified in the attack model rather than inserting large amount of extraneous network traffic that would ultimately cause network delays. This is important because from the perspective of security and resilience of large-scale

Table 8.1   Attack libraries in SURE

Attack type	Description
Cyber attacks	
DOS	Disable a controller, or network component
Disable network	Disable communication within the network
Delay	Delay packets when they are routed between components
Integrity	Change packet values before they reach destination
Data corruption	Make packets unreadable
Reply	Retransmit packets
Out of order	Send transmitted packets in the wrong order
Network filter	Filter out traffic between given source and destination subnets
Sniffer	Listen to communicated traffic
Routing table manipulation	Redefine the network routes
Physical attacks	
Lane closure	Close a road or lane of a road
Vehicle failure	Cause a vehicle to stall
Traffic light failure	Cause a traffic light to stop operating
Vehicles crash	Cause vehicles to crash within the simulation
HIL attacks	
DOS/DDOS	Transmit bulk traffic from multiple nodes
Side Channel	Reverse engineer components based on behavior
Spoofing	Transmit fake messages

Table 8.2 Example of attacks, impacts, and recovery actions

Type of attack	Description	Impact in the city	Potential recovery actions
Denial-of-Service (DOS) attack on a traffic light at a key intersection	A cyber-attack that makes the traffic light controller (responsible to switch traffic light states) unreachable	Long queues of vehicles in the lane where the traffic light remains 'Red' and no waiting at the intersection where the traffic light remains 'Green'	1. Switch the traffic light to default controller which turns light into 'blinking-yellow' state – a suboptimal solution but fast and easy to implement 2. Divert the incoming traffic in alternate routes, while fixing and restoring the traffic light damaged by the attack 3. Deploy security mechanisms on city traffic lights to prevent future attacks
Lane closure attack on a key road segment	A physical attack (e.g., downed tree, or breaking of a bridge) that makes certain roads or lanes unusable	Quick accumulation of road traffic around the blocked road or lanes.	1. Generate and install traffic diversions to ensure traffic does not accumulate 2. Dispersion of already accumulated traffic through rerouting and lane changing areas 3. Removal of the blockages and restoration of traffic 4. Installation of monitors that can quickly warn agencies about the attacks 5. Deployment of diversion and rerouting gear and personnel near key roads and lanes for quick recovery in future attacks.
Spoofing of traffic sensors at a key intersection	A hardware attack that takes over the data sent by traffic sensors to traffic controllers	Unwarranted and unfair of use of roads and lanes by attackers (e.g., a shipment company spoofing traffic light sensors in the city to ensure non-stop flow of their delivery trucks)	1. Detection of irregular traffic flows by sensor-fusion methods on multiple geographically distributed traffic sensors. 2. Override capability on traffic controllers when under spoofing attack. 3. Installation of fallback controllers while original controllers are restored from the attack.

systems, such as the city-wide road traffic management, the most important consideration is how different types of attacks will impact the road traffic and its control and ultimately impact the city's resilience in maintaining acceptable traffic flows amidst these attacks. A few examples of using these attacks, along with the impact they achieve in disrupting the road traffic and potential recovery actions to alleviate the disruptions are given in Table 8.2.

6.3 Simulation for Prediction with Uncertainty

Real-world systems have to deal with numerous uncertainties that arise due to complex network of components, their inter-dependencies, and various other social and geo-political factors that affect their operations. In addition, the adversaries may impact the system operations by attacking its components at any time in many different ways. Therefore, an intelligent agent tasked for resilience and recovery of these systems must take uncertainties into account in order to better prepare for and handle emerging situations as they occur. In the SURE platform, we use integrated simulations for evaluating security and resilience of systems under normal conditions as well as when under attack. In addition, the platform provides ways to inject uncertainty into the scenario designs and tools to execute a *Design of Experiments* over different parametric combinations. These parametric variations can also take into account different combinations of attack plans and security mechanisms. Below are a few examples of introducing uncertainty and handling their impact:

1. Uncertainty in Traffic Demand: Traffic scenarios in the SURE platform are used for evaluating many security and resilience methods and algorithms. In these scenarios, we allow introduction of uncertainties by randomly varying traffic patterns. The traffic demand is determined by the quantity and timing of vehicles going between all source and destination pairs. Here, we allow randomization for varying both the number of vehicles and their start times. The cloud deployed backend and the large-scale scenario-based experimentation in SURE, allows scaling experiments and exercising these variations in order to determine how systems are going to operate in these situations.
2. Uncertainty in Attack Plans: The course of action (COA) modeling language incorporates several workflow/scenario atomic elements that allow random values for their configurations. For example, the *Random Duration* element can be placed within the workflow to delay its execution (when the execution path has reached this workflow element) for a random duration. Another interesting example in the COA language is *Probabilistic Choice* element. This is essentially a fork in the workflow where several alternative branches can be executed, but each of the branch has an associated probability with it. The branch that gets chosen for execution depends on the probabilistic value chosen during COA execution. This enables testing Cyber COAs for uncertain timing and paths.
3. Situationally Aware Active Defense Strategies: One of the key defense strategies is to keep an adversary guessing of potential defense actions that defender might take. For example, the US nuclear forces use a declaratory policy of ambiguity to keep enemy guessing of its intentions and response as a way to ensure deterrence. In SURE platform, the Cyber COAs not only has means to deploy different attacks and defense actions at different times, but it also allows introspection of executing scenarios and adjustment of defense strategies based on observations made during scenario execution. This capability transforms Cyber COAs from mundane static experimentations to highly dynamic and adaptive evaluations. As an example, if an adversary knows modus operandi of how the defender

is going to institute security mechanisms in different attack situations, it can deploy counterattack plans to further exacerbate the disruption. These types of situations involving counter attacks and counter-counterattacks can be easily programmed using Cyber COAs, which along with random elements described above brings in significant capability to evaluate cyber resilience with uncertainties.

7 Recovery COA Verification

With the simulation platform, we predict the city's future states with the requested COAs. However, it is challenging to check whether the predicted time series from a large scale of locations satisfy the safety requirements, especially with various city requirements. Therefore, we introduce recovery COA formal verification into our design. We first formalize the city requirements using Signal Temporal Logic with Uncertainty (STL-U) (Ma et al., 2021), then verify the simulated prediction results for each recovery COA option using STL-U. This section presents STL-U's formal definition, syntax, and semantics, then formalizes security and safety requirements in smart cities using STL-U and verifies these requirements with confidence guarantees.

To start with, we formally define the signals as *flowpipes* that characterize the prediction results (i.e., the predicted future states of smart cities from the simulation) with uncertainty.

Definition 1(Flowpipe) A flowpipe signal Ω is defined over a finite discrete time domain $\mathbb{T}$ such that $\Omega[t] = \Phi_t$ at any time $t \in \mathbb{T}$, where Φ_t is a Gaussian distribution $\mathcal{N}\left(\theta_t, \sigma_t^2\right)$.

Given a confidence level $\epsilon \in [0, 1] \subseteq \mathbb{R}$, the flowpipe at time t is bounded by a confidence interval $\left[\Phi_t^-(\epsilon),\ \Phi_t^+(\epsilon)\right]$ with the lower bound $\Phi_t^-(\epsilon) = \theta_t - \delta \cdot \dfrac{\sigma_t}{\sqrt{N}}$, where N is the number of samples that the Gaussian distribution is estimated from, and δ s a parameter obtained from the quantile function of Gaussian distribution Φ_t based on the confidence level ϵ. In the special case where the Gaussian distribution's variance $\sigma_t = 0$, the lower and upper bounds of the confidence interval concide (i.e., $\Phi_t^-(\epsilon) = \Phi_t^+(\epsilon) = \theta_t$), thus the flowpipe becomes a single trace signal. We then present the syntax of STL-U which is used to formalize city requirements on the city's future states. Please refer to Ma et al. (2021) for the detailed definition.

Definition 2 (STL-U Syntax) The syntax of a STL-U formula φ over ω is defined by the grammar

$$\varphi := \mu_x(\epsilon) \,\big|\, \neg\varphi \,\big|\, \varphi_1 \wedge \varphi_2 \big|\, \varphi_1 \mathcal{U}_I \varphi_2$$

where, $\omega : \mathbb{T} \to \{\Omega\}^n$ a multi-dimensional flowpipe signal, where $\mathbb{T} = [0,d) \subseteq \mathbb{R}$ represents for a finite discrete time domain and $n = |X|$ for a finite set of (independent) *real* variables X, $I \subseteq \mathbb{R}^+$ is a time interval, and $\mu_x(\epsilon)$ is an atomic predicate over a real variable x with confidence level ϵ whose value is determined by the sign of a function of an underlying flowpipe signal Ω_x, that is, $\mu_x(\epsilon) \equiv f(x) > 0$ for $x \in \left[\Phi_t^-(\epsilon), \Phi_t^+(\epsilon) \right]$ with $\Phi_t = \Omega_x[t]$. (We assume that $f(x) = \lambda - x$ where $\lambda \in \mathbb{R}$ is a constant).

The above syntactic definition of STL-U is minimal and includes only basic operators. We can derive other operators, for example, *eventually* denoted by $\Diamond_I \varphi \equiv$ true $\upsilon_I \varphi$, and *always* denoted by $\Box_I \varphi \equiv \neg \Diamond_I \neg \varphi$. Using STL-U syntax, we can specify a requirement on Air Quality Index (AQI) "with 95% confidence level, the AQI should never exceed 100 in the next 10 hours" as "$\Box_{[0,10]}(\mathrm{AQI}_{95\%} < 100)$".

To verify the predicted flowpipe with its requirement, we present the Boolean semantics of a STL-U formula φ over a multidimensional flowpipe signal ω at time t by two indices: *strong satisfaction*, denoted by $(\omega, t) \vDash_s \varphi$, and *weak satisfaction*, denoted by $(\omega, t) \vDash_w \varphi$.

Definition 3 (STL-U Strong Satisfaction)

$$(\omega, t) \vDash_s \mu_x(\epsilon) \Leftrightarrow f\left(\Phi_t^+(\epsilon)\right) > 0$$

$$(\omega, t) \vDash_s \neg \varphi \Leftrightarrow (\omega, t) \nvDash_w \varphi$$

$$(\omega, t) \vDash_s \varphi_1 \wedge \varphi_2 \Leftrightarrow (\omega, t) \vDash_s \varphi_1 \ and \ (\omega, t) \vDash_s \varphi_2$$

$$(\omega, t) \vDash_s \varphi_1 \mathcal{U}_I \varphi_2 \Leftrightarrow \exists t' \in (t+I) \cap \mathbb{T}, (\omega, t') \vDash_s \varphi_2 \ and \ \forall t'' \in (t, t'), (\omega, t'') \vDash_s \varphi_1$$

Definition 4 (STL-U Weak Satisfaction)

$$(\omega, t) \vDash_w \mu_x(\epsilon) \Leftrightarrow f\left(\Phi_t^-(\epsilon)\right) > 0$$

$$(\omega, t) \vDash_w \neg \varphi \Leftrightarrow (\omega, t) \nvDash_s \varphi$$

$$(\omega, t) \vDash_w \varphi_1 \wedge \varphi_2 \Leftrightarrow (\omega, t) \vDash_w \varphi_1 \ and \ (\omega, t) \vDash_w \varphi_2$$

$$(\omega, t) \vDash_w \varphi_1 \mathcal{U}_I \varphi_2 \Leftrightarrow \exists t' \in (t+I) \cap \mathbb{T}, (\omega, t') \vDash_w \varphi_2 \ and \ \forall t'' \in (t, t'), (\omega, t'') \vDash_w \varphi_1$$

Intuitively, the strong satisfaction means that all the flowpipe signal values bounded within the confidence interval with a certain confidence ϵ should satisfy the requirement φ; while the weak satisfaction means that the flowpipe signal at least partially satisfies φ. In the smart city, the strong semantics can be applied to monitor safety critical requirements, e.g., the fire risk, accidents, and the weak semantics can be applied to monitor less-strict performance requirements, e.g., the noise levels, illumination of streetlights. We present examples of formalized city requirements in recovery planning in Table 8.3.

Table 8.3 City requirements formalization using STL-U

Domain	City requirements	Formal specification
Safety & Security	Maximum disconnection time of device and AICA is 5 min	$\text{Disconnect}(\text{device})\mathcal{U}_{(0,5)}(\neg\text{Disconnect}(\text{device}))$
	At least one of the two data centers should remain active	$\Box_{(a,b)}(Active(C_1) \bigvee Active(C_2))$
	At least 80% of signal lights should maintain active status	$\Box_{(a,b)}(Active_e(\text{signals}) < 80\%)$
	The sensing coverage should not be reduced to less than 50% per block	$\Box_{(a,b)}(Active_e(\text{sensors}) < 50\%)$
Transportation	No vehicle collision should occur	$\Box_{(a,b)} \neg\, Collision(i)$
	Number of vehicles should never exceed limit	$\Box_{(a,b)}(\text{VehicleNumber(lane)} < \text{Capacity(lane)})$
	Any lane on the main street should not be closed for more than 2 h	$\text{Closed}(\text{lane})\mathcal{U}_{(0,120)}(\neg\text{Closed}(\text{lane}))$
Emergency	Emergency vehicles should not wait for more than 10 s at an intersection	$\Box_{(a,b)}(EmergencyWaitTime_e(i) < 10)$
	Emergency vehicles should not be directed to a blocked lane or area	$\Box_{(a,b)} \neg\, (\text{EmergencyDirection(lane)} \land \text{Blocked(lane)})$
	The highway blocked by an emergency accident should be unblocked within 30 min	$\text{Blocked}(\text{lane})\mathcal{U}_{(0,30)}(\neg\text{Blocked}(\text{lane}))$
Environment	The noise level in a lane should always be less than 70 dB	$\Box_{(a,b)}(Noise_e(\text{lane}) < 70)$
	The particulate matter (PMx) emission in a lane should always be no more than 0.2 mg	$\Box_{(a,b)}(PMx_e(\text{lane}) < 0.2)$

8 Recovery Scenarios

In this section, we present two recovery scenarios using simulation-based predictive monitoring. These two scenarios demonstrate how our system supports recovery from random attacks in normal days and planning for the potential attacks under special city events, respectively. We present these scenarios using the street network and communication network on Vanderbilt campus, as shown in Fig. 8.8.

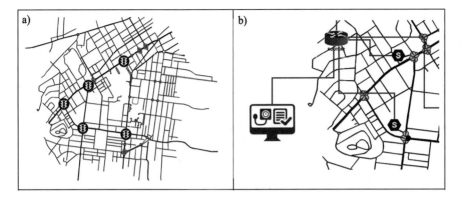

Fig. 8.8 (**a**) Vanderbilt Campus street network (**b**) Communication network model

8.1   Recovery Scenario 1

In the first recovery scenario, assume the city was under both physical and cyber-attacks, which lead to lane closure and signal lights failures. As shown in Fig. 8.8, due to the attacks, at the intersections with signal lights, long queues of vehicles in the lane where the traffic light remains "Red" and no waiting at the intersection where the traffic light remains "Green". Meanwhile, there is a quick accumulation of road traffic around the blocked road or lanes.

Therefore, the goal of our recovery planning is to generate optimal recovery COAs to restore the signal lights and release the traffic congestion without violating city requirements. We illustrate the major steps of our system with an example of COAs from 2 recovery agents. To be noted, the scenarios could be much more complex in practice (e.g., there are over 50 intersections in Fig. 8.8), and our solution is general and scalable.

Step 1: In this case, multiple COAs are generated by different agents and services based on their recovery goals. Our system first gathers all the COAs from recovery agents. For example, traffic service S1 requests seven traffic signals to stay green for 5 min. These requested actions are denoted as $\{a_1, ..., a_7\}$. If action a_3 is not accepted, the service also allows an alternative action (denoted by a_8) to keep the corresponding signal green only for 3 min. Suppose that, at the same time, an emergency recovery service S2 requests three green different traffic signals for 3 min, which has conflicts with previous actions because they share a crossroads. These new actions are denoted $\{a_9, a_{10}, a_{11}\}$. We know that actions a_9 and a_{10} are interdependent. Action a_{10} is contradicting with actions a_3 and a_8. We also assume actions requested by the emergency recovery service S2 has a higher priority weight than the traffic service S1. Let the weight value for S2 actions be 2 and the weight value for S1 actions be 1.

Step 2: Next, we generate subsets of COAs using ILP. We write an ILP as follows:

$$\underset{\mu_i \in \{0,1\}}{maximize} \sum_{1 \leq i \leq 8} \mu_i + \sum_{9 \leq i \leq 11} 2\mu_i$$

Subject to

$$\mu_3 + \mu_{10} \leq 1$$

$$\mu_8 + \mu_{10} \leq 1$$

$$\mu_9 - \mu_{10} = 0$$

$$\mu_3 + \mu_8 \leq 1$$

Step 3: We rank solution results based on their objective function values. The top 3 resolution options are as follows:

Option 1: Reject a_3 and a_8, accept other actions.
Option 2: Reject a_3, a_8, and a_{11}, accept other actions.
Option 3: Reject a_8, a_9, and a_{10}, accept other actions.

Step 4: We simulate the state of the city over time with each subset in the simulation. In the simulation, we simulate not only the performance at the intersections but also the states of traffic, sensors, pedestrians, communications, etc., on the lanes and intersections nearby. By considering the uncertainty and disturbance (as described in Sect. 6.3), the simulator returns sequences of city states as flowpipes.

Step 5: To verify the safety of the predicted performance with different set of COAs, we formalize safety and security requirements using STL-U. Below are some examples of requirements:

- R1: The sensing coverage should not be reduced to less than 50% per block.
- R2: Any lane on the main street should not be closed for more than 2 h.
- R3: From location A to B, there should be at least more than 1 lane unblocked.
- R4: At least 80% of signal lights should maintain active status.
- R5: Pedestrians should not be blocked at an intersection for more than 10 min.
- R6: No system compromise should be caused by COAs.

Step 6: We verify the flowpipes against all the formalized requirements and return satisfaction degrees with confidence guarantees. Then we find the optimal solution by comparing the verification results. In cases that none of the options satisfy all the requirements, we present the dashboard of trade-offs with violation degrees (as shown in Fig. 8.9) to the decision makers.

Fig. 8.9 An example dashboard displaying the trade-off between three resolution options in terms of the percentage of time violating R1–R4

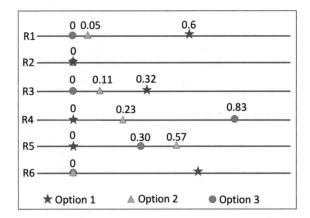

8.2   Recovery Scenario 2

Different from the first recovery scenario, which focuses on the random attacks after they are detected, in the second recovery scenario, we present how to make recovery plans for potential attacks before special city events. The city infrastructure, traffic, and communication networks are vulnerable to attacks at the same time. In advance of the attacks, it is of great significance to anticipate and prepare recovery plans to deal with potential attacks.

Assuming there is a football game on campus on Friday, city planners will make special arrangements for the traffic and parking to handle a large number of audiences. For example, some bi-direction lanes are changed to single-direction lanes, some streets are blocked, and important routes are constrained for emergency usage only.

In this scenario, the goal of our system is to support the city to prevent potential attacks from happening or prepare recovery plans to mitigate the influence of unavoidable attacks. To start with, taking advantage of our SURE simulator, we first generate simulation scenarios using real-world data (e.g., traffic volume, pedestrians, city event policies, etc.) from past football games. Next, we simulate different types of cyber-attacks, physical attacks, HIL attacks, and combinations of them.

We first simulate the city under Denial-of-Service (DOS) attack on a traffic light at several key intersections (as shown in Fig. 8.8a). When simulating the attacks, we incorporate uncertainty under attack plans which generate several workflows (i.e., cyber scenarios) with random variables in their configurations. As a result, long queues of vehicles form in the lane where the traffic light remains "Red." Since the traffic is already under stress due to the football game, the DOS attack worsens the situation. Next, the recovery agents react to this attack and generate COAs for our system to evaluate. As shown in Table 8.2, potential COAs may include,

- Switch the traffic light to default controller which turns light into 'blinking-yellow' state.
- Divert the incoming traffic in alternate routes, while fixing and restoring the traffic light damaged by the attack.
- Deploy security mechanisms on city traffic lights to prevent future attacks.

Different from Scenario 1, the system also considers long-term plans to prevent multiple future attacks and their combinations using attack COAs. Following the steps in Recovery Scenario 1, we verify and identify the optimal set of COAs for recovery. Similarly, we simulate and test the other types of attacks in Table 8.1 and generate optimal COAs for them. The goal is to improve the readiness of critical infrastructures to handle future, potential attacks.

We continue running the system to detect and generate recovery plans for security attacks during the event. With the precautions implemented, some types (or combinations) of attacks that have been tested under this particular context should be prevented or detected easily. The system proceeds for unseen types of attacks as presented in Recovery Scenario 1.

In summary, the recovery scenarios demonstrate the effectiveness of our system in recovery planning. It supports the city in finding the optimal COAs to recover from the attacks and prepares the city for potential attacks ahead of time.

9 Summary and Conclusion

This chapter discusses the problem, challenges, and solutions of recovery planning in cyber-physical systems. There is a high demand for an autonomous intelligent cyber defense agent for planning a rapid recovery. When the threat has been neutralized or deactivated, AICA will attempt to return the system to adequate working conditions through the most appropriate COAs. However, it is challenging to automatically identify the optimal COAs in recovery planning for cyber-physical systems due to the complex safety and security requirements and uncertainty in the impact of different sets of COAs. In this chapter, we first show various aspects of recovery planning regarding cyber-physical systems, including device recovery, communication system recovery, and data recovery. Targeting these challenges, many recovery techniques have been developed for each aspect. We discuss how several essential techniques - simulation, prediction with machine learning, and formal methods – support evaluating recovery plans and making recovery decisions.

Furthermore, we create a system for recovery planning using simulation-based predictive monitoring to recover the system from attacks (cyber, physical, or hardware) and disruptions automatically. The recovery planning system first evaluates the impact of system degradation and generates recovery courses of actions (COAs) efficiently. Then, it evaluates recovery COAs through integrated heterogeneous simulations considering uncertainty. By formalizing security and safety requirements, it formally verifies recovery COAs with confidence guarantees, and obtains the optimal recovery COAs. We present two recovery scenarios in smart cities to demonstrate the effectiveness of our recovery planning system.

In the future, we envision extending the recovery planning systems in several ways. First, we will consider adding new attacks in our attack libraries to be able to test for system's resilience more widely. Secondly, we plan to incorporate deep learning models for prediction (data-driven) and integrate it with integrated simulations allowing us to develop autonomous monitoring agents capable of detecting deviations in observed traffic patterns and generating advance alarms for initiating recovery planning. Finally, we envision scaling up the system capabilities to develop it into a real-time autonomous decision-making system which can form the foundation of creating a fully autonomous intelligent agent deployed for resilience and recovery in the real-world.

References

Akbar, A., Khan, A., Carrez, F., & Moessner, K. (2017). Predictive analytics for complex IoT data streams. *IEEE Internet of Things Journal, 4*, 1571–1582. https://doi.org/10.1109/JIOT.2017.2712672

Al-Hamadi, H., & Chen, I. R. (2017). Trust-based decision making for health IoT systems. *IEEE Internet of Things Journal, 4*. https://doi.org/10.1109/JIOT.2017.2736446

Chong, S., Guttman, J., Datta, A., et al. (2016). Report on the NSF workshop on formal methods for security. arXiv preprint arXiv:160800678.

Christakou, C., Vrettos, S., & Stafylopatis, A. (2007). A hybrid movie recommender system based on neural networks. *International Journal on Artificial Intelligence Tools, 16*. https://doi.org/10.1142/S0218213007003540

Fekade, B., Maksymyuk, T., Kyryk, M., & Jo, M. (2018). Probabilistic recovery of incomplete sensed data in IoT. *IEEE Internet of Things Journal, 5*. https://doi.org/10.1109/JIOT.2017.2730360

Gurobi. (2021). *Gurobi optimization*. https://www.gurobi.com/

Han, S. N., Lee, G. M., Crespi, N., et al. (2014). DPWSim: A simulation toolkit for IoT applications using devices profile for web services. In *2014 IEEE World Forum on Internet of Things, WF-IoT 2014*.

IEEE Std 1516-2010. (2010). IEEE Standard for Modeling and Simulation (M&S) High Level Architecture (HLA) – Framework and Rules.

Indiana State Government. (2021). *Disaster recovery – Indiana Office of Technology*. https://www.in.gov/iot/security/disaster-recovery/

Issariyakul, T., & Hossain, E. (2012). Introduction to network simulator NS2.

Kim, S., Eun, Y., & Park, K. J. (2021). Stealthy sensor attack detection and real-time performance recovery for resilient CPS. *IEEE Transactions on Industrial Informatics, 17*, 7412–7422. https://doi.org/10.1109/TII.2021.3052182

Kott, A., & Theron, P. (2020). Doers, not watchers: Intelligent autonomous agents are a path to cyber resilience. *IEEE Security and Privacy, 18*, 62–66. https://doi.org/10.1109/MSEC.2020.2983714

Koutsoukos, X., Karsai, G., Laszka, A., et al. (2018). SURE: A modeling and simulation integration platform for evaluation of SecUre and REsilient cyber-physical systems. *Proceedings of the IEEE, 106*, 93–112. https://doi.org/10.1109/JPROC.2017.2731741

Krajzewicz, D., Erdmann, J., Behrisch, M., & Bieker, L. (2012). Recent development and applications of {SUMO – Simulation of Urban MObility}. *International Journal on Advances in Systems and Measurements, 5*, 128–138.

Li, N., Liu, D., & Nepal, S. (2017). Lightweight mutual authentication for IoT and its applications. *IEEE Transactions on Sustainable Computing, 2*, 359–370. https://doi.org/10.1109/TSUSC.2017.2716953

Ma, M., Stankovic, J. A., & Feng, L. (2018). Cityresolver: A decision support system for conflict resolution in smart cities. In *2018 ACM/IEEE 9th International Conference on Cyber-Physical Systems (ICCPS)*.

Ma, M., Stankovic, J., Bartocci, E., & Feng, L. (2021). Predictive monitoring with logic-calibrated uncertainty for cyber-physical systems. *ACM Transactions on Embedded Computing Systems, 20*, 1–25.

Maróti, M., Kecskés, T., & Kereskényi, R., et al. (2014). Next generation (Meta)modeling: Web- and cloud-based collaborative tool infrastructure. In *CEUR workshop proceedings*.

Matlabworks Simulink is for Model-Based Design. https://www.mathworks.com/products/simulink.html

Min, S. H., & Han, I. (2005). *Recommender systems using support vector machines*. In Web Engineering: 5th International Conference, ICWE 2005, Sydney, Australia, July 27–29, 2005. Proceedings 5, pp. 387–393. Springer Berlin Heidelberg.

Mohsin, M., Anwar, Z., Husari, G., et al. (2017). IoTSAT: A formal framework for security analysis of the internet of things (IoT). In *2016 IEEE Conference on Communications and Network Security, CNS 2016*.

Neema, H. (2018). Large-scale integration of heterogeneous simulations. PhD Dissertation, Vanderbilt University.

Neema, H., Potteiger, B., Koutsoukos, X., et al. (2018). Integrated simulation testbed for security and resilience of CPS. In *Proceedings of the ACM symposium on applied computing*.

Neema, H., Sztipanovits, J., Steinbrink, C., et al. (2019). Simulation integration platforms for cyber-physical systems. In *DESTION 2019 – proceedings of the workshop on design automation for CPS and IoT*.

Österlind, F., Dunkels, A., Eriksson, J., et al. (2006). Cross-level sensor network simulation with COOJA. In *Proceedings – Conference on Local Computer Networks, LCN*.

Piccialli, F., Casolla, G., Cuomo, S., et al. (2020). Decision making in IoT environment through unsupervised learning. *IEEE Intelligent Systems, 35*. https://doi.org/10.1109/MIS.2019.2944783

Spinellis, D. (2012). Git. *IEEE Software, 29*, 100–101.

Sridhar, S., & Smys, S. (2017). Intelligent security framework for IoT devices: Cryptography based end-to-end security architecture. In *Proceedings of the International Conference on Inventive Systems and Control, ICISC 2017*.

Varga, A. (2019). A practical introduction to the OMNeT++ simulation framework. In: A. Virdis, & M. Kirsche (eds) *Recent Advances in Network Simulation. EAI/Springer Innovations in Communication and Computing.* Springer, Cham. https://doi.org/10.1007/978-3-030-12842-5_1.

Westergaard, M., & Kristensen, L. M. (2009). *The access/CPN framework: A tool for interacting with the CPN tools simulator*. In Applications and Theory of Petri Nets: 30th International Conference, PETRI NETS 2009, Paris, France, June 22–26, 2009. Proceedings 30, pp. 313–322. Springer Berlin Heidelberg.

Woo, M. W., Lee, J. W., & Park, K. H. (2018). A reliable IoT system for Personal Healthcare Devices. *Future Generation Computer Systems, 78*, 626–640. https://doi.org/10.1016/j.future.2017.04.004

Zhang, D., Wang, Y., Suh, G. E., & Myers, A. C. (2015). A hardware design language for timing-sensitive information-flow security. *ACM SIGPLAN Notices, 50*, 503–516. https://doi.org/10.1145/2775054.2694372

Chapter 9
Strategic Cyber Camouflage

Christopher Kiekintveld, Aron Laszka, Mohammad Sujan Miah, Shanto Roy, and Nazia Sharmin

1 Introduction

From the earliest history of conflict, stealth and deception tactics have been a critical way to gain strategic advantage on the battlefield. While the details vary, the goal is always to control the information space, preventing the adversary from gaining useful information and creating false or misleading beliefs in some cases. Camouflage is one example of this; it has a long history of use in physical environments as a method to make the presence or actions of an entity difficult to detect against the backdrop of the environment. In cyber warfare the control of information is even more central, and the ability to perform (or hinder) effective reconnaissance will likely be decisive in many engagements. Therefore, developing effective methods for implementing and strategically deploying camouflage in a cyber context is an important research objective for cyber operations.

In the particular context of an Autonomous Intelligent Cyber-defense Agent (AICA), we identify three primary reasons why cyber-camouflage techniques are important:

C. Kiekintveld (✉) · M. S. Miah · N. Sharmin
University of Texas at El Paso, El Paso, TX, USA
e-mail: cdkiekintveld@utep.edu; msmiah@miners.utep.edu; nsharmin@miners.utep.edu

A. Laszka
College of Information Sciences and Technology, Pennsylvania State University,
University Park, PA, USA
e-mail: aql5923@psu.edu

S. Roy
University of Houston, Houston, TX, USA
e-mail: shantoroy@ieee.org

- An AICA may be tasked with implementing and deploying camouflage actions for a network or individual host to make reconnaissance more difficult for the adversary
- An AICA may need to conceal it's own presence or actions from the adversary to evade detection
- An AICA may need to detect and identify threats that are using camouflage tactics to conceal their own activities, so the agent would need to be able to mitigate camouflage tactics of the opponent

In this chapter we present an overview of some common methods for implementing camouflage tactics in the cyber environment. We then present some basic mathematical frameworks based in game theory that have been developed to model the strategic aspects of how to use and optimize camouflage in the cyber environment. We go into detail on three particular models. The first two use game theory to formulate specific optimization problems, and the last one shows how we can extend these models using machine learning to implement more effective decoy objects (e.g., honeypots or fake traffic) that are difficult for adversaries to detect. Finally, we review some of the ways in which camouflage (and more generally, deception methods) have been evaluated so far in the research literature. While we cannot cover all of the important topics on cyber-camouflage here, we present some fundamental concepts and models that can be adapted to address many key challenges for AICA, and provide references for additional study.

2   Implementing Camouflage

The goal of cyber camouflage is to take actions that make the presence, actions, and intentions of systems or artificial agents more difficult for an adversary to correctly perceive. This can be achieved using a wide variety of specific techniques for manipulating information depending on the context and objectives. We begin by introducing some representative methods from the literature for implementing camouflage at a technical level to give a sense of what types of actions can potentially be used to manipulate the information space. We focus our discussion on two broad categories of actions: obfuscation (hiding information) and deploying decoys (a form of deception). More thorough coverage and discussion can be found in related survey articles (e.g., Han et al., 2018; Fraunholz et al., 2018).

2.1   Obfuscation Techniques

One of the most basic goals for cyber camouflage for AICA agents is to conceal the presence of an agent in the first place, or to conceal specific actions or objectives. Cyber attackers use a wide variety of methods to conceal their activities, such as stealthy scanning, obfuscated malware, obfuscated command and control communications, and specific actions to cover the tracks of an attack. Many of these are also relevant for cyber defense to make it more difficult for attackers to perform basic system reconnaissance as well as to conceal the nature of cyber defenses. However, cyber defense has typically placed less emphasis on effective conceal-ment and obfuscation of information for several reasons, including potential impacts on legitimate users, the complexity of implementing such strategies broadly on a network, and the desire not to rely entirely on obfuscation for security. However, as automated agents for both attack and defense become more sophisticated, it is both possible and necessary to focus more attention on defensive obfuscation to gain advantages early in the cyber kill chain by hindering attacker reconnaissance and planning efforts Hosseinzadeh et al. (2015). We now briefly introduce some existing methods for defensive obfuscation at different levels.

Network Layer Basic properties of the network topology and configuration can be obscured by manipulating the data plane in various ways to limit the accuracy of passive and active network scanning methods. This can include intercepting and modifying path tracing probes directly Meier et al. (2018), route obfuscation utiliz-ing ranking-based route mutation Bin-Yahya and Shen (2022), utilizing honey links and hiding important links in a large network Liu et al. (2021), delaying identified probe packets to hinder Network Topology Inference Hou et al. (2020), etc. New methods for obfuscation are actively being developed that make use of AI tech-niques such as adversarial machine learning to more effectively obfuscate the char-acteristics of network traffic Verma et al. (2018), Datta et al. (2018).

System Layer Attackers also use fingerprinting methods to identify specific soft-ware or configuration details for individual systems, such as operating system ver-sions. Information is often leaked by protocols and services, but information can be either redacted or modified to limit or mislead fingerprinting attempts (Anderson & McGrew, 2017; Hosseinzadeh et al., 2015).

Application Layer The application layer encompasses many different applica-tions that could be running on a host, as well as their configurations, associated data, and user activities. This includes security applications, including AICA agents. Examples of application-level obfuscation include the framework proposed by Perez et al. that identifies and obfuscates user data using metadata and related obfus-cation strategies (Perez et al., 2018). Software or application data can also be obfus-cated level by level to achieve layered security (Xu et al., 2020). Other examples have used adversarial learning to obscure data without compromising semantic attributes (Bertran et al., 2019).

2.2 Decoy Technologies

Moving beyond obfuscation, deception methods aim to explicitly create false beliefs, rather than just hiding or changing the characteristics of existing systems or data. One of the most common forms of deception is using decoy objects (e.g., host, files, tokens, etc.) that can be used to distract and confuse attackers, as well as to improve detection and monitoring of malicious activities (Rauti & Leppanen, 2017). Han et al. provides a layered categorization for different deception techniques (Han et al., 2018). Effectively deploying decoys may be an important task for AICA agents, who may also do this dynamically in response to detected attacker activities (e.g., deploying a new honeynet in response to specific scanning activities). AICA agents may also use decoys to try to distract opponents from their own presence or activities.

Network Layer Network traffic sniffing, scanning, and fingerprinting major attacks in the network layer, which involve capturing and analyzing existing network packets, or generating malicious and fingerprinting packets. The system can deceive the attacker by redirecting attack traffic (e.g., ICMP/TCP packets) to a honey network or fake virtual machines (Sharma & Kaul, 2018), generating vulnerability-driven honey traffic to prevent optimal fingerprinting or packet analysis (Anjum et al., 2020), etc. These methods may also lead the attacker to form incorrect beliefs and plan ineffective attacks or target fake systems rather than real ones.

System Layer Attackers typically want to compromise internal systems one after another and plan for the next attacks. To deceive adversaries from attacking a real system, honeypots are widely used in the industry. A honeypot is a fake system that may or may not resemble the original hosts. Recent applications of honeypot include VANET Cloud (Sharma & Kaul, 2018), industrial cyberphysical systems (Sun et al., 2020), real-time intrusion detection (Baykara & Das, 2018), defending IoT based botnet DDoS attacks (Vishwakarma & Jain, 2019; Du & Wang, 2019), capturing CPE and IoT zero days (Vetterl & Clayton, 2019), and classifying botnet attacks (Lee et al., 2021).

Application Layer Application layer reconnaissance includes software and application vulnerability scanning. Both native and web-based applications are targeted by the attackers. Several fake entities of software and applications can be utilized to detect and monitor malicious activity (Rauti & Leppanen, 2017). Software decoys are widely used to prevent counter-intelligence (Ferguson-Walter et al., 2021). Other application-level decoys include honeytokens (Ferguson-Walter et al., 2019), honeypermissions for insider threat detection (Kaghazgaran & Takabi, 2015), and honeyfiles such as automated decoy documents (Voris et al., 2015).

3   Optimizing Camouflage Strategies

We have given some examples of specific actions and tactics that can be used to achieve the broad goals of cyber camouflage. Now we turn to the question of how to deploy these camouflage techniques and actions *effectively*, taking into account the costs and possible impacts on resource utilization, activities of real users, etc. The details of these decisions will vary depending on the purpose of the camouflage, the techniques being used, specific costs and constraints, and assumptions about the adversary. However, the literature provides a set of fundamental principles, models, and algorithms that are abstract enough that they can be used for decision support and automation across a broad range of cyber camouflage and deception situations. We now introduce some basic models for optimizing cyber camouflage decisions using game theoretic models, and provide references for further reading on more advanced models.

3.1 Optimizing Decoy Resource Allocation

One area where game-theoretic approaches have been very successful in finding optimal strategies for allocating limited deceptive resources to detect and distract attackers (Carroll & Grosu, 2011; Kiekintveld et al., 2015). One example is the *Honeypot Selection Game* (HSG) (Píbil et al., 2012; Kiekintveld et al., 2015) that models the problem of allocating honeypots to a network. In a real network, not all systems are equally important. A database server may be much more valuable than a user laptop or mobile device. A strategy for deploying honeypots should take this into account when deciding what kinds of systems to create as decoys. The HFG model uses a zero-sum game to optimize the importance values of honeypots to deploy to increase the likelihood that an attacker will target a honeypot rather than a real system. Durkota et al. (2015) extends this model by using attack graphs to determine the attacker's optimal attack plans against the defender strategy, where the defender strategy modifies the attack graph by adding honeypots to interdict attacker actions. The attack graphs allow the attacker to attack sequentially, with costs and probabilities of success or failure associated with each attempt. Anwar et al. (2021) also determine the optimal strategy for deploying honeypots on the attack graphs in a dynamic environment where the attacker and defender interact and can make changes based on observations of the other player. Wang et al. (2017) uses Bayesian games to explore honeypot strategies in the smart grid to prevent denial of service attacks. La et al. (2016) also optimizes honeypot deployment for mitigating denial-of-service attacks in the Internet-of-Things domain. Du et al. (2017) uses Bayesian game modeling to solve a similar problem for honeypots in the social networking domain. Anjum et al. (2020) use a Stackelberg game to deploy honey flows (fake network traffic) optimally to confuse the attacker in distinguishing real and fake vulnerabilities.

3.2   Optimizing Feature Obfuscation

In addition to deploying deceptive objects, there is also a significant body of work in optimizing strategies to obfuscate features of particular objects. This can be used both to make more effective decoys (by making them look more realistic) and to disguise or camouflage real objects (by hiding information or making them look fake). For example, and AICA agent may want to disguise the features of a binary or network traffic to make it look like a normal application.

The Cyber Deception Game (CDG) (Schlenker et al., 2018) computes an optimal deception strategy for concealing specific characteristics of network hosts. This game focuses on invalidating an attacker's information in the reconnaissance phase by deciding what signals the defender wants to send about the type of the host. The defender can respond with obfuscated messages when the attacker probes network hosts, but the model is limited to zero-sum settings. The Cyber Camouflage Games (CCG) (Thakoor et al., 2019) extends the CDG model by considering a general-sum setting. This model also considers uncertainties in the defender's knowledge of the attacker's valuations of different network hosts. Miah et al. (2020) present a Bayesian game model to find the optimal strategy for obfuscating the observable characteristics of either real or fake objects, making it difficult to distinguish between them. Guan et al. (2001) camouflages payload traffic components, such as the communication system, location, diversity of hosts, network topology, etc., such that their pattern is unrelated to the operational status of applications to an observer. However, this method is inefficient and can result in significant network overhead.

While there are various methods for obfuscating network traffic, Ciftcioglu et al. (2017) use a game model to obfuscate network traffic, considering that defender has limited resources and obfuscation has network overhead. The water-filling algorithm is another efficient method for finding traffic obfuscation strategies for a given budget (Ciftcioglu et al., 2018). Machine learning methods have also been used for optimizing feature obfuscation, making use of the gradient of the loss function for generating a perturbation (Carlini & Wagner, 2017; Szegedy et al., 2013). Verma et al. (2018) present an adversarial machine learning approach that uses a post-processing procedure on the resulting distributions to manipulate network traffic. However, the proposed method sometimes generates incorrect perturbations and does not correspond to real-world scenarios. Granados et al. (2020) impose more generalized constraints for obfuscating traffic samples and generate valid perturbation and distribution.

4   Example Methods for Optimizing Camouflage

This section presents three examples of cyber camouflage optimization techniques from the literature in more detail. The first model determines an optimal strategy for disguising network configurations using a game-theoretic model for optimizing signaling strategies. The second model uses game theory to determine how to modify individual features of both real and deceptive objects to make them more effective as decoys, or confusing real objects. The final approach brings in a different set of techniques in machine learning to address similar questions of how to modify features in a more scalable way. All of these models can be generalized to different cyber camouflage problems by considering different action spaces and objective functions.

4.1 Disguising Network Attributes

A network topology comprises multiple systems, each with it's own set of attributes such as the operating system, running services, antivirus protection measures, etc. A system's true configuration (TC) could be any combination of these attributes, and systems have different TCs. An attacker can employ network scanning to learn about each system's characteristics before attempting to exploit a target. This reconnaissance reveals potential weak points, such as open ports, operating services, subnetworks, user information, etc. Then the attacker uses specific vulnerability information to find a strategy for system exploitation. However, if the network defender obfuscates the information collected by an attacker, the likelihood of a successful attack decreases. A defender can benefit from using a combination of truthful, false, and obscured responses to the attacker's network probes. For example, consider a network with one system running NGINX web serber and two systems running a Tomcat proxy server. The attacker has a specific NGINX exploit and examines all systems using NGINX before deploying the exploit. If the defender can deceive the attacker about the webserver, the attacker needs to exploit all systems to infiltrate the network. The attacker's network infiltration is delayed by this deception strategy, giving the defender more time to detect an attack. The defender might also use deception techniques to reveal parts of a system's observable attributes that are not true configuration, such as changing the TCP/IP stack or spoofing a running service on a port. Determining deception strategies to alter an attacker's perception is challenging for the defender and also associated with cost.

Cyber Deception Game The Cyber Deception Game (CDG) (Schlenker et al., 2018) addresses this problem and determines the optimal strategies to optimize the defender's deception strategy. The CDG is a two-player zero-sum Stackelberg game between a defender and an attacker. The defender moves as a leader and determines how to respond to the attacker's scanning activity. The attacker moves as a follower and chooses a system to attack based on the observations. The model assumes that when an attacker probes a system, the defender controls the attacker's perception of observed configuration (OC). Masking a true configuration TC with an OC incurs a cost for the defender. The true configuration TC of a system is associated with a utility that is the attacker's reward and an equal loss for the defender. Therefore, the defender's objective is to determine optimal strategies to mask TCs with OCs to minimize the attacker's expected utility while considering deception costs. The following is a formal description of the game notation:

- χ and $\bar{\chi}$ represents all possible TCs and OCs respectively.
- The true state of the network (TSN) is a vector $v = (v_x)_{x\in\chi}$, where v_x is the number of systems on the network with a TC $x \in \chi$.
- Similarly, the attacker's observed state of the network (OSN) is a vector $\bar{v} = (\bar{v}_{\bar{x}})_{\bar{x}\in\bar{\chi}}$. Here, two systems with the same $\bar{x}$ as their OC are indistinguishable from the attacker's perspective.
- Λ is the feasibility constraint as a (0,1)-matrix that defines whether or not x can be masked with $\bar{x}$, with 1 denoting feasibility.
- $\zeta(x, \bar{x})$ denotes the defender cost of masking a TC x with an OC $\bar{x}$

Defender Strategies The CDG considers that the defender knows the TSN, all possible TCs and OCs, costs, total budget and feasibility constraints. The defender strategy Θ is to determine how many of the v_x systems having TC x, should be assigned to the OC $\bar{x}$. Therefore, all possible strategies are a $|\chi| \times |\bar{\chi}|$ matrix where $\Theta_{x,\bar{x}}$ representing the number of systems having TC x is masked with OC $\bar{x}$. Θ must satisfy the following constraints:

- Any entry $\Theta_{x,\bar{x}}$ of $|\chi| \times |\bar{\chi}|$ matrix must be a non-negative integer
- The total number of systems having any TC x and OC $\bar{x}$ must be equal to v_x since the CDG assumes that the TSN v_x is fixed.
- The Θ must satisfy feasibility constraints. The defender is not allowed to mask any TC x with any OC $\bar{x}$ if the entry $\Lambda_{x,\bar{x}}$ of (0,1)-matrix Λ is 0.
- Finally, the total masking cost must be less than or equal to the cost budget.

Attacker's Strategies Following the defender's move, the attacker observes the OSN $\bar{v}$ and tries to attack the OC $\bar{x}$ that gives the highest expected utility. The attacker is indifferent in attempting an attack against all such $\bar{v}_{\bar{x}}$ because all the systems with the same OC $\bar{x}$, are indistinguishable. Therefore, when he selects an OC $\bar{x}$, he means that he attacks all systems with an OC $\bar{x}$ with the same probability.

Utility The defender aims to protect a set of systems Ns from potential exploits where each system is associated with a utility that is the attacker's reward for attacking it. This utility depends on the TC of a system where Ψ_x denotes the utility of each $x \in \chi$. The Ψ_x might be negative when a system's security level is high, or the attacker receives incorrect information. If the defender's strategy is Θ, the attacker's expected utility $\bar{\Psi}_{\bar{x}}$ for attacking an OC $\bar{x}$ with $\bar{v}_{x>\bar{0}}$ is defined by:

$$\bar{\Psi}_{\bar{x}} = \sum_{x\in\chi} \frac{\Theta_{x,\bar{x}}}{\bar{v}_{\bar{x}}} \Psi_x$$

The equation denotes that $\bar{v}_{\bar{x}}$ systems having an OC $\bar{x}$, $\Theta_{x,\bar{x}}$ have a TC x. When the attacker attacks $\bar{x}$, the defender's expected utility is $-\bar{\Psi}_{\bar{x}}$ since the game is zero-sum. Here, the attacker is restricted to attack an OC $\bar{x}$ when $\bar{v}_{\bar{x}} = 0$ because it leads his expected utility to $-\infty$.

Small Example Figure 9.1 shows a example of a small network that comprises a set of systems $N = \{n_1, n_2, n_3, n_4\}$, a set of TCs $\chi = \{x_1, x_2, x_3\}$ (Shown in Fig. 9.1 as the gray boxes) and set of OCs $\bar{\chi} = \{\bar{x}_1, \bar{x}_2\}$ (Shown in Fig. 9.1 as the blue boxes). Let $\chi_{\bar{x}1} = \{x_1, x_2\}$ and $\chi_{\bar{x}2} = \{x_2, x_3\}$ be feasibility constraints sets. According to Fig. 9.1, the following are the TCs:

$$x_1 = \left[[os]L, [web]N, [files]S \right] x_2$$
$$= \left[[os]W, [web]T, [files]I \right] x_3$$
$$= \left[[os]W, [web]T, [files]P \right]$$

Also, the following are the OCs:

$$\bar{x}_1 = \left[[os]L, [web]T \right]$$
$$\bar{x}_2 = \left[[os]W, [web]N \right]$$

Let the utilities be $\Psi_{x1} = 5$, $\Psi_{x2} = 0$, and $\Psi_{x3} = 6$. For simplicity, let all the costs $\zeta((x, \bar{x}))$ be 0 with no budget constraint. According to Fig. 9.1, the true state of the network $(v_x)_{x \in \chi}$ is $(2, 1, 1)$, and the defender strategy Θ is given by

$$\bar{x}_1 \bar{x}_2$$
$$x_1^{"} \; 2 \; 0 \#$$
$$x_2 \; 0 \; 1 \; x_3 \; 0 \; 1$$

Now, if the attacker attempts to attack $\bar{x}_1$, his expected utility is $\bar{\Psi}_{\bar{x}1} = (2 \times 5)/2 = 5$. On the other hand, the expected utility of attacking $\bar{x}_2$ is $\bar{\Psi}_{\bar{x}2} = (0 + 6)/2 = 3$. Therefore, attacking $\bar{x}_1$ is the best response for the attacker and the defender loses an equal amount.

4.2   Feature Selection Game

The Feature Selection Game (FSG) (Miah et al., 2020) addresses a different aspect of the camouflage problem, deciding how exactly to modify the features of real or fake objects to achieve a specific goal (e.g., making fake objects appear more realistic). The FSG is modeled as a general-sum two-player extensive form imperfect information game between an attacker and defender. The defender's goal is to strategically modify both real and fake objects so that the attacker can't tell the difference. Objects are associated with observable feature vectors that can provide useful

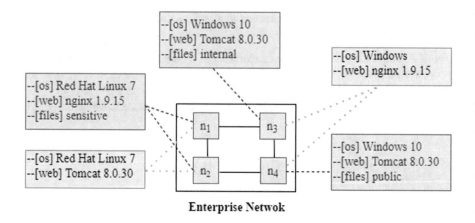

--[os] Windows 10
--[web] Tomcat 8.0.30
--[files] internal

--[os] Windows
--[web] nginx 1.9.15

--[os] Red Hat Linux 7
--[web] nginx 1.9.15
--[files] sensitive

--[os] Red Hat Linux 7
--[web] Tomcat 8.0.30

--[os] Windows 10
--[web] Tomcat 8.0.30
--[files] public

n_1 — n_3

n_2 — n_4

Enterprise Netwok

Fig. 9.1 Example of an enterprise network

information to the attackers, allowing them to distinguish objects more accurately. To make classification difficult, the defender changes the observable features of real and fake samples, which we call 2-sided deception. The FSG can be formally defined by the tuple $FSG = (K, v^r, v^h, P^r, P^f, \tau, \chi)$. Here, K represents the complete set of real and fake samples. P^r and P^f are the probability distributions over feature vectors of real and fake samples where the nature player generates the configurations based on these distributions. Samples $x_r = (x_1, \ldots, x_k)_k$ are generated according to the joint distribution P^x where $P^x(x) = \prod_{i=1}^{r} P^r(x_i) \times \prod_{i=r+1}^{k} P^f(x_i)$. The defender examines a sample $x \in X$, where X represents all possible samples, and then takes steps to change each object's features. An action $d \in D$ results a new configuration $x' \in X$, which the attacker observes and uses as an information set $I \in \tau$. In each I, the attacker perceives any permutation of configurations in the same way. Therefore, he cannot reliably detect real and fake objects in a feature vector. The data set for the attacker is the all possible combinations of object configurations where attacker's action a' is to detect real and fake objects in each information set I.

The utility functions in this game are calculated based on the importance values of the objects and the cost of changing the features. The attacker gets positive rewards when he correctly detects real and fake objects, but he receives a penalty for misclassifying. In particular, if an attacker's action a in the information set I corresponds to a real object, then the utility function $U(x,j,a) = v^r$, whereas, if it corresponds to a fake object, then $U(x,j,a) = -v^f$ where v^r and v^f are the importance values for real and fake objects, respectively. The defender loses the same amount as the attacker's positive reward, but the situation is reversed when the attacker misclassifies. This part of the utility function represents the zero-sum component of the game. However, the defender need to pay additional cost to change the characteristics, which makes the game model non-zerosum. The defender's action in a sample x that produces an information set I, where different actions in different network samples can result in the same I. Then, in each $I \in \tau$, the attacker plays the best response where the defender's objective is to maximize his utility, considering feature modification costs. In principle, the FSG game allows us to determine optimal camouflage strategies for the defender to modify the appearance of different objects. However, in practice this model has limited scalability due the exponential growth in the strategy spaces as the number of features grows. This leads us to consider a machine learning variation that can approximate this type of strategy in the next section.

4.3 Two-Sided Feature Deception Using Adversarial Learning

The Two-Sided Generative Adversarial Network (TS-GAN) solves the two-sided feature deception problem in a complex and large feature space by using adversarial learning techniques. It generates fake samples that look like real samples and real samples that look like fake samples. This model consists of two parts: the attacker and the defender. The defender contains two modules, and both are neural networks. One of the networks is a generator that generates fake data, which is represented as G_θ with θ parameters. The G_θ uses a latent space z from an l-dimensional spherical Gaussian distribution P_g to create a fake sample $x' = G_\theta(z)$. It learns to estimate the distribution from which the real training data is drawn to generate fake samples. The objective of G_θ is to minimize the probability of a generated sample being detected as fake by the attacker. The defender's second neural network is the Obfuscator, which refers to O_θ with θ parameters. The O_θ takes the original instance x as input and generates a perturbation $O_\theta(x)$. The dimensions of the input data and output perturbed data of this network are identical. Then $x + O_\theta(x)$ will be passed to the attacker. The learning goal of O_θ is to create a perturbed adversarial example that is indistinguishable from a fake sample.

The attacker or Discriminator (D_θ) is also a neural network and learns to detect as well as possible between the real and fake samples. The problem can be formulated as follows: Let $(x_1, \ldots, x_n)$ represent the training instances and (x_i, y_i) is the ith instance in the training set, which is made up of feature vectors $x_i \in \chi$ where $\chi \subseteq R^n$ represents the feature space and y_i corresponding real class label (1). Also, let $G_\theta(z_1), \ldots, G_\theta(z_r)$ be a collection of r examples from the generated distribution Pg that are corresponding fake class label (0) and represented by ($x'_1, \ldots, x'_n$) where.

$x'_i \in \chi$. Similarly, assume, $O_\theta(x_1), \ldots, O_\theta(x_n)$ is a set of perturbation generated from $(x_1, \ldots, x_n)$ where $x_i + O_\theta(x_i) = x^{adv}_i \in \chi$ is the ith adversarial example, such that $D_\theta(x^{adv}_i) = t$ (target attack) where t is the target class (0). The attacker's learning goal is to learn a classifier $D_\theta: \chi \to Y$ from the domain χ to the set of classification outputs $Y \in \{0, 1\}$, where $|Y|$ represents the number of classification outputs. Figure 9.2 shows the basic architecture of TS-GAN.

The TS-GAN model can be considered as a game between a defender and an attacker where the defender uses two networks G_θ and O_θ to minimize the detection

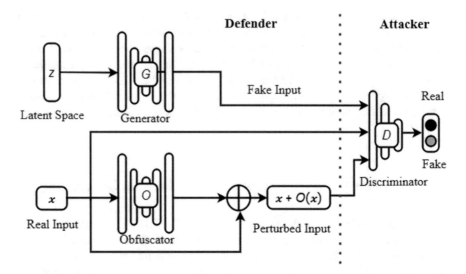

Fig. 9.2 Two-sided generative adversarial network architecture

success of the attacker and forms a minimax game between the attacker and the defender.

5 Evaluating Camouflage

We now discuss some general strategies for measuring and evaluating the effectiveness of cyber camouflage and deception. There are several frameworks for cyber camouflage that have evaluated their work based on effectiveness (e.g., optimal defender utility in game-theoretic models (Anwar et al., 2020, Miah et al., 2020), expected number of attacks deceived (Rawat et al., 2019)) and cost (e.g., reducing defender's cost (Anwar et al., 2020), deceived attacks with respect to deception deployment time (Rawat et al., 2019)). We divide the evaluation of camouflage models primarily based on two approaches: theoretical and experimental and discuss some metrics that have been used to evaluate existing models.

5.1 *Theoretical Evaluation*

Theoretical evaluation is one of the first steps in assessing the potential benefits of camouflage strategies. These evaluations assess performance within the context and assumptions of a particular model, and usually present an optimistic view of the potential impact in a realistic setting. They are relatively easy to do, and a useful first step in evaluating different approaches. We present some examples of these types of evaluation from the literature.

Non-game-Theoretic Evaluation Jajodia et al. argued that attackers could map system configurations (e.g., type of operating systems, applications, or services) for a particular node in the network (Jajodia et al., 2017). The authors propose a belief state model that considers an interval of probabilities for specific configurations and then tightens the interval over time. The authors proposed two algorithms (Naive-PLD and Fast-PLD) to keep the attacker away from the valuable nodes by answering a scan query that minimizes the damage. They estimated the average damage against the attacker's steps when applying these algorithms. Sugrim et al. utilize Bayesian inference to update the attacker's belief for an individual node property (e.g., IP address) (Sugrim et al., 2018). The authors quantified the attacker's updated belief over the increasing number of operations. They also measured the attacker's belief error, yield, and footprints.

Game-Theoretic Evaluation Game theoretic models evaluate each player's (attacker and defender) strategies, and current works focus on optimizing strategies for the defender. In a typical Cyber Camouflage Game, computing the optimal defender strategy is NP-hard (Thakoor et al., 2019; Milani et al., 2020), where the first model masks each machine with different observable configurations in a zero-sum game setting, and the second model alters the perceived structure of the attack graph, respectively. The authors proposed approximation algorithms (e.g., MILP, NAS, etc.) to calculate optimal defender strategies. Additionally, there are several honeypot allocation games over the attack graphs in cyber deception or camouflage games (Anwar et al., 2020).

Milani et al. quantified average defender utility for different proposed algorithms achieved against the number of nodes in the network (Milani et al., 2020). The authors compared the performances of these algorithms by calculating the average defender utility over time. One of the essential evaluation metrics is the run time of proposed algorithms to approximate an optimal solution and how these algorithms handle the scaling of a network. For example, a typical experiment could be quantifying the algorithm run time against the increasing size of the network (Anwar et al., 2020). Similarly, Thakoor et al. calculated the run time of the proposed MILP with cuts against the strategy space size. Another metric is each player's cost estimation. The goal is always to increase the attack cost or maintain the defender's cost as low as possible. For example, Anwar et al. estimated the defender reward at Nash Equilibrium (optimal allocation) and random allocation at different attack costs (Anwar et al., 2020).

Here, we show an example game-theoretic measurement presented by Miah et al. (2020), where the authors calculated defender's utility in different scenarios 3. The authors showed that the defender can benefit significantly through utilizing the two-sided feature deception model when the unmodifiable features are different in real and honeypot hosts. Figure 9.3a considers two-sided feature deception while calculating the defender's utility. Figure 9.3b presents a comparison between a

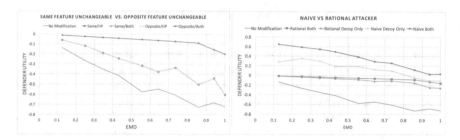

Fig. 9.3 Game-theoretic model evaluation (comparison of defender utility) (Miah et al., 2020). (**a**) When some features cannot be modified. (**b**) Naïve attacker versus a fully rational attacker

rational and naïve attacker. The author confirms that the best case is when the defender can perform two-sided deception against a naïve attacker and the worst case is when the defender ignores deception against a fully rational attacker.

5.2 Experimental Evaluation

Theoretical models may not always correspond to the results obtained from a real-world scenario for a variety of reasons. Therefore, it is important to also conduct evaluations using experiments in more realistic settings, ideally using real-world architectures, data, etc. as much as possible.

Automated Adversaries Automated evaluation depends on particular objectives in a predefined scenario, such as a particular type of attacker or a typical vulnerability/exploit choice. Simulation can be used to evaluate strategies based on a predefined automated attacker, which has the advantage of consistency and speed. For example, Rawat et al. evaluated performance of deception system for deceiving cyber adversaries in adaptive virtualized wireless networks (Rawat et al., 2019). The authors quantified the expected number of attacks and deceived attacks with respect to deception deployment time. They also plotted the successful attack time with respect to the deception deployment time.

Human Adversaries In many cases the ideal evaluation is done using humans, including penetration testers, read teams, or ethical hackers to evaluate the impact of strategies in a realistic scenario. Evaluation using humans can account for how humans may really make decisions (including imperfect ones), which could vary considerably from perfect models in cyber deception scenarios. However, human data is also limited and expensive, and humans can exhibit a wide variety of behaviors and their responses may depend heavily on background knowledge and expertise, especially in very technical domains.

Shade et al. performed an experimental evaluation of host-based deception that involved 30 participants in choosing any host to attack (Shade et al., 2020). The authors measured the ratio of successful task completion, the proportion of successful commands, and time to task completion. They also estimated the total time to complete, time wasted on decoys, reported surprises, etc.

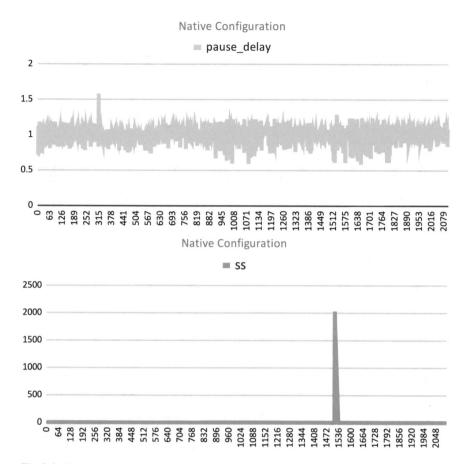

Fig. 9.4 Ping delays in Native configuration (Acosta et al., 2021)

Acosta et al. designed a cyber deception experimentation system (CDES) where the authors proposed an on-demand honeypot instantiation approach (Acosta et al., 2021). Here the honeypots are dynamically instantiated and presented before an identified attacker. They proposed three types of configurations: *no inst* configuration where the honey VM is instantiated beforehand, *pause resume* configuration where VMs are usually in a suspended state and activated only when resumed, and *save state* case where the VMs are offloaded, but their state is saved and restored based on the requirement. Figure 9.4 compares the ping delays using CDES in *pause resume* and *save state* configurations. Here, the the *Native* setup uses a separate laptop to run CDES. The authors also experimented with the *In-VM* setup, which uses the CORE emulator within a virtual machine. Later, the authors estimated the CPU and memory usage (Fig. 9.5) while executing these frameworks.

The primary goals of evaluating camouflage frameworks are to estimate optimal defender's strategy and cost while minimizing the affect in network or system

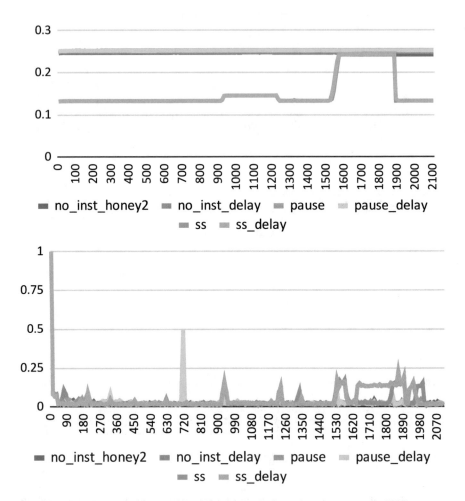

Fig. 9.5 Utilization during the execution of the three configurations (Acosta et al., 2021)

performance. Even though there are several theoretical models, it is necessary to test the effectiveness of the models or frameworks with experimental setups and human evaluation to evaluate outcomes in more realistic settings.

6   Summary and Conclusions

This chapter has discussed several different aspects of strategic cyber camouflage, including implementation, modeling, optimization, and evaluation. All of these are key considerations for an Autonomous Intelligent Cyber-defense Agent (AICA), both for taking actions to disguise a network and to conceal the activities of the

AICA agent. In the basic form, cyber camouflage is about hiding information from an adversary, making their reconnaissance less effective. However, more advanced forms can also use deception tactics to introduce false information and beliefs, such as the use of decoy objects (hosts, traffic, etc.) into a network. These tactics can all achieve goals including confusing the attacker and increasing uncertainty, delaying attacks, creating additional opportunities for detection, etc. An AICA can implement decoy and obfuscation technologies at different layers (network, system, and application) and can choose the best strategies based on an optimal solution. The game theory and machine learning models presented here are examples that can be used as the basis for implementing AI strategies for using camouflage, but they are only a starting point, and many additional factors can be taking into account in developing more advanced strategies. In addition, we have presented some initial evaluations but there is much work to be done to evaluate different cyber camouflage tactics deployed by real AICA agents in realistic networks, particularly in the presence of adversarial agents.

References

Acosta, J. C., Basak, A., Kiekintveld, C., & Kamhoua, C. A. (2021). Lightweight ondemand honeypot deployment for cyber deception. In *The 12th EAI International Conference on Digital Forensics & Cyber Crime (EAI ICDF2C), Singapore*.

Anderson, B., & McGrew, D. (2017). Os fingerprinting: New techniques and a study of information gain and obfuscation. In *2017 IEEE Conference on Communications and Network Security (CNS)* (pp. 1–9). IEEE.

Anjum, I., Miah, M. S., Zhu, M., Sharmin, N., Kiekintveld, C., Enck, W., & Singh, M. P. (2020). Optimizing vulnerability-driven honey traffic using game theory. *arXiv preprint*, arXiv:2002.09069.

Anwar, A. H., Kamhoua, C. A., & Leslie, N. (2020). Honeypot allocation over attack graphs in cyber deception games. In *2020 International Conference on Computing, Networking and Communications (ICNC)* (pp. 502–506). IEEE.

Anwar, A. H., Kamhoua, C. A., Leslie, N., & Kiekintveld, C. D. (2021). Honeypot allocation games over attack graphs for cyber deception. *Game theory and machine learning for cyber security* (pp. 62–76).

Baykara, M., & Das, R. (2018). A novel honeypot based security approach for real-time intrusion detection and prevention systems. *Journal of Information Security and Applications, 41*, 103–116.

Bertran, M., Martinez, N., Papadaki, A., Qiu, Q., Rodrigues, M., Reeves, G., & Sapiro, G. (2019). Adversarially learned representations for information obfuscation and inference. In *International conference on machine learning* (pp. 614–623). PMLR.

Manaf Bin-Yahya and Xuemin Shen. Secure and energy-efficient network topology obfuscation for software-defined wsns. IEEE Internet of Things Journal, 2022.

Carlini, N., & Wagner, D. (2017). Towards evaluating the robustness of neural networks. In *2017 IEEE symposium on security and privacy (sp)* (pp. 39–57). IEEE.

Carroll, T. E., & Grosu, D. (2011). A game theoretic investigation of deception in network security. *Security and Communication Networks, 4*(10), 1162–1172.

Ciftcioglu, E. N., Hardy, R. L., Scott, L. M., & Chan, K. S. (2017). Efficient chaff-aided obfuscation in resource constrained environments. In *MILCOM 2017-2017 IEEE Military Communications Conference (MILCOM)* (pp. 97–102). IEEE.

Ciftcioglu, E., Hardy, R., Chan, K., Scott, L., Oliveira, D., & Verma, G. (2018). Chaff allocation and performance for network traffic obfuscation. In *2018 IEEE 38th International Conference on Distributed Computing Systems (ICDCS)*.

Datta, T., Apthorpe, N., & Feamster, N. (2018). A developer-friendly library for smart home iot privacy-preserving traffic obfuscation. In *Proceedings of the 2018 workshop on IoT security and privacy* (pp. 43–48).

Du, M., & Wang, K. (2019). An SDN-enabled pseudo-honeypot strategy for distributed denial of service attacks in industrial internet of things. *IEEE Transactions on Industrial Informatics, 16*(1), 648–657.

Du, M., Li, Y., Lu, Q., & Wang, K. (2017). Bayesian game based pseudo honeypot model in social networks. In *International conference on cloud computing and security* (pp. 62–71). Springer.

Durkota, K., Lisý, V., Kiekintveld, C., & Bošansky, B. (2015). Game-theoretic algorithms for optimal network security hardening using attack graphs. *Database, 20*, 4xPC.

Ferguson-Walter, K., Fugate, S., Mauger, J., & Major, M. (2019). Game theory for adaptive defensive cyber deception. In *Proceedings of the 6th annual symposium on hot topics in the science of security* (p. 4).

Ferguson-Walter, K.J., Major, M. M., Johnson, C. K., & Muhleman, D. H. (2021). Examining the efficacy of decoy-based and psychological cyber deception. In *30th USENIX Security symposium (USENIX Security 21)* (pp. 1127–1144).

Fraunholz, D., Anton, S. D., Lipps, C., Reti, D., Krohmer, D., Pohl, F., Tammen, M., & Schotten, H. D. (2018). Demystifying deception technology: A survey. *arXiv preprint*, arXiv:1804.06196.

Granados, A., Miah, M. S., Ortiz, A., & Kiekintveld, C. (2020). A realistic approach for network traffic obfuscation using adversarial machine learning. In *International conference on decision and game theory for security* (pp. 45–57). Springer.

Guan, Y., Xinwen, F., Xuan, D., Shenoy, P. U., Bettati, R., & Zhao, W. (2001). Netcamo: camouflaging network traffic for QOS-guaranteed mission critical applications. *IEEE Transactions on Systems, Man, and Cybernetics-Part A: Systems and Humans, 31*(4), 253–265.

Han, X., Kheir, N., & Balzarotti, D. (2018). Deception techniques in computer security: A research perspective. *ACM Computing Surveys (CSUR), 51*(4), 1–36.

Hosseinzadeh, S., Rauti, S., Hyrynsalmi, S., & Leppanen, V. (2015). Security in the internet of things through obfuscation and diversification. In *2015 International Conference on Computing, Communication and Security (ICCCS)* (pp. 1–5). IEEE.

Hou, T., Qu, Z., Wang, T., Lu, Z., & Liu, Y. (2020). Proto: Proactive topology obfuscation against adversarial network topology inference. In *IEEE INFOCOM 2020-IEEE conference on computer communications* (pp. 1598–1607). IEEE.

Jajodia, S., Park, N., Pierazzi, F., Pugliese, A., Serra, E., Simari, G. I., & Subrahmanian, V. S. (2017). A probabilistic logic of cyber deception. *IEEE Transactions on Information Forensics and Security, 12*(11), 2532–2544.

Kaghazgaran, P., & Takabi, H. (2015). Toward an insider threat detection framework using honey permissions. *Journal of Internet Services and Information Security, 5*(3), 19–36.

Kiekintveld, C., Lisý, V., & Píbil, R. (2015). Game-theoretic foundations for the strategic use of honeypots in network security. In *Cyber warfare* (pp. 81–101).

La, Q. D., Quek, T. Q. S., Lee, J., Jin, S., & Zhu, H. (2016). Deceptive attack and defense game in honeypot-enabled networks for the internet of things. *IEEE Internet of Things Journal, 3*(6), 1025–1035.

Lee, S., Abdullah, A., Jhanjhi, N., & Kok, S. (2021). Classification of botnet attacks in IOT smart factory using honeypot combined with machine learning. *Peer Journal of Computer Science, 7*, e350.

Liu, Y., Zhao, J., Zhang, G., & Xing, C. (2021). Netobfu: A lightweight and efficient network topology obfuscation defense scheme. *Computers & Security, 110*, 102447.

Meier, R., Tsankov, P., Lenders, V., Vanbever, L., & Vechev, M. (2018). {NetHide}: Secure and practical network topology obfuscation. In *27th USENIX Security symposium (USENIX Security 18)* (pp. 693–709).

Miah, M. S., Gutierrez, M., Veliz, O., Thakoor, O., & Kiekintveld, C. (2020). Concealing cyber-decoys using two-sided feature deception games. In *HICSS* (pp. 1–10).

Milani, S., Shen, W., Chan, K. S., Venkatesan, S., Leslie, N. O., Kamhoua, C., & Fang, F. (2020) Harnessing the power of deception in attack graph-based security games. In *International conference on decision and game theory for security*.

Perez, B., Musolesi, M., & Stringhini, G. (2018). You are your metadata: Identification and obfuscation of social media users using metadata information. In *Twelfth international AAAI conference on web and social media*.

Píbil, R., Lisý, V., Kiekintveld, C., Bošanský, B., & Pěchouček, M. (2012). Game theoretic model of strategic honeypot selection in computer networks. In J. Grosslags & J. Walrand (Eds.), *Decision and game theory for security*. GameSec 2012 (Lecture notes in computer science) (Vol. 7638, pp. 201–220). Springer. https://doi.org/10.1007/978-3-642-34266-0_12. URL: https://link.springer.com/chapter/10.1007/978-3-642-34266-0_12

Rauti, S., & Leppanen, V.. (2017). A survey on fake entities as a method to detect and monitor malicious activity. In *2017 25th Euromicro international conference on Parallel, Distributed and Network-based Processing (PDP)* (pp. 386–390). IEEE.

Rawat, D. B., Sapavath, N., & Song, M. (2019). Performance evaluation of deception system for deceiving cyber adversaries in adaptive virtualized wireless networks. In *Proceedings of the 4th ACM/IEEE symposium on edge computing* (pp. 401–406).

Schlenker, A., Thakoor, O., Xu, H., Fang, F., Tambe, M., Tran-Thanh, L., Vayanos, P., & Vorobeychik, Y. (2018). Deceiving cyber adversaries: A game theoretic approach. In *Proceedings of the 17th international conference on autonomous agents and multiagent systems* (pp. 892–900). International Foundation for Autonomous Agents and Multiagent Systems.

Shade, T., Rogers, A., Ferguson-Walter, K., Elsen, S. B., Fayette, D., & Heckman, K. E. (2020). The moonraker study: An experimental evaluation of host-based deception. In *HICSS* (pp. 1–10).

Sharma, S., & Kaul, A. (2018). A survey on intrusion detection systems and honeypot based proactive security mechanisms in vanets and vanet cloud. *Vehicular Communications, 12*, 138–164.

Sugrim, S., Venkatesan, S., Youzwak, J. A., Chiang, C.-Y. J., Chadha, R., Albanese, M., & Cam, H. (2018). Measuring the effectiveness of network deception. In *2018 IEEE international conference on Intelligence and Security Informatics (ISI)* (pp. 142–147). IEEE.

Sun, Y., Tian, Z., Li, M., Shen, S., Xiaojiang, D., & Guizani, M. (2020). Honeypot identification in softwarized industrial cyber–physical systems. *IEEE Transactions on Industrial Informatics, 17*(8), 5542–5551.

Szegedy, C., Zaremba, W., Sutskever, I., Bruna, J., Erhan, D., Goodfellow, I., & Fergus, R. (2013). Intriguing properties of neural networks. *arXiv preprint*, arXiv:1312.6199.

Thakoor, O., Tambe, M., Vayanos, P., Xu, H., Kiekintveld, C., & Fang, F. (2019) Cyber camouflage games for strategic deception. In *International conference on decision and game theory for security* (pp. 525–541).

Verma, G., Ciftcioglu, E., Sheatsley, R., Chan, K., & Scott, L. (2018). Network traffic obfuscation: An adversarial machine learning approach. In *MILCOM 2018–2018 IEEE Military Communications Conference (MILCOM)* (pp. 1–6). IEEE.

Vetterl, A., & Clayton, R. (2019). Honware: A virtual honeypot framework for capturing CPE and IOT zero days. In *2019 APWG symposium on electronic crime research (eCrime)* (pp. 1–13). IEEE.

Vishwakarma, R., & Jain, A. K. (2019). A honeypot with machine learning based detection framework for defending IOT based botnet DDOS attacks. In *2019 3rd International Conference on Trends in Electronics and Informatics (ICOEI)* (pp. 1019–1024). IEEE.

Voris, J., Jermyn, J., Boggs, N., & Stolfo, S. (2015). Fox in the trap: Thwarting masqueraders via automated decoy document deployment. In *Proceedings of the eighth European workshop on system security* (pp. 1–7).

Wang, K., Du, M., Maharjan, S., & Sun, Y. (2017). Strategic honeypot game model for distributed denial of service attacks in the smart grid. *IEEE Transactions on Smart Grid, 8*(5), 2474–2482.

Xu, H., Zhou, Y., Ming, J., & Lyu, M. (2020). Layered obfuscation: A taxonomy of software obfuscation techniques for layered security. *Cybersecurity, 3*(1), 1–18.

Chapter 10
Adaptivity and Antifragility

**Anton V. Uzunov, Bao Vo, Hoa Khanh Dam, Charles Harold,
Mohan Baruwal Chhetri, Alan Colman, and Saad Sajid Hashmi**

1 Introduction

Like all systems, AICA systems are susceptible to various kinds of faults and attacks. AICA systems need to survive and fight-through these faults and attacks so as to maintain effective operation and continue to defend their target environments.

In terms of fragility, software systems can reside on a spectrum ranging from *fragile*, where the system is easily broken; *robust*, where the system operates until a breaking point, after which it becomes fragile once again; *resilient/survivable* (Linkov & Kott, 2019; Dobson et al., 2019), where the system can "bounce back" from failures or attacks; and *antifragile* (Hole, 2022), where the system can not only bounce back but also formulate improved responses for when similar or related

A. V. Uzunov (✉)
Cyber and Electronic Warfare Division, Defence Science and Technology Group
Edinburgh, Australia
e-mail: anton.uzunov@defence.gov.au

B. Vo
School of Science, Computing and Engineering Technologies, Swinburne University of
Technology, Hawthorn, Australia

H. K. Dam · S. S. Hashmi
School of Computing and Information Technology, University of Wollongong,
Wollongong, Australia

C. Harold
Department of Computer Science and Software Engineering, Swinburne University of
Technology, Melbourne, Australia

M. Baruwal Chhetri · A. Colman
Data61, CSIRO, Clayton, Australia

adverse events are encountered. Resilience and antifragility in particular can be achieved by:

1. Using various architectural principles and patterns during design-time, such as modularity, redundancy, and diversity (Hole, 2016; Nygard, 2018);
2. Employing active defense mechanisms during run-time, including (self-oriented) intrusion detection and response (Yuan et al., 2014); and
3. Enabling the system to learn, re-organize and adapt to change (Atighetchi & Pal, 2009; Baruwal Chhetri et al., 2018).

All of these approaches are important; however, in this chapter the focus will be on the last of these: re-organizing and adapting to change via self-management and self-improvement. Specifically, our focus is on effecting distributed self-management and self-improvement via collections of intelligent software agents (henceforth *self-* or simply *S* agents*) that either complement and reside alongside AICA agents or are themselves special AICA agents with the requisite S* functionality. In the following, we outline several assumptions about: (i) the nature of S* agents; (ii) the nature of AICA systems; (iii) inter-agent communication; and (iv) the relation between S* and AICA agents in achieving resilience and antifragility.

1.1 S* Agents

Adapting from (Wooldridge & Jennings, 1995), we define an S* agent as a computational entity situated in some environment and capable of *flexible* action in order to meet its self-management design objectives, where flexibility is further characterised by the following three properties: autonomy, adaptivity and interactivity. *Autonomy* refers to the agent's ability to control its own internal state and behaviour without external intervention. A system capable of (self-)*adaptivity* has the ability to adjust itself to changes. This adjustment can simply be the system's response when encountering or anticipating changes, but it can also imply the ability to learn and (implicitly) improve itself. As S* agents are typically co-situated in an environment with other agents, *interaction* with other agents locally and globally, via message-passing mechanisms, is a critical skill. An *S* multi-agent system* is made up of a collection of S* agents that interact within an evolving, exogenously or endogenously defined organizational structure.

1.2 AICA Systems and Agents

We assume an AICA system may be composed of tens, hundreds, or possibly even thousands of intelligent software agents that are co-situated and operate across a heterogeneous set of execution environments on different platforms and/or devices (see (Theron et al., 2018) and Chap. 2 of this volume on alternative AICA architectures), with each AICA agent fulfilling some cyber defense or supportive AI functionality. These agents have the ability to cooperate with other types of intelligent agents in a secure team structure. There are good reasons for making this assumption. Firstly, decomposition and decentralization of functionality and control across separate software units is now standard industry practice in distributed systems. A single, isolated AICA agent per environment would not reflect current engineering best-practices (cf. the arguments behind micro-service architectures (Newman, 2021). Secondly, a single AICA agent per environment would be a single point of failure – a well-known resilience anti-pattern. Thirdly, it is sometimes necessary and more efficient to break down a problem into smaller, more manageable parts, and to solve the resulting sub-problems in parallel via multiple agents (as argued in the distributed AI/multi-agent systems communities). Finally, a single AICA agent per environment would severely limit or even disable the system's options for adaptivity, as monoliths are inherently tightly coupled and inflexible.

1.3   Relation Between S* and AICA Agents

We assume that AICA agents are designed to fulfill their cyber defense functions but do not provide system-wide self-management capabilities and are not inherently able to survive faults or fight-through attacks – that is, they are not in themselves able to deal with changes that may threaten survival or negatively affect performance. This is the function that S* agents are designed to fulfil by evaluating their own state and behaviour, the state and behaviour of related AICA agents, and (as a collective) the state and behaviour of the whole system, and subsequently executing various reconfiguration/regulatory actions. S* agents could be realized as part of a complementary S* multi-agent system residing alongside the AICA system, or as special AICA agents within the AICA system itself – e.g., AICA support agents designed for self-management but not cyber defense *per se* – in either case forming an *S* management (sub-)system*. For the sake of simplicity, we will assume S* agents reside alongside AICA agents, and refer to S* and AICA agents separately, even if S* agents are realized as special AICA agents. Whatever the realization, the collective aim of S* agents is to provide the combined <AICA + S* > system with various *self-* properties*, including self-management and self-improvement, which are the premise for achieving resilience and antifragility. We discuss self-* properties in the next section.

1.4   Agent Communication

Both AICA and S* agents interact and communicate with each other in two ways: internally, within the same execution environment; or externally, across different environments. We outline our assumptions with respect to these ways of communicating below.

- **Internal**: our first assumption with respect to communication is that internal communications enabling the interaction between multiple agents are necessary, trusted, and reliable within a secure team structure. Various military vehicle standards, e.g., the GVA (Bergamaschi et al., 2010) and AS GVA, rely on a service-oriented architecture paradigm where multiple services interact internally to a vehicle; hence this assumption is reasonable. While internal communications can lead to (unwanted) on-platform discovery of AICA agents, we assume AICA architectures are designed to eschew the infamous "security by obscurity" anti-pattern, and that adaptation can ensure the functionality provided by any discovered agents is not denied (this is the value of antifragility).
- **External**: We assume external communications is not reliable due to the nature of the contested battlespace, and may need to be minimized in certain circumstances, e.g., to avoid geo-location. At the same time, we also recognize that communications in the future battlespace will become ubiquitous, with devices and software units of various types exchanging vast amounts of information between each other and across different networks; hence it may not be a matter of how much, but in what way agents communicate. Regardless of the situation, we make the assumption that both AICA and S* agents use a special *stealth communications middleware* (see also Chap. 9 of this volume), e.g. akin to a stealthy version of ZeroMQ or JMS, that is able to encrypt and suitably blend agent communications (for example, by generating interleaved dummy messages, a technique that is well documented since the 1980s) whenever the relevant links are available.

With these assumptions in mind, we next describe a number of core self-* properties required to realize self-management and self-improvement.

2   Self-* Properties

2.1   Definitions

In accord with the definitions of (Berns & Ghosh, 2009), *self-management* can be seen as both a vision and a top-level self-* property pertaining to autonomous adaptation. Other, lower-level self-* properties include *self-healing* (Schneider et al., 2015), which is the ability of a system to recover from failures by diagnosing and localizing faults and taking corrective actions without manual intervention; and *self-optimization*, which is the ability of the system to adjust and improve its performance, or to otherwise optimize some aspects of its functioning based on a local or global objective function. These properties are in turn based on *self-awareness* via self-monitoring, and *self-configuration*. Berns and Ghosh also put forward self-stabilization, self-adaptation, self-protection and self-scaling as separate self-* properties in terms of system behaviours and maintained predicates (system properties) in the face of adversary actions. However, most research uses and focuses only on the four self-* properties mentioned earlier – sometimes also called self-CHOP (configuration, healing, optimization, protection) – due to their long history stemming from initial work by IBM on autonomic computing, *circa* 2002 (Kephart & Chess, 2003; Lalanda ct al., 2013). Readers are referred to (Salehie & Tahvildari, 2009) for another perspective on self-* properties and another, though similar, property hierarchy. Regardless of the schema or hierarchy used, all self-* properties support self-management in some way, which in turn supports resilience.

Besides these properties, there is a special, meta-level property called *self-improvement* (Krupitzer et al., 2016), which enables a system to learn, improve the realization of other self-* properties and become more resilient over time, thereby achieving antifragility. Following Baruwal Chhetri et al. (2019), self-improvement relies on perturbing the system online in a controlled fashion in order to find the "unknown unknowns", which allows the system to prepare for 'black swan' events before they occur in full measure. Black swan events are those for which the system has no ready responses, and hence has to partially or fully improvise responses and learn from experience. In this way unknown unknowns can become known unknowns or even known knowns. Clearly this implies the need for learning, which we discuss later.

2.2   Realization Approaches

There are two main ways in which the self-* properties enumerated in the previous sub-section can be realized: *internalized*, where management and business functionalities are blended; and *externalized*, where management and business functionalities are partitioned using a separate (self-)management (sub-)system.

Each of these approaches has advantages and disadvantages. With respect to AICA, a separate set of S* agents complementing the AICA agents can facilitate both the modification of the AICA system's own functionality (or the way this is realized – execution control), and also maintain operation under duress (antifragility aspect). However, separation of the S* agents also implies the possibility of contention and conflict, as some decisions made by S* agents may not align with those made by AICA agents, for example, with respect to the same set of resources (an AICA agent blocks a network connection, while an S* agent enables the same connection to adjust throughput). Despite this disadvantage, separation of S* agents and AICA agents provides much stronger separation of concerns, which from an engineering perspective is almost always desirable – not least because in the AICA context it will allow the independent (co-)development of cyber security and self-* functionalities. Moreover, internalized realization approaches do not entirely avoid contention, since the same decisions will need to be made within a given agent or set of agents and will likewise require algorithmic resolution. Thus, we argue that externalized self-management and self-improvement using S* agents in a separate (sub-)system is the better of the two approaches.

3 S* Multi-Agent Systems for Adaptivity & Antifragility

In the externalized approach to self-* property realization, adaptation becomes the responsibility of computational entities outside the target system, which in this chapter is the AICA cyber defense system. For these entities to be capable of self-management and self-improvement, we argue that they need precisely the core properties of intelligent software agents which we discussed earlier: autonomy, adaptivity and interactivity (cf. also Tesuaro et al., 2004). Subsequently, an externalized realization of self-management/improvement for an AICA system implies defining various S* agents whose main responsibility will be to manage the <AICA + S* > system. In the following two subsections, we provide a high-level overview of a conceptual framework that enables S* agents to be properly defined. The conceptual framework is composed of two parts, spanning the micro- and macro-levels of an S* multi-agent system: (i) an abstract reference architecture of an S* agent, and (ii) a set of flexibly applicable concepts for multi-agent system design. Taken together, these two parts of the framework provide the key design abstractions for defining a self-managing/improving system for AICA and for allocating self-management/improvement concerns to various S* agents.

3.1 S* Agent Reference Architecture (Conceptual Framework, Part 1)

Building on the generic architecture of intelligent software agents as distilled in AICA (Kott et al., 2018) (cf. Chap. 2 of this volume) – which in turn builds on Russell and Norvig's (2016) abstract agent definition – and inspired by the ideas of Lesser (1998) and Sabatucci et al. (2018), we require each S* agent in an S* management (sub-)system to have at least ten core skill-sets captured as notional components or modules: a *sensing element* (SE), an *interaction element* (IE), a *memory element* (ME), a *coordination element* (CE), an *organization design element* (ODE), an *awareness element* (AE), a *detection & diagnosis element* (DDE), an *adaptation response element* (ARE), a *meta-adaptation element* (MAE), and a *learning element* (LE).

The SE enables the S* agent to perceive relevant data (percepts) from the environment and the systems (i.e., the AICA cyber defense system) for which the agent provides self-* capabilities. The IE allows the S* agent to execute the actions it has decided to perform, which take on the form of communicating and interacting with the environment and other agents to effect necessary changes to the <AICA + S*> system. The ARE provides the core reasoning and decision-making functions pertaining to self-management, which can be based on simple rules or more complex model- and metric-driven approaches. The ME provides structured local storage of beliefs, goals, ongoing interactions, organizational relationships and other state that is used by other skill-sets. The CE provides first-class interaction abstractions that facilitate coordination of information (beliefs, adaptation decisions, partial models, etc.) for related skill-sets (ARE, LE, MAE, ODE). The ODE specifically defines how the S* agent participates in one or more relevant agent organizations, and through the coordination element can reach agreement on these organization structures in order to support the ARE. The AE continually builds up situational awareness of the S* agent itself, as well as related AICA agents and the environment, and stores the resulting models in the ME for future use, allowing the S* agent to make suitable adaptation decisions via the ARE. The DDE provides an analysis function on the awareness information, which can diagnose problems either in parallel to the ARE or as a precursor to the ARE generating responses. The MAE by itself can adapt the ARE by providing meta-reasoning functionality or by building new strategies in conjunction with the LE.

Finally, the MAE, DDE and LE together provide the S* agent with the ability to achieve self-improvement. More specifically – in terms of Russell and Norvig's (2016) concept of a learning agent – an MAE acts as a *problem generator* responsible for suggesting interactions in the form of perturbations that will lead to new and informative experiences; the DDE acts as a *critic* that provides feedback in terms of how successful these interactions were with respect to a given adaptation-performance standard; while the LE acts as a *learning subsystem* responsible for

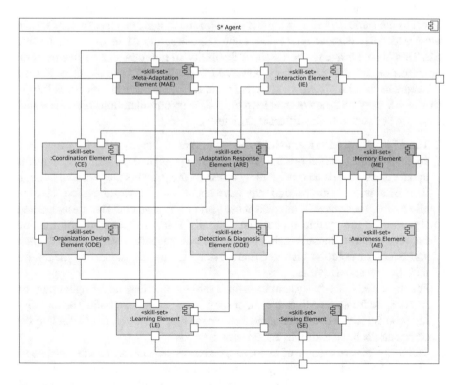

Fig. 10.1 Abstract reference architecture of an S* agent

evolving the ARE and other skill-sets, so that the S* agent and (with the use of the CE) S* system can become more competent than the agent's/system's initial knowledge and skills alone might allow.

A simple UML model of the S* agent architecture is shown in Fig. 10.1. More sophisticated models can be defined by detailing the skill-sets and adding associated internal structures pertaining to reasoning and decision-making where appropriate (Ye et al., 2018).

For S* agents to fulfill their responsibility of achieving resilience and antifragility for the AICA cyber defense system, their SE component must be able to observe the status and performance of AICA agents, and their IE component must be able to make changes to AICA agents. That is, S* agents will have certain control authority over AICA agents so that they can intervene in the AICA agents' configurations and activities in a timely fashion to prevent and manage task failures or other adverse events. Observe also that the above structure of the S* agents does not significantly deviate from the MAPE-K loop proposed by autonomic computing researchers (Kephart & Chess, 2003) that has been widely adopted by the self-adaptive systems community (see e.g. Villegas et al., 2017; Weyns, 2020). In particular, the M, A, P and E activities approximately correspond to the S* agent's SE + AE ($\rightarrow$ M), DDE ($\rightarrow$ A), ARE ($\rightarrow$ P) and IE ($\rightarrow$ E) skill-sets, while the K in the MAPE-K loop is localized to the S* agent's ME.

It should be noted that not all skill-sets will need to be implemented in all S* agents to the same degree. A simple S* agent, for example, can have a very simple rule-based ARE without a complex knowledge-base stored in its internal state/ ME. This gives S* agents the essential flexibility so that they can be deployed on low-resource devices (e.g., battery-powered IoT devices) if/when required. For the S* agents to fulfill their self-management and self-improvement objectives for the <AICA + S*> system, however, at least the following considerations need to be kept in mind when realizing the different skill-sets:

1. The S* agents need to maintain models of the parts of the systems for which they are responsible (including other AICA and S* agents) in their ME. The S* agents update these models as time goes by based on the percepts they receive through their SEs, and the knowledge they have about how the world evolves and the effects their actions will have on those parts of the system. This decentralized structure of the system model can naturally lead to conflicting information between different models maintained by different agents. Thus, communication and conflict resolution via the CE are needed for the S* agents to synchronise their beliefs and activities.
2. For the <AICA + S*> system to exhibit self-* properties, an S* agent may be responsible for some AICA agents, or for other S* agents, or both. The underlying premise is that every component of the <AICA + S*> system (including the S* agents) is looked after by at least one S* agent.
3. The S* agents are capable of improving their own self-management mechanisms via the MAE and LE. An S* agent can itself discover the improvement based on its learning capability. On the other hand, every S* agent (with or without a full

LE realization) can also acquire improved adaptation mechanisms discovered by other agents via transfer learning when appropriate (LE using CE).

4. As S* agents operate over a long time-span, they are exposed to continuous streams of information generated by the system/environment or via an integrated, in-system perturbation capability consisting of S* agents with suitably realized MAE + LE skill-sets. When new knowledge and/or experience arrives, the S* agents should continue learning "on-the-fly" from the new knowledge/ experience while keeping previously learned experiences. This capability is referred to as online, continual or lifelong learning. The S* agents incrementally obtain new knowledge from the continuous stream of input, and fine-tune existing knowledge. The S* agents should acquire the new information in such a way that it does not interfere substantially with their existing learned knowledge, creating the so-called "catastrophic forgetting" (McClelland et al., 1995) phenomenon in learning.

3.2 S Multi-agent System Design Concepts (Conceptual Framework, Part 2)*

In addition to the agent architecture, we summarize below a number of design concepts that can be used to both elaborate the various (micro-level) architecture elements and guide the macro-level architectural design of S* multi-agent systems. These concepts are a distillation of the AWaRE2-MM meta-model proposed in our previous work (Uzunov et al., 2021a), which in turn is inspired by several existing multi-agent meta-models (see Beydoun et al., 2009 for a combined summary of such meta-models) and existing self-management systems.

The first set of concepts are *goal, contract,* and *team*. Similar to AICA agents, S* agents are autonomous, cooperative and goal driven. Hence, they are capable of intelligently selecting actions to fulfill the goals they have adopted. The goal concept can support traditional planning as well as other decision-making processes (Bulling, 2014) as part of an agent's ARE and MAE realizations; and it can also be refined further and used to support goal-driven self-adaptation (Uzunov et al., 2021b). Contracts express relationships and specify the responsibilities an agent has toward other components of the systems (including the AICA agents and other S* agents). Finally, teams provide the system with clear boundaries for the S* agents or groups of agents in terms of their responsibilities and authority.

The second set of concepts are *capability* and *role*. Capabilities capture the notion of an atomic skill for a given agent and can be aggregated to form capability-sets – the equivalent of skill-sets. These capabilities can be used to realize all or parts of the various S* agent elements discussed previously. Roles aggregate one or more capability-sets to define the overall responsibility or type of an S* agent.

The third and final set of concepts are *activity, change* and *abstract quality*. Activities refer to the sets of actions generated through the use of various capabilities, which can include adaptation actions (recomposition and reparameterization), monitoring actions, coordination-related actions and others. Changes occur at various scales within the combined <AICA + S*> system as well as its environment. Capturing these changes explicitly allows for a definition of the S*/AICA variability space, thereby defining the space of "known unknowns". Change can also refer to the results of the adaptation actions, since they seek to change both the S* system as well as the AICA system. Finally, abstract qualities can define constraints on, or otherwise characterize, other concepts, including goals, capabilities, activities, etc.

The UML model in Fig. 10.2 captures a set of default relationships between the various design concepts, including S* agents (modelled abstractly). Since the concepts are meant to be flexibly applied across the macro- and micro-levels of an S* multi-agent system – including when designing S* agent element realizations, which are not shown in the figure – it would be perfectly reasonable for some of these relationships to change across different system and/or agent architectures.

3.3 Generic Self-Management and Self-Improvement (S-M/I) Approach

Self-management and self-improvement can be undertaken across 3 scopes: (i) within individual S* agents, which can reconfigure their own capabilities; (ii) within agent teams; and (iii) globally, spanning the whole <AICA + S* > system. We make this process more precise via the concept of *levels of adaptation and learning*, which we present in this sub-section. The concept, in essence, is to explicitly stratify the different algorithms which the system will use to adapt and learn, depending on the context (where context is equivalent to environmental conditions and internal system state), in a subsumption-style hierarchy. The levels of this hierarchy are as

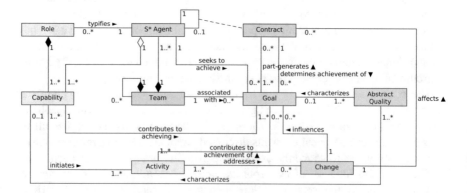

Fig. 10.2 Default relations of S* multi-agent system design concepts

follows, described in terms of the design concepts from our S* conceptual framework:

- *Level one (L1) – agent-self:* each S* agent changes its own state or capabilities, provided it does not violate any existing contracts/relationships it has with other agents. In doing so, it also learns from its adaptation actions and the resulting effects.
- *Level two (L2) – peer-to-peer relationship:* ensures that pair-wise compositions of agents within the system are operating as expected: repairing minor faults as they appear. For example, if two S* agents controlling AICA agents have a contract stating that certain quality-of-service agreements must be maintained, and this contract is violated, then they may try to re-negotiate the terms such that both sides can fulfill their obligations under the contract. The adaptation is non-violating in the sense that this peer-to-peer negotiation should not cause other contracts to become violated, which would lead to cyclic negotiations or "adaptation thrashing". Through these adaptations, the S* peers learn to evolve and improve their relationship, for example in response to changes in their individual capabilities.
- *Level three (L3) – intra-team:* re-configures multiple contracts/relationships within a team to meet the goals of the team. Specifically, if two S* agents are unable to resolve the failure of their contract (which may represent some contract failure condition for corresponding AICA agents), then the condition of the management goal associated with the contract will likewise fail, meaning that one or more higher-level goals will be unfulfilled. In this case the failure is escalated to a higher level of control. One or more S* agents may agree to reform all the contracts associated with sub-goals of the unfulfilled goal in order to fulfil this goal again – re-decomposing the problem based on other hypothetically available capability-sets of agents within the system and re-allocating capabilities and agents within the given team – or they may otherwise change the goal itself. While it is easiest to conceptualize this as a single team leader making these decisions, there is no reason it cannot be done in a distributed way. Through repeated intra-team adaptations, the team can learn to improve its decision-making across all team-based activities including negotiation and coordination activities, as well as the adaptation activities related to an S* agent's different skill-sets, leading to better team management.
- *Level four (L4) – inter-team:* the system is partitioned into teams (if not already organized this way) and S* agents from each team attempt to agree on a globally optimal or satisfactory configuration by triggering various adaptation strategies from the lower levels in a coordinated fashion. While L4 adaptation is clearly the most complex, it need not always result in large-scale system reconfigurations. For example, in some situations all that may be required is re-assignment of roles across two teams instead of one team (L3 adaptation, twice); or contracting of agents across teams (L2 adaptation, once per team). This is also dependent on the realization of team boundaries, if any, which may dictate allowable information sharing and scope of control, among other factors. Learning at L4 is similar to that at L3, except that it occurs across teams.

Material to this concept is that the scope of control of decision-making and learning expands from more local to more global. At the lower levels, fine-grained adaptations have local effect (assuming they are designed to be side-effect-free) and the learning is limited to the local level. At higher levels, adaptations necessitate reconfiguration of multiple parts of the system; similarly, learning occurs across multiple parts of the system. In this hierarchical approach, goal adaptation resides higher in the hierarchy of levels than adapting contracts to fulfill those goals – the details of how the goal is realized – as well as making subsidiary adjustments – such as load balancing at the network or hardware layers, memory refresh-rate tuning – and countless other adaptations the system could make that do not affect the higher levels. Thus, each level is responsible for maintaining the resilience and contributing to the antifragility of the system at its "level of granularity". The objects of control in each case are internal to agents (L1); between peer agents (L2); within agent teams (L3); and across agent teams/whole system (L4). Within a team, an S* agent might have the ability to tweak its contract in consultation with the other party, but likewise the higher-level adaptation by another S* agent might have the ability to rewrite the terms of that same contract to achieve higher-level goals. In effect, each of these levels have their own MAPE-K loop. From the viewpoint of the SOTA model of Abeywickrama et al. (2012) – where each configuration of the system is a point in a high dimensional space with a utility attached to it – lower-level adaptations exploit the current configuration space, while higher-level adaptations explore points further away.

The cause of the adaptations can be adverse systemic/environmental changes, or perturbations introduced by S* agents. These perturbations can also follow the hierarchical structure: local first, and increasingly more global.

In terms of process, applying the levels of adaptation and learning concept implies that adaptation typically starts with the lowest level and proceeds up through the levels whenever each adaptation strategy at a given level fails to account for the adverse changes. Once higher-level adaptations are triggered, they may initiate lower-level adaptations – though with greater knowledge available from the increased system scope. For example, as a result of L4 adaptation, capabilities that are not available in one team but available in another team can lead to simple re-contracting – L2 adaptation – with a remote team member (assuming the team concept is realized to support such team-transparency); L2 adaptation alone would not have been sufficient to discover the remote team member. The exception is responding to changes when realizing self-optimization, which can be initiated at the higher levels first. Learning occurs across all levels of adaptation, although the knowledge gained is greater at the higher levels.

The levels of adaptation and learning concept has several key advantages:

1. *Timeliness*: Adaptation responses can be rapid, since they are initiated at the lowest level first, which involves simple processes utilizing small amounts of knowledge. If these lower-level adaptations cannot address the change which necessitated the adaptation, higher-level adaptations (which are increasingly slower by necessity) can "step-up".

2. *Run-time decoupling*: Assuming lower-level adaptation strategies are designed properly, the use of the adaptation levels helps to reduce run-time dependencies between the S* agents executing higher−/lower-level adaptations.
3. *Potential for scalability*: The knowledge created during the execution of lower-level adaptation strategies (including when initiated as part of higher-level adaptation), can be used to inform and expedite higher-level adaptations, thus increasing their scalability over time.

Below we provide several examples of what can be adapted in an <AICA + S*> system by using the various levels of adaptation as part of the self-management process.

- *Agents (L3 and L4 triggering L3)*: the number and types of agents in a secure team structure, as well as their internal capabilities (L3 triggering L1 adaptation). A self-optimization mechanism could spawn more agents of a particular type that has been previously shown to prevent attacks (e.g., load balancing agents against repeated DDoS attacks).
- *Communications (L1, L4 triggering L1)*: the amount and nature of the communications. For example, the number of messages allowed can be dynamically adjusted to the "right" amount in any given situation via a self-configuration mechanism (per agent, L1); and threats such as link jamming can be mitigated via a self-healing mechanism that allows the communications to be run over alternative channels, such as SATCOM (system-wide, L4).
- *QoS Agreements (L2)*: the service-levels between agents and other software infrastructure, e.g., related data stores. Interconnections can be modelled as contracts and dynamically re-negotiated according to fluctuations in throughput and performance to ensure, for example, that cyber threat data collection is uninterrupted; that the relevant data flows optimally throughout the system; and that this data is optimally stored (scaling storage infrastructure based not only on need – which existing commercial/open-source systems can easily do by themselves – but based on data analysis/domain information).

3.4   Reifying the S* Conceptual Framework and Generic S-M/I Approach

The conceptual framework and generic self-management/improvement approach presented above can be reified in various ways. Specifically, as discussed previously, the S* agents can be either part of a separate S* multi-agent system, or special AICA agents, which can each undertake adaptation/learning across different levels. In all cases, it will be necessary to support the agents with a specific agent-based platform or middleware framework (Regli et al., 2009), which supports agent deployment on a variety of platforms and devices. This framework can be rudimentary or comprehensive, even to the point that it provides some of the S* system functionality *a priori*, leaving as the only requirement to fill in some of the agent skill-sets/capabilities. We describe such a framework, called AWaRE, in the next section.

4 The AWaRE Framework

In this section we provide an overview of AWaRE (Baruwal Chhetri et al., 2018; Uzunov et al., 2021a; Uzunov et al., 2021b) as an example of a concrete, in-progress system and middleware framework for antifragility, which also aims to be anti-fragile itself. We begin by briefly discussing the principles and concepts underpinning the current version of AWaRE, AWaRE 2.0 – *inter alia* showing their relation to the S* conceptual framework in the previous section; and then briefly outline the AWaRE 2.0 architecture, focusing on the contracting approach, goal reasoning, and adaptation strategies.

4.1 AWaRE Principles

AWaRE 2.0 is based on four inter-related principles:

- *Virtualization* refers to the formation of a "live" model of a domain system (e.g., AICA system) at the AWaRE level by creating proxies that represent the relevant domain services (meant in a broad sense).
- *Transitivity* refers to the management/adaptation of this "live" model as part of managing/adapting AWaRE itself, which in turn should translate into the management of the domain system. In other words, by managing itself, AWaRE also seeks to manage the domain system.
- *Duality* refers to the use of meta-reasoning across abstraction levels to achieve genuine self-* behaviours (sometimes also referred to as meta-adaptation or "self-self" behaviours Bouchenak et al., 2011).
- *Intentionality* refers to the approach of capturing the intent (requirements as goals) of a domain system as well as AWaRE itself at a high level of abstraction, translating the resultant goal models appropriately, and employing goal reasoning to drive the decision-making relating to the adaptation strategies at various levels of adaptation.

The first three principles above relate to the externalized/internalized approaches discussed earlier; namely, AWaRE seeks to realize self-* properties in an external-ized fashion by realizing these properties in an internalized fashion, i.e. AWaRE manages itself (and from the framework/system perspective, only itself) so that it can manage the given domain system.

4.2   AWaRE Concepts

The AWaRE 2.0 architecture is underpinned by the AWaRE2-MM meta-model (Uzunov et al., 2021a). Below we provide a brief summary of how the core concepts of this model have been instantiated.

- *Agent-service*: AWaRE 2.0 adopts the concept of an agent-service (Baruwal Chhetri et al., 2019) as its realization of an S* agent. An agent-service abstraction combines the desirable characteristics of an intelligent software agent with the modularity and reusability of service-based interactions, following service-oriented architecture (SOA) style. Notionally, it has a core agent part and a service interaction shell, so that it can indeed be regarded as an agent which can interact with other agents as well as services. The hybrid nature of an agent-service also enables it to have varying levels of autonomy, being more "agent-like" (proactive agent) or "service-like" (reactive agent).
- *Requirement* and *Goal*: Requirements for both the domain services and AWaRE agent-services, respectively, can be captured as goals using a domain-specific language called AGML (AWaRE Goal Modelling Language) – see Uzunov et al. (2021b). AGML supports design-time goals and two types of run-time goals: *achieve* and *maintain* (see (Van Riemsdijk et al., 2008) for an explanation of these goal types). Goals can be updated, added and removed at run-time as a result of change events.
- *Capability*: Capabilities (henceforth *a-caps*) represent the skills or behaviours that an agent-service possesses, and hence mirror the relevant design concept discussed in the previous section. A-caps fulfil run-time achieve goals, either directly or by dispatching (achieve) goals to be handled by other capabilities. The matching of goals to capabilities is done at run-time as a form of dynamic means-end analysis. Every agent-service has a baseline set of a-caps encompassing goal reasoning, contract formation, interaction, and others. A-caps are composable and swappable at run-time, ensuring that an agent-service's internal structure and control flow are flexible. Some a-caps are *internal* to the agent-service, while others – referred to as *consumable capabilities* – may be discovered and utilized by other agent-services, just like "small-scale" services or functions.
- *Role*: In AWaRE, a role is an aggregation of a-caps that typifies an agent-service. Roles in AWaRE can be classified by domain or management concerns. Differently from our S* conceptual framework, there is only one core role per agent, for a given role type. A special management role type allows agent-services to aggregate arbitrary a-caps without regard for typification. The a-caps provided by a core (management or domain) role augment the baseline a-caps possessed by every agent-service.
- *Team* and *Template*: A team in AWaRE directly corresponds to the S* conceptual framework team concept, capturing the notion of a localized agent organization. Agent-service teams can be formed in one of two ways: (i) by deriving the required sub-goals from the top-level goals and contracting them out to

agent-services that possess the required capabilities, or (ii) using a team template that maps teams of agent-services to goals/sub-goals in a given goal model.

- *Contract*: Like teams, contracts are the same as the corresponding contracts in the S* conceptual framework – expressing peer-relationships between agent-services.   Contracts support the principle of duality via meta-reasoning: one agent-service acts at a meta-level with respect to its contract-managing contracted peer, and conversely.
- *Change*: A key requirement for AWaRE is that it should be capable of managing domain systems deployed in a variety of environments by managing itself (transitivity principle). As described before, AWaRE takes the hierarchical layers of adaptation approach, with the adaptation strategies captured as a-caps triggered via goal matching. Changes are not modelled explicitly, though they can generate change events on occurrence.
- *Abstract Quality Metrics*: Goals and capabilities in AWaRE are qualified by abstract quality metrics – qualities with an associated metric. This allows agent-services to reason about and manage themselves by matching not only functional descriptions of goals and a-caps but also corresponding quality (non-functional) specifications.

4.3   AWaRE Architecture

Conceptual View

A high-level conceptual view of the AWaRE 2.0 technical architecture is shown in Fig. 10.3. Note that only a sub-set of all viable contract links is represented, and team boundaries – as well as the number of services and agent-services – are purely illustrative.

AWaRE defines various core management roles, such as a Goalkeeper (G), encompassing a-caps for looking after goals for a team; a Team Commissioner (TC), encompassing a-caps for team management; an Architecture Optimizer (AO), which is responsible for analyzing the criticality of agents and any performance bottlenecks; a Replication Manager (RM), which is responsible for creating/destroying agents; and a Marketplace (not shown in the figure), which is connected to all other agent-services and acts as an a-cap registry supporting discovery and the goal reasoning process across all agents in a given team. There is a single core domain role, called a Double (Dn in the figure) for performing proxying/domain service virtualization in a one-to-one fashion.

At the time of this writing, AWaRE 2.0 supports a simple realization of the sensing, interaction and adaptation response elements (SE, IE, ARE) in each agent-service as sets of a-caps, with sensing being restricted to contract monitoring and actuation being restricted to effecting adaptation actions via capability executions. The ARE of each agent-service currently consists of goal reasoning and adaptation-specific functionality, which also spans a separate Changemaster management role possessed by a single agent per team. Contract formation – partially supporting the

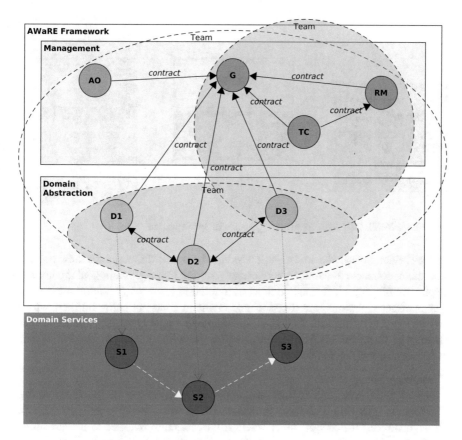

Fig. 10.3 AWaRE 2.0 Technical Architecture: Conceptual View (Illustrative)

organization design element (ODE) – is realized via an implementation of the Contract-Net Protocol (CNP) and LAP+ (a light-weight extension of LAP – Lambert & Lambert, 2012), both distilled in baseline a-caps common to all agent-services.

Since AWaRE is a generic framework, *semantic specialization* is required to "attach" it to a domain system. There are several different elements of AWaRE that require this specialization (see Fig. 10.4). For example, plugins – finer-grained modules associated with an a-cap – are used to interface with domain services and external technologies facilitating adaptation actions. As new domain services require management, or new technologies become available (e.g., Kubernetes instead of Nomad for orchestration), then new plugins would need to be written. At present, plugins are only associated with an a-cap belonging to a Double core domain role.

Execution View

AWaRE 2.0 employs the levels of adaptation approach to self-management (self-improvement is left for the next AWaRE iteration). After bootstrapping the system via an agent-service with a Bootstrapper core management role, a Goalkeeper

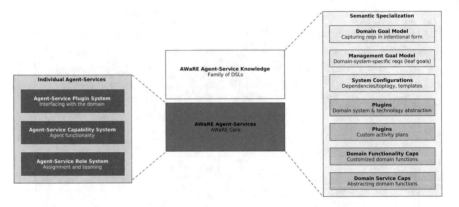

Fig. 10.4 AWaRE 2.0 Elements Requiring Semantic Specialization

agent-service ingests the AGML-specified goal models, disseminates them to team members, connects the domain services as required by the domain goal model, and begins monitoring all formed contracts. Adaptation is currently contract-driven, in that contract violations lead to associated maintain goals not being fulfilled, which in turn triggers change events that are first handled via L1 and L2 adaptation a-caps inside a given agent, and then via an agent-service with a Changemaster role, which possesses L3 and L4 adaptation a-caps.

Technology View

AWaRE 2.0 has been rapidly prototyped in Java on top of the Jadex/Active Components platform (Pokahr & Braubach, 2013), with the implementation of most (though not all) aspects of the AWaRE 2.0 architecture realized to a functioning level. HashiCorp's Nomad can be used to (self-)deploy AWaRE by deploying Jadex platforms across a network. Apache Ignite is used for publish/subscribe messaging and reliable data storage. AGML, as well as a simple domain-specification language allowing a-caps to be specified outside of Java (useful when specifying Double a-caps that nominally belong to a domain service but do not actually carry any domain functionality – i.e. they merely enable discovery via Marketplace agents), are defined using Xtext. The whole technology stack used to realize AWaRE 2.0 is shown in Fig. 10.5.

4.4   AWaRE 3.0 – Micro-service Integration

Work is currently being undertaken on extending the AWaRE framework to a new version – AWaRE 3.0. Besides incorporating self-improvement and the remaining elements of the S* reference architecture, a core aim is to enable the integration of AWaRE with micro-service technologies (cf. Collier et al., 2019), thereby fully realizing the vision of agent-services adhering to both multi-agent and service-oriented

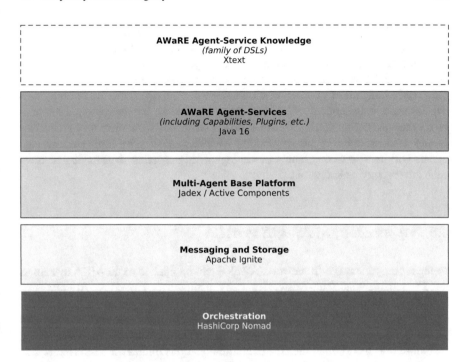

Fig. 10.5 AWaRE 2.0 Technical Architecture: Technology View

architectural styles (Baruwal Chhetri et al., 2019). Although they lack autonomy, micro-service systems are becoming the de-facto standard for developing highly distributed software systems. Micro-services are typically deployed independently on their own container that provides full-stack functionality. All inter-service communications occur via network calls. This independence facilitates agile development using DevOps methodologies and CI/CD (continuous integration/continuous deployment) toolchains (Newman, 2021). Micro-service deployment on containers can be orchestrated using tools such as Kubernetes,[1] which not only provide flexibility over how service instances are deployed across clusters of containers, but also support inherent reliability through capabilities such as load balancing, health checks and automated recovery. Service meshes such as Istio[2] build on top of container orchestrators to provide enhanced observability and control over the infrastructure level via 'sidecar' proxies. It is precisely this observability and control that is needed in MAPE-K loops. Meshes also provide high-level control over service routing enabling ready reconfiguration of service networks (L3 adaptation as described earlier).

AWaRE 3.0 will provide the option of deploying agents as micro-services in an industry standard service mesh, in addition to using Jadex/Active Components. The

---

[1] https://kubernetes.io/

[2] https://istio.io/latest/

ability of agents to control their own deployment, as well as the deployment of other agents (as micro-services) and domain services, via powerful underlying technologies will provide a new dimension of flexibility, control and antifragility to both AWaRE and the target domain system(s) being managed. Service meshes also provide ready integration with application integration services such as routing, message brokers, data services, DNS and Internet gateways. By abstracting away a lot of the complexity of the application integration code, we anticipate that service meshes will make the implementation of AWaRE agent control logic simpler, e.g., agents will be able to communicate via logical names rather than having to know each other's service endpoints.

4.5   Applicability of AWaRE to AICA

Being a comprehensive framework, AWaRE can be applied to an AICA system as an S* management (sub-)system, thereby acting as an overlay. Alternatively, AWaRE could be used as an agent platform/middleware framework for AICA agents, in which case AWaRE agent-services would reside alongside AICA and would technically be special AICA agents. In both cases, changes to AWaRE would be required to incorporate the stealth communications middleware referred to earlier. However, since AWaRE 3.0 is being designed to be as technology-agnostic as possible, this should not pose considerable difficulty. The greater challenge would be to incorporate more sophisticated self-* functionality into AWaRE (as per the next section), which requires maturation of the research ideas as well as ongoing development efforts.

5   Challenges and Recommendations

There are a number of R & D challenges associated with realizing externalized self-management and self-improvement. Many overlap with the challenges outlined in this book pertaining to AICA agents. In this section we focus on two sets of challenges associated with learning – related to realizing an S* agent's LE – and agent coordination and teaming – related to realizing an S* agent's CE and ODE, and outline recommendations on how they could be addressed.

5.1   Learning and Self-Improvement

Adversarial Search and Opponent Learning:
One challenge is to model the contested nature of an <AICA + S* > system and its adversaries. One recommended approach is viewing the system and its environment

as an adversarial game. There may be multiple adversaries in a contested environment, however, we can abstract all possible adversarial attacks as actions taken by *"the environment player"*. This abstraction enables us to view the cyber defense-versus-attack setting as a 2-player game between the AICA-based system and the environment player. This model enables the <AICA + S*> system to compute steps ahead of its adversaries by exploring possibilities of attacks and resilience pathways. The environment player's behaviour is maximally adversarial in the worst case in that it seeks to impede the behaviour of the system as much as possible. The S* management (sub-)system computes the most robust and resilient responses to the environment player's actions by deploying game-tree search techniques (e.g., Monte Carlo Tree Search).

This approach depends on building a model of the environment player's behaviour (cf. Chap. 6 of this volume). As the adversaries' action space is unknown to us, one solution is to model this behaviour in terms of effects on our system. This behaviour can be learnt from a history of interactions and observed effects. Given an ongoing interaction, this opponent learning model aims to answer three important questions:

1. *Is this an unintentional event or a planned attack?* Anomaly detection and classification techniques need to be developed to detect if an event is abnormal, and if it is unintentional or part of a plan underlying the attack.
2. *What would be the next effect on our system?* We need to develop techniques that can learn from previous attacks and their effects on the system, and use this knowledge to predict, giving an ongoing attack, what the next impact would be (cf. the proactive antifragility paradigm introduced in (Uzunov et al., 2019)). This is related to policy reconstruction techniques in opponent agent modelling.
3. *If a planned attack, what would be the goal of this attack? What would be the plan underlying this attack?* This is the most advanced and challenging form of opponent modelling. The emphasis is on predicting the intended end-effect (goal) and the sequence of immediate effects (plan). We need to develop plan recognition techniques that can predict the opponent agent's top-level plans based on its observed effects on the system. An abductive-reasoning model would be needed to infer plans that best explained observed effects. Plan recognition may also need the capability in Question (1) above to filter out non-intentional events from planned attack events.

This game-tree search approach requires a simulation that enables the system's ability to "look-ahead" in the search, training/learning through, e.g., log mining, representation learning and reinforcement learning, and testing.

Meta-Learning for Self-Improvement:

As we have discussed earlier, to be antifragile, an AICA system needs self-improvement. Self-improvement can be achieved through learning so that the system can operate better in both known and unknown situations. Earlier in the chapter we discussed learning from adaptations caused accidentally (adverse events) and purposefully (in-system perturbations) across different levels. Another S* agent skill-set that we suggest would support self-improvement is the ability of *learning to learn (i.e., meta-learning),* which is the process of improving a learning algorithm over a number of learning episodes. Meta-learning will provide an <AICA + S* > system with a learning capability that can generalize across tasks such that each new task is learned better than the previous one. For example, meta-learning will enable the knowledge learnt from observed attacks to be used for adapting responses to unseen attacks. Meta-learning could also help improve the agent's adaptation to maintain interoperability and/or shared understanding.

5.2 Agent Teaming and Negotiation

Another critical challenge for a combined <AICA + S*> system as outlined in this chapter is the coordination and organisation of the various agents, i.e., how they can cooperate and reach consensus agreements given their distributed, autonomous nature, with different agents having different (possibly conflicting) goals and maintaining different beliefs about the world state. There are two major paradigms used to organize agents within multi-agent systems (Picard et al., 2009): (i) the top-down paradigm, in which the entire organisational structure and coordination patterns are designed by a system architect and the autonomous agents then coordinate their local behaviours and interactions with other agents according to the rules or norms imposed by the organisation; and (ii) the bottom-up (self-organization) paradigm, in which individual agents with local behaviours are capable of interacting with other agents via communication and possibly some pre-defined interaction protocols. In the bottom-up paradigm, the required global functions of the multi-agent system are supposed to emerge as a result of the individual agents' interaction and the agents organise themselves into organisational structures, such as teams, accordingly.

As self-organisation is one of the important properties of a self-* system, S* agents should have the ability to autonomously form teams when there is a need for a complex global function that requires multiple agents to work together. Clearly, the challenges then lie in the roles each agent plays within the team and the relationship between the agents. An equally challenging problem is how the agents collectively evolve their roles and relationships within an organisation/team when there are changes to the environment, to the requirements, and/or to the agents' availability and capabilities. Nevertheless, we also recognise the importance of some predefined organisational structures such as a *marketplace* or *registry* to enable the discovery of agents' services and capabilities as well as the requirements and goals an agent or organisation may have. Furthermore, pre-defined interaction protocols can enable the agents to successfully coordinate their local behaviours and to reach consensus.

As individual S* agents autonomously make adaptation-related decisions, their decisions and actions can make changes to the environment and subsequently affect the decisions and adaptation activities carried out by other agents. To prevent the agents (including both the AICA and S* agents) from making conflicting decisions, they may need to engage in negotiations with other agents to reach agreements regarding goals, world and system states and execution of plans. Since contracts between agents are a fundamental construct employed by S* agents, the agreements between agents can be captured in the contracts. There are several research challenges associated with agent negotiations and contract-enabled agreement technologies:

1. *Many-to-many negotiation*: Existing works on automated negotiation typically considers bilateral negotiations or one-to-many negotiation. However, in an <AICA + S* > system, an agent typically has to collaborate and negotiate with multiple other agents who in turn also engage with many other agents. This presents a non-trivial challenge as, on the one hand, an agent would like to reach an agreement quickly to finalise its contract with another agent; and on the other hand, it would also need to manage other contracts that might have some relations with the contract the agent is trying to finalise.

2. *Levelled commitment contracting*: The simplest mechanism for contract-based agreement requires contracts to be binding. However, in self-adaptive systems changes can occur quickly, and binding contracts do not accommodate such changes. While contingency contracts (Raiffa, 1982) present a possible option, they are typically very complex and require the anticipation of potential future changes. Levelled commitment contracts (Sandholm & Lesser, 2001) that set penalties for different contract breaches can be considered an attractive option. While levelled commitment contracting is particularly suitable for agreements between self-interested agents, the agents in an <AICA + S* > system are generally cooperative and share common goals. Thus, the challenge is in adapting levelled commitment contracting mechanisms to enable S* and AICA agents to reach agreements that can accommodate future events.

6 Summary and Conclusions

The focus of this chapter was on endowing AICA systems with the qualities of resilience and antifragility through distributed self-management and self-improvement, which entails the realization of various self-* properties pertaining to autonomous adaptation, failure recovery, and refinement of individual agent or collective functionality after encountering stressors. We explained that this could be accomplished by employing collections of S* agents that form an S* multi-agent system residing alongside, and interacting with, AICA agents. We discussed how these S* agents can be realized, and argued for an externalized approach where the self-management/improvement and business/cyber defence functionalities in a combined <AICA + S*> system are partitioned, with the former being the sole responsibility of S* agents, i.e., of a separate S* management (sub-)system.

Subsequently, we introduced a two-part conceptual framework providing the necessary design abstractions for developing an S* management (sub-)system/S* multi-agent system. The first part of this conceptual framework encompasses a reference architecture for S* agents, which stipulates that S* agents must possess at least ten core skill-sets for enabling interaction, information sharing, awareness, adaptation and meta-adaptation reasoning and decision-making, and the coordinated design of agent organizations. The second part of the conceptual framework encompasses a number of concepts for multi-agent system design across both a macro- and micro-level. We then presented an accompanying multi-scope/multi-level adaptation and learning approach for self-management/improvement.

As a concrete example of an S* multi-agent system realizing self-management/improvement using an externalized approach, we outlined the AWaRE autonomous middleware framework, focusing on the architectural design of AWaRE's current iteration, AWaRE 2.0. AWaRE can be applied to an AICA system as an overlay or be used as a middleware framework for AICA agents.

Going forward, we discussed two sets of R & D challenges related to incorporating advanced self-* functionalities in an <AICA + S*> system: one set pertaining to learning, and the other to agent organization and coordination. With respect to learning, a key challenge is to predict the next effect and the goal of an ongoing attack on an <AICA + S*> system. This will enable an <AICA + S*> system to deploy counter-measures before the full impact of the attack becomes manifest. The adaptation of an agent can be improved via meta-learning, where an agent learns a task by learning from the output of other tasks. With respect to agent organization and coordination, a key challenge is to define mechanisms for agents to negotiate with each other and reach consensus. These mechanisms need to support agents in forming teams and discovering their roles and relationships within a team structure in a dynamic environment.

Acknowledgements The authors would like to thank Ryszard Kowalczyk (UniSA, SmartSat CRC) for his feedback on earlier drafts of this chapter. Some of the work presented was undertaken within the "Autonomic Cyber Resilience and Antifragility" Collaborative Research Project, supported by the Australian Department of Defence – Next Generation Technologies Fund initiative (Cyber theme).

References

Abeywickrama, D. B., Bicocchi, N., & Zambonelli, F. (2012). SOTA: Towards a general model for self-adaptive systems. In *Proceedings of 21st IEEE international workshop on enabling technologies: Infrastructure for collaborative enterprises* (pp. 48–53). IEEE.

Atighetchi, M., & Pal, P. (2009). From auto-adaptive to survivable and self-regenerative systems successes, challenges, and future. In *Proceedings of 8th IEEE international symposium on network computing and applications* (pp. 98–101). IEEE.

Baruwal Chhetri, M., Uzunov, A. V., Vo, Q. B., Kowalczyk, R., Docking, M., Luong, H., Rajapakse, I., & Nepal, S. (2018). Aware – Towards distributed self-management for resilient cyber systems. In *Proceedings of 23rd international conference on engineering of complex computer systems (ICECCS)* (pp. 185–188). IEEE.

Baruwal Chhetri, M., Uzunov, A. V., Vo, B., Nepal, S., & Kowalczyk, R. (2019). Self-improving autonomic systems for antifragile cyber defence: Challenges and opportunities. In *2019 IEEE international conference on autonomic computing (ICAC)* (pp. 18–23). IEEE.

Bergamaschi, F., Conway-Jones, D., & Peach, N. (2010). Generic vehicle architecture for the integration and sharing of in-vehicle and extra-vehicle sensors. In *Ground/air multi-sensor interoperability, integration, and networking for persistent ISR* (Vol. 7694, p. 76940B). International Society for Optics and Photonics.

Berns, A., & Ghosh, S. (2009). Dissecting self-* properties. In *Proceedings of 3rd IEEE international conference on self-adaptive and self-organizing systems* (pp. 10–19). IEEE.

Beydoun, G., Low, G., Henderson-Sellers, B., Mouratidis, H., Gomez-Sanz, J. J., Pavon, J., & Gonzalez-Perez, C. (2009). FAML: a generic metamodel for MAS development. *IEEE Transactions on Software Engineering, 35*(6), 841–863.

Bouchenak, S., Boyer, F., Claudel, B., De Palma, N., Gruber, O., & Sicard, S. (2011). From autonomic to self-self behaviors: The JADE experience. *ACM Transactions on Autonomous and Adaptive Systems, 6*(4), 1–22.

Bulling, N. (2014). A survey of multi-agent decision making. *KI-Künstliche Intelligenz, 28*(3), 147–158.

Collier, R. W., O'Neill, E., Lillis, D., & O'Hare, G. (2019). MAMS: Multi-Agent Micro-Services. In *Companion proceedings of the 2019 world wide web conference* (pp. 655–662). Association for Computing Machinery.

Dobson, S., Hutchison, D., Mauthe, A., Schaeffer-Filho, A., Smith, P., & Sterbenz, J. P. (2019). Self-organization and resilience for networked systems: Design principles and open research issues. *Proceedings of the IEEE, 107*(4), 819–834.

Hole, K. J. (2016). Principles ensuring anti-fragility. In *Anti-fragile ICT Systems* (pp. 35–43). Springer.

Hole, K. J. (2022). Tutorial on systems with antifragility to downtime. *Computing, 104*(1), 73–93.

Kephart, J. O., & Chess, D. M. (2003). The vision of autonomic computing. *Computer, 36*(1), 41–50.

Kott, A., & Linkov, I. (Eds.). (2019). *Cyber resilience of systems and networks*. Springer International Publishing.

Kott, A., Théron, P., Drašar, M., Dushku, E., LeBlanc, B., Losiewicz, P., Guarino, A., Mancini, L., Panico, A., Pihelgas, M. & Rzadca, K. (2018). Autonomous intelligent cyber-defense agent (AICA) reference architecture, Release 2.0. *arXiv preprint arXiv:1803.10664.*

Krupitzer, C., Roth, F. M., Pfannemüller, M., & Becker, C. (2016). Comparison of approaches for self-improvement in self-adaptive systems. In *2016 IEEE international conference on autonomic computing (ICAC)* (pp. 308–314). IEEE.

Lalanda, P., McCann, J. A., & Diaconescu, A. (2013). *Autonomic computing: Principles, design and implementation*. Springer Science & Business Media.

Lambert, D. A., & Lambert, A. G. (2012). The legal agreement protocol. In *High-level information fusion management and systems design* (pp. 173–190). Artech.

Lesser, V. R. (1998). Reflections on the nature of multi-agent coordination and its implications for an agent architecture. *Autonomous Agents and Multi-Agent Systems, 1*(1), 89–111.

McClelland, J. L., McNaughton, B. L., & O'Reilly, R. C. (1995). Why there are complementary learning systems in the hippocampus and neocortex: Insights from the successes and failures of connectionist models of learning and memory. *Psychological Review, 102*, 419–457.

Newman, S. (2021). *Building microservices*. O'Reilly Media, Inc.

Nygard, M. (2018). *Release it!: Design and deploy production-ready software* (2nd ed.). Pragmatic Bookshelf.

Picard, G., Hübner, J. F., Boissier, O., & Gleizes, M. P. (2009). Reorganisation and self-organisation in multi-agent systems. In *1st International workshop on organizational Modeling (ORGMOD)* (pp. 66–80).

Pokahr, A., & Braubach, L. (2013). The active components approach for distributed systems development. *International Journal of Parallel, Emergent and Distributed Systems, 28*(4), 321–369.

Raiffa, H. (1982). *The art and science of negotiation*. Harvard University Press.

Regli, W. C., Mayk, I., Dugan, C. J., Kopena, J. B., Lass, R. N., Modi, P. J., Mongan, W. M., Salvage, J. K., & Sultanik, E. A. (2009). Development and specification of a reference model for agent-based systems. *IEEE Transactions on Systems, Man, and Cybernetics, 39*(5), 572–596.

Russell, S., & Norvig, P. (2016). *Artificial intelligence: A modern approach* (3rd ed.). Pearson.

Sabatucci, L., Seidita, V., & Cossentino, M. (2018). The four types of self-adaptive systems: A metamodel. In *International conference on intelligent interactive multimedia systems and services* (pp. 440–450). Springer.

Salehie, M., & Tahvildari, L. (2009). Self-adaptive software: Landscape and research challenges. *ACM Transactions on Autonomous and Adaptive Systems, 4*(2), 1–42.

Sandholm, T. W., & Lesser, V. R. (2001). Leveled commitment contracts and strategic breach. *Games and Economic Behavior, 35*(1-2), 212–270.

Schneider, C., Barker, A., & Dobson, S. (2015). A survey of self-healing systems frameworks. *Software: Practice and Experience, 45*(10), 1375–1398.

Tesauro, G., Chess, D. M., Walsh, W. E., Das, R., Segal, A., Whalley, I., Kephart, J. O., & White, S. R. (2004, July). A multi-agent systems approach to autonomic computing. In *Proceedings of 3rd international joint conference on autonomous agents and multiagent systems* (pp. 464–471).

Theron, P., Kott, A., Drašar, M., Rzadca, K., LeBlanc, B., Pihelgas, M., Mancini, L. & Panico, A. (2018, May). Towards an active, autonomous and intelligent cyber defense of military systems: The NATO AICA reference architecture. In *2018 International conference on military communications and information systems (ICMCIS)* (pp. 1–9). IEEE.

Uzunov, A. V., Nepal, S., & Baruwal Chhetri, M. (2019). Proactive antifragility: A new paradigm for next-generation cyber defence at the edge. In *Proceedings of 5th IEEE international conference on collaboration and internet computing (CIC)* (pp. 246–255). IEEE.

Uzunov, A. V., Brennan, M., Baruwal Chhetri, M., Vo, Q. B., Kowalczyk, R., & Wondoh, J. (2021a). AWaRE2-MM: A meta-model for goal-driven, contract-mediated, team-centric autonomous middleware frameworks for antifragility. In *Proceedings of 28th Asia-Pacific software engineering conference (APSEC)* (pp. 547–552). IEEE.

Uzunov, A. V., Baruwal Chhetri, M., & Wondoh, J. (2021b). GOURMET: A methodology for realizing goal-driven self-adaptation. In *2021 ACM/IEEE international conference on model driven engineering languages and systems companion (MODELS-C)* (pp. 197–202). IEEE.

Van Riemsdijk, M. B., Dastani, M. & Winikoff, M. (2008). Goals in agent systems: A unifying framework. In *Proceedings of 7th International Joint Conference on Autonomous Agents and Multi-Agent Systems (AAMAS)* (pp. 713–720).

Villegas, N. M., Tamura, G., & Müller, H. A. (2017). Architecting software systems for runtime self-adaptation: Concepts, models, and challenges. In *Managing trade-offs in adaptable software architectures* (pp. 17–43). Morgan Kaufmann.

Weyns, D. (2020). *An introduction to self-adaptive systems: A contemporary software engineering perspective*. John Wiley & Sons.

Wooldridge, M., & Jennings, N. R. (1995). Intelligent agents: Theory and practice. *The Knowledge Engineering Review, 10*(2), 115–152.

Ye, P., Wang, S., & Wang, F. Y. (2018). A general cognitive architecture for agent-based modeling in artificial societies. *IEEE Transactions on Computational Social Systems, 5*(1), 176–185.

Yuan, E., Esfahani, N., & Malek, S. (2014). A systematic survey of self-protecting software systems. *ACM Transactions on Autonomous and Adaptive Systems, 8*(4), 1–41.

Chapter 11
Collaboration and Negotiation

Samrat Chatterjee, Arnab Bhattacharya, Ashutosh Dutta, Aowabin Rahman, Thiagarajan Ramachandran, Satish Chikkagoudar, and Ramesh Bharadwaj

1 Background and Objective

Collaboration and Negotiation is a critical high-level function of an Autonomous Intelligent Cyber-Defense Agent (AICA) in contested operational cyber defense environments. This function contributes to collaborative mission planning by enabling communication among agents, central cyber C2, and human operators. Since an AICA agent must be stealthy, solving problems autonomously, and collaborating as needed, maintaining the Confidentiality, Integrity, and Availability (CIA) triad is key during world state identification, planning, or action selection phases (Kott et al., 2018; Théron & Kott, 2019; Kott & Théron, 2020). Therefore, the underlying AICA infrastructure must enable rapid deployment and coordination of distributed processing elements and on-the-fly customization and

S. Chatterjee (✉)
Physical and Computational Sciences Directorate, Pacific Northwest National Laboratory, Richland, WA, USA
e-mail: samrat.chatterjee@pnnl.gov

A. Bhattacharya · A. Rahman · T. Ramachandran
Energy and Environment Directorate, Pacific Northwest National Laboratory, Richland, WA, USA
e-mail: arnab.bhattacharya@pnnl.gov; aowabin.rahman@pnnl.gov; thiagarajan.ramachandran@pnnl.gov

A. Dutta
National Security Directorate, Pacific Northwest National Laboratory, Richland, WA, USA
e-mail: ashutosh.dutta@pnnl.gov

S. Chikkagoudar · R. Bharadwaj
Center for High Assurance Computer Systems, U.S. Naval Research Laboratory, Washington, DC, USA
e-mail: satish.chikkagoudar@nrl.navy.mil; ramesh.bharadwaj@nrl.navy.mil

reconfiguration, in the face of changing situations and mission needs. Within the AICA context, the presence of multiple decision-making agents with possibly different goals, suggests that the domain of multi-agent autonomous systems learning may provide a strong foundation for operationalizing the collaboration and negotiation functions (Shoham & Leyton-Brown, 2008; Russell & Norvig, 2010; Weiss, 2013; Singh, 2015; Sutton & Barto, 2018; Bertsekas, 2021). Securing AICA agents includes maintaining the CIA triad against threats targeting the systems or agent (Hedin & Moradian, 2015). For example, system level threats may include the compromise of the central cyber C2 by an adversary (human or AICA agents) resulting in malicious information transfer among agents; however, agent level threats may include unauthorized access to AICA agents by an adversary (human or AICA agents) via compromise of communication links and/or message injection attacks. As a result, secure and trustworthy communication among AICA agents is paramount for mission success in autonomous cyber defense settings.

In a contested multi-agent environment, mission tasks may arise at the *global level* (e.g., involving coordination among multiple teams or platoons of AICA agents) and *local level* (e.g., confined to multiple AICA agents within a team or platoon), necessitating collaboration among agents under information uncertainties and/or partial knowledge. These information uncertainties may correspond to an AICA agent's perception of the environment based on interaction with other agents, central cyber C2, and/or human operators, which may be limited by design and/or operational need to communicate. Since active response and recovery is key for *cyber resilience* – defined by the U.S. National Academy of Sciences as "the ability to prepare and plan for, absorb, recover from, or more successfully adapt to actual or potential adverse events" (National Research Council, 2012), an AICA agent must exhibit autonomy and intelligence with varying degree of information and knowledge, especially under attack while minimizing risks from unintended consequences (Kott & Linkov, 2019; Kott & Théron, 2020; Ligo et al., 2021). Since AICA agents are designed to process information and collaboratively generate executable COA solutions, explainability and interpretability of autonomous actionable decisions become important to assess trustworthiness (Linkov et al., 2020).

Figure 11.1 presents an overarching communication architecture among AICA agents, central cyber C2, and human operators. In this figure, bi-directional communication links are depicted between pairs of entities among the AICA layer, central cyber C2, and human operator (i.e., AICA-AICA, AICA-C2, AICA-Human, and C2-Human). Further, the AICA layer is decomposed into a two-tier hierarchical structure representing distributed levels of agents with different roles defined as: (1) *level 1 learners* that lead a team of agents in pursuit of high-level mission goals or sub-goals, and (2) *level 2 learners* that identify low-level actions supporting identified goals or sub-goals. Further, there may be an ensemble of AICAs pursuing varying mission objectives in a contested setting. As a result, jointly identifying and executing a Course of Action (COA) solution becomes extremely important. Negotiating to achieve consensus toward a COA solution is further complicated by the need for an AICA agent to remain stealthy, verify information received with possibly limited resources, and actively learn in contested mission environments.

Fig. 11.1 High-level communication architecture among agents, central cyber C2, and human operators

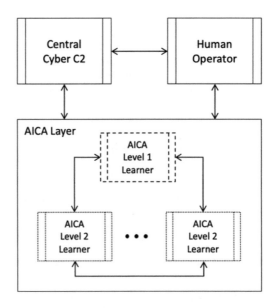

The two-tier hierarchical architecture within the AICA layer in Fig. 11.1 also poses challenges with handling information uncertainties associated with the environment. Thus, AICA agents must be able to generate actionable policies by solving multi-agent stochastic games with imperfect knowledge using robust optimization methods (Zhang et al., 2020).

The rest of this chapter is organized as follows. The next section discusses AICA agent levels and their learning objectives including goals and actions in support of mission tasks. This is followed by a discussion of AICA agent properties critical for enabling secure communication including policy optimization, safety verification, and deception techniques for stealthiness. Thereafter, promising algorithmic approaches for multi-agent coordination are outlined including resilience by design via federated learning and resilience by operational need via randomized information sharing protocols. A representative simulation example comprised of a multi-agent navigation and communication environment is described next. Finally, thoughts for future development are discussed.

2 AICA Agent Levels

Within the AICA layer, levels of agents may be coordinated based on *distributed* and/or *decentralized* architectures. Distributed settings may involve centralized training at the global level followed by policy execution at the local level. After deployment on a distributed infrastructure, each AICA agent must be automatically notified of events of interest; thereafter, processing of an event by an agent or agents in turn may generate new events which are propagated to other (relevant) agents.

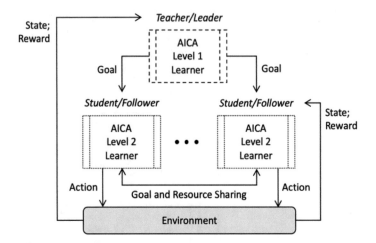

Fig. 11.2 Levels of AICA agents with goal and action learning objectives

Distributed agents may also rely upon the central cyber C2 to provide reliable and fault-tolerant services including virtual synchrony, data integrity, confidentiality, and provenance. However, in decentralized settings, both training and policy execution may occur at the local level. Depending on operational needs, hybrid learning architectures with distributed and decentralized training and action execution schemes may be needed to meet AICA agent goals.

Figure 11.2 presents an expanded overview of the AICA layer in Fig. 11.1 with a two-tier hierarchical structure comprised of a *level 1 learner* (i.e., teacher or leader) and *level 2 learners* (i.e., student or follower). In this case, level 1 learners learn mission goals to convey further to the level 2 learners. Thereafter, level 2 learners learn optimal actions to meet the goals via collaborative goal and resource sharing. Execution of learned actions may result in changes to the environment state and rewards that are conveyed back to AICA agents for identifying future COA plans. Leader agents may also communicate as needed with other leader agents for goal sharing. Collective intelligence is demonstrated here via joint COA plans based on negotiation and consensus building across levels of AICA agents.

Given such an AICA layer architecture, multi-agent hierarchical reinforcement learning (HRL) provides a well-grounded mathematical foundation for developing autonomous and cooperative multi-level decision agents (Barto & Mahadevan, 2003; Sutton & Barto, 2018; Nachum et al., 2018). Reinforcement learning addresses one of the major challenges in agent design and development by affording the possibility of agent synthesis, based on actions and rewards. Moreover, learning can be dynamic, online, and self-directed. This is a major advance which may prove to be a game changer in agent creation and operation. In an HRL setting, AICA agents can learn atomic tasks through interaction with the environment and/or through experience acquired from observed data. Deep reinforcement learning (DRL) algorithms have been proposed recently to address challenges in developing high-dimensional cyber defenses that are dynamic and adaptive (Nguyen & Reddi, 2019). These DRL algorithms can be broadly categorized into *model-free* (i.e., learn direct mapping from states to actions) and *model-based* (i.e., learn predictive model of the environment and then derive actions) methods. To develop autonomous and assured cyber defense solutions for AICA at scale under uncertainty, additional research on combining elements from model-free strategies and model-based planning is needed with safety and security guarantees, especially across multi-modal system operational regimes. Furthermore, DRL with transfer learning may need to be employed to evaluate diverse hierarchical learning architectures via dynamic reconfiguration of agent interactions. This may require leveraging recent work on DRL-based autonomous cyber defense agent architecture and computational workflow with constraint satisfaction (Dutta et al., 2021) and explainable RL (Puiutta & Veith, 2020), as well as uncertainty-tolerant methods for data-driven sequential decision optimization and cybersecurity risk modeling (Chatterjee et al., 2015, 2016, 2021; Saha et al., 2016; Tipireddy et al., 2017; Bhattacharya et al., 2019; Chatterjee & Thekdi, 2020).

3 AICA Agent Properties for Secure Communication

The objective of an AICA agent is to optimize decision-making while satisfying the safety and stability requirements of the environment. Modern cyber systems are complex and dynamic with numerous correlated and stochastically evolving factors. As a result, the agent cannot predict future environmental conditions from the beginning, which makes action planning infeasible. For computing context-aware optimal decisions in such a dynamic environment, an agent needs to understand the current environment condition prior to executing the next action. Therefore, we formulate each AICA agent's decision-making problem as a sequential decision process (SDP) (Braziunas, 2003). In SDP, the agent divides the time-horizon into discrete time-steps, where, at each time t, the agent infers the current environment condition based on current observation, executes an action, and receives feedback from the environment.

Figure 11.3 illustrates the architectural components and workflow of an AICA agent. The inputs for an AICA agent are: (1) state space, S, consisting of all possible conditions of the environment, (2) action space, A, enlisting all possible actions, and (3) safety properties defining the business, mission, or operation related constraints and requirements. In general, human operators are responsible to provide these inputs. Our AICA agent aims to actively learn the optimal policy based on interactive experience while satisfying all the safety constraints. Next, we will discuss how an AICA agent learns policy in an online/active manner and guarantees the satisfiability of safety requirements by describing the different components of AICA agent depicted in Fig. 11.3.

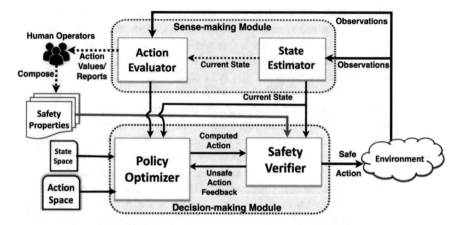

Fig. 11.3 AICA agent architecture and operational workflow for secure communication. (Note: *Human Operators* are a part of the environment and may change set of safety properties. *Safety Verifier* contains environment information such as network topology and device status)

3.1 Active Learning

To deploy context-aware optimal action, the AICA agent has two main capabilities: (1) *sense-making*, that tries to infer the current environment condition, currently adopted attack strategy, and others; and (2) *decision-making*, that tries to compute optimal action based on current sense-making.

Sense-Making

In Fig. 11.3, the *Sense-making* module consists of a *State Estimator* and *Action Evaluator*. At the start of each time t, the agent observes the current symptoms of the environment, based on which, the *State Estimator* infers the current state, $s \in S$. For an environment where each agent has complete information of the rest (fully observable), the agent may directly map the current observation to the current underlying state (Braziunas, 2003). However, in case of partial observability, the current observation cannot be directly mapped to a specific state due to incomplete and imperfect information. In such cases, if the agent knows the correlations of observations and state, it can infer the current state probabilistically using a belief matrix that can address the incomplete and imperfect observability (Braziunas, 2003). One example of such correlation is $p(s|o)$ defining the likelihood of s as the current state for the current observation o. Otherwise (i.e., unknown $p(s|o)$), the policy optimization algorithm generally relies on the reward function to address such uncertainties (Schulman et al., 2017).

The other component, *Action Evaluator*, tries to compute the reward, $R(s', s, a)$, to quantify the payoff or consequences of the last executed action $a \in A$ in state

$s' \in S$ and transitioning to a new state $s \in S$. Moreover, the *Action Evaluator* is responsible to provide reports which, for example, may describe the outcome of different actions in a specific condition. These reports help the human operators to modify, introduce, or remove safety properties; assuming that the operators may not certainly determine all safety properties initially due to not having complete knowledge. As shown in Fig. 11.3, the *Sense-making* module pass the reward $R(s', s, a)$ alongside the current state to the decision-making module at each t.

Decision-Making

The *decision-making* module consists of the *Policy Optimizer* and *Safety Verifier*. The *Policy Optimizer* aims to compute the optimal policy to recommend the optimal action for the current state. As mentioned before, the agent formulates the decision-making problem as SDP, to be deployed in a stochastic environment. Notably, if the agent knows the behavior (e.g., state transition probabilities) of the environment, it can apply Markov Decision Process (MDP) or partially observable MDP (POMDP) models for a fully or partially observable environment (Braziunas, 2003), respectively. In this chapter, we assume that the AICA agent does not know the environment behaviors/dynamics initially; hence, the AICA agent solves the SDP using model-free deep reinforcement learning (DRL).

RL is an approach of learning the optimal policy in a stochastic environment through synchronously acting on and receiving feedback on action consequences from the environment (Kaelbling et al., 1996). In DRL, deep neural networks are used to optimize the RL policy. RL is a tuple of (S, A, O, R, γ), where S is the state space, A is the action space, O is the observation space, R is the reward function, and γ is the discount factor (weights the future impact of an action). At each time t, the agent executes an action $a_t \in A$ on the environment for the current state $s_t \in S$, that induces new observations. The agent observes the current observation $o_t \in O$ to infer the next state s_{t+1} (by *State Estimator*) and computes the reward $R(s_t, s_{t+1}, a_t)$ (by *Action Evaluator*). Based on $R(s_t, s_{t+1}, a_t)$, the agent refines the current policy by tuning its policy parameters. One of the challenges of any RL algorithm is to balance the trade-off between exploration (i.e., executing less-explored actions to understand their consequences) and exploitation (i.e., executing actions based on the current policy). We apply ϵ-greedy algorithm which, as exploration, executes least-explored actions with the likelihood of ϵ (i.e., ϵ cases out of 100) that generally reduces with the passage of time.

Below are three primary approaches for policy optimization:

1. **Value Iteration:** In value iteration, the agent estimates the value, $V(s_t, a_t)$, of each action $a \in A$ for state $s \in S$, which specifies the accumulated rewards when a_t is executed at s_t. $V(s_t, a_t)$ is determined using the following equation:

$$V\left(s_t,a_t\right)=\left(1-\alpha\right)V\left(s_t,a_t\right)+\alpha\left(R\left(s_t,s_{t+1},a_t\right)+\gamma \max_a V\left(s_{t+1},a_{t+1}\right)\right) \quad (11.1)$$

where, α is the learning rate.

At any state $s \in S$, the action with maximum $V(s_t, a_t)$ is chosen as the optimal action a^*. In DRL, the agent determines this value using a deep neural network, and Deep Q Network (DQN) is an example of such value iteration based DRL (Mnih et al., 2015). DQN incrementally updates its DNN parameters based on new experience, using the following loss function:

$$\text{loss} = \left(R\left(s_t, s_{t+1}, a_t\right) + \gamma \max_a V\left(s_{t+1}, a_{t+1}\right) \right) - V\left(s_t, a_t\right) \tag{11.2}$$

In the loss function, the first term is called the target value, and the second term ($V_t(s, a)$) is the predicted value. Another DQN variant, Double DQN, uses separate DNNs for the target and predicted value (Van Hasselt et al., 2016).

2. **Policy Iteration:** In policy iteration based DRL, the DNN predicts the action distribution directly for the current state. REINFORCE is an example of policy iteration based DRL (Sutton et al., 1999). Based on new experience, the agent updates the DNN parameters, θ, based on policy gradients, $\nabla J(\pi_\theta)$, using the following equation:

$$\theta = \theta + \alpha \nabla J\left(\pi_\theta\right) \tag{11.3}$$

where,

$$\nabla J\left(\pi_\theta\right) = \nabla E_{\pi_\theta}\left[\sum_{t=1}^{T} G\left(s_t, a_t\right)\right] = \nabla E_{\pi_\theta}\left(\sum_{t=1}^{T} \nabla_\theta \log \pi_\theta\left(a_t \mid s_t\right) G\left(s_t, a_t\right)\right),$$

$G(s_t, a_t)$ is the accumulated rewards, and $\pi_\theta(a_t \mid s_t)$ defines the action distribution for the current state s_t.

3. **Actor-Critic Approach:** This approach combines both value iteration and policy iteration. Here, an *actor agent* with a policy network determines the action distribution and updates the policy using policy iteration algorithm. Whereas a *critic agent* assesses the value of the recently computed action and updates the DNN using the value iteration algorithm. There can be multiple critics exploring different environment conditions/samples in parallel to expedite the training convergence. Advantage actor-critic (A2C) is an example of such RL algorithm (Mnih et al., 2016), which replaces the value function with the following advantage function:

$$A\left(s_t, a_t\right) = V\left(s_t, a_t\right) - V\left(s_t\right) \tag{11.4}$$

In this advantage function, $V(s_t)$ is the baseline value introduced to keep the variance low and make the DRL more stable.

3.2   Safety Verification

The RL exploration in a real operational setting may cause devastating impacts due to the execution of undesired actions under specific environmental conditions, which makes active RL learning very challenging. To address this, our AICA agent deploys a *Safety Verifier* that verifies whether the RL-computed action violates any given safety property/constraint or not. If the action violates any constraint, the module interrupts the action and sends feedback to the optimizer, which can be in the form of a penalty (i.e., negative incentive/reward). Otherwise, the *Safe Action* is executed on the environment that triggers new observations. Thus, the AICA agents are guaranteed to avoid execution of irrelevant and dangerous actions despite the RL exploration or evolving operational safety requirements.

The safety verifier can be categorized into two different types based on their objectives and RL strategy. The objective of the first type is to find a configuration (fine-grained actions) that can deploy RL recommended action (generally coarse-grained) without violating any constraint. To clarify, let assume a scenario where the agent wants to monitor network communication to detect compromised devices. There are n number of detectors, where each detector represented by a Boolean variable, d_i, can be enabled ($d_i = 1$) or disabled ($d_i = 0$). Notably, each enabled detector inspects traffic of a particular subset of communication links. A specific configuration, $C^k = \{d_o^k, d_1^k, \ldots, d_{n-1}^k\}$, defines which subset of detectors to be enabled (e.g., $d_1^k = 1$) or disabled (e.g., $d_1^k = 0$). Let assume that at a specific time t, the RL recommends doubling the monitoring for each of the device, which imposes the constraint:

$$\forall b \in V, l_b^t \geq \min\left(2l_b^{t-1}, l_b^M\right) \tag{11.5}$$

where, V is the set of network device, l_b^M is the number of links of the device b, and l_b^t is the number of b's links monitored by enabled detectors at t. This constraint specifies that the number of monitored links for each of the device should be twice of the number of previously monitored links. Moreover, there is another constraint specifying that the consumed energy due to traffic inspection by enabled detectors must not exceed the user-given threshold. This constraint can be formalized using the following equation:

$$\sum_{i=0}^{|D|} d_i \times E\left(T_i^t\right) < E_I \tag{11.6}$$

where, D is the set of detectors, $E\left(T_i^t\right)$ is the power consumption a detector i due to inspecting traffic of its assigned links, and E_I is the tolerable maximum energy consumption at any specific time.

Therefore, to deploy the RL recommended action (i.e., doubling the link monitoring), the first type of *Safety Verifier* aims to find a C^k that satisfies both constraints (Dutta et al., 2021). By contrast, the second type of *Safety Verifier* just checks whether the RL recommended action can be deployed without violating the maximum energy constraint (Alshiekh et al., 2018). Understandably, for the second type, the RL action must be fine-grained specifying which detectors to be switched on or off, which may make the RL action space unscalable. This module formulated as Constraints Satisfaction Problem (CSP) can be developed using satisfiability modulo theories (SMT) (Barrett & Tinelli, 2018). Importantly, this module decoupled from the policy optimizer enables the AICA agent to support multi-control cyber resiliency requirements or diversified user or business requirements without exploding the problem space (Dutta & Al-Shaer, 2019a, b).

3.3 Stealthiness

In a collaborative and distributed setting, an attacker can utilize a compromised agent's credibility to access or corrupt other agents' data, send fake/bad messages, or hamper availability. Therefore, stealthiness is a critical feature of AICA to deter attack propagation. One possible approach for agent's stealthiness is to impose the reachability constraint, specifying that an agent will always have to request to specific authoritative servers (e.g., C2 servers) to initiate communication with other agents. If permitted, the agent can reach to another agent only for a fixed interval or until ending the ongoing communication session. After that interval or session, the agent will have to request again to establish new communication session. This can be achieved by implementing IP-mutation with the help of a centralized/distributed C2 servers in a SDN network or using proxies. IP-mutation is a moving target defense (MTD) approach, where IP addresses of agents will be changed in a periodic manner (Jafarian et al., 2015). The advantage of this approach is two-fold; firstly, even if the attacker knows IP address of an agent by reconnaissance, it will become obsolete after a certain interval – that will compel the attacker to go to C2 servers. Secondly, to propagate or initiate attack, the attacker will require to communicate with C2 servers, that may increase the detection likelihood due to abnormal request patterns.

In the IP-mutation approach, agents' communications are conducted using virtual IP addresses (vIPs) instead of real IP addresses (rIPs). The agents will not know rIPs of itself and of other agents. At a specific time interval, the C2 servers will allocate an unique vIP for each of the agent from a pool of vIP, which will be changed again after the end of the interval. To initiate a communication a session, an agent will ask the C2 server about the vIP of the recipient agent (identified by unique name or ID). To prevent attacker's sniffing of these replies, all communication can be encrypted or spatial mutation can be deployed (i.e., different vIPs for the same destination agent from different locations (Jafarian et al., 2014)). The C2 servers will send the mapping among vIPs and rIPs to all SDN switches or proxies, to transform vIPs to rIPs at source end and rIPs to vIPs at receiver end. To keep the ongoing long session (longer than the interval) alive, two possible approaches can be adopted: (1) vIPs of participant agents of that session will remain active until terminating the session, or (2) these vIPs will be valid only for participating agents of this session. Therefore, IP-mutation can increase the attacker's time-to-compromise by deterring the attack reachability or detection likelihood by forcing the attacker to initiate unusual request/access patterns.

In situations where agents have low communication bandwidths and the team cannot communicate with a central C2, then agents can enforce local stealthiness by executing a randomization strategy to decide who to communicate within its local communication neighborhood, as depicted in Fig. 11.4. This is a highly effective tactic in decentralized operational settings where an agent can reduce the impact of adversarial messages sent by some of its neighbors. Typically, in many multi-agent settings, the number and identity of neighboring agents constantly changes over time as a sequence of sub-tasks are completed to accomplish the final mission. If a team has already been compromised and communication with C2 is not available, then this random select and communicate strategy allow agents to reduce the impact of possible interference by adversarial agents in their neighborhood. While AICA's performance will slightly degrade using this randomization strategy if there are no adversarial agents in the neighborhood, it will always be better than the case when an agent unknowingly communicates with adversarial agents in its neighborhood.

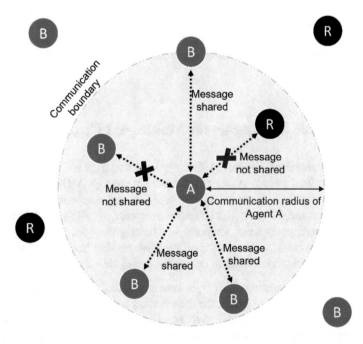

Fig. 11.4 AICA agent communication via randomization for stealthiness. Here, B indicates a friendly "blue" agent, R is an adversarial/compromised "red" agent and A is the agent under consideration. This real-time stealthiness tactic is highly relevant in operational scenarios where the team has already been compromised and communication bandwidth is low

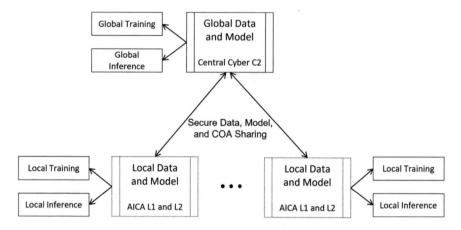

Fig. 11.5 Federated learning architecture for AICA operations

Finally, stealthiness in AICA can be further enhanced by using a federated learning-based design architecture for communication and control, as depicted in Fig. 11.5. Federated learning distributes model training among a multitude of agents, who, guided by privacy concerns, perform training and inference using their local data but share only model parameter updates, for iterative aggregation at the central C2 coordination level. In such a setup, local agents do not share their observational data with any other agents but only shares their inference and model-update outcomes with the central coordinator, who maintains a global model used by agents for autonomous operations.

4   Algorithmic Approaches for Multi-agent Coordination

The key to collaboration between AICA agents lies in their ability to safely communicate, negotiate, and act in adverse operational settings. AICA agents with different capabilities can leverage system-wide complementarity, diversity, and redundancy to accomplish complex missions. However, not all agents interact in the same way as a variety of spatial, temporal, and functional dependencies arise during missions. We can classify the team-level decision-making behavior of agents into three main categories: coordination, cooperation, and collaboration.

(i) *Coordination* achieves additive performance gains for a team of agents via communication. For example, the time it takes for a surveillance team to scour an area of interest decreases linearly as more agents join the team, provided the agents coordinate with a global objective in mind. In coordination strategies, agents at the same level need not always share goals amongst themselves (although a Level 1 learner can share goals to Level 2 learners) as agents are separately rewarded for their individual performance. However, team performance may suffer (exhibit sub-additive performance gains) if smaller coalitions of agents with different objectives are formed within the team.

(ii) *Cooperation* considers teamwork that achieves super-additive performance ('whole is greater than the sum of its parts'). Cooperating agents share their intentions amongst themselves at all levels (resulting in increased communication) to help improve team performance. However, the effect of cooperation on team performance becomes substantial only after a threshold is reached. For example, it may require a certain threshold fraction of interacting cooperating agents to communicate continually to execute a highly efficient search-and-rescue mission. Until this threshold is reached, performance may increase very slightly even with an increasing number of interacting agents.

(iii) *Collaboration* involves interactions between a set of heterogenous agents with complementary capabilities that leads to super-additive performance. In contrast to cooperation, collaboration requires specific types of agents to work together due to task requirements. The resulting team performance is often a step function: performance only reaches a satisfactory level when all the different capabilities are leveraged. For example, a search and rescue mission in a remote environment may leverage teamwork between aerial and ground agents. The aerial agents localize and map the geographical area from a birds-eye view, which is then communicated to the ground vehicles for target retrieval.

The desired team behavior can be accomplished using a control architecture that prescribes how agents should communicate and navigate in adverse conditions to accomplish their goals. The control architecture used often depends on the type of agent-agent interactions, mission goals, available communication resources, and operational conditions. Here, we will discuss three main categories of control architecture: decentralized, centralized and hybrid.

(i) *Decentralized control* is used when an agent takes actions using local information recorded by its sensing module and information received from other neighboring agents within a predefined communication radius. For example, two AICA agents heading towards their separate target locations interacts to avoid colliding when they are too close to each other. Decentralized control is also used when local information needs to be disseminated via repeated agent-agent interactions. One common example of such a scenario is the rendezvous problem, where different agents stationed at different locations in a geographical region seek to meet at a target location within this region. A common decentralized solution to this problem involves each agent moving consenting to move towards the centroid of its visible neighbors that leads to global consensus (Amirkhani & Barshooi, 2021). Decentralized control is typically used in missions requiring coordination and in some special cases, even cooperation. The main advantage of using decentralized control is the reduced need for sensing and communication as most decisions utilize only local information. However, decentralized control is prone to imprecise navigation trajectories and is vulnerable to information distortion by adversarial agents that can destabilize global consensus.

(ii) *Centralized control* is used when global system-wide information is needed for agents to efficiently accomplish a mission objective. A key example of such a mission is consensus-based formation control, where local information is insufficient to maintain a strict formation even if an agent knows the shape of the formation beforehand. Such class of problems is typically solved using the well-known Hungarian method (Wang et al., 2018), where a central coordinator assigns each agent a position in the formation that minimizes their travel time and fuel costs. A key advantage of centralized control is the increased efficiency obtained using a central coordinator that can access the local state of each agent to effectively coordinate their actions. Almost all multi-agent tasks can be deployed in a centralized manner and is, therefore, often the default choice when decentralized control is not feasible. However, the central coordination mechanism is susceptible to interference or sabotage of the communication channels between the agents and the coordinator (Hsu et al., 2020).

(iii) *Hybrid control* systematically blends centralized and decentralized control mechanisms to a wide variety of tasks, such as coverage control, rendezvous to a target location, and search-and-rescue. For example, in coverage control, agents are responsible to optimally scour a given area using a probabilistic density measure that captures the importance of different locations within that area. This density measure is a global piece of information that is used by all the agents to decide their coverage strategy. However, once this global density is accessed, agents can identify regions they are responsible for by observing the behavior of their neighboring agents (Santos et al., 2018; Huang et al., 2020). Leader-follower agent configurations also typically use a hybrid control architecture where certain agents, designated as the leader, obtain global information by communicating with a central coordinator, while the follower agents coordinate their actions based on the leader's behavior. A hybrid control approach blends the best attributes of both centralized and decentralized control with reduced communication requirements as most interactions occur between the agents rather than between the agents and the central controller. However, team performance can be severely affected in certain scenarios where critical agents in the team are prone to vulnerabilities.

5 Representative Multi-agent Navigation and Communication Simulation Example

We consider a simulation-based multi-agent navigation and communication example of decentralized collaboration and negotiation between a set of AICA agents that have no access to a central C2 for path planning and action selection. Specifically, the agents are tasked to carry out a strategic *search and rescue* mission where they need to collectively scour a surveillance area of interest to locate missing assets whose locations are not known precisely at the start of the mission. The agents can be a team of unmanned ground or aerial vehicles (or both), but for this example, we assume a homogenous team of agents with similar sensing and navigation capabilities. The team's mission is deemed to be successful when all the missing assets can be precisely located in the shortest possible time. It is assumed that the mission is carried out in a remote location where agents must autonomously navigate and bypass obstacles and uncertain terrain without any communication with C2 or human operators. However, agents can communicate with each other at regular intervals sharing relevant local information of the navigation environment and coordinates of the missing assets, if located.

A key challenge here is the fact that the number of missing assets is usually very small compared to the size of the surveillance area. In the parlance of multi-agent systems and active learning, this is often referred to as the sparse rewards problem, where the team receives a joint reward (or utility) only when all the goal states (location of missing assets) have been explored. Therefore, for a successful mission, agents must strategically coordinate their local exploration strategies to avoid redundant visits to non-informative locations by different agents at different points in time. It would be much more sensible for the agents to execute a communication-based, "divide-and-conquer" collaboration strategy where local sensing information can be exchanged to determine estimates of where the missing assets can be found with high probabilities (Figura et al., 2021). Moreover, there is a need for negotiation between the agents to optimize task allocation with regards to exploration of different regions of the surveillance perimeter in the shortest possible time. In our setup, it is assumed that the agents have inference capabilities that allow them to concurrently learn from past experiences (local observations, action selections) and agent-agent interactions in a decentralized fashion to inspect surveillance regions that are less explored.

5.1   Algorithmic Approach

To overcome the drawbacks of independent exploration by the agents, it is important for agents to adaptively coordinate and learn different exploration modalities that can maximize their chance to locate the missing targets successfully. Such a strategy requires consistent communication between the agents and a mechanism to devise local rewards (or utilities) for agents to avoid visiting redundant and non-informative locations. The algorithmic approach we present here is based on the paper by Iqbal and Sha (2019), which used a soft actor-critic multi-agent reinforcement (MARL) algorithm (Haarnoja et al., 2018). In reinforcement learning (RL) parlance, actor-critic models comprise of two learning components: (i) a critic that learns the expected long-term utility of executing a joint team action for a given set of local observations, and (ii) an actor that learns the action-selection strategy (or policy) of each agent in the team. Similar to other RL algorithms, actor-critic methods learn the optimal collaboration behavior by updating the actor and critic estimates (represented by neural networks) iteratively from multiple simulations of possible agent-agent interactions, location visitations, and total team rewards accrued over a surveillance period. The soft actor-critic algorithm, however, promotes exploration of different states as it favors a probabilistic action-selection strategy for the entire team compared to standard actor-critic methods. To overcome the challenge associated with sparse rewards, one needs to characterize an intrinsic reward mechanism, which measures an agent's implicit reward of exploring a given state (location). This intrinsic reward value is calculated based on other agents' evaluation of how informative the state is based on their previous visits to that state. The mathematical form of the intrinsic rewards is chosen in a way that promotes coordinated team exploration. For example, if an agent on visiting a particular location deems it to be non-informative (in the absence of any missing target), then the intrinsic rewards for other agents visiting that location should not increase to prevent over-exploration. In a more extreme case, if a visiting agent labels a certain location (or areas close to it) to have no chance of finding missing targets (fully non-informative), then the agent's intrinsic reward of visiting that location should be zero irrespective of what other agents broadcast; this prevents the agent to repetitively explore the same region at the persuasion of other agents. In this example, we consider the following three types of agent exploration strategies for which the intrinsic rewards are defined:

(i) **Covering strategy** rewards an agent more for exploring locations that it considers more informative than an average agent. This strategy results in agents being more selective about exploring new locations; only exploring those areas where an agent believes have a higher chance of locating missing assets.

(ii) **Burrowing strategy** rewards an agent for exploring locations that it considers less informative than the average agent. While this strategy may seem counterintuitive, such a reward scheme encourages agents to further explore areas that have been less visited with the hope that potential dead-ends can be identified quickly to reduce overall exploration time.

(iii) **Minimum strategy** rewards an agent for exploring locations based on the most conservative agent's estimate. This strategy is a more extreme version of the Burrowing strategy that leads to agents exploring locations that no other agents have explored.

However, for our search and rescue example, it is not immediately clear which type of exploration results in the mission being successful in the shortest amount of time. Moreover, as mentioned previously, agents may adaptively change their exploration strategies that result in different intrinsic rewards for different locations in the surveillance area. To account for these challenges, a two-tier hierarchical learning strategy is proposed to simultaneously learn the team's exploration strategy, where:

(i) A collection of lower-level soft actor-critic RL models are trained to learn team strategies (joint action selection) for all different intrinsic reward types (and associated agent exploration strategies) using a common pool of observations from all the agents (global state of the system).

(ii) An upper-level selection strategy that chooses the learnt lower-level team strategy for different reward types to accomplish the mission in the shortest possible time (i.e., reaches the target goal states in smallest time duration). The upper-level selection strategy, referred to as the meta-policy learning, provides team consensus in choosing among a set of possible exploration strategies (with different intrinsic rewards) to attain optimal collaboration leading to mission completion.

The algorithm considers that agents communicate their observations at time t, which consist of their own locations, information about the surrounding (in a grid-world, this will be whether a surrounding wall exists in each of the four edges) and whether an agent has found any missing asset at that location. Thus, the state of each agent is the global state containing the above-mentioned information. The rewards assigned to an agent could be "extrinsic" – when an agent achieves the main objective of locating missing asset; or "intrinsic", when we assign rewards to an agent for exploring novel regions. The reward also contains a time penalty, to motivate the agents to complete the tasks quickly. The following steps are used to train the agents using the two-tier HRL algorithm:

- Set the initial locations (states) of the agents and the missing targets.
- Initialize the actor-critic model for each type of intrinsic-reward based team exploration strategy; also, initialize the upper-level meta-policy model.
- For each of the lower-level models, start a training episode (an episode refers to a temporal sequence of states, actions, and rewards of the agents observed at each time step until all goal states have been explored).

  - If the current episode has not terminated (i.e., the goal states have not been reached)

    ○ Sample an action for each agent from their current exploration strategy
    ○ Record the new locations of the agents after sampled actions are executed
    ○ Determine the intrinsic rewards accrued by the agents at each time step
    ○ Store the current state, action, reward, and next state for each agent in a set storing the history of agent-agent and agent-environment interactions for all the lower-level models
    ○ Continue to the next time step

  - Once the current episode has terminated, update the actor-critic model parameters concurrently for a fixed number of iterations using data from the history set. This updates the action-selection strategy of each agent for a given intrinsic reward type.

- Once all the actor-critic models are updated, we update the upper-level policy selection model parameters and updates the policy choosing a combination of exploration strategies that minimize the time to find all the missing assets.
- Repeat the steps until the parameters of the upper-level model converge.

It is important to note that such a two-tier learning strategy belongs to the class of Centralized Training with Decentralized Execution (CTED) type RL algorithms. The CTED paradigm allows for agents to train while sharing information during model training that is usually not available during online exploration, which depends only on agents' local observations. A CTED based learning strategy may lead to emergent team behaviors in decentralized decision-making problems that maybe otherwise difficult to learn if only local observations were used during training.

5.2   Simulation Environment

For demonstrative purposes, we use a discrete 2D grid-world environment to represent the surveillance area. Specifically, we used a grid with 20 rows and 20 columns, where each row-column combination depicts a specific location or state. Some of the grid-world states cannot be reached by any agent, which denotes obstacles in the environment. It is assumed that the surveillance agents start from a common terminal at the start of the mission. The missing assets are in one of the reachable grid-world states; however, their locations are not known *a priori* to the agents. Each state of the grid-world has an associated intrinsic reward that depends on the current exploration strategy pursued by the team. In this example, the agents have 4 potential actions to choose from to navigate around the grid: going left, right, up, or down. It is instructive to note that in this example, agents do not stay in one location in consecutive time periods. This is because surveillance is a time-sensitive operation, and agents seek to complete the mission as early as possible. In our setup, we have two surveillance agents (indicated by circles) and two missing assets (indicated by stars). For discussion purposes, we will refer to the asset on the left-side of the grid as Asset A, while the other one is referred to as Asset B. Similarly, we will refer to the agent on the left as agent 1, and the agent on the right as agent 2. During model training, we keep the initial starting point of the agents fixed and run simulations to iteratively learn the best collaborative strategy to find the unknown missing assets. The episodes end whenever both the missing targets have been discovered by the agents. The entire code was executed in *Python* and an *OpenAI-Gym* environment was used for both training and testing the algorithms. We trained the model on 50,000 timesteps. Figure 11.6 describes the initial location of the agents before training and the final states of the agents once the model has been trained. For evaluation, we considered the flowtime metric, which, in the context of this problem, is the average number of timesteps it takes for the agents to locate both missing assets.

5.3   Discussion

To assess the performance of the trained agents, we consider the same 20 × 20 grid-world with the same initial location of the agents but with new target locations of the missing assets. Figure 11.7 depicts the strategies used by the agents in this scenario. As observed from the state visits of the two agents, each agent starts to take a separate path to a different missing asset. Now that we have trained the model, how does

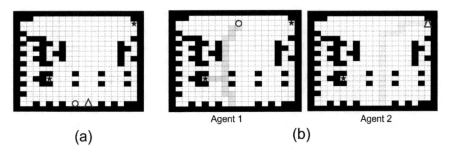

(a) (b)

Fig. 11.6 (**a**) Initial states of the agents (circle and triangle) in the 20 × 20 grid-world during training. The locations of the missing assets (stars) are unknown to the agents a priori; (**b**) final states of the agents at the end of training the RL model

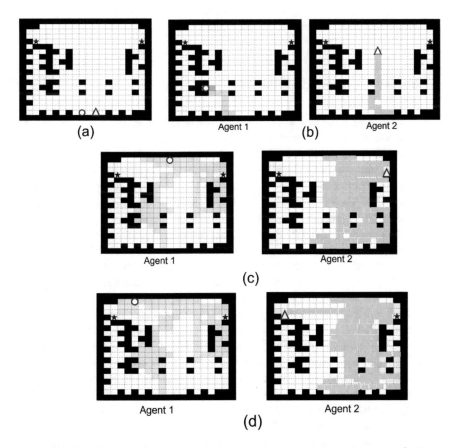

Fig. 11.7 (**a**) Initial state of agents during testing. (**b**) and (**c**) show intermediate states; (**b**) shows that initially, the agents directly go to the original locations of the treasures, i.e., locations of the missing assets in the training phase, using a burrowing approach. (**c**) As the location of the treasures have changed, the agents now switch to "covering" approach to maximize exploration. (**d**) shows the final state at which both missing assets have been found by the agents

it generalize for a case in which the locations of the missing people/items are different to those on which the model was trained on. Figure 11.7a presents the initial state of the agents for the evaluation scenario. In Fig. 11.7b, we see that the agents directly move towards the original locations of the missing assets in line with what was observed during training (Fig. 11.6b). As asset A is not in the original location used during training, the agents switch from a burrowing to a covering strategy, to minimize redundancy in exploration, as observed in Fig. 11.7c. While we do observe that there is small degree of overlap in the states visited by the two agents in Fig. 11.7c, mostly the sub-regions explored by the two agents are disparate. Finally, Fig. 11.7d shows the terminal states when both missing assets have been located. We observe that while agent 2 had discovered both missing assets, its collaboration with agent 1 was critical in retrieving the assets quickly. As the agents follow a covering strategy, agent 2 is more likely to visit a state that is less frequented by agent 1, resulting in a more efficient exploration. Across 12 parallel threads, the mean flowtime was computed to be 903 timesteps.

6   Summary and Conclusions

This chapter describes steps toward operationalizing the *collaboration and negotiation* function of an AICA agent using multi-agent autonomous systems learning as a core foundational element. We start by representing a two-tier hierarchical AICA layer architecture with different levels of agent teams pursuing goal and action learning to collaboratively develop joint COA plans to support cyber defense missions. Key AICA agent properties including stealthiness, safety verification, and active learning for secure communication are presented in the context of a reinforcement learning paradigm. Promising algorithmic approaches are also outlined for multi-agent coordination and consensus with hierarchical and federated learning principles. Based on a representative simulation example for a search and rescue mission, we demonstrate the benefits of adaptive multi-agent collaboration within an autonomous and decentralized operational setting.

In this representative example, three types of multi-agent exploration strategies were considered: (1) *covering* — rewards an agent for being more selective about exploring new locations relative to an average agent; (2) *burrowing* — rewards an agent for being less selective about exploring new locations relative to an average agent; and (3) *minimum* — rewards an agent for exploring locations that no other agent has explored or are visited the least. A two-tier hierarchical learning strategy was implemented where a lower-level soft actor-critic RL model is used to learn team strategies (joint action selection), and an upper-level meta-policy learning scheme is adopted to determine consensus among a set of possible exploration strategies. This two-tier learning strategy is a class of CTED type RL algorithms leading to emergent collaborative team behaviors among AICA agents. Simulation experiments with a 2D grid-world environment involving a *search and rescue* mission was implemented in a customized Python-based OpenAI-Gym learning environment.

The simulation results reveal that stochasticity in asset locations can trigger changes in collaboration strategies among agents to improve overall mission performance. Future development opportunities for further enhancing the AICA *collaboration and negotiation* function may include: (1) *scalable multi-agent consensus methods* to learn emergent behaviors within and across diverse AICA agent teams with heterogenous capabilities; (2) *dynamic threat inference at system and agent levels* to ensure secure information exchange while maintaining stealthiness and robust operations; (3) *safe transfer of collaborative strategies* learned in low-dimensional settings to high-dimensional operational environments; (4) *explainability of learning outcomes and algorithmic traceability* to instill AICA agent trustworthiness via actionable information sharing; (5) *blended data-driven and domain-aware learning* to account for sparse communication with limited situational awareness in contested settings; and (6) *resilient response and proactive messaging schemes* to maintain consensus under evolving system constraints and limited communication resources.

Acknowledgments The research described in this book chapter is part of the Mathematics for Artificial Reasoning in Science Initiative at Pacific Northwest National Laboratory (PNNL). It was conducted under the Laboratory Directed Research and Development Program at PNNL, a multi-program national laboratory operated by Battelle for the U.S. Department of Energy under contract DE-AC05-76RL01830.

References

Alshiekh, M., Bloem, R., Ehlers, R., Könighofer, B., Niekum, S., & Topcu, U. (2018). Safe reinforcement learning via shielding. In *Proceedings of the AAAI conference on artificial intelligence* (Vol. 32, No. 1).

Amirkhani, A., & Barshooi, A. H. (2021). Consensus in multi-agent systems: A review. *Artificial Intelligence Review*, 1–39.

Barrett, C., & Tinelli, C. (2018). Satisfiability modulo theories. In E. M. Clarke et al. (Eds.), *Handbook of model checking* (pp. 305–343). Springer.

Barto, A. G., & Mahadevan, S. (2003). Recent advances in hierarchical reinforcement learning. *Discrete Event Dynamic Systems, 13*(1), 41–77.

Bertsekas, D. (2021). *Rollout, policy iteration, and distributed reinforcement learning*. Athena Scientific.

Bhattacharya, A., Bopardikar, S. D., Chatterjee, S., & Vrabie, D. (2019). Cyber threat screening using a queuing-based game-theoretic approach. *Journal of Information Warfare, 18*(4), 37–52.

Braziunas, D. (2003). *POMDP solution methods*. University of Toronto. https://www.techfak.uni-bielefeld.de/~skopp/Lehre/STdKI_SS10/POMDP_solution.pdf

Chatterjee, S., & Thekdi, S. (2020). An iterative learning and inference approach to managing dynamic cyber vulnerabilities of complex systems. *Reliability Engineering & System Safety, 193*, 106664.

Chatterjee, S., Halappanavar, M., Tipireddy, R., Oster, M., & Saha, S. (2015). Quantifying mixed uncertainties in cyber attacker payoffs. In *2015 IEEE international symposium on Technologies for Homeland Security (HST)* (pp. 1–6). Best Paper Award (Cyber Security).

Chatterjee, S., Halappanavar, M., Tipireddy, R., & Oster, M. (2016). Game theory and uncertainty quantification for cyber defense applications. *SIAM News, 49*(6).

Chatterjee, S., Brigantic, R. T., & Waterworth, A. M. (Eds.). (2021). *Applied risk analysis for guiding homeland security policy and decisions*. Wiley.

Dutta, A., & Al-Shaer, E. (2019a, April). Cyber defense matrix: A new model for optimal composition of cybersecurity controls to construct resilient risk mitigation. In *Proceedings of the 6th annual symposium on hot topics in the science of security* (pp. 1–2).

Dutta, A., & Al-Shaer, E. (2019b, June). "What", "Where", and "Why" cybersecurity controls to enforce for optimal risk mitigation. In *2019 IEEE conference on Communications and Network Security (CNS)* (pp. 160–168). IEEE.

Dutta, A., Al-Shaer, E., & Chatterjee, S. (2021). Constraints satisfiability driven reinforcement learning for autonomous cyber defense. *arXiv preprint*, arXiv:2104.08994. In Proceedings of the 1st international conference on Autonomous Intelligent Cyber-Defence Agents (AICA) 2021.

Figura, M., Lin, Y., Liu, J., & Gupta, V. (2021). Resilient consensus-based multi-agent reinforcement learning with function approximation. *arXiv preprint*, arXiv:2111.06776.

Hedin, Y., & Moradian, E. (2015). Security in multi-agent systems. *Procedia Computer Science, 60*, 1604–1612.

Hsu, C. D., Jeong, H., Pappas, G. J., & Chaudhari, P. (2020). Scalable reinforcement learning policies for multi-agent control. *arXiv preprint*, arXiv:2011.08055.

Huang, W., Mordatch, I., & Pathak, D. (2020). One policy to control them all: Shared modular policies for agent-agnostic control. *In International conference on machine learning* (pp. 4455–4464).

Haarnoja, T., Zhou, A., Abbeel, P., & Levine, S. (2018, July). Soft actor-critic: Off-policy maximum entropy deep reinforcement learning with a stochastic actor. *In International conference on machine learning* (pp. 1861–1870).

Iqbal, S., & Sha, F. (2019). Coordinated exploration via intrinsic rewards for multi-agent reinforcement learning. arXiv preprint arXiv:1905.12127.

Jafarian, J. H. H., Al-Shaer, E., & Duan, Q. (2014, November). Spatio-temporal address mutation for proactive cyber agility against sophisticated attackers. In *Proceedings of the first ACM workshop on moving target defense* (pp. 69–78).

Jafarian, J.H., Al-Shaer, E., & Duan, Q. (2015, April). Adversary-aware IP address randomization for proactive agility against sophisticated attackers. In *2015 IEEE conference on computer communications (INFOCOM)* (pp. 738–746). IEEE.

Kaelbling, L. P., Littman, M. L., & Moore, A. W. (1996). Reinforcement learning: A survey. *Journal of Artificial Intelligence Research, 4*, 237–285.

Kott, A., & Linkov, I. (Eds.). (2019). *Cyber resilience of systems and networks* (pp. 381–401). Springer.

Kott, A., & Théron, P. (2020). Doers, not watchers: Intelligent autonomous agents are a path to cyber resilience. *IEEE Security & Privacy, 18*(3), 62–66.

Kott, A., Théron, P., Drašar, M., Dushku, E., LeBlanc, B., Losiewicz, P., Guarino, A., Mancini, L., Panico, A., Pihelgas, M. et al. (2018). *Autonomous Intelligent Cyber-defense Agent (AICA) reference architecture*. Release 2.0. arXiv preprint arXiv:1803.10664.

Ligo, A. K., Kott, A., & Linkov, I. (2021). Autonomous cyberdefense introduces risk: Can we manage the risk? *Computer, 54*(10), 106–110.

Linkov, I., Galaitsi, S., Trump, B. D., Keisler, J. M., & Kott, A. (2020). Cybertrust: From explainable to actionable and interpretable artificial intelligence. *Computer, 53*(9), 91–96.

Mnih, V., Kavukcuoglu, K., Silver, D., Rusu, A. A., Veness, J., Bellemare, M. G., & Hassabis, D. (2015). Human-level control through deep reinforcement learning. *Nature, 518*(7540), 529–533.

Mnih, V., Badia, A. P., Mirza, M., Graves, A., Lillicrap, T., Harley, T., & Kavukcuoglu, K. (2016). Asynchronous methods for deep reinforcement learning. In *International conference on machine learning* (pp. 1928–1937).

Nachum, O., Gu, S. S., Lee, H., & Levine, S. (2018). Data-efficient hierarchical reinforcement learning. *Advances in Neural Information Processing Systems, 31*, 3303–3313.

National Research Council. (2012). *Disaster resilience: A national imperative*. The National Academies Press. https://doi.org/10.17226/13457

Nguyen, T. T., & Reddi, V. J. (2019). Deep reinforcement learning for cyber security. *IEEE Transactions on Neural Networks and Learning Systems*. https://doi.org/10.1109/TNNLS.2021.3121870

Puiutta, E., & Veith, E. (2020). Explainable reinforcement learning: A survey. In *International cross-domain conference for machine learning and knowledge extraction* (pp. 77–95). Springer.

Russell, S., & Norvig, P. (2010). *Artificial intelligence: A modern approach* (3rd ed.). Pearson.

Saha, S., Vullikanti, A. K. S., Halappanavar, M., & Chatterjee, S. (2016). Identifying vulnerabilities and hardening attack graphs for networked systems. In *2016 IEEE symposium on Technologies for Homeland Security (HST)* (pp. 1–6). IEEE.

Santos, M., Diaz-Mercado, Y., & Egerstedt, M. (2018). Coverage control for multirobot teams with heterogeneous sensing capabilities. *IEEE Robotics and Automation Letters, 3*(2), 919–925.

Schulman, J., Wolski, F., Dhariwal, P., Radford, A., & Klimov, O. (2017). Proximal policy optimization algorithms. *arXiv preprint*, arXiv:1707.06347.

Shoham, Y., & Leyton-Brown, K. (2008). *Multiagent systems: Algorithmic, game-theoretic, and logical foundations*. Cambridge University Press.

Singh, M. P. (2015). Cybersecurity as an application domain for multiagent systems. In *AAMAS* (pp. 1207–1212).

Sutton, R. S., & Barto, A. G. (2018). *Reinforcement learning: An introduction* (2nd ed.). MIT press.

Sutton, R. S., McAllester, D., Singh, S., & Mansour, Y. (1999). Policy gradient methods for reinforcement learning with function approximation. *Advances in Neural Information Processing Systems, 12*.

Théron, P. & Kott, A. (2019). When autonomous intelligent goodware will fight autonomous intelligent malware: A possible future of cyber defense. In *2019–2019 IEEE Military Communications Conference (MILCOM)* (pp. 1–7). IEEE.

Tipireddy, R., Chatterjee, S., Paulson, P., Oster, M., & Halappanavar, M. (2017). Agent-centric approach for cybersecurity decision-support with partial observability. *In 2017 IEEE international symposium on technologies for Homeland Security (HST)* (pp. 1–6).

Van Hasselt, H., Guez, A., & Silver, D. (2016, March). Deep reinforcement learning with double q-learning. In *Proceedings of the AAAI conference on artificial intelligence* (Vol. 30, No. 1).

Wang, H., Shi, D., & Song, B. (2018, October). A dynamic role assignment formation control algorithm based on Hungarian method. In *2018 IEEE SmartWorld, Ubiquitous Intelligence & Computing, Advanced & Trusted Computing, Scalable Computing & Communications, Cloud & Big Data Computing, Internet of People and Smart City Innovation* (SmartWorld/SCALCOM/UIC/ATC/CBDCom/IOP/SCI, pp. 687–696). IEEE.

Weiss, G. (2013). *Multiagent systems* (Intelligent robotics and autonomous agents series) (2nd ed.). MIT Press.

Zhang, K., Sun, T., Tao, Y., Genc, S., Mallya, S., & Basar, T. (2020). Robust multi-agent reinforcement learning with model uncertainty. *Advances in Neural Information Processing Systems, 33*, 10571–10583.

Chapter 12
Human Interactions

Eric Holder, Jessie Y. C. Chen, Kristen Liggett, Phillip Bridgham, Neil Briscombe, Thomas Eskridge, Marco Carvalho, and Lavinia Burski

1 Introduction

Human interactions with an Autonomous Intelligent Cyber-defense Agent (AICA) need to be systematically considered across all stages of design and employment including: conceptual design; iterative design of software, hardware and interfaces; marketing and sales; system training; operational use; and the system updating and adaptation stages (Holder et al., 2021). The AICA system will include various occasional cyber defender users such as analysts, updaters or system trainers, incident responders, maintainers, programmers and others, typically working in a remote and secure location and with some degree of cyber defense expertise and/or artificial intelligence or machine learning (AI/ML) expertise. What makes the AICA

E. Holder (✉)
Army Research Directorate, DEVCOM U.S. Army Research Laboratory,
Sierra Vista, AZ, USA
e-mail: eric.w.holder4.civ@army.mil

J. Y. C. Chen
Army Research Directorate, DEVCOM U.S. Army Research Laboratory, Orlando, FL, USA
e-mail: yun-sheng.c.chen.civ@army.mil

K. Liggett
711 Human Performance Wing, Air Force Research Laboratory,
Wright-Patterson AFB, OH, USA
e-mail: kristen.liggett@us.af.mil

P. Bridgham
Mission Systems, Northrop Grumman, McClellan Park, CA, USA
e-mail: Phillip.bridgham@ngc.com

N. Briscombe
Mission Systems, Northrop Grumman, Cheltenham, UK
e-mail: neil.briscombe@euro.ngc.com

© The Author(s), under exclusive license to Springer Nature Switzerland AG 2023
A. Kott (ed.), *Autonomous Intelligent Cyber Defense Agent (AICA)*, Advances in Information Security 87, https://doi.org/10.1007/978-3-031-29269-9_12

conceptualization unique is that one of the primary users and stakeholders impacted by AICA actions, and the main focus of this chapter, is not really a cyber defender at all.

This unique user group is the frontline users that operate the equipment and systems with one or more embedded AICAs programmed to defend their systems from attacks. The autonomous agents will make decisions and take actions that can alter the frontline users' operational capability and real-time decisions. The ACIA system is an automated cyber defense system and the frontline user is unlikely to have dedicated cyber defense personnel embedded that really understand cyber defense and the nuts and bolts of AICA's functioning or decisions (Kott et al., 2019). As argued by Kott et al. (2019) for the Department of Defense use cases, in the future battlespace, communication and reachback to these cyber defender stakeholders also cannot be assumed, or relied on either, leaving this frontline user group to interact, interpret and decide largely on their own how to deal with AICA and AICA's decisions and actions. This lack of anytime access to AICA experts or developers is expected for civilian and industrial applications as well. What the frontline users have training and expertise on is the employment of their systems in the operational context as it is, and predicted to be into the foreseeable future, and they need to maintain their ability to function and act, with the ACIA serving as an intelligent agent replacement for an embedded human cyber defender. In essence, this makes ACIA more like an embedded, mostly-automated, cyber defender teammate with some control over the functioning of their systems. One doesn't have to look far to see how human cyber/network defender decisions, even simple things such as resetting a service or unannounced outages, can impact the daily work of those on the systems impacted and the breakdowns and workarounds that this can create. The frontline users, such as military, safety critical, or emergency personnel, may also be operating in a context where these real-time matches and mismatches in goals and decision outcomes between humans and agents can mean mission success or failure and life or death. The effective design of AICAs with the human in mind can help to minimize these frictions and this user-centered process can't wait until the later stages of the design process to be added.

A high-risk example to highlight the importance of human interactions would be a military unmanned aerial vehicle (UAV) with embedded AICA(s). Decisions and actions by the AICA might impact the unit's ability to move, shoot and communicate and the UAV's ability to provide persistent surveillance or overwatch of humans

T. Eskridge
L3Harris Institute for Assured Information, Florida Institute of Technology, Melbourne, USA
e-mail: teskridge@fit.edu

M. Carvalho
Computer Engineering and Sciences, Florida Institute of Technology, Melbourne, FL, USA
e-mail: mcarvalho@fit.edu

L. Burski
AECOM, Hertfordshire, UK

in danger zones or reliable weapons support. In time critical phases of combat there might be reasons to accept more or less temporary cyber risk in order to achieve overall mission success or complete a maneuver. Further, these risk assessments might be based on knowledge that humans uniquely possess. These operations typically can't be halted for any extended period of time to sort out the automation. This chapter will argue that the design and employment of any AICA application will need to:

- Identify and understand its stakeholders, workflows, and information and decision requirements
- Leverage this information to design the AICA interdependencies, interactions and interfaces to support usability, transparency and explainability where needed across the design and operational use lifecycle
- Identify and employ measures and methods to evaluate design success and impact, and
- Manage expectations and perception of the AICA(s) and its capabilities and limitations to ensure effective use and calibrated trust.

This introduction was intended to emphasize the importance of the human and human interactions for successful deployment of AICA on real-world applications, embedded in real-world equipment. This chapter will provide an overview of considerations and methods to apply to ACIA design to help ensure that the ACIA-enabled equipment and systems put into use enable, rather than hinder, operational success. This chapter also provides a proposed approach to apply to AICA designs to synch human and agent mental models based on real-world examples, along with guidance on how to measure the impact.

2 Human Interaction Considerations and Techniques

2.1 Trust and Transparency

In recent years, various expert groups have consistently identified transparency as a key area of research that is critical to achieve trustworthy AI and effective human-agent teaming (e.g., the IEEE P 7001 Design Standard on Transparency, see Winfield et al., 2021). Indeed, empirical studies have shown that transparency information can help human operators properly calibrate their trust in machine agents (Stowers et al. 2020), although there is also evidence that high levels of transparency may lead to over-trust (Bhaskara et al., 2021). Furthermore, studies show that that there may be costs associated with greater system transparency (particularly information about uncertainty) in terms of increased operator workload and, additionally, decision response times could be impacted due to the large amount of information to be processed associated with transparent interfaces (Kunze et al., 2019). However, the same result of increased operator workload was not observed in other transparency studies (Bhaskara et al., 2021; Stowers et al., 2020) suggesting that transparent design needs to be tailored to the users, the workflow and the information required for decisions. AICA design needs to find the optimal level of relevant transparency using human factors design and evaluation techniques.

As intelligent systems become increasingly sophisticated and are capable of learning/evolving either based on their learning algorithms or access to information from other networks, it is imperative to examine the implications of these agent capabilities/behaviors on operator trust in the systems. Since predictability is a critical aspect of trust development and maintenance, agent behaviors that change over time (e.g., because of learning, updates, or new inputs from another network) may prevent operators from properly maintaining accurate mental models of agent capabilities, which are crucial for effective trust calibration. As a result, human-agent team performance can be negatively impacted due to the misalignment of human mental models and agent capabilities (Bansal et al., 2019). Computation-driven trust modeling and update methods that ensure compatibility of updates with human mental models are promising approaches that promote effective joint human–agent system performance (Bansal et al., 2019).

Effects of individual differences on cognitive task performance and interaction with automation have been well documented in the literature (Chen & Barnes, 2014), and research findings suggest that for human–technology interaction designs (including their associated training requirements), factors such as human variations in their characteristics and abilities should be taken into account. For example, Ingram et al. (2021) found that participants with a higher propensity to trust (as measured by their responses to the Propensity to Trust Machine Questionnaire) were more likely to trust an image classifying agent than their lower-propensity counterparts, particularly when the agent was incorrect or under uncertain situations (e.g., poor image quality). At the cultural level, Chien et al. (2020) found that agent transparency had an impact on the participants' interaction with an intelligent agent (i.e. compliance with agent's recommendations) in a simulation-based experiment, but the effects of agent transparency were significantly influenced by participants' culture. These results suggest that when transitioning intelligent systems from one culture to another, user interface modifications and training interventions may be required due to the effects of cultural differences on system reliance related to agent transparency. AICA designers need to understand the target user populations and sub-populations to enable effective design.

2.2 Transparency-Based Approaches to Human-Agent Interaction

There are a number of agent transparency frameworks that have received attention since the 2010's. While most of these frameworks are focused on robotic systems (e.g., the Human-Robot Transparency Model by Lyons and the Coactive System

Model by Johnson), the Situation awareness-based Agent Transparency (SAT) framework (Chen et al., 2018) is more general and has been applied to AI-based agents in numerous joint human-AI decision making contexts. The SAT framework, based on Endsley's (1995) situation awareness (SA) model, consists of three levels of information requirements from one agent (e.g. an AI agent) to its partner (e.g. a human operator) to support the partner's perception of the agent's current actions and plans (Level 1), comprehension of its underlying logic (Level 2), and projections of future outcomes based on the agent's predicted end-states of current actions and plans (e.g. likelihood of success/failure), and any uncertainty associated with the projections (Level 3). The SAT framework, after its initial introduction in 2014 (Chen et al., 2014), was updated in 2018 (Chen et al., 2018) to incorporate bidirectional communications and teaming-related aspects between human and machine agents (see Fig. 12.1). A number of research groups that conducted HAT research based on the SAT model use "what if" simulation as a Level 3 item, which can support humans' prediction of future outcomes through interactive/bidirectional human-agent transparency (Cabour et al., 2021). The SAT model is one method that can be effectively used to capture the information that needs to be shared between the humans and agents to support AICA design.

An emerging area of research related to transparency is eXplainable AI (XAI). XAI systems can be delivered via various techniques (e.g., feature- or policy-based explanation, causal link, contrastive explanation, simplification and local explanation techniques such as LIME, "what if" simulation, etc.) and modalities (e.g.,

Situation Awareness-based Agent Transparency

Level 1: Goals & Actions
Agent's current status/actions/plans
- Purpose: Desire (Goal selection)
- Process: Intentions (Planning/Execution); Progress
- Performance
- Perception (Environment/Teammates)

Level 2: Reasoning
Agent's reasoning process
- Reasoning Process (Belief/Purpose)
- Motivations
  - Environmental & other constraints/affordances

Level 3: Projections
Agent's projections/predictions; uncertainty
- Projection of future outcomes
- Uncertainty and potential limitations; Likelihood of success/failure
- History of performance

Fig. 12.1 Updated SAT model. (Reproduced with permission from Chen et al., 2018)

visual, language/dialogue, multimodal) (see review articles by Miller, 2019; Rawal et al., 2021). While transparency and explainability are used interchangeably by some, it is important to note that transparency is a broader concept that can be achieved by various techniques such as XAI and interpretable models. Transparency is also inherently more proactive, while explainability implies post-hoc explanations. Cabour et al. (2021) propose the Abstracted Explanation Space framework — with all three SAT (Chen et al., 2014) levels embedded in the architecture — and present a case study of a human-machine interface (HMI) design for an anomaly detection agent based on the architecture. In the cyber domain, Holder and Wang (2021) apply the SAT model in the HMI design of a "junior cyber analyst," which is an XAI-based agent that can assist human analysts in cyber protection team mission planning (see Fig. 12.2 for an overview).

In high stakes environments such as cyber warfare, transparent HMIs capable of justifying recommendations are particularly beneficial for humans to determine whether to accept the agent's input. It is critical to note that the transparency and explainability have to be translated or phrased in a way that each user can understand. Indeed, the draft IEEE P 7001 Design Standard on Transparency (Winfield et al., 2021) identifies five categories of stakeholders (end users/operators; general public/bystanders; certification agencies; incident/accident investigators; legal personnel), each of whom may have similar yet distinct transparency requirements. In fact, even the user/operator group may include individuals with widely different backgrounds and expertise. AICA designers need to have a base understanding of the trust and transparency factors that will impact how the system interacts with different groups of stakeholders; they also need to identify the translation requirements that support each group's needs given their task, information requirements and way of thinking and communicating. Methods such as SAT should be used early in the

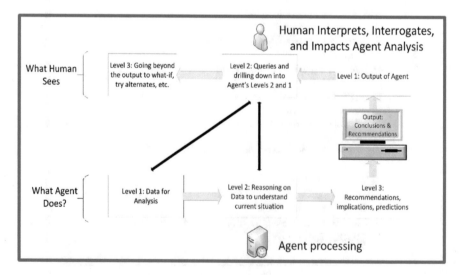

Fig. 12.2 Overview of the SAT modeling process used to define an XAI junior cyber analyst. (Reproduced with permission from Holder & Wang, 2021)

design process to map out the information requirements. This analysis can guide design behaviors and even the algorithmic approaches that are optimal and valid for the application in terms of being able to provide the required information or explanations.

2.3 Human Factors Design Process

At the most basic level, the Human Factors Design Process is a user-centered design (UCD) process. UCD is a design approach that definitively places the user at the center of all design activities. According to William Hudson (2022) of the Interaction Design Foundation, UCD is "an iterative design process in which designers focus on the users and their needs in each phase of the design process. UCD calls for involving users throughout the design process via a variety of research and design techniques so as to create highly usable and accessible products for them" (see Fig. 12.3). The process starts with a deep understanding of the users, their needs for

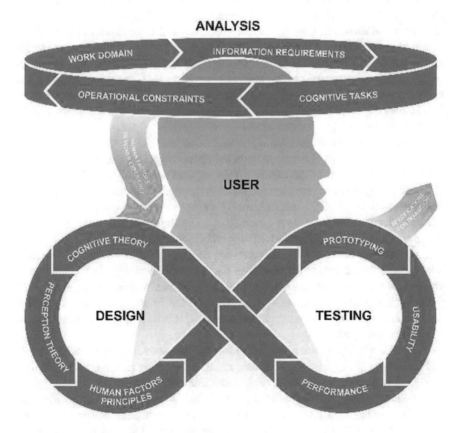

Fig. 12.3 User-centered design process

performing their work, and their constraints and limitations from both a work perspective and a human capabilities perspective. This analysis feeds an iterative design and evaluation process that again requires working with users to obtain feedback. Keeping users involved throughout the design process helps ensure that the final product will be both useful and usable.

As shown in Fig. 12.3, the user-centered design process or human factors design process (HFDP) begins with analysis. Effective analysis is crucial to the success of the design process as it provides a foundation to support all subsequent design activities. The Analysis Phase establishes the relationship between the design team and the end-users of the product being developed. The design team employs human factors methods and techniques such as unstructured and structured interviews, observations, and specific techniques such as goal-directed task analyses in order to elicit information about the work and work context. Analysis techniques such as workflow diagramming are used to validate the information and determine gaps in understanding for iterative knowledge elicitation. These activities supply the design team with a valuable understanding of the work domain that includes the overall goal of the work; tasks currently done to accomplish it; objectives, order, and dependencies of those tasks; information requirements; etc. The analysis enhances the team's knowledge of stakeholders; tasks, information and decisions to be supported; sources of information; gaps in current processes and information; constraints of time and environment; and the objectives of the work. For example in the Holder and Wang (2021) work on XAI as a junior cyber analyst, the analysis phase produced tables of information requirements, based on SAT concepts, mapping the agent's level 1, 2, or 3 SA with the data used, reasoning performed and human interactions expected mapped out for each information type (e.g., incidents, vulnerabilities, threats, etc.).

An important requirement for supporting effective HAT is the identification of interdependence points that enable team members to support and assist each other in the accomplishment of the mission. This requires analyzing the structure of the HAT according to the information and task interdependencies that can be supported. The performance of HATs are defined by the interaction of cooperating entities tasked with common goals. These include not only the cyber offense/defense goals of the agent, but teamwork goals that support human situation awareness and sensemaking such as observability, directability, and predictability (Johnson & Vera, 2019). Hard interdependence describes the relationship where one teammate is waiting for the output of another teammate to continue: without the completion of the other teammate's work, the current goal will not be reached. Soft interdependence holds when help from others could be used if offered but is not necessary to complete a task goal.

While identifying interdependencies is most often done at design time, Tummala and Eskridge (2022) describe a technique for interpreting an agent's hierarchical task specifications to identify and exploit task interdependencies for improved team performance. These interdependencies are extracted from task sub goals and preconditions found in a task analysis to determine how agents can assist and be assisted by other teammates. The interdependence information also constrains information sharing among team members to be specifically relevant to those team members that can be of assistance in an interdependent task.

The most challenging step in the HFDP is the conversion of domain knowledge obtained during the Analysis Phase into initial design concepts (represented by the arrow from the Analysis Phase to the Iterative Design and Testing Phases in Fig. 12.3). This step requires the integration of information gathered in the Analysis Phase with foundational empirical knowledge of human perception (vision theory, color theory, etc.) and cognition (encoding theory, memory theory, information processing theory, multiple resource theory, attention theory, etc.) guided by human factors design principles that represent decades of empirical research to determine the most effective ways to display information for different uses (see Fig. 12.3). This foundational knowledge and experience in applying it to design prevents the creation of complex designs that overtax users' perception and cognition. For example, Liggett and Thomas (2015) found that transforming thousands of rows of intrusion detection system (IDS) log files into a parallel coordinates visualization allowed IDS analysts to use their pattern matching skills to detect potential cyber attacks by looking for attack signatures versus reviewing the rows of raw data individually (see Fig. 12.4). Design teams must also determine sources of required data to support the interfaces and visualizations and consider methods of effectively accessing those data. Through these activities, a design team can provide an effective tool that will guide users to information they need when they need it, and training and documentation needs will be minimal.

During the Iterative Design and Testing phase, products are tested, refined, and tested again as needed to ensure maximum utility and usability. The thoroughness

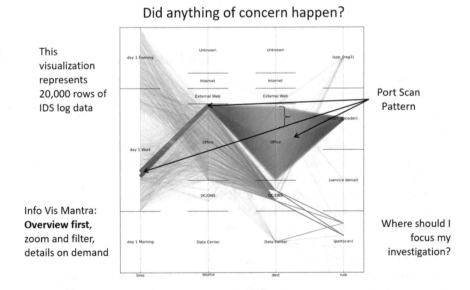

Fig. 12.4 Parallel coordinates visualization of IDS log files

of the analysis and the skill, experience and knowledge of the designer will affect the number of iterations that will be required. Later evaluations should include user-in-the-loop testing with operationally representative scenarios in order to verify that the design is effective. User involvement has the added advantage of ensuring user buy-in. Users often end up preferring things that are best for them when they feel they have been allowed an adequate amount of input into the design process.

Research supports that early consideration of work processes reduces situations in which unanticipated requirements are encountered by users at or after development, requiring high-cost design adaptations or, worse yet, retrofitting or shelving of developed systems.

3   An Example Approach for AICA Applications

3.1   Applying Lessons Learned for Human Interactions in AICA-Relevant Systems

This section presents an applied approach for addressing some of the core challenges related to designing for human interaction in AICA-enabled systems and tailored to the AICA reference architecture currently available. The following guidance has been curated through hands-on experimentation and includes lessons-learned, technical approaches, and multiple human interaction user interface techniques for supporting HATs (human-autonomy teams) from applied projects with agent-based interactions supporting various Intelligence, Surveillance and Reconnaissance (ISR) applications.

3.2   Implementation Strategies Aligning Human and Agent Mental Models

As described above the need to establish an alignment of a human mental model to the agent capabilities is paramount. This necessary alignment will enable both human and agent to perceive and comprehend events in the environment using the same criteria and vocabulary. Once the alignment is established, knowledge and decision making can be shared between humans and agents in a human-centric fashion enabling the primary requirement of effective human-machine teaming. A strategy for this alignment, selected for its applicability to AICA design and called the Human-Agent Mental Model, is presented in Fig. 12.5 below.

Reading from bottom to top, the Human-Agent Mental Model begins with a representation of the human mental model, indicated in blue. This layer of the conceptual map aligns the levels of human situational awareness. As discussed above, the SAT model is proposed to capture the information required to enable

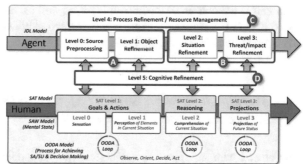

Fig. 12.5 Human-agent mental model: alignment of human mental model and agent capabilities

bidirectional transparency between humans and agents. Each SAT level represents an opportunity for synchronizing discrete levels of understanding across HAT members. The underlying Situation AWareness (SAW) ontology model alignment is included as a means to capture the current mental state and to further illustrate the progression of mapping from human to agent and illustrate one mechanism of transparency.

Moving up to the agent layer, indicated in green, we show the corresponding computational and software design-oriented model. This mapping considers an agent's capabilities of sensing and reasoning as its "mental model". The Joint Directors of Laboratories (JDL) information fusion model (Steinberg & Bowman, 2017) is applied here to provide a functional decomposition of the agent's capabilities. The reason for selecting an information fusion model is because agent-based architectures are sensor based and sensor-based architectures rely on information fusion techniques to establish and maintain situational knowledge, or state estimation. Additionally, the latest JDL information fusion model is comprehensive and includes cognitive refinement (level 5 in Fig. 12.5) that is well suited for alignment of concerns for HATs. Using this model of agent information processing and decision-making, the conceptual mapping aligns the JDL information fusion levels to the SAT levels, completing the alignment of agent and human mental models. This alignment can be achieved through several different strategies, leveraging techniques described in prior sections to gather the required information. These strategies can be applied to agent design using techniques ranging from more simplistic agent processing implementation of classifying information as it is processed within a message or event based processing strategy, to more complex semantic classification algorithms for alignment to semantic ontological knowledge representations.

The resulting alignment, in its entirety, not only provides a mental state mapping between agent and human, but also provides a mapping to specific agent functional elements, namely the agent's ability to sense and reason with information fusion levels. We have successfully used this approach in past projects to orchestrate agent capabilities that work and interact in alignment with human mental models supporting usability and explainability (Allen & Steiner, 2018). The OODA Model alignment at the bottom of the human layer, as well as the red markers, will be discussed in detail later in this chapter when addressing how to apply this approach for developing effective AICA solutions.

3.3 An Implementation Strategy Applied to the AICA Reference Architecture (AICA RA)

Now armed with an approach for human mental models and agent capabilities alignment, we modify the AICA reference architecture (Kott et al., 2019) to set the stage to design for effective human interactions. Using a sensemaking control loop model suitable for both human and machine cognition allows understanding and annotation of decisions within HATs. The OODA model (Boyd, 1987) is ideally suited as a human mental model that is also fit for autonomous agent capability alignment and has been demonstrated to provide agent capability orchestration (Allen & Steiner, 2018). Additionally, by applying the OODA model to a cognitive agent-based framework, agent capabilities of sensing, orienting/planning, deciding, and acting are able to drive specialized and concurrent development activities focused in these areas. The OODA loop occurring for human processing is shown on the bottom of Fig. 12.5 and is also now aligned to the AICA reference architecture, including the mapping of the agent capabilities in terms of information fusion.

The red labels from Fig. 12.5 represent the agent capabilities from a conceptual perspective and are aligned and labeled here in Fig. 12.6 within the AICA RA's functional areas to provide guidance as to where and how they can be implemented and integrated into a working solution. The information Level 0 and Level 1, Level 2 and Level 3, and Level 4 (from Fig. 12.5) are mapped to the AICA reference architecture functions as indicated by the A, B, and C notations. The JDL information fusion Level 4, process refinement and resource management, has been mapped to the AICA reference architecture collaboration and negotiation function. Additionally, information fusion Level 5, user/cognitive refinement, has been mapped to the AICA

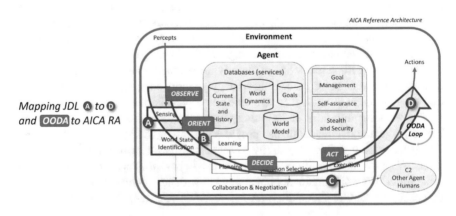

Fig. 12.6 Alignment of information fusion and OODA model within AICA RA

reference architecture cognitive loop because this feature definition includes activities related to refining human-machine conceptual alignment and processes.

As indicated earlier, the OODA constructs provide an opportunity to support both human interaction and agent capability development in a transparent way based on common ground overlap of the OODA steps between agent and human tasks and understanding. A close look at the AICA reference architecture cognitive loop in Fig. 12.6 shows an alignment of the OODA constructs of Observe, Orient, Decide, and Act. These activities are shown loosely mapped within the agent cognitive loop. The opportunity for establishing a more formal adoption of the OODA loop within the AICA reference architecture cognitive loop is expanded upon next to help address transparency and explainability requirements.

The functional diagram above is an extension of the AICA reference architecture with modifications indicated with red. The AICA Reference Architecture's cognitive loop is shown with the addition of the OODA loop constructs provided as the OODA Service. The OODA Service is a cross-functional capability that acts as a proxy between the core knowledge management and agent functions. In other words, the OODA service classifies interactions into bins that both the agent and human can relate to. This is illustrated in Fig. 12.7 by how it wraps around the knowledge management service and knowledge domains and mediates access to and from these knowledge sources. The OODA Service is event-oriented and provides opportunities for AICA core components to exchange events with cognitive context described as an OODA Trace (similar to an agent epoch). As an example, when a percept is received and processed by the core component "Sensing", an OODA Trace instance will be created and the sensing information will be saved and categorized as "Observe" events within this OODA Trace. As the agent performs World State Identification and Planning, the resultant information gain and state estimations will be categorized as "Orient" events and recorded as part of the same OODA Trace. This OODA Trace processing continues with the resulting "Decide" and "Act" events. These OODA traces will be the key element of the human-agent interactions.

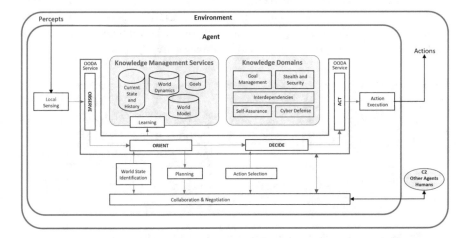

Fig. 12.7 Integrating the cognitive OODA loop within the AICA reference architecture

This extended AICA Reference Architecture is now capable of exposing the details of OODA Traces through the "Collaboration & Negotiation" function illustrated at the bottom of Fig. 12.7. An additional modification of the AICA Reference Architecture is that the "Sensing" block (left side of diagram) has been changed to "Local Sensing" to distinguish between an agent's ability to sense using its local sensing capabilities vs. exchanging knowledge using more advanced OODA Trace constructs via collaboration and communication. Due to the complexities inherent in cyber defense, as well as team coordination in general, the "Cyber Defense" and "Interdependencies" knowledge domains were added. It is expected that an agent's knowledge domain requirements change depending on their tasking and so this portion of the reference architecture is subject to change.

3.4   Example 1: Applying the OODA Trace Method as a Web Interface

The OODA Service within the AICA Reference Architecture provides opportunities for orchestration of agent capabilities when implemented as an events-driven solution. As an example, the Orient process may be implemented using complex event processing techniques where event filters can be defined to "look for event conditions". Such an approach would provide a natural way for humans to define conditions of interest, while minimizing the agent complexity. This can support effective bi-directional interactions between the human and agent. Not only does the OODA Service enhance an agent's cognitive process orchestration, but also helps to address some challenges associated with transparency, explainability, and trust in AI.

The ability to classify agent events and maintain OODA traces has substantial benefits for explainability. Because the OODA model is human-centric, it provides a natural way to structure communications between human and AICA team mates. With the OODA service enhancement to the AICA reference architecture and OODA Trace content accessible via the Collaboration & Negotiation service, there are new opportunities for implementing human-centric interfaces supporting elements of explainability (see Fig. 12.8 for examples of how a web-based interface could provide shareable common ground information items).

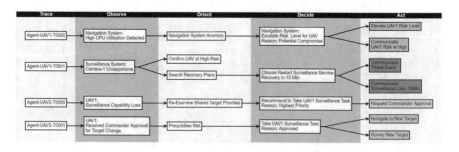

Fig. 12.8   Example 1: OODA trace supporting web-based human interaction

Example 1 presented here is a screen shot of a proof-of-concept browser-based web interface that exposes OODA Traces to end-users for providing insight for humans to better understand agent-based decision making. The example here illustrates information that might be available to an operator controlling multiple AICA-enabled UAVs during their post mission debrief. Each construct of Trace, Observe, Orient, Decide, and Act are aligned to a unique swim lane. Each instance and relationships across individual traces are then presented as a horizontal graph, from left-to-right. There is a natural sequence of events occurring from top-to-bottom. The dataset used in this example and shown in the web-interface illustrates the following sequences of events for our autonomous UAV example in a debrief session after a mission:

1. UAV1 Agent starts a new trace when anomalous CPU utilization is observed.
2. UAV1 Agent elevates the risk level for this UAV platform and communicates this to the HAT.
3. UAV1 Agent starts a new trace when it is observed that Camera-1 becomes unresponsive.
4. UAV1 Agent confirms that this platform is already at high risk, searches for applicable recovery plans, and decides to restart the surveillance service and this will take 10 minutes.
5. UAV1 Agent executes the service restart and communicates to the HAT of the capability loss.
6. UAV2 Agent observes the UAV1 capability loss and compares target priorities and need for persistent surveillance on priority targets.
7. UAV2 Agent notifies Commander of intent to change targets.
8. Commander views data from UAV1 and the decision process from UAV2 in the web interface and approves the change of targets.
9. UAV2 Agent receives approval from Commander and takes over UAV1's target and begins navigation and surveillance activities.

This particular example captures HAT communication as a cognitive activity, meaning that communication is integrated into the OODA cognitive loop and results in an action event, accessible in the updated world model for reasoning or review. This example also illustrates how agent collaboration and change in priorities may be explained across the HAT at a human-centric level.

3.5   Example 2: Applying to OODA Trace Method to Natural Language Interfaces

Effective human-machine teaming can be accomplished by leveraging and integrating into already established human-centric communication channels for seamless HAT interactions, especially natural language interfaces. Both voice and chat interfaces represent good candidates for providing natural human-centric interfaces on top of an OODA cognitive loop. It is envisioned that such techniques would interact

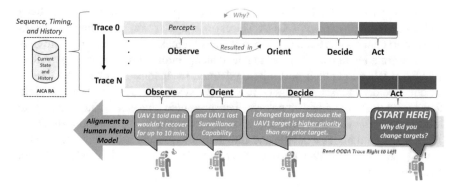

Fig. 12.9 OODA trace supporting a natural language interface

with the AICA's OODA Trace Service to provide end-user interaction. These interactions can be tailored to the intended user's mental model, context, workflow and terminology. An illustration of how the UAV example may be explained using OODA Traces and a natural language interface is illustrated below.

As illustrated above in Fig. 12.9, reading right to left, the human operator may inquire about why an action was taken, or proposed, and receive an explanation from the agent with details regarding what was observed, how this was interpreted, and what decisions were made. This technique also works reading left to right to query the agent on what it would do in certain circumstances. This also allows the human to set pre-conditions in the OODA process to trigger confirmation by the human or other pre-conditioned behaviors. As an example, a human-in-the-loop condition may be able to set a condition that all target changes require human approval in the decision stage before acting. Using this technique, the human is able to explore the potential interaction space and HAT decision making process and criteria when time allows, as well as receiving tailored direct action messages when more appropriate for the context.

As mentioned above, communication and collaboration is a cognitive activity that takes advantage of the complete HAT cognitive loop. One of the advantages of this is that communication needs may be tracked and learned about and as the OODA loop refines the world model and assesses interdependency needs, information may now be pushed vs. pulled. This technique results in effective proactive and team-oriented communication and collaboration.

4 Evaluating AICAs' Operational Effectiveness

Measurement using meaningful and valid measures, metrics, methods, contexts and events (e.g., cyber threats or injects) is critical to the successful design and deployment of fielded systems regardless of the exact approach taken or nuances of that specific application. Establishing a continual measurement process is also essential when the task requirements or context changes and/or system algorithms and behaviors are continually adapting, updating or learning as this impacts both how the system and its agents perform and the human's interactions with those systems. Embedded AI systems, like the AICA, require a fundamental change to the typical evaluation approach to ensure both AICA cyber defense system test and evaluation factors, as well as measures of operational usability and utility of the AICA-embedded systems, are included and integrated.

Kott et al. (2019) do a good job of laying out many of the AICA use cases and system evaluation factors so the focus here will be on how to integrate those with human-centered operational measures. What this means is that the impact of AICA performance on team, or task, outputs and overall effectiveness for the teams using the industrial machine, military system, or other AICA-embedded systems needs to be evaluated and there is a need to bridge the approach and understanding of two, or more, typically disparate groups. The operational communities that are conducting system evaluation and human systems integration, or are training and evaluating individuals or teams on using these systems, often have established metrics and measures (e.g., Gunnery tables, task or productions standards) and scenarios they run to evaluate performance and qualify systems, students or users. What these communities typically lack is cyber-specific injects and data to be able to integrate and really test the ability of AICA to add value and support operational success during scenarios that are realistically impacted by cyber and other electronic attacks.

In contrast, the groups that understand how to implement the cyber events of interest to AICA will typically lack the understanding of the operational requirements, scenarios and evaluation methods for the overall systems that AICA will be embedded in. These two groups will have to come together in order to create implementable, integrated test events where operational users perform their core tasks realistically while also dealing with realistic cyber threats, attacks and incidents by interacting with both AICA agents and the impact of AICA actions while completing their tasks. This will require a mechanism to force this integration, along with testing personnel and resources to see it through. See Li et al. (2022) for a relevant example for Platooning under cyber attacks to illustrate steps in the combined scenario direction. The other AICA cyber-defender user groups can, and should, be integrated in some of these test cases as warranted but as noted are not the primary focus of this chapter.

A quick discussion of applicable measures should include consideration of both objective and subjective measures of performance and utility. At the core of objective measures are the impacts on process and task outcomes with, and without, AICA support and can include constructs such as efficiency (timing and process flow) and effectiveness (task success measures) and embedded measures of constructs, such as situation awareness or resilience among others. Subjective measures can include satisfaction and willingness to use measures, as well as the impact of AICA on situation awareness, trust, resilience, attention allocation, workload, mission success and other human factors and usability measures. See Charlton and O'Brien (2019) for more detailed discussion of various measures and note that there are some standard measures used but every evaluation usually requires adaptation and tailoring to capture relevant performance measures for that application and context. A hybrid set of measures involves creating, and confirming with operators, understandable AICA system performance specifications (e.g., readme files) that inform the frontline users on AICA capabilities and limits by contextual factors and result in informed use. This would be like the performance specification and tolerances sheets you'd expect for mechanical or weapons systems but tailored to the complex performance nuances of an AICA.

A number of organizations have published their guidance on designs of systems with transparent HMIs (Winfield et al., 2021). Specific assessment methods have also been proposed to evaluate system transparency levels. For example, multiple sets of metrics have been proposed by XAI researchers to assess the effectiveness of XAI systems (Rawal et al., 2021). The metrics largely focus on four aspects of the XAI systems: correctness and robustness; usefulness, understandability, and processing difficulty for the human; congruity (congruence between human's and machine's mental models); generalizability, adaptability, and versatility (Miller, 2019). A survey, the Explanation Satisfaction Scale, has been developed to evaluate XAI users' experience (Hoffman et al., 2018) with a focus on assessing congruence between the AI systems output and the human's mental model of the problem space. Sanneman and Shah (2022) propose the SA-Framework for XAI (SAFE-AI) to assess transparency of agents' XAI-based explanations and how well they supports humans' SA.

There are a few additional considerations for the measurement of human interaction factors for the AICA-embedded systems. How will the systems be validated at various stages, to include before release to a user group, for any variations in scenario or contexts, and any revalidation after algorithm learning and adapting based on experience with operations? Will there also be a way to learn from the cases where the system was destroyed or failed, or are we losing critical data and limiting the training pipeline? How will additional user feedback and context-relevant training data be fed back into the AICA learning process? It is also critical to understand that these testing and training events should not be solely based on canned data and cases where everything works perfectly as that is not likely the reality of how the operational use of the system will be. The users, and also evaluators, need to have realistic understanding and expectations of impacts, possible malfunctions or odd actions, and off normal conditions early in the process, rather than experiencing them after the system is in operational use. The need for realistic expectations extends beyond training and testing to include realistic marketing to the stakeholders that buy the systems which are often not the actual end users. How the AICA is presented, framed and understood by the end users will also impact how they perceive and interact with the system, particularly when it makes errors, and especially errors that a human would not make. It is important to align the user's mental models and expectations with the realistic capabilities and limits of the AICA system (Holder et al., 2021).

5   Future Interaction Considerations

We have identified key requirements for supporting human interaction with AICA, including human factors approaches; core HAT considerations such as transparency, bi-directional communication and interdependencies; the need for a structure to capture that information and guide design as shown with the Human-Agent Mental Model and OODA trace methodology; and suggested measurement options and approaches. In this final section, we forecast where advanced interaction techniques may be used to enhance human interaction with AICA to heighten operator awareness and increase overall team performance.

There have been recent significant advances in technologies that enable viewing and interacting with software and automation outside of the typical computer desktop metaphor. Some of these advances include the viewing of information in unconstrained 3D space, utilizing Virtual Reality (VR), Augmented Reality (AR), and tangible interfaces, where users manipulate physical devices to interact with software systems. These new technologies offer opportunities for the development of novel user interfaces that permit users to have richer interaction with complex information while taking advantage of new techniques to make this information more accessible, meaningful, and retainable. This is relevant to HATs when considering that agents are capable of tracking, aligning, and analyzing much more data than humans.

We have mostly ignored the cyber defender stakeholders in AICA use. Future work needs to consider these users as well to include troubleshooting or improving AICA performance, as well as AICA algorithm training and updating the agents' intended tasks and contexts. These users can be prime candidates for advanced visualization techniques. The screen shot above in Fig. 12.10 shows a prototype 3D web view. This view extends an interface called Cyber Looking Glass (CLG) on top and adds an interactive 3D model of underlying interconnected information (Carvalho, et al., 2016). This is an example of increasing information sharing between human and agent for training, diagnostics, and with editing capabilities included, bi-directional information sharing.

Another area for future development is to expand on the ability for the ACIA Reference Architecture to support two-way OODA Traces not just for agents, but for human team members as well. An agent-sourced OODA Trace may be represented as a data set that is capable of being re-computed by another agent with similar domain knowledge representation that would result in the agent making the same decision. However, several challenges exist for capturing and using an OODA Trace that is human-sourced. The first challenge is capturing the OODA Trace elements in such a way that does not impede performance, so that the operator is not forced to create a diary of their actions. The second challenge is codifying the information that can lead to consistency and repeatability of reasoning across humans and agents. A third challenge is documenting those traces where one or more of the Observe, Orient, Decide, and Act steps are informed by the operator's creativity and curiosity. In such cases, the operator may be exploring the space of possible

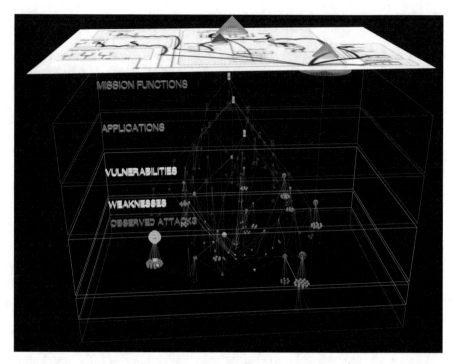

Fig. 12.10 Three dimensional data using 3D web technology

solutions within a cyber situation, but it would be difficult to precisely specify a set of repeatable conditions for the operator actions, making reproduction of their behavior by other AICA or human teammates difficult. One promising effort would be to establish at least human-to-agent OODA Traces such that HATs interfaces can provide reinforcement learning to agents in a seamless manner. Future techniques for automatically capturing natural language and human interface inputs into, and behaviors on, the system and the related context may also help automatically produce OODA traces from the human that the AICA agents can access and integrate.

6   Summary and Conclusions

This chapter laid out the base tool box AICA developers should bring in to explore and create effective human interactions and measure their success. This included an overview of the core human factors and iterative design considerations and a deeper dive into transparency and trust-related considerations. When AICA outputs and decisions are impacting the human user's ability to operate their systems these trust and transparency factors will play a central role in informed use and utility. This foundational toolbox was then grounded in a practical example of how these techniques might be applied to AICA design based on a modified version of the current AICA reference architecture, with an embedded OODA service layer as the common ground between humans and agents.

The Human-Agent Mental Model approach was provided to capture the human "architecture" to set the stage to map out the information requirements for each AICA system that is developed, providing a framework to hang that information on to support the human-agent interactions and teaming using a common language. The core of this approach was to foster alignment and understanding on sensemaking constructs across human and software agent models. It is recommended to use the techniques and considerations provided to create the information, interaction and interdependency understanding needed to build an architecture, such as the Human Agent Mental Model and OODA Trace proposed. This supports the approach of designing systems in a human understandable way rather than forcing humans to conform to the machines. The architecture can then be used to advance the design of the system, using iterative user-centered design techniques and measures as provided to ensure the system provides operational utility for its intended user population dealing with realistic cyber threats.

The chapter also provided guidance on how to measure the success of the AICA design to support human interactions, grounded in operational context and scenarios. The discussion also provided ideas on where some of the directions that interaction concepts may expand towards in future use cases and design considerations for those as well. The exact application of each technique or approach listed may require some adaptation for any specific AICA application as is always the case but the core building blocks and knowledge to accomplish this goal are provided.

References

Allen, H., & Steiner, D. (2018). Creating and maintaining a world model for automated decision making. In *Computational context* (Vol. 2018, pp. 107–136). CRC Press.

Bansal, G., Nushi, B., & Kamar, E. (2019). Updates in human-AI teams: Understanding and addressing the performance/compatibility tradeoff. In *Proceedings of the AAAI Conference on Artificial Intelligence*.

Bhaskara, A., Duong, L., Brooks, J., et al. (2021). Effect of automation transparency in the management of multiple unmanned vehicles. *Applied Ergonomics, 90*, 103243.

Boyd, J. (1987). *A discourse on winning and losing* (Vol. 1). Air University Press. MU43947 Brief.

Cabour, G., Morales, A., Ledoux, E. et al. (2021). Towards an explanation space to align humans and explainable-AI teamwork. *arXiv:2106.01503*.

Carvalho, M., Eskridge, T. C., Atighetchi, M., & Paltzer, C. N. (2016). Semi-automated wrapping of defenses (SAWD) for cyber command and control. In *MILCOM 2016–2016 IEEE military communications conference 2016*.

Charlton, S. G., & O'Brien, T. G. (2019). *Handbook of human factors testing and evaluation* (2nd ed.). CDC Press.

Chen, J., & Barnes, M. (2014). Human-agent teaming for multirobot control: A review of human factors issues. *IEEE Transactions on Human-Machine Systems, 44*, 13–29.

Chen, J., Procci, K., Boyce, M., et al. (2014). *Situation awareness-based agent transparency (ARL-TR-6905)*. DEVCOM Army Research Lab.

Chen, J., Lakhmani, S., Stowers, K., et al. (2018). Situation awareness-based agent transparency and human–autonomy teaming effectiveness. *Theoretical Issues in Ergonomics Science, 19,* 259–282.

Chien, S., Lewis, M., Sycara, K., et al. (2020). Influence of culture, transparency, trust, and degree of automation on automation use. *IEEE Transactions on Human-Machine Systems, 50,* 205–214.

Endsley, M. (1995). Toward a theory of situation awareness in dynamic systems. *Human Factors, 37,* 32–64.

Hoffman, R., Mueller, S., Klein, G. et al. (2018). Metrics for explainable AI: Challenges and prospects. *arXiv:1812.04608.*

Holder, E., & Wang, N. (2021). Explainable artificial intelligence (XAI) interactively working with humans as a junior cyber analyst. *Human-Intelligent Systems Integration, 3,* 139–153.

Holder, E., Huang, L., Chiou, E., Jeon, M., & Lyons, J. (2021). *Designing for Bi-directional transparency in human-AI-Robot teaming.* Paper and presentation in the proceedings for the 65th Annual Human Factors and Ergonomics International Meeting

Hudson, W. (2022). *User centered design.* Retrieved February 25, 2022 from https://www.interaction-design.org/literature/topics/user-centered-design

Ingram, M., Moreton, R., Gancz, B., et al. (2021). Calibrating trust toward an autonomous image classifier. *Technology, Mind, and Behavior, 2,* 1.

Johnson, M., & Vera, A. (2019). No AI is an Island: The case for teaming intelligence. *AI Magazine, 40*(1), 16–28. https://doi.org/10.1609/aimag.v40i1.2842

Kott, A.S., Theron, P.T., Drasar, M.D., et al. (2019). Autonomous intelligent cyber-defense agent (AICA) reference architecture, release 2.0. In *Technical Report for the DEVCOM Army Research Laboratory (ARL-SR-0421).*

Kunze, A., Summerskill, S., Marshall, R., et al. (2019). Automation transparency: Implications of uncertainty communication for human-automation interaction and interfaces. *Ergonomics, 62,* 345–360.

Li, F., Wang, C., Mikulski, D., Wagner, J., & Wang, Y. (2022). Unmanned ground vehicle platooning under cyber attacks: A human-robot interaction framework. *IEEE Transactions on Intelligent Transportation Systems, 23*(10), 18113–18128. https://doi.org/10.1109/TITS.2022.3150745

Liggett, K. K., & Thomas, G. F. (2015). Determining the effectiveness of visualization techniques for representing intrusion detection system log files. In *Proceedings of the human factors and ergonomics society 50th annual meeting.* HFES.

Miller, T. (2019). Explanation in artificial intelligence: Insights from the social sciences. *Artificial Intelligence, 267,* 1–38.

Rawal, A., McCoy, J., Rawat, D., & Sadler B. (2021). Recent advances in trustworthy explainable artificial intelligence: Status, challenges and perspectives. *IEEE Transactions on Artificial Intelligence, 3*(6), 852–866.

Sanneman, L., & Shah, J. (2022). The situation awareness framework for explainable AI (SAFE-AI) and human factors considerations for XAI systems. *International Journal of Human-Computer Interaction, 38*(18–20), 1772–1788.

Steinberg, A. N., & Christopher, L. B. (2017). Revisions to the JDL data fusion model. In *Handbook of multisensor data fusion* (pp. 65–88). CRC press.

Stowers, K., Kasdaglis, N., Rupp, M., et al. (2020). The IMPACT of agent transparency on human performance. *IEEE Transactions on Human-Machine Systems, 50,* 245–253.

Tummala, V. and Eskridge, T.C. (2022). *Exploiting Interdependence for Ad Hoc Teams, submitted.*

Winfield, A., Booth, S., Dennis, L., et al. (2021). IEEE P7001: A proposed standard on transparency. *Frontiers in Robotics and AI, 8,* 665729.

Chapter 13
Testing and Measurements

Toby J. Richer and Maxwell Standen

1 Introduction

This chapter first discusses the aspects of performance that determine effective cyber defence agents. With any cyber defence system, the goals of confidentiality, integrity and availability must be balanced appropriately for the role of the system or systems being defended. The goal of preventing any access by an attacker is a simple clear goal which lends itself to a simple solution; blocking all potentially malicious inputs at the system boundary., However, blocking all possible attack vectors is difficult if not impossible. This approach presents the end users with few options once an attacker does gain entry. Depending on the importance of the system mission, a quality cyber defence agent may be required to respond appropriately to an attacker who has gained access – by restricting further access, delaying and misdirecting an attacker, or balancing the attacker's access against the need to keep critical systems operational.

Another key aspect of performance is robustness and reliability. Robustness requires a cyber-defence system to handle new attacks that it may not have seen in training. For an autonomous system to do this, it must first have some capacity to assess its performance independently of the model it has been trained on; as an example, a robust malware detection system would require methods of detecting software that was determined to be benign, but then has malicious effects on the system. Therefore the question of how to accurately measure the performance of autonomous systems is key to determining, and thus improving, robustness. Reliability, the ability of an autonomous system to consistently make appropriate decisions, is made more difficult with the increased use of techniques such as Deep

T. J. Richer (✉) · M. Standen
Defence Science and Technology Group, Australian Department of Defence,
Edinburgh, SA, Australia
e-mail: toby.richer@defence.gov.au; max.standen1@defence.gov.au

© The Author(s), under exclusive license to Springer Nature Switzerland AG 2023
A. Kott (ed.), *Autonomous Intelligent Cyber Defense Agent (AICA)*, Advances in
Information Security 87, https://doi.org/10.1007/978-3-031-29269-9_13

Learning, as it can be difficult to explain how such techniques arrive at a decision once they are trained. Given that subverting security tools is a common technique of cyber attackers, a human cyber defender may shut down an autonomous cyber defence agent that is acting in an unreliable or inexplicable manner rather than risk a compromised (or poorly functioning) agent taking actions that make the system more vulnerable.

A major obstacle to the widespread deployment of AICA is convincing cyber professionals that these agents will improve their work. While an advantage of autonomous cyber agents would be their ability to adapt to the cyber environment they are deployed to, it needs to be demonstrated that cyber agents trained and tested in synthetic environments can translate effectively to the complexity and variety of real-world networks and the abilities of their adversaries. This problem, known as the 'reality gap', has been addressed previously in autonomous research, but the gap between synthetic and real environments in cybersecurity is significant and unique. To design effective agents that have credibility with the professionals who will work with them requires that the testing and measurement processes for these agents must address the reality gap and demonstrate the potential to handle real-world problems in a broad range of cyber environments.

The chapter will discuss all of these issues, drawing upon real-world examples from cybersecurity to present some potential measures of performance. The definition of effective performance will be highly dependent on the type of system being defended, and the circumstances in which this is occurring, but this can hopefully act as a starting point for measuring the effectiveness of AICA.

The chapter then presents a summary of existing work in the field. Several testbeds have been developed and released for testing autonomous cyber defence algorithms, with significant differences in approach for the cyber problem being tested, the methods used to model or implement it, or the metrics currently used for success. We will present a more detailed case study of the CybORG Cyber Operations Gym developed by DST Group and used in the TTCP CAGE Challenge. The chapter ends with a summary of the current state of the field and proposals for important areas of future work.

2   Background

Cybersecurity presents unique issues of trust to the human users of autonomous systems, as discussed in previous chapters. For measurements of AICA systems to be useful, both the measurements themselves and the methods of measurement need to be designed with these issues of trust in mind.

Artificial Intelligence for Cyber Security combines issues of some of the most difficult problems in AI. In particular, it combines a complex action environment with clever adversaries. The cybersecurity environment can require information on the environment down to its physical components, as exploits such as Rowhammer (Kim et al. 2020) exploit the physical properties and proximity of memory.

Autonomous cybersecurity systems need to work with human defenders, and also be able to respond to adversaries who can not only detect and make use of novel attacks, but employ deception to turn an autonomous cyber agent against the system it is intended to defend. An effective autonomous cyber system must be robust to both the vagaries of complex physical environments and the attempts of human adversaries to undermine them. Therefore, any attempt to measure the effectiveness of such systems must also address these factors.

Given that it is vital autonomous cyber systems be measured in terms of their resilience to adversaries, a key issue in measuring their effectiveness is the nature of the adversary their actions are measured against.

2.1 Robustness

Robustness is defined as the ability of cyber defence systems to respond to novel attacks. The leading approach in developing autonomous cyber systems, as with developing autonomous agents in other domains, is the use of deep reinforcement learning. While such systems are able to learn and implement complex strategies with minimal human involvement, a drawback of such systems is their brittleness. While they can be tolerant to changes in problem configuration, changes in goal often cause them to fail catastrophically (Stooke et al., 2021). Given the rate at which computers and networks change configuration, an autonomous cyber defence system that is not robust, and able to respond to changes in environment or in adversary, is simply not useful as an autonomous cyber agent.

There is a wide range of research in training agents to be reliable in complex environments, with two particularly promising areas of research being curriculum learning and domain randomization. Domain randomization adds randomness to either the data or the scenario that is used for agent training. Successful agents will be flexible enough to make correct decisions in spite of this randomness. Curriculum learning (Bengio et al., 2009) trains an agent on simple scenarios and then increases the complexity of the scenarios as training progresses.

2.2 The Reality Gap

The Reality Gap (Mouret and Chatzilygeroudis 2017) is a term from autonomous robotics, created to address a problem which is key to that field but also has applications to autonomous cyber. Deep reinforcement learning and other reinforcement learning approaches require large numbers of iterations through a scenario in order to build appropriate sets of behaviours to achieve a goal. Physical systems are not suited to the large amount of iteration required, so simulators have become a popular method in robotics of applying reinforcement learning in a feasible amount of time. The problem is that any simulation of the real world is not going to perfectly match real world physics. The behaviours learned in such simulators may not perform as well when instantiated in physical robots, due to the 'reality gap.' In robotics, a number of researchers have investigated methods of reducing the gap between simulations of motion and real motion (Zhao et al. 2020). Creating solutions to this for autonomous cyber is still very much an ongoing question, but this chapter will discuss some early attempts.

2.3   The CIA Triad

The CIA triad (Samonas and Coss 2014) defines the security of a system in terms of its confidentiality, integrity and availability. Key to effective cyber defence is the ability to weigh each of these against the others to result in a security posture that best matches the needs of the system. The most effective way of maintaining system confidentiality is to block all access to sensitive systems; an approach that will clearly have major negative effects on availability. Human cyber operators develop the ability to balance the triad through familiarity, both with the tools available to secure systems and the real-world usage of the system being defended. Being able to balance these goals is a requirement for an effective autonomous cyber defence agent, and therefore needs to be integrated into the measurement of such agents.

Confidentiality is the most straightforward part of the CIA triad to measure, as it can be measured purely in terms of an attacker's access to systems. The more systems an attacker has access to, the less confidential the activities of the systems' users are and therefore the worse it performs according to this metric.

Integrity is not generally addressed by existing research in AICA, as research into autonomous cyber agents has focused on the denial of access to attackers. The actions taken once access or control is established are not discussed in much detail, and in many current systems training runs end once a side has developed full control of the network. Therefore, while AICA systems may prevent attacks on system integrity by preventing unauthorised access, they do not directly prevent or cause integrity changes and therefore do not rely on integrity to measure the effectiveness of an autonomous system.

Availability is measured in some cases as part of the effectiveness of autonomous cyber agents. As stated above, most existing literature has focused on system access and control, though some work focused on autonomous network defence has proposed Quality of Service as a metric of agent effectiveness.

2.4   Reliability

In terms of an autonomous cyber agent, reliability refers to the ability of an autonomous agent to consistently make effective decisions. One reason that a learning process can lead to inconsistent decisions is if the data set or scenario used to train it, or the algorithms used for training, do not capture the complexity of the real-world problem. This is a key aspect of the 'reality gap' issue described above. Another reason that agents may not perform reliably in the cybersecurity domain is that an algorithm, while able to learn well, is susceptible to being deceived by input data that is manipulated by an attacker. A third aspect is the reliability of the data provided to an autonomous agent, and the ability of an agent to interpret that data effectively.

An approach to improve reliability is to ensure test scenarios or data sets are as close as possible to the scenarios or data dealt with in real systems. Some of the frameworks for training and testing autonomous cyber defence agents are described later in this chapter; several of these frameworks allow for agents to be tested on both models of a scenario and instantiations of scenarios in virtual infrastructure. The difference between results in each case can be used to refine models and develop more reliable agents.

(Bengio et al. 2009)The area of Adversarial Machine Learning, or AML, is beginning to develop approaches for measuring the reliability of learning techniques used in machine learning or artificial intelligence in the face of attack. Researchers have proposed metrics such as CLEVER that measure the ease with which an adversarial example can be constructed for a neural network (Nicolae et al., 2018).

However, there could be some issues in the application of these metrics to autonomous cyber defensive agents. The majority of this research focuses on adversarial examples for classifiers, such as those used in writing and image recognition. Such classifiers do not generally incorporate state over multiple observations, unlike an autonomous agent.

The complexity of the observations provided to an autonomous cyber agent may introduce obstacles to adversarial machine learning but can also undermine the effectiveness of the agent itself. The use of machine learning and analytics in the detection of malicious activity is a more mature field than the autonomous response field, with many companies releasing cyber threat intelligence tools that use machine learning (Samtani et al., 2020), but false positives still occur. Using a machine learning system as the input to an autonomous agent runs the risk of compounding errors introduced by the machine learning system.

A potential way around this problem is active defence, in which system defenders present false information on system vulnerabilities or configuration (Zhang and Thing 2021). This false information is in areas that should be ignored by normal users, but may provoke a response from an attacker. This response is therefore an indication of malicious activity that is more reliable than attempting to infer maliciousness from large bodies of ambiguous data. If incorporated in the input of an autonomous cyber defence agent, it should reduce the degree to which initial errors in sensing can lead to greater errors in response.

2.5   Resilience

The definition of resilience, as applied to autonomous systems, is the ability of the system to respond to and recover from novel attacks. Unlike reliability, which indicates that the system responds appropriately to threats with a high degree of confidence, resilience covers the ability of the system to recover from and adapt to attacks that it is unable to block. An extension of resilience is the concept of antifragility, the ability for a system to become more effective in defence as the result of breaches.

Measuring resilience requires the testing of autonomous cyber systems in situations where they have already failed – where an attack has not been blocked and the systems they are defending have been compromised. A key issue in military focused AICA research is the ability for systems to 'fight through', or to continue to fulfil their mission in spite of interference or compromise. The traditional enterprise approach to compromise, to shut down systems and re-image, could have disastrous consequences if applied to mission critical military systems or military platforms. It is particularly important if military systems are in a conflict, as not only is this the situation in which systems are most likely to be under sustained cyber-attack, but it is also when there will be serious consequences if systems are not functioning. Part of a cyber defence agent's resilience is its ability to deal with the consequences of a breach once it occurs and remediate compromised systems with minimal effect on the system mission.

In summary, since autonomous systems are designed to make decisions with an independence and flexibility that automated systems lack, the measurement of such systems needs to cover a broader range of scenarios. This includes the broadening of the inputs to the system, firstly by the favouring of interactive scenarios over static data sets and the randomization of starting conditions. It also includes the broadening of the metrics of success, by requiring agents to balance the different aspects of the CIA triad and to evaluate the ability of agents to both prevent compromise and remediate compromised systems as appropriate. Finally, it requires the measurement of such systems to account for the 'reality gap', and test that the valuation of an agent in training translates well to the application of that agent in a real-world scenario.

3   Existing Test Systems

Researchers have already developed a range of frameworks for the training of autonomous cyber defence agents. These frameworks attempt to measure the reliability of autonomous agents by determining their behaviour in an interactive scenario rather than against a static data set. Some of these frameworks address the reality gap through the use of full operating systems and real-world tools rather than, or alongside, lower-fidelity simulations.

CyberBattleSim (Team 2021) is a simulation-only approach to developing red agents that can perform post breach lateral movement in a windows enterprise environment. It measures the effectiveness of agents as a rate, based on a weighted percentage of the number of systems controlled by the red agent. The weighting applied to systems is based on an assessment of the system's criticality. Full control of all systems counts as a 'win' for Red.

CyAMS (Brown et al., 2016) is a tool for addressing the reality gap, via the development of frameworks to test cyber scenarios. In simulation, it uses finite state machines to model the program state whereas in emulation it uses real software. The intent of experimentation in it is to refine methods so that the simulation and emulation match. The measurement used to compare simulation and emulation is a single scenario-relevant metric rather than a range of measures.

FARLAND (Molina-Markham et al., 2021) is a system for network-based simulation and emulation of cybersecurity scenarios for the development of agents. While the valuation of agent effectiveness is based on whether the agent succeeds in its goals, similar to CyberBattleSim, FARLAND introduces a range of other features that can measure reliability and resilience. They propose the use of domain randomization and curriculum learning. Domain randomization can serve as a method of measuring and improving reliability, as the performance of an agent can be measured for reliability in terms of its ability to maintain performance as the level of randomness in the domain is increased. Curriculum learning involves the gradual increase of problem complexity as an agent learns; measurements of agent effectiveness as a problem increases in complexity will serve as a measure of agent reliability.

GALAXY (Schoonover et al., 2018) uses full operating systems and finite state machines representing the state of these systems to test and train agents, thereby addressing the reality gap. One issue that is raised in the design of GALAXY is that the measurement of agent effectiveness in an emulated environment relies on network traffic that itself may be observed and acted upon by an agent. This could potentially result in the measurement of agent behaviour affecting the agent behaviour, something to be avoided if measurement is to be accurate. In GALAXY's case, this is addressed by using separate networks for measurements and network activity that is part of the scenario.

Vine (Eskridge et al., 2015) is an emulation framework that allows the use of hardware in the loop, a unique feature not shared by the other frameworks for agent development. One particular use is for the attachment of traffic generators for use in testing. Traffic Generators can generally provide more detailed traffic more rapidly than software systems. Vine is designed as a framework for a wide range of cybersecurity scenarios, provides an example that measures the Quality of Service measure for a user, which is a reasonable method for measuring network availability.

4   Case Study: CybORG

This section presents a detailed analysis of the Cyber Operations Research Gym or CybORG (Standen et al., 2021b). This framework is designed for simulation and emulation of military-relevant cybersecurity scenarios. One area that has been investigated in its design, both in the general framework and the scenarios created within it, is fight-through and maintaining mission success. This section presents a detailed discussion of the CybORG system and describe how the scenarios within it measure effectiveness.

4.1   CybORG Design

CybORG is designed to implement a cybersecurity scenario for the training or testing of autonomous cyber agents. The CybORG tool implements a scenario based on a pre-generated description, initialises a set of agents to perform roles within that scenario, then implements their actions and assesses their effectiveness. CybORG runs the scenario in a series of discrete steps. At each step, each agent selects an action to perform from its action space. An agent's action space is a subset of the overall available set of actions, dependent on the role of the agent and defined as part of the scenario. Once each agent has selected an action, it is performed. The agent receives an observation of the updated state of the scenario. The scenario is run until it reaches its termination condition, which is either a limit on the number of steps, or the achievement of an agent's goal. At this point, the agents receive any final information on the state of the scenario. The scenario can be reset for further training or testing.

The same agent can interact with a scenario modelled in a finite state machine (defined here as simulation) or fully implemented in virtual infrastructure (defined here as emulation). To implement CybORG's two levels of fidelity, the scenarios and actions used by CybORG are defined at two levels. The scenario definition contains the required information to simulate the scenario. It also contains the system images required to emulate the scenario. Each action used by CybORG is defined twice. For simulation, each action is defined as a state transition. For emulation, each action defines a command (with appropriate parameters) that can be executed to achieve the desired effect.

4.2   Scenarios

A CybORG scenario defines the environment that agents are aiming to solve or compete in, and the means by which they succeed or fail. The scenario defines what agents exist, what actions they may perform, what information they begin the game with, and how their reward is calculated. It defines the configuration of each host and the network connections between them.

To deploy a particular scenario, the CybORG user must specify whether it will be simulated or emulated and provide a scenario description file in the data-serialization format YAML. The scenario description file includes details for config-uring the environment including hosts, networking and subnet information, and the set of actions available to red and blue agents. The scenario files are deliberately simple, requiring a minimum of information and employing many default behav-iours to reduce the burden on users when creating files.

The information provided for each host includes the host's operating system, services, processes, users and other system information. The scenario file also con-tains an identifier for a deployable image to be used in emulation. The process information includes the process id, the parent id, process network connections, the process owner and the process name. The user information includes usernames, UIDs, groups, GIDs, passwords, and password hashes. The system information includes the operating system type, distribution, version, and patches, and the hard-ware architecture.

4.3   Simulation

The simulator represents the scenario as a finite state machine, where the current state represents the state of all systems and networks in the scenario. Actions use the values in the current state to determine the next state, update the values inside of the current state such that they match the next state, and then return the observable sub-set of this updated state to the agent.

Simulated actions are defined by their preconditions and effects. The precondi-tions of an action are the state conditions that must be satisfied for the action to be successful. The effects define how the action will change the state of the environ-ment if the action is successful.

To reduce the chance of the simulator model diverging from the behaviour of the emulator (in particular, allowing actions to succeed where they would not in real systems) the state includes details such as the creation or deletion of individual files or the making and breaking of network connections.

The simulator provides a reward to agents at each step. Agents receive an overall valuation based on their cumulative reward over a run. For the scenarios that have been developed so far, the run has a fixed length rather than terminating when a particular condition has been met.

4.4   Emulation

The emulator uses Amazon Web Services (AWS) with virtual machines to create a high fidelity cyber security environment with which an agent can interact.

The emulator uses the description of the scenario from the YAML scenario files to deploy and configure a virtual network in Amazon Web Services (AWS) (as well as for tearing them down). It does this by using SSH to access a virtual gateway server in a private AWS cloud and then deploying and configuring environments using AWS's Command Line Interface (CLI) on that virtual (master) host. CybORG is capable of rapidly and concurrently deploying independent clusters of hosts and subnets, allowing multiple instantiations of a scenario to be run in parallel.

To implement actions, the CybORG emulator uses a series of actuator objects. These connect to VMs using SSH or specialised session handlers for third party tools. Third-party tools currently used in CybORG include the Metasploit Framework (Kennedy et al., 2011) and Velociraptor (Cohen, 2022). Other session handlers can be added as required. These actuator objects interact with security tools and systems either through APIs or terminal commands. The results of these actions are then filtered and merged to present a single observation back to an agent. This control method allows for multiple adversarial agents to act simultaneously in the environment, and will potentially allow human operators to interact within the emulator in parallel with agents.

Through the approach described above, CybORG is able to implement a novel capability for cyber autonomy; the ability to train and test the same agent, using the same body of code, at differing levels of fidelity. Agents can be trained, using standard learning approaches, in the simulator. The effectiveness of these agents can then be validated on virtual infrastructure. In the next section, we describe a scenario implemented within CybORG for the development of an autonomous penetration testing agent using RL.

The initial experiments with CybORG were designed to test its ability to address the 'reality gap'. Following this, CybORG formed the basis of a public challenge to develop blue agents to defend a set of connected networks. A second challenge, using the same scenario but with modifications to the available actions, was released in April 2022.

4.5   Experiment One: Reality Gap Test

Our initial test scenario is shown in Fig. 13.1. While only having three hosts for an attacker to access, it is of sufficient complexity and detail to capture examples of most attacker behaviours within the cyber kill chain, as first defined in (Hutchins et al., 2011).

The scenario consists of 3 hosts split into 2 subnets. The attacker host runs a Metasploit server that allows the agent to perform all parts of the kill chain. The

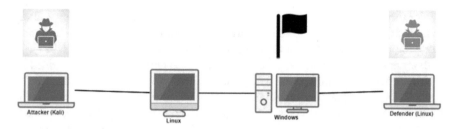

Fig. 13.1 Network for initial CybORG tests

attacker is in its own subnet, which does not block any traffic and allows packets to be sent to hosts in the other subnet.

The other two hosts are the Internal and Gateway hosts that sit in the internal subnet. The Gateway host is an Ubuntu 18 host that has an open SSH port. The Internal host is a Windows 2008 server with open SSH and SMB ports. The SSH services have sufficiently simple sets of credentials for the server to be vulnerable to a brute force attack; the Gateway host has the username "pi" and password "raspberry", and the Internal host has the username "vagrant" and password "vagrant". The SMB service is vulnerable to the Eternal Blue (MS17–010) exploit.

There is a single red agent in the scenario. The goal of the red agent is to get a session on the Internal host as the System user, and thereby have full access to the internal host's file system. In order to achieve this goal, the agent must be able to perform reconnaissance on hosts, exploit these hosts, establish meterpreter sessions and use a meterpreter session to pivot between machines. An effective red agent will be able to select appropriate actions, with correct parameters, to complete each of these sub-goals in the proper order.

To model these actions, and then implement these actions in the Emulator, we use the Metasploit Framework and Meterpreter as the actuators and sensors for the agent. The actions available to the red agent are: SSH Bruteforce, Portscan, Pingsweep, Upgrade to Meterpreter, IPConfig, MS17-010-PSExec, Autoroute, and Sleep. Each of these actions has associated parameters, for which the agent must learn the correct values.

The red agent receives a large reward for starting a session on the Internal host as the System user. The agent also receives moderate rewards for gaining user sessions on the Internal and Gateway hosts, and minor rewards for discovering new information about the network. For this simple scenario the reward did not take into account any action costs.

In order to demonstrate the transferability of training from the simulator to the emulator, an RL agent is initially trained on the simulator then run on the emulator.

This RL agent uses a Deep Q-Network (Mnih et al., 2015) to learn a policy which maps the current state of the environment to the discounted rewards for each action. Learning this policy, over a large series of training runs, allows the agent to select an action at each step that will produce the highest reward.

For this scenario, the agent will be unable to learn an effective policy without remembering key features of the scenario. This memory is implemented through a Long Short Term Memory, as described in Hochreiter and Schmidhuber (1997).

For approaches such as Deep RL the observation and action space provided by CybORG require modification. We construct a suitable observation space for the agent using a wrapper around CybORG. This wrapper turns the elements of the observation into a single vector of floating point numbers with a fixed size. This is the input required for Deep Q-learning as used here. We also use a wrapper that takes a vector of integers from the RL agent and converts them into an action (and parameters, if required) that can be performed in CybORG.

To select the action and parameters, our agent uses a neural network that takes in an observation, constructs a feature vector from that observation, interprets it through an LSTM module, then splits into branches which each output a Q-value for either an action or a parameter. As some of the parameters, such as IP address, are discovered incrementally, we mask the parameter values that would be valid but the agent would have no method of discovering through their previous actions. This improves the realism of the scenario and the convergence rate of the agent.

Each RL agent was trained in the simulator for up to 2500 iterations. This was selected as it was well above the average number of iterations for a successful run in initial testing, but short enough for multiple training runs to be conducted on our hardware in a reasonable amount of time. Each iteration took a maximum of 20 steps. An iteration was stopped if an agent could get access to the Windows host using the System account. If an agent was able to achieve this within 10 steps, then that agent was deemed to be successful and the training run was finished; otherwise the agent was deemed not successful. A minimum of 7 steps was required for an agent to get System access on the Windows host. With these parameters, we were able to generate an effective red agent on every training run.

To test the ability of these agents to transfer to the emulator, we took a selection of these trained agents and reran them on CybORG in emulation mode. In this case, they ran exploits using the Metasploit framework on virtual hosts within our testing network.

The initial training produced 21 independent RL agents. Each RL agent was evaluated in the emulator 10 times. The total number of successful tests was 139, giving a 66% rate of success.

Figure 13.2 shows the distribution of success rates across independently trained RL agents. Almost half of the trained agents were successful on every emulator run. Four trained agents were never successful on emulator runs, with the rest having a varying numbers of successes.

These results demonstrate that the underlying concept of CybORG is feasible; that a simulation can be used to train an agent which can then run effectively on virtualised infrastructure using professional security tools. While there were a significant number of failures to transfer trained agents from simulator to emulator for this scenario, these failures were sometimes associated with deficiencies in the simulator model or in the emulator's interface between the agent and the emulation environment. These deficiencies could be detected and used to refine CybORG for

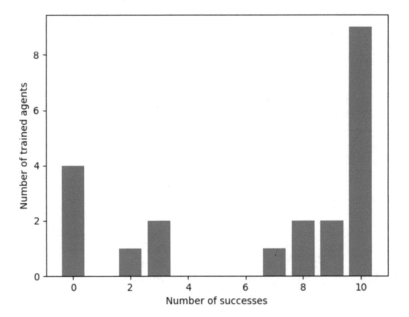

Fig. 13.2 Distribution of success rates across independently trained agents

future training, thus demonstrating the feasibility of the approach of combining simulator and emulator in order to refine the simulator model or emulator interface.

4.6   Experiment 2: CAGE Challenge One

CAGE Challenge One was a public challenge run using the CybORG framework (Standen et al., 2021a). This challenge is designed for teams to create a blue (defensive) agent to defend a set of connected networks against a red (offensive) agent. The network is illustrated below in Fig. 13.3. It is divided into three subnets. Subnet 1 consists of user hosts that are not critical. Subnet 2 consists of enterprise servers designed to support the user activities on Subnet 1. Subnet 3 contains the critical operational server and three user hosts.

Each scenario run is a fixed number of steps representing a fixed period of time. An episode will terminate only once the time expires. At each step, the red and blue agents each choose one action from a set of high-level actions that are described in Fig. 13.2. CybORG will take the chosen action and select a context-appropriate low-level action, such as modelling the behaviour of an operating system-specific exploit in response to a high-level exploit action by the red agent. This is designed to reduce the action space and make a wider range of learning approaches tractable.

The red agent starts each scenario run with an initial foothold: access to one of the user machines in Subnet 1. The red agent can then choose actions to perform

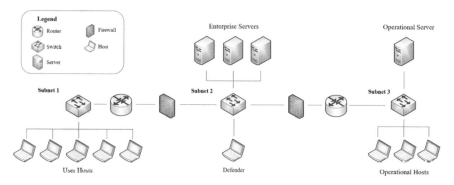

Fig. 13.3 Network for CAGE challenge one

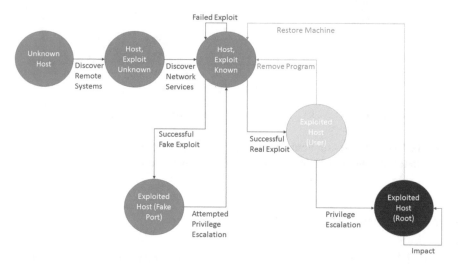

Fig. 13.4 Action set and transitions for cage challenge one

reconnaissance on hosts in the enterprise network (Subnet 2) and then exploit these hosts and perform privilege escalation. Once they have exploited the server in the enterprise network that has the operational server IP address on it, they can access the operational network (Subnet 3). The operational server maintains a service that is key to the system owners' operations; the goal of the red agent is to disrupt this service for as long as possible through the Impact action (Fig. 13.4).

In order to create a more robust blue agent, two red agents have been implemented, each with its own unique strategy. The first has prior knowledge of the network layout and compromises hosts that will enable it to reach and compromise the operational server in the shortest number of turns. The other explores the network one subnet at a time, seeking to gain privileged access on all hosts in a subnet before moving on to the next one, eventually arriving at the operational Server.

The blue agent is assumed to start each scenario run with monitoring tools installed on all the user and server hosts. It automatically receives data on new events that occur on these hosts. It can use actions to perform more detailed analysis of hosts, giving it improved knowledge as to whether particular activity on a system is due to malicious activities of the red agent or benign activities of a green agent. It can remove red access to hosts, or restore a system back to a standard configuration. Removing red access only works if the red agent has not escalated their privilege on the system, as at this point it is assumed the red agent has sufficient access and persistence to recover from deleted processes or files. Restoring a system is guaranteed to remove red agent activity, but restoring a system from a previously-generated image is assumed to disrupt user activities on that system. The red agent cannot be removed from the initial foothold system, even by the restore action – this assumption is made both as a means of ensuring the game lasts for the entire period, and to reflect the difficulty of eliminating a threat that has successfully phished credentials.

The Misinform action enables a decoy service, on a nominated host, which is vulnerable to exploitation by the red agent. The probability of a red agent exploiting the decoy service versus a real service is given a fixed value of 75%.

The decoy service is assumed to be monitored and secured such that an exploit of it does not allow further access to the host by the red agent. Privilege Escalation actions using an exploited decoy service will automatically fail and will result in the removal of the red agent from that host. To effectively exploit the system, the red agent must re-exploit the host via a non-decoy service.

The effect of each action on the state of a targeted host is summarised in Fig. 13.2.

The green agent only performs the discovery action, and does not exploit hosts. It should prevent the blue agent from assuming all network activity is due to the red agent.

The order in which the agents choose and enact actions is blue, then green then red. Before acting again, the blue agent receives an observation and reward based on the events that occurred as a result of the green and red actions.

The blue agent receives a negative reward any time the red agent gets administrator access to a system. They continue to receive negative rewards as long as the red agent maintains administrator access. The amount of each reward is dependent on the relative importance of that host to the confidentiality or availability of the entire system: -0.1 and -1.0 for low and high importance systems respectively (see Table 13.1). They also receive a negative reward if the red agent successfully uses the Impact action on the operational server (-10) or the blue agent uses the restore

Table 13.1 Blue rewards for red administrator access (per turn)

Subnet	Hosts	Blue reward for red access (per turn)
Subnet 1	User hosts	-0.1
Subnet 2	Enterprise servers	-1
Subnet 3	Operational server	-1
Subnet 3	Operational hosts	-0.1

Table 13.2 Blue rewards for successful red actions (per turn)

Agent	Hosts	Action	Blue reward (per turn)
Red	Operational server	Impact	−10
Blue	Any	Restore	−1

action on any host (−1) (see Table 13.2). The final score for a blue agent is the cumulative reward received by the agent over the course of the scenario run.

The results of the challenge are available at http://www.github.com/cage-challenge/cage-challenge-1/.

4.7 Analysis of Measurement in CybORG

One of the key goals behind the design of CybORG was to foster the development of cyber agents that will work in the real world. To work in the real world requires good performance across all the metrics described above – reliability, resilience, the CIA triad and the ability to translate all these qualities to a real situation.

The first experiment targeted the last of these factors by measuring the relative effectiveness of the same agent in simulation and emulation. The results of the experiment showed the potential of this approach as a means of measuring agent reliability. However, this scenario was for a simple red agent, and therefore the effectiveness of the CIA triad was not measured as part of this work.

Having established a methodology for measuring and bridging the reality gap, the scenarios tested within CybORG were extended to start addressing the other metrics. The first CAGE challenge was scored based on a mix of confidentiality and availability. This mix was determined based on an analysis of the system mission. While resilience and reliability were not explicitly measured as part of this challenge, aspects of the scenario were chosen to introduce concepts of resilience – in particular, the use of a scenario where the blue agent had to re-establish control once compromised, rather than ending the scenario once red established control.

5 Future Work

There is plenty of scope – and need – to expand the scenarios and metrics for cyber agent learning. The examples above are still on networks much smaller than real-world enterprise networks, and look at only a narrow slice of potential defensive actions. One simple method of expanding the applicability of these measurements is to expand them to enterprise scale, and to broaden the range of attacks and defences to match those used by cyber professionals.

One underlying assumption that was made for CybORG, which would need to be critically examined as the system develops, is the ability of blue agents to detect and analyse attacks. The probabilities of detection require further empirical analysis, so that the agents work from real-world data. Even with these probabilities, the ability of a defensive system to effectively detect attacks is dependent on the attack itself and the detection pipeline.

One potential way to short-circuit this approach, and produce a more resilient system, is the use of active or deceptive defences such as canaries or honeypots. These defences replace numerous but low-probability indicators of attack with a single high-probability indicator of attack. These defences are also more resilient to zero-day attacks, as they detect the results of an attack rather than the attack itself.

The measurement of reliability or resilience of a blue agent is still a new field, with no agreement on what metrics accurately measure it. This is partly because the development of autonomous cyber defence agents is still new. At this stage, the quickest way to advance the field is to develop more advanced scenarios, then develop more advanced agents to succeed given the current metrics for those scenarios. The use of cyber defence agents in situations with increasing realism will be the best way of identifying shortcomings in the current approaches and bring the overall maturity of the field forward.

6 Summary and Conclusions

This chapter discusses the importance of appropriate testing and measurement techniques to the development of autonomous cyber defence agents. Cybersecurity is a particularly difficult domain for reinforcement learning, as the domain is complex and evolving and requires autonomous systems to be effective against clever and innovative human adversaries. Testing and measurement of autonomous cybersecurity systems must address the 'reality gap' – the differences between models on which an autonomous system is trained and the real system in which the system must be effective. It must also exhibit robustness to changes in the model or system it is instantiated in, as cyber-attacks often rely on the detection and exploitation of differences between the assumed behaviour of a system and its actual behaviour. The measurement of the effectiveness of a cyber-defence system is generally not a single metric, but a balance between opposed factors as described in the CIA triad. A system that preserves confidentiality at the expense of availability is unsuccessful, as it cannot achieve its mission. Finally, a real-world cyber defence system must be resilient to failure, both because new breaches can be developed and because being able to recover from breaches is a key part of the role of human cyber defenders. A range of frameworks for developing and testing autonomous cyber agents have been developed. Common amongst these are the twin use of simulation and emulation to address the reality gap. Other techniques used are hardware-in-the-loop, repeated use of simulation and emulation to refine both the model and the resulting agent behaviour, and use of scenario randomization in order to improve robustness.

Finally, this chapter presents a case study of CybORG, a system intended to address these issues to develop effective cyber defence agents. CybORG has been used in initial experiments to develop agents in simulation and transfer them to virtual infrastructure. It has then been used as the basis for the TTCP CAGE Challenge to develop a range of approaches to autonomous cyber defence in a competitive manner. The range of existing approaches are promising, and have settled on key methods to effectively measure and test the performance of autonomous cyber agents, but these methods require further refinement through the development and testing of cyber agents in more varied and realistic scenarios.

References

Bengio, Y. et al. (2009). Curriculum learning. In *Proceedings of the 26th annual international conference on machine learning*.

Brown, S., et al. (2016). Validation of network simulation model and scalability tests using example malware. MILCOM 2016-2016. In *IEEE military communications conference*. IEEE.

Cohen, M. (2022). *Velociraptor – Endpoint visibility and collection tool*. From https://github.com/Velocidex/velociraptor

Eskridge, T. C., et al. (2015). VINE: A cyber emulation environment for MTD experimentation. In *Proceedings of the second ACM workshop on moving target defense*. ICSE.

Hochreiter, S., & Schmidhuber, J. (1997). Long short-term memory. *Neural Computation, 9*(8), 1735–1780.

Hutchins, E. M., et al. (2011). Intelligence-driven computer network defense informed by analysis of adversary campaigns and intrusion kill chains. *Leading Issues in Information Warfare & Security Research, 1*(1), 80.

Kennedy, D., et al. (2011). *Metasploit: The penetration tester's guide*. No Starch Press.

Kim, J. S., et al. (2020). Revisiting rowhammer: An experimental analysis of modern dram devices and mitigation techniques. In *2020 ACM/IEEE 47th annual international symposium on computer architecture (ISCA)*. IEEE.

Mnih, V., et al. (2015). Human-level control through deep reinforcement learning. *Nature, 518*(7540), 529–533.

Molina-Markham, A., et al. (2021). Network environment design for autonomous cyberdefense. *arXiv preprint arXiv:2103.07583*.

Mouret, J.-B. and K. Chatzilygeroudis (2017). 20 years of reality gap: a few thoughts about simulators in evolutionary robotics. In *Proceedings of the genetic and evolutionary computation conference companion*.

Nicolae, M.-I., et al. (2018). Adversarial robustness toolbox v1. 0.0. *arXiv preprint arXiv:1807.01069*.

Samonas, S., & Coss, D. (2014). The CIA strikes back: Redefining confidentiality, integrity and availability in security. *Journal of Information System Security, 10*(3), 21–45.

Samtani, S. et al. (2020). Cybersecurity as an industry: A cyber threat intelligence perspective. In *The Palgrave Handbook of International Cybercrime and Cyberdeviance* (pp. 135–154).

Schoonover, K. et al. (2018). Galaxy: a network emulation framework for cybersecurity. In *11th USENIX Workshop on Cyber Security Experimentation and Test (CSET 18)*.

Standen, M., et al. (2021a). *Cyber autonomy gym for experimentation challenge 1*. Github.

Standen, M. et al. (2021b). Cyborg: A gym for the development of autonomous cyber agents. In *IJCAI-ACD 2021: IJCAI First International Workshop on Adaptive Cyber Defense*.

Stooke, A. et al. (2021). Open-ended learning leads to generally capable agents. *arXiv preprint arXiv:2107.12808*.

Team, M. (2021). *CyberBattleSim*. Created by Christian Seifert, Michael Betser, William Blum, James Bono, Kate Farris, Emily Goren, Justin Grana, Kristian Holsheimer, Brandon Marken, Joshua Neil, Nicole Nichols, Jugal Parikh, Haoran Wei.

Zhang, L., & Thing, V. L. (2021). Three decades of deception techniques in active cyber defense- retrospect and outlook. *Computers & Security, 106,* 102288.

Zhao, W., et al. (2020). Sim-to-real transfer in deep reinforcement learning for robotics: A survey. In *2020 IEEE symposium series on computational intelligence (SSCI)*. IEEE.

Chapter 14
Deployment and Operation

Benjamin Blakely, William Horsthemke, Daniel Harkness, and Nate Evans

1 Introduction

Deploying and operating autonomous intelligent agents for cyber defense present unique opportunities and challenges for traditional network defenses. At the core of their utility is the premise that human operators and statically configured defensive systems (even if augmented with threat feeds and signatures) will increasingly be outpaced by malicious software, or even human adversaries, who act at "machine speed" with adaptive attack strategies. For this reason, Kott & Theron (2020) and others have suggested that a passive "observer" role is no longer sufficient for cyber systems in defending themselves. Anti-virus, logging, alerting, etc. are all cases where activity on a host or network is monitored and/or analyzed, but ultimately relies on some other human or system to respond as appropriate.

While systems such as heuristic-based anti-virus or increasingly intelligent boundary protection services (e.g., Cloudflare) are much more capable of taking preventive actions and potentially identifying threats through statistical analysis, they might still find it difficult to adapt to truly novel threats, or attackers who are engaged in an active back-and-forth with the defender. What is needed (or will be soon) are systems capable of defending themselves and their peers. However, deploying such systems creates concerns regarding how to ensure their behaviors are acceptable and "net-positive", and how are they to be monitored and controlled.

In this chapter, we will discuss threat scenarios where an autonomous agent might have an advantage. We will then discuss how learning and cooperation are critical elements of deployments to combat those risks. Finally, we will consider several deployment scenarios and the operational implications of autonomous agents in each.

B. Blakely (✉) · W. Horsthemke · D. Harkness · N. Evans
Strategic Security Sciences, Argonne National Laboratory, Lemont, IL, USA
e-mail: bblakely@anl.gov; horst@anl.gov; dharkness@anl.gov; nevans@anl.gov

2   Advantageous Scenarios

Most of the scenarios where an autonomous cyber defense agent might have an advantage relate to the potential advantages of systems that can operate without the delay introduced by needing to consult with a human operator or wait for approval to act. In these scenarios, if risk models can be built to account for these specific advantages, while accounting for the potential negative repercussions of autonomous action, the cost-benefit tradeoffs can be quantified and used to drive agent behavior (Booker & Musman, 2020). This approach has seen some success already, such as in countering botnets by treating them as an adversarial multi-agent system and responding with agents built in a MAS paradigm (Kotenko et al., 2012).

2.1   Interacting with an Adversary

The first category of advantages concerns the fact that cyber adversaries may be adaptive in nature. While simple attacks might simply be "fire and forget" – e.g., malicious email attachments, mass scans for vulnerabilities – many attacks are likely better represented by a "game theoretic" framing. That is, attacks and defenders are engaged in a back-and-forth interaction where each's knowledge of each other's actions has an impact on their subsequent responses. In such an exchange, being able to mask or misrepresent one's intentions can lead to an advantage against an intelligent attacker. Unpredictability is an advantage, but misdirection is even more valuable (Huang & Zhu, 2018).

Pawlick et al. (2019) define six different types of deception that can be employed for protecting security and privacy: perturbation of data (e.g., differential privacy), moving target defenses (making the "attack surface" non-static to make it more difficult to find and exploit vulnerabilities), obfuscation (masking sensitive data with "noise" – i.e., distractors for the attacker), mixing of data (e.g., in the manner of traffic traversing the Tor network), honey-x (deploying apparently vulnerable systems to lure attackers into wasting their time and revealing their intentions), and attacker engagement (treating interactions with an attacker as multi-phased games). Though some of these approaches are more relevant to a dataset than a network or host, others are potential options for incorporation into interactions with an adversary. An autonomous agent, or a collaborative "swarm" of them, could proactively create honeypot services or virtual hosts to collect data, make changes to network or host configuration on the fly in response to perceived or predicted threats, or return extraneous or misleading data to an attacker. These might also assist with situations where an attacker has compromised a system but not been detected (van Dijk et al., 2013), by making the job of moving laterally, escalating privileges, or making heads or tails of discovered information more difficult.

Moving beyond just deception, one can of course consider situations in which a defender takes a more aggressive approach and launches a counterattack against the identified threat. These are potentially the highest-risk scenarios to consider for deploying autonomous agents. It requires a very well-defined and -understood set of rules restricting the behavior of the agent(s) to ensure they don't accidentally cause unintended harm, or unnecessarily escalate a situation. If we are to employ machine learning solutions, often assumed when discussing autonomous systems, it's important to be aware of the increasing sophistication of adversarial machine learning, as well as the potential for poisoning of training datasets in online learning systems or exploiting boundary regions in learned parameters.

A particularly interesting advantage that could be leveraged by autonomous agent deployments is the automated exploitation of vulnerabilities in an adversary system. This is clearly an offensive action, so is not a capability to add without due consideration. There have been early successes in this area. In 2016, MAYHEM won the DARPA Cyber Grand Challenge by finding a vulnerability in the source code used by it and its adversary, patching the vulnerability in its own code, and then exploiting it in the adversary (Avgerinos et al., 2018). Granted, this was a highly constrained environment with a purpose-written programming language.

2.2 Dynamic Threat Environments

The second category of advantages pertain to the fact that many aspects of systems and networks are not static in nature, or at least might not be in some network environments. Systems come and go (or turn on and off); software is installed, patched, and uninstalled; vulnerabilities are discovered and remediated; networks are reconfigured and rearchitected; and attackers' tools and tactics constantly shift. This means that yesterday's vulnerabilities (and those of decades ago!) still need to be defended against, but defenders also need to concern themselves with undiscovered vulnerabilities and threats not in existing threat models and risk assessments.

This means defenders systems and networks need to be resilient and capable of adapting their defenses to new threats. Kott et al. (2021) referred to this as "Resilience by design" – the concept that systems should be built to account for the kinds of adaptability that will allow them to tolerate adversarial actions in a graceful manner, with minimal impact to their function or mission. Making systems "self-reorganizable" is one way proposed to do so. Autonomous agents can learn about their network environment, perceive threats, and "reorganize" themselves or their configurations to minimize the impact of an attack – even if it cannot be fully rendered neutral. In fact, Hammar & Stadler (2020) had success in using reinforcement learning over Markov games for defending systems to automatically find effective security strategies to prevent intrusions. A challenge in doing so, as in many machine learning paradigms, is quickly or reliably converging to an optimal strategy, but the potential is there, nonetheless.

If we can connect this sort of adaptation to a changing environment with the adversarial interactions discussed above, we can then envision an agent capable of predicting future actions of the attacker and proactively deploying appropriate resilience-building measures (Cam, 2020). Not only simple adaptations such as proactively configuring network filtering devices but potentially staging purpose-built deceptions, spinning up additional resources to soften the blow of a denial-of-service attack, rotating out a host for one using a different operating system or type of daemon, etc. In this way the defender could turn the dynamic nature of the threat environment to its advantage.

2.3 Human-in-the-Loop

Due to the inherent difficult in building and training autonomous systems that can make perfect cybersecurity decisions, it's likely that human-in-the-loop strategies will continue to be important. This is especially true if we are allowing systems to take offensive actions (Ligo et al., 2021). However, this can be turned to an advantage if systems are designed to appropriately complement automated reasoning with human analysis. If automated systems can do the major of the work of observing the network, correlating observed events, making friend or foe determinations, etc., then a human operator is freed up to make only those decisions that require human intuition, additional external analysis, or interaction with external systems (technical or non-technical, such as chains of command). However, for this to be effective, humans must be able to understand and trust their autonomous defender counterparts. We need to ensure that we can explain the way automated reasoning systems make decisions, can interpret what they learn and output, and have the information be sufficiently actionable to be worthwhile (Linkov et al., 2020).

3 Learning and Cooperation

As we deploy autonomous agents to different types of environments, it's likely they will benefit from collaboration among themselves. Differing agents may have different perspectives on activity occurring, visibility of other agents on the network that others cannot see, heterogeneity in operations to avoid overtraining, and may be able to compensate if one agent becomes compromised and its observations or decisions are no longer trustworthy. These might rely upon a centralized coordinator agent or be fully decentralized (Andreadis et al., 2014) but we are particularly interested in the resilience of fully decentralized agents. Two ways we might approach such collaborative efforts are federated machine learning and swarm intelligence.

3.1 Federated Machine Learning

Federated machine learning is an approach whereby computations are decentralized to avoid sharing of "raw" observations or data, leverage the collective local computing power and diversity of all participating systems, and share derived model parameters with the full community in a manner which allows convergence to a globally optimal solution. This allows for additional assurance regarding privacy of sensitive datasets, can minimize the computational load on any given participant, and broadens the reach of observations. It also helps avoid underfitting or overfitting by adding the natural variance that can come with differing systems generating local models that are then aggregated.

This can however create additional challenges. Primary among them is that we are not guaranteed that the community will converge to an optimal global model, or even converge at all. We might end up in a worse state upon trying to aggregate many locally trained models than if we had collected all the data and performed a centralized computation. Second is that even though we are reducing the computational requirements from a single, large-dataset training approach, even training small models can be intensive – especially without a graphical processing unit (GPU). Deploying this sort of learning to low-powered devices such as found in SCADA networks or "Internet of Things" (IOT) scenarios might not be feasible or might require careful selection of algorithms suitable to such constraints. Third, is that an inherent level of trust in the contributing nodes must be held, otherwise we risk poisoning of the globally trained model. Last is the reliance upon a central coordinating agent to aggregate data from participating nodes. Work towards fully peer-to-peer methods of federated machine learning are needed for maximal resilience.

While these challenges do require research investment to overcome, there are still opportunities to be realized in using federated machine learning for AICA-like purposes. AICA agents are very likely to exist in a multi-agent environment, with differing configurations, attack surfaces, and environmental conditions. This makes them a natural fit for a collaborative learning model. Given the intended use cases, the observations of each agent are likely to be sensitive, and thus sending this to another system for analysis may present untenable security concerns (or the data might be too burdensome for a low power device, or a device with limited connectivity, to transmit in this way). Building AICA agents to learn as much as they can locally, and then share those "learnings" with the broader network of agents, may be an optimal compromise in such environments.

3.2 Swarm Intelligence

Swarm intelligence algorithms are related to federated machine learning in that they seek to leverage multiple nodes in a collaborative manner. However, these methods are significantly different in that they rely on emergent behavior arising from varying levels of simplistic local decision making. Holland (n.d.) categories these levels of agent complexity as type 0 (no emergent behavior), type 1 (nominal - local-to-global feedback, no coordination), type 2 (moderated – global to local feedback), type 3 (multiple – combines stable and unstable type 2 behaviors to achieve global stability), and type 4 (evolutionary – agents can alter their own governing principles). Maier (2014) further classifies emergent properties into four levels: simple (readily predicted by a simplified model of components), weak (readily reproduced in simulations of the system), strong (consistent with known properties but not consistently reproduced in any simplified model of the system), and spooky (inconsistent with known properties of the system, not reproduced in models of the system of equal complexity). These two rating scales give a large variety of potential swarming algorithm possibilities, and indeed in algorithmic optimization literature many nature-inspired algorithms continue to be developed. The applications to an AICA-like multi-agent system, however, is not quite so straightforward. Rauf et al. (2019) suggest that biological inspirations might be useful for overcoming limitations current network security devices, including: difficulty obtaining a global network picture, poor device self-awareness, a tendency toward error-prone and time-consuming configuration, and multi-party management making diagnosing issues or resolving conflicts difficult.

On one hand, a properly constructed swarm intelligence multi-agent system would be able to respond to adversarial behaviors not envisioned by its designers. With the right set of local governing behavioral rules, a very low-powered device could make decisions that contribute to the security of the overall swarm and adapt if the environmental parameters change. Generalizing away from specific signatures or indicators toward patterns of activity can add resilience to such systems.

On the other hand, such behavior is inherently difficult to predict, and thus may not be well-suited for safety- or security-critical applications. Such simplistic rule-sets, while they may serve biological entities well, might fail to capture and respond to the complexity and game-theoretic realities of a cyber conflict. Most challenging is determining what rules we should even build into our system. An approach akin to genetic algorithms may yield results here, but then under what conditions do we "train" our system?

4 Deployment Environments

We turn now to considerations of the different types of environments in which an AICA agent might be deployed. Exhaustively covering all possible environments is of course not a feasible undertaking, so we will start with a taxonomy under which we might consider possible environments, and then discuss several of particular interest that might be well-suited for further analysis and experimentation (Table 14.1).

Table 14.1 Deployment dichotomies

Non-ideal deployment environment	Ideal deployment environment
Mobile Platform	Stationary Platform
Safety-critical Environment	Non-safety-critical Environment
Low-quality Connectivity	High-quality Connectivity
Independent Nature	Cooperative Nature
Resource-consumption Sensitive	Resource-consumption Tolerant
Proprietary/Custom Platform	Commodity Platform

4.1 Dichotomies as Environmental Classifications

We will use a series of either-or distinctions as a simplifying approach to discussing the operational scenarios in which agents might be deployed. These are intended to capture those most salient considerations as regards the practicalities of using an AICA-like agent in a production system.

First, we can distinguish between platforms which are mobile in nature versus mobile. Mobile systems have additional constraints and considerations – for example connectivity to other agents or broader networks, computational capability, power usage, dynamic exposure to hostile actors in the physical domain, and potential safety considerations on appropriate behaviors of the system. They are also more likely to use an operating system outside of a common consumer platform. Conversely, stationary systems are less likely to have these restrictions, but might present more of a "sitting duck" target for adversaries and might have more significant stores of valuable data or computational capacity.

We can thus also consider whether agents are designed to operate in safety-critical environments versus non-safety critical. This not only has implications on the restrictions that must be placed on their behavior, but also on how they are designed and evaluated before deployment. Safety-critical systems may need to default more heavily to not intervening in otherwise-stable decision-making strategies or performing more conservatively when detection potential attacks requiring retaliation. They may also be required to weigh the potential safety risks of intervention against the safety or security risks of inaction.

Next, we can consider whether the agents have quality connectivity (low-latency, high-bandwidth, high-uptime) to each other and the outside world, or whether they must be able to operate independently. Some agents might have intermittent connectivity, such as during certain windows (or not during certain windows). Other agents might have highly constrained connectivity due to physical limitations or cost. Agents that cannot rely on practically unfettered communication with other agents, human controllers, or central control systems must be designed quite differently from those than can.

To this point, we can consider whether agents are intended to operate in a cooperative manner, or in a more autonomous mode. While it is largely envisioned that AICA agents would be collaborative in nature, much of the automated situational awareness, decision making, and response capability could be deployed independently but would lack the benefit of additional insight from other nodes or emergent defensive strategies. Independent agents, or those needing to operate for periods of time in an independent manner, might require additional "pre-training", more complex static rulesets, or more conservative decision parameters to compensate for a lack of possible human intervention.

The power consumption and computational capacity of agents is also of primary concern, as mentioned above. A system without restrictions on energy usage, and/or with high-capability CPU or GPU resources does not need to concern itself with performance beyond preventing mission impact through resource consumption. An agent on a low-energy or -capability system however must minimize computationally intensive tasks, rely heavily on pre-computation or static rulesets as much as possible, and explicitly account for the resource expenditure of potential response actions in its decision-making calculus.

Likewise, we must consider the cross-platform compatibility of developed agent software. In typical Information Technology (IT) environments, it might be sufficient to support Microsoft Windows, MacOS, and two or three common Linux distributions. Though this does create additional complexity, technologies such as containerization, abstracted languages such as Java, or large-degrees of cross-platform library availability (such as in the Python ecosystem) can make this feasible. However, if considerations are needed for highly customized, very simplified, or non-standard/proprietary operating systems AICA agent software will require additional development (or different architectural decisions) to be deployable.

Finally, a closely related consideration to the platform used in an environment is the cycle-time under which we can assume changes can be made to the running system. In conventional IT systems, systems are reasonably accessible – virtually or physically – should new versions of software need to be deployed, configuration changes made, etc. However, in many environments systems may not be frequently accessible, may have long cycle times for validation and testing of any changes, or may simply not be readily modified after deployment due to hardware or logistical practicalities. Such systems would need to rely much more heavily on collaborative and dynamic behaviors, and less on preconfigured rulesets or datasets.

We will now consider several deployment scenarios that illustrate the distinctions above. For each we will discuss how the fit into this taxonomy, what sorts of threats are typical, what sorts of situational awareness are likely to be required or feasible, and how threats might be detected or countered.

4.2   Unmanned Aircraft Systems (UAS)

UAS and other autonomous vehicles have garnered much attention over the past decade. They have many advantages, primary among them keeping operators out of harm's way, but also allowing increased speed of decision-making in real-time operations, and even enabling new missions that might not otherwise be possible (David & Nielsen, 2016). The environment in which they operate is unique, especially when deployed at a long distance from their operators or others capable of servicing them. From the list of dichotomies, we can consider these systems to be:

- Mobile (a given)
- Potentially disconnected for short periods of time from operators (or requiring safe return to operator functionality if connectivity cannot be restored)
- Currently they are often deployed solo but increasing interest has been show in cooperative swarms
- Safety-critical by nature – whether due to the vehicle-as-a-weapon/hazard concerns or potentially the armaments or payloads they carry

- Likely to be resource constrained due to mission priorities, on-board energy reserves, and/or the computational capacity of onboard systems
- Likely to use special purpose/proprietary operating systems
- Generally easy to modify or update between missions, though not during

The threats to a UAS are tightly coupled to the type of mission it is performing, but generally focused on the mobility and kinetic aspects. An attacker able deny or spoof positioning (e.g., GPS) information could cause the system to veer off course, deploy its capabilities to the wrong location, or trigger safety protocols causing the system to return to the operator or conduct an emergency landing. Similarly, denial of environmental sensing (e.g., LiDAR, visual, altimeters, compass) could have a similar affect or cause the system to impact terrain or structures. Any interruption to the communication signals with operators might have negative mission impacts, especially if conducted at critical times of the mission, worst-case being takeover of the system from the operators. In such a case, initiation of kinetic action (vehicle-as-weapon or ordinance) or theft of imagery, surveilled signals, location history, or other data from the system presents significant risk.

From a situational awareness perspective, environmental considerations are paramount, but network considerations are also important. Environmental inputs might include direct (e.g., visual, RADAR, thermal) detection of potential adversarial systems or forces, sensory information about the environment (e.g., LiDAR, acoustic, thermal), derived information (e.g., object recognition, mapping), and vehicle communications and diagnostics through protocols such as CANBUS or OBDII. Correlating observations from these with in-built models of the environment or known-hazard indicators would be a valuable approach to an AICA agent detecting potential threats.

Network considerations would include observed wireless signals – whether terrestrial (e.g., cellular, point-to-point microwave/optical links, or Wi-Fi), from nearby deployed systems, or earth-to-satellite (and vice versa) communications. Most relevant is likely to be communications from nearby systems in terms of identifying potential inbound threats, but the others might serve a broader mission purpose or allow monitoring of potential attackers in the network environment if appropriately targeted. Network traffic broadcasted on the same control network might be of interest, though this would require a compromise of that channel. More likely valuable is active scanning of the control network or other accessible networks to identify nodes and conduct friend-or-foe determinations.

4.3 Power Grids

The generation, transmission, and distribution of electricity relies heavily on instrumentation and control. This leverages a variety of SCADA systems, which are ubiquitous but the degree to which they are kept up to date varies widely due to concerns about changes impacting stability of these critical systems. This makes approaches that can mitigate vulnerabilities without having to make changes to the underlying systems particularly appealing (Davidson & Andel, 2016; Hu et al., 2021). However, applying an AICA-like multi-agent system must be done with great care due to the real-time constraints that must be met for the underlying system's operation (Abbas et al., 2015). Approaches such as reinforcement learning (Cao et al., 2020) and moving target defenses (Pappa et al., 2017) have been applied to the programs of optimizing or protecting grid resources successfully. From the list of dichotomies, we can consider these systems to be:

- Stationary, due to their close coupling with energy systems mobility is not likely to be encountered
- Connected to a broader network, though the quality of that connection might vary based on deployment location. Older systems might have local communications that are performed through non-routable protocols that are then mediated or relayed by connected systems.
- Though there is potential for collaboration between nodes, their deployment to remote field sites (in many cases) means that the primary focus will be on "lone wolf" operation.
- Safety-critical, due to the potential for impacting operations of the grid
- Likely deployed on systems without problematic resource constraints, but this could vary when considering simpler IOT-type devices.
- A combination of commodity and special-purpose operating systems. For many of the SCADA controllers and human-machine interfaces, they are likely to run on Windows or a common Linux distribution. However, lower-level devices are likely to use embedded and/or real-time operating systems.
- Unlikely to be easily modifiable. This could be due to inaccessibility in particular remote sites, but more so the risks of making changes to these networks require very careful evaluation. This means cycle times between updates to an AICA agent are likely to be long.

Threats to these systems are primarily concerned with the control systems and safety aspects. Denial or spoofing of time signals (network-based, GPS-originated, etc.) could interfere with phase synchronization and reporting mechanisms. Denial or spoofing of phase, voltage, and amperage measurements back to a control center could prevent the grid from being appropriately calibrated – leading to unsafe or unstable conditions. Impeding the ability of an operator to interact with a system in the field could prevent the routine or emergency operations necessary to keep components operating properly. Spoofing operator actions could cause faults such as tripped breakers, disconnected lines, imbalances in supply and demand, or other misconfigurations. Due to the stationary, exposed, and remote nature of many of these systems, we must also be concerned with potential physical threats.

Situational awareness once again is a combination of network and environmental inputs. Broadcasted traffic on the same network segment may give indications to online nodes or servers, and active scanning of local or non-local network segments can reveal additional information about what else is active. Appropriately positioned agents could also monitor traffic between nodes on the network, or between the network and external hosts. Since these environments are likely to be more static in nature and configured according to common IT conventions, log files from the host(s) on which the agent resides or in an aggregated form can provide additional detail about ongoing activity. Environmental awareness can leverage the many sensors required to monitor systems of this type. In addition to basic readings such as temperature, we could expect to have access to electrical information about the grid such as voltage, phase, current, or breaker/line status. Comparing such values with expected values or known anomaly threshold could be a valuable indicator of activity requiring attention.

4.4 Orbital or Deep-Space Platforms

An information systems domain that is particularly unique is that of communications to or between orbital or deep-space (beyond Earth orbit) systems. The number of systems deployed to outer space is growing exponentially as more nationally- and privately- funded programs mature their capabilities. These missions are enormously expensive, high-risk by nature, and may have significant national security implications (or at least national reputation). From the list of dichotomies, we can consider these systems to be:

- Generally mobile, except for any future permanent/stationary operating bases on the Moon, Mars, or otherwise (and ground stations on Earth)
- Though these platforms typically do have connectivity to Earth (such as through NASA's Deep Space Network), this connectivity may have extraordinarily high latency, very low bandwidth, and may have prolonged blackout periods. Thus, it is critical that AICA-like agents deployed to outer space (especially deep space) can operate in a disconnected state.
- Given this fact, it also follows that such system must be able to operate in a "lone wolf" mode. However, as the number of devices continues to expand, it's possible that even without terrestrial connectivity collaboration between nodes could continue. This is challenged by the long cycle times and large deltas in system technologies between missions but may become more feasible as large constellations of systems are deployed within shorter time spans.
- These systems are not safety-critical in most cases (the exception being when deployed as part of or near manned missions). They may require a similar level of diligence given the large potential loss if the system becomes in operable after deployment, but risk to human life is minimal. Special consideration must be given to systems which are deployed using nuclear power sources.
- There are likely to be very tight constraints on energy usage, computational capability (largely limited by weight and space considerations), and the criticality of ensuring resources are allocated to the primary mission. In the current environment, it would be hard to justify sidelining any resources for the purpose

of detecting and responding to hostile actors, but we expect this to change as space becomes more crowded.

- The operating systems on these devices are likely to be highly customized or proprietary in nature, or they might be composed of multiple platforms/instruments that function semi-independently. Software deployed for usage in these environments would need to be largely custom-built for a given mission profile.

- The cycle time on changes to the systems is essentially infinite insofar as it requires any physical interaction or high-bandwidth data transfer. Reusable launch vehicles have become common, but to date except for the Space Shuttle Orbiters there are no instances of a system deployed being returned, modified, and reused (and no such instances of deep space vehicles). Thus, the deployed configuration is very likely to be the final configure except for any small modifications, and focus must be given to adaptive responses in situ.

Like UASs, threats to these systems largely consist of impact to their mission, or theft of sensitive information collected. We can distinguish between threats that can be conducted from Earth versus those that require a presence in physical proximity (on a space scale, which is to say potentially still a significant distance). On Earth, threats consist of attacks on ground stations, communications between those ground stations, or tampering with control systems or signals sent to spacecraft. Interruptions to or modifications of communications with operators at vital times could have catastrophic effects on the ability of a craft to reach its intended destination or maintain a defined position – and subtle changes could potentially escape detection until the cost to correct them becomes large. Such instructions might interfere with maneuvers, deployment or operation of instruments, waste fuel or energy, or even be intended to cause collisions or other damage. As the value of these missions and the information they generate can be enormously valuable to the science or national security communities, even "hacktivist"-type activities might be of concern even if information is not stolen.

Threats that might require proximity to a deployed platform include interfering with instruments required for positioning or sensing, detecting the physical location of sensitive systems, surveilling communications to/from the platform, or obtaining sensitive information from this platform (this last could also be potentially achieved from Earth). One can consider the situation where a deployed platform in a communications blackout is targeted by a hostile platform of an adversary. By the time a human operator even becomes aware of the encounter, it might be too late to do anything about it. The only indication something has happened could be the inability to communicate with the system, or there might be no indication whatsoever. For this reason, it's critical that future space systems have capabilities to detect and respond to hostile actions autonomously.

Situational awareness for these platforms will also look like UASs. For deep-space systems there is unlikely to be much of a demand for network-based observation, at least in the near future. Communications are largely point-to-point and the likelihood of another devices in close enough proximity to communicate via non-directional communications is minimal. However, orbital systems are increasingly deployed in large constellations that might communicate not only with ground stations but with each other. Though optical point-to-point communications are a primary focus due to the bandwidth that can be achieved, there is still the possibility for a hostile device to be near enough to be detected through RF/microwave sensing. If work on permanent settlements and communication systems on the Moon or Mars advances significantly in coming years, this is likely to begin to look very similar to the UAS case.

For the time being, environmental sensing is probably a more important focus for space systems. Visual, RADAR, thermal, or other direct detection of nearby devices (and projection of their trajectories) is a vital element of maintaining situational awareness. Position, velocity, and acceleration data is also critical. Depending on the mission profile, other sensors might be available to conduct other direct measurements – but the degree to which they're available for non-mission purposes might vary. Metrics regarding communication links with ground stations, relays, or other craft may also help a system detect the presence of possible threats.

4.5   Large-Scale Computational Arrays

The last deployment scenario we'll consider is perhaps the most familiar for those in the information technology space. On varying scales, we can consider arrays of systems built for the purposes of cloud computing, high-performance computing, or even normal business/mission operations. Such systems might use technologies such as software-defined network (SDN) which can be protected via autonomous means with reinforcement learning (Han et al., 2018), containerized workloads (e.g., Docker, Kubernetes) that lend themselves well to moving target defense approaches (Jin et al., 2021), or an easy traversable network architecture that could enable "roaming" agents (Prosser & Fulp, 2020). From the list of dichotomies, we can consider these systems to be:

- Stationary in nature, though potentially distributed across multiple geographic locations.
- Typically connected to the broader internet (except for high-security air-gapped systems) and with good connectivity to operators and other agents.
- Well-suited for cooperative agents due to the potential quantity and connectivity of systems on which agents could be deployed.
- In most deployments, excluding critical infrastructures such as power systems (as discussed above), these are not likely to be safety critical. Some ambiguity might exist in domains such as healthcare or emergency services.
- These systems are unlikely to be constrained in their energy usage (beyond cost and environmental considerations) and can essentially be built with whatever computational capacity is necessary to achieve their objectives with the scope of available budgets.

- The vast majority of the time, these systems will use commodity hardware and operating systems. General purpose agents designed for these platforms are likely to have a high potential for reuse between environments. Some exceptions exist, such as very large cloud providers who build their own hardware or HPC environments with special purpose operating systems.
- It is likely to be comparatively easy to make modifications to these types of systems, and automation might even exist to do so at scale with minimal effort. More incremental approaches to deployment and configuration are possible.

Threats to these types of environments are reasonably well understood (if not always effectively combatted). Like any IT system, concerns regarding the theft of confidential information from any of the constituent nodes is a concern. Additionally, deletion or corruption is often a concern – whether due to impact to business processes or harm to consumers. In the HPC context, such modifications might require re-computation and impact overall performance, or could lead to incorrect or poor-quality results. Similarly, interruption of communications between system could impact the delivery of services or interfere with coordination of distributed workloads. Lower-level attacks might physically damage hardware, create anomalous power or cooling loads, or interfere with processing of other users on shared resources.

Situational awareness in such a context is largely limited to network-based considerations. Though some basic environmental parameters such as local temperatures, voltages, or the current draw of various components is typically accessible, there are not typically any other environmental sensors. Thus, awareness of network communications, reachable or adjacent nodes, and analysis of local or aggregated logs are the primary signals of interest.

5   Summary and Conclusions

Autonomous intelligent cyber-defense agents have great potential to enable new forms of defense and counter the types of attacks that may become common place soon – attacks that are automated, adaptive, and high velocity. Human defenders will be increasingly at a disadvantage, even beyond the current typical times to detect and respond to security incidents. However, it will be critical that such agents are designed for the appropriate deployment scenario to ensure that they take appropriate advantage of the environment, but also do not cause unnecessary risk or harm to the systems they are intended to protect. Further research and field trials are needed not only in the fundamental considerations of how to construct AICA-like agents and enable their reasoning and collaborative capabilities, but also to determine how to make it possible to deploy them effectively to a variety of environments. The considerations of mobility, safety-criticality, connectivity, independence, resource constraints, and platform uniqueness are perhaps not fully exhaustive, but are important aspects to consider as such work continues.

Acknowledgements The work presented in this paper was partially supported by the U.S. Department of Energy, Office of Science under DOE contract number DE-AC02-06CH11357. The submitted manuscript has been created by UChicago Argonne, LLC, operator of Argonne National Laboratory. Argonne, a DOE Office of Science laboratory, is operated under Contract No. DE-AC02-06CH11357. The U.S. Government retains for itself, and others acting on its behalf, a paid-up nonexclusive, irrevocable worldwide license in said article to reproduce, prepare derivative works, distribute copies to the public, and perform publicly and display publicly, by or on behalf of the Government.

References

Abbas, H. A., Shaheen, S. I., & Amin, M. H. (2015). On the adoption of multi-agent systems for the development of industrial control networks. *ArXiv:1506.05235 [Cs]*. http://arxiv.org/abs/1506.05235

Andreadis, G., Klazoglou, P., Niotaki, K., & Bouzakis, K.-D. (2014). Classification and review of multi-agents Systems in the Manufacturing Section. *Procedia Engineering, 69*, 282–290. https://doi.org/10.1016/j.proeng.2014.02.233

Avgerinos, T., Brumley, D., Davis, J., Goulden, R., Nighswander, T., Rebert, A., & Williamson, N. (2018). The Mayhem cyber reasoning system. *IEEE Security & Privacy, 16*(2), 52–60. https://doi.org/10.1109/MSP.2018.1870873

Booker, L. B., & Musman, S. A. (2020). A model-based, decision-theoretic perspective on automated cyber response. *ArXiv:2002.08957 [Cs]*. http://arxiv.org/abs/2002.08957

Cam, H. (2020). Cyber resilience using autonomous agents and reinforcement learning. In T. Pham, L. Solomon, & K. Rainey (Eds.), *Artificial intelligence and machine learning for multi-domain operations applications II* (p. 35). SPIE. https://doi.org/10.1117/12.2559319

Cao, D., Hu, W., Zhao, J., Zhang, G., Zhang, B., Liu, Z., Chen, Z., & Blaabjerg, F. (2020). Reinforcement learning and its applications in modern power and energy systems: A review. *Journal of Modern Power Systems and Clean Energy, 8*(6), 1029–1042. https://doi.org/10.35833/MPCE.2020.000552

David, R. A., & Nielsen, P. (2016). Defense science board summer study on autonomy. Defense Science Board Washington United States. https://apps.dtic.mil/sti/citations/AD1017790.

Davidson, C., & Andel, T. (2016). Feasibility of applying moving target defensive techniques in a SCADA system. In *11th international conference on cyber warfare and security*. https://doi.org/10.13140/RG.2.1.5189.5441.

Hammar, K., & Stadler, R. (2020). Finding effective security strategies through reinforcement learning and self-play. *ArXiv:2009.08120 [Cs, Stat]*. https://doi.org/10.13140/RG.2.2.14128.38405.

Han, Y., Rubinstein, B. I. P., Abraham, T., Alpcan, T., De Vel, O., Erfani, S., Hubczenko, D., Leckie, C., & Montague, P. (2018). Reinforcement learning for autonomous defence in software-defined networking. In L. Bushnell, R. Poovendran, & T. Başar (Eds.), *Decision and game theory for security* (pp. 145–165). Springer International Publishing. https://doi.org/10.1007/978-3-030-01554-1_9

Holland, O. T. (n.d.). Taxonomy for the modeling and simulation of emergent. *Behavior Systems, 1*, 9.

Hu, Y., Zhu, P., Xun, P., Liu, B., Kang, W., Xiong, Y., & Shi, W. (2021). CPMTD: Cyber-physical moving target defense for hardening the security of power system against false data injected attack. *Computers & Security, 111*, 102465. https://doi.org/10.1016/j.cose.2021.102465

Huang, L., & Zhu, Q. (2018). Analysis and computation of adaptive Defense strategies against advanced persistent threats for cyber-physical systems. In L. Bushnell, R. Poovendran, & T. Başar (Eds.), *Decision and game theory for security* (pp. 205–226). Springer International Publishing. https://doi.org/10.1007/978-3-030-01554-1_12

Jin, H., Li, Z., Zou, D., & Yuan, B. (2021). DSEOM: A framework for dynamic security evaluation and optimization of MTD in container-based cloud. *IEEE Transactions on Dependable and Secure Computing, 18*(3), 1125–1136. https://doi.org/10.1109/TDSC.2019.2916666

Kotenko, I., Konovalov, A., & Shorov, A. (2012). Agent-based simulation of cooperative defence against botnets. *Concurrency and Computation: Practice and Experience, 24*(6), 573–588. https://doi.org/10.1002/cpe.1858

Kott, A., & Theron, P. (2020). Doers, not watchers: Intelligent autonomous agents are a path to cyber resilience. *IEEE Security & Privacy, 18*(3), 62–66. https://doi.org/10.1109/MSEC.2020.2983714

Kott, A., Golan, M. S., Trump, B. D., & Linkov, I. (2021). Cyber resilience: By design or by intervention? *Computer, 54*(8), 112–117. https://doi.org/10.1109/MC.2021.3082836

Ligo, A. K., Kott, A., & Linkov, I. (2021). Autonomous Cyberdefense introduces risk: Can we manage the risk? *Computer, 54*(10), 106–110. https://doi.org/10.1109/MC.2021.3099042

Linkov, I., Galaitsi, S., Trump, B. D., Keisler, J. M., & Kott, A. (2020). Cybertrust: From explainable to actionable and interpretable artificial intelligence. *Computer, 53*(9), 91–96. https://doi.org/10.1109/MC.2020.2993623

Maier, M. W. (2014). The role of Modeling and simulation in system of systems development. In *Modeling and simulation support for system of systems engineering applications* (pp. 11–41). Wiley. https://doi.org/10.1002/9781118501757.ch2

Pappa, A., Ashok, A., & Govindarasu, M. (2017). Moving target Defense for security smart grid communications: Architecture, Implementation & Evaluation. In *Power & Energy Society Innovative Smart Grid Technologies Conference* (pp. 3–7). https://doi.org/10.1109/ISGT.2017.8085954

Pawlick, J., Colbert, E., & Zhu, Q. (2019). A game-theoretic taxonomy and survey of defensive deception for cybersecurity and privacy. *ACM Computing Surveys, 52*(4), 1–28. https://doi.org/10.1145/3337772

Prosser, B. J., & Fulp, E. W. (2020). A distributed population management approach for Mobile agent systems. In *2020 IEEE international conference on autonomic computing and self-organizing systems (ACSOS)* (pp. 102–108). https://doi.org/10.1109/ACSOS49614.2020.00031

Rauf, U., Mohsin, M., & Mazurczyk, W. (2019). Cyber regulatory networks: Towards a bio-inspired auto-resilient framework for cyber-Defense. In A. Compagnoni, W. Casey, Y. Cai, & B. Mishra (Eds.), *Bio-inspired information and communication technologies* (pp. 156–174). Springer International Publishing. https://doi.org/10.1007/978-3-030-24202-2_12

van Dijk, M., Juels, A., Oprea, A., & Rivest, R. L. (2013). FlipIt: The game of "stealthy takeover.". *Journal of Cryptology, 26*(4), 655–713. https://doi.org/10.1007/s00145-012-9134-5

Chapter 15
Command in AICA-Intensive Operations

Arne Norlander

1 Introduction and Challenges: The AICA-Inhabited Operational Environment Is Contested, Nonlinear, and Dynamic

Operating in a contested mission environment requires comprehensive operational awareness, with the ability to accurately and rapidly perceive and interpret relevant events and circumstances. In order to provide the context, insight and foresight is required for effective decision-making. Complex multi-domain operations are of particular concern; while some operational tasks necessarily would employ a human component, other tasks can only be accomplished through non-human intelligent entities, acting autonomously within the socio-technical enterprise, defined by Kott et al. (2019) and in previous chapters in this volume as Autonomous Intelligent Cyberdefense Agents (AICA).

A complex system is any system in which the parts of the system and their interactions together represent a specific behavior, such that an analysis of all its constituent parts cannot explain the behavior. In such systems, the cause and effect cannot necessarily be related, and relationships are non-linear –a small change could have a disproportionate impact. In other words, as Aristotle said: 'the whole is greater than the sum of its parts'. This requires adaptive and versatile principles and concepts for complex multi-domain operations along with high-performance human, technological and organizational architectures (Norlander, 2019a).

Operational success is strongly linked to effective interaction and collaboration within and between the physical, information and cognitive domains. Cyber-Physical Systems (CPS), different organizational cultures, people with different

A. Norlander (✉)
NORSECON AB, Stockholm, Sweden
e-mail: arne.norlander@norsecon.se

© The Author(s), under exclusive license to Springer Nature Switzerland AG 2023   311
A. Kott (ed.), *Autonomous Intelligent Cyber Defense Agent (AICA)*, Advances in
Information Security 87, https://doi.org/10.1007/978-3-031-29269-9_15

backgrounds, education and experience rely heavily on collectively managing and maintaining operational availability, versatility and efficiency. In many situations the desired effects cannot be linearly planned and reliably predicted, but must be anticipated to emerge from shaping the Operational Environment (OE) and influencing the agents operating in the OE.

There are several issues concerning the use of mission-specific and contextual information and knowledge for judgment, decision, and choice, as well as the information-coupled activities leading to supervisory control of a complex, partly or completely automated process, and the more obvious control of the involved technological systems. This also concerns the degree of automation needed to achieve flexible task and resource allocation, and relates to all kinds of Human-Machine interaction concerns and management tasks at every organisational level. There is a monitoring or feedback portion of the efforts required to execute supervisory control and the need for functions enabling learning and adapting over time, but also a feedforward part that is crucial to ensure rapid and reliable, autonomous response in routine decision situations. DARPA's Mosaic Warfare concept (Congressional Research Service, 2022; DARPA, 2020) is an ambitious endeavor into Human-Machine capabilities in extensively, sometimes entirely, autonomous warfighting.

Additionally, success in AICA-intensive operations requires Comprehensive Operational Awareness. Cyber operations are of particular concern; while some cyberspace operational tasks necessarily would employ human agents, other tasks can only be accomplished through non-human intelligent entities, acting autonomously and with machine speed within the socio-technical enterprise. This requires adaptive and versatile principles and concepts for Joint Systems Operations along with high-performance human, technological and organizational architectures.

Finally, the turbulent environment in which AICA-intensive operations take place stresses the need for Organizational Agility (OA), to be adaptable and resilient without having to change (Dyer and Shafer, 1998). The goal is to keep internal operations at a level of fluidity and flexibility that matches the degree of turmoil in external environments, a principle known as requisite variety (Ashby, 1956). This requires adaptive and versatile principles and concepts for management and decision-making along with agile high-performance organizational structures, illustrated in Fig. 15.1.

The number and diversity of the entities required to interact and collaborate in AICA-intensive operations, the set of operational sub-domains in which these entities operate, the interdependencies between and among operations in these domains and the effects they create, all pose significant challenges not yet fully anticipated nor appreciated.

Fig. 15.1 A model of agile
organizational capability.
(Adapted from Dyer &
Shafer, 1998, p. 11)

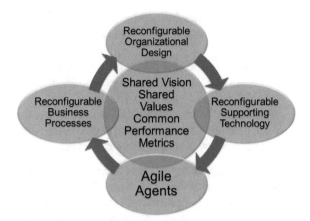

2   Developing AICA Command Capabilities: A Command Layer of the AICA Architecture

In multifunctional and multi-organizational operations, we must have multiple perspectives and an ability to undertake missions in all environments, including the cyberspace domain (Norlander, 2019b). The Stuxnet worm that was spread in 2010 marked a watershed in cyber warfare revealing a level of destructive power with computer code previously reserved for kinetic bombings and physical sabotage (Rosenbaum, 2012). Different types of offensive cyberspace operations threaten the cyber domain and defensive cyberspace operations are the tools to defend against these threats. It is important to develop capabilities for executing cyberspace operations. The problem with commanding cyberspace operations is already recognized; One example was formulated by Carvelli (2018), "The United States should delegate cyber-attack authority to operational commanders, but it should impose restrictions on the authority based on the attack's effects". How does this new domain's conditions affect our chosen command philosophy? This chapter examines the C2 capability in general and especially for command in relation to AICA-intensive operations. A crucial factor in achievement of the objectives in AICA-intensive operations is that all actors and partners can be consolidated into an architecture that is:

1. Generic – represents all relevant capabilities, artificial and human alike,
2. Scalable – across all capability categories (or business areas) and organizational levels,
3. Shared – accepted and used by all agents, commanders and stakeholders.

Each one of the three requirements of the AICA capability architecture is fulfilled by a combination of operational characteristics, enabling development of the agile AICA-enabled force and its essential operational capabilities:

- **Efficiency** defines the possibilities to both develop and operate AICA-enabled capabilities as well as to deploy and support them in theatre with optimal resource utilization.
- **Versatility** defines the possibilities to operate in all dimensions and operational levels of risk. Most operations include an, at times, unpredictable mix of offensive, defensive and stabilizing elements.
- **Availability** defines the possibilities to deploy AICA-enabled capabilities at the right time and to carry out operational activities during the time required with regard to policy and operational objectives.

Primary and supporting fields of study are found in other chapters in this volume: Architectures; Machine Learning; Perception of threats in the Operational Environment (OE); Situational Understanding (SU); Defense, Response and Recovery planning; Adaptivity and Antifragility; Development, Deployment and Operation of AICA capabilities; Team formation and Human Interaction; Risk and Trust Issues; and several case studies. These studies are conducted in a multitude of organizations: government, industry, healthcare, education and aid organizations to name a few. What all have in common is the need for a strategy and vision for developing these capabilities. Based on these studies and with the support from other fields of study – Computerized Automation, Cognitive Systems, Complex Adaptive Systems, High-Reliability Organizations, Leadership and War studies – we have devised a number of strategy elements as part of an essence of command for AICA-intensive operations.

3 Joint Cognitive Systems

The research field of cognitive systems engineering (CSE) (Rasmussen, 1983, 1986; Hollnagel & Woods, 1983, 2006; Smith & Hoffman, 2017) offers such a perspective in terms of "joint cognitive systems" (JCS) which, using concepts from cybernetics (Wiener, 1961; Ashby, 1956), cognitive psychology and perception (Neisser, 1976), and systems thinking (Senge, 1990) as points of departure, view purposeful constellations of humans and technology as "joint systems" capable of adaptive behavior. The underlying logic of the Joint Cognitive Systems (JCS) perspective is to look at any constellation of humans and technology asking the questions "what goals are being pursued by this system?" and "what control relationships exist within the system and between the system and its environment?"

Originally, the JCS concept was developed to overcome the duality of traditional human-machine research, focusing on better understanding what people actually do with technology rather than what functions belong to the machine and what functions belong to the human. Instead, the JCS perspective suggests that the important issue is to understand whether the human-machine system can achieve its goal(s) by analyzing in what way the JCS can affect or influence its target processes and in what way it is influenced or affected by its environment. Norlander (2014) developed a theoretical and methodological foundation for analyzing Tactical JCS in military and emergency management missions, derived from the fields of CSE, Systems Theory/ Cybernetics, Command and Decision theory, and Psychophysiology.

A cognitive system operates by using knowledge about itself and its environment to plan and modify its actions based on that knowledge (Rasmussen et al., 1994). As for complex systems, such knowledge is imperative. For example, in military missions a multitude of autonomous and intelligent sensor systems, communication systems, together with human operators, and specific Tactics, Techniques and Procedures (TTPs) are all elements of a 'wider' (total) operational system (Norlander, 2014). The total operational capability is built from a set of capability elements: Doctrine, Organization, Training, Materiel, Leadership, Personnel, Facilities and Interoperability (abbreviated as DOTMLPFI).

Employing the cognitive systems paradigm also for AICA-intensive operations permits the integration of all capability elements into an adaptive distributed system that can achieve a mission safely and efficiently.

4 Complex Adaptive Systems (CAS)

The research literature describes the broader aspects of defense systems in terms of Complex Adaptive Systems (CAS) (Holland, 1995, 2006; Norlander, 2011) in the sense that military or crisis management organizations demonstrate CAS properties, and identify adaptive mechanisms at the levels of adaptive systems, capability development and collective/society, which adjust through learning, evolutionary development and cultural change to fulfill an externally imposed purpose. CAS has characteristics of self-learning, emergence, and evolution among the entities of the complex system. The entities or agents in a CAS demonstrate heterogeneous behavior. The key characteristics for a complex adaptive system are:

- The behavior or output cannot be predicted simply by analyzing the parts and inputs of the system.
- The behavior of the system is emergent and changes with time. The same input and environmental conditions do not always guarantee the same output.
- The entities or agents of a system are self-learning and change their behavior based on the outcome of their previous experiences.

The CAS framework has its parallels of course, not only to the theoretical foundation of cybernetics, but also to the field of neuroscience. The law of required model-regulatory identity stipulates that every good regulator of a system must be a model of that system (Conant & Ashby, 1970). It states that any regulator able to confine the variations in the system to be controlled, must not only have adequate amounts of variety available to control that system, but also be a homomorphic representation of that system. It is a more rigorous version of the law of requisite variety, originally formulated by Ashby (1956), which states that the variety of a controller of a dynamic system has to be equal to or greater than the variety of the system itself.

Homomorphisms are important for verifying whether one system is a model of another, and for investigating which original system properties are retained in the model. It means that the regulator must be a many-to-one mapping, representing a pattern in the mapping domain by a simpler pattern in its range.

5 Intelligent Collaboration: An Emergent Feature of Artificial and Human Agents

5.1 A Functional Perspective on Intelligent Collaboration

In the case of AICAs, we need to understand how a unit consisting of both humans and AICAs can reach their goals and how control, rather than functions, is allocated in the human-machine system. Further, both humans and AICAs are bounded in their rationality, although by different characteristics, deciding how control should be allocated between humans and AICAs depending on context and current goals.

The discussion benefits from this as it takes place in a hypothetical zone where the exact technical components cannot be described, as they do not yet exist. However, we can describe what an AICA is/should be in terms of what it can do (its functional properties), which is in line with the JCS perspective that emphasizes *what a system does, rather than what it is*. Below, we elaborate on why an AICA can be seen as a cognitive system in its own right, and how the JCS approach can be used to better understand the human-autonomy system in different situations and contexts.

The AICA concept is integrated with the central premise of the human operator and decision maker as a capability component in the cognitive domain, operating symbiotically within and between the physical and information domains through technological artifacts (Norlander, 2014). Human operators are constantly collecting and building knowledge about themselves, other agents and the operational environment. They apply skills, rules and heuristics to plan and modify their actions based on that knowledge. Every commander and every human and artificial agent must develop a capability for sensemaking to enable a comprehensive detailed system insight, leading to safe and efficient mission accomplishment (Weick et al., 2005).

AICA entities must possess corresponding inherent capabilities and characteristics to successfully manage the mission spectrum. This involves an ability to interact with human operators, operate effectively and create emergent effects through highly capable Human-AICA Command (HAC), illustrated in Fig. 15.2.

An AICA is, in this chapter, defined as an adaptive artificial entity that is capable of autonomously engaging with its environment in direct interaction and interdependency with other artificial entities and human operators in order to meet a specific objective. Besides deciding and acting on an individual basis, both the human operators and the artificial entities complement each other's decision-making

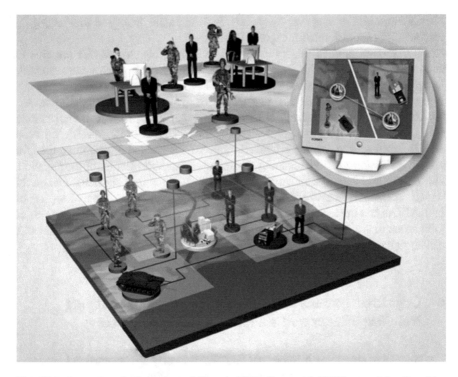

Fig. 15.2 A conceptual illustration of Human-AICA Command (HAC) as a Joint Cognitive System (JCS). (Adapted from Norlander, 2014)

processes and actions and jointly solve problems, in many respects analogous to the concept of cognitive work of Rasmussen et al. (1991). In order to do so, they must possess a sufficient level of Situation Understanding (Noel and Swarup, this volume) to enable effective and efficient collaboration through

1. Understanding complex ideas and concepts (relative to the activity),
2. Adaptation effectively to a dynamic environment, and
3. Combining task related with social and interactive skills and capabilities.

5.2 Standardized Automation Concepts Do Not Capture Intelligent Collaboration

Previous research on autonomy has largely focused on understanding how different "levels" of automation changes the working conditions for human operators (Sheridan & Verplank, 1978; Parasuraman et al., 2000). This view largely prevails today, as can be seen in the development of self-driving cars. Future applications of robotics and autonomous capabilities suggest a world were different robotic or software entities are integrated in society, fulfilling many tasks and even taking on responsibility for different managerial tasks.

As described later in this chapter, this calls for technologies that are able to autonomously engage with its environment, without continuous human surveillance. In terms of perspectives that can provide some theoretical context for such a future, this can be seen as a case of a socio-technical system. Additionally, success in AICA-intensive Operations requires highly capable Mission Understanding (MU), based on an accurate perception and interpretation of the specific situation and circumstances in order to provide the context, insight and foresight required for effective decision-making, enabling a comprehensive appreciation of the situation. However, while socio-technical aspects of human-autonomy constellations are of importance, we need also to focus understanding towards the cognitive aspects of both AICAs and humans in order to better grasp the possibilities and limitations of joint human-autonomy system in terms of performance and the types of tasks that can be supported by AICAs.

6 Cognitive Systems and Autonomous Agents: Learning from Experience and Adapting to Circumstances

The concept of autonomy is important for AICAs, as they are assumed to have capabilities for performing their tasks independently or interdependently and to have capabilities for reasoning and interaction that are needed for collaboration. The term "autonomy", however, needs more clarification as it may be used in multiple ways. Autonomy in relation to robotics is sometimes conflated with automation. An autonomous/automated system, then, "performs its actions without human intervention". It can be fully pre-programmed and may have no choices about its action execution.

Nevertheless, from a more philosophical perspective, this interpretation of autonomy as automation is questionable. AI researchers have imposed requirements on autonomous systems regarding their internal reasoning, decision-making and SA dynamics (National Academies of Sciences, Engineering, and Medicine, 2022; Ziemke et al., 2017; Endsley, 2015). Furthermore, an autonomous system is not necessarily independent; it may allow external influences (e.g. human guidance), as long as it explicitly accepts these influences. This notion is important in the context of AICAs, as it combines social and collaborative capabilities in autonomous systems. Lastly, autonomy of artificial systems, just as in the case of humans, is dependent on operational circumstances. A physical autonomous system, such as a UAV, or a virtual one, like an AICA, may be autonomous in the sense that it can operate without guidance during conventionally planned and executed missions, much like a human being, but it will only be autonomous in certain operational contexts and in relation to specific goals. If these conditions are changed, then the system is no longer "autonomous" in any of perspectives presented above. From this point of view, the idea of a "cognitive system" actually fits the description of what we generally refer to as "autonomous agents".

In reality, no systems to be considered for military usage should be truly autonomous, as even when tasked to do something that requires autonomy in a specific situation and context, the autonomous unit should only present agency within the frames of the task given to it.

As pointed out above, an autonomous unit like an AICA fits the definition of a "cognitive system". Hollnagel (1999) defines a cognitive system as a system that "can modify its pattern of behavior on the basis of past experience in order to achieve specific anti-entropic ends". This definition fits any organism or system that is to prevail in a dynamic environment.

The conclusion from this is that an AICA must possess three fundamental capabilities to act as a cognitive system, defined by Worm (2000) as cornerstones of modern complex cognitive systems science:

1. A cognitive system is capable of adaptation to the varying conditions of the surrounding environment;
2. A cognitive system is capable of prediction of how the surrounding environment evolves over time;
3. A cognitive system is capable of regulation in order to reach an equilibrium that matches the current conditions of the surrounding environment.

These capabilities are well in line with observed properties of any category of complex systems. If we view the role of AICAs in the context of Multi-Domain Operations, the AICAs must be able to apply these capabilities in relation to a multitude of organizational entities; human and artificial operators, sensor systems, communication systems, doctrine and networks are all elements of the total operational system. Analogous to the findings of Conant and Ashby (1970), the conclusion of this is that an AICA has to be capable to adapt, predict and regulate to a level at least in line with human decision-making process and action to be able to complement each other.

The adaptive capability of an AICA can be understood in the light of the CSE definition provided above. Additionally, recent work by Prof. Tom Malone's research group in the realm of Superminds (Malone, 2018), suggest that human and artificial entities can jointly utilize Artificial Intelligence and Hyperconnectivity to form learning loops, constituting strategic planning and decision-making capabilities of business corporations, government agencies and global organizations. Combining the JCS, CAS, Autonomy and Superminds conceptual structures lead to four corollaries to the AICA capabilities definitions above, characterizing AICAs as Autonomous Adaptive Agents (AAAs), originally defined by Worm (2000):

1. An autonomous adaptive agent can sense the environment through observation and measurement and act on the environment through its inherent actuators or other collaborating agents;

2. An autonomous adaptive agent has an internal information management and decision-making capability, and can classify and anticipate future states and possibilities, based on internal models;
3. An autonomous adaptive agent's internal models are often incomplete and/or incorrect due to the dynamic characteristics of the agent itself or the surrounding environment, and must be updated and restructured through observation and measurement;
4. An autonomous adaptive agent's anticipatory ability often significantly alters the aggregate behavior of the system of which an agent is part.

Besides constituting an autonomous intelligent adaptive agent, an AICA is also designed as a team member, meaning it is able when executing its tasks to complement the human decision-making process and task execution. Effective human-AICA teams are capable of exploiting the unique abilities of both humans and AI, while overcoming the known challenges and limitations of each team member. Recent advances in Human-AI Teaming (HAT) support the idea that an optimally balanced human-AICA team ultimately augments human capabilities and raises performance beyond that of either entity (National Academies of Sciences, Engineering, and Medicine, 2022). Hence, AICAs will, when integrated with humans in mission teams, be more perceived as team members than a collection of tools, algorithms and artifacts.

Mission success is strongly linked to effective interaction and collaboration within and between different organizational cultures, between people with different backgrounds, education and experience, and on managing and maintaining operational availability, versatility and efficiency (Norlander, 2019a).

In many business domains – industry or government, civilian or military – it is widely acknowledged that the principal drivers of evolution reciprocate between scientific progress and operational experience (Alberts & Hayes, 2006). Science advances theory, providing options for analysis and development. Theory advances technology, providing opportunities for future capabilities. Operational experience advances the state of the practice, improving adaptability and generating strategies for managing change in missions and environments. This experience can be formalized into requirements for future AICA capabilities through an evidence-based analytical framework.

An integrative approach to studying this through the lenses of Systems Theory, Cognitive Systems Engineering and Psychophysiology was made by Norlander (2010), supported by findings in the areas of Complex Adaptive Systems; Cognitive Systems; Critical skills of individual operators and teams; Mission Critical resource management; Agile Command and Control and distribution of authority and responsibility; Leadership, decision-making and operational performance.

7   Executing High-Risk Missions with AICAs as Part of High-Reliability Organizations

In most day-to-day business operations, operational reliability, availability and high technical performance at the lowest possible cost are persisting overall objectives, and risk awareness in the organization is often limited. On the other hand, more specialized operational domains i.e. aviation, space, maritime, intensive care, nuclear power and military systems, require extraordinary risk awareness and risk management (Rasmussen, 1997). These cases can be classified as complex endeavors, and the costs of incidents, attacks and breakdowns are valued not only in economic terms but also in human lives.

Ligo et al. (2021) argued that human intervention should not include the direct operation of AICAs, but rather team up with autonomous cyber agents in a hierarchical command arrangement. Kott and Alberts (2017) conclude that the superior response time and data processing of cyber systems might be combined with human judgment of safety or ethical consequences. Ligo et al. (This volume) analyze risks associated with AICA inherent complexity, that might emerge when AICA are part of a defense strategy. They discuss three approaches to mitigating and managing complexity-induced risk, and where human operators cannot acquire the necessary Situation Awareness (SA) and/or react accordingly in the time and scale required:

1. Human-centered strategies that shape AICA behavior before action selection and execution.
2. Specific machine learning algorithms such as reinforcement learning and generative adversarial networks (GAN) applied to AICA behavior.
3. General algorithmic principles that constrain AICA actions and outcome spaces (e.g. Asimov rules of robotics).

In a joint system the artificial components would quickly produce purely autonomous responses to attacks, and human operators could evaluate such responses (probably not in real time) and adjust the system to produce responses in the future with lower risk of negative outcomes.

Additionally, the concept of risk in joint systems is indivisibly unified with trust, a topic that is treated in depth by Reason (1997), Parasuraman et al. (2014) and in other chapters of this volume. For the AICA-intensive operational spectrum, there is an analogous concept for managing this type of risk and utilizing human performance as a component of security, defense and other complex endeavors: High-Reliability Organizations (HRO), which rest on an organizational culture that aims to achieve error-free performance and safety in every procedure, every time—all while operating in complex, high-risk or hazardous environments, identifying and preventing potentially catastrophic incidents before they happen.

Weick and Sutcliffe (2015) identified five central principles for HROs that can be used to support development and implementation of a vision for AICA-enabled capabilities:

1. Sensitivity to operations (i.e. heightened awareness of the state of relevant systems and processes), achieved via monitoring);
2. Reluctance to simplify (i.e. acceptance that work is complex, with the potential to fail in new and unexpected ways);
3. Preoccupation with failure (i.e., to view 'near misses' as opportunities to improve, rather than proof of success and learning from incidents);
4. Deference to expertise (i.e., to value insights from staff with the most pertinent safety knowledge over those with greater seniority);
5. Practicing resilience (e.g., to prioritize training for many unlikely, but possible, system failures).

Finally, the concept of responsibility is a factor that cannot be ignored in AICA capability development. Responsibility is primarily a doctrinal and regulatory concept influencing every dimension of high-risk operations.

> Responsibility is a unique concept... You may share it with others, but your portion is not diminished. You may delegate it, but it is still with you... If responsibility is rightfully yours, no evasion, or ignorance or passing the blame can shift the burden to someone else.
>
> – Admiral Hyman. G. Rickover, United States Navy, known as the "Father of the Nuclear Navy" due to his role in developing the first nuclear-powered submarine.

8 Command Characteristics for AICA-Enabled Capabilities

The world is changing and so are the conditions for the command and execution of military, crisis management and business operations. Command approaches that worked well in the past may not be appropriate today (Alberts, 2018). The celebrated Mission Command concept evolved from high-intensity kinetic warfare (van Creveld, 1985; Lind, 1985), but its relevance to a wider spectrum of operations such as operations in the information and cognitive domains must be thoroughly examined.

8.1 Command in AICA-Intensive Operations Requires an Agility Mindset That Embraces Uncertainty

On Command and Leadership Under VUCA Circumstances

An Agility mindset represents adaptability to a variety of challenges and a readiness to act effectively and timely. It requires a global perspective with a focus on managing a wide range of interdependent agents and events, in remote, austere and hostile conditions (Norlander, 2019b; McChrystal et al., 2015), and where Volatile, Uncertain, Complex and Ambiguous (VUCA) circumstances are the norm rather than the exception (Barber, 1992). AICA-intensive operations under these circumstances warrant the following command and leadership characteristics:

- **Volatility** is amplified by accelerating change, in a world in which social, cultural, and technological progress is exponentially increasing in ever-shorter intervals of time. In such an ecosystem, it is not enough to stay informed about the latest trends and data. Savvy commanders understand that there is now a mandate toward staying ahead of growth curves, and having the foresight to both know how to find breakthroughs to handle the inherent enterprise dynamics and, ultimately, create the future.
- **Uncertainty** pushes commanders to demonstrate more agility and active engagement. In addition to technology driving the complexity of today's environment, societal, economic, environmental, and political drivers converge to create new challenges and, more importantly, new opportunities. Progress in algorithmic technologies and cognitive systems enables a significant growth in the amount of information available for judgment and decision-making. Even the highest quality information will generally be associated with considerable uncertainty, ambiguity, inaccuracy and other deficiencies.
- **Complexity** compels commanders to remain focused on what's next. To gain greater visibility about the future requires an instrument for building resilience, adaptability, and opportunity through recognition of emerging patterns. The number and diversity of the entities required to respond, the set of operational sub-domains in which they operate, the interdependencies between and among operations in these domains and the effects they create, all pose significant operational challenges is yet to be fully identified and appreciated.
- **Ambiguity** raises a number of leadership, trust and agency concerns regarding the needs, characteristics, interdependencies, and abilities of the involved human agents, AICAs, and joint systems. Ambiguity forces leaders to cope with poorly structured and imprecise knowledge, by employing a diversity of problem solving activities. In some cases the results are interpreted and converted into physical control signals to control and influence some physical process. In other cases the results are implemented as policy or directives (Tessensohn et al., 2018), containing plans, orders, tactics, techniques and procedures for other human agents or AICAs to follow.

On Risk vs. Uncertainty

Risk is the probability of loss, injury or other negative results and this can be managed by being quantifiable and controlled. This is the reason why the insurance industry exists, and the basis of all risk management and vulnerability assessment schemes, in industry as well as in government. Scholarly work on risk in the insurance industry led to the development of the theory of asymmetric information by Joseph Stiglitz, who shared the Nobel Prize in economics in 2001 (Nobel Foundation, 2001) with George Akerlof and Michael Spence.

An application of risk and probability theory that is of particular interest in the context of this volume is Bayes' Theorem, and how it is utilized in Machine Learning. In short, Bayes' Theorem is a method for calculating *conditional probabilities*, or the likelihood of one event occurring if another has previously occurred. A conditional probability can lead to more accurate outcomes by including more data. In order to obtain correct estimations and probabilities in Machine Learning, Bayesian classifiers are widely regarded as simple but high-accuracy approaches. Given their increasing prevalence across a wide range of domains, it's critical to comprehend the importance of Bayesian inference algorithms in AICA-enabled operations, that are critically dependent on high-performance Machine Learning.

Uncertainty is a different animal, though, as it cannot be precisely quantified. The theory of uncertainty was not formalized until the twentieth century by Knight (1921). The central characteristic of Knightian uncertainty is: *The higher the uncertainty, the more possible outcomes, both positive and negative.*

One thing that characterizes very successful entrepreneurs and innovators is the ability to identify the difference between uncertainty and risk, and exploit it for success. They see value in uncertainty because they earn profits when the profits are significantly greater than what is generally expected. Information and influence operations, futures studies and forecasting are examples of exploiting and/or counteracting uncertainty. This kind of information asymmetry is also a vital component in military operations, intelligence acquisition, and stock markets worldwide.

If higher uncertainty can provide strategic benefits, how will Human-AICA Command benefit from it? By exploring the uncertainty in domains that can have great potential while limiting possible losses. The essential point is that risk must be managed while uncertainty can be successfully explored, tested, validated and exploited. Another important thing is that this ability can be acquired through training and experience.

Cyber defense and the agents that depend on cyber security can be considered as components of a very complex sociotechnical system. The socio-technical perspective spans studies of end-user security and integrity (where improving human interaction with software and hardware tools will improve security and reduce the likelihood of successful attacks), to the activities of business actors and government entities responsible for overall national cyber defense.

Closing the cognitive human-machine knowledge and performance gap – embedding new behaviors, learning, and shared understanding as part of culture and normal activities – is a huge task, but it is ultimately the best defense against cyber attacks.

On Exaptation vs. Adaptation
Cognitive systems and agents employ different approaches to problems and the way in which they subjectively converge to a set of "useful" hypotheses forming the current internal system model. Through this iterative procedure, adaptation to environmental characteristics takes place as the agents or cognitive systems learn which hypotheses are most appropriate.

The conventional wisdom is heuristic search for an adaptive solution, searching for good combinations in a vast space of alternatives. An alternative approach is recursive, recombinant and multistage – or, in short, *exaptive* – driven by effectual behaviors that create a permissive local context that increases the likelihood for exaptation to occur (Weitzman, 1998). Exaptation has a direct bearing on the radical repurposing of artifacts, technologies, processes, skills, organizations, and resources for emergent uses that they were not (initially) designed for. The potential for exaptation in AICA missions arises from the combination of heuristics, diversity and connectivity as influencing factors on the frequency and quality of exaptation.

Another aspect of exaptation is what really happens after an exaptive possibility arises (Dew et al., 2004; Dew & Sarasvathy, 2016), connecting technologies to market niches by building those niches. This is a variant of organizational agility – how organizational entities shape their environments and create favorable circumstances for continued operations. This story of niche construction is theoretically less well developed however, particularly with regard to its behavioral aspects. These new advances offer exaptation opportunities for radical repurposing of theories and artifacts to new fields. Exaptation innovations can have considerable real-world impact. Innovation with an origin in exaptation would include autonomous intelligent agents and robotics in military missions and health care applications, nuclear energy operations, critical infrastructure and transportation technologies from the ocean floor to outer space.

The role of decision-making logic (effectual versus causal) and evolutionary morphology (exaptation versus adaptation) are critical drivers of disruptive innovation since they influence organizational mindsets, operations and strategies. It would be worthwhile to study the logics and impact of these business models and evolutionary forces on disruptive innovation. It is suspected here that disruptive opportunity may be better created by 'controlling' uncertain future through effectuation strategies (where Knightian uncertainty is assumed) than 'predicting' the uncertainty via causation strategies (where quantifiable risk is assumed).

The competing forces between adaptation (i.e. Darwinian natural selection) and exaptation.

(i.e. radical repurposing or unintended selection) create instabilities and disequilibria that result in Knightian uncertainty in the trajectory of the AICA mission. It is suggested here that the clash between the two main morphologies of evolutionary processes is an important causal mechanism that leads to disruptive innovation. The processes can also be described as the leveraging of existing knowledge to new applications, or "cross domain application", with significant innovations as the result (Banerjee, 2008).

A New Agility Mindset – And New Policy to Support it

This change of mindset must be instilled at all levels: the individual agent, the collective and the organisation/nation, utilizing this new mindset as an enabler of agile and adaptive behavior in AICA-intensive operations, and characterized by:

- Cognizance – Evidence-based, developed from both research, development and innovation with sufficient breadth and depth that coalesces into knowledge;
- Competencies – Based on quality, productivity and innovation;
- Context – Operational experience, domain understanding and an effects-focused value perspective;
- Creativity – Challenging established thought patterns and solves complex problems through adaptation, exaptation and learning.

Building AICA-enabled capabilities requires a mental shift – striving towards an Agility mindset that permeates security and defence policy, legal and financial frameworks, science and technology agendas, strategy and operations. Visner (this volume) concludes that it will be necessary for policy makers and national security strategists to understand and be prepared for pursuing certain activities that will not be under their direct control, with consequences that may prove to be difficult to manage. Otherwise, this urgently required implementation of new methods, procedures, technologies or organisational structures will not be sustainable.

8.2 Studies on Command, Systems Safety, Agents, Network Theory and Learning: A Foundation for AICA-Enabled Capabilities

Mission Command in Cyber Operations
Josefsson et al. (2019) explored the conditions for mission command in conducting cyber operations in two real-world cases: Stuxnet and NotPetya. They conclude that the distinction between war and peace has blurred and adversaries, both state and non-state, threatening the stability in many western countries. Mission command can be seen both as a philosophy and a method. The fundamental principles for mission command as a philosophy are trust, intent focus, initiative and common ground.

Dangerous Digitalization
Norlander (2019b) investigated four authentic cases ranging from vehicle accidents and natural disasters, to digitalized intensive care and antagonistic influence operations, all exacerbated or in some cases even directly enabled through dysfunction or failure of cyber-reliant safety, security and defence capabilities. Each case was analyzed with regards to agility characteristics and rated to what degree they were fulfilled, and how human, technological and organizational agility influenced operational performance and consequences of systemic failure.

The AICA Reference Architecture
Kott and Theron (2020) formulate a vision of future opportunities of cyber defense tools, citing recent progress made by a NATO research task group IST-152, which developed an AICA reference architecture Kott et al. (2019) as a foundation for the way forward. This reference architecture is founded on the growing recognition of, and extensive use of, partially autonomous agents that actively patrol the friendly network, detecting and reacting to hostile activities far more rapidly than the reaction time of a human operator. The suggested architecture framework for future cyber defense should be able to detect, decide and act before the hostile malware is able to inflict any major damage, evading or destroying friendly agents. This requires cyber-defense agents with a significant degree of intelligence, autonomy, self-learning, and adaptability. The report focuses on the following questions:

- In what computing and tactical environments would such an agent operate?
- What data would be available for the agent to observe or ingest?
- What actions would the agent be able to take?
- How would such an agent plan a complex course of actions?
- Would the agent learn from its experiences, and how?
- How would the agent collaborate with humans?
- How can we ensure that the agent will not take undesirable destructive actions?

The cyber OE is a relatively new domain, with its unique characteristics. AICA-intensive operations that must counter the effects of cyber adversaries are forced to generate successful operational outcomes in milliseconds. Operating in the cyber OE amplifies the importance of joint operations, multiple perspectives, and collaboration. Hybrid warfare, and the grey zone between peace and conventional war, has gained the western world's attention for more than a decade (Pogoson, 2018; Wirtz, 2017).

The Power of Networks
The interconnectivity paradigm is ubiquitous, proven and resilient, in many domains apart from the cyber OE. According to Barabási (2009), the unarguable scale-free nature of networks of key scientific interest, from human-guided social networks, to evolution-originated protein interactions and interlinked documents that make up the WWW to the interconnected hardware behind the Internet, has been firmly established. Many robust, real-life networks, from the cell to the Internet, independent of their origin, function, and scope, converge to similar, universal architectures. This has allowed researchers from different disciplines to embrace network theory as a common frame of reference. The evidence comes not only from better maps and data sets but also from the agreement between empirical data and analytical models that predict the network structure (Caldarelli, 2007; Dorogovtsev & Mendes, 2003).

> Today the understanding of networks is a common goal of an unprecedented array of traditional disciplines: Cell biologists use networks to make sense of signal transduction cascades and metabolism, to name a few applications in this area; computer scientists are mapping the Internet and the WWW; epidemiologists follow transmission networks through which viruses spread; and brain researchers are after the connectome, a neural-level connectivity map of the brain. Although many fads have come and gone in complexity, one thing is increasingly clear: Interconnectivity is so fundamental to the behavior of complex systems that networks are here to stay.
>
> – Albert-László Barabási

The Character and Composition of Human-AICA Command Capabilities
Human-AICA Command is contingent on policy, setting the framework for these contingencies and, not the least, for strategic, operational and tactical decision-making. In fact, decisions are only made within the realm of what is seen, understood and accepted, and Norlander (2019b) asserts that *decisions are made* at policy level, as this is where the conditions and circumstances are determined, whereas *decisions are taken* within the organization, with adherence to the framework set by the policy level.

Table 15.1 Characteristics of human-AICA command capabilities

Multiple Perspectives, Flexibly Managed Capabilities	Multifunctional, multi-organizational and multi-domain interaction towards a common objective
	Working with intermittent teams and temporary coalition partners in joint, interagency, multinational and multi-dimensional operations
	An ability to undertake missions and tasks in all operational environments, applying flexible methods and procedures for planning and execution
	Understanding of the situation's driving forces, and of the role of self and others in the overall campaign, its objectives, stakeholders and resources
Trusted, Distributed, Cognitive Capabilities	Trusted capabilities, where human and AICA entities and teams are vital components of an "Edge Organization" where decision rights and autonomy are granted to local operators to effectively cope with uncertainty, situational complexity and dynamics
	Distributed capabilities, with a high degree of "Edge Computing", i.e. local intelligence processing capability to provide data mining, data reduction, and reasoning from massive amounts of data
	Cognitive capabilities, characterized by "Edge Cognition", constituted by network-enabled information exchange, shared situational awareness, mission understanding and self-synchronization, when in a collective or coalition environment, to generate the intended effects
Adaptive, Exaptive and Learning Capabilities	Adaptation includes the ability to perceive, understand and deal with change requirements under time-, risk- and resource-critical conditions. This enables the force to develop during ongoing operations through its mission agility against variations in environment, mission, organisation and resource availability
	Exaptation includes radical re-purposing under conditions of stress. driving an evolving, emergent system that is characterized by qualitative, structural change. It anchors success in the future on the tolerance and understanding of serendipitous perspectives, views, and ideas, since it is through the future implementation of some of these that survival will be achieved
	Learning includes analysis of performance and conclusions of experiences from ongoing and completed campaigns are translated into action. Unexpected irregular threats and events are tackled through critical thinking, comprehensive analysis, rapid testing and experiments to improve efficiency and shorten the time from discovery to implementation

Operations in the grey zone are persistent and unending, and trusted cognitive capabilities are essential for managing such elusive and adaptive threats in the information age. In multifunctional and multi-organizational operations, we must be able to adapt, learn and re-purpose on the fly to be able to undertake missions in all environments, including the cyberspace domain (Norlander, 2019b). Table 15.1 illustrates the characteristics of Human-AICA Command capabilities, based on a modified analytical model originally developed by Norlander (2019a).

9 Defining Command in AICA-Intensive Operations

To be able to define command in AICA-intensive operations, we must first decouple Command from Control, as was suggested by Pigeau and McCann (2002) and later by Teske et al. (2018). The fundamental distinction between Command and Control rests on two critically important and uniquely human characteristics: creativity and will. The central proposition in this chapter is based on the premise that only humans command, but that both artificial and human agents continuously control and execute mission and tasks. Pigeau and McCann suggested the following definition of Command:

The creative expression of human will necessary to accomplish the mission

Practical experience and historical examples suggests that creativity and anticipation is one of the most important requirements for Command. Control in the cybernetic sense involves perception, processing, action, and a feedback mechanism by which the real outcome is compared with the formulated goal, a mechanism that minimizes the difference. However, Control in military operations comprises more than such mechanisms. It implies the collaboration and interaction between personnel, facilities and procedures for planning, directing and coordinating resources in the accomplishment of the mission. In the context of AICA-intensive operations we find the definition of Control suggested by Pigeau and McCann to be well suited for supporting the development of AICA-specific command:

The act of enabling command and of managing risk using existing structures and processes

Because we assume that Command is performed by humans but supported by both human and artificial agents, we choose to define four fundamental components of Command capabilities in AICA-intensive operations separate from Control with its inherent dependencies on organizational structures, processes, technology, etc. The fundamental components of a Command capability for AICA-intensive operations are founded on original work by Pigeau and McCann (2000, 2001), further developed by Norlander (2011) and adapted for AICA-intensive operations by this author, comprising: Competency, Authority, Responsibility and Situation Awareness, illustrated in Fig. 15.3.

Competency
Commanders at all echelons need skills and abilities for accomplishing missions.

- *Physical competency* includes physical strength to fulfill the mission but also sophisticated sensory motor skills, good health agility and endurance.
- *Intellectual competency* includes using reasoning, critical thinking, creativity, flexibility, ability to constructive thinking and willingness to learn.
- *Emotional competency* includes resilience, hardiness and the ability to cope under stress. The ability to keep an overall emotional balance and perspective on the situation is critical.

Fig. 15.3 The four fundamental components of Command in AICA-Intensive Operations: Generating Effects through executing Missions in the Operational Environment (OE)

- *Interrelational competency* is essential for interacting effectively with subordinates, peers, superiors, the media and other government organizations. It includes social skill with attributes of trust, respect, perceptiveness and empathy.

Authority

Authority is the degree to which a commander is empowered to act. There is a distinction between

- *Legal authority,* which is *assigned* from superior command and the degree of formal power given to an individual agent by the commanding organization, specifically, the formal power over resources and other agents.
- *Individual authority,* which is *earned,* for example, through reference or reputation, performance, integrity, experience, strength of character and example, by virtue of individual credibility; it is the degree of informal power given to an individual agents by other agents, including subordinates, peers and superiors.

Responsibility

Responsibility addresses the degree to which an individual agent accepts the legal and moral liability commensurate with command. As with authority, there are two components to responsibility, one externally imposed and the other internally generated:

- *Extrinsic responsibility,* involving the obligation for public accountability. Extrinsic responsibility is the degree to which an individual feels accountable both up to superiors and down to subordinates.
- *Intrinsic responsibility,* which is the degree of self-generated obligation that one feels towards the current mission. It is a function of the resolve and motivation that an individual brings to a problem — the amount of ownership taken and the amount of commitment expressed.

Situation Awareness

To be able to project events, decide on course of action and exploit in situations, within an operational environment, commanders need Situation Awareness (SA). SA is basically about knowing what is going on around you (Endsley, 1995), indicating that the commander has to be able to observe, assess, interpret and engage in operational objectives. Noel and Swarup (This volume) further explore Situation Understanding (SU) in AICA-specific environments and missions. We mean that SA or SU also means that the commander must understand the effects and consequences of actions that are to be decided, through "action oriented understanding" as Brehmer (2006) defined it.

The principal concepts of the combined Pigeau-McCann-Norlander Command framework, including the concepts of explicit and implicit intent, the command dimensions, control support for command and the dependence on adequate SA have been assessed and applied in comprehensive cyber operations analysis (Josefsson et al., 2019). The framework has been proven to have excellent effectiveness for assessing command challenges, providing insights into contemporary and prospect command themes, and generating understanding of the command aspects of complex multi-domain operations, like cyber defense. Also, the framework is considered to have wide-ranging validity for wide application to real world cyber defense situations, and thus would be useful to operators, policy makers, requirement analysts, training coordinators, boards of inquiry and strategic planners.

Communicating Intent Over Time, Space and Situational Dynamics

The significance of successful communication and understanding of the intent and standards of a mission, from the commander/manager to all subordinates/agents, is generally acknowledged in professional communities. Remote commanders have no other means to control a process except through the actions of local agents. Plans and procedures are too brittle to effectively guide the situation understanding and decision-making of these agents.

An on-site commander with high-level, systemic knowledge and a clear understanding of operational objectives would effectively adapt plans and procedures based on local conditions. Remote commanders, however, must remain in a position where they can retain a comprehensive system understanding and avoid exposure due to operational safety and security reasons (Shattuck & Woods, 2000). Since they cannot be physically present and execute with the same dynamics as local agents, they need to impart their presence to optimally influence the adaptation, exaptation and learning capabilities of all local agents.

When remote commanders impart their presence, they are equipping local agents with the strategic-level objectives, constraints, and tradeoffs of the system. Imparted presence empowers a local agent to make decisions similar to those that the commander would make if the commander had been temporally and physically present. This interconnectivity also induces interdependence, a prerequisite for accurate collective prediction of course of events, intra- and inter-unit co-ordination of actions and mission resource management. It is difficult to practice what is preached, however.

Chatterjee, et al. (this volume) present an overarching communication, multi-level architecture comprising AICA agents, central cyber Command & Control, and human operators. They propose two main architectural components for an AICA agent:

1. A sense-making module, containing a state estimator and an action evaluator, and
2. A decision-making module, containing a policy optimizer and a safety verifier.

The architecture approach proposed by Chatterjee et al. is an instructive example of how to develop communication architectures for AICA collaboration and negotiation. Their Multi-Agent coordination and cooperation algorithms, and the related control architecture categories: decentralized, centralized, and hybrid, are of particular interest for studying, developing and implementing recursive Joint Cognitive Systems, containing both human and artificial intelligent agents, collaborating intensively but with a high level of autonomy. This is further elaborated upon from a AICA Command capability perspective below.

A Recursive Perspective of Command Dynamics in AICA-Intensive Operations

Rapidly unfolding events, actions by other (friendly or hostile) agents, and VUCA situational dynamics in the OE can jeopardize Human-AICA operations through loss of control. According to Worm (2000), situational dynamics are determined by large and transitory variations in the unit's capability to accomplish its mission regarding:

1. Gathering, processing, utilization and distribution of available and relevant information indicative of the mission, the actions taken and the operational environment, i.e. *observation, communication and interaction.*
2. Rapid and accurate generation and sustainment of a coherent and cohesive situation understanding at the individual agent and team levels resulting in an accurate and shared mission model, i.e. *situation assessment, state determination and system representation.*
3. How agents, control functions and commanders manage, anticipate and control the course of events during the mission, and construct and select alternative actions when the situation changes in an unanticipated way, i.e. *adaptation, prediction and co-ordination.*
4. Utilisation, deployment, protection and sustainability of available human, technological, organisational and logistical resources, and determination of outcome and effect of the mission related to the resources put into action, i.e. *mission resource management and mission efficiency.*

The previously referred case studies by Josefsson et al. (2019) and Norlander (2019b), and the cases described in this volume represent different aspects of emergent crisis dynamics in the command function, i.e. the commander and support functions temporarily losing their ability to think ahead and anticipate the forthcoming course of events, *disabling command and succumbing to risk due to existing structures and processes,* to paraphrase Pigeau and McCann.

According to Beer (1981), already the expectation of losing control counts as a crisis, requiring commander guidance and intervention. Beer (1981) defined a comprehensive recursive model called the Viable Systems Model (VSM) based on cybernetic principles and organization theory. VSM represents a system of systems perspective in different levels of Command and has a Control component on each level.

In this context we need to use a model that describes Command, Operational Environment, Missions and Emergent Effects at different echelons. We base our work on an execution and control model developed by Worm (2000, 2001) and Norlander (2011, 2014), which we further developed into a recursive multilevel Mission Execution and Command Model (MECOM), adapted to represent Command and generation of Emergent Effects through executing Missions in the Operational Environment in AICA-Intensive Operations. The model is depicted in Fig. 15.4. The recursive structure illustrates the fact that Command capabilities are used in a hierarchy with several echelons of Command.

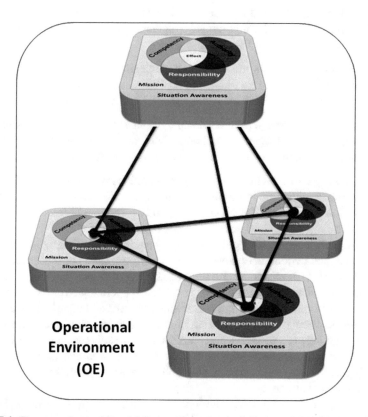

Fig. 15.4 The recursive multilevel Mission Execution and Command Model (MECOM) of Command in AICA-Intensive Operations, generating emergent effects in the operational environment. (Adapted from Norlander, 2014)

10 Recommendations: Developing an Essence of Command for AICA-Intensive Operations

A conflict situation within or with operational reach into the cyber domain can rapidly escalate or change character in fractions of a second, and this requires adequate response times. This is beyond the ability of humans, hence requiring the use of high-performance, automated cognitive cyber capabilities such as AICAs. Furthermore, without the appropriate distribution of information, and the necessary decision rights to the AICAs that match their required level of autonomy, the decisions and actions needed for success in AICA-intensive operations will not be achieved in a timely manner. Reduction of response times enables losses of cyber capability to be minimized, or restored more quickly if degraded. This would indicate that command approaches that can respond more rapidly to changes in circumstances (e.g., a loss of cyber capability or an unforeseen cross-domain system shock) would be more appropriate for operating in a contested operational environment.

In addition to the ability to act in a timely manner to exploit or manage rapidly changing circumstances, the requirement to interact and collaborate in Joint Systems Operations call for command approaches that:

1. Utilize multiple paths for information dissemination,
2. Adapt its interactions to changing circumstances, and
3. Dynamically delegate decision rights between AICA and human agents.

We propose formulating a future-oriented essence of Multi-Domain Cognitive Command, with equal relevance and applicability on human operators and AICAs. The following is a first attempt, with six overarching conceptual mainstays:

1. Command in future security and defense operations will be complex, laborious and in many cases mission-critical, requiring unprecedented vigilance, awareness and determination. Decision-makers and operators will frequently encounter uncertainty, risks, time-criticalities and resource shortages.
2. Operational characteristics will be highly dynamic and non-linear; Minor events, decisions and actions may have serious and irreversible consequences for the entire mission. Success in future security and defense operations requires extraordinary capabilities to operate in contested operating environments, and to master the Command challenges of complex systems and interdependencies.
3. Mission success is strongly linked to effective interaction and collaboration within and between different organizational cultures, between people with different backgrounds, education and experience, non-human autonomous and intelligent systems, and on managing and maintaining operational availability, versatility and efficiency.
4. Operating in a contested mission environment requires Comprehensive Operational Awareness, with the abilities to accurately and rapidly perceive and interpret relevant events and circumstances in order to provide the context,

insight and foresight required for effective decision-making, enabling every commander and operator to develop a wide-ranging appreciation of the situation.

5. Joint Systems Operations are of particular concern; while some operational tasks necessarily would employ human agents, other tasks can only be accomplished through non-human intelligent entities, acting autonomously within the socio-technical enterprise. This requires adaptive and versatile principles and concepts for Joint Systems Operations along with high-performance human, technological and organizational architectures – cognitive mission architectures.

6. The turbulent environment in which Joint Systems Operations play out stresses the need further for Organizational Agility, to be adaptable and resilient without having to change. The goal is to keep internal operations at a level of fluidity and flexibility that matches the degree of turmoil in external environments, a principle known as requisite variety.

The number, characteristics and diversity of AICA and human agents, the operational domains and sub-domains in which these entities operate, the interdependencies between and among operations in these domains, and the emergent effects they create, constitute efficient performance-influencing factors on an operational unit's tolerance of capability degradation before any significant loss of mission capability is manifested. However, maintaining performance through actively measuring, interpreting and regulating these factors pose significant challenges not yet fully anticipated nor appreciated – a major Scientific, Technological and Operational challenge.

Based upon an analysis of the empirical evidence from case studies, and theoretical concepts from Human Factors, systems safety, risk management, autonomy and Machine Learning, and supported by organizational agility theory, we conclude that developing and implementing agile AICA Capabilities, with its inherent competencies, methods, technologies, procedures and structures, depends heavily on adaptation, exaptation, learning and collaboration (*Cognition-Centric*), traits that are at the core of AICA-intensive Operations.

Management commitment is required, all the way through policy and doctrine to Tactics, Techniques and Procedures. Organizations need to be able to employ a Multi-Domain Operational approach, understanding when different approaches are appropriate (*Context-Centric*), coupled with decision rights enabling timely and efficient transition between approaches (*Decision-Centric*).

Organizational Culture is the personality of the organization, and needs to be based on flexibility, deliberate risk-taking, openness to change and tolerance for error (i.e. a learning culture). We are advocating agility and adaptability as guiding principles since an adaptive organization requires a philosophy of leadership comprising curiosity, learning, boldness and dynamism, where initiative is rewarded and the bar is set high towards excellence.

11 Summary and Conclusions

This chapter examines command capability in general and command in AICA-intensive operations in particular, and emphasizes three principal characteristics of Cognitive Command, with equal relevance and applicability for human operators and artificial agents: A) Make Uncertainty and Awareness your Allies, B) Stagnation Equals Defeat, and C) Cognitive Command is Multi-Domain Joint Systems Command. A crucial factor in achievement of mission objectives in AICA-intensive operations is that all actors and partners can be consolidated into an architecture that is:

1. Generic – represents all relevant capabilities, artificial and human alike,
2. Scalable – across all capability categories (or business areas) and organizational levels,
3. Shared – accepted and used by all agents, commanders and stakeholders.

Operating in a contested mission environment requires comprehensive situational awareness, with the ability to accurately and rapidly perceive and interpret mission-relevant events and circumstances, in order to provide the context, insight and foresight required for effective decision-making and action. Complex multi-domain operations are of particular concern; while some operational tasks necessarily would employ a human component, other tasks can only be accomplished through non-human intelligent entities, acting autonomously within the socio-technical enterprise.

The Joint Cognitive Systems (JCS) body of research was utilized to overcome the duality of traditional human-machine research, focusing on better understanding what people actually do with technology rather than what functions belong to the machine and what functions belong to the human. The Complex Adaptive Systems (CAS) body of research contributed with characteristics of self-learning, emergence, and evolution among the entities of the complex system, demonstrating heterogeneous and adaptive behavior. According to the body of research for Autonomous Adaptive Agents (AAAs), an agent is also viewed as a team member, meaning it is able to autonomously complement human decision-making when executing its tasks.

Building AICA-enabled capabilities requires a mental shift – striving towards an Agility mindset that permeates security and defence policy, legal and financial frameworks, science and technology agendas, strategy and operations. Employing the JCS, CAS and AAA paradigms for AICA-intensive operations permits the integration of all capability elements into an adaptive distributed system that can achieve a mission safely and efficiently. Based on these studies and with the support from other fields of study, we devised a number of strategy elements as part of an essence of command for AICA-intensive operations.

Finally, we brought together the above AICA-relevant body of knowledge into a recursive, multilevel Mission Execution and Command Model (MECOM), adapted to represent Command Competency, Authority, Responsibility and Situational Awareness in AICA-Intensive Operations.

References

Alberts, D. S. (2018). Cyberspace operations: Is a non-traditional C2 approach required? In *Proceedings of 23th International Command and Control Research and Technology Symposium (ICCRTS)*, 6–9 Nov, 2018.

Alberts, D. S., & Hayes, R. E. (2006). *Understanding command and control.* US DoD Assistant Secretary of Defense Command & Control Research Program. ISBN 1-893723-17-8.

Ashby, W. R. (1956). *An introduction to cybernetics.* Chapman & Hall.

Banerjee, P. (2008). Leveraging existing technology: The role of alliances in cross-application. *Strategic Management Review, 2*(1), 1–22.

Barabási, A. L. (2009). Scale-Free Networks: A Decade and beyond science 325(5939) 412–413 10.1126/science.1173299.

Barber, H. F. (1992). Developing strategic leadership: The US army war college experience. *Journal of Management Development, 11*(6), 4–12.

Beer, S. (1981). *Brain of the firm* (2nd ed.). Wiley.

Brehmer, B. (2006). One loop to rule them all. In *Proceedings of the 11th international command and control research and technology symposium (ICCRTS)*.

Caldarelli, G. (2007). *Scale-free networks: Complex webs in nature and technology.* Oxford University Press.

Carvelli, M.P. (2018). *A smarter approach to cyber attack authorities.* Joint Force Quarterly (JFQ). 4th Quarter 2018 (pp. 67–73).

Chatterjee, S., Bhattacharya, A., Dutta, A., Rahman, A., Ramachandran, T., Chikkagoudar, S., & Bharadwaj, R. (This volume). Collaboration and Negotiation.

Conant, R. C., & Ashby, W. R. (1970). Every good regulator of a system must be a model of that system. *International journal of System Science, 1*, 89–97.

Congressional Research Service. (2022). *Joint all-domain command and control: Background and issues for congress.* United States Congress. Report No. R46725.

DARPA. (2020). Defense advanced research projects agency. In *Creating cross-domain kill webs in real time: DARPA decision-aid software, integration tool key to recent advanced battle management system demo,* Press release, September 18, 2020, https://www.darpa.mil/news-events/2020-09-18a.

Dew, N., & Sarasvathy, S. D. (2016). Exaptation and niche construction: Behavioral insights for an evolutionary theory. *Industrial and Corporate Change, 25*(1), 167–179.

Dew, N., Sarasvathy, S. D., & Venkataraman, S. (2004). The economic implications of exaptation. *Journal of Evolutionary Economics, 14*, 69–84.

Dorogovtsev, S. N., & Mendes, J. F. (2003). *Evolution of networks: From biological nets to the internet and WWW.* Oxford university press.

Dyer, L., & Shafer, R.A. (1998). *From human resource strategy to organizational effectiveness: Lessons from research on organizational agility.* CAHRS Working Paper. Ithaca.

Endsley, M. R. (1995). Towards a theory for situation awareness in dynamic systems. *Human Factors, 37*, 32–64.

Endsley, M. R. (2015). *Autonomous horizons: System autonomy in the air force: A path to the future.* US Air Force Office of the Chief Scientist.

Holland, J. H. (1995). *Hidden order: How adaptation builds complexity.* Basic Books.

Holland, J. H. (2006). Studying complex adaptive systems. *Journal of Systems Science and Complexity, 19*(1), 1–8.

Hollnagel, E. (1999). Modelling the controller of a process. *Transactions of the Institute of Measurement and Control, 21*(4/5), 163–170.

Hollnagel, E., & Woods, D. D. (1983). Cognitive systems engineering: New wine in new bottles. *International Journal of Man-Machine Studies, 18*, 583–600.

Hollnagel, E., & Woods, D. D. (2006). *Joint cognitive systems: Patterns in cognitive systems engineering.* CRC Press.

Josefsson, A., Anderson, J., Norlander, A., & Marcusson, Björn. (2019). Mission command when waging cyber operations. In *Proceedings of the 24th international command and control research and technology symposium (ICCRTS)*. (pp. 29–31) October 2019, Laurel.

Knight, F. H. (1921). *Risk, uncertainty and profit*. Houghton Mifflin.

Kott, A., & Alberts, D. S. (2017). How do you command an army of intelligent things? *Computer, 50*(12), 96–100.

Kott, A., & Theron, P. (2020). Doers, not watchers: Intelligent autonomous agents are a path to cyber resilience. *IEEE Security & Privacy, 18*(3), 62–66.

Kott, A., et al. (2019). *Autonomous intelligent cyber-defense agent (AICA) reference architecture*, Release 2.0," CCDC Army Research Laboratory. Adelphi, MD 20783–1138. ARL-SR0421.

Ligo, A. K., Kott, A., & Linkov, I. (2021). Autonomous cyberdefense introduces risk: Can we manage the risk? *Computer, 54*(10), 106–110.

Ligo, A. K., Kott, A., Dozier, H., Igor Linkov, I. (This volume). Risk management of AICA.

Lind, W. S. (1985). *Maneuver warfare handbook*. Westview Press.

Malone, T. W. (2018). *Superminds: How hyperconnectivity is changing the way we solve problems*. Simon and Schuster.

McChrystal, S., Collins, T., Silverman, D., & Fussell, C. (2015). *Team of teams: New rules of engagement for a complex world*. Penguin Random House.

National Academies of Sciences, Engineering, and Medicine. (2022). *Human-AI teaming: State-of-the-art and research needs*. The National Academies Press. https://doi.org/10.17226/26355

Neisser, U. (1976). *Cognition and reality*. W. H. Freeman and Company.

Nobel Foundation. (2001). *The Sveriges Riksbank prize in economic sciences in memory of Alfred Nobel 2001*. https://www.nobelprize.org/uploads/2018/06/advanced-economicsciences2001. pdf. Accessed 17 May 2022.

Noel, S., & Swarup, V. (This volume) Situational understanding and diagnosis.

Norlander, A. (2010). Analysis of tactical missions: Integrating systems theory, cognitive systems engineering and psychophysiology. In *Proceedings of the human factors and ergonomics society 54th annual meeting*. The Human Factors Society.

Norlander, A. (2011). Cognitive systems modeling and analysis of command & control systems. In *Proceedings of the MODSIM world 2011 conference and expo*. National Aeronautics and Space Administration. NASA/CP-2012-217326.

Norlander, A. (2014). Analyzing tactical cognitive systems: Theories, models and methods. In P. Berggren, S. Nählinder, & E. Svensson (Eds.), *Assessing command and control effectiveness – Dealing with a changing world*. Ashgate. ISBN: 978-1-4724-3696-2.

Norlander, A. (2019a). Strategies for developing agile crisis management capabilities. In *Proceedings of the 30th international training and education conference*. Stockholm.

Norlander, A. (2019b). Societal security: How digitalization enables resilient, agile and learning capabilities. In R. Teigland & A. Larsson (Eds.), *The digital disruption of public services: An investigative study of the societal impact in Sweden and beyond*. Center for Strategy and Competitiveness (CSC), Stockholm School of Economics (SSE).

Parasuraman, R., Sheridan, T. B., & Wickens, C. D. (2000). A model for types and levels of human interaction with automation. *IEEE Transactions on systems, man, and cybernetics-Part A: Systems and Humans, 30*(3), 286–297.

Parasuraman, R., De Visser, E., Wiese, E., & Madhavan, P. (2014). Human trust in other humans, automation, robots, and cognitive agents: Neural correlates and design implications. In *Proceedings of the Human Factors and Ergonomics Society* (pp. 340–344) 2014–January. https://doi.org/10.1177/1541931214581070.

Pigeau, R., & McCann, C. (2000). Redefining command and control. In C. McCann & R. Pigeau (Eds.), *The human in command* (pp. 163–184). Kluwer Academic/Plenum Publishers.

Pigeau, R., & McCann, C. (2001). What is a military commander? In P. Essens, A. Vogelaar, E. Tanercan, & D. Winslow (Eds.), *The human in command: Peace support operations* (pp. 394–413). Mets & Schilt.

Pigeau, R., & McCann, C. (2002). Re-conceptualizing command and control. *Canadian Military Journal, 3*(1), 53–64.

Pogoson, A. I. (2018). Issues, trends and challenges in an emerging global power structure. *Canadian Social Science, 14*(2), 5–15.

Rasmussen, J. (1983). Skills, rules, and knowledge: Signals, signs, and symbols, and other distinctions in human performance models. *IEEE Transactions on Systems, Man, and Cybernetics, SMC-13*, 257–266.

Rasmussen, J. (1986). *Information processing and human-machine interaction: An approach to cognitive engineering*. North-Holland.

Rasmussen, J. (1997). Risk management in a dynamic society: A modelling problem. *Safety Science, 27*(2–3), 183–213.

Rasmussen, J., Brehmer, B., & Leplat, L. (Eds.). (1991). *Distributed decision making: Cognitive models for cooperative work*. Wiley.

Rasmussen, J., Pejtersen, A. M., & Goodstein, L. (1994). *Cognitive systems engineering*. Wiley.

Reason, J. (1997). *Managing the risks of organizational accidents*. Ashgate.

Rosenbaum, R. (2012). *Richard Clarke on who was behind the Stuxnet attack*. Smithsonian Magazine. Received from: https://www.smithsonianmag.com/history/richard-clarke-on-who-was-behind-the-stuxnet-attack-160630516/

Senge, P. M. (1990). *The fifth discipline – The art and practice of the learning organisation*. Currency and Doubleday.

Shattuck, L. G., & Woods, D. D. (2000). Communication of intent in military command and control systems. In C. McCann & R. Pigeau (Eds.), *The human in command: Exploring the modern military experience* (pp. 279–292). Kluwer Academic/Plenum Publishers.

Sheridan, T. B., & Verplank, W. L. (1978). *Human and computer control of undersea teleoperators*. Massachusetts Institute of Technology. Cambridge Man-Machine Systems Lab.

Smith, P. J., & Hoffman, R. R. (Eds.). (2017). *Cognitive systems engineering: The future for a changing world*. CRC Press.

Teske, K., Miller, M.. Guerin, P., & Lauver, J. (2018). Decoupling command from control – making the term C2 Stronger. In *Proceedings of 23th international command and control research and technology symposium (ICCRTS)*, 6–9 Nov, 2018.

Tessensohn, T. L., van der Vecht, B., & Eikelboom, A. R. (2018). How to cooperate with intelligent machines: Lessons for defence operations from the integration of AI and robotics across multiple domains. In *Proceedings of The 23rd international command and control research and technology symposium (ICCRTS)*.

van Creveld, M. (1985). *Command in war*. Harvard University Press.

Visner, S. S. (This volume). Policy issues related to autonomous intelligent cyber-defense agents.

Weick, K. E., & Sutcliffe, K. M. (2015). *Managing the unexpected: Sustained performance in a complex world*. Wiley.

Weick, K. E., Sutcliffe, K. M., & Obstfeld, D. (2005). Organizing and the process of sensemaking. *Organization Science, 16*(4), 409–421.

Weitzman, M. L. (1998). Recombinant growth. *Quarterly Journal of Economics, 113*(2), 331–360.

Wiener, N. (1961). *Cybernetics or control and communication in the animal and the machine*. The M.I.T. Press.

Wirtz, J. J. (2017). Life in the "Gray zone": Observations for contemporary strategists. *Defense & Security Analysis, 33*(2), 106–114.

Worm, A. (2000). *On control and Interaction in Complex Distributed Systems and Environments*. Linköping Studies in Science and Technology, Dissertation No. 664, Linköping University, Linköping, Sweden. ISBN 91–7219–899-0.

Worm, A. (2001). On systems analysis and performance assessment in complex, high-risk work environments. *International Journal of Risk Assessment and management, 2*(3/4), 276–287. Inderscience, United Kingdom.

Ziemke, T., Schaefer, K. E., & Endsley, M. (2017). Situation awareness in human-machine interactive systems. *Cognitive Systems Research, 46*, 1–2.

Chapter 16
Risk Management

Alexandre K. Ligo, Alexander Kott, Haley Dozier, and Igor Linkov

1 Introduction

Risk management is an important topic in research and practice of cybersecurity (Hubbard & Seiersen, 2016; Oltramari & Kott, 2018). One situation of interest involves the assessment of risks that a certain system or mission is exposed to, followed by an analysis of possible strategies to mitigate those risks. For a given mitigation strategy, one can evaluate how much of the risks assessed initially are eliminated or reduced. However, we must not forget to account for new risks that might be introduced by mitigation strategy itself.

A. K. Ligo (✉)
Environmental Laboratory, US Army Corps of Engineers, Engineer Research and Development Center, Concord, MA, USA

Engineering Systems & Environment, University of Virginia, Concord, MA, USA

US Army, University of Virginia, Concord, MA, USA

A. Kott
Environmental Laboratory, US Army Corps of Engineers, Engineer Research and Development Center, Concord, MA, USA

Engineering Systems & Environment, University of Virginia, Concord, MA, USA
e-mail: alexander.kott1.civ@army.mil

H. Dozier
Information Technology Laboratory, The U.S. Army Engineer Research and Development Center, Vicksburg, MS, USA
e-mail: Haley.R.Dozier@erdc.dren.mil

I. Linkov
Environmental Laboratory, US Army Corps of Engineers, Engineer Research and Development Center, Concord, MA, USA
e-mail: Igor.Linkov@usace.army.mil

© The Author(s), under exclusive license to Springer Nature Switzerland AG 2023   341
A. Kott (ed.), *Autonomous Intelligent Cyber Defense Agent (AICA)*, Advances in Information Security 87, https://doi.org/10.1007/978-3-031-29269-9_16

This chapter is a discussion of risks that might emerge when AICA are adopted as part of a defense strategy. These risks can be associated with AICA inherent complexity. The concept and reference architecture of AICA was developed by NATO for military missions. Earlier in this book, Norlander notes that the military and other critical domains require extraordinary awareness and management of risk. This is because in these domains a successful cyberattack can result in death, injuries, or catastrophic material damage – a well-known example is the impact that the Stuxnet malware caused on Iran's nuclear program and its probable weapon capability (Kott & Linkov, 2019). In contrast, Norlander argues that in commercial operations objectives such as operational reliability, availability, and high technical performance at the lowest possible cost have priority over risk mitigation. Nevertheless, even in such commercial applications the use of AICA-like defenses may become essential. For example, intrusion detection and prevention systems tend to be increasingly autonomous given the rise in sophistication and frequency of cyberattacks, as well as the potential financial loss these attacks cause. Manual or semi-automated defenses will not be able to respond in required time, scale, and accuracy.

The inherent complexities of AICA in military missions and AICA-like systems in commercial applications introduce new kinds of risk. Norlander's chapter argues that AICA fits the definition of a cognitive system as one that can" modify its pattern of behavior on the basis of past experience in order to achieve specific anti-entropic ends". This would introduce specific risks may be related to AICA malfunction or AI bias, unintended effects arising from swarm-like behavior, communications or coordination failures among agents, or even attacks targeting AICA themselves. In this chapter we introduce the types of new risks, their consequences, and possible ways to mitigate them while preserving the AICA mission.

2 Types of Risks Introduced by AICA

Vast amounts of historical data about cyber activity are increasingly available. These data include logs of login attempts, domain resolution or webpage requests, application programming interface (API) calls, network traffic, and other activities. It is expected that AICA make use of these data to enhance AI algorithms by training machine learning (ML) models that detect future attacks (Kott & Theron, 2020). The enhanced AI capability translate into unsupervised actions that bring both opportunities and new risks. Some of these risks include flawed AICA actions due to wrong AI predictions. "Black box" AI models (discussed earlier in this book by Fitzpatrick) make it hard to prevent AI errors (Linkov et al., 2020). Likewise, data that are biased or contaminated with measurement errors may also result in wrong AICA predictions or actions (see Drasar's chapter on perception). Moreover, intentional hacking or destruction of the AICA themselves is also a risk.

Another type of new risks is related to collective AICA action. First, multiple agents may be required to cooperate with each other to achieve the scale or scope required for a given defense. Communications failures due to packet loss, poor signal-to-noise ratio, or network congestion impair coordination and action. Second, communications between AICA may be intentionally corrupted by malicious agents. Finally, a group of AICA might exhibit swarm behavior that differ from the action of individual agents in unpredictable ways.

3 Consequences of Risks Introduced by AICA

Risks arising from AICA may have harmful consequences of functional, safety, security, ethical, or moral nature. Such consequences can be imposed on parties who do not benefit from the AICA actions or do not agree to accept the respective risks (Morgan, 2017). Types of consequences from AICA-specific risks include:

- Functional consequences: AICA might inadvertently impair the system's mission or functionality. One example is AICA needlessly shutting down service to avert an attack.
- Safety consequences: AICA might injury or kill system's operators or communities. For example, AICA take action against a cyberattack on an oil refinery, but the defense might inadvertently disable critical control systems and cause an explosion killing residents nearby (Ligo et al., 2021a).
- Security consequences: AICA might inadvertently create vulnerabilities that enable unauthorized access or data breaches, with consequences similar to the breach of Equifax data in 2017 that followed from vulnerabilities in Apache software (Federal Trade Commission, 2022).
- Ethical, moral or unfair consequences: AICA algorithmic biases might result in defenses that produce questionable results or prioritize certain groups over others. This includes considerations about whether AICA should maximize benefits for immediate stakeholders over social welfare at large. For example, should a self-driving car prioritize the safety of its occupants even if it exposes nearby pedestrians to increased risk?

The awareness of the nature of AICA-related risks or the possible consequences of these risks does not make AICA safer or more effective. Moreover, mitigating these risks is likely a challenging task. Nevertheless, understanding the nature and consequences of new AICA-related risks is a required step towards an evaluation of the net benefit of deploying AICA. In other words, are the risks mitigated by AICA more important than the new ones that are introduced? A different but related question is how these new AICA-related risks can be mitigated, which you increase the net value of AICA.

In the next sections we discuss possible mitigation strategies in deploying AICA that enhance cybersecurity and cyber-resilience while minimizing new risks. In particular, we discuss the human role in the design and control of defenses, as well as design or algorithmic strategies. While this discussion is non-exhaustive, it provides possible directions of research in risk management for AICA.

4   Human-Centric Approaches with Real-Time Cooperation

The natural remedy to mitigate the novel risks of harm caused by AICA is to have them team up with humans. This collaboration is essential not only from a risk perspective but also to ensure effective mission accomplishment, as noted by Norlander previously in this chapter for military operations – where he articulates the concept of Joint Cognitive Systems (JCS) for the interaction between humans and AICA.

However, having AICA depend on real-time human action may not help and in fact may cause other problems for certain cyber-defense scenarios. The vision for AICA includes their ability to respond faster than humans, or at a larger scale. Hence, human intervention may be detrimental to the autonomous defense. For example, intrusion prevention systems (IPS) may be able to autonomously avert data breaches in a fraction of a second. However, this is not the case if the IPS is part of a semi-automated workflow when human operators are required to review alerts or approve blocking of requests and addresses. Moreover, even a well-trained and alert human operator may slow down defenses against large scale attacks that target several points of the system simultaneously.

Another problem is that a human taking over during an attack (after AICA initiated maneuvers) may not have the level of situational awareness required for adequate defense and ruin it (Kott et al., 2014). Consider the related and perhaps familiar context of autonomous driving described in (Ligo et al., 2021a). The Society of Automotive Engineers defines a five-level scale of vehicle automation (Automated Vehicles 3.0 – Preparing for the Future of Transportation, 2018). In all but level 5, a human driver is expected to take control over the machine during an emergency. Consider the scenario of a self-driving car in level 3 or 4, thus having a human driver in stand-by, when a child runs into the street from between parked cars. If the human tries to retake control to swerve and miss the child in its path the vehicle could override the driver. If the vehicle senses the child and begins a collision-avoidance maneuver, then any human operator action may ruin the automated system's plan for avoiding a collision, or the person's reaction time may be dangerously longer than the time taken by the machine. If neither the human nor the vehicle does anything, there will be a dead child and liability for all involved. As long as the probability of error by the vehicle is sufficiently low, the best course of action is that the human driver does **not** interfere with the autonomous operation after the collision-avoidance maneuver starts.

The car example has similarities with autonomous cyber-defenses teaming with humans. For example, both types of systems require quick and accurate decision making. If machine action (either assisted by human or not) is not effective, negative consequences from AICA may follow. However, there is a key difference between driving and AICA action. Autonomous cars are designed to replace a human ability – driving. Therefore, a trained human driver can usually take the wheel and achieve currently acceptable driving performance if enough time is available. On the other hand, autonomous cyber-defenses may need to perform "super-human" defenses with respect to response times, volume of data processed, or scale of response. These attributes of AICA make it impossible for humans to intervene appropriately.

Therefore, humans should avoid interfering with the operation of AICA after they determine and start a course of action. This is especially true in situations when there is not enough time for the human to acquire situation awareness, decide, and respond.

Should we *never* have human-in-the-loop in real time? If humans should not interfere with AICA when a planned course of action is underway, are there any exceptions? There is no single solution that satisfies every situation. If AICA take risky or harmful action but the human alternative is not safer nor less damaging, then there is no value in overriding the AICA. However, in practice evaluating which action is preferred – machine or human – is not straightforward. Perhaps there is no time to evaluate because a cyberattack is already underway, or there is not enough information, or the AICA course of action is not entirely explainable. In these situations, it is not entirely clear when humans should override AICA, it at all.

5   Human-Centric Approaches with Data-Driven Intervention

With unknown risks and challenges of determining human-machine cooperation during cyber-defense operation, it is beneficial to consider some form of "offline" cooperation, or ways in which modelers can shape AICA behavior *before* agents are deployed. There are at least a few general approaches for such offline intervention. One is related to the data engineering processes involved in training machine learning models.

Machine learning algorithms are often categorized with three general types: unsupervised, supervised, and reinforcement learning. Unsupervised machine learning refers to the type of algorithms that identify patterns in data. For example, unsupervised learning algorithms such as *k-means* clustering could be applied to historical data from cyberattacks to learn classes of malware with respect to their signatures, impacts or other features that might be present in the data. This might be useful when AICA respond uniquely to different types of malware.

In contrast, supervised machine learning is a type of algorithms that depend on previously labeled data that represent an outcome of interest. These labels are often provided by humans to enable the algorithm to train a model that represents the relationship between features in the data and the outcome. For example, in email spam detection features may include the relative frequency of upper-case letters, number, symbols or other clues that distinct spam from legitimate messages. In this example the outcome is whether a given message is spam. The goal of the algorithm is to use labeled data (i.e., messages that were previously classified as spam or not spam, typically with human assistance) to fit the model's parameters (Goodfellow et al., 2020).

In general, the majority of AI algorithms is based on supervised learning. This prevalence is likely to be true in AICA as well, as supervised learning algorithms are building blocks of cybersecurity and autonomy to monitor user activity and traffic to detect malware and attacks. This is a major opportunity for humans to shape AICA behavior and mitigate their specific risks. Data scientists and engineers provide labeled training samples that ideally represent the population of individuals, or in our case, cyber-events of interest.

However, this opportunity is highly dependent on the availability of labeled data that is representative of the future scenarios of AICA action. Quality data is scarce or expensive. For AICA-induced risks of functional, safety and security consequences, it is probably unknown the exact extent to which insufficient data increase such risks. Moreover, regarding AICA-specific risks of ethical, moral or unfair consequences, there is a growing body of literature on how biased data can lead to algorithmic bias, or ML models that produce outcomes that are racist or otherwise exacerbate inequality (Ligo et al., 2021b; Linkov et al., 2020; Vincent, 2018). These biases are again caused by labelled examples that are insufficient or not representative.

Another challenge is measuring how much of AICA-specific risk is mitigated with improved labeling. In today's systems, the influence of labeled data on performance of machine learning models is assessed and the data updated on a regular basis. For example, an intrusion detection system may include a supervised learning algorithm trained with historical data from attacks. The trained model will probably have high classification precision – able to detect most of the intrusions with a small number of legitimate users flagged as malware (false positives). However, it is not uncommon for the precision of these classification systems to fade over time. This is because malware and attack characteristics change over time, as do legitimate applications, causing the number of misclassifications to increase over time (false positives of legitimate use being classified as intrusion and false negatives of attacks being classified as normal use). As AICA become more autonomous, it is likely that an increasingly greater number of more sophisticated supervised learning models will be deployed. This will imply that AICA will require more and more up-to-date labeled data to re-train the algorithms more frequently than today's spam or fraud detection systems. Research will be needed to fully understand how much new labeled data and at what frequency will be needed by AICA, and how much risk mitigation can be achieved per byte of fresh data.

Besides, no amount of labeled data can account for "black swans." Taleb defines those as events that are so unlikely and impactful that they are impossible to predict (Taleb, 2007) – think about 9/11. People naturally collects lots of data and derive conclusions after black swans occur, but their unique nature prevent the use of data about past black swans to accurately predict the next one. For example, the emergence of the Internet is a life-changing but singular data point – knowing its history does not allow to predict when the next life-changing technology will emerge nor what its impact will be. Likewise, AICA based on supervised machine learning is good only to defend against attacks that are similar to previous ones.

6 Human-Centric Approaches Based on Algorithm Design

Because of the challenges mentioned in the previous section, human intervention should go beyond providing labeled data for supervised machine learning. A second and perhaps more direct approach for human control of AICA relates to resilience by design (Kott et al., 2021) and refers to the choice and development of machine learning algorithms themselves.

One possibility is reinforcement learning (Sutton & Barto, 2020), which is a promising choice for AICA algorithms (Cam, 2020). Reinforcement learning (RL) is the category of machine learning algorithms that interacts with an environment or simulation in a recurrent way. This typically involves models that perform a series of tasks over time while managing a balance between long and short-term objectives. In this way, an RL-based AICA can try a certain course of action and measure the outcome based on how well the objectives were met and relative to how "important" those objectives are thought to be. If the outcome contributes to a long-term goal (for example, avert a cyberattack or restore service), then a relatively strong reward input is fed back to algorithm as a signal that the current course of action should be kept. On the other hand, if the outcome does not contribute to the long-term goal (e.g., there is no significant restoration), then the reward is relatively lower or negative to signal that the algorithm needs to change its course of action. As a cyber-defense example, consider a combat scenario in which AICA are deployed to defend a series of targets. The long-term and highest rewarded goals of such a scenario would be for all targets to remain intact as well as for the mission to be carried by the targets as planned. Additional goals may be set for desirable, but less important, outcomes (e.g., minimizing resource use) and when met, can be marginally rewarded.

Cam provides a conceptual model that is applicable to AICA, in which RL is used to predict actions from attackers and enable agents to counterattack appropriately (Cam, 2020). However, the proposed model does not include mitigation of specific AICA-related risks. Nevertheless, RL opens the possibility for design choices in which the optimization of the long-term goal of the algorithm could include the minimization of AICA risks. If probability or consequence of these risks can be measured over time, then they can be incorporated into the reward of the RL algorithm to minimize long term AICA risk over time.

One possible design choice might be to have an RL-based agent to control AICA-specific risk as a separate agent from the AICA themselves. In other words, this would be a design of agents controlling other agents – AICA performing the main cyber-defense mission and coexisting with other agents specialized in monitoring AICA courses of action, estimating risk, and acting either to change AICA operation or to remedy whatever damage the AICA cause. This hypothetical architecture highlights another data challenge. Data about rare cybersecurity events is… well, rare. Data from autonomous agents that allow the inference of the incremental risk and negative impact of the agent's actions should be even scarcer. Furthermore, to our knowledge human-labeled data of actions, risks, and negative impacts of agents is probably non-existent.

Another possibility of human intervention with AICA to mitigate risk through algorithmic design could be inspired by generative adversarial networks (GAN). Conceptually, a GAN is a pair of "competing" machine learning algorithms (Goodfellow, 2016). One is a "generative" neural network that is trained to determine its parameters to approximate an unknown distribution of examples that are fed to the generative system; it then generates synthetic examples that are as similar as possible to the original data. The other algorithm is a "discriminative" neural network that is trained to classify whether given examples come from the original data or are synthetic examples output by the generative algorithm. The result of the classification by the discriminative system are fed back to the generative algorithm for improvement. The two networks are then trained simultaneously. Ideally, the networks interact until the generative model outputs examples for which the discriminative network would assign the same probability as for real examples, meaning that the discriminative network can no longer differentiate the output from the generative network from the original data.

We hypothesize that algorithms like GANs could be used for incremental risk mitigation. Data would be provided from a set of possible AICA courses of action that result in acceptable functional, safety, security, ethical, and moral consequences. AICA would play the role of the generative part of this GAN-like system, meaning that AICA would approximate acceptable courses of action as close as possible. On the other hand, a discriminative algorithm would be fed both the data on acceptable actions and data about AICA actions and try to discriminate the origin of the fed data. The output of the discriminative algorithm would be fed back to AICA in order to re-adjust their actions and make them as similar as possible to the acceptable courses of action (Ligo et al., 2021a). Once again, this concept implies a data challenge. Available data on acceptable actions needs to be collected and curated (probably by humans) to be fed both the AICA and the discriminative algorithms.

7 Simulation of Strategies

Most of the strategies discussed so far for mitigation of AICA-related risks involve gathering, labeling and/or curation of data by humans at some degree. AI algorithms in cybersecurity, computer vision, natural language processing and other applications are based on deep learning algorithms, which are particularly known to demand massive amounts of data (Goodfellow et al., 2016). What is worse is that data about risks, consequences and/or acceptable courses may simply not exist. Moreover, strategies based on historical data will not work for novel threats and situations.

This limitation in data urges the exploration of other opportunities. One general way to manage risk is to anticipate outcomes by simulation. AICA-specific risks could then be inferred by a simulation of outcomes that are synthetized and labeled for supervised learning algorithms of AICA. There are advantages and disadvantages with this approach. One advantage is that while real data is limited to historical events that were recorded and labeled, synthetic data is limited only by human imagination – new attacks, disasters or accidents can be conceived and simulated. Disadvantages of simulated data include simulation models that are simplistic or unrealistic representations of systems or attackers. For example, simulations of cyber events can be simple tabletop exercises where the scale and complexities of the real system, attacks and AICA are not considered. These exercises are useful to review human procedures, but the data resulting from the simulation may not be useful to train AICA's supervised learning models.

Another possibility is if AICA have a built-in (or have remote access to) a simulation system that estimates risks and likely outcomes of a given course of action *before* AICA triggers that action. Estimation the optimal course of action is likely to be extremely complex, as noted by Ma in the chapter about recovery planning using simulation. Therefore, it is probable that a simulation of outcomes needs to be a digital twin – a high-fidelity and probably expensive representation of both the AICA and its environment (i.e., the system being defended). In any case, the reliability of the simulated outcomes is a risk in itself – a wrong estimate of risks and outcomes would result in overconfidence about the chosen course of action, which may lead to negative consequences.

The feasibility of use of simulation with AICA depends on a trade-off between fidelity, scenario complexity, and computational cost. A "physical" example of the advantages and disadvantages of simulation for risk assessment and reduction is demonstrated in the Operational Analysis community through the use of simulation software, such as the Advanced Framework for Simulation, Integration, and Modeling, or AFSIM (Clive et al., 2015; Dozier, 2021). AFSIM is a framework that can be leveraged to develop and visualize either high or low fidelity combat engagements (Fig. 16.1). For example, in a simulation an air combat platform can be represented simply as a point in space traveling along a vector or as a

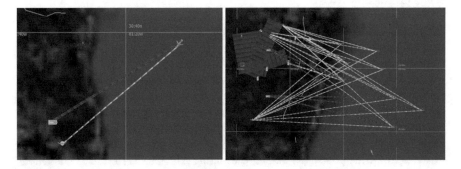

Fig. 16.1 An example of a simple (left) and more complex (right) simulation within AFSIM involving air and ground units. The computational expense of the simulation in the right figure is much higher due to many factors including the number of platforms in the engagement, missile tracking, communications between platforms, radar, and routing

six-degree-of-freedom (6-DOF) model with the ability to realistically change speed, altitude, and direction using the AFSIM physics engine. With high fidelity models, AFSIM users are able to gain an accurate assessment of the success of the simulated mission, but this level of fidelity comes with a high computational cost. The expense of complex, high fidelity simulations and models prohibits the use of simulation in real-time, and therefore limits "on the spot" engagement outcome evaluation. Therefore, when simulation results are required quickly, lower fidelity simulations with less accurate outcomes must be utilized.

8 Software-Centric Strategies: Constraints to AICA Algorithms

We have discussed the use of several types of machine learning algorithms as ways for humans to intervene with AICA at design time, aiming to mitigate the risk of negative consequences arising from AICA actions. Another form of human intervention through algorithmic design might involve an explicit design of constraints. The obvious analogy is Asimov's three laws of robotics (Asimov, 2004): (1) robots may not injure humans; (2) robots must obey orders given by humans unless they violate (1); and (3) robots must protect themselves unless the protection violates (1) or (2). The analogy might look silly when considering the complexity of AI systems. However, it is illustrative of the use of rules explicitly defined by humans, as opposed to rules learned by AICA and derived from the data available, sometimes in a non-explainable way.

Constraints are imposed at the design phase in such a way that if the behavior learned from data by the AICA violates those rules, then the agent's course of action is aborted or reversed. For example, the AICA might learn to shut down an oil pipeline in the event of unauthorized access. But what if that line is critical for heating to a certain community in a cold day? An explicit rule could cancel or remedy the action executed by AICA.

While the idea of constraints may look simple, rule-based programming can be challenging and has limitations. Defining rules for every single condition is impractical for certain applications. Consider a search engine, for example. If one implemented it exclusively with rules like "if the search term is X then return Y", they would need to code an "if" statement for every possible search term. This is impractical to code and maintain because the number of "if" statements would be in the order of billions, if not trillions (it is estimated that Google processes 1.2 trillion searchers per year) (Internet Live Stats, 2022). Nevertheless, it may be possible to design generic case-based rules or principles that can be coded to limit the degrees of freedom for the courses of action, preventing AICA to learn or execute actions that violate pre-defined functional, safety, security, ethical, or moral limits for the outcomes. Of course, no rule is able to avoid outcomes that are unknown, but this problem is present with any of the other approaches as well.

9 Summary

In this chapter we discussed how AICA may introduce new risks. These risks might overshadow the cyber-defense improvement brought by the intelligent agents. Types of new risks include flawed AICA actions caused by faulty algorithms or training data that is biased or tampered, or flaws arising from collective AICA behavior that is not observed from individual agents. These AICA-introduced risks may produce harmful outcomes of functional, safety, security, ethical, moral or equity nature. Such consequences demand mitigation strategies that prevent AICA risks to surpass their benefits.

An intuitive approach is to consider human cooperation and oversight of autonomous agents. However, human intervention in real-time during AICA action or operation is not recommended in some situations because it may make the harm worse. This includes situations in which humans cannot respond within the time or scale required to absorb or recover from the attack or disaster, or when humans cannot acquire the situational awareness required for the action.

There are options of human-centered strategies that allow humans to shape AICA behavior before they choose and execute a course of action. One option is to provide labeled data for the training of supervised learning algorithms of AICA that mitigates risk. One challenge is to determine the amount of training data required to mitigate risk, or even gather historical data that is representative of cyber-defense scenarios that are relevant for AICA training. Another challenge is how to measure risk mitigation itself, including the determination of how frequently the assessment of AICA-related risks should be executed. Finally, training AICA exclusively on historical data restricts their behavior to what has already happened in the past and is of no help to mitigate risks that are totally new.

A second strategy is to focus on the choice and design of machine learning algorithms such as reinforcement learning and generative adversarial networks applied to AICA. Again, one likely challenge of this approach is the availability of data about risks and outcomes of each algorithm. Simulation might be possible approach to overcome the data limitations of both strategies above, as it may be able to help estimate risks (historical or not) and possible mitigation strategies before AICA perform any action on production systems. However, simulation approaches must consider the trade-off between fidelity and computational cost of simulation scenarios.

A third strategy is to focus on general algorithmic rules or principles that constrain AICA actions (e.g. Asimov rules of robotics), regardless of ML training. This could leverage the power of AI and machine learning while minimizing risks by explicitly constraining the space of possible outcomes.

AICA represent a necessary, and perhaps unique, response to cyber threats that have been increasing in frequency, scale, and autonomy. Therefore, AICA-related risks should not be an obstacle to their deployment. Rather, effective risk mitigation strategies must be developed and implemented such as the benefits of AICA can be fully experienced.

References

Asimov, I. (2004). *I, robot*. Random House Publishing Group.

Cam, H. (2020). Cyber resilience using autonomous agents and reinforcement learning. In T. Pham, L. Solomon, & K. Rainey (Eds.), *Artificial intelligence and machine learning for multi-domain operations applications II* (Vol. 11413, p. 35). SPIE. https://doi.org/10.1117/12.2559319

Clive, P. D., Johnson, J. A., Moss, M. J., Zeh, J. M., Birkmire, B. M., & Hodson, D. D. (2015). Advanced Framework for Simulation, Integration and Modeling (AFSIM). In *International conference on scientific computing CSC'15*.

Dozier, H. (2021). Machine-assisted Mission engineering: An exploration of reinforcement learning with the advanced framework for simulation, integration, and Modeling (AFSIM). *ERDC/ITL SR, 21*(4), 28.

Federal Trade Commission. (2022). *Equifax data breach settlement*. https://www.ftc.gov/enforcement/refunds/equifax-data-breach-settlement

Goodfellow, I. (2016). NIPS 2016 tutorial: Generative adversarial networks. In *Conference on neural information processing systems*. http://arxiv.org/abs/1701.00160

Goodfellow, I., Bengio, Y., & Courville, A. (2016). Deep learning. *MIT Press*.. https://www.deeplearningbook.org

Goodfellow, I., Pouget-Abadie, J., Mirza, M., Xu, B., Warde-Farley, D., Ozair, S., Courville, A., & Bengio, Y. (2020). Generative adversarial networks. *Communications of the ACM, 63*(11), 139–144. https://doi.org/10.1145/3422622

Hubbard, D. W., & Seiersen, R. (2016). *How to measure anything in cybersecurity risk*. Wiley.

Internet Live Stats. (2022). *Google search statistics*. https://www.internetlivestats.com/google-search-statistics/

Kott, A., & Linkov, I. (2019). Cyber resilience -of systems and networks. In A. Kott & I. Linkov (Eds.), *Cyber resilience of systems and networks*. Springer. https://doi.org/10.1007/978-3-319-77492-3

Kott, A., & Theron, P. (2020). Doers, not watchers: Intelligent autonomous agents are a path to cyber resilience. *IEEE Security and Privacy, 18*(3), 62–66. https://doi.org/10.1109/MSEC.2020.2983714

Kott, A., Buchler, N., & Schaefer, K. E. (2014). Kinetic and cyber. In A. Kott, C. Wang, & R. F. Erbacher (Eds.), *Cyber defense and situational awareness*. Springer International Publishing Switzerland. https://doi.org/10.1007/978-3-319-11391-3_3

Kott, A., Golan, M. S., Trump, B. D., & Linkov, I. (2021). Cyber resilience: By design or by intervention? *Computer, 54*(8), 112–117. https://doi.org/10.1109/MC.2021.3082836

Ligo, A. K., Kott, A., & Linkov, I. (2021a). Autonomous Cyberdefense introduces risk: Can we manage the risk? *Computer, 54*(10), 106–110. https://doi.org/10.1109/MC.2021.3099042

Ligo, A. K., Rand, K., Bassett, J., Galaitsi, S. E., Trump, B. D., Jayabalasingham, B., Collins, T., & Linkov, I. (2021b). Comparing the emergence of technical and social sciences research in artificial intelligence. *Frontiers in Computer Science, 3*, 653235. https://doi.org/10.3389/fcomp.2021.653235

Linkov, I., Galaitsi, S., Trump, B. D., Keisler, J. M., & Kott, A. (2020). *Cybertrust: From explainable to actionable and interpretable artificial intelligence*. IEEE Computer.

Morgan, M. G. (2017). *Theory and practice in policy analysis*. Cambridge University Press.

Oltramari, A., & Kott, A. (2018). Towards a reconceptualisation of cyber risk: An empirical and ontological study. *The Journal of Information Warfare, 17*(1), 1–22. http://www.nist.gov/cyberframework/

Sutton, R. S., & Barto, A. G. (2020). *Reinforcement learning: An introduction* (2nd ed.). MIT Press.

Taleb, N. N. (2007). *The black swan: The impact of the highly improbable* (Vol. 2). Random House.

U.S. Department of Transportation. (2018). *Automated Vehicles 3.0 – Preparing for the Future of Transportation*.

Vincent, J. (2018). *Google 'fixed' its racist algorithm by removing gorillas from its image-labeling tech*. The Verge. https://www.theverge.com/2018/1/12/16882408/google-racist-gorillas-photo-recognition-algorithm-ai

Chapter 17
Policy Issues

Samuel Sanders Visner

1 Introduction – AICA and the Changing Information Technology Eco-System

This chapter contextualizes the use of the use of Artificial Intelligent Cyber-defense Agents (AICA) within today's policy environment and the one taking shape around us. We try in this chapter to frame the overarching policy issues that AICA users and designers will face in the hope that their understanding of these policy issues will strengthen AICA effectiveness and safety, while enhancing their general acceptability by the people they are meant to protect.

AICA should be considered within a rapidly changing global information eco-system, one in which digital technology and connectivity are almost ubiquitous. Over 62% of the world's population of some 7.6 billion people have routine access to cyberspace, with Internet penetration rates ranging from 98% in Northern Europe, 92% in North America, and 73% in East Asia, to a low of 24% in Middle Africa.[1] The growth rate of Internet traffic is astonishing; one estimate puts the growth of such traffic between 2000 and 2020 at 1266%, with some 332 billion emails sent per day in 2022.[2] American alone are estimated to account for 3,138,420 GB of Internet traffic.[3] By 2020, over 50% of Internet traffic originated from or was sent to mobile

---

[1] See: https://www.statista.com/statistics/269329/penetration-rate-of-the-internet-by-region/ Accessed March 21, 2022.

[2] See: https://www.broadbandsearch.net/blog/internet-statistics Accessed March 21, 2022.

[3] Ibid.

S. S. Visner (✉)
MITRE Labs, The MITRE Corporation, Washington, DC, USA
e-mail: svisner@mitre.org

© The Author(s), under exclusive license to Springer Nature Switzerland AG 2023
A. Kott (ed.), *Autonomous Intelligent Cyber Defense Agent (AICA)*, Advances in Information Security 87, https://doi.org/10.1007/978-3-031-29269-9_17

devices,[4] and the rise of global 5G networks, combined with the practically unlimited number of Internet Protocol (IP) addresses being made possible by IP version 6 (IPv6) is likely to expand the number of people and devices connected globally. SpaceX's Starlink constellation is expected to comprise as many as 12,000 low earth orbiting (LEO) satellites, and possibly as many as 42,000 satellites to be lofted,[5] connected to a global cloud infrastructure, creating a new kind of "hyperscalar". Similar plans exist for Blue Origin Plans to launch over 3,200 satellites,[6] connected to the Amazon Web Services cloud infrastructure. China plans to loft a similar, albeit smaller 5G orbital network,[7] evidence of the continued expansion of the global information eco-system. One telecommunications carrier estimates that some 24 billion Internet of Things (IoT) devices will be connected by 2030, with IoT densities likely of up to one million devices per square kilometer.[8] This new information technology eco-system, and its massive connectivity, will service every industry, business sector, and critical infrastructure. Civil government and military operations alike depend increasingly on either the global information infrastructure, or separate infrastructures that share the same basic Internet architecture used globally.

In addition, new, "smart cities" and smart infrastructures will arise as the global information eco-system expands. While various architectures exist and have been offered for such smart cities, these architectures consist generally of:

- A common information technology infrastructure
- Numerous IoT devices to sense, capture, and transmit data relating to everything from water pressure to public transportation loading, from power consumption to the needs for policing resources
- Machine Learning (M/L) and artificial intelligence (AI) applications to recognize activity patterns and make decisions about the allocation of resources (e.g., water, power, transport, policing)
- And the infrastructures themselves in which these IoT devices are embedded, allowing the decisions derived from AI applications to be realized.

The adoption of this smart cities architecture approach can be used a across a broad range of infrastructures, and possibly even for military operations.

Overall, the growth of the global information eco-system and the complex infrastructures that inhabit them represent a growing challenge for cyber defense. Large, complex infrastructures serving millions, if not billions of IoT devices, present expanding and ever-changing attack surfaces in which new vulnerabilities can emerge without warning and can be difficult to detect.

---

[4] Ibid.

[5] See: https://en.wikipedia.org/wiki/Starlink Accessed March 21, 2022.

[6] See: https://orbitaltoday.com/2021/11/19/jeff-bezos-kuiper-holding-llc-seeks-permission-to-launch-4538-more-satellites/ Accessed March 21, 2022.

[7] See: https://techstory.in/china-to-start-building-5g-satellite-network/ Accessed March 21, 2022.

[8] See: https://www.verizon.com/business/resources/articles/s/5G-device-density-and-the-industries-it-will-impact/ Accessed March 21, 2022.

Such infrastructures represent important opportunities for the application of AICA, as well as policy challenges to their application. AICA can be used to detect anomalous behavior in complex networks; it can also be used to detect and possibly mitigate emerging vulnerabilities, and to adjust dynamically automated cyber defenses. AICA can be used also to detect prospective and actual malicious activity on adversary networks, and possibly to preempt or block such activity before it leaves those networks. Such approaches, known generally as "defend forward," signals the use of AICA on network we do not own or control.

2 The Changing Concepts of Cyber-Defense

"Traditional" cybersecurity consists of three inter-related operational concepts pertinent to today's integrated computer networks, the building blocks of the global information infrastructure:

- Computer Network Defense – the defense of a network, its data, its systems, and the infrastructures that depend on that data and those systems
- Computer Network Exploitation – the penetration of a network, generally to steal data or otherwise gain access to its systems and the infrastructures that depend on that data and those systems
- Computer Network Attack – the ability to damage data, hold it at risk (possibly for ransom), or to damage information systems, or the infrastructures that depend on that data and those systems.

In other words, the defense of our systems includes both the ability to defend them and to intervene and interfere with adversaries, to disrupt their operations, and to hold at risk their data, systems, and infrastructures.

The convergence of such defensive and potentially offensive cyber defense concepts continues to evolve. New approaches have been given impetus by the development by the U.S. National Security Agency (NSA) of more active forms of cyber defense. According to the NSA:

Active Cyber Defense (ACD) is a component of the Department of Defense's (DoD) overall approach to defensive cyber operations.

> *Its elements complement preventative and regenerative cyber-defense efforts by synchronizing the real-time detection, analysis and mitigation of threats to critical networks and systems. The concept is applicable to the defense of all U.S. Government and critical infrastructure networks, not just those owned and operated by DoD. While ACD is active within the networks it protects, it is not offensive and its capabilities affect only the networks where they have been installed by network operators and owners.*
>
> *Real-time detection and mitigation at every tier in every cyber environment require the seamless integration of cyber-defense services across program and network boundaries and the application of standards for messaging and Command and Control (C2). ACD elements*

complement preventative and regenerative cyber-defense efforts by synchronizing the real-time detection, analysis, and mitigation of threats to critical networks and systems.[9]

The concept of "hunt forward," which deploys "cyber warriors" overseas, allows U.S. military personnel to work overseas with foreign military personnel to hunt for cyber vulnerabilities and exploits on their networks. Hunt forward is related closely to the "Defend Forward" doctrine of the U.S. Department of Defense, which is described by Dr. Erica Borghard of the Congressional Solarium Commission as:

the proactive observing, pursuing, and countering of adversary operations and imposing costs in day-to-day competition to disrupt and defeat ongoing malicious adversary cyber campaigns, deter future campaigns, and reinforce favorable international norms of behavior, using all the instruments of national power.[10]

Overall, these approaches to cyber defense exist within the umbrella concept of "persistent engagement," a concept defined by the United States Cyber Command (USCYBERCOM) as

continuously engaging and contesting adversaries and causing them uncertainty wherever they maneuver.[11]

In addition, the Deputy Commander of the United States Cyber Command (USCYBEROM) described persistent engagement in the following terms:

(W)e want to be in constant contact with our adversaries. We want to be in a proactive posture and not in a reactive posture.[12]

The Congressional Cybersecurity Solarium Commission, established in 2019, was directed to "develop a consensus on a strategic approach to defending the United States in cyberspace against cyber attacks of significant consequences."[13] The Commission described a comprehensive cybersecurity approach, one that calls for hunt forward, defend forward, and persistent engagement using a wide range of tools. For the United States, the Commission called for a wide range of ambitious goals, including:

1. Reform the U.S. Government's Structure and Organization for Cyberspace
2. Strengthen Norms and Non-Military Tools
3. Promote National Resilience
4. Reshape the Cyber Ecosystem
5. Operationalize Cybersecurity Collaboration with the Private Sector

---

[9] See: https://apps.nsa.gov/iad/programs/iad-initiatives/active-cyber-defense.cfm Accessed March 21, 2022.

[10] See: https://cyber.forum.yale.edu/blog/2021/7/20/defend-forward-adapting-offense-and-defense-strategy-to-cyberspace Accessed March 21, 2022.

[11] "Achieve and Maintain Cyberspace Superiority," Command Vision for US Cyber Command, April 2018.

[12] See: https://www.defense.gov/News/News-Stories/Article/Article/2840284/persistent-engagement-strategy-paying-dividends-cybercom-general-says/ Accessed March 21, 2022.

[13] See: https://www.solarium.gov/home Accessed March 21, 2022.

6. Preserve and Employ the Military Instrument of National Power.[14]

Several of these goals, particularly those relating to national resilience, reshaping the cyber eco systems, and operationalizing cybersecurity collaboration with the private sector, are likely to be fertile grounds for the use of AICA. AICA will surely prove promising in understanding and defeating adversary cyber activity, on the networks of the adversaries themselves. In addition, the Commission's calls for stronger cyber deterrence requires both strong cyber defense, i.e., "deterrence by denial," and the ability to detect, attribute, and respond appropriately to malicious cyber activity. Again, AICA will play a strong and increasing role.

3 Existing Policies and Considerations

The emergence of cybersecurity norms is likely to influence significantly the policy framework that shapes our use of AICA. Efforts to create cybersecurity norms have been sporadic, though progress in recent years has been noteworthy. The United Nations *Ad hoc* Panel of Experts has worked to create a consensus regarding the conduct in cyberspace of U.N member countries.[15]

Overall, policy- and decision-makers should understand current national and international policy and doctrine as it relates to the information technology eco-systems in which AICA will operate. While relevant, existing policy and doctrine relates principally to the conduct of military operations, the use of information technology for the private sector and critical infrastructure, and to safeguard citizens' privacy, the development of policy and doctrine relating to the use of AICA in the information eco-system is nascent. Nonetheless, some existing policy and doctrine are instructive and may provide the framework for which AICA is employed ultimately. In general, policy and doctrine exist in the following domains:

- Military operations and the laws of war
- US national security and foreign policy
- Personal privacy and Constitutional protections
- The safety and security of national infrastructure.

Responsibility for the use of most technology is vested generally with those that employ it. AICA, in contrast, presents a challenge to policymakers because its employment is affected – and perhaps determined – by the computer scientists and software engineers who create it. Their judgment, understanding of legal and other constraints, and (perhaps) their values may play an as important a role in the use of AICA as those who employ AICA directly. In fact, an important policy consideration in the use of AICA will be to establish who is responsible for a tool's

---

[14] Ibid.

[15] See: https://www.un.org/securitycouncil/sanctions/2374/panel-of-experts/work-mandate Accessed March 21, 2022.

behavior, as well as its ultimate effect, the designer, the user, or both, and for each party, to what extent. This concern looms over any policy consideration.

In broad terms, salient policy issues relating to AICA exist in the following areas:

- In wartime, for the defense of our systems and for offensive cybersecurity regarding adversary systems
- In peacetime, where we practice "hunt forward" on adversary systems
- The effects on and possible disruption of US policy vis a vis allies, partners, and other countries
- Also in peacetime, where privacy frameworks such as Europe's General Data Protection Requirements (GDPR) and the California Consumer Privacy Act (CCPA), which require accountability in relation to privacy and the relationship between a commercial enterprise and its customers
- And, in the context of the 4th Amendment of the Constitution of the United States, ensuring that AICA does not violate the Amendment's protections.

In addition, one may consider also the question of policy as it relates to the continued development of Artificial Intelligence generally, and AICA specifically.

3.1   Wartime Policy Considerations – Some Examples

Perhaps the most salient question of policy relates to the use of AICA under wartime conditions. Wartime conditions can be highly dynamic under which friendly (or "blue") and adversary (or "red") forces may be in proximity, operating in each other's cyberspace, or in common cyberspace.

Military operations take place under conditions constrained by several policy components, including doctrine, proportionality, and international agreements, *de jure* and *de facto* that may constrain operations. AICA tools are designed to operate, in some cases without direct human supervision, in situations that are dynamic and may not conform to pre-determined doctrine, operational objectives, or even accepted international policies and practices. A particular potential complication arising from the use of AICA relates to attribution and proportionality. Proportionality in wartime (defined in international law as a component of *jus in bello*) relates to the need to observe:

> the balance to be struck between the achievement of a military goal and the cost in terms of lives.[16]

Proportionality can also be used in the justification for armed conflict, balancing the grievance suffered with the intensity of the response (defined in international law as *jus ad bellum*).

---

[16] See: "Proportionality and Force in International Law," Judith Gail Gardam, The American Journal of International Law, Vol 87. No 3, July, 1993, Pages 391–413.

We can regard proportionality as one of the most important challenges to the use of AICA, and possibly one of its strongest opportunities. Proportionality constrains attacks and armed responses, sometimes in conformance with the 1907 Hague Convention.[17] Article 23(e) prohibits employing "arms, projectiles, or material calculated to cause unnecessary suffering." Article 25 apples the "principle of distinction," which prohibits direct attacks against non-military targets. Article 27 requires attacks to spare buildings with religious or cultural significance. More precision regarding conduct during wartime was conveyed by the Geneva Convention of 1977 which prohibits:

(a) An attack by bombardment by any methods or means which treats as a single military objective a number of clearly separated and distinct military objectives located in a city, town, village or other area containing a similar concentration of civilians or civilian objects; and

(b) An attack which may be expected to cause incidental loss of civilian life, injury to civilians, damage to civilian objects, or a combination thereof, which would be excessive in relation to the concrete and direct military advantage anticipated.[18]

In other words, efforts should be undertaken to constrain operations, at least regarding military objectives and regarding collateral damage. However, effective implementation of proportionality relies on attribution. AICA tools that may be used to respond "intelligently" to cyber-attacks or exploits, particularly in a world of "persistent engagement" and "defend forward" must be informed by reliable attribution. Without such attribution, AICA responses could react to or even retaliate against the wrong target, causing inadvertent and possibly unjustified damage to information, information systems, and infrastructures. AICA developers, therefore, must bear the additional burden of building into their capabilities the means to relate attribution to the responses of which their tools may be capable.

Efforts are underway to improve our understanding of proportionality in cyberspace. In recent years, the Tallinn Manual[19] was developed by the NATO Cooperative Cyber Defence Centre of Excellence.[20] The Tallinn Manual:

(h)as become an influential resource for legal advisers and policy experts dealing with cyber issues.[21]

While non-binding the Manual is intended:

(t)o provide an objective restatement of international law as applied in the cyber context.[22]

---

[17] See: https://besacenter.org/proportionality-in-the-modern-law-of-war-an-unenforceable-norm-or-the-answer-to-our-dilemma/ Accessed, March 27, 2022.

[18] Ibid.

[19] See: https://ccdcoe.org/research/tallinn-manual/ Accessed March 27, 2022.

[20] See: https://ccdcoe.org/ Accessed March 27, 2022.

[21] Ibid.

[22] Ibid.

The Tallinn Manual exists as an example of notional restraints on the use of cyber-security tools, particularly regarding offensive cyber tools. For example, Section 1, Rule 10 of the Manual notes:

> *A cyber operation that constitutes a threat or use of force against the territorial integrity or political independence of any State, or that is in any other manner inconsistent with the purposes of the United Nations is unlawful.*[23]

Other aspects of the Manual discuss prohibitions regarding attacks against civilian infrastructures or attacks that harm or kill non-combatants. While the Manual does not reflect international law, and cannot be enforced through legal means, the United State and other countries may adopt policies regarding the use of cybersecurity tools that conform to the Tallinn Manual's precepts. For each wartime operation, those employing defensive and offensive cybersecurity tools must understand which Tallinn Manual rules are encompassed by current policy. They might ask, for example, if their forces are required to abide by Tallinn Manual proscriptions against damage to civilian infrastructures. If so, AICA programming must reflect this pol-icy, implying that such tools can recognize civilian cyber targets and avoid them. Conversely, AICA must also be able to identify friendly civilian infrastructure tar-gets, and be prepared to defend them, should an adversary choose not to abide by policies that would avoid damage to such targets. In either case, AICA programmers would share with users responsibility for the performance of such tools, and the effects they achieve.

The cybersecurity operations of the United States Armed Forces have developed and continue to develop doctrines and operational concepts that will affect AICA. The U.S. Army (like the other Armed Services), both defends its own networks, conduct-ing Defensive Cyber Operations-Internal Defense Measures (DCO-IDM), as well as operations external to Army networks, or Defensive Cyber Operations-Response Actions (DCO-RA). Again, the use of AICA requires an understanding on the part of operators and programmers of policy and doctrine associated with every operation, particularly those operations taken to defend the Army on networks it does not own or control necessarily. In this instance, desired effects must be calibrated carefully to conform to desired outcomes without, for example, causing collateral damage. As networks undergo increasingly convergence in which, for example, US forces rely on non-US networks, or energy and transportation networks are managed in common, the need for finely grained cyber defenses, including offensive cybersecurity, will require increasingly "intelligent" AICA.

Finally, national defense policy regarding AI generally continues to evolve. The Department of Defense adopted in 2020 a statement of principles for the use of AI, all of which are applicable to AICA. These principles include the need for AI appli-cations to be:

> **Responsible**. *DoD personnel will exercise appropriate levels of judgment and care, while remaining responsible for the development, deployment, and use of AI capabilities.*

---

[23] Ibid.

Equitable. The Department will take deliberate steps to minimize unintended bias in AI capabilities.

Traceable. The Department's AI capabilities will be developed and deployed such that relevant personnel possess an appropriate understanding of the technology, development processes, and operational methods applicable to AI capabilities, including with transparent and auditable methodologies, data sources, and design procedure and documentation.

Reliable. The Department's AI capabilities will have explicit, well-defined uses, and the safety, security, and effectiveness of such capabilities will be subject to testing and assurance within those defined uses across their entire life-cycles.

Governable. The Department will design and engineer AI capabilities to fulfill their intended functions while possessing the ability to detect and avoid unintended consequences, and the ability to disengage or deactivate deployed systems that demonstrate unintended behavior.[24]

Overall, these principles point to the need for AI tools development and use to be transparent, both in their development and in their use. AICA tools that adhere to these policies must reflect the ability of developers to adhere to policies regarding acceptable use, the need for users to employ these tools in a manner that does not exceed intended consequences.

3.2 AICA in the "Grey Zone"

AICA may be seen in the application of armed force prior to war, or in "grey zone" operations, situations that can be described as "not war" and "not peace."[25] Such operations represent intersecting and overlapping application of cyber, diplomatic, political, economic, and military power short of open armed conflict. Important to such operations is the careful calibration of the application of any instrument such that only specific effects are achieved, effects that do not lead to escalation or, in some cases, attribution. Within the realm of cybersecurity, the "defend forward" component of U.S. Department of Defense cyber strategy is an important aspect of such grey zone operations. As the Honorable Patrick J. Murphy and Dr. Erica Borghard describe "defend forward:"

(d)efend forward rests on the premise that to deter and defeat adversary threats to national security, the US could not solely rely on responding to malicious behavior after the fact. Rather, the DoD should be proactive in maneuvering outside of US cyberspace to observe and understand evolving adversary organizations and, when authorized, conduct operations to disrupt, deny, or degrade their capabilities and infrastructure before they reach the intended targets.[26]

---

[24] See: https://www.defense.gov/News/Releases/Release/Article/2091996/dod-adopts-ethical-principles-for-artificial-intelligence/ Accessed May 6, 2020.

[25] Antulio J. Echevarria II, "Operating in the Gray Zone: An Alternative Paradigm for U.S. Military Strategy," United States Army War College Press, United States Army War College, 2016.

[26] Op cit. page 1.

Overall, these tools are designed to both coerce another state's compliance or, in some cases, to deter another state's actions. In all cases, calibration of effects and outcomes must be considered carefully by those who use cyber tools and, in the case of AICA, those who program their "intelligence," consistent with policymakers' objectives.

3.3   US National and Economic Security Policy

Artificial intelligence is considered to be an important aspect of US national and economic security. A 2020 report[27] from the National Science and Technology Council and the Office of Science and Technology Policy noted that artificial intelligence is vital for the protection of United States critical infrastructure. According to the report, AI can be used to detect malicious code, find anomalous behavior in complex networks, and even "synthesize defensive patches."[28] The report also noted that AI systems can be evaded, or even fooled, through a variety of techniques, while also calling for the development of tools for autonomous cyber defense. From a policy perspective, the Final Report of the National Security Commission on Artificial Intelligence[29] called for a comprehensive investment and organizational policy to advance the state of AI for cybersecurity, as well as the need to mitigate risks associated with autonomous cyber tools and weapons systems. In particular, the report notes that more must be done to establish confidence in AI systems. Specifically:

> To establish justified confidence, the government should focus on ensuring that its AI systems are robust and reliable, including through research and development (R&D) investments in AI security and advancing human-AI teaming through a sustained initiative led by the national research labs.[30]

3.4   Consumer Privacy

The passage of the Cybersecurity Information Sharing and Protection Act (CISPA) of 2015, as part of the 2015 National Defense Authorization Act, signaled the need to balance the cybersecurity of the nation's business and critical infrastructure with

---

[27] Artificial Intelligence and Cybersecurity: Opportunities and Challenges Technical Workshop Summary, a report by the Networking and Information Technology Research and Development Subcommittee and the Machine Learning and Artificial Intelligence Subcommittee of the National Science and Technology Council and the Office of Science and Technology Policy (Executive Office of the President), March 2020.

[28] Ibid.

[29] Final Report, National Security Commission on Artificial Intelligence, 2021.

[30] Ibid.

the privacy of its citizens. Passed after several years of vigorous debate between cybersecurity, intelligence, and civil liberties actors, the Bill encourages cybersecurity reporting to the United States Government but constrains the scope and manner of reporting to safeguard personally identifiable information (PII).[31] Civil liberties and privacy concerns regarding cybersecurity are important to the development of AICA, given the need to ensure that intelligent agents neither "invade" information technology infrastructures that contain PII, nor report PII by mistake to the United States Federal Government. Privacy concerns will likely become more acute. The General Data Protection Regulation (GDPR) of the European Union constrains the holding of PII by commercial enterprise. GDPR also requires such enterprises to be able to disclose to their customer how and where their data is held, while giving these same customers the right to have that data deleted and how such deletion can be verified. GDPR Article 25, paragraph 2, is illustrative, referring to a commercial enterprise's "controller:"

> The controller shall implement appropriate technical and organizational (sic) measures for ensuring that, by default, only personal data which are necessary for each specific purpose of the processing are processed. That obligation applies to the amount of personal data collected, the extent of their processing, the period of their storage and their accessibility. In particular, such measures shall ensure that by default personal data are not made accessible without the individual's intervention to an indefinite number of natural persons.[32]

The California Consumer Protection Act (CCPA) echoes GDPR-like concerns, defining:

- The right to know about the personal information a business collects about them and how it is used and shared;
- The right to delete personal information collected from them (with some exceptions);
- The right to opt-out of the sale of their personal information; and
- The right to non-discrimination for exercising their CCPA rights.[33]

GDPR and CCPA, and possibly other, similar policies in prospect will require AICA developers to ensure that the actions of autonomous cyber defense agent to not "scrape" PII unnecessarily, particularly when safeguarding complex business infrastructures. The privacy concerns that underly GDPR and CCPA make incumbent that the automation of cyber defense be accompanied by the need to discriminate between network data, analysis of which is important to defending a network, and PII that may be associated with network data, but which would compromise the rights GDPR and CCPA attempt to defend.

---

[31] See: National Institutes of Standards and Technology Special Publication 800–122 "Guide to Protecting the Confidentiality of Personally Identifiable Information (PII)."

[32] See: https://gdpr-info.eu/art-25-gdpr/

[33] See: https://www.oag.ca.gov/privacy/ccpa

3.5   Constitutional Protections

The Constitution of the United States provides powerful protection for "United States Persons." The Constitution's Fourth Amend is short, but eloquent:

> *The right of the people to be secure in their persons, houses, papers, and effects, against unreasonable searches and seizures, shall not be violated, and no Warrants shall issue, but upon probable cause, supported by Oath or affirmation, and particularly describing the place to be searched, and the persons or things to be seized.*[34]

While debate will likely continue regarding what constitutes "persons, houses, papers, and effects," those who operate and design AICA must remain mindful constantly that information needed to safeguard our citizens' networks generally, and critical infrastructures specifically, cannot compromise Fourth Amendment protections. As our infrastructures become more complex, so too will be the intricacies of automating the monitoring of the networks on which these infrastructures depend, identifying anomalous behavior, mitigating breaches, while ensuring that the private information of the people remain secure.

4   Policy Issues for the Future

4.1   National Security

From a national security perspective, AICA operators and developers are faced with complex issues. The examples above make clear that the design and use of AICA must conform to policy objectives, often situationally unique, as well as the doctrine that integrates the use of AICA specifically, and cyber defense generally with other instruments of state power, including military, diplomatic, political, economic, and other components. We will need, as the previous Army discussion shows, to be able to operate effectively on our own networks, and on networks we do not own or control necessarily.

What can we expect in the future?

First, we can expect our national security to be more dependent on complex information systems and the infrastructures that employ them. These information systems will reside and operate in environments heavily contested in wartime, peacetime, and during grey zone conflicts. The global information infrastructure will be characterized by increasing competition, likely to make necessary the use of AICA on dynamic networks not subject to "friendly" configuration control. The rise of IPv6, 6G and "NextG," coupled with AI-mediated "smart infrastructures" will foster the emergence complex behaviors in which anomalies may be difficult to spot and mitigate without AICA. At the same time, such networks are interdependent;

---

[34] See: https://constitution.congress.gov/constitution/amendment-4/

avoiding collateral damage may become even more difficult, particularly in interconnected, "smart" infrastructures. The ability to "defend forward" on such network will require both effective AICA and programming that constrains the effects caused to specific policy objectives.

We can also expect that our competitive ability to develop and employ AICA will be regarded as an element of national power, a concept made clear by the National Security Commission on Artificial Intelligence.[35] We should expect the emergence of more robust, and possibly better funded research agendas for the creation of AICA, as well as national guidelines for their employment.

4.2 Homeland Security and Privacy

Even as we seek to defend our own, increasingly complex, "smart" infrastructures, privacy concerns, both in the context of the relationship of citizens to commercial enterprises (evidenced by GDPR and CCPA), and for the preservation of our Constitutional protections, will continue to gain visibility and importance. Commercial enterprises may be engaged to managed critical infrastructures in smart cities. Such infrastructures, encompassing millions of IoT devices, will require AICA that is effective and inspires the confidence of those cities' residents. As the intelligence and military services of other countries probe our critical infrastructures for vulnerabilities they can exploit or attack, policy makers will be challenged to harden the cybersecurity of those infrastructures. To the extent that they do so, policies associated with the use of AICA that improves cybersecurity *and* protect privacy will likely emerge, even as the national discussion regarding the mix of security and privacy policies continues.

As we close this discussion regarding policy, we note that other countries may not share our policy concerns regarding AICA, nor adhere to the prohibitions we choose to impose on ourselves. As Caitríona H. Heinl noted at a 2014 workshop of the NATO Cooperative Cyber Defense Center of Excellence:

> *Cyber capabilities in particular are inherently difficult to prevent from being created and such regulatory solutions might not deter malicious actors. In addition, non-state actors will not necessarily feel morally or legally bound in the same way and state actors may not always play by the same "version of the rules." A combination of technical and legal safeguards is required but further research is still needed to examine whether more could be done, while also ensuring that innovation is not suppressed disproportionately.[36]*

---

[35] Op cit.

[36] Proceedings of the 6th International Conference on Cyber Conflict, P. Brangetto, M. Maybaum, J Stinissen (Eds.), NATO Cooperative Cyber Defense Center of Excellence, 2014.

5   Summary and Conclusions

The use of AICA, while promising in terms of defending new, increasingly complex networks, poses important policy and doctrinal challenges. Emerging interdependent networks (serving, for example, energy and transportation systems) can make difficult identifying reliably a valid cyber threat or attributing that threat accurately. The interdependence of such networks, weaving together several critical infrastructures, will require that AICA actions that protect one infrastructure, while not leaving vunlerable other infrastructures. The autonomous nature of AICA means that responsibility for safeguarding the privacy of our citizens, as well as for any unintended consequences, will shift somewhat, and possibly decisively from the AICA users and operators to those who create and program AICA tools. Should AICA be used in pursuit of "persistent engagement," "defend forward," and "hunt forward" cyber defense activities, policy makers, and possibly national security strategists will need to understand and be prepared for possible activities, some extra-territorial, they cannot control directly, the consequences of which may be difficult to manage.

The emergence of AICA should be accompanied by an active research agenda, one that constrains as much as possible the use of AICA to the consequences policymakers, decision-makers, and operators, intend. Such research should encompass an understanding of the rapid evolution of the global information technology ecosystem, including the deployment of global 5G (and possibly next-G) networks, new, space-based telecommunications backbones, IoT device densities approaching and even exceeding one million devices per square kilometer, and new "smart" cities and other infrastructures that depend on machine learning and artificial intelligence to mediate infrastructure resources and behavior. Research activities should include the participation of those charged with developing national and homeland security policy, and those charged with safeguarding our citizens' privacy, given that their constitutional and operational concerns may set the boundaries in which AICA can be allowed to operate effectively.

Chapter 18
AICA Development Challenges

Shouhuai Xu

1 Chapter Motivation

The envisioned potential of AICA has been described in (Kott et al., 2018; Kott & Théron, 2020; Théron & Kott, 2019) and earlier chapters (e.g., "Introduction and Overview"). Independent of (Kott et al., 2018; Kott & Théron, 2020; Théron & Kott, 2019), the term of *active cyber defense*, which is essentially the same idea as AICA, and its associated active cyber defense dynamics, have been investigated in (Xu et al., 2015a, b; Lu et al., 2013; Zheng et al., 2015). The notion of active cyber defense dynamics is one indispensable pillar of the Cybersecurity Dynamics framework (Xu, 2014a, b, 2019, 2020), on par with *preventive and reactive* cyber defense dynamics (Li et al., 2007, 2011; Xu et al., 2012a, b; Xu & Xu, 2012; Zheng et al., 2018; Lin et al., 2019; Han et al., 2021; Chen et al., 2018), *adaptive* cyber defense dynamics (Xu et al., 2014), and *proactive* cyber defense dynamics (Han et al., 2014; Chen et al., 2021). These studies characterize the global (i.e., network-wide) effectiveness of employing certain cyber defenses against certain cyberattacks. In particular, it is now known that active cyber defense is advantageous to the other kinds of defenses, where the advantage can be quantified by a factor that reflects the connectivity property of a mathematical matrix corresponding to the preventive cybersecurity policies in question (more precisely, the factor is a function of the largest eigenvalue of the matrix) (Xu et al., 2015a, b; Lu et al., 2013). Nevertheless, active cyber defense may render cybersecurity unmanageable in terms of measuring and predicting the evolution of the global cybersecurity state because of the chaotic nature of active cyber defense dynamics under certain circumstances (Zheng et al., 2015); fortunately, there are technical means to avoid such situations (Zheng et al.,

S. Xu (✉)
Department of Computer Science, University of Colorado Colorado Springs,
Colorado Springs, CO, USA
e-mail: sxu@uccs.edu

© The Author(s), under exclusive license to Springer Nature Switzerland AG 2023   367
A. Kott (ed.), *Autonomous Intelligent Cyber Defense Agent (AICA)*, Advances in
Information Security 87, https://doi.org/10.1007/978-3-031-29269-9_18

2015). In order to capitalize on these advantages of AICAs or active cyber defense, we must materialize such systems. This turns out to be challenging. This chapter systematically explores the development challenges towards fulfilling the vision of AICAs and active cyber defenses.

Chapter Contributions Given the complexity of AICAs, we propose dividing its development challenges into *engineering* challenges and *research* challenges, following the methodology of "divide-and-conquer" in a sense. These two kinds of challenges are not necessarily complementary to each other; instead, tackling the engineering challenges requires to tackling the research challenges because engineering often needs to leverage technological breakthroughs which typically come from fundamental research. More specifically, in this chapter we make three contributions. First, we articulate and systematize the engineering challenges posed by AICAs, which must be adequately tackled before fulfilling the vision of AICAs. These engineering challenges are centered at what we call "the AICA engineering ecosystem". We suggest approaches to tackling these engineering challenges. Second, we articulate and systematize the research challenges in a broader context. Addressing these research challenges will assure success of AICAs. We also suggest approaches to tackling these research challenges. Third, we show how tackling the research challenges will help address the engineering challenges, by presenting a mapping between the former and the latter. It is worth mentioning that the mapping is not one-to-one because engineering and research often follow different ways of thinking; moreover, research often aims at a broader context so that the resulting knowledge can be widely applied.

Chapter Terminology To simplify terminology, we will use AICA to represent both AICA and active cyber defenses throughout the present chapter. AICAs are often employed into a *network* of interest, which is broadly defined to include enterprise Information Technology networks, networks of cyber physical systems, battlefield networks, and national critical infrastructures. Such a network consists of many computers and networking devices, which are referred to as *computers* in general but include low-power Internet-of-Things (IoT) devices. These networks may employ traditional defense mechanisms, such as firewalls and intrusion detection systems, which are preventive and/or reactive defenses and therefore are complementary to the defenses enabled by AICAs.

2   AICA Engineering Ecosystem

As shown in Fig. 18.1, we propose dividing the AICA engineering ecosystem into six components: design; implementation; individual test & certification; composition; composite test & certification; and deployment. We will use this ecosystem to guide the exploration of the engineering challenges associated with AICAs. The ecosystem-based approach is arguably systematic, so are the resulting challenges.

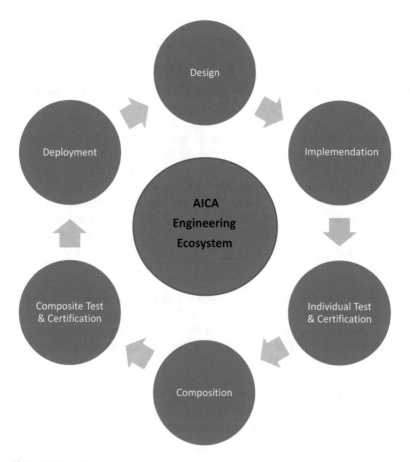

Fig. 18.1 AICA engineering ecosystem

Design This deals with the design of AICA systems, including not only the AICAs themselves, but also the environments they interact with. The design should include the requirements and the constraints that must be accommodated while satisfying the requirements. This is important because existing systems, including their architectures, may need to be revisited to incorporate AICAs. It would be ideal to create a body of standardizations for the interfaces between the AICAs themselves and between the AICAs and the environment systems with which they interact.

Implementation This deals with the realization of the designs so that the resulting software, and hardware (if applicable), can be executed on various platforms. This includes the choice of programming languages or the design of new programming languages if necessary.

Individual Test & Certification This deals with the test and certification of individual AICAs as a standalone entity in the environments specified by the design requirements and constraints. This is important because pure theoretical analysis, simulation, and/or emulation would not be sufficient for demonstrating the effectiveness of the AICAs and their environment systems, partly because the assumptions that are made in those studies may not be realistic. Given the potential impact of AICAs, their effectiveness must be tested and certified in real-world environments with realistic attack-defense experiments.

Composition The effectiveness of AICAs would grow possibly nonlinearly with the number of cooperating AICAs, assuming that they are well coordinated and orchestrated to accomplish missions. This is relevant because AICAs may have to be specialized, rather than making each AICA versatile. This calls for "optimal" composition of AICAs into "troops", in a fashion similar to (for example) how many soldiers and what kinds of weapons should compose a squadron. The way of AICAs cooperating with each other matters because it determines the resulting emergent property, which cannot be derived from the behaviors of individual AICAs (Xu, 2014b).

Composite Test & Certification This deals with testing and certifying the capability or effectiveness of a composition of AICAs which cooperate with each other. Unlike individual test & certification, which can be simply geared towards design specifications, this would be much more challenging because of the emergent property (Xu, 2014b) mentioned above.

Deployment This deals with the employment of AICAs in real-world systems, such as DoD networks. We envision that deployment must be done in an automated or autonomous fashion. This also imposes a range of challenges, especially from a cybersecurity perspective.

3   AICA Engineering Challenges

The AICA engineering ecosystem guides us to characterize a range of engineering challenges, which are inspired by, and extend while re-structuring, the five engineering challenges presented in Théron and Kott (2019), namely architecture; certification; test and simulation; compatibility; and assurance.

3.1   Challenges on AICA Design

A good design starts with a competent specification. However, there is no well-accepted specification for AICAs. This requires us to address the following problems, ranging from requirements (including metrics and constraints) to threat models.

First, we must understand the requirements of AICAs. (i) One requirement deals with the functionalities of AICAs, including its purposes and security assurance. This provides a basis for test & certification. (ii) Another requirement deals with the specification on the support that must be provided by the environment for AICAs to function correctly and securely. Supporting AICAs may incur necessary changes to the current system and/or security architectures of the underlying infrastructures. Therefore, we must understand the impact of such changes. (iii) Another requirement deals with the interactions between AICAs and the interactions between AICAs and the environments where they execute. This would mandate the standardization of interfaces between AICAs and the interfaces between AICAs and the environments with which they interact, such as the demand of computational support that should be provided by the environment. For example, an AICA may offload a certain computational task to the environment with a demand of a certain amount of CPU cycles, memory space, and possibly a hardware-assured trusted execution environment or TEE—such as Intel SGX or Arm TrustZone. (iv) Yet another requirement deals with the security properties of the communications between AICAs and the communications between AICAs and the environments where they execute. All these requirements need to be specified with well-defined and ideally quantitative metrics, which can be readily measured.

Second, we must have a clear definition of threat models against AICAs. There might be a hierarchy of threat models, each of which may be relevant under specific circumstances (e.g., dealing with cyber criminals vs. nation-state adversaries). This hierarchy of threat models justifies the need of a spectrum of AICA designs. The requirements and constraints mentioned above must be specified with respect to specific threat models.

The preceding discussion leads to:

Insight 1: We must deeply understand the requirements (including metrics and constraints) and threat models to design optimal, or at least cost-effective AICAs.

Pertinent to this challenge, the chapters entitled "Alternative Architectural Approaches", "Perception of Environment", "Perception of Threat", "Situational Understanding and Diagnostics", "Learning about the Adversary", "Response Planning", "Recovery Planning", "Adaptivity & Antifragility", "Negotiation and Collaboration", and "Human Interactions" present detailed discussions on the state-of-the-art from specific perspectives.

3.2   Challenges on AICA Implementation

Having specified the requirements (including metrics and constraints) and the threat models, we need to implement or realize AICAs and the environments where they execute. There are many aspects that need to be considered, such as the following. (i) In what environment should AICAs execute? For example, should they execute in virtual machines, containers, or hardware-assured TEE such as Intel SGX or Arm

TrustZone? Alternatively, should we create a new kind of environment that is tailored to satisfy the needs of AICAs? (ii) What programming language(s) should be used to implement AICAs? Different languages have different features and incur different vulnerability surfaces. Do we need to design new programming languages to accommodate the special requirements of AICAs? (iii) How should we secure the communications between AICAs and the communications between AICAs and the environments in which they execute? What kinds of cryptographic mechanisms are necessary and sufficient for assuring such secure communications? (iv) How can we minimize the trust that must be assumed when implementing AICAs, if not assuring zero-trust? This is important because many incidents demonstrate that a huge damage can be caused when trust is intentionally or unintentionally abused; a recent example is the SolarWinds attack (US GAO, 2021). This is relevant to supply-chain security, for example when an implementation reuses some pieces of code from third parties, let alone the globalization in manufacturing computer hardware.

The preceding discussion leads to:

Insight 2: The implementation requirements of AICAs remain to be understood.

Pertinent to this challenge, the chapters on "Command in AICA-intensive Operations", and "Case Study" present a discussion of the state-of-the-art from certain perspectives of implementation.

3.3   Challenges on AICA Individual Test & Certification

This deals with the test and certification of AICAs as if they will be used standalone. While we should pursue theoretical analysis and/or simulation and/or emulation (e.g., rigorously proving security properties of the employed cryptographic protocols), we must admit that such an analysis often makes assumptions which may be hard to validate (Xu, 2021). Moreover, such an analysis is often conducted in an abstract model, while assuming away the implementation which however can introduce vulnerabilities. Therefore, given the specification of requirements (including metrics and constraints) and a threat model, the AICA implementation or software can be tested and certified with respect to the requirements and the threat model.

The competency of test & certification depends on several factors: (i) the completeness of the requirements, which is important because failure in including a necessary requirement may render the certified assurance useless if not doing more harm than good; (ii) the accuracy of the threat model, which is important because a missed threat can render the certified assurance useless if not doing more harm than good; (iii) the completeness of testing scenarios, which is often a large space—possibly exponential—and thus infeasible to test each and every case. For example, when we use static analyses and/or dynamic analyses to test and certify that an implementation of an AICA does not contain vulnerabilities (because rigorously proving that a software of reasonable size contains no vulnerabilities is beyond the reach of the current technology), the static analysis approach (Li et al., 2018a, b,

2022a, b; Zou et al., 2021a, b) is limited by the representativeness of the training data. Whereas, the dynamic analysis approach may not be able to cover all possible execution paths (Li et al., 2018a, b). These highlight that we must be conscious about the limitations of test & certification.

The preceding discussion leads to:

Insight 3: We must be aware of the limitations on the AICA properties that are being tested and certified.

3.4   Challenges on AICA Composition

The most useful scenarios of AICAs would not be that they are used standalone; rather, we should team AICAs to form "troops". Indeed, there are two extremes in designing and implementing AICAs. One extreme is to make each and every AICA possess all possible functionalities. This has several weaknesses, such as: compromising one AICA would expose the entire AICA design to the attacker; the AICA software is too large to remain stealthy. The other extreme is to make each AICA embody a single basic functionality. This may make it unnecessarily difficult to team AICAs to accomplish even relatively simple missions. We envision that there should be a good trade-off which resides somewhere in between these two extremes.

Given a specific set of AICAs with certain functionalities, it is important to team them up to accomplish a given mission. For example, the mission of defeating ransomware attacks may require one set of functionalities than the mission of defeating denial-of-service attacks. Moreover, different missions may require different kinds of collaborations between AICAs of different functionalities and different collaborations between AICAs and their environments. This calls for "optimal" composition of AICAs into "troops", which is similar to (for example) how soldiers and weapons should be composed to form squadrons. This is also reminiscent of the Joint All Domain Operations that have been pursued by the United States Department of Defense, which essentially aim to optimize the collective use of all kinds of forces.

Insight 4: Mission-driven optimal teaming between AICAs and optimal interactions between AICAs and environments are key to maximizing the usefulness of AICAs.

3.5   Challenges on AICA Composite Test & Certification

This extends the test and certification of individual AICAs (i.e., individual test & certification). We distinguish these two because they have different focuses, they are at different levels of abstractions, and they face different challenges. For example, composite test & certification would demand AICAs to make effective and autonomous decisions, possibly in scenarios where they cannot communicate with their respectively trusted parties (e.g., their respective commanders or headquarters). This poses as a big challenge because of the notion of emergent property (Xu, 2014b), which means that different kinds of interactions between AICAs and different kinds of interactions between AICAs and their environments may lead to different outcomes, such as success vs. failure in accomplishing missions. The problem becomes even more challenging when some AICAs or environments may have been compromised by the attacker. To the best of our knowledge, this problem is little understood. The preceding discussion leads to:

Insight 5: The problem of testing and certifying properties which are jointly assured
    by a set of AICAs and environments is yet to be systematically investigated, especially so when some AICAs and environments are compromised.

3.6   Challenges on AICA Deployment

The deployment process of AICAs themselves can be exploited by the attacker to compromise AICAs, as illustrated by the SolarWinds attack (US GAO, 2021). Therefore, it is critical to assure security of the AICA deployment process. We characterize the deployment process from a security perspective, by focusing on two challenges corresponding to two orthogonal issues: *cryptography assurance* and *software integrity*. First, the deployment process must be done in an automated or autonomous fashion because for example, it is not feasible or even possible for soldiers to manually install AICAs in scenarios like battlefields. This means that there must be trustworthy mechanisms for authenticating AICAs. While cryptographic mechanisms can be used for such purposes, this assurance assumes that the cryptographic keys in question or the corresponding cryptographic services are not compromised. Unfortunately, this assurance can be invalidated in realistic scenarios where compromises of cryptographic keys or services may not be detected until after a long delays (Xu & Yung, 2009; Xu et al., 2011, 2019; Dai et al., 2012; Dodis et al., 2003). Second, even if the cryptographic assurance is warranted, it does not necessarily guarantee that the AICA software cannot be compromised. Indeed, the SolarWinds attack (US GAO, 2021) demonstrates that software, and systems in general, can be compromised even though the cryptographic services (e.g., digital signatures) for attesting them are not.

The preceding discussion highlights the importance of practicing zero-trust, including cryptographic assurance and software integrity from legitimate sources. This leads to:

Insight 6: It is important and challenging to deploy AICAs while assuring zero-trust.

Pertinent to this challenge, the chapter entitled "Deployment and Operation" presents a state-of-the-art exploration.

4   AICA Research Ecosystem

To tackle the engineering challenges outlined above, we must conduct research. However, research often has a different way of thinking than engineering. This prompts us to propose the AICA research ecosystem. As highlighted in Fig. 18.2, we divide the AICA research ecosystem into six components, which are different from the six components in the engineering ecosystem, including: models; architectures; mechanisms; test & certification; operations; and social, technical, and legal. We will use this ecosystem to guide the exploration of research challenges.

Models In principle, we must adequately understand, and quantitatively characterize, the effectiveness or assurance of a new cybersecurity policy, architecture, or mechanism before employing it in the real world. This is important because it gives the decision-maker a sense on "what to expect", at least in any scenario that is accommodated by the model in question. Putting into the context of AICAs, we must build models to quantify their cybersecurity effectiveness. As shown by what will be elaborated below, this imposes a range of challenges that must be adequately addressed.

Fig. 18.2 AICA research ecosystem

Architectures A competent architecture is necessary to make AICAs succeed in practice. Ideally, we should quantitatively and precisely characterize the effectiveness of candidate architectures when incorporating certain mechanisms into architectures to build systems. Given the nature of AICAs, a good architecture should be scalable because AICAs in principle can be equally applied to tactical networks (e.g., Army Internet of Battlefield Things or AIoBT) or national critical infrastructures (e.g., financial networks or cyber-physical networks). As what will be elaborated below, this imposes another range of challenges that must be adequately addressed.

Mechanisms Effective mechanisms must be designed by taking into consideration of the constraints and features that are inherent to the AICAs and the environments with which they interact. For example, the AICA mechanisms that are designed for employment in AIoBT might be very different from the AICA mechanisms that are designed for employment in national critical infrastructures because the latter can leverage rich compute resources and a large communication bandwidth. We will explore the challenges in designing AICA mechanisms.

Testing and Certification Pure theoretical analysis and/or simulation and/or emulation would not be sufficient for characterizing the effectiveness or assurance of a new kinds of defenses, including AICA, partly because the assumptions that are made in those studies may not be valid. Given the potential impact of AICAs, its effectiveness or assurance must be tested and certified in real-world environments with realistic attack-defense experiments. This also imposes a range of research challenges.

Operations Since AICAs are inherently, and by default, autonomous, their operations should not demand human interferences. Nevertheless, the current Artificial Intelligence/Machine Learning (AI/ML) technologies may not be able to support 100% autonomy, meaning that some kind of human-AICA interactions may be needed. In this case, as described in the chapter entitled "Human Interactions", human operators may need to approve or amend the actions recommended by AICAs. Even if human-AICA interaction is not necessary, the autonomous operation of AICAs imposes yet another range of challenges.

Social, Ethical, and Legal AICAs inevitably encounter many social, ethical and legal challenges, simply because they may become the norm of future warfare and they must leverage AI/ML technologies as enablers. This means that the social, ethical and legal aspects of traditional kinetic warfare need to be revisited to accommodate AICAs. This also means that all the social, ethical, and legal issues associated with AI/ML naturally apply to AICAs. We will focus on exploring the challenges that are unique to AICAs, while referring the broader challenges to the literature (Vought, 2020; US DoD, 2020; Practical Law Intellectual Property & Technology, 2022).

5   ACIA Research Challenges

The AICA research ecosystem guides us to characterize the challenges that are centered at it. The resulting challenges substantially extend, and restructure, the five decision-making challenges (i.e., modeling, individual agent decision-making, collective agents decision-making, learning, and cooperation) and the two resilience challenges (i.e., stealth and resilience) described in Théron and Kott (2019). The ecosystem-based approach is arguably systematic, so are the resulting challenges.

5.1   Challenges on AICA Models

We use the term "models" (rather than "model") to indicate that a single model might not be able to adequately accommodate all relevant aspects of AICAs, owing to their complexities. Moreover, a single kind of models (e.g., analytic models) may not be adequate because they may have limited capabilities in deriving rich results (e.g., analytic models are often difficult to analyze and may not lead to as many analytic results as we wanted).

As highlighted in Fig. 18.3 and elaborated below, the complexity is attributed to the involvement of the following components. (i) Operation Technology (OT) components, which are often the physical systems that are integral to the networks in question, such as the Tanks in AIoBT and the various kinds of controllers in national critical infrastructures. (ii) Information Technology (IT) components, which are the computing and networking devices that are used in a network. This largely corresponds to traditional network warfare. (iii) Psychological Technology (PT) components, which, when applicable, are the human factors that can be exploited by attackers to manipulate the human operators to benefit the attacker, such as misoperating devices (Rodriguez et al., 2020, 2022; Longtchi et al., 2022). This largely corresponds to what is known as information warfare, including the exploitation of

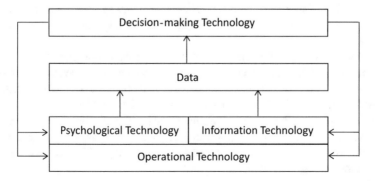

Fig. 18.3 The components that should be adequately accommodated in AICA models

misinformation and/or disinformation in Internet and social networks to influence operations. (iv) The Data components, which are the basis for AICAs decision-making and therefore their trustworthiness is key to the success of AICAs. (v) The Decision-making Technology (DT) components, which are the algorithms, AI/ML-based or not, that are used by AICAs or human-AICA to make decisions in response to observed changes in the environment (e.g., adversarial behaviors). This is critical because decision-making often uses the observed data as input and a decision leads to actions by some OT, IT, and/or PT components.

The components mentioned above inherently interfere with each other. For example, the compromise of IT or OT components can cause that the Data collected by AICAs is misleading as the data reflects what the attacker wants the defender to see; this can cause the DT components to make wrong decisions to benefit the attacker. When applicable, this is also true when PT components are exploited to cause human operators to apply wrong operations. As another example, the DT components should be able to quantify the confidence of the decisions they recommended (e.g., AI/ML trustworthiness) and explain why they make certain decisions (e.g., AI/ML explainability), so that human decision-makers, if applicable, can decide whether to adopt a recommendation or not.

There are a number of challenges associated with the modeling of AICA systems:

- *Security quantification.* This is to quantify the security of network defended by AICAs (Pendleton et al., 2017), which serves as a starting point. Our more recent research (Xu, 2021) puts it into a broader and more systematic context.
- *Agility quantification.* This is to quantify the agility of AICAs in adapting to new threats imposed by attackers and the agility for attackers to adapt to counter AICAs and other defenses (Mireles et al., 2019; Xu, 2021).
- *Resilience quantification.* This is to quantify how resilient AICAs are in resisting attacks, which often attempt to disrupt the entire AICA defense system by compromising a small fraction of AICAs (Cho et al., 2016, 2019; Kott & Linkov, 2021; Xu, 2021).
- *Risk quantification.* This is to quantify the risk associated with AICAs. This is a challenging task because risk is often associated with the inherent uncertainty regarding threats and limited defense or detection capabilities (Xu, 2021; Ligo et al., 2021). The chapter entitled "Risk Management" discusses the risks that may be encountered by AICAs and the approaches that may be leveraged to mitigate such risks.
- *Trustworthiness quantification.* This is to quantify the degree of trust one can put on the decisions or recommendations made by an AICA system. This brings a new dimension of challenges as discussed in (Cho et al., 2016, 2019). The chapter entitled "Testing and Measurements" discusses some closely related matters, including that quality of defense and resilience must be tested and measured in a rigorous and quantitative manner. Trustworthiness can be leveraged to reduce the trust one has to assume, towards achieving zero-trust in decision-making.

To quantify cybersecurity from these perspectives, there are many challenges (Xu, 2014a, b, 2019, 2020), such as the scalability challenge encountered when dealing with large-scale networks, the transient behavior challenges (Chen et al., 2018, 2021) (in contrast to characterizing the asymptotic behavior of the global cybersecurity state of a network), the dependence challenge between random variables (Da et al., 2014; Fang et al., 2021; Xu et al., 2015a, b, 2017, 2018), rather than assuming away the due dependence as it can cause misleading results. One interesting future work is to analyze the four AICA prototype systems presented in the "Case Study" chapters according to the models mentioned above.

The preceding discussion leads to the following:

Insight 7: To adequately model AICAs and analyze their effectiveness or assurance, a model should be as holistic as possible in terms of accommodating the OT, IT, PT, Data, and DT components in both the system model and the threat model. Moreover, we might need to systematically and collectively use analytic, numerical, simulation, emulation, and experimental models to quantify the effectiveness or assurance (of combinations) of defense policies, architectures and mechanisms.

5.2 Challenges on AICA Architectures

While the chapter entitled "Alternative Architectural Approaches" provides a few alternative architectures and there has been some earlier investigation (Kott et al., 2018; De Gaspari et al., 2016), we do not know what architecture would be ideal, meaning that we need to quantitatively compare the effectiveness of different AICA architectures. For this purpose, we need to build competent models, as described above, to quantify the effectiveness of each architecture. One promising approach is to adapt the analytic models described in the Cybersecurity Dynamics framework (Xu, 2014a, b, 2019, 2020), especially those *active cyber defense dynamics* models (Xu et al., 2015a, b; Lu et al., 2013; Zheng et al., 2015) to quantitatively characterize the effectiveness of AICA architectures. This approach is relevant because: (i) it explicitly considers the time dimension, which is important because the effectiveness of AICAs evolves with time; and (ii) both cyber attacks and cyber defenses evolve with time because attackers and defenders frequently adapt their behaviors.

Another particular research direction we propose to pursue is what we call the "cyber neuroimmune system" architecture, which is inspired by, and mimics, the human neuroimmune system architecture. The subject of neuroimmunology studies how human-body's immune system and nervous system interact with each other. It is known that the immune system and the nervous system work together to coordinate in detecting and responding to dangers against human body (Steinman, 2004; Kraus et al., 2021). This analogy is appropriate because of the following interactions between the central nervous system and the immune system as follows (Steinman, 2004; Schiller et al., 2021): (i) The central nervous system acts reciprocally with the immune system, meaning that the immune system and the nervous system function in close association with each other. The nervous system, especially the brain, maintains the human-body's homeostasis while the immune system restores the homeostasis after pathogenic attacks. (ii) The central nervous system drives immunity in response to recognized dangers or threats. The nervous system, especially the brain, predictively perceives and assesses threats against the human body before the threats actually hurt the human body, which enables the human body to proactively prepare for incoming challenges (e.g., behavioral or cellular changes). (iii) The immune system regulates the central nervous system; for example, infection incurs the immune system to signal the brain to respond to threats or dangers that may be caused by bacteria, parasites, or viruses. (iv) The nervous system and the immune system operate at different speeds or time scales because the nervous system can react to situations swiftly (e.g., within milliseconds) but the immune system often reacts to situations slowly (i.e., taking minutes or even weeks to make defense take effect).

The proposed "cyber neuroimmune system" architecture is highlight in Fig. 18.4. The key idea is to (i) design and build a "cyber nervous system" to rapidly orchestrate decentralized AICA defenses and (ii) design and build decentralized autonomous AICA defenses at individual computers. The envisioned "cyber neuroimmune

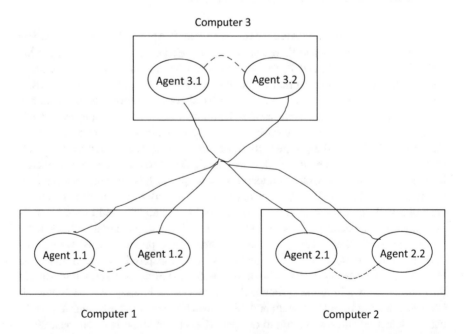

Fig. 18.4 Illustration of the envisioned "cyber neuroimmune system" architecture for AICAs, where AICAs (i.e., the agents) mimic the human immune system, the solid curves illustrate the "cyber nervous systems" which connect AICAs for coordinating their activities, and the dashed curves represent the communication channels between the AICAs in a computer

system" architecture needs to support or achieve the following set of challenging requirements or properties:

- **Intelligent orchestration**. The envisioned cyber nervous system needs to rapidly orchestrate defenses across multiple scales, such as: (i) orchestrating nation-state level defenses between autonomous defense systems at the enterprise levels; and (ii) orchestrating enterprise-level defenses between autonomous AICAs employed at individual computers.
- **Swift detection**. The architecture can swiftly detect new threats, like the human nervous system. Moreover, the architecture should equip AICAs with capabilities in predicting incoming threats or provide early-warning to the largest extent possible.
- **Quick response**. The architecture can automatically and autonomously quarantine compromised computers, and possibly the computers that are suspected to have been compromised. This means that the false-positives associated with the detection system should be controlled below a tolerable threshold; otherwise, this technique may be exploited by attackers to cause denial-of-service attacks.
- **Adaptive defense**. The architecture should facilitate AICAs' capabilities in learning attacker's evolution and adapting to the evolution of threats. This is fundamentally related to the notion of *learnability*. This adaptation capability is a salient characteristic of human immune system. As mentioned above, human immune system is slow in learning new threats (e.g., taking days to learn) and takes a longer period to eliminate threats (e.g., weeks). This means that AICAs must operate at a much smaller time scale to take effect.
- **Proactive defense**. The architecture should facilitate the AICA's capabilities in predicting the evolution of attacks. This is fundamentally related to the notion of *predictability*. This prediction capability of AICAs may be able to go beyond the reach of human neuroimmunological system, in a fashion similar to how AI has defeated human Go players.
- **Resilient defense**. The architecture should be resilient, meaning that the compromise of some AICAs should not render the other AICAs useless, let alone doing more harm than good. For this purpose, the architecture should naturally be decentralized and should embrace Byzantine fault-tolerance techniques. There are discussions on achieving resilience by design vs. dynamic adaptation (Kott et al., 2021; Bagchi et al., 2020). It is our position that both are needed because they are reminiscent of innate immunization and adaptive immunization, respectively. One approach to resilience-by-design is to leverage program synthesis techniques to automatically generate software programs (Bagchi et al., 2020). One approach to resilience by dynamic adaptation is to detect anomalies and adapt to them (Bagchi et al., 2020).
- **Autonomous defense**. The architecture should support autonomous defense, meaning that each AICA should have its own OODA Loop, while a swarm or "troop" of AICAs can collectively run a virtual OODA Loop for joint intelligent decision-making.

The preceding discussion leads to:

Insight 8: Cyber neuroimmune system, mimicking the neuroimmune system in the human body, might be the ideal architecture of AICAs, even though the details need to be investigated in future work.

5.3   Challenges on AICA Defense Mechanisms

AICA brings a range of challenges at the mechanisms level. We propose dividing AICA mechanisms into three categories: *surviving*, *adapting*, and *fight*. In what follows we explore these challenges.

The *surviving* mechanisms are those which can be employed to survive AICAs from malicious attacks. This is important because an attacker, once penetrating a computer, would attempt to disable or compromise the AICA(s) executing in the computer. We highlight three surviving mechanisms.

- **Stealth mechanism**. This mechanism is to make AICAs stealthy, which has been discussed elsewhere (Théron & Kott, 2019). The goal is to make it harder for the attacker to detect the presence of AICAs; even if the attacker knows the presence of AICAs (because they are widely employed), it is still hard for the attacker to figure out which process(es) and/or thread(s) and/or virtual machines are acting as AICAs. For this purpose, we propose leveraging the techniques that have been exploited by stealthy malware, possibly including adversarial example techniques that can be used to evade malware detectors (Li et al., 2023). Our position is the following: We can leverage the stealth techniques to hide AICAs from malware and leverage the detection techniques that are exploited by attackers to detect stealthy AICAs to detect stealthy malware. To the best of our knowledge, this idea of "leveraging attack techniques to defend against attacks" has not been systematically investigated in the literature and therefore can become an effective mechanism for defending AICAs. Of course, the details of such mechanisms need to be investigated in future work.
- **Attack-resistance mechanism**. This mechanism is to leverage operating system and/or computer architectural features to help AICAs survive malware attacks. This is possible by making an operating system to pay special attention to the integrity of AICAs, for example by frequently checking that they are not compromised by malware. To make AICAs as stealthy a possible, this mechanism should not expose AICAs to malware, which may be monitoring the activities of operating systems. For this purpose, the operating system may act equally and frequently on evaluating the integrity (i.e., "health condition") of programs including AICAs. Of course, care must be taken to deal with potential side-channel leakages that a malware can determine whether or not one program is an AICA (or contains the functionality of AICA).
- **Agents diversification**. This mechanism asks if there should be one kind of agents or multiple kinds of agents. We propose diversifying agents in two senses.

(i) There should be multiple kinds of agents, as mentioned above. This is partly inspired by how human immune system operates: B-cells, which are developed in human's bone marrow, are charged with the functionality of recognizing harms (i.e., antigens or foreign materials), but T-cells specialize in attacking the cells that are infected with viruses; moreover, T-cells can be divided into multiple sub-categories (e.g., "killer" vs. helper T-cells) (Clark, 2008). Similarly, we advocate designing different kinds of agents. (ii) Even for the same kind of agents, the implementation should be diversified; otherwise, the compromise of a single agent will cause the compromise of all agents.

The *adapting* mechanisms are those which can be employed to make AICAs autonomously adapt to the evolution of threats. We highlight the following mechanisms:

- **Dynamic learning**. This mechanism is for AICAs to dynamically learn the evolution of cyber threats and the environment to which they interact, as what have been described in the chapters entitled "Perception of Environment", "Perception of Threats", "Situational Understanding and Diagnostics", and "Learning about the Adversary". This is critical because cyber attacks, such as malware, are dynamically evolving with time to evade cyber defenses. Moreover, the learning function must be robust against deception which may be exploited by attacks.
- **Self-adaptation**. This mechanism is for AICAs to autonomously adapt to the evolution of cyber threats, as described in the chapter entitled "Adaptivity & Antifragility". Ideally, this should be achieved without relying on assistance from the other defense systems. As an intermediate solution, this may be achieved by leveraging a non-AICA defense system; for example, there may be a network-wide defense system leveraging data collected from the entire network to learn the evolution of threats and then inform AICAs with the learned threats evolution and possibly strategies to adapt their defenses, so that the AICAs can leverage such "advice" to adapt.
- **Autonomous defense-in-depth**. This mechanism is for AICAs to achieve autonomous defense-in-depth. This is inspired by the human body defense system, which consists of the skin, the physiological conditions, the innate immune system (for inheriting defenses against recognized threats), and the adaptive immune system (for building capabilities to defend against newly encountered threats).

The *fight* mechanisms are those which can be employed to disrupt attackers' malware. We highlight the following mechanisms.

- **Deception mechanism**. This mechanism aims to deceive malware into making wrong decisions as described in the chapter entitled "Cyber Camouflage", which is one form of cyber deception for hindering the attacker's reconnaissance and other activities. Traditionally, cyber deception has been providing misleading environmental information to malware (Lu et al., 2020; Al-Shaer et al., 2019; Wang & Lu, 2018). In the context of AICAs, we propose leveraging AICAs to feed malware with misleading information. This is possible when malware of the same attacker or different attackers need to communication with each other to coordinate their attacks; in this case, it is possible to make AICAs impersonate the malware that have been reverse-engineered to communicate with the yet-to-be-detected malware, feeding them with misleading information, and making them make the decisions that can benefit the defenders (e.g., revealing their attack intents or plans). This is another manifestation of "leveraging attack techniques against attackers".

- **Friend or foe mechanism** (Théron & Kott, 2019). For AICAs to form a squadron or corps of "soldiers", they must be able to communicate with each other to coordinate activities. As described in the chapter entitled "Negotiation and Collaboration", it is important to make "friend or foe" mechanisms robust against malware which may attempt to exploit this mechanism to identify other AICAs. Two kinds of techniques can be used. The first technique is to preserve the anonymity of AICAs until after being certain about the identity of two or multiple interacting AICAs; otherwise, malware could participate in unsuccessful "friend or foe" interactions to identify AICAs. For this purpose, the cryptographic notion of two-party or multi-party secret handshakes (Xu & Yung, 2004, 2007; Tsudik & Xu, 2006) can be used for this purpose. Even with such techniques, malware may still be able to identify AICAs by purely observing who is interacting with whom via such protocols, unless many programs adopt this paradigm of "interacting agents" or "multiagent programming". Since this paradigm of "interacting agents" has not been widely used in IT/OT/DT systems, hiding the presence of secret handshakes needs to be investigated in future work. This manifests one impact of AICAs on the environments where they execute, which is described as one engineering challenge above.

- **Autonomous malware detection**. This mechanism is to autonomously recognize malware. While malware detection has been investigated extensively in the literature, the problem remains largely open as evidenced by the prevalence of malware. This can be attributed to the endless "arms race" between malware writers and malware detectors, including the use of adversarial examples against AI/ML-based malware detectors (Li et al., 2021a, b, 2023). This problem becomes even more challenging in the setting of AICAs because such detection functionalities may have to be conducted by AICAs, which are less powerful than the current generation of server- or cloud-based malware detectors. In order to tackle this challenge, new ideas need to be investigated, such as: How can AICAs leverage server- or cloud-based malware detectors without exposing themselves to malware (e.g., stealthy communications with server- or cloud-based malware detectors)?

- **Autonomous cleanup**. This mechanism is to autonomously eliminate malware that have been detected. This turns out to be a big challenge because the current cyber defense tools are mainly "watchers, rather than doers" (Kott & Théron, 2020). That is, the cleanup of compromised computers and devices are largely manual rather than automated, let alone autonomous. To achieve this, we might have to resort to new operating system and/or computer architecture features, such that when an AICA detects a malware, it can trigger the operating system and/or computer architectural features to run some sort of "privileged instructions" to clean up the malware. We stress that this technique is a double-edged sword because once compromised, a malware can exploit it to remove legitimate programs including AICAs. This highlights the importance of designing attack-resistant authentication mechanisms, ideally with minimal if not zero trust assumptions, for authenticating legitimate and uncompromised AICAs to such privileged instructions, while allowing the operating system to detect compromised AICAs such that their requests will be ignored and these compromised AICAs may be removed from the system in an autonomous fashion.

- *Leveraging attackers to cope with attackers*. This mechanism is to leverage the presence of multiple attackers, namely leveraging one attacker against another (i.e., leveraging one attacker's malware against another). This is possible when multiple attackers are competing against each other, as demonstrated in (Xu et al., 2012a, b). The intuition is the following: when the defender does not have technique to cope with attacker A's malware, the defender may leverage attacker B's malware to "kick out" attacker A's malware (assuming it can indeed achieve it) and then cope with attacker B's malware. This would go much beyond the current technology, which is that one attacker's malware can "patch" the vulnerability it exploited so that the vulnerability cannot be exploited by another attacker's malware anymore (Xu et al., 2012a, b).

The preceding discussion leads to:

Insight 9: There are many challenges when designing and developing mechanisms to support AICAs, for tackling which some technical directions are discussed above.

5.4   Challenges on AICA Testing and Certification

For AICAs to be successful in systems like national critical infrastructures and military systems, there must be an adequate testing and certification process. This is important because the aforementioned modeling and quantification studies often assume away the other functionalities that are related to the mission of AICAs, which is natural in taming complex systems. However, these assumed-away assumptions may interfere with the missions of AICAs in a fashion that may not be related to AICA missions. For example, the crash of an operating system at a certain time may prevent it from providing the due support to AICAs, which may be exploited by a malware to compromise an AICA; this compromise may not be detected until after a significant delay. This highlights the importance of testing and certification.

Testing aims to evaluate the effectiveness of AICAs in realistic environments, which may go much beyond the analytic, simulation, and emulation models whereby effectiveness of AICAs is evaluated as mentioned above. Testing often conducts penetrations by red-teams that have the skills similar to what are possessed by attackers, including their malware planning and writing skills. Testing also evaluates whether AICAs interfere with, or are interfered by, other software systems that will co-exist with AICAs. It is important to recognize that AICAs are a new approach to cyber defense, which cannot disrupt the functionalities of the computers or networks that are defended by them.

Certification aims to decide whether AICAs comply with industrial standards before they can be considered for incorporation or employment. This is particularly relevant to governmental or military systems, largely owing to their complexity. As mentioned above, certification cannot be done without conducting extensive testing of AICAs in real-world networks. Certification of AICAs is expected to be a complex task (Théron & Kott, 2019).

The preceding discussion leads to the following:

Insight 10: Both extensive testing and certification of AICAs are expected to be challenging tasks.

5.5   Challenges on AICA Operations

Once tested and certified, AICAs are deployed to operate in real-world systems. The chapter entitled "Deployment and Operation" discussed several scenarios of AICA deployment and operations. In general, the operation of AICAs poses a big challenge because they are essentially on their own in terms of surviving attacks from malware and fighting against malware, despite that they may receive some assistance from the operating system and/or computer architectural features mentioned above. We propose equipping AICAs with their own Observation-Orientation-Decision-Action (OODA) Loop, which is inspired by the military notion of OODA Loop introduced by Air Force Colonel John Boyd. Figure 18.5 highlights the ACIA OODA Loop, which is elaborated below.

- **Challenges on Observation**. Observation aims to collect data to adequately reflect the situation awareness and the historic data over a past period of time. As hinted in the Modeling component of the AICA research ecosystem, there are multiple challenges associated with data. (i) The adequacy of the collected data

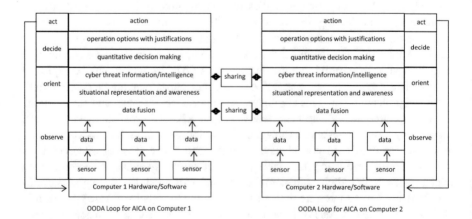

Fig. 18.5 AICA OODA loop

in reflecting the situational awareness. This is related to answering the following fundamental questions: What must be observed? How can the defender observe what must be observed? (ii) The adequacy of the collected data in reflecting the history and modeling purposes, such as the length of the past period of time during which the data will be collected and maintained. For example, if statistical forecasting or predictive AI/ML models will be applied to historic data, a good trade-off will be made in terms of the time windows for modeling purposes; the longer the time window, the more resources will be needed to store the historic data and possibly a bigger challenge in securing and maintaining the historic data. (iii) The trustworthiness of the collected data. The collected data may be poisoned before being collected; for example, malware may compromise the sensors that read and/or collect data. The collected data may also be poisoned after being collected, for example during its storage.

- *Challenges on Orientation*. Orientation aims to process the collected data for understanding the current situation and the trend in the evolution of the situation, ideally also the evolution of attack strategies and tactics. This incurs a number of challenges. (i) How can AICAs correctly perceive the environment? How can we be sure the AICAs are not misled by malware when comprehending the environment? (ii) How can AICAs correctly perceive the threats and their evolutions, such as the attack strategies or tactics that are used by attackers? This is particularly important for "knowing the enemy". (iii) How can AICAs collaborate with each other in the orientation process? This is important because each AICA may only see some aspect of a system or network, meaning that they need to collaborate with each other to "piece together" a holistic picture of the situation.

- *Challenges on Decision*. Decision aims to identify the best responses to threats, by leveraging the current situation and the historic evolution as reflected by the outcome of the Orientation process. In addition to what are described in the chapters entitled "Response Planning" and "Recovery Planning", there are multiple challenges associated with the Decision process. (i) The decision-making of individual AICAs (Théron & Kott, 2019), including: How can we quantify the trustworthiness of a decision made by an AICA? To answer this question, we need to quantify the uncertainty associated with the decision-making process of an AICA. Some initial investigation has been conducted in the context of adversarial malware detection in (Li et al., 2021a, b). How can we interpret why an AICA makes a particular decision or recommendation? In general, this relates to AI/ML explainability and interpretation. (ii) The decision-making of a group of AICAs (Théron & Kott, 2019). This is important because no single AICA sees the entire picture of the current situation or the historic information, which highlights the importance of collective decision-making by AICAs. This is nontrivial because of the following dilemma: If too many AICAs are involved in the collective decision-making process, the process may not be efficient enough while increasing the risk of exposing AICAs (to malware that may be observing network communication activities); if few AICAs are involved in the collective decision-making process, the resulting decision may not be trustworthy because these AICAs collectively may not be able to see the entire situation. Identifying an appropriate subset of AICAs is challenging, especially because AICAs are autonomous, meaning that we may not be able to pre-determine which AICAs should be designated as decision-making AICAs. This reiterates the importance of designing competent collaboration mechanisms for AICAs to securely identify their peers that have the right kinds of information for effective decision-making.

- **Challenges on Action**. Action includes cleaning up compromised computers or devices. As described above, this may require new operating system and computer architectural features to help AICAs to autonomously clean up compromised computers. Also as mentioned above and discussed elsewhere (Kott & Théron, 2020), our understanding on this matter is very limited because the current defense technology is primarily "watchers, rather than doers" (Kott & Théron, 2020).

The preceding discussion leads to the following:

Insight 11: AICAs require the support of autonomous OODA Loop, which goes much beyond what can be achieved by the current generation of defense technology.

5.6   Challenges on Social, Ethical, and Legal Aspects

AICAs are fundamentally based on autonomy, which heavily uses AI/ML technologies. As a consequence, all of the social, ethical, and legal challenges associated with AI/ML technologies naturally apply to AICAs. Moreover, AICAs may become the norm in future warfare, this means that the doctrines for warfare might need to be revisited to accommodate this new form.

- The social challenges include the acceptance of AICAs to the society. This includes (Vought, 2020): assuring public trust in AI in the context of AICAs; assuring public participation; assuring scientific integrity and information quality; assuring adequate risk management; assuring fairness and non-discrimination; and assuring disclosure transparency.
- The ethical challenges include what AI/ML technologies may or may not be ethical to use. For example, the AI/ML technologies potentially harming privacy may not be used even for AICA purposes. The United States Department of Defense adopts the following principles for ethical AI/ML (US DoD, 2020): responsible AI; equitable AI; Traceable AI (for accountability); reliable AI; and governable AI.
- The legal challenges deal with both domestic laws and international laws. The former has a broad impact (Practical Law Intellectual Property & Technology, 2022), concerning: (i) risk allocation provisions in commercial transactions when AI is involved; (ii) products liabilities when AI is involved; (iii) data protection and privacy issues when AI is involved; (iv) intellectual property protections when AI is involved; (v) bankruptcy issues when AI is involved; (vi)

discriminations and biases when AI is used in workplace; (vii) issues related to health plans, HIPPA compliance, and retirement plans when AI is involved; (viii) antitrust issues when AI is involved. The latter copes with international cyber-enabled warfare. This is particularly important when studies show that certain cyber attacks, such as the cyberspace counterpart of "atomic bombs", cannot be adequately defended by cyber technological means, we may have to resort to international treaties to prohibit the use of such attacks, which is similar to the international treaties in prohibiting the use of atomic bombs.

The chapter entitled "Policy Issues" further discusses concerns from ethical, governance, social and legal perspectives. In general, we can draw the following:

Insight 12: Social sciences should play an important role in regulating the use of AICAs in cyberspace.

6   Mapping Between the Engineering Ecosystem and the Research Ecosystem

Having described the engineering ecosystem and the research ecosystem as well as their associated challenges, we now present a mapping between them to highlight how the engineering ecosystem can be supported by the research ecosystem, namely how the engineering challenges can be resolved by leveraging the results in tackling the research challenges.

The relationship between the AICA engineering ecosystem and the AICA research ecosystem are highlighted in Fig. 18.6. We make the following observations. First, investigating models in the research ecosystem is fundamental to the

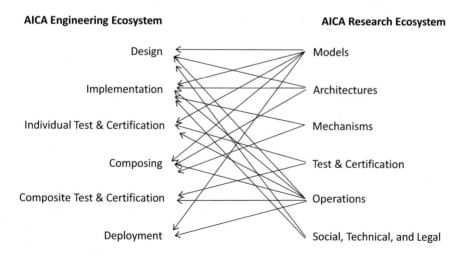

Fig. 18.6 Mapping between the AICA engineering ecosystem and the AICA research ecosystem, where "A → B" means that tackling A will contribute to tackling B

success of AICAs, because it will contribute to tackling every aspect of the engineering system. This is because models provide a clean way of thinking in coping with the complexity encountered when dealing with complex problems like AICAs, including the assumptions that need to be made (e.g., minimal if not zero trust assumptions). A good model would guide: (i) cost-effective, if not optimal, design, implementation, and composition of AICAs; (ii) both individual and composite test & certification in terms of what can be tested and certified; and (iii) the deployment while assuring the desired security properties. Second, investigating architectures will contribute to optimizing or fine-tuning the design, and will guide the implementation and the composition of AICAs. For example, it would automatically recommend an architecture with associated mechanisms with respect to a given mission. Third, investigating mechanisms will guide the implementation of AICAs because an AICA needs to use specific mechanisms, and will guide the composition of AICAs because different mechanisms may be employed together to accomplish a given mission. Fourth, investigating test & certification in abstract models and possible experimental environments will directly contribute to achieving both individual and composite test & certification. Fifth, investigating operations will also contribute to the optimization of the design, implementation, composition, deployment, and individual and composite test & certification, because each of them has an impact on operations. Sixth, the social, technical, and legal aspect in the research ecosystem will have an impact on the design and implementation of AICAs. This is because, for example, certain technologies may be prohibited from being incorporated into AICAs as regulated by international treaties as mentioned above.

7 Summary and Conclusions

AICAs, or active cyber defenses, have a great potential to become a game-changer technology for cybersecurity. In particular, it can eliminate an asymmetry which benefits the attacker. The asymmetry is inherent to the following discrepancy: On one hand, the effect of attacks can be automatically amplified by the mathematical property (i.e., the largest eigenvalue) of a certain matrix, which encodes the network connectivity and the preventive cyber defense policies that are employed to defend the network (Xu et al., 2012a, b, 2015a, b; Lu et al., 2013; Zheng et al., 2015, 2018; Lin et al., 2019; Han et al., 2021); on the other hand, the effect of other kinds of defenses (i.e., preventive defenses, reactive defenses, adaptive defenses, proactive defenses (Xu, 2014a, b, 2019, 2020) are not amplified by any network effect as such. This highlights that AICAs must be employed when the other kinds of defenses are not effective against capable cyber attacks.

While attractive and promising, AICAs impose many development challenges, which we decompose into two kinds: the *engineering* challenges vs. the *research* challenges. The former are associated with the AICA *engineering* ecosystem we propose and the latter are associated with the AICA *research* ecosystem we propose. The AICA engineering ecosystem consists of six components: *design*;

implementation; *individual test & certification*; *composition*; *composite test & certification*; and *deployment*. The AICA research ecosystem also consists of six components: *models*; *architectures*; *mechanisms*; *testing and certification*; *operations*; and *social, ethical, and legal aspects*. In order to tackle the engineering and research challenges, we draw insights into the gaps between the state-of-the-art technology and the desired ultimate goals and propose research directions to bridge them. Moreover, we make connections between the engineering challenges and the research challenges, by describing how tackling the research challenges would contribute to tackling the engineering challenges.

Given the potential gain of AICAs, we strongly suggest that the academia, industry, and government to work together to tackle the engineering and research challenges described above because these challenges cannot be tackled by any single community. We hope the research directions outlined in the present chapter will serve as a roadmap in guiding future development efforts towards making AICAs a full-fledged solution for real-world employment. One issue we want to highlight is that AICAs, or active cyber defenses, may render cybersecurity *unmanageable* in terms of measuring and predicting the evolution of the global cybersecurity state, which is attributed to the fact that active cyber defense dynamics can exhibit the chaos phenomenon under certain circumstances (Zheng et al., 2015). In principle, there are technical means to avoid such situations (Zheng et al., 2015), but more research needs to be conducted in taming the chaos phenomenon.

Acknowledgement We thank Dr. Alexander Kott for his constructive feedbacks that guided us in revising the content. The work was supported in part by ARO Grant #W911NF-17-1-0566, NSF Grants #2122631 and #2115134, and Colorado State Bill 18-086.

References

Al-Shaer, E., Wei, J., Hamlen, K., & Wang, C. (2019). *Autonomous cyber deception – Reasoning, adaptive planning, and evaluation of HoneyThings*. Springer. ISBN 978-3-030-02109-2.

Bagchi, S., Aggarwal, V., Chaterji, S., Douglis, F., El Gamal, A., Han, J., Henz, b., Hoffmann, H., Jana, S., Kulkarni, M., Lin, F., Marais, K., Mittal, P., Mou, S., Qiu, X., & Scutari, G. (2020). Vision paper: Grand challenges in resilience: Autonomous system resilience through design and runtime measures. *IEEE Open Journal of the Computer Society, 1*, 155–172.

Chen, H., Cho, J., & Xu, S. (2018). Quantifying the security effectiveness of firewalls and DMZs. HotSoS 2018, pp. 9:1–9:11.

Chen, H., Cam, H., & Xu, S. (2021). Quantifying cybersecurity effectiveness of dynamic network diversity. Accepted to IEEE Transactions on Dependable and Secure Computing.

Cho, J., Hurley, P., & Xu, S. (2016). Metrics and measurement of trustworthy systems. MILCOM 2016, pp. 1237–1242.

Cho, J., Xu, S., Hurley, P., Mackay, M., Benjamin, T., & Beaumont, M. (2019, November). STRAM: Measuring the trustworthiness of computer-based systems. *ACM Computing Surveys, 51*(6), Article No.: 128, 1–47. https://doi.org/10.1145/3277666

Clark, M. (2008, February 4). *Defense of self: How the immune system really works* (Illustrated ed.). Oxford University Press. ISBN-13: 978-0195335552, ISBN-10: 0195335554.

Da, G., Xu, M., & Xu, S. (2014). A new approach to modeling and analyzing security of networked systems. HotSoS 2014, p. 6.

Dai, W., Parker, T., Jin, H., & Xu, S. (2012). Enhancing data trustworthiness via assured digital signing. *IEEE Transactions on Dependable and Secure Computing, 9*(6), 838–851.

De Gaspari, F., Jajodia, S., Mancini, L., & Panico, A. (2016). AHEAD: A new architecture for active defense. SafeConfig@CCS 2016, pp. 11–16.

Dodis, Y., Katz, J., Xu, S., & Yung, M. (2003). Strong key-insulated signature schemes. Public Key Cryptography 2003, pp. 130–144.

Fang, Z., Xu, M., Xu, S., & Hu, T. (2021). A framework for predicting data breach risk: Leveraging dependence to cope with sparsity. *IEEE Transactions on Information Forensics and Security, 16*, 2186–2201.

Han, Y., Lu, W., & Xu, S. (2014). Characterizing the power of moving target defense via cyber epidemic dynamics. HotSoS 2014, p. 10.

Han, Y., Lu, W., & Xu, S. (2021). Preventive and reactive cyber defense dynamics with ergodic time-dependent parameters is globally attractive. *IEEE Transactions on Network Science and Engineering, 8*(3), 2517–2532.

Kott, K., & Linkov, I. (2021). To improve cyber resilience, measure it. *Computer, 54*(2), 80–85.

Kott, A., & Théron, P. (2020). Doers, not watchers: Intelligent autonomous agents are a path to cyber resilience. *IEEE Security and Privacy, 18*(3), 62–66.

Kott, A., Théron, P., Drašar, M., Dushku, E., LeBlanc, B., Losiewicz, P., Guarino, A., Mancini, L., Panico, A., Pihelgas, M., & Rzadca, K. (2018). Autonomous Intelligent Cyber-defense Agent (AICA) reference architecture. Release 2.0. arXiv:1803.10664.

Kott, A., Golan, M., Trump, B., & Linkov, I. (2021). Cyber resilience: By design or by intervention? *Computer, 54*(8), 112–117.

Kraus, A., Buckley, K., & Salinas, I. (2021, April). Sensing the world and its dangers: An evolutionary perspective in neuroimmunology. *eLife, 10*, e66706. https://doi.org/10.7554/eLife.66706

Li, X., Parker, P., & Xu, S. (2007). Towards quantifying the (in)security of networked systems. AINA 2007, pp. 420–427.

Li, X., Parker, P., & Xu, S. (2011). A stochastic model for quantitative security analyses of networked systems. *IEEE Transactions on Dependable and Secure Computing, 8*(1), 28–43.

Li, J., Zhao, B., & Zhang, C. (2018a). Fuzzing: A survey. *Cybersecurity, 1*(1), 6.

Li, Z., Zou, D., Xu, S., Ou, X., Jin, H., Wang, S., Deng, Z., & Zhong, Y. (2018b) VulDeePecker: A deep learning-based system for vulnerability detection. Proceedings of NDSS'2018.

Li, D., Li, Q., Ye, Y., & Xu, S. (2021a). A framework for enhancing deep neural networks against adversarial malware. *IEEE Transactions on Network Science and Engineering, 8*(1), 736–750.

Li, D., Qiu, T., Chen, S., Li, Q., & Xu, S. (2021b). Can we leverage predictive uncertainty to detect dataset shift and adversarial examples in android malware detection? ACSAC 2021, pp. 596–608.

Li, Z., Zou, D., Xu, S., Chen, Z., Zhu, Y., & Jin, H. (2022a). VulDeeLocator: A deep learning-based fine-grained vulnerability detector. IEEE TDSC 2022, to appear.

Li, Z., Zou, D., Xu, S., Jin, H., Zhu, Y., Chen, Z., Wang, S., & Wang, J. (2022b). SySeVR: A framework for using deep learning to detect software vulnerabilities. IEEE TDSC 2022, to appear.

Li, D., Li, Q., Ye, Y., & Xu, S. (2023, January). Arms race in adversarial malware detection: A survey. *ACM Computing Survey, 55*(1), Article No.: 15, 1–35. https://doi.org/10.1145/3484491

Ligo, A., Kott, A., & Linkov, I. (2021). Autonomous cyberdefense introduces risk: Can we manage the risk? *Computer, 54*(10), 106–110.

Lin, Z., Lu, W., & Xu, S. (2019). Unified preventive and reactive cyber defense dynamics is still globally convergent. *IEEE/ACM Transactions on Networking, 27*(3), 1098–1111.

Longtchi, T., Rodriguez, R., Al-Shawaf, L., Atyabi, A., & Xu, S. (2022). SoK: Why have defenses against social engineering attacks achieved limited success? arXiv preprint arXiv:2203.08302.

Lu, W., Xu, S., & Yi, X. (2013). Optimizing active cyber defense. GameSec 2013, pp. 206–225.

Lu, Z., Wang, C., & Zhao, S. (2020). Cyber deception for computer and network security: Survey and challenges. CoRR abs/2007.14497.

Mireles, J., Ficke, E., Cho, J., Hurley, P., & Xu, S. (2019). Metrics towards measuring cyber agility. *IEEE Transactions on Information Forensics and Security, 14*(12), 3217–3232.

Pendleton, M., Garcia-Lebron, R., Cho, J., & Xu, S. (2017). A survey on systems security metrics. *ACM Computing Surveys, 49*(4), 62:1–62:35.

Practical Law Intellectual Property & Technology. (2022). *Artificial intelligence key legal issues: Overview.* https://content.next.westlaw.com/Document/Ibc68c39002d611e9a5b3e3d9e23d7429/View/FullText.html?transitionType=Default&contextData=(sc.Default)&firstPage=true. Accessed 3 Jan 2022.

Rodriguez, R., Golob, E., & Xu, S. (2020, September). Human cognition through the lens of social engineering cyberattacks. *Frontiers in Psychology, 30.* https://doi.org/10.3389/fpsyg.2020.01755

Rodriguez, R., Atyabi, A., & Xu, S. (2022). Social engineering attacks and defenses in the physical world vs. cyberspace a contrast study. Invited book chapter to "Cybersecurity and Cognitive Science".

Schiller, M., Ben-Shaanan, T., & Rolls, A. (2021). Neuronal regulation of immunity: Why, how and where? *Nature Reviews Immunology, 21,* 20–36. https://doi.org/10.1038/s41577-020-0387-1

Steinman, L. (2004). Elaborate interactions between the immune and nervous systems. *Nature Immunology, 5,* 575–581. https://doi.org/10.1038/ni1078

Théron, P., & Kott, A. (2019). When autonomous intelligent goodware will fight autonomous intelligent malware: A possible future of cyber defense. MILCOM 2019, pp. 1–7.

Tsudik, G., & Xu, S. (2006). A flexible framework for secret handshakes. Privacy Enhancing Technologies 2006, pp. 295–315.

U.S. Government Accountability Office. (2021, April 22). *SolarWinds cyberattack demands significant federal and private-sector response (infographic).* https://www.gao.gov/blog/solarwinds-cyberattack-demands-significant-federal-and-private-sector-response-infographic. Accessed on 22 Mar 2022.

United States Department of Defense. (2020). *DOD adopts ethical principles for artificial intelligence.* https://www.defense.gov/News/Releases/Release/Article/2091996/dod-adopts-ethical-principles-for-artificial-intelligence/

Vought, R. (2020). *Guidance for regulation of artificial intelligence applications.* https://www.whitehouse.gov/wp-content/uploads/2020/01/Draft-OMB-Memo-on-Regulation-of-AI-1-7-19.pdf

Wang, C., & Lu, Z. (2018). Cyber deception: Overview and the road ahead. *IEEE Security and Privacy, 16*(2), 80–85.

Xu, S. (2014a). Cybersecurity dynamics. HotSoS 2014, p. 14.

Xu, S. (2014b). Emergent behavior in cybersecurity. HotSoS 2014, p. 13.

Xu, S. (2019). Cybersecurity dynamics: A foundation for the science of cybersecurity. In C. Wang & Z. Lu (Eds.), *Proactive and dynamic network defense* (Advances in information security) (Vol. 74). Springer. https://doi.org/10.1007/978-3-030-10597-6_1

Xu, S. (2020). The cybersecurity dynamics way of thinking and landscape. In *The 2020 ACM workshop on moving target defense,* pp. 69–80.

Xu, S. (2021). SARR: A cybersecurity metrics and quantification framework (Keynote). SciSec 2021, pp. 3–17.

Xu, M., & Xu, S. (2012). An extended stochastic model for quantitative security analysis of networked systems. *Internet Mathematics, 8*(3), 288–320.

Xu, S., & Yung, M. (2004). k-anonymous secret handshakes with reusable credentials. ACM CCS 2004, pp. 158–167.

Xu, S., & Yung, M. (2007). K-anonymous multi-party secret handshakes. Financial cryptography 2007, pp. 72–87.

Xu, S., & Yung, M. (2009). Expecting the unexpected: Towards robust credential infrastructure. Financial cryptography 2009, pp. 201–221.

Xu, S., Li, X., Parker, P., & Wang, X. (2011). Exploiting trust-based social networks for distributed protection of sensitive data. *IEEE Transactions on Information Forensics and Security,* *6*(1), 39–52.

Xu, S., Lu, W., & Xu, L. (2012a). Push- and pull-based epidemic spreading in networks: Thresholds and deeper insights. *ACM Transactions on Autonomous and Adaptive Systems,* *7*(3), 32:1–32:26.

Xu, S., Lu, W., & Zhan, Z. (2012b). A stochastic model of multivirus dynamics. *IEEE Transactions on Dependable and Secure Computing, 9*(1), 30–45.

Xu, S., Lu, W., Xu, L., & Zhan, Z. (2014). Adaptive epidemic dynamics in networks: Thresholds and control. *ACM Transactions on Autonomous and Adaptive Systems, 8*(4), 19:1–19:19.

Xu, M., Da, G., & Xu, S. (2015a). Cyber epidemic models with dependences. *Internet Mathematics, 11*(1), 62–92.

Xu, S., Lu, W., & Li, H. (2015b). A stochastic model of active cyber defense dynamics. *Internet Mathematics, 11*(1), 23–61.

Xu, M., Hua, L., & Xu, S. (2017). A vine copula model for predicting the effectiveness of cyber defense early-warning. *Technometrics, 59*(4), 508–520.

Xu, M., Schweitzer, K., Bateman, R., & Xu, S. (2018). Modeling and predicting cyber hacking breaches. *IEEE Transactions on Information Forensics and Security, 13*(11), 2856–2871.

Xu, L., Chen, L., Gao, Z., Fan, X., Doan, K., Xu, S., & Shi, W. (2019). KCRS: A blockchain-based key compromise resilient signature system. BlockSys 2019, pp. 226–239.

Zheng, R., Lu, W., & Xu, S. (2015). Active cyber defense dynamics exhibiting rich phenomena. HotSoS 2015, pp. 2:1–2:12.

Zheng, R., Lu, W., & Xu, S. (2018). Preventive and reactive cyber defense dynamics is globally stable. *IEEE Transactions on Network Science and Engineering, 5*(2), 156–170.

Zou, D., Wang, S., Xu, S., Li, Z., & Jin, H. (2021a). μVulDeePecker: A deep learning-based system for multiclass vulnerability detection. *IEEE Transactions on Dependable and Secure Computing, 18*(5), 2224–2236.

Zou, D., Zhu, Y., Xu, S., Li, Z., Jin, H., & Ye, H. (2021b). Interpreting deep learning-based vulnerability detector predictions based on Heuristic searching. *ACM Transactions on Software Engineering and Methodology, 30*(2), 23:1–23:31.

Chapter 19
Case Study A: A Prototype Autonomous Intelligent Cyber-Defense Agent

Benjamin Blakely, William Horsthemke, Nate Evans, and Daniel Harkness

1 Introduction

Throughout 2021 an international group of collaborators, the AICAproto21 consortium, collaborated under the auspices of the NATO NCIA to develop a prototype of the AICA architecture for demonstration purposes. This work succeeded, largely due to the focus on a "minimum viable" initial demonstration, and in this chapter, we will outline the considerations that went into it, the technical details of its construction, the test scenario performed, and how such an agent prototype can be extended for use in supporting the research and innovation described in the remainder of this book.

2 Related Work

2.1 Frameworks and Methodologies

The question of how to approach the technical architecture of an autonomous agent has a number of potential answers, and in fact there are a number of works relevant to this topic. Our implementation is based upon the AICA Reference Architecture (Kott et al., 2018, 2020).

The first angle to consider is the methodologies behind designing the agents. A foundational concept is that of agent-oriented design, proposed as part of the GAIA framework in Wooldridge et al., 2000. Similar work includes the FAME Agent-oriented Modeling Language (FAML), a generic agent-oriented metamodel

B. Blakely (✉) · W. Horsthemke · N. Evans · D. Harkness
Strategic Security Sciences, Argonne National Laboratory, Lemont, IL, USA
e-mail: bblakely@anl.gov; horst@anl.gov; nevans@anl.gov; dharkness@anl.gov

proposed as a candidate for an agent modeling language, akin to UML (Universal Markup Language). – a widely adopted modeling language in software engineering (Beydoun et al., 2009). Tropos is an object-oriented methodology spanning requirements analysis to implementation for developing agent-oriented software systems (Bresciani et al., 2004). It is constructed around models of key agent-related concepts: actors, goals, plans, resources, dependencies, capabilities, and beliefs using existing standard tools and methodologies such as interaction diagrams and UML. The ASPECS holonic (agents composed of agents) organization metamodel proposes a recursive design methodology as the basis for an agent-oriented process for engineering complex systems (Cossentino et al., 2010). In this way agent functionality can be recursively modeled as subcomponents to drive simplicity in the models. This is very similar to the methodology used to build out AICAproto21, though we have used the term "micro-agents" to indicate these "subagent" components and generally only go to one level of recursion. Prometheus is a methodology for designing multiagent systems intended for use by non-experts (Padgham & Winikoff, 2003). It introduces the concept of a data coupling diagram showing where information is produced and consumed within the agent's capabilities. This type of coupling serves as the basis for communication between the micro-agents in the AICA prototype.

There are a number of ways a testbed environment for these agents could be built. Standen et al., 2021 proposes the CybORG environment built atop Amazon Web Services (AWS), generating the environment and scenario from YAML files in an automated manner. Another focused on creating an environment with a focus on reinforcement learning for cyber defenses (Molina-Markham et al., 2021). Due to financial constraints, we were not able to leverage AWS until late in the prototype phase and thus our implementation was built in a containerized architecture. We were, however, able to successfully deploy this to AWS on a Linux Docker host. Utilizing AWS services (e.g., Elastic Container Registry (ECR), Elastic Container Service (ECS), and various database services) would have made the implementation simpler but would have required more in-depth architectural changes at a late stage of implementation.

We then turn to concepts that are relevant to AICAproto21, but perhaps not fully implemented in the initial demonstration. INGENIAS is a software development methodology composed of a visual language for multi-agent systems development, an integration with software development methodologies, and an analysis/design environment (Pavón & Gómez-Sanz, 2003). The overall design methodology is very similar to our approach, and at the conclusion of the prototype phase, we find ourselves thinking about the elements in the "elaboration" phase of the design workflow – specifically modeling tasks and goals and "mental state patterns" (i.e., decision making and reasoning). SEMMAS is an integration of intelligent agents and semantic web services based on a shared ontology for communication interfaces (García-Sánchez et al., 2009). This is very similar to work to define the knowledge and decision-making capabilities through software-development methodologies (e.g., Shiang & Sterling, 2008). If all participants in an automated defense system had a shared ontology, it could ease some of the technical burdens of intercommunication. This is the reason we propose STIX/TAXII as potential intercommunication and knowledge representation methods below. A framework has also been proposed for agents to cooperatively explore domain-specific and situational information and share it to the group's mutual benefit (Kendrick et al., 2018).

2.2   Moving Target and Proactive Defenses

A related area of research is that of moving target and proactive defenses (MTD/PD). These are mechanisms and algorithms built to allow information systems to take autonomous action to either make their "attack surface" (i.e., the profile of a system relevant to an interested attacker) more difficult to discern or respond to perceived attacks in a way that makes the attack more expensive or defeats it entirely. The overlap in this work — as can be seen in e.g., Briskin et al., 2016 — makes it worth considering various implementations of MTD/PD and their evaluation. A full coverage of the topics of designing (e.g., Blakely et al., 2019; Pawlick et al., 2019; Xu et al., 2014) or evaluating (Zaffarano et al., 2015) MTD/PD defenses is better left to more detailed works, but we will provide a high-level overview of the commonalities.

Zhuang et al., 2014 provides an overall theory of moving-target defenses. It discusses how we can change the configuration states of a system in response to (adaption) or anticipation of (diversification) cyber-attacks. It also provides formal definitions for the problems that must be solved for an MTD: choosing the next configuration state or a series of adaptations to achieve it given constraints on time and cost. These problems are also relevant to automated cyber-defense agents, though perhaps in a more general form. Instead of just determining a configuration state, an AICA-like agent must determine a course of action that could be an adaptation but could also be a direct response to an adversary or collaborator.

A challenge in MTD/PD that is likely to also be relevant to AICA-type agents is where to locate the agents. Should they run as "patrol" agents on networks of interest, akin to white blood cells? Or should they be integral to the functioning of the protected systems, even if those systems are highly complex, run on proprietary operating systems, or are not open to additions of this kind without direct collaboration with a manufacturer. The AHEAD architecture for active defense advocates instrumenting production systems in place of ancillary honeypot systems (De Gaspari et al., 2016). Though this adds complexity and cost to the system, it provides the best vantage point for observing attacker activity.

2.3   Application Libraries

There has been a fair amount of existing work into developing software packages to evaluate the performance of various automated agent algorithms. Generally, these can be divided into those designed to allow for simulation of agent behavior and environment, and those intended to serve as the basis for operational usage (i.e., actual deployment of a functional agent).

Simulations of agent behavior may be useful in quickly evaluating alternative methodologies prior to fully implementing them in the operation agent. There are several well-known tools of this type. NetLogo is a Scala modeling environment used primarily for education and research purposes (Wilensky, 1999). MASON is another modeling environment of a similar type written in Java (Luke, 2019). Mesa is similar, but designed for the Python community (Kazil et al., 2020).

Actual agent development frameworks are also available. OsBrain is a Python implementation (OsBrain - 0.6.5 — OsBrain 0.6.5 Documentation, n.d.). JADE is a Java implementation that conforms to the FIPA (Foundation of Intelligent Physical Agents, IEEE Computer Society[1]) standards for agent-based technology (Bellifemine et al., 2001). PADE is another Python implementation developed for research into use on smart grids (Melo et al., 2019). SPADE is yet another Python implementation (no apparent relation to PADE) but utilizing XMPP (Jabber) for inter-node communication (2006). These agents vary greatly in their age, however at least a few appear to still be active projects. Ultimately, we chose to forgo tools such as these to permit a more flexible approach.

A key consideration for deciding to adopt an existing framework or develop a new one was whether it would be possible to quickly create a foundational prototype flexible enough to meet potentially unknown future needs. As discussed below, this led to the decision to use "stock" open-source components in a containerized architecture instead of an existing library. This will also allow for easier cross-platform compatibility and maximal ability to add, remove, or swap components as needed for experimentation. It does, however, mean that the agent is much heavier weight (i.e., resource requirements and installed footprint) than a monolithic process or application. For that reason, and for the other advantages purpose-built application environments might provide, it might be desirable to move back to one of these later, likely one of the Python-based options given the desire to maintain any work done on the existing prototype. However, they did not provide enough capabilities for the prototype without significant additional work.

Standardization of the knowledge representation ontology and sharing interfaces, to the extent possible, will also increase interoperability and accelerate development. For this reason, our intent (as the prototype continues to mature) is to leverage the STIX and TAXII standards for knowledge representation and threat intelligence sharing (Introduction to STIX, n.d.; Introduction to TAXII, n.d.).

---

[1] http://www.fipa.org/

3   Guiding Principles for Prototype Development

In building an initial demonstration prototype of the AICA reference architecture, it was important to define a manageable scope that would allow for successful completion in a reasonable amount of time. To this end, tradeoffs needed to be made between desired functionality and achievable outcomes. The following describes the primary objectives of the work, as well as the limitations on the scope that were defined.

The initial prototype, AICAproto21, was built for demonstration to the NATO Communications and Information Agency (NCIA) in collaboration with our partners in the AICA International Working Group (https://www.aica-iwg.org). This was the first implementation of the AICA reference architecture, and the objective was to build a technical framework that demonstrated the basic concepts of "micro-agent" interaction and operation in a simulated environment, while providing a foundation for future research work that could also be grown into an operational system for use in production systems.

The group decided early on that the work developed under this working group would be licensed under the LGPL (https://www.gnu.org/licenses/lgpl-3.0.en.html). It was desired that the AICA prototype be of maximum value to the research community and serve as a catalyst for future collaboration, and thus the group felt strongly that it should be open source in nature. However, the group did not want to prevent the use of developed technologies in future proprietary applications, should that become useful and appropriate. The code developed for this prototype is available at https://github.com/aica-iwg/aica-agent.

The group wanted to maximize time spent on innovative research topics, and minimize time spent on "solved" problems of architecture and intercommunication. Many of the available frameworks, as discussed above, are focused on simulation only and do not provide the sorts of interactions with external systems that are required for an operational agent. Additionally, using existing well-known components decreases the time required for new contributors, who may not be familiar with the more simulation- and research-oriented tools available and rather may already have familiarity with common open-source tools, to become familiar with the agent. Combining these considerations, it was determined that the agent would be built in a containerized (Docker) architecture and would maximize the use of existing open-source components.

Building a fully functional autonomous cyber-defense agent, as can be inferred from the breadth of topics in this book, would have been much too ambitious of an undertaking for this single prototype. Accordingly, a few simplifying scope limitations were adopted.

First, the intent of this prototype was to demonstrate the functioning framework of micro-agents. The intent was not to demonstrate a sophisticated attack detection, threat response, learning, or collaboration capability. For this reason, the demonstration scenario was constrained to a simple network-based port scan and firewall modification example. This is detailed in the section below. Additional scenarios, such as malware detection or interaction with human adversaries, are saved for follow-on work.

Second, though many types of platforms are relevant and of interest for eventual deployment, the prototype was only tested in a Linux (Ubuntu) x86 environment. The use of Docker maximizes options for cross-platform portability to other commodity operating systems, but considerations for non-consumer operating systems were not validated.

Third, though a primary research interest to the group is the application of automated learning, reasoning, and collaboration capabilities, this was scoped out of this initial demonstration. This demonstration focused on a static set of rules regarding detection and response.

4   Technical Details of Prototype

The selection of Docker as the basis of the prototype implementation allowed for maximal re-use of existing components with minimal effort. Combined with Docker Compose, it also allows for different contributors to quickly instantiate their own test instance on Linux, MacOS, or Windows base operating systems and reproduce the demonstration test cases with only a few commands. Last, it allowed for integration of the development process with a continuous integration and deployment (CI/CD) pipeline so that each new change submitted by a contributor is tested and reviewed before being merged into the main branch, and then can be automatically deployed to demonstration instances.

The overall architecture of the agent and its simulated environment is show in Fig. 19.1. The left side of the diagram depicts the agent itself, and the right side shows the environmental components included in the demonstration. The

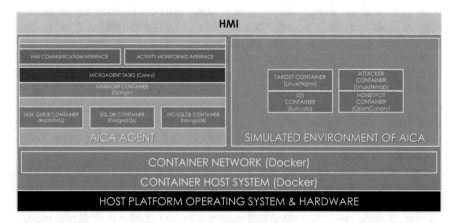

Fig. 19.1 AICAproto21 technical architecture. (Credit: Paul Theron and the AICA Prototype 2021 Consortium)

Human-Machine Interface (HMI) for the agent is built in the Django Python web framework (with a Gunicorn web frontend) and forms the basis of the Manager container. This is a commonly used framework with a broad community of contributors and users, allows for integrations with a number of other components, and provides an overall model-template-view pattern that lends itself to easily building HMI components as necessary. It is integrated with the Celery task queue system (in the same container) for dispatching individual agent tasks as necessary in an asynchronous and multi-threaded manner.

Micro-agents within the AICA architecture are defined as Python classes which are either called directly by the Manager or dispatched as Celery tasks (depending on whether asynchronous processing is required). Celery also supports scheduling of tasks for any repetitive actions that must be done without being explicitly invoked by the manager or another micro-agent. Upon startup of the agent, Gunicorn and Celery are started. The initial Celery task starts the Offline Loader micro-agent, which loads static configuration files (or eventually other data sources) and then calls the main Decision-Making Engine loop. This may instantiate other tasks (in our example monitoring for intrusion detection system (IDS) alerts), as required. Micro-agents defined include:

- Offline Loader – upon instantiation of an agent, this loads any pre-configured or cached information needed by the agent. For the prototype this read from a YAML file to configure an action of "honeypot" for any signature indicated in an IDS alert.
- Decision Making Engine – the primary task for the agent that instantiates other "startup" tasks and is notified by other agents when an important event is observed so that it can coordinate decisions about potential actions, evaluate their acceptability, and determine the best course of action.
- Behavior Engine – defines and/or adjudicates acceptable behaviors for the agent. In the prototype, this simply defines all responses as acceptable except for any activity which would break the prototype by blocking internal network communications.
- Knowledge Base – serves as the nexus for retrieving and storing information necessary to maintain world-state and configuration. In the prototype this interacted with the NoSQL instance (see below) to retrieve acceptable actions for observed events.
- Online Learning – this will serve as the nexus for all dynamic attributes of the agent as pertains to updating "intelligent" behaviors based on observed events. It was only implemented as a stub in the prototype and no actual functionality was implemented.
- Collaboration – provides mechanisms to interact with external systems and other AICA agents. In the prototype, this was limited to monitoring IDS alerts and initiating honeypot redirect actions, but no inter-agent collaboration was implemented.

The manager relies on three other containers to perform agent tasks. The first is a task queue, which is closely integrated with the Celery system above. RabbitMQ is used for this system, as it is again a common and well-supported tool for this purpose. Though in this prototype it is used only for task queuing, it provides the ability to facilitate additional inter-agent message queues in the future as required. The second is a relational database, used both to support the Django application and for any other relational storage required to support the agent's operations (i.e., storing configuration or knowledge data). In the prototype demonstration, the well-known database PostgreSQL was chosen. Third, as some types of data are more appropriate for storage without a relational structure (i.e., dictionaries or other key-value-type stores), a MongoDB "NoSQL" (or DocumentDB) container is instantiated. These three containers will also be complimented by a GraphDB mechanism such as Neo4J as the prototype continues to be developed.

5   Demonstration Scenario and Results

The AICA agent is written in a way to lend itself to external integrations, but for prototype demonstration purposes a self-contained environment was desired. The scenario to be used was an attacker port-scanning a target webserver, an IDS detecting the scan, the AICA agent observing the IDS detection, and the agent informing the victim to redirect all traffic from the origin of the port scan to a honeypot system. This is a simple scenario, to be sure, but serves to demonstrate most of the components of the AICA agent without requiring separate lines of inquiry into more speculative or research-focused capabilities. This scenario is outlined in Fig. 19.2.

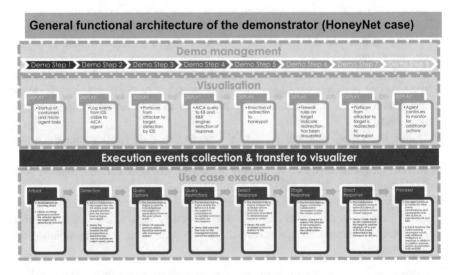

Fig. 19.2 AICAproto21 demonstration scenario. (Credit: Paul Theron and the AICA Prototype 2021 Consortium)

To facilitate this scenario, as shown in Fig. 19.1, several additional containers were created in the containerized test environment. The attacker was an Alpine Linux container with nmap. This simply allows the operator to invoke a shell (from the Makefile) and manually run scans. While the invocation of scans could have been automated, it was desired to have control over this to ensure demonstrations could be paced appropriately.

The target was an Alpine Linux container with Nginx (an HTTP daemon), iptables, and ipset. Nginx merely hosted its default webpage; no customization was done. The iptables firewall served as the basis for the redirection capability, which was achieved by creating a group in ipset for origin hosts to be redirected that expired after 5 min. In this way, ipset can be used to add or remove hosts from redirection without any changes to the iptables ruleset, which would be difficult to track and keep in a consistent state.

The IDS was an Alpine Linux container with the Suricata IDS. This was configured to update its rules from the Emerging Threats database upon startup, as well as setting the HOME_NET variable in Suricata's configuration file to include only the target host. This container shared a /var./log/suricata volume with the Manager container. In this directory, the eve.json file contained any output from Suricata regarding detected events, including signature alerts. In this way the Manager was able to watch for these alerts without any additional network configuration or application program interface (API) development.

The Honeypot was an Alpine Linux container with OpenCanary. Minimal configuration changes were made to this instance for demonstration purposes, though this is a highly extensible tool. It could be configured to emulate several different types of hosts and services, instead of the Synology network-attached storage (NAS) presented by default. Upon initial startup, using Secure Shell Protocol (SSH) port redirection proxied via the Attacker container, the operator can browse to the Target container's website and get the default Nginx webpage. After giving Suricata a couple of minutes to finish initializing, the operator then runs an nmap scan from the attacker. If the eve.json Suricata log is being observed manually during this time, the alert message can be observed (though it might require output filtering to catch due to the volume of output in this log!). When this alert is logged, the Collaboration micro-agent also sees it. It is configured to watch for any 'alert' events in this file and pass them on to the Decision-Making Engine via the handle_alert method.

The handle_alert method passes the alert object (which is formatted in JSON in the Suricata output and represented as a dictionary in Python) to the Knowledge Base micro-agent to query for available response actions for this type of event. For demonstration purposes, the only available action is defined as "honeypot" and is returned as the only recommendation action option for all signature identifications (IDs) presented from Suricata alert events. This could return multiple options in future iterations. The Decision-Making Engine receives this response and queries the Behavior Engine for each response option (only one here) to determine if it should proceed with that option. Based on the recommendation options that are approved, the Decision-Making Engine then determines the best among them. In future iterations this would likely interact with the online learning, knowledge base, and collaboration micro-agents at this phase for determining the best option; for the demonstration it simply takes the first approved action – i.e., redirect the "attacker" to the honeypot. The Decision-Making Engine then invokes the Collaboration micro-agent redirect_to_honeypot_iptables tasks with the attacker and target internet protocol addresses (IPs) indicated in the alert.

The Collaboration micro-agent creates an SSH connection to the target (authentication keypairs are set up at startup of the agent), and then sends a single command to add the attacker's IP address to the honeypot-redirect list using ipset. This will persist for five minutes unless triggered again. Although the realism of a target handling redirection of an attacker is low, this avoided the need for a more complicated software-defined network configuration or intermediate router/firewall container. If the operator then browses to the Target again from the same attacker-proxied connection, the Synology NAS website from OpenCanary is returned.

This level of functionality is what might be referred to as a "minimum viable product" in the software industry. It is still a long way from a fully functioning AICA implementation but provides the basis to validate the basic micro-agent interactions, demonstrate the concept to collaborators and sponsors for feedback, and make architectural or implementation changes without incurring large losses of completed work. It also "stubs out" all of the interfaces where more advanced functionality will be incorporated in a way that can be modularly developed by a community of collaborators with minimal interdependencies that might add friction to parallel lines of research and development. It is a foundation upon which future development can easily build.

6   Future Capabilities

As work on this prototype continues, there are three primary areas of focus. First is to expand beyond just commodity Linux (or, in theory Windows/MacOS given Docker compatibility) systems on consumer hardware and evaluate the functionality of an AICA agent on different platforms. An easy next step would be "fleets" of endpoints or servers as it would be a direct extension of the existing functionality and provide ample opportunities for evaluation of collaborative strategies. However, the current container-based architecture might be too heavy to be reasonable installed on systems with other primary purposes, so a decision must be made as to whether to build a more monolithic and "lightweight" agent for deployment to these systems or focus on installing AICA "patrol agents" into key vantage points in defender networks.

A slightly further extension would be to critical infrastructure (CI) systems, including embedded systems. A portion of CI systems would run on platforms very similar, if not the same, as the endpoint and server devices above. Embedded devices present new challenges in terms of low resource availability but are likely to run on

Linux-based platforms, so compatibility is not a concern. Still, the prevention of impact to CI systems is paramount due to their safety-critical nature, so that would need to be a primary focus. Critical infrastructure networks might also lack reliable connectivity for agents to intercommunicate or communicate with human operators. Getting test hardware for these applications will require collaborations with manufactures due to cost and licensing, but simulation may also be a reasonable alternative.

A similar challenge would be deploying AICA agents to unmanned autonomous system (UAS) such as drones or automated vehicles. Again, they are safety-critical and have unreliable connectivity, but they might have higher processing capabilities than a CI-type (i.e., industrial control system (ICS) or internet of things (IOT) system. This of course depends greatly on the type of device in question. A consumer-grade drone is unlikely to have much processing power (or energy storage) to spare, but a passenger vehicle, commercial vehicle, or military drone potentially could. Again, access to hardware is likely to be an obstacle to this line on inquiry. An extension of this area would be into weapons platforms which would have very similar needs, but of course much higher requirements for safe operation; and of course, the difficulty procuring such platforms is likely to be high as well.

A scenario that incorporates many of the challenges above but is of primary interest to the authors is that of space-based platforms. As the proliferation of governmental, commercial, academic, and privately-owned devices in space continues to increase, the threat of adversarial action cannot be ignored. They combine multiple attributes of the systems above: they may have unreliable communications (or very high latency), may have very low resource availability or energy budget, might run on proprietary platforms, and are likely to be difficult to obtain and evaluate. However, lower-cost options such as "microsatellites" might be a good place to start to get an initial feeling for this area, and the communication oddities of space can be largely simulated.

The second major area of focus for additional development will be the incorporation of knowledge representation, learning and decision making, and more complex definitions of rules and objectives. In the current prototype, a static ruleset is used with a very simple decision-making process. Incorporating knowledge graphs and semantic reasoning capabilities will be a very valuable line of research. Investigating current frontiers in machine learning research such as graph-based neural networks and the application of convolutional neural networks (CNNs) to intrusion detection is also likely to pay dividends.

Third, a taxonomy of detection and response agents, their actions, and their interfaces is needed to build out the interfaces between an AICA agent and its environment. We desire to expand supported interactions beyond the IDS/Honeypot scenario to incorporate (e.g.) malware, user interaction, moving-target defenses, or active defenses. This will help overcome some of the integration challenges, namely that it is difficult to generalize from system to system when developing interfaces, and that one must have a tight definition of the interface and expectations for possible actions and responses.

7 Summary and Conclusions

The development of this prototype, and a more full-featured testbed environment, will provide the basis for collaborative research into this area going forward. Early testing shows that commodity components can be readily combined to create a basic framework for this work, and simple, static cases of behavior rules and response behaviors can be constructed without great effort. A central question as the authors look ahead to production deployments is whether these savings in effort (and gains in flexibility) offset the potential performance and compatibility issues of running a multi-container deployment on defender systems or networks.

Examples of how this prototype can support research into other areas of this book are described in Table 19.1. To fully realize the potential of this prototype

Table 19.1 AICAproto21 as a testbed for ideas in this book

Architectural Approaches	AICAproto21 demonstrates just one potential architecture. The modular nature of its development and deployment into the containerized environment will allow alternate approaches to be evaluated.
Perception of Environment, Situational Understanding and Diagnostics	The virtualized nature of the AICA agent and the general framework including the online learning and collaboration micro-agents will allow for various environmental scenarios and co-resident systems to be tested and incorporated into the AICA agent's capabilities.
Perception of Threat, Learning about the Adversary, Defense by Deception	The virtualized nature of the AICA agent and the CI/CD development methodology will allow for hostile and even destructive actions to be evaluated in the environment, with the ability to easily reset and rebuild the environment from scratch before each experiment.
Response Planning, Recovery Planning, Adaptivity & Antifragility, Negotiation & Collaboration, Forming Effective Teams	The architecture of the AICA agent and its simulated test environment lends itself well to the execution of predefined scenarios – whether automatically or manually executed. The Django web frontend provides an easy foundation on which to build additional instrumentation for the agent itself, and a wide variety of other tools can be obtained from Dockerhub or installed onto a Linux-based container.
Human Interactions, Command in AICA-intensive Operations	The developed prototype utilizes Django as a human-machine interface (HMI) framework. This will allow extensible implementations of input and output capabilities, as well as API integrations with other tools.
Development Challenges, Deployment and Operation	The developed architecture has been designed with extensibility and low-friction deployment in mind. It will lend itself well to incorporation with modern software development best practices and methodologies, and easily be extensible (even if through a fork) to enable deployments to different environments, as needed.
Risk Management, Developing Trust, Policy Issues	The key to developing the trust needed to allow policy formation around automated agents comes down to being able to quantify the risks of the technology through technical validation. Having this agent framework, and extending it overtime, will allow the types of experimentation needed to add clarity to these discussions and develop the appropriate standards, guidelines, and safeguards.

technology, it will be necessary to example its capabilities to include more sophisticated learning and reasoning, inputs and outputs, and evaluate its potential for varying deployment scenarios.

Acknowledgements The work presented in this chapter was partially supported by the U.S. Department of Energy, Office of Science under DOE contract number DE-AC02-06CH11357. The submitted manuscript has been created by UChicago Argonne, LLC, operator of Argonne National Laboratory. Argonne, a DOE Office of Science laboratory, is operated under Contract No. DE-AC02-06CH11357. The U.S. Government retains for itself, and others acting on its behalf, a paid-up nonexclusive, irrevocable worldwide license in said article to reproduce, prepare derivative works, distribute copies to the public, and perform publicly and display publicly, by or on behalf of the Government.

References

Bellifemine, F., Poggi, A., & Rimassa, G. (2001). Developing multi-agent systems with JADE. In C. Castelfranchi & Y. Lespérance (Eds.), *Intelligent agents VII agent theories architectures and languages* (pp. 89–103). Springer. https://doi.org/10.1007/3-540-44631-1_7

Beydoun, G., Low, G., Henderson-Sellers, B., Mouratidis, H., Gomez-Sanz, J. J., Pavon, J., & Gonzalez-Perez, C. (2009). FAML: A generic metamodel for MAS development. *IEEE Transactions on Software Engineering, 35*(6), 841–863. https://doi.org/10.1109/TSE.2009.34

Blakely, B., Horsthemke, W., Poczatec, A., Nowak, L., & Evans, N. (2019). Moving target, deception, and other adaptive defenses. In C. Rieger, I. Ray, Q. Zhu, & M. A. Haney (Eds.), *Industrial control systems security and resiliency: Practice and theory* (pp. 95–118). Springer. https://doi.org/10.1007/978-3-030-18214-4_6

Bresciani, P., Perini, A., Giorgini, P., Giunchiglia, F., & Mylopoulos, J. (2004). Tropos: An agent-oriented software development methodology. *Autonomous Agents and Multi-Agent Systems, 8*(3), 203–236. https://doi.org/10.1023/B:AGNT.0000018806.20944.ef

Briskin, G., Fayette, D., Evancich, N., Rajabian-Schwart, V., Macera, A., & Li, J. (2016). Design considerations for building cyber deception systems. In S. Jajodia, V. S. Subrahmanian, V. Swarup, & C. Wang (Eds.), *Cyber deception: Building the scientific foundation* (pp. 69–80). Springer International Publishing. https://doi.org/10.1007/978-3-319-32699-3

Cossentino, M., Gaud, N., Hilaire, V., Galland, S., & Koukam, A. (2010). ASPECS: An agent-oriented software process for engineering complex systems: How to design agent societies under a holonic perspective. *Autonomous Agents and Multi-Agent Systems, 20*(2), 260–304. https://doi.org/10.1007/s10458-009-9099-4

De Gaspari, F., Jajodia, S., Mancini, L. V., & Panico, A. (2016). AHEAD: A new architecture for active defense. In *Proceedings of the 2016 ACM workshop on automated decision making for active cyber defense* (pp. 11–16). https://doi.org/10.1145/2994475.2994481

García-Sánchez, F., Valencia-García, R., Martínez-Béjar, R., & Fernández-Breis, J. T. (2009). An ontology, intelligent agent-based framework for the provision of semantic web services. *Expert Systems with Applications, 36*(2), 3167–3187. https://doi.org/10.1016/j.eswa.2008.01.037

Introduction to STIX. (n.d.). Retrieved February 21, 2022, from https://oasis-open.github.io/cti-documentation/stix/intro

Introduction to TAXII. (n.d.). Retrieved February 21, 2022, from https://oasis-open.github.io/cti-documentation/taxii/intro.html

Kazil, J., Masad, D., & Crooks, A. (2020). Utilizing python for agent-based modeling: The mesa framework. In R. Thomson, H. Bisgin, C. Dancy, A. Hyder, & M. Hussain (Eds.), *Social, cultural, and behavioral modeling* (pp. 308–317). Springer International Publishing. https://doi.org/10.1007/978-3-030-61255-9_30

Kendrick, P., Criado, N., Hussain, A., & Randles, M. (2018). A self-organising multi-agent system for decentralised forensic investigations. *Expert Systems with Applications, 102*, 12–26. https://doi.org/10.1016/j.eswa.2018.02.023

Kott, A., Thomas, R., Drašar, M., Kont, M., Poylisher, A., Blakely, B., Theron, P., Evans, N., Leslie, N., Singh, R., Rigaki, M., Yang, S. J., LeBlanc, B., Losiewicz, P., Hourlier, S., Blowers, M., Harney, H., Wehner, G., Guarino, A., et al. (2018). Toward intelligent autonomous agents for cyber defense: Report of the 2017 Workshop by the North Atlantic Treaty Organization (NATO) Research Group IST-152-RTG. *ArXiv:1804.07646 [Cs]*. http://arxiv.org/abs/1804.07646

Kott, A., Théron, P., Mancini, L. V., Dushku, E., Panico, A., Drašar, M., LeBlanc, B., Losiewicz, P., Guarino, A., Pihelgas, M., & Rzadca, K. (2020). An introductory preview of autonomous intelligent cyber-defense agent reference architecture, release 2.0. *The Journal of Defense Modeling and Simulation, 17*(1), 51–54. https://doi.org/10.1177/1548512919886163

Luke, S. (2019). *Multiagent simulation and the MASON library*. George Mason University. https://cs.gmu.edu/~eclab/projects/mason/manual.pdf

Melo, L. S., Sampaio, R. F., Leão, R. P. S., Barroso, G. C., & Bezerra, J. R. (2019). Python-based multi-agent platform for application on power grids. *International Transactions on Electrical Energy Systems, 29*(6), e12012. https://doi.org/10.1002/2050-7038.12012

Molina-Markham, A., Winder, R. K., & Ridley, A. (2021). Network Defense is not a game. *ArXiv:2104.10262 [Cs]*. http://arxiv.org/abs/2104.10262

OsBrain—0.6.5—OsBrain 0.6.5 documentation. (n.d.). Retrieved February 21, 2022, from https://osbrain.readthedocs.io/en/stable/

Padgham, L., & Winikoff, M. (2003). Prometheus: A methodology for developing intelligent agents. In F. Giunchiglia, J. Odell, & G. Weiß (Eds.), *Agent-oriented software engineering III* (pp. 174–185). Springer. https://doi.org/10.1007/3-540-36540-0_14

Pavón, J., & Gómez-Sanz, J. (2003). Agent oriented software engineering with INGENIAS. In V. Mařík, M. Pěchouček, & J. Müller (Eds.), *Multi-agent systems and applications III* (Vol. 2691, pp. 394–403). Springer. https://doi.org/10.1007/3-540-45023-8_38

Pawlick, J., Colbert, E., & Zhu, Q. (2019). A game-theoretic taxonomy and survey of defensive deception for cybersecurity and privacy. *ACM Computing Surveys, 52*(4), 1–28. https://doi.org/10.1145/3337772

Shiang, C. W., & Sterling, L. (2008). Analysis and design of multi agent knowledge development process. In *19th Australian Conference on Software Engineering (Aswec 2008)* (pp. 402–411). https://doi.org/10.1109/ASWEC.2008.4483229

Standen, M., Lucas, M., Bowman, D., Richer, T. J., Kim, J., & Marriott, D. (2021). CybORG: A Gym for the development *of autonomous cyber agents*. *ArXiv:2108.09118 [Cs]*. http://arxiv.org/abs/2108.09118

Wilensky, U. (1999). *NetLogo. Center for connected learning and computer-based modeling, Northwestern University*. Northwestern University. https://ccl.northwestern.edu/netlogo/

Wooldridge, M., Jennings, N. R., & Kinny, D. (2000). The Gaia methodology for agent-oriented analysis and design. *Autonomous Agents and Multi-Agent Systems, 3*(3), 285–312. https://doi.org/10.1023/A:1010071910869

Xu, J., Guo, P., Zhao, M., Erbacher, R. F., Zhu, M., & Liu, P. (2014). Comparing different moving target defense techniques. In *Proceedings of the first ACM workshop on moving target defense* (pp. 97–107). https://doi.org/10.1145/2663474.2663486

Zaffarano, K., Taylor, J., & Hamilton, S. (2015). A quantitative framework for moving target defense effectiveness evaluation. In *Proceedings of the second ACM workshop on moving target defense* (pp. 3–10). https://doi.org/10.1145/2808475.2808476

Zhuang, R., DeLoach, S. A., & Ou, X. (2014). Towards a theory of moving target defense. In *Proceedings of the first ACM workshop on moving target defense* (pp. 31–40). https://doi.org/10.1145/2663474.2663479

Chapter 20
Case Study B: AI Agents for the Tactical Edge

Pierre Trepagnier and Allan Wollaber

1 Introduction to the Tactical Edge

What is the tactical edge? It is commonly described as the "tip of the spear (Joint Staff, 2005)," where combat actually takes place. The tactical edge is thus obviously of immense importance in warfighting. However, so far relatively little attention has been given in academic literature to the study of AI agents there. One can easily sympathize with this state of affairs. Academic research tends to take place in what we shall refer to as "the center," as opposed to "the edge." In the center, computing resources and network connectivity are both plentiful, and researchers are generally concerned with pushing forward the state-of-the-art rather than considering how to make do with limited resources. It is the purpose of this chapter to make a small effort to rectify the situation, by first considering the edge and its limitations as opposed to the center, and then presenting a specific example of an AI Agent which can be deployed there. We begin by contrasting "the edge" with "the center" in a number of relevant dimensions. Note that we will be using "the center" in this discussion in an overloaded sense, referring to both to "center-academic", where academic research takes place, as mentioned above, and to "center-warfighter" where large scale units are based, as will be discussed below. In both cases, at the center resources are generally plentiful, and so there is no need to lift the degeneracy. When necessary, however, we will be careful to make the distinction clear.

P. Trepagnier (✉)
Cyber Security and Information Sciences Division, MIT Lincoln Laboratory,
Lexington, MA, USA
e-mail: ptrepagnier@ll.mit.edu

A. Wollaber
Artificial Intelligence Technology, MIT Lincoln Laboratory, Lexington, MA, USA
e-mail: allan.wollaber@ll.mit.edu

In warfare, the "center" is characterized large units (corps and above) and permanent or semi-permanent bases and concomitant infrastructure, as opposed to the "edge," which consists of smaller units, transient basing, and higher mobility. More important, from the point of view of AI agents, is the character of the computing resources on which they depend. We will explore these resources in greater detail.

MITRE has produced a Tactical Edge Characterization Network (Dandashi et al., 2007) which, although somewhat dated, is still very valuable, as they pay close attention to the computational and networking issues which limit and define the roles of AI agents the tactical edge. MITRE enumerates the four major dimensions which constrain the environment as (Dandashi et al., 2007)

- Network characteristics

  - Connectivity fraction
  - Bandwidth
  - Latency

- Resource availability

  - Processing power
  - Storage capacity
  - Size, Weight, and Power (SWaP)

- Information assurance
- User interface considerations

However, MITRE's scope is broader than ours; we will concentrate on the first two major dimensions, as they are the key drivers of AI agents' characteristics at the edge, at the expense of the information assurance and user interface considerations.

1.1 Network Characteristics

The first key insight is that as one gets further from the center and towards the edge, all three network characteristics degrade. In a center environment with enterprise-type connectivity, connectivity will be >99%; outages will be exceptional events. Bandwidth will be at the gigabit/s level. Latency will be less than a millisecond. None of these levels will be present at the tactical edge. Connectivity and bandwidth will in general be dependent on radio frequency (RF) rather than wired physical layers, reducing both. Connectivity will be supplied by means such as satellite communication, cell phones, point-to-point radio, or high frequency radio for over-the-horizon communications if satellite communication is not available. However, all of these methods of supplying communication to the edge will be degraded in each of the sub-dimensions of connectivity fraction, bandwidth, and latency as compared to what is available at the center.

1.2   Computing Resources

Turning our attention to resource availability, we note the edge is in a similarly disadvantaged state relative to the center as was the case with network characteristics. The center has access to enormous amounts of processing power and storage capacity, which can be scaled as necessary (for example AWS). Size, weight, and power (SWaP) is not generally an issue at all at the center; because of the high connectivity and bandwidth mentioned earlier, the actual resources can be located remotely in purpose-built data centers with access to cheap power. The edge's disadvantages in network characteristics spills over into resource availability; because of spotty connectivity and low bandwidth the edge needs to have its resources physically at hand in order to guarantee availability. Thus, compute power may be limited to a few rack units (U)s of server space in the case of mobile units, and even less for dismount (i.e. foot) units.

Another key aspect of the tactical edge is that, disadvantaged as it is in peacetime, in terms of network characteristics it becomes even more so in times of actual combat. Connectivity, latency, and bandwidth may all suffer at the tactical edge in current stressing adversarial scenarios. As a prudential aspect of planning, connectivity to the center should be assumed to be seriously impacted or eliminated entirely for substantial periods of time in the case of actual hostilities. In short, AI at the tactical edge is important to the warfighter, but the conditions there are far from ideal for AI, and are becoming more precarious over time. Figure 20.1, which is a re-work and simplification of work presented in (Schulz & Trepagnier, 2020), summarizes the situation. Here it is necessary to lift the "center" degeneracy mentioned above. Note that we assume that hostilities are not taking place on US soil, and thus that network characteristics are unaffected for that part of the center, which included

Evaluation Category	CENTER		EDGE	
	CONUS	OCONUS Base	Mobile	Dismount
Peacetime				
Connectivity	High	High	Intermittent	Poor
Bandwidth	High	High	Medium	Low
Latency	Low	Low	Medium	Higher
Processing Power	Very Large	Very Large	Small Servers	Handhelds
Storage Capacity	Very Large	Very Large	Few Terabytes	Few Gigabytes
SWaP	Unlimited	Unlimited	Cu Yd/Small Generators	Cu Ft/Batteries
Increasing Tension to Active Hostilities				
Connectivity	High	Medium	Poor	Very Low/Zero
Bandwidth	High	Medium	Degraded	Very Low/Zero
Latency	Low	Medium	Increased	High
Processing Power	Very Large	Large	Small Servers	Handhelds
Storage Capacity	Very Large	Large	Few Terabytes	Few Gigabytes
SWaP	Unlimited	Limited	Cu Yd/Small Generators	Cu Ft/Batteries

Fig. 20.1 Comparison of network and computing resources available to Tactical Edge vs. Center. Center is subdivided into CONUS and OCONUS Base, reflecting the fact that as tensions rise, even large bases outside the continental US may be impacted

both the center-academic and part of the center-warfighter. However, bases outside of the US, even if normally considered as part of the center-warfighter, may be impacted as tensions rise. Thus, we break the center into CONUS (within the continental US) and OCONUS (outside it). The forgoing assumption of CONUS immunity may be optimistic for adversaries with sophisticated offensive cyber capabilities, but the edge, not the center, is the focus of this chapter. We also assume that local computing resources at the edge, as opposed to network resources, remain unchanged.

2   AI Agents at the Tactical Edge

In order to design any autonomous agent at the tactical edge, it is useful to consider the framework of Fig. 20.2, which depicts a hierarchical framework building towards true AI autonomy (automated, consequence-informed decision-making) or human-machine teaming (HMT) and is an adaptation of the well-known DIKW (Data, Information, Knowledge, Wisdom) hierarchy. "Data" and "basic visibility" form the foundation of the problem and capability, and "AI" with "autonomy" or "HMT" form the peak. In the information age, it is easy to become seduced by the idea that one could jump from mission data to autonomy.

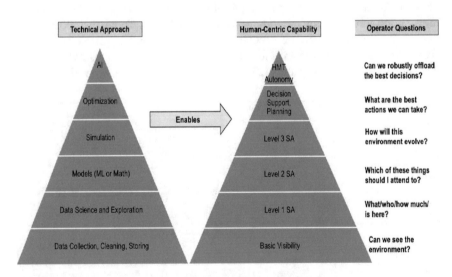

Fig. 20.2 Notional hierarchy relating human-centric capabilities (and corresponding operator questions) that are enabled by increasingly sophisticated technical approaches. The Situation Awareness (SA) levels on the right correspond to the 3-level Endsley model, which roughly signify an ability to discern elements in the environment, to comprehend the current situation, and to forward-project the current conditions, all of which require more sophisticated technical capabilities, with an AI agent becoming possible no earlier than the "Models" or "Level 2 SA" level

However, we believe that any tactical edge capability first needs to consider the potential impact to operators or stakeholders in that environment, as is evidenced by the "Operator Questions" at the right in Fig. 20.2. If operators at the tactical edge do not have deployed sensors and data collection, they are operating blind.

The first step in the technical approach is to instrument the environment and regularize the data, which is a task for data engineers. Achieving this step allows development to move up the pyramid into the realm of data science, which can begin to provide what is indicated as "Level 1 Situation Awareness (SA)". The listed SA levels (Endsley, 1995) correspond to the 3-level Endsley model of situation awareness (SA) (Shakarami et al., 2020), in which level 1 signifies perception of elements in the environment, level 2 signifies comprehension of the current situation, and level 3 signifies an ability to project the current conditions into a future status.

From the perspective of the capabilities in Fig. 20.2, these capabilities correspond to an ability to discern and track interacting entities from their data signals, assign them relevance and priorities, and forecast what may happen given the current situation, respectively. Having achieved an ability to track entities, it then becomes possible to deploy mathematical models or train machine learning (ML) models to provide functions that can associate the entities with contexts, such as whether an entity has been seen before, whether it is has features that are known to be "good" or "bad". This is the first level at which ML analytics or dashboards become useful, although operators retain full responsibility for taking any response actions.

At the next level, some form of "simulation" can enable level 3 SA, although this does not necessarily imply a full time-dependent model if consequences can reasonably be estimated by allowing discovered, "bad" entities from level 2 SA to persist. Arguably, this is the first level at which an AI agent (in the simplest sense) can begin to operate, and we will focus on capabilities from this level and up for the remainder of the paper. An example of this would be an antivirus software, pretrained on malware behaviors, detecting a suspicious executable and preemptively sandboxing it from access to the network.

Moving up one more level, having an ability to forward-project hypothetical scenarios with potential differences via simulation enables optimization approaches according to a mission-relevant metric. This can help the operator choose a best approach among several options and determine an optimal course-of-action (COA), either during a planning phase or in real time. Alternatively, this optimization approach can become the basis of a reinforcement learning (RL) procedure to train an AI agent that is equipped with an ability to perform response actions either on its own or alongside the operator in a human-machine team, which represents the peak technical approach in Fig. 20.2.

2.1 AI Characteristics Relevant to the Tactical Edge

In general, one cannot develop and deploy the entire framework on the tactical edge given the resource and time constraints, and the alert reader should recognize that several assumptions are naturally embedded within the course of development from the base to the peak of this framework. One is that a substantial fraction of the data at the base level must be (in some sense) stationary or invariant, in order for any of the above structure to retain meaning between development time and deployment (Endsley, 1995). All models possess an inherent time constant, Δt, over which they can remain valid before they "go stale"; this property can be highly domain dependent, particularly for cyber or EW applications. Returning to the example of malware, one can consider the time scale for a specific set of malware signatures as compared with models that label network protocols: new malware and software patches are developed every day, such that a months-old malware library could become mostly irrelevant, but network protocols tend to be developed over months or years. If Δt is sufficiently small (e.g., on the order of hours or days), it can become impractical or impossible to deploy a trustworthy AI agent, although one may still offer marginal utility.

Another factor is that the data and models used to build up the technical approaches needs to be transferable to the specific environment on the tactical edge, whether that be through transfer learning in the usual sense (Schulz et al., 2019) or fine tuning (Weiss et al., 2016). Note that transfer learning can be quite general in that networks trained on image classification tasks can be adapted for cybersecurity problems such as malware classification using ResNet50 (Guo et al., 2018). As an example of "fine tuning", consider a deep neural network (DNN) classifier that accurately learns to associate radio-frequency (RF) signals with a large variety of specific devices; this would be considered a "pre-training" step. If the model were deployed to a location with novel RF emitters, it is necessary to add these labels and retrain a subset of the DNN weights, thereby fine-tuning the DNN to the new, but related task. Chen et al. (2019) elucidate an example of this approach for cyber-physical transportation systems (Rezende et al., 2017). However, deep neural networks (DNN)s can easily outstrip available compute resources for learning (and even inference) on the tactical edge, with recent pre-trained language models such as GPT-3 famously reaching hundreds of billions of parameters.

2.2 Tactical Edge Conditions and Resultant Needs

In considering deployment scenarios on the tactical edge, we envisage scenarios constrained by Space, Weight and Power (SWaP) limitations, an inability to operate at scale, and extremely limited connectivity to data centers. Examples include space and underwater applications, as well as networking equipment at remote outposts. It is worth pointing out that in certain scenarios, depending on the severity of these constraints, it is possible to judiciously offload certain tasks to "cloud" or "fog" computing capabilities (Endsley, 1995), making use of internet-of-things (IoT) or mobile edge computing devices (Li et al., 2018), but we do not focus on those scenarios here. We also presume that we cannot defer tactical edge deployments until revolutionary technologies such as neuromorphic computing (with its potential to vastly reduce SWaP requirements) are extant (Marković et al., 2020). The fundamental requirements, then, are to design AI agents that are as robust and resilient as is achievable over their deployment period, require minimal compute resources, and degrade gracefully. Because these requirements can be at odds with each other, a balance must be struck.

By robustness, we consider the definition in the initial draft of the NIST framework, which includes assessing a model's "sensitivity in uncontrollable factors", as well as "error measurements on novel datasets."(NIST, 2022) In particular, we stress that any deployed edge model must also be trained to be aware of its uncertainties with respect to "out-of-distribution" (OOD) data, i.e. data it has never seen before and in-distribution data, i.e. data similar to those on which it has been trained. That is, the models must aware enough of their own ignorance to reduce the likelihood of over-confident predictions on novel data, and their predictions on in-distribution data should be accompanied with calibrated probabilities (Hüllermeier & Waegeman, 2021). Recent advances in machine learning have made this possible. This is one mechanism by which a deployed AI agent can degrade gracefully, as it can signal to operators the prevalence of any drift due to data staleness or relevant examples of datapoints that are highly uncertain. Robustness also implies that there should be an ability to "move up the pyramid" in Fig. 20.2, which should help the model finetune in its deployed scenario, likely with human assistance in the near future to ensure model resilience.

Resilience refers to the ability of a model to withstand not only data drift or novelty, but adversarial attack (NIST, 2022) Uncertainty quantification alone is likely insufficient to address this vulnerability. However, it is possible to "red team" a model before deployment with a suite of known adversarial attacks, which should enhance resilience. Fortunately, fewer-parameter models (i.e., models that are less susceptible to overfitting) tend to be more resilient, which also helps with SWaP constraints by reducing required memory and computation. Active or unsupervised learning implementations must be considered carefully in such environments as a motivated and patient adversary could eventually learn a way to poison the model.

2.3   Discussion

In general, if warfighters at the edge are to be confident that they have AIs they can depend on in times of conflict, they require AIs running on equipment also at the edge and under their direct control. Maximal resilience at the edge depends on not attempting to use AI agents that require significant compute power or any but the most minimal communications. Cloud computing, for instance, is out of the question.

There are additional subtleties having to do with model training and stability as well as compute power. A stable model that requires large resources to train is not problematic if it can be trained at the center and then run at the edge with available data and compute power. The following technical illustration will provide a concrete example of many of these issues.

3 Technical Illustration: AI Agents for Blue Force RF Situational Awareness (BFSA)

3.1 Introduction

As a technical illustration of the concept of AI agents at the tactical edge, this section will discuss the automation of Blue Force Spectrum Awareness (BFSA).[1] In this context, we will use "BFSA" to refer to situational awareness in the radio frequency (RF) domain. In many aspects of warfare, warfighters will communicate using RF, which adversaries can pick up and use against them. Thus warfighters require a real-time RF monitoring capability to effectively manage modern adversary threats. Experience has shown that RF emissions can leak important information about activities and plans to an adversary if not monitored. Questions of particular importance at the tactical edge include

- Are my actual emissions consistent with communication plans?
- Are anomalous emissions present?
- Am I under attack?

Before turning to our example, however, it behooves us to tie BFSA back to the concept of cyber AI agents. Consider the Cyber/Electronic Warfare (EW) matrix shown in Fig. 20.3.

AI agents in warfare are normally concerned with the lower right cell, in which the domains of action and effect are both cyber. In the case of BFSA, the cell of interest is lower left. AI agents will be having effects in the RF domain. As discussed in the first section, this approach is a consequence of the disadvantaged nature of the tactical edge, in which RF bears most or all of the communications burden. Accordingly, AI Agents need leave their natural realm in cyber to cause effects in the EW domain.

---

[1] For those unfamiliar with US military terminology, "Blue" refers to our forces; "Red" refers to adversary forces. "Own Force Spectrum Awareness" is occasionally seen as a synonym for BFSA.

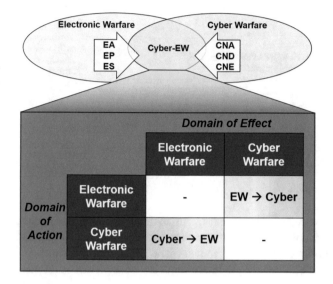

Fig. 20.3 Cyber and EW matrix of possibilities

3.2 State of the Art Prior to AI

Current practice is to utilize specially trained personnel and special equipment to conduct BFSA. It generally requires a combination of Signature Management (SIGMAN) and Signals Intelligence (SIGINT) personnel to gather energy across the RF spectrum and evaluate it for answers to the three questions outlined above. There are obvious limitations to this approach. The most important are

- It does not scale, as it requires manual operation and interpretation by limited numbers of trained personnel
- It is not suited to the tactical edge, which is characterized by limited numbers of warfighters in geographically separated units. These would be ill-served by a central SIGMAN platoon.
- In a tension to openly hostile situation, the SIGINT personnel's attention will have likely shifted away from BFSA leaving the SIGMAN personnel unserved.

3.3 Program Goal

In order to mitigate this problem, MIT Lincoln Laboratory is currently participating in a program to automate BFSA, utilizing an AI–based approach. The goal of the program is to permit an inexperienced user to easily check for compliance with expected RF emissions, thereby getting rapid situational awareness of the RF space. The AI agent will convey the current status as compared to plan, plus indications of

Event: New Unexpected Detection

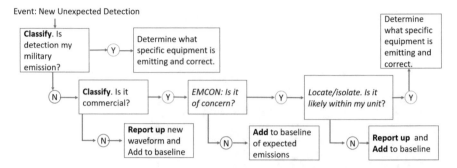

Fig. 20.4 BFSA flow for unexpected emission

what is wrong if the current status is non-conformant. In this initial implementation, however, the AI agent will not take remediation actions on its own initiative. Rather the unit will report issues up the chain of command. The general flow of this business process is shown in Fig. 20.4 for the interesting case when something unexpected is found.

The process begins at upper left with a two-step Classification action, first deciding if the detection is military or not, then what kind of commercial emission it might be if not military. (Unintended commercial emissions in the unit may correspond to illicit cell phone use). This is the key AI assisted action, as the inexperienced user will not in general be in a position to classify observed radio emissions. The other aspect is reporting up the chain of command detected emissions. Rule-based AI agents can assist in this process as well by packaging the reports in a proper schema and adding technical details which the inexperienced user may misinterpret or get wrong. In our initial implementation, only the boxes with **bolded** verbs are done by the AI agent and roman text by the human operator. Italic text could be done by either, depending on the situation. To give some examples.

- The "*Is it of concern*" step depends on the emission control (EMCON) status. If radio silence is being kept, anything is of concern, and the step could be performed by an AI Agent
- The domain of AI action could also be extended by adding a drone to perform the "*Locate/isolate. Is it likely within my unit?*" step.

3.4 Architecture

Having established the utility of AI agents for BFSA at the tactical edge, let us move on to discussing the architecture in a little more detail.

As shown in Fig. 20.5, the AI-agent-assisted BFSA can be conceptualized as a pipeline, but one with a hierarchy of levels. The levels incorporate varying levels of AI. The first level, Aggregation, is not dependent on AI, but consists of classical

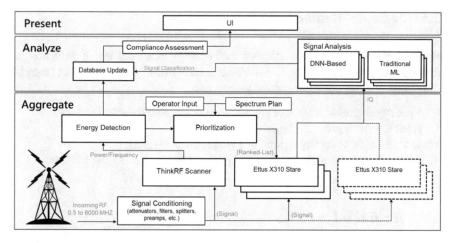

Fig. 20.5 Architecture of AI-assisted BFSA

radio frequency engineering. At the bottom left, an antenna picks up incoming ambient RF. The signals are then conditioned and sent to both a real-time spectrum analyzer manufactured by ThinkRF[2] and to a bank of software-defined radios (SDRs), manufactured by Ettus.[3] Detections from the real-time spectrum analyzer are then prioritized, depending on inputs supplied by the operator and the expected emissions defined by a spectrum plan, and sent to the SDRs, which acquire signals as raw .iq files.

From the Aggregate level, the signals move up to the Analyze level, where they are classified by either "traditional" classifiers involving signal processing and rule-based AI, and/or deep neural net (DNN) based classifiers. The use of both types of classifiers is a design tradeoff caused by the intended austere tactical edge environment in which SWaP and compute power is at a premium. This tradeoff will be discussed in more detail below, but it may be quickly motivated by observing that if the BFSA is receiving a commercial radio station transmitting on its assigned frequency, you wish to dedicate the minimum of scarce resources necessary to remove it from your compliance calculations. From the classifiers, the output moves to a database, and then compliance is assessed by comparing the detected signals with expected ones.

The result of the compliance assessment then goes finally to the Presentation level, where the naïve user is presented with the results of BFSA. The user will then correct anomalous emissions for which s/he is directly responsible, and report other ones up the chain of command utilizing metadata and formatting generated by the BFSA.

---

[2] ThinkRF R5550. https://thinkrf.com/products/real-time-spectrum-analyzers/

[3] Ettus X310. https://www.ettus.com/all-products/x310-kit/

3.5   Software Methodology

Here we briefly mention the software methodology and tools which were used to develop the BFSA capability. These are not central to the AI agent issue but may be of interest to other practitioners and developers.

- Agile development methodology was employed, with two-week sprints
- Version control provided by git
- Analysis code generally written in Python; UI in Javascript
- Docker containers were employed to package the constituent applications

3.6   Tactical Edge Issues

Let us return to consider our previous discussion in Sect. 2 of how the general characteristics of an AI agent are influenced by the environment of the tactical edge and see how it applies to the specific case of AI as developed for the BFSA solution. To put it in a more Darwinian way, how the evolutionary pressure of life at the tactical edge shapes the development of AI agents. We noted in Sect. 2 that life at the tactical edge was characterized by

- Lack of high-performance computing hardware
- Inability to operate at scale
- Poor connectivity to center
- Fuzzy borders between cyber, physical, and EW domains

and that these environmental pressures would cause the selection of AI agents characterized by

- Robust and long-lived models (or models adapted to transfer learning)
- Models which do not require a lot of computing power at run time
- Modest ambitions
- Graceful degradation
- Graceful interactions with non-cyber

Let us consider each of the above predictions in turn.

- Robust and long-lived models (or models adapted to transfer learning)

Our BFSA DNN classifiers are trained on common commercial and military protocols, which they can then recognize at run time. Training the classifier requires significant computing resources, but these can be applied at the center in advance. Military and commercial protocols change slowly, with characteristic times on the order of years.

In addition to the DNN classifiers, as indicated in Fig. 20.5, support for traditional signal-processing-and-ML-based classifiers is also included in the architecture. These also take advantage of the stability of RF waveforms and can provide information even if the DNN classifier cannot be used, as will be discussed below

- Models which do not require a lot of computing power at run time

Although DNN classifiers require both significant compute power and extensive memory resources at training time, at run time they are much less demanding. GPU-enhanced embedded systems such as the Nvidia Jetson family of modules can run them[4] and may draw as little as 40 watts. Of course, the development of these modules was driven by demand in the commercial marketplace for AI applications at the edge in fields such as robotics and transportation. However, they can find a home at the tactical edge as well.

- Modest ambitions

We wish to emphasize that the automated BFSA under development is only designed and intended to monitor and control own force tactical emissions. Although it may provide benefits by capturing adversarial emissions, these are out of scope as design requirements. Hence no provision is required for considerations such as novel adversarial war reserve RF modes, which would require model retraining on the fly and hence violate our assumption of poor or nonexistent connectivity to the center with its many resources.

- Graceful degradation and interactions with non-cyber

As shown above in Fig. 20.5, the signal analysis portion of the Analyze layer contains room for both DNN and traditional (signal processing) ML based classifiers. The latter classifiers yield lower level information such as modulation type, as opposed to advanced DNN classifiers which use their greater breadth to reach higher up the stack and return protocol-level classifications. However, even in the event the DNN classifiers became unusable during action, the lower-level information would still yield helpful information on own force emissions, given the knowledge that forces have about their own plans and capabilities. Even more degradation is possible without losing all functionality. The energy/frequency detections which come from the ThinkRF scanner in the Aggregate layer and are entered into a database in the Analyze layer can give useful information about what is happening in the RF spectrum in the event that classification capability had been completely degraded. That is, because, energy detection and signal processing are less likely to be fooled than neural nets, degraded capabilities will still be present in case the neural net is somehow poisoned by a clever adversary. The DNN-dependent AI agent portion of BFSA could fail completely, but useful information is still available to be presented directly to the user via the UI.

---

[4] See, for example. https://www.nvidia.com/en-us/autonomous-machines/jetson-store/ and https://www.nvidia.com/en-us/autonomous-machines/embedded-systems/jetson-orin/

3.7   Technical Illustration Recapitulation

In this section we have both given a specific example of an AI agent working at the tactical edge, and demonstrated how this agent conforms and adapts to the limitations on AI agents which arise from the particular conditions existing there, as introduced in Sect. 1 and further developed in Sect. 2.

4   Thoughts and Recommendations

4.1   Thoughts on Future Evolution

Due to the disadvantaged nature of the tactical edge as compared to the center, it is reasonable to suppose that the evolutionary pressures previously mentioned will continue to shape AI there. In particular (barring revolutionary as opposed to evolutionary developments), it will continue to have access to less compute power than state-of-the-art technologies in the center, and it will continue to require models with a larger time constant ΔT than is the case at the center. Nonetheless, although the tactical edge's relative position will remain disadvantaged with respect to the center, its absolute position relative to what exists today will continue to advance.

In particular, technologies with commercial drivers, such as the Jetson embedded GPU systems developed for commercial edge applications mentioned in Sect. 3, and advances in battery technology driven by climate change considerations, as well as general improvements in compute power due to the workings of Moore's Law, will increase the capabilities of AI agents at the tactical edge.

Let us return to the hierarchy of situational awareness presented in Fig. 20.2 to place the increased capabilities in context. As described, the BFSA project described in Sect. 3 has achieved Basic Visibility ("can we see the environment?") and is working in Level 1 SA ("what/who/how much is there?"). The next level is Level 2 SA ("Which of these things should I attend to?"). These possibilities are within sight, given the increased compute power and battery capacity currently on the horizon. Thus, returning to the paradigmatic example shown in Fig. 20.4, one might predict that the activities in italic and Roman fonts could eventually be performed by AI agents, working in concert with human warfighters.

A key enabling technology for replacing simple, rule-based risk assessment garnered from SME rules-of-thumb with more sophisticated modern ML approaches, however, is the availability of large training sets. Large data sets generally precede AI breakthroughs, and are conspicuously lacking in the tactical edge context. We conclude this section, therefore, with a suggestion that obtaining them should be high priority in the cause of advancing AI at the tactical edge. Their scarcity is likely to be limiting factor relatively soon.

4.2 Concluding Remarks

To conclude, up to now the tactical edge has been, due to its austere environment, largely an AI backwater. This situation is now changing. Recent advances in techniques and equipment have made it possible to deploy effective AI there, and we have provided a specific example in BFSA. As technology brought about largely by commercial forces is deployed there and increases the scope for effective AI we expect continued improvement. We must caveat our optimism with two observations, however. The first is that the disadvantaged nature of the edge relative to the center will persist and provide evolutionary pressure which developers cannot ignore. The second is that while relatively recent advances in AI technology have satisfied the preconditions for AI-assisted Level 1 Situational Awareness at the edge, advances beyond that will depend on gathering appropriate training data. Unlike the happy situation which obtained with Facebook and image recognition, it is difficult to imagine the relevant training data appearing organically; it will require effort and planning. Nonetheless, even without the AI breakthroughs which generally accompany large data set, the AI agent sketched out in Sect. 3 represents a significant advance for warfighters at the edge over the current status quo, an advance which may be expected to increase as newer technology is deployed.

Distribution Statement A Approved for public release. Distribution is unlimited. This material is based upon work supported by the Dept of the Navy under Air Force Contract No. FA8702-15-D-0001. Any opinions, findings, conclusions or recommendations expressed in this material are those of the author(s) and do not necessarily reflect the views of the Dept of the Navy.

References

Chen, Y., Zhang, Y., Maharjan, S., Alam, M., & Wu, T. (2019). Deep learning for secure mobile edge computing in cyber-physical transportation systems. *IEEE Network, 33*(4), 36–41. https://doi.org/10.1109/MNET.2019.1800458

Dandashi, F., Higginson, J., Hughes, J., Narvaez, W., Sabbouh, M., Semy, S., & Yost, B. (2007). *Tactical edge characterization framework* (MITRE Technical Report MTR070331) (Vol. 1). MITRE.

Endsley, M. R. (1995). Toward a theory of situation awareness in dynamic systems. *Human Factors, 37*(1), 32–64. https://doi.org/10.1518/001872095779049543

Guo, Y., Shi, H., Kumar, A., Grauman, K., Rosing, T., & Feris, R. (2018). *SpotTune: Transfer learning through adaptive fine-tuning*, p. 10. arXiv:1811.08737.

Hüllermeier, E., & Waegeman, W. (2021). Aleatoric and epistemic uncertainty in machine learning: An introduction to concepts and methods. *Machine Learning, 110*(3), 457–506. https://doi.org/10.1007/s10994-021-05946-3

Joint Staff. (2005). *Net-centric operational environment joint integrating concept*. Department of Defense.

Li, H., Ota, K., & Dong, M. (2018). Learning IoT in edge: Deep learning for the internet of things with edge computing. *IEEE Network, 32*(1), 96–101. https://doi.org/10.1109/MNET.2018.1700202

Marković, D., Mizrahi, A., Querlioz, D., & Grollier, J. (2020). Physics for neuromorphic computing. *Nature Reviews Physics, 2*(9), Art. No. 9. https://doi.org/10.1038/s42254-020-0208-2

NIST. (2022, March 17). *AI risk management framework: Initial draft*. [Online]. Available: https://www.nist.gov/system/files/documents/2022/03/17/AI-RMF-1stdraft.pdf. Accessed 31 Mar 2022.

Rezende, E., Ruppert, G., Carvalho, T., Ramos, F., & de Geus, P. (2017). *Malicious software classification using transfer learning of ResNet-50 deep neural network*. In *2017 16th IEEE international conference on machine learning and applications (ICMLA)* (pp. 1011–1014). https://doi.org/10.1109/ICMLA.2017.00-19

Schulz, A., & Trepagnier, P. (2020, September). AI at the tactical edge. In *IEEE high performance extreme computing conference 2022*, BRAIDS Special Session.

Schulz, A., Aubin, E., Trepagnier, P., & Wollaber, A. (2019). *Cyber baselining: Statistical properties of cyber time series and the search for stability*. In *2019 IEEE High Performance Extreme Computing Conference (HPEC)* (pp. 1–7). https://doi.org/10.1109/HPEC.2019.8916350

Shakarami, A., Ghobaei-Arani, M., & Shahidinejad, A. (2020). *A survey on the computation offloading approaches in mobile edge computing: A machine learning-based perspective*. *Computer Networks, 182*. https://doi.org/10.1016/j.comnet.2020.107496

Weiss, K., Khoshgoftaar, T. M., & Wang, D. (2016). A survey of transfer learning. *Journal of Big Data, 3*(1), 9. https://doi.org/10.1186/s40537-016-0043-6

Chapter 21
Case Study C: Sentinels for Cyber Resilience

Peter A. Beling, Tim Sherburne, and Barry Horowitz

1 Introduction

This chapter describes an approach to cyber resilience-by-design in which the system is engineered to include processes, called *sentinels*, that monitor for the symptoms of cyber-attacks. In the event of a detection, a sentinel will attempt to reconfigure the system by engaging alternate sets of hardware and software designed to permit continued operation in spite of the attack. Sentinel-based resilience finds most of its application in cyber-physical systems, such as vehicles and weapons systems, rather than in pure cyber and networking systems, such as enterprise information technology systems.

Figure 21.1 provides a representation of a sentinel-based system architecture for resilience against cyber attack. In this basic design pattern, the sentinel monitors data associated with critical system functions, using rule-based or statistical methods to judge whether these functions are being performed at an acceptable level. In the event of anomalous or unacceptable function, the sentinel will initiate a system reconfiguration to engage a *resilient mode* of operation that uses different hardware and software to perform the affected function at an acceptable if not ideal level. Typically, resilient modes of operation are designed using components that are redundant in terms of function but come from different manufacturers, thus facilitating recovery from attacks that are idiosyncratic to a manufacturer.

Sentinels are typically implemented by adding to the system dedicated software and sensing, computing, and communication hardware. In some systems, internal

P. A. Beling (✉) · T. Sherburne
Virginia Tech, National Security Institute, Intelligent Systems Division, Blacksburg, VA, USA
e-mail: beling@vt.edu

B. Horowitz
Crozet, VA, USA
e-mail: beling@vt.edu

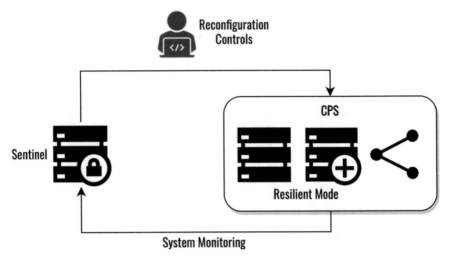

Fig. 21.1 Sentinel-based system for resilience against cyber atack

data may be available As such, sentinels can represent potential targets for attack and pathways that an attacker might use to access other subsystems. To minimize that risk, sentinels should be designed to be far more secure than their host system. While the sentinel-based cyber-attack detection process is expected to be automated, the level of reconfiguration automation may vary across system functions.

The following sections describe how sentinels detect attacks, what they do after detection, and how to choose where to put them. The discussion covers several specific engineering patterns for sentinels and resilient models of operation, as well as more general topics including operational and life cycle issues in sentinel-based cyber resilience and the roles of humans vs. autonomy (e.g. manual, semi-automated, automated) in controlling sentinels and reconfiguration actions. The chapter concludes with a case study on a hypothetical weapons system.

Figure 21.2 provides a detailed representation of sentinel functions. As illustrated in the figure, the sentinel receives the data to support its monitoring function through interfaces to the system functions or sensors monitoring those functions. These interfaces may be wired or wireless. The sentinel must then condition the diverse sets of collected data so that they can be integrated and used as the basis for analysis and, ultimately, decision making. Data conditioning includes setting data rates and formats, as well as communication protocols for internal use in the sentinel. Once the data is conditioned, the sentinel analyzes the data to detect and localize cyberattacks. A wide set of analytical methods might be employed, ranging from simple threshold mechanisms, to statistical methods that aim to detect anomalies in multivariate data based on deviation from mean, to machine learning methods. Upon detecting an attack, the sentinel must alert system users and provide information on the detected attack and the steps required to reconfigure the system for continued operation. Depending on the level of automation designed into the

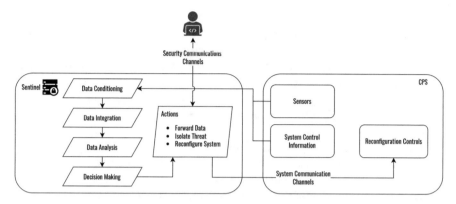

Fig. 21.2 Detailed representation of sentinel functions

resilience response, the sentinel may also engage in communication and computer control of the subsystems involved in the resilience-related reconfiguration solution. The level of automation will depend on system design that may vary across a spectrum, including the following cases:

- Totally automated: Sentinel determines reconfiguration to be performed and either directly engages with control elements or informs operators who will execute the reconfiguration.
- Semiautomated: System operators receive automated attack alerts and reconfiguration recommendation(s) from the sentinel and select reconfiguration actions based on fusing that input with their own understanding of the system context, such as mission priorities or other information sources.
- Manual: System operators receive automated attack alerts from the sentinel and select reconfiguration actions using their own understanding of the system and its context.

In addition, the sentinel must prepare and disseminate its results for users engaged in more strategic roles such as forensics and systems adaptation related to managing resilience over longer time cycles.

There are a wide variety of possibilities for the hardware/ software design of sentinels that are dependent on the system being supported. For example, implementation can be through a single computing node or through a highly distributed set of nodes, and selection of the design should be highly dependent on the methods of security that can be applied for protection of the sentinel. To provide quality and cost advantages, the design approach ideally would be based on reusable design patterns. Examples of patterns for detecting cyberattacks include:

- Discovery of data inconsistencies within the system with no other explainable cause (e.g., operator system control inputs are different from the inputs received by the related controlled subsystems, diverse sensors provide inconsistent measurements).

- Detection of changes of system operational parameters without authorized and operationally correct procedures, resulting in significant performance consequences.
- Recognizing significant unexplainable incompatibilities between internal system communication levels and the presentation of situation awareness information provided to system operators (e.g., air defense system operators are provided with low levels of traffic information, but sensors are observed to be communicating information that should be presented at high rates).
- Rules and thresholds – physical principals, binary notions like tampering.
- Statistical anomaly detection based on deviations from mean values.
- Advanced methods for anomaly detection, such as machine learning models trained on data sets for which ground truth of attack status is known.

While each of these examples applies to a wide variety of physical systems, the implementation of specific solutions will vary across different systems. The authors' own research has included development of prototype designs that employed some of the above patterns for detecting cyberattacks on UAVs, police cars, 3D printers, and military systems (Babineau et al., 2012; Carter et al., 2019; Fleming et al., 2021; Horowitz et al., 2017; Horowitz et al., 2018; Bakirtzis et al., 2022). Note that the consequences of a cyberattack can vary significantly depending upon the actual system being attacked, so risk-based decisions are required in terms of which design patterns reduce the risks of attack most significantly. Furthermore, as noted previously, resilient system efforts must be directed toward achieving designs that are highly secured.

The following sections describe how sentinels detect attacks, what they do after detections of an attack, where to put them, and how to test them. The chapter concludes with a case study on a hypothetical weapons system.

2 How Sentinels Detect Attacks

A set of design patterns for sentinel detection of abnormal system behavior is defined in this section. Detecting abnormal system behavior is an indication of potential cyber attack. A logical architecture for each pattern is presented, a message flow is described, as well as a discussion of the system architecture which is appropriate for the application of the sentinel pattern.

2.1 Changing Control Input

The logical architecture for the changing control input pattern is shown in Fig. 21.3. The sentinel monitors the control path through a hierarchy of controllers to ensure consistency of control actions. For example, Control Action B is logical given

Fig. 21.3 Changing
control input pattern for
detection of cyber attacks

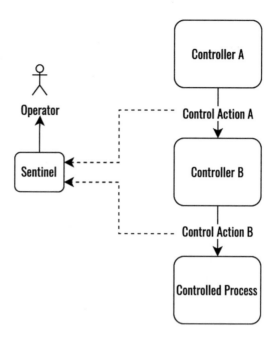

previous Control Action A. This pattern is useful for detecting cyber tampering of
Controller B or the control path for Control Action B. Cyber physical systems with
hierarchical control structures can benefit from this detection pattern.

2.2 Resource Introspection

The logical architecture for the resource introspection pattern is shown in Fig. 21.4.
The sentinel monitors controller/controlled process resource utilization (cpu, memory, link, etc.) to ensure consistency with current operating state/mode of the system. For example, the throughput of feedback messages is consistent with the CPU
utilization of the controlled process which is the expected source of the feedback
messages. Cyber physical system architectures with well understood resource utilization semantics can benefit from this detection pattern.

2.3 Attestation Using TPM

The logical architecture for the attestation using a Trusted Platform Module (TPM)
is shown in the Fig. 21.5. During controller boot, secure hashes (SHA256) of partitions of software and configuration are performed and extended to platform configuration registers (PCR) of a trusted platform module (TPM) . Typically, the

Fig. 21.4 Resource introspection pattern for detection of cyber attacks

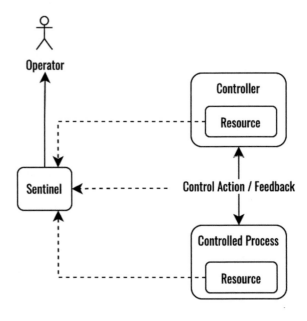

Fig. 21.5 Attestation using a Trusted Platform Module (TPM) pattern for detection of cyber attacks

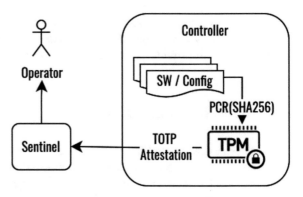

firmware which performs the initial partition hash is from a write-once memory location. Upon completion of the boot sequence, if all PCR values hold correct SHA256 values a shared secret is released within the TPM that allows calculation of a time-based one-time-password (TOTP). The TOTP is reported to the Sentinel which attests (via prior knowledge of the controller shared secret) that all partitions of controller software and configuration have not been tampered. Cyber physical systems which include regular deployment or maintenance phases provide an opportunity for tampering of software or configuration and can benefit from this detection pattern.

3   What Sentinels Do After Detecting an Attack

A set of design patterns for system resilience are described in this section. Upon detection of abnormal system behavior, a Sentinel will recommend a resilient mode of operation that remediates the abnormal system behavior. A logical architecture for each pattern is presented, a message flow is described, as well as a discussion of the system architecture which is appropriate for the application of the resilience pattern.

3.1   Example Sentinel Pattern: Diverse Redundant Controller

The logical architecture for the diverse redundant controller resilience pattern is shown in Fig. 21.6. Depending on mission requirements, the sentinel may automatically initiate the switch of the active controller, or the operator may manually initiate the switch. The diversity of implementation/supplier makes it unlikely that the detected abnormal system behavior will be propagated to the redundant controller. Cyber physical system controllers that support mission critical functions can benefit from this resilience pattern.

3.2   Example Sentinel Pattern: Path Diversity

The logical architecture for the path diversity resilience pattern is shown in Fig. 21.7. Depending on mission requirements, the sentinel may automatically initiate the switch of the active path, or the operator may manually initiate the switch. The diversity of the path technology makes it unlikely that the detected abnormal system

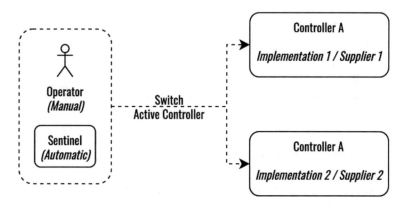

Fig. 21.6 Diverse redundant controller resilience pattern

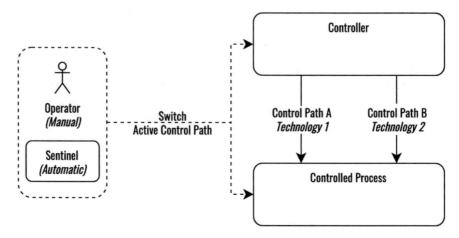

Fig. 21.7 Path diversity resilience pattern

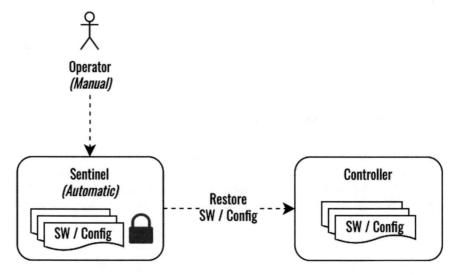

Fig. 21.8 Protected restore resilience pattern

behavior will be propagated to the redundant path. Cyber physical system control paths that support mission critical messaging can benefit from this resilience pattern.

3.3 Example Sentinel Pattern: Protected Restore

The logical architecture for the protected restore resilience pattern is shown in Fig. 21.8. Depending on mission requirements, the sentinel may automatically initiate the restore of software/configuration for a controller, or the operator may manually initiate the restore. The restore of a protected backup can interrupt a cyber attacker's access into a controller and restore a controller to a known state of operation. Cyber physical systems which include regular deployment or maintenance phases provide an opportunity for tampering of software or configuration and can benefit from this resilience pattern.

The anticipated value of employing this type of resilience solution is that it requires the cyberattacker both to understand how the system to be attacked is designed and to develop and employ multiple attacks on diversely redundant subsystems to sufficiently disrupt the targeted system. This, in turn, should impact the cost, time, technical complexity, and risk for creating the desired cyberattacks, with the objective of deterring attackers from going ahead with their desire to be disruptive. Of course, the resilience solution must be sufficiently low cost, timely, low risk, and effective to make it an attractive option.

As illustrated earlier in discussing reusable design patterns for cyberattack detection, designs that exploit diverse redundancy for continuing operation also are reusable, but implementation and risk reduction value depend upon the actual system to be protected. In addition, diverse solutions typically do not perform as well as the normal mode of system operation, although they are potentially acceptable for continuing operation. Examples of diverse redundancy opportunities include the following:

1. use of diverse sensors for providing situation awareness information (e.g., radar, infrared, audio, video, and many other technologies that can potentially be used as the basis for surveillance subsystems)
2. use of diverse navigation subsystems (e.g., GPS, inertial navigation)
3. use of relatively common sub-systems, but designed and produced with different hardware and software by different manufacturers (e.g., different operating systems, application software, microelectronics components, communications switches).

As a result, designers of resilient systems must evaluate the losses in performance that could result when the protected system is reconfigured and the operational acceptability of such losses. Resilience can also be achieved through the integration of multiple approaches for achieving diversity that serve both detection of attacks and reconfiguration responses. For example, one of the design patterns derived from the authors' research efforts is referred to as configuration hopping with voting (Babineau et al., 2012). An experimental application of this design pattern, utilizing multivariant programming via the use of three diversely manufactured communication switches and through comparison of message content going into and coming out of the switches, could determine if there was an inappropriately performing switch. If so, the improperly performing switch could be taken out of service while continuing system operation.

In addition, to make matters more complex for a cyber-attacker intent on changing message content, the design pattern included the use of a moving target technique, dynamically changing which switch is to be operationally employed once every few seconds, with the use of randomly selected times for moving the potential targets (Babineau et al., 2012). Since the diversely implemented switches were not closely synchronized in terms of order of messages and their timing, use of moving target defense brought with it the potential to create problems due to the timing of message processing within the diverse switches. To address this problem, message content comparisons were done in a batched manner at sufficiently spaced intervals to reduce the percentage of deviating messages due to timing. The sentinel detection algorithms were designed to permit missing messages as a normal situation when the deviations occurred close to the switching times, and the operational system depended on its existing communication protocols to assure that missing messages due to dynamic changing of the switch in operation were either resent in a timely manner or were acceptable for loss at low rates. Operational prototype-based experiments related to control of a ship's propulsion system were conducted to measure message loss rates. Results indicated that the number of lost messages due to a 20-hop/s resilience design was acceptably low (Babineau et al., 2012).

4   Where to Place Sentinels

Systems Theoretic Accident Model and Processes (STAMP) is a safety analysis method that is based on causation (Leveson & Thomas, 2018; Young & Leveson, 2014; Young & Porada, 2017). Causation in STAMP is modeled through hierarchical control, which models each level of a system as a control process, where unsafe control actions can occur. This layered approach to safety has the advantage that unsafe control actions at each level percolate upwards or downwards in the hierarchy that in turn provides a notion of consequence within the safety model. STAMP works in contrast to linear failure modes, where unsafe actions form a chain of events. In STAMP, by contrast, safety violations emerge from the interacting control layers governing the system. Specifically, STAMP is a hazard analysis technique based on an extended model of accident causation. In addition to component failures, STAMP assumes that accidents can also be caused by unsafe interactions of system components, none of which may have individually failed. For this reason, STAMP further asserts that emergent properties, for example safety and security, cannot be assured by examining subsystems in isolation. As illustrated in Fig. 21.9, the System Theoretic Process Analysis (STPA) is one variant of STAMP modeling that is primarily used to proactively identify hazardous conditions and states. STPA-Sec is an extension of STPA with the intention of transitioning the benefits of loss-oriented safety assessment to security (Young & Porada, 2017).

The first step of STPA is to define the system boundary and purpose of the analysis in the form of losses and hazards. The losses are prioritized by the mission/system owners and are used to drive the system architecture tradespace analysis. The next step is to model the hierarchical control structure for the system's key behaviors. Based on this control structure, a methodical analysis considers how unsafe or hazardous control actions could lead to hazardous states and system losses. Finally, scenarios are considered to understand reasons why unsafe or hazardous actions could occur including intentional cyber security attacks.

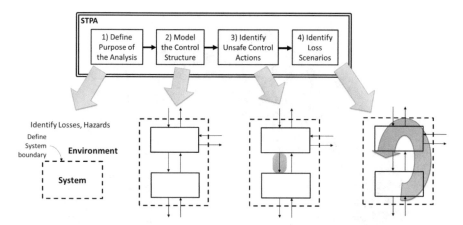

Fig. 21.9 System Theoretic Process Analysis (STPA) overview. (Source (Leveson & Thomas, 2018): STPA Handbook)

The identified scenarios are evaluated to determine remediation mechanisms which effectively minimize the loss using sentinel detection patterns and resilience architecture patterns. The architectural tradespace incorporates the set of sentinels and resilience modes which mitigate the most likely cyber attacks which could lead to the highest priority mission losses that are within the programmatic constraints of development time and budget.

5   How to Test Sentinels

Cyber resilience also presents special challenges with regard to test and evaluation. Typically, system requirements can be specified in terms of technology function and can be tested through manipulation of the systems operational environment, controls, or inputs. Cyber resilience is a high-level property and lacks commonly accepted definitions in terms of system requirements and associated test metrics. Moreover, by design, resilience behaviors are exhibited only when the system has lost critical functions. The implication is that the test and evaluation of requirements for operational resilience will involve creating, emulating, or reasoning about the internal systems states that might result from successful attacks. The implication is that the definition, development, and test and evaluation of requirements for operational resilience will involve creating and emulating functional models, then reasoning about the internal systems states that might result from disruptions caused by system failures or successful attacks.

The Framework for Operational Resilience in Engineering and System Test (FOREST) is a process meta-model that provides a decomposition of operational resilience into the principal mechanisms, options, information flows, and decisions that arise as attacks and resilience responses play out in systems. As illustrated in

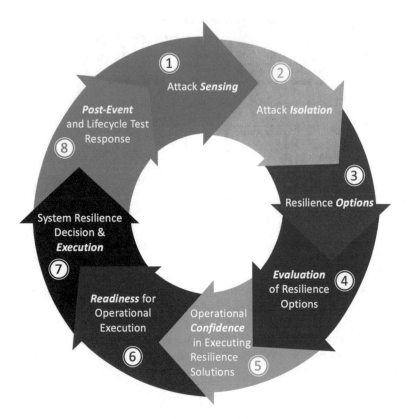

Fig. 21.10 Overview of the Framework for Operational Resilience in Engineering and Systems Test (FOREST)

Fig. 21.10, the framework is composed of eight elements known as Testable Requirements Elicitation Elements (TREEs) and are described in the table below. The first TREE embodies the notion that there is active sensing to detect loss of function or abnormal behavior in the system. Next, the framework considers the task of isolating a detected incident and the use of diagnostic information as the basis for choosing resilience mode responses. From that point, FOREST expands to include consideration of operator response and supporting technology. For instance, would an operator have confidence in resilience solutions being employed, or does the system provide the operator with the ability to run tests or exercise control to help in gaining confidence in resilience modes of operation. Finally, the framework considers decision support and archiving to allow for post-event analysis and adaptation (Table 21.1).

There is significant complexity to the TREEs, and many of them overlap intentionally and deal with issues at the intersections of technology, doctrine, and people. As their name implies, TREEs provide a view of resilience that supports the development of test plans, and associated measures and metrics, for both the technological and operational aspects of the system.

Table 21.1 Testable Requirements Elicitation Elements (TREE)

TREE	ID	Description
Attack **Sensing**	T.1	This element of resilience provides the basis for discovering a successful cyber-attack and informing the system operators about the attack.
Attack **Isolation**	T.2	This element of resilience solutions addresses identification of the part of the system that has been successfully attacked.
Resilience **Options**	T.3	This element of resilience solutions addresses the reconfiguration solution(s) for the attacks under consideration as well as the immediate containment of safety-related consequences.
Evaluation of Resilience Options	T.4	This part of the framework calls for documentation that provides explanations for the selection of solutions, the anticipated performance of the reconfigured system (including time to reconfigure), and the basis for deciding that the resulting operational capabilities are satisfactory.
Operational **Confidence** in Executing Resilience Solutions	T.5	The framework calls for documentation of the basis for achieving high enough confidence and the related test and evaluation methods.
Readiness for Operational Execution (Real-time Mission Context)	T.6	The framework will expect explanation of the basis for the system design approach regarding test support for addressing operator roles and anticipated performance.
System Resilience Decision & **Execution**	T.7	The framework will look for the rationale for who decides on what, and the training and tech support required for decision-makers.
Post-Event and Lifecycle Test Responses	T.8	This portion of the framework addresses identification of information reporting and re-use of development test support capabilities to address system re-testing regarding potential improvements based upon actual results derived from executing resilience solutions in response to cyber-attacks.

6 Silverfish Case Study

This section describes the application of sentinel-based resilience concepts to *Silverfish*, a fictional system-of-systems (Beling et al., 2019, 2022). The use case shows from tabletop analysis exercises, requirements and functional architecture definition, design and test, and then developmental and operational test and evaluation.

6.1 Pre-resilience Architecture

As illustrated in Fig. 21.11, the Silverfish System is a rapidly deployable set of 50 individual ground-based weapon platforms (referred to as obstacles) controlled by a single operator. The purpose of the system is to deter and prevent adversaries from

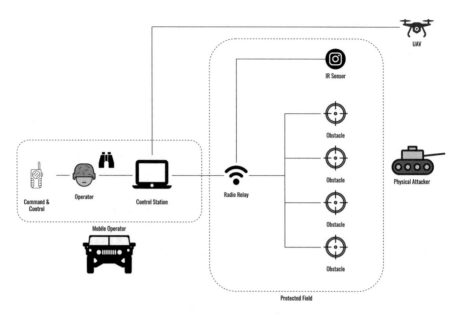

Fig. 21.11 Silverfish Case Study – Pre-Resilience Architecture

trespassing into a designated geographic area that is located near a strategically sensitive location. The system includes a variety of sensors to locate and classify potential trespassers as either personnel or vehicles. An internal wireless communication system is used to support communication between the sensors and the operator and supports fire control communications between the operator and the obstacles. The sensors include obstacle-based seismic and acoustic sensors, infrared sensors and an unmanned aerial vehicle-based surveillance system to provide warning of potential adversaries approaching the protected area. The operator, located in a vehicle, operates within visual range of the protected area. The operator is in communication with a higher-level command and control (C2) system for exchange of doctrinal-related and situation awareness information.

6.2 MA – Cyber Tabletop

The SE team begins the cyber tabletop exercise by defining the Silverfish hierarchical control structure shown in Fig. 21.12.

Silverfish is built from a Control Station, Obstacles and IR Sensors. The Obstacle is built from Munitions and Sensors. External actors include the Operator, Technician, C2, UAV and the Physical Attacker. Control Actions & Feedback Items are shown on the arcs between components and Control Actions are summarized in Table 21.3.

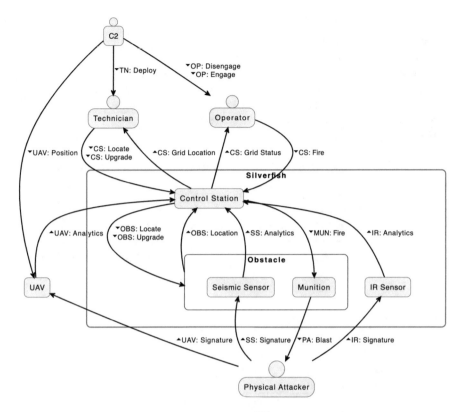

Fig. 21.12 Silverfish Hierarchical Control Structure (▼Control Action ▲Feedback)

Next the system operators/mission owners perform an operational risk assessment. The Silverfish operational risk assessment identifies four losses with an assigned mission priority (see Table 21.4). Three hazards are identified (see Table 21.5) which can lead to the losses.

There are four ways (variation type) a control action can be hazardous:

1. Not providing the control action leads to a hazard.
2. Providing the control action leads to a hazard.
3. Providing a potentially safe control action but too early, too late, or in the wrong order
4. The control action lasts too long or is stopped too soon (for continuous control actions, not discrete ones).

Three examples of hazardous control actions are identified, which are variations of system control actions, and which can lead to a system hazard state (see Table 21.6).

Table 21.3 Silverfish Control Actions

Control Action	Description
CS:Position	Technician request to set location during deployment.
CS:Upgrade	Technician request to upgrade SW before deployment.
MUN:Fire	Control Station message to Obstacle Munition to initiate firing.
OBS:Position	Control Station message to set equipment field position.
OBS:Upgrade	Control Station message to upgrade component SW.
OP:Disengage	Command & Control voice instruction to disengage (hold fire) against physical attackers.
OP:Engage	Command & Control voice instruction to engage (allow fire) against physical attackers.
OP:Fire	Operator request to Fire one or more munitions.
PA:Blast	Munition kinetic blast towards physical attacker.
TN:Deploy	Command & Control voice instruction to deploy Silverfish.
TN:UnDeploy	Command & Control voice instruction to un-deploy Silverfish.
UAV:Position	Command & Control navigation control to position UAV at protected field location.

Table 21.4 Silverfish STPA Losses

Loss ID	Title	Priority	is caused by: Hazard
L.1	Loss of life or serious injury to military.	1	H.1,H.2,H.3
L.2	Loss of life or serious injury to civilians.	1	H.1
L.3	Loss of protected area assets.	2	H.1,H.2
L.4	Loss of classified mission HW/SW.	3	H.3

Table 21.5 Silverfish STPA Hazards

Hazard ID	Title	Description	leads to: Loss	is caused by: Hazardous Action
H.1	Weapon Misfire	Incorrect, or no weapon, is fired.	L.1,L.2,L.3	HCA.1,HCA.2
H.2	Slow Deploy	Excessive time and/or personnel to deploy the system.	L.1,L.3	HCA.3
H.3	Slow Un-Deploy	Excessive time and/or personnel to un-deploy system.	L.1,L.4	

Next the cyber security experts perform a vulnerability assessment. The Silverfish vulnerability assessment identifies four example loss scenarios (see Table 21.7) which can lead to hazardous control actions and can be protected by a sentinel instance. The Silverfish case study includes two sentinels, one deployed within the operator vehicle and one deployed into the protected field.

Table 21.6 Silverfish STPA Hazardous Control Actions (HCA)

HCA ID	Title	Description	Variation Type	leads to: Hazard	is variation of: Control Action
HCA.1	Incorrect Fire	Something other than the operator selected munition/ obstacle is fired.	Providing	H.1	MUN:Fire
HCA.2	No Fire	Operator does not fire munition/obstacle when physical attack is imminent.	NotProviding	H.1	OP:Fire
HCA.3	Unable to set Location	During deployment, the location can not be set.	NotProviding	H.2	OBS:Position

Table 21.7 Silverfish STPA loss scenarios

Loss scenario ID	Title	leads to: Hazardous Control Action	is protected by: Sentinel
LS.1	Manipulated Fire Command	HCA.1	SEN.1: Vehicle
LS.2	Situational Injection	HCA.2	SEN.2: Field
LS.3	Situational Delay	HCA.2	SEN.2: Field
LS.4	Tampered Deployment	HCA.4	SEN.1: Vehicle

6.3   MA – Resilience Analysis

Based upon the cyber tabletop, the SE team next considers system resilient modes (see Table 21.8), which provide reconfigure for the identified loss scenarios and alternate operation for affected components.

The process iterates until an acceptable baseline system description is achieved that is acceptable to the SE team, system operators/mission owners, and cyber security analysts.

6.4   MA – Requirements Elicitation

Based on the identified loss scenarios and remediations (sentinels) a set of cyber resilience system requirements can be elicited. A set of Silverfish constraint and functional requirements, with reference to the elicited by loss scenario, are listed in Table 21.9. These requirements constrain the system structure to provide the identified monitoring mechanisms and related resilient modes. Additionally, system requirements are elicited that refine the system behavior to enable management (enable/disable/self-test, etc.) of the related resilient modes. Finally, a sample set of sentinel (Table 21.9) and test support system (Table 21.10) requirements are elicited that specify the performance for the FOREST quality attributes that achieve the Mission MOPs (Table 21.11).

Table 21.8 Silverfish Resilient Modes

Resilient Mode ID	Title	provides reconfiguration for: Loss Scenario	provides alternate operation for: Component
RM.1	Diverse Redundant Radio Relay	LS.2,LS.3	Control Station, IR Sensor, Obstacle, Radio Relay
RM.2	Diverse Redundant Control Station	LS.1	Control Station
RM.3	Diverse Redundant IR Sensor	LS.3	IR Sensor
RM.4	Obstacle Restore	LS.4	Obstacle

Table 21.9 Silverfish Loss Scenario Elicited Requirements

Requirement	Type	elicited by: LS
SF.600.1 Silverfish shall provide fire control action monitor.	Constraint	LS.1 Manipulated Fire Command
SF.600.2 Silverfish shall provide fire control timing monitor.	Constraint	LS.5 Delayed Fire Command
SF.600.3 Silverfish shall provide situational sensor report consistency monitor.	Constraint	LS.2 Situational Injection
SF.600.4 Silverfish shall provide situational sensor report timing monitor.	Constraint	LS.3 Situational Delay
SF.600.5 Silverfish shall provide measured boot monitor.	Constraint	LS.4 Tampered Deployment
SF.600.10 Silverfish shall provide component self test operations.	Functional	LS.1 Manipulated Fire Command LS.2 Situational Injection LS.3 Situational Delay LS.4 Tampered Deployment LS.5 Delayed Fire Command
SF.600.11 Silverfish shall provide fire control redundancy management controls.	Functional	LS.1 Manipulated Fire Command LS.5 Delayed Fire Command
SF.600.12 Silverfish shall provide fire control self test operations.	Functional	LS.1 Manipulated Fire Command LS.5 Delayed Fire Command
SF.600.13 Silverfish shall provide IR sensor redundancy management controls.	Functional	LS.2 Situational Injection LS.3 Situational Delay
SF.600.14 Silverfish shall provide obstacle restore management controls.	Functional	LS.4 Tampered Deployment
SF.600.15 Silverfish shall provide radio relay redundancy management controls.	Functional	LS.2 Situational Injection LS.3 Situational Delay LS.5 Delayed Fire Command
SF.600.16 Silverfish shall provide situational aware self test operations.	Functional	LS.2 Situational Injection LS.3 Situational Delay

Table 21.10 Sentinel Loss Scenario Elicited Requirements

Requirement	Type	elicited by: LS	refines: Requirement
SEN.602.1 Vehicle Sentinel shall sense LS.1: Manipulated Fire Command Loss Scenario within .5 seconds.	Performance	LS.1 Manipulated Fire Command	T.1.5 TREE. Sense – Time Spec
SEN.602.2 Vehicle Sentinel shall sense LS.1 Manipulated Fire Command with 99% accuracy.	Performance	LS.1 Manipulated Fire Command	T.1.6 TREE. Sense – Accuracy Spec
SEN.602.3 Vehicle Sentinel shall isolate C.3.1:Fire Control Station as the source of LS.1: Manipulated Fire Control Loss Scenario within .5 seconds.	Performance	LS.1 Manipulated Fire Command	T.2.3 TREE. Isolate – Time Spec
SEN.602.4 Vehicle Sentinel shall isolate C.3.1:Fire Control Station as the source of LS.1: Manipulated Fire Control Loss Scenario with 99% accuracy.	Performance	LS.1 Manipulated Fire Command	T.2.4 TREE. Isolate – Accuracy Spec
SEN.602.5 Vehicle Sentinel shall abort SF.1.1: Fire Munition Function upon sensing LS.1: Manipulated Fire Command Loss Scenario.	Functional	LS.1 Manipulated Fire Command	T.3.2 TREE. Option – Abort Unsafe

Table 21.11 Test support system elicited requirements

Requirement	Type	elicited by: LS	refines: Requirement
TSS.603.1 Test Support System shall provide an operator 'composability' rating for RM.2: Diverse Redundant Fire Control	Performance	LS.1 Manipulated Fire Command	T.3.3 TREE. Option – Composability Rating
TSS.603.2 Test Support System shall provide an operator 'failure transparency' rating for RM.2: Diverse Redundant Fire Control.	Performance	LS.1 Manipulated Fire Command	T.4.2 TREE. Evaluate – Recoverability Rating
TSS.603.3 Test Support System shall provide and operator 'usability' rating for RM.2: Diverse Redundant Fire Control	Performance	LS.1 Manipulated Fire Command	T.4.3 TREE. Evaluate – Useability Rating
TSS.603.4 Test Support System shall measure 'timeliness' of operator evaluation of RM.2: Diverse Redundant Fire Control.	Performance	LS.1 Manipulated Fire Command	T.4.4 TREE. Evaluate – Time Spec

6.5 Post-Resilience Architecture

Based on the MA-Cyber Tabletop and MA-Resilience Analysis, the post resilience Silverfish architecture is shown in Fig. 21.13. Resilience artifacts are highlighted in red.

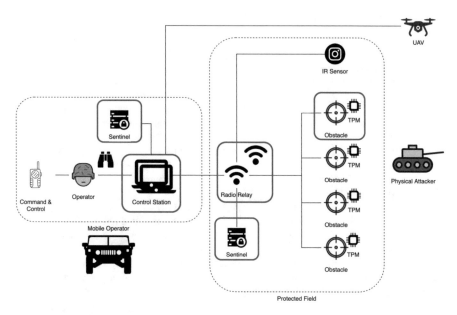

Fig. 21.13 Silverfish case study – post-resilience architecture

7 Conclusions

The sentinel approach to resilience described in this chapter can be effective in preserving critical system function under cyber attack. However, it is important to emphasize that attack detection is only part of the equation. The system must be able to mitigate the attack by reconfiguring its operation using diverse redundant subsystems or other techniques, as described in the chapter. Clearly, there are limits to scalability to an approach that involves adding hardware and software to a system. Resilience engineers are advised to engage in structure processes, involving system owners and other stakeholders, to identify critical functions and to define a trade space between the monetary cost, operational impacts, and benefits of engineered resilience responses.

References

Babineau, G. L., Jones, R. A., & Horowitz, B. (2012). A system-aware cyber security method for shipboard control systems with a method described to evaluate cyber security solutions. In *2012 IEEE conference on Technologies for Homeland Security (HST)* (pp. 99–104).

Bakirtzis, G., Sherburne, T., Adams, S., Horowitz, B. M., Beling, P. A., & Fleming, C. H. (2022). An ontological metamodel for cyber-physical system safety, security, and resilience coengineering. *Software and Systems Modeling, 21*(1), 113–137.

Beling, P., Horowitz, B., Fleming, C., Adams, S., Bakirtzis, G., Carter, B., Sherburne, T., Elks, C., Collins, A., & Simon, B. (2019). *Model-based engineering for functional risk assessment and design of cyber resilient systems*. Systems Engineering Research Center Technical Report.

Beling, P., McDermott, T., Sherburne, T., Clifford, M., & Horowitz, B. (2022). *Developmental test and evaluation and cyberattack resilient systems*. Systems Engineering Research Center Technical Report.

Carter, B., Adams, S., Bakirtzis, G., Sherburne, T., Beling, P., Horowitz, B., & Fleming, C. (2019). A preliminary design-phase security methodology for cyber–physical systems. *Systems, 7*(2), 21.

Fleming, C. H., Elks, C., Bakirtzis, G., Adams, S., Carter, B., Beling, P., & Horowitz, B. (2021). Cyberphysical security through resiliency: A systems-centric approach. *Computer, 54*(6), 36–45.

Horowitz, B., Beling, P., Fleming, C., Adams, S., Carter, B., Vemuru, K., Elks, C., Bakker, T., Cios, K., Bakirtzis, G., & Collins, A. (2017). *Security engineering fy17 systems aware cybersecurity*. Systems Engineering Research Center Technical Report.

Horowitz, B., Beling, P., Fleming, C., Adams, S., Carter, B., Sherburne, T., Elks, C., Bakirtzis, G., Shull, F., & Mead, N. R. (2018). *Cyber security requirements methodology*. Systems Engineering Research Center Technical Report.

Leveson, N. G., & Thomas, J. (2018). *STPA Handook*. Available online: https://psas.scripts.mit.edu/home/get_file.php?name=STPA_handbook.pdf

Young, W., & Leveson, N. G. (2014). An integrated approach to safety and security based on systems theory. *Communications of the ACM, 57*(2), 31–35.

Young, W., & Porada, R. (2017, March). System-theoretic process analysis for security (STPA-SEC): Cyber security and STPA. In *2017 STAMP Conference*.

Printed in the United States
by Baker & Taylor Publisher Services